MW00640012

WITHDRAWN

THE COLLECTED WORKS OF W. B. YEATS

*George Mills Harper and George Bornstein,*
*General Editors*

VOLUME I THE POEMS
*ed. Richard J. Finneran*

VOLUME II THE PLAYS
*ed. David R. Clark and Rosalind E. Clark*

VOLUME III AUTOBIOGRAPHIES
*ed. William H. O'Donnell and Douglas N. Archibald*

VOLUME IV EARLY ESSAYS
*ed. George Bornstein and Richard J. Finneran*

VOLUME V LATER ESSAYS
*ed. William H. O'Donnell*

VOLUME VI PREFACES AND INTRODUCTIONS
*ed. William H. O'Donnell*

VOLUME VII LETTERS TO THE NEW ISLAND
*ed. George Bornstein and Hugh Witemeyer*

VOLUME VIII THE IRISH DRAMATIC MOVEMENT
*ed. Mary FitzGerald and Richard J. Finneran*

VOLUME IX EARLY ARTICLES AND REVIEWS
*ed. John P. Frayne and Madeleine Marchaterre*

VOLUME X LATER ARTICLES AND REVIEWS
*ed. Colton Johnson*

VOLUME XI MYTHOLOGIES
*ed. Jonathan Allison*

VOLUME XII JOHN SHERMAN AND DHOYA
*ed. Richard J. Finneran*

VOLUME XIII A VISION (1925)
*ed. Margaret Mills Harper and Catherine Paul*

VOLUME XIV A VISION (1937)
*ed. Margaret Mills Harper and Catherine Paul*

# THE COLLECTED WORKS OF W. B. YEATS

## VOLUME IV

*Francesca and Paolo.* After the rare engraving
by William Blake (*Inferno* V)

# W. B. YEATS

# *Early Essays*

EDITED BY
George Bornstein and Richard J. Finneran

Scribner
NEW YORK LONDON TORONTO SYDNEY

SCRIBNER
1230 Avenue of the Americas
New York, NY 10020



For information about special discounts for bulk purchases,
please contact Simon & Schuster Special Sales:
1-800-456-6798 or business@simonandschuster.com

Text set in Sabon

Manufactured in the United States of America

1 3 5 7 9 10 8 6 4 2

Library of Congress Cataloging-in-Publication Data
Yeats, W. B. (William Butler), 1865–1939.
Early essays / W. B. Yeats ;
edited by George Bornstein and Richard J. Finneran.
p. cm.—(The collected works of W. B. Yeats ; v. 4)
Includes bibliographical references (p. ) and index.
I. Bornstein, George. II. Finneran, Richard J. III. Title.
PR5900.A2 F56 1989 vol. 9
821'.8—dc22 88-027365

ISBN-13: 978-0-684-80729-4
ISBN-10: 0-684-80729-7

*To the memory of*
*Richard J. Finneran*
*and*
*to our children:*
*Ben, Rebecca, and Josh Bornstein*
*Rich and Kate Finneran*

# CONTENTS



## Early Essays

### IDEAS OF GOOD AND EVIL

THE CUTTING OF AN AGATE

## Yeats's Prefaces and Dedication



## Appendices



## Textual Matters and Notes

# EDITORS' PREFACE AND ACKNOWLEDGMENTS

This volume contains the first scholarly edition of Yeats's two most important volumes of criticism written during his youth and middle age, *Ideas of Good and Evil* and *The Cutting of an Agate,* both included by him in the 1924 volume *Essays* and from 1961 until recently available chiefly through the posthumous *Essays and Introductions* compilation. The front matter contains lists of abbreviations and illustrations, followed by the editors' introduction. The essays themselves then follow, first *IGE* and then *COA*. After that come first Yeats's own prefaces to *COA* and his dedication of *Essays* (1924). A series of appendices presents a chronological list of essays by date of first publication, the omitted "The Pathway," and omitted sections from seven other essays, including the illustrations that originally accompanied "William Blake and His Illustrations to *The Divine Comedy.*" The final section, "Textual Matters and Notes," begins with an explanation of our textual policies and procedures, followed by lists of textual emendations and corrections. Explanatory notes include first background notes on fourteen frequently cited writers, followed by headnotes for each essay and identification of quotations and direct allusions in Yeats's texts. Finally, an index facilitates finding writers, works, and other topics referred to in the text.

Completing a project like this requires assistance from a variety of sources. We are pleased to acknowledge generous help from the following scholars: Morris Eaves, Neil Fraistat, Linda Gregerson, Margaret Harper, K. P. S. Jochum, Declan Kiely, Kerry Larson, Jerome McGann, James McGuire, William O'Donnell, James Olney, Jonathan Price, Ann Saddlemyer, and H. Wayne Storey. We owe a special debt to Jon Alan Lanham, who provided us with a copy of his doctoral dissertation, "A Critical Edition of *Ideas of Good and Evil* by W. B. Yeats" (PhD diss., University of Toronto, 1976), which proved helpful throughout our work.

We are also pleased to acknowledge help from librarians and curators at the following collections: Boston Museum of Fine Arts (Joan Cummins), British Museum (Richard Blurton, Michael Boggan, Timothy Clark, Christopher Fletcher, Antony Griffiths, Peter Higgs), Harry Ransom Humanities Research Center at University of Texas at Austin (Elizabeth Garver, Kurt Heinzelman, Tom Staley), National Library of Ireland (Catherine Fahy, Peter Kenny, Dónal Ó Luanaigh), New York Public Library (Berg Collection: Isaac Gewirtz), University of London Library (Alun Ford), University of Michigan Library (Kathryn Beam, Peggy Daub, Franki Hand), University of New York at Stony Brook Yeats Archive (Kristen J. Nyitray), University of North Carolina Library (Charles Macnamara).

We have been fortunate to have exceptionally enthusiastic and competent research assistants. Richard Finneran acknowledges help from Brian Gempp, Jesse Graves, and Lauren Todd Taylor at the University of Tennessee. George Bornstein acknowledges help from Olivia Bustion, Russell McDonald, Jamie Olson, and Jenny Sorensen at the University of Michigan. The University of Michigan also provided timely research support through the Office of the Vice President for Research, the Horace H. Rackham School of Graduate Study, the College of Literature Science and Arts, and the Department of English. The University of Tennessee did so through the John C. Hodges Better English Fund.

THE EDITORS

After a two-year struggle against cancer, Richard Finneran—co-editor of this volume and of the Collected Works of W. B. Yeats—passed away while *Early Essays* was in press. His passing is a great loss to many both professionally and personally. The dedication of this edition to our children follows our original plan. I have added his own name to the dedication in tribute to his memory and friendship.

GEORGE BORNSTEIN

# ABBREVIATIONS

| | |
|---|---|
| *Au* | *Autobiographies*. Edited by William H. O'Donnell and Douglas N. Archibald. New York: Scribner, 1999. |
| AV-B | *A Vision*. London: Macmillan, 1937. |
| Berg | Berg Collection, New York Public Library. |
| *Bibliography* | Allan Wade, *A Bibliography of the Writings of W. B. Yeats*. 3rd edition, revised and edited by Russell K. Alspach. London: Rupert Hart-Davis, 1968. |
| BL | British Library Additional Manuscript |
| Bornstein | George Bornstein, *Yeats and Shelley*. Chicago and London: University of Chicago Press, 1970. |
| Clark | *Shelley's Prose; or, The Trumpet of a Prophecy*. Corrected edition, edited by David Lee Clark. Albuquerque: University of New Mexico Press, 1966. |
| *CL1* | *The Collected Letters of W. B. Yeats: Volume One, 1865–1895*. Edited by John Kelly and Eric Domville. Oxford: Clarendon, 1986. |
| *CL2* | *The Collected Letters of W. B. Yeats: Volume Two, 1896–1900*. Edited by Warwick Gould, John Kelly, and Deirdre Toomey. Oxford: Clarendon, 1997. |
| *CL3* | *The Collected Letters of W. B. Yeats: Volume Three, 1901–1904*. Edited by John Kelly and Ronald Schuchard. Oxford: Clarendon, 1994. |
| *E&I* | *Essays and Introductions*. London: Macmillan, 1961. |
| *EAR* | *Early Articles and Reviews*. Edited by John P. Frayne and Madeleine Marchaterre. New York: Scribner, 2004. |
| Ellis-Yeats | *The Works of William Blake: Poetic, Symbolic, and Critical*. Edited by Edwin John Ellis and William |

| | |
|---|---|
| | Butler Yeats. London: B. Quaritch, 1893. O'Shea #220. Unless otherwise noted, citations are to volume 3. |
| Erdman | *The Complete Poetry and Prose of William Blake.* Newly revised edition, edited By David V. Erdman. New York: Random House (Anchor Books), 1988. |
| *Essays* | *Essays.* London: Macmillan, 1924. |
| *Essays* (NY) | *Essays.* New York: Macmillan, 1924. |
| *Ex* | *Explorations.* Selected by Mrs. W. B. Yeats. London: Macmillan, 1962. |
| Foster | R. F. Foster, *W. B. Yeats: A Life—I: The Apprentice Mage, 1865–1914.* Oxford and New York: Oxford University Press, 1997. *II: The Arch-Poet, 1915–1939.* Oxford and New York: Oxford University Press, 2003. |
| HRC | Harry Ransom Humanities Research Center, University of Texas, Austin |
| Hutchinson | *Shelley: Poetical Works.* Edited by Thomas Hutchinson. New edition, corrected by G. M. Matthews. London and New York: Oxford University Press, 1970. |
| *IDM* | *The Irish Dramatic Movement.* Edited by Mary FitzGerald and Richard J. Finneran. New York: Scribner, 2003. |
| *InteLex* | *The Collected Letters of W. B. Yeats,* Oxford University Press (InteLex Electronic Edition), 2002. |
| *L* | *The Letters of W. B. Yeats.* Edited by Allan Wade. London: Rupert Hart-Davis, 1954. |
| Lanham | "A Critical Edition of *Ideas of Good and Evil* by W. B. Yeats, with Complete Collation, Notes and Commentary." Edited by Jon Alan Lanham. Dissertation, University of Toronto, 1976. Listed in *DAI* 39.3 (September 1978): 1551–52A. |
| *LAR* | *Later Articles and Reviews.* Edited by Colton Johnson. New York: Scribner, 2000. |
| *LE* | *Later Essays.* Edited by William H. O'Donnell. New York: Scribner, 1994. |
| *Letters* | *The Collected Letters of John Millington Synge.* |

Three volumes. Edited by Ann Saddlemyer. Oxford: Clarendon Press, 1984.

*LNI* — *Letters to the New Island.* Edited by George Bornstein and Hugh Witemeyer. New York: Macmillan, 1989.

*Mem* — *Memoirs.* Edited by Denis Donoghue. London: Macmillan, 1972.

*Myth* — *Mythologies.* London: Macmillan, 1959.

NLI — National Library of Ireland

O'Shea — Edward O'Shea, *A Descriptive Catalogue of W. B. Yeats's Library.* New York: Garland, 1985. Cited by item number.

*P* — *The Poems.* 2nd edition. Edited by Richard J. Finneran. New York: Scribner, 1997.

*P&I* — *Prefaces and Introductions.* Edited by William H. O'Donnell. New York: Macmillan, 1988.

*Pl* — *The Plays.* Edited by David R. Clark and Rosalind E. Clark. New York: Scribner, 2001.

*Plays* — J. M. Synge, *Collected Works. Plays: Book I. Plays: Book II.* Edited by Ann Saddlemyer. Gerrards Cross, Bucks: Colin Smythe; Washington, D.C.: Catholic University of America Press, 1982.

*Poems* — J. M. Synge, *Collected Works. Poems.* Edited by Robin Skelton. Gerrards Cross, Bucks: Colin Smythe; Washington, D.C.: Catholic University of America Press, 1982.

Princeton — Princeton University Library

*Prose* — J. M. Synge, *Collected Works. Prose.* Edited by Robin Skelton. Gerrards Cross, Bucks: Colin Smythe; Washington, D.C.: Catholic University of America Press, 1982.

SB — Yeats Archives, State University of New York at Stony Brook

*SB* — *The Speckled Bird: An Autobiographical Novel, with Variant Versions.* New edition. Edited by William H. O'Donnell. London: Palgrave Macmillan, 2003.

Shakespeare — *The Norton Shakespeare.* Edited by Stephen Greenblatt et al. New York and London: Norton, 1997.

*SR* *The Secret Rose, Stories by W. B. Yeats: A Variorum Edition.* 2nd edition. Edited by Warwick Gould, Phillip L. Marcus, and Michael J. Sidnell. London: Macmillan, 1992.

*TB* *Theatre Business: The Correspondence of the First Abbey Theatre Directors: William Butler Yeats, Lady Gregory, and J. M. Synge.* Edited by Ann Saddlemyer. Gerrards Cross, Bucks.: Colin Smythe, 1982.

TCD Trinity College Dublin Library

*UP1* *Uncollected Prose by W. B. Yeats—1: First Reviews and Articles, 1886–1896.* Edited by John P. Frayne. New York: Columbia University Press, 1970.

*UP2* *Uncollected Prose by W. B. Yeats—2: Reviews, Articles, and Other Miscellaneous Prose, 1897–1939.* Edited by John P. Frayne and Colton Johnson. New York: Columbia University Press, 1976.

*VP* *The Variorum Edition of the Poems of W. B. Yeats.* Edited by Russell K. Alspach. New York: Macmillan, 1957; corrected 3rd printing, 1966.

*VPl* *The Variorum Edition of the Plays of W. B. Yeats.* Edited by Russell K. Alspach. New York: Macmillan, 1966; corrected 2nd printing, 1966.

# ILLUSTRATIONS

# EDITORS' INTRODUCTION

This volume of *The Collected Works of W. B. Yeats* contains Yeats's own winnowing of his most important critical essays written during his first fifty years and selected by him for inclusion in the two volumes *Ideas of Good and Evil* (first published 1903) and *The Cutting of an Agate* (first published 1912; revised 1919). They number twenty-nine if we count as one the twenty-one separate short sections that he published under the heading "Discoveries"—nineteen in *Ideas of Good and Evil* and eventually ten more in *The Cutting of an Agate.* They embrace a wide range of topics, including Irish nationalism, magic and mysticism, Japanese Noh drama, essays on contemporaries such as Lady Gregory's nephew John Shawe-Taylor and her and Yeats's collaborator John Synge, and studies of previous poets such as Edmund Spenser, William Shakespeare, William Blake, Percy Bysshe Shelley, and William Morris. The volume also includes in appendices Yeats's original prefaces to both the 1912 and 1919 editions of *The Cutting of an Agate,* the essay "The Pathway" once associated with that grouping, and the most interesting major excisions made by Yeats to the essays, usually when revising them from first publication for inclusion in one of the two volumes (it does not include the original opening essay of *The Cutting of an Agate,* "Thoughts on Lady Gregory's Translations," which may be found in the *Prefaces and Introductions* volume of the present collected edition). *Early Essays* also reproduces fifteen images, including facsimiles of the original covers of these important collections and, for the first time since their initial appearance in *The Savoy* magazine for 1896, of the Blake designs that first accompanied "William Blake and His Illustrations to *The Divine Comedy.*" The documentary record for the construction of both volumes allows for an exceptionally full account of the evolution of these two important works.

## I. IDEAS OF GOOD AND EVIL (1903)

Yeats had planned an edition of his critical prose as early as November 1893, when he told an interviewer that he projected "a collection of essays, and lectures dealing with Irish nationality and literature, which will probably appear under the title of the 'Watch, Fire'" (*UP*1, 302).[1] On 15 February 1898, he told George W. Russell (AE) that "I expect presently to have a book of essays largely on Celtic subjects but partly on mystical subjects . . ." (*CL*2, 188). There is no further reference to such a collection in Yeats's correspondence until 13 April 1901, when he told Lady Gregory that his essay on Shakespeare "will go into the book of essays rather well" (*CL*3, 59). On 22 December 1901, Yeats informed Lady Gregory that the publisher A. H. Bullen had agreed to take "the book of essays" to satisfy the fifty pounds advanced him for the still unfinished (and never to be completed) novel *The Speckled Bird*, under contract since 1896 (*CL*3, 138).

By 9 June 1902, Yeats could tell Lady Gregory, "I am putting my essays together for Bullen" (*CL*3, 199). He must have submitted some material almost at once, as on 19 June 1902, he told Bullen, "I will send you more manuscript for the book of essays from Lady Gregorys, where I shall be after next Monday [23 June]" (*CL*3, 205). On 27 June 1902, he sent Bullen "a lot more of the book of essays," suggesting Blake's engraving of *Francesca and Paolo* as frontispiece (*CL*3, 210–11), a suggestion belatedly honored in the present edition. On 3 July 1902, Yeats sent Bullen his own copy of "The Way of Wisdom" (later "The Pathway") from *The Speaker,* 14 April 1900, though in the end this was not included in *Ideas of Good and Evil.* On 20 November 1902, he wrote Lady Gregory that the edition would be delayed until the publication of "The Happiest of the Poets," which did not appear in *The Fortnightly Review* until March 1903: "I am going to add the Essays I had sketched out in the rough and one or two new little essays" (*CL*3, 257).[2] On 16 December 1902, he told Lady Gregory that he would shortly "wind up the [book?] of which I have dictated some new little essays" (*CL*3, 279). By 15 January 1903, he was "about to correct proofs of essays" (*CL*3, 304). On 6 February 1903, Yeats wrote John Quinn,

"I am very busy just at present, correcting proofs of my book of essays which should be out in March . . ." (*CL*3, 313). On 18 March 1903, he asked Sydney Cockerell, Morris's associate at the Kelmscott Press until its demise, for "advice about the binding" of *Ideas of Good and Evil*: "I should like to have it bound in boards, grey or blue, a white back, bound round with real cords, like one of the examples you showed me" (*CL*3, 331).[3] Despite Yeats's preferences, the book was eventually bound in green paper boards with a darker green spine (see fig. 2). Yeats took the title itself from the "Rossetti Manuscript," where Blake entered the title "Ideas of Good and Evil" facing the first emblem (Ellis-Yeats 1: 202; Erdman, 694). On 5 April 1903, Yeats reminded Bullen not to send the volume for review in Ireland: "Reviews in Dublin papers sell no copies & I don't see why I should give them the oppertunity [*sic*] of attacking me" (*CL*3, 341–42).[4]

As he did with his poems, Yeats took considerable care with the arrangement of his essays for publication and avoided a merely chronological ordering of contents. On the contrary, the two essays published first—"The Moods" and "The Body of Father Christian Rosencrux," both from 1895—came fourteenth and fifteenth in the volume order, while four of the essays published last—"What Is 'Popular Poetry'?," "Speaking to the Psaltery," "Magic," and "The Happiest of the Poets" came first, albeit in different order, with the very last published piece, "Emotion of Multitude," coming also at the very end of the volume. He thus began the collection with a characteristic broadside on the relation of nationalism to popular poetry before moving into more esoteric experiments in speaking verse to music and with magic itself before reaching the heart of the collection, with its essays on Morris, Shelley, Shakespeare, and Blake. After a response to Matthew Arnold's views on Celticism in literature, the volume moved on to consider esoteric doctrines and a fugitive play before concluding with another meditation on Ireland and the arts and then two short pieces, one on Lady Gregory and the other on drama. And while Yeats did not revise the essays as much as he did some of his poems, he did make major changes from earlier published versions, including dropping an entire brief section from "At Stratford-on-Avon," excising all of the illustrations and accompanying brief commentary from "William Blake and His Illustrations

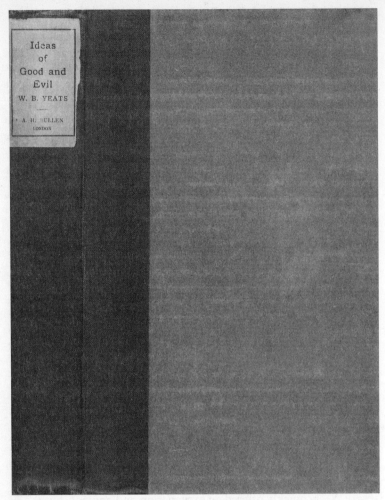


Cover of *Ideas of Good and Evil* (1903)

to *The Divine Comedy,*" and cutting other chunks from "Symbolism in Painting" and "*The Return of Ulysses*" (all of which are reproduced in appendices here, along with original dates of separate publication). He would later add more of his own notes as well as two whole sections to "Speaking to the Psaltery" and tinker with wording throughout.

On 1 May 1903, Yeats told Lady Gregory, "The essays are to be published on May 7th & bound copies should be ready to-day or tomorrow" (*CL*3, 352). *Ideas of Good and Evil* was published by A. H. Bullen in an edition of 1,490 copies, including 520 with an American imprint of the Macmillan Company. There was a second edition of 1,090 copies in 1903, probably in late September or early October (*CL*3, 426, 781); a third edition in 1907 (with Maunsel and Company listed as the Dublin publisher); and a fourth edition in 1914. In 1916 the remainder of the edition was transferred to Macmillan (London). Some sheets of the second edition were issued in Dublin by Maunsel and Company in 1905, and some copies of the second and third editions were also sent to America, where a second edition was published in 1903 as well.[5]

Shortly after publication Yeats regretted the inclusion of part of his introduction to William Thomas Horton's *A Book of Images* (1898) as "Symbolism in Painting." Since he had not asked permission of E. J. Oldmeadow, the publisher of *A Book of Images,* Oldmeadow demanded and got what Yeats called an "exhorbitant" royalty of ten pounds as well as an acknowledgment in the second edition (*CL*3, 379–80).[6] Perhaps worse, Horton was infuriated that Yeats had omitted the third section of the introduction dealing with his work and had indeed not mentioned his name anywhere in the essay. Yeats quickly offered an explanation and apology, but the rift was not quickly—and never fully—healed (*CL*3, 400).[7]

*Ideas of Good and Evil* attracted more than two dozen reviews, most of which stressed the book's affinities with Symbolism, with esotericism, and with Irish nationalism and folk materials. Most reviewers treated *Ideas of Good and Evil* positively, though some were mixed and a few frankly hostile. The first review that Yeats saw, from the *British Weekly* for 21 May, raised his spirits in calling the book "full of profound thought and searching criticism, expressed in a style wonderfully simple and translucent" (*CL*3, 369). Journals that Yeats had written for, such as *The Athenaeum* and *The Monthly Review,* also welcomed the book, the first calling Yeats "a poet with a philosophy" and the second wryly noting that "so exquisite is the English in which he tells us what prosy folk the English are."[8] As might be expected from Yeats's friend Arthur Symons, the *Athenaeum* review stressed Yeats's symbolist side, though Symons allowed himself a brief outburst at Yeats's cavalier attitude toward accuracy in quotation: "Mr. Yeats shares with Coleridge a memory of unfailing and often enlightening inaccuracy; he rewrites his quotations, remodels the title of every second book of which he speaks, and respells the name of any third writer to whom he refers" (808). *The Times Literary Supplement* review was positive though doubtful that Yeats and the symbolists could accomplish all that they promised, while on the other side of the water *The New York Times* in its *Saturday Review of Books and Art* waxed more enthusiastic in praising "the extraordinary beauty of his accomplishment" even while hoping that Yeats would discard some of his more obscure mysticism.[9] Irish reviewers came across perhaps the most harshly. *The Irish Times,* for example, began by observing that "Mr. Yeats is not at his happiest in this small volume of essays" but also praised him for getting "to the core of the matter" about "popular poetry" and cited a "great" passage from "Ireland and the Arts" that "every artist, however humble, should lay to heart." The predictably hostile *The Leader* provided perhaps the nadir of invective, with "Imaal" (J. J. O'Toole) deploring that so much of the book had been published as articles and declaring, "So far as Mr. Yeats and his followers (if he really has any) are concerned, I should say that they are a feather-headed set of pseudo-'originals' . . ."[10]

As so often, Yeats himself served as one of his most acute critics, and his insights illuminate his astonishing development and self-revision over an active career of so many years. On 14 May 1903, he forwarded a copy of the volume to AE with the following comment:

> I send you "Ideas of Good and Evil" a book which will I think have an interest. The only review that has been [published] as yet is as enthusiastic as one could have wished. The book is only one half of the orange for I only got a grip on the other half very lately. I am no

> longer in much sympathy with an essay like the Autumn of the Body, not that I think that essay untrue. But I think I mistook for a permanent phase of the world what was only a preparation. The close of the last century was full of a strange desire to get out of form to get to some kind of disembodied beauty and now it seems to me the contrary impulse has come. I feel about me and in me an impulse to create form, to carry the realisation of beauty as far as possible. The Greeks said that the Dionysisic [*sic*] enthusiasm preceeded the Apollonic and that the Dionysisic was sad and delirious, but that the Apollonic was joyful and self sufficient. Long ago I used to define to myself these two influences as the transfiguration on the mountain and the incarnation, only the Transfiguration comes before the Incarnation in the natural order. I would like to know what you think of the book, and if you could make your Hermitists read it. I have a notion that it would do them a world of good. (*CL*3, 369–70).[11]

Writing to John Quinn the next day, Yeats offered a similar assessment of his work:

> Tomorrow I shall send you my new book "Ideas of Good and Evil". I think you will like it, for it is certainly thoughtful. I feel that much of it is out of my present mood. That it is true but no longer true for me. I have been in a good deal better health lately and that and certain other things has made me look upon the world I think with somewhat more defiant eyes. The book is, I think, too lyrical, too full of aspirations after remote things, too full of desires. Whatever I do from this out will, I think, be more creative. I will express myself so far as I express myself in criticism at all, by that sort of thought that leads straight to action, straight to some sort of craft. I have always felt that the soul has two movements primarily, one to transcend forms, and the other to create forms. Niet[z]sche, to whom you have been the first to introduce me, calls these the Dionysic and the Apollonic respectively. I think I have to some extent got weary of that wild God Dionysius, and I am hoping that the Far-Darter will come in his place. (*CL*3, 372).[12]

## II. THE COLLECTED WORKS IN VERSE AND PROSE (1908)

As early as 30 May 1905, Yeats discussed a comprehensive edition of his canon with A. H. Bullen, telling Lady Gregory that he had agreed "to put off the expensive collected edition until next year" (*L,* 449). The project began to move forward in 1907, helped by a surety from Annie Horniman.[13] As of 12 July 1907, a five-volume edition was projected, but by 26 September 1907, the project had grown to seven volumes. By then Bullen had copy in hand for four volumes, including *Ideas of Good and Evil* (*L,* 494). Eventually the project was published in eight volumes. *Ideas of Good and Evil* comprised volume six, published in November 1908 by the Shakespeare Head Press. Inscribing John Quinn's copy, Yeats noted, "I think the best of these Essays is that on Shakespeare. It is a family exasperation with the Dowden point of view, which rather filled Dublin in my youth. There is a good deal of my father in it, though nothing is just as he would have put it" (*Bibliography,* 90). Volume eight consisted of *Discoveries,* first collected under that title in a limited edition by the Cuala Press on 15 December 1907, and other essays; this collection, published in December 1908, would form the basis for the 1912 *The Cutting of an Agate.*[14]

The 1908 *Collected Works* attracted at least fifteen reviews. Because the overall edition included Yeats's poetry, drama, and other works, the sixth volume containing *Ideas of Good and Evil* received extended mention in only a few of them. Most reviewers responded positively but with occasional ambivalence or reservation, and many highlighted Yeats's Celticism. The anonymous reviewer for *The Saturday Review of Politics, Literature, Science, and Art,* for example, judged that "A great part of the critical work in the sixth volume is admirably sane, though tinged inevitably with the romantic predilection." But the reviewer went on to term the prose "singularly immune from such vapours as we might look for in so 'temperamental' a writer." In a five-page review for *The Month,* Edward Garnett quoted a long passage from "Ireland and the Arts" to support his view that "Mr. Yeats's genius is the latest blossoming and fruiting of the ancient, most persistent roots of Irish feeling in literature."

James Huneker penned one of the most rapturous responses in his collection *The Pathos of Distance,* where he also perceptively noticed the conjunction of Blake and Nietzsche in Yeats's essays. "The artistic creeds of Mr. Yeats are clearly formulated in his collection of prose essays, Ideas of Good and Evil—a very Nietzsche-like title," he wrote. "In this book Blake and Nietzsche are happily compared."[15]

## III. THE CUTTING OF AN AGATE (1912)

The first edition of *The Cutting of an Agate* was published only in the United States. The earliest mention of it is found in a letter of 28 July 1911 to E. M. Lister, secretary to A. H. Bullen:

> If Mr. Bullen does not think it would injure the collected edition I would get out *in America* while the company are there a volume of essays containing (1) *J. M. Synge and the Ireland of his Time* (just published by my sister) (2) *Discoveries* (3) *Literature and Tradition* (4) Essay from the *Mask* (5) *Edmund Spenser.* Let me [know] at once about this. I think it might have a large sale as the players would be there. (*L,* 561)[16]

In the event, *The Cutting of an Agate* would be published in time for the American tour by the Abbey Players of December 1912–May 1913.[17]

By the time the galley proofs were prepared, most likely in July or early August 1912, the contents of *The Cutting of an Agate* had expanded. The extant though incomplete set of galleys in the Berg Collection allows for reconstructing the original contents and order:

"Discoveries"
"Poetry and Tradition"
"J. M. Synge and the Ireland of his Time"
"Thoughts on Lady Gregory's Translations"
"Preface to the First Edition of the *Well of the Saints*"
"Preface to the First Edition of John M. Synge's *Poems and Translations*"
"John Shawe-Taylor"
"Edmund Spenser"
"The Tragic Theatre"

From the two sheets of the first page proofs that survive, dated 26 August 1912, it is apparent that this arrangement had been followed (at least as far as the opening position of *Discoveries*). At this point Yeats may have been queried by the publisher about the order of the essays, as (like the previous collection) it did not follow the accompanying dates; or Yeats may have decided on a revised order on his own. In any case, a second partial set of page proofs, undated, shows (at least up though *Discoveries*) a revised order for the 1912 edition:

Thoughts on Lady Gregory's Translations
Preface to the First Edition of the *Well of the Saints*
Discoveries
Poetry and Tradition
Preface to the First Edition of John M. Synge's *Poems and Translations*
J. M. Synge and the Ireland of his Time
The Tragic Theatre
John Shawe-Taylor
Edmund Spenser

The 1912 collection was more chronological in its ordering than its predecessor *Ideas of Good and Evil* but not wholly so. According to the dates provided, "The Tragic Theatre" (dated "August, 1910") followed rather than preceded "J. M. Synge and the Ireland of his Time" (dated "September 14th, 1910"). Furthermore, "John Shawe-Taylor" (dated "July 1, 1911") was followed by the final piece in *The Cutting of an Agate,* "Edmund Spenser" (dated "October, 1902"), which chronologically came first.[18] The resultant volume thus emphasized Irish material throughout: it began with an account of Lady Gregory's translations from the Irish, moved on to consideration of the work of John Synge and of poetry and tradition in general, and concluded with Lady Gregory's nephew John Shawe-Taylor, with even the final essay on Spenser emphasizing Irish aspects of his life and work. Although the contents of the volume would be rearranged and expanded for the 1919 edition, "Edmund Spenser" would remain the final piece.

As with the earlier volume, Yeats again revised the essays for inclusion in book form. For example, he omitted sections I and II from "Thoughts on Lady Gregory's Translations," omitted several paragraphs at the end of "The Tragic Theatre," and omitted a letter from Synge and his short poem "The Curse" from the "Preface to the First Edition of John M. Synge's *Poems and Translations*" (again, major deletions are contained in appendices or in notes to the essays themselves). Minor corrections continued on the galley proofs. The galleys are corrected in red ink by a copy editor and in black ink by Yeats. Yeats's revisions are relatively minor in comparison with his usual practice. He corrects misprints, and adds or revises punctuation, but makes only a few changes of wording. In "Thoughts on Lady Gregory's Translations," for example, the statement that "the Greeks called myths the activities of the dæmons" changes to "some Greek writer."[19] Likewise, in "Poetry and Tradition" the "'recklessness' or negligence which Castiglione thought necessary in good manners" becomes but "'recklessness.'"

Although only two pages of the first page proofs survive, they make clear that Yeats reviewed this state of the text. However, having just corrected the galleys he was unlikely to have made significant changes. The second partial set of page proofs is uncorrected by Yeats. *The Cutting of an Agate* was eventually published by Macmillan in New York on 13 November 1912. Yeats had copies in hand no later than 4 December 1912, when he inscribed one to Allan Wade (Indiana University). There was no English edition, and notices of the American one were sparse. Stuart P. Sherman's review in *The Nation* focused wholly on Synge and queried Yeats's view of Synge's evolution as a writer, while James W. Tupper's in *The Dial* also stressed Synge though was more open to Yeats's account of his development.[20] Unexpectedly, the volume also inspired a laudatory sonnet by Amy Lowell, "On 'The Cutting of an Agate' by W. B. Yeats," that closed with the couplet "A little handful of this harvesting / Would make most poets an ample covering."[21]

## IV. THE CUTTING OF AN AGATE (1919)

An English edition of *The Cutting of an Agate* followed in 1919. In preparing copy for that version, Yeats decided to omit "Thoughts on Lady Gregory's Translations," which would not be published again in his lifetime.[22] He replaced it with "Certain Noble Plays of Japan,"

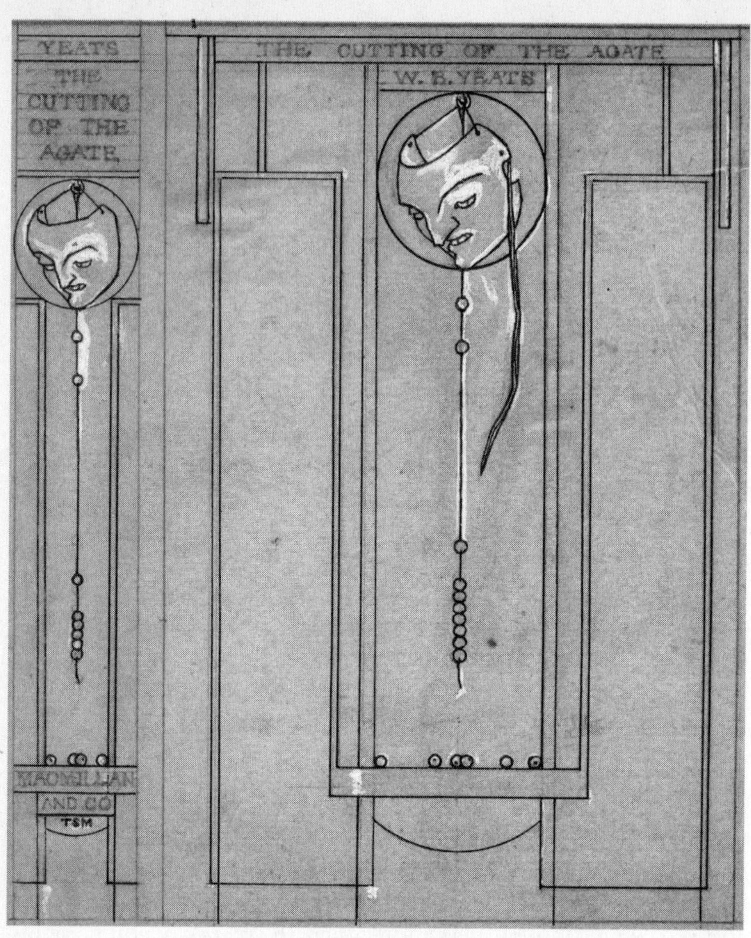


T. Sturge Moore's design for the cover of
*The Cutting of an Agate* (1919)
[Senate House Library, University of London,
MS 978/65/54 (ii)]

first published as the introduction to the Cuala Press *Certain Noble Plays of Japan* (1916) and reprinted in *The Drama* for November 1916. The order of the essays was also rearranged, with chronology now being all but irrelevant:

Certain Noble Plays of Japan
The Tragic Theatre
Poetry and Tradition
Discoveries
Preface to the First Edition of the Well of the Saints
Preface to the First Edition of John M. Synge's Poems and Translations
J. M. Synge and the Ireland of his Time
John Shawe-Taylor
Edmund Spenser

By replacing the discussion of Lady Gregory's translations from the Irish with that of Ezra Pound's adaptations of Japanese drama before moving on to Irish materials and then Spenser, Yeats internationalized the volume and made it one of implicit parallels between East and West.

The cover design reinforced the East/West theme. On 18 December 1918, Yeats wrote Macmillan, "May I ask Mr Sturge Moore to make a design for cover of 'Cutting of an Agate'? He is doing one as you know for 'The Wild Swans at Coole'" (BL, 55003/54). Macmillan agreed to that request in a letter of 20 December 1918, "on the understanding that he would supply it for his usual fee of three guineas" (BL, 55551/294). Moore's design was stamped in gold on the blue front cover and spine (see fig. 3). It featured an Asian mask with a broken rosary hanging from it. The design thus brought East and West together and accorded greater prominence to the essay on Noh drama than that work otherwise would have had.

Although Macmillan told Yeats on 22 February 1919, "We hope to publish 'The Cutting of an Agate' on March 11" (BL, 55552/515), the volume was eventually published on 8 April 1919, in an edition of 1,500 copies. Just as there was no British edition of the 1912 *COA*, so this time was there no American edition of the revised work. Reviews were again mixed. Francis Bickley in *The Bookman* perceptively noted Yeats's penchant for ongoing self-fashioning:

"Of this remaking, his prose essays offer as good evidence as the revisions of his verse." In contrast, the anonymous review in *The Nation* castigated the book repeatedly with comments like "We can think of no other poet whose prose so ill expresses the airy perfection of his genius."[23] Reviews by two well-known poets were again mixed, perhaps with World War I clashing in their minds with Yeats's more exotic tendencies. Walter de la Mare admired many aspects of Yeats but thought that "He engraves his fine prose for a little clan." Most damningly of all, T. S. Eliot declared in *The Athenaeum* that "Mr. Yeats . . . as much in his prose as in his verse, is not 'of this world'—*this* world, of course, being our visible planet with whatever our theology or myth may conceive as below or above it."[24]

## V. ESSAYS (1924)

*Ideas of Good and Evil* and *The Cutting of an Agate* were revised and included with *Per Amica Silentia Lunae* (1918) in *Essays* (1924). In addition to providing several footnotes, Yeats added to "Speaking to the Psaltery" in *Ideas of Good and Evil* two new sections, first published in the 1908 *Collected Works*; and he expanded *The Cutting of an Agate* to ten essays by including as the penultimate item "Art and Ideas," first published in *The New Weekly* for 20 and 27 June 1914. The new sections of the first essay highlighted the contributions of Florence Farr; indeed, the final new section (part V) bore the title "Note by Florence Farr upon Her Settings." Adding "Art and Ideas" to *Agate* provided a major recent meditation on Yeats's evolving view of art, one that again subordinated opinion and ideas to energy and spiritual unity.

*Essays* was the fourth in the six-volume collected edition of the works published by Macmillan from 1922 to 1926.[25] Yeats had been anxious for some time about such a project, which had been a part of his agreement with Macmillan on 27 June 1916 (BL, 54898/138). Early in January 1922, Yeats sent to his agent A. S. Watt (who had succeeded his father at the agency A. P. Watt & Son) a plan for a six-volume collected works, with *Essays* as the fifth volume (BL, 54848/55). Watt forwarded Yeats's letter to Macmillan on 10 January 1922; Macmillan replied to Watt on 12 January 1922, suggesting a meeting the following day (BL, 55576/106).

In the event, Watt was again not especially successful in convincing Macmillan of the wisdom of Yeats's proposal. On 18 January 1922, Macmillan wrote to Watt offering to publish only three volumes of poems and plays:

> We cannot however undertake at this point to publish any further volumes, and it must be distinctly understood that we are not to announce or bind ourselves in any way to issue more than the poetical and dramatic works. There is of course nothing to prevent the publication of three or four more volumes of prose in time to come if it seems reasonable (BL, 55576/243).

Watt replied on 20 January 1922, reminding Macmillan of the 1916 agreement (BL, 54898/138). But the publishers were adamant: responding on 23 January 1922, they offered two reasons for the refusal to undertake a larger edition:

> In the first place, if we were to announce an edition containing the prose works it would at once put out of action all the separate editions of the prose works which are now on sale and of which, as you know, we have a very considerable stock. Secondly, it would be impossible for us to publish as a complete work, and ask payment for it, the Large Paper Edition of the Poetical and Dramatic Works if, as you suggest, the publication of the prose works was announced but not immediately carried out.[26]

Further, Macmillan argued that "Unless I am very much mistaken Mr. Yeats himself suggested in a letter which he wrote about a year ago that the present publication should consist of the Poetical and Dramatic Works, so our proposal is not in any way new" (BL, 55576/381).[27]

Watt apparently replied on 6 February 1922 with a further suggestion from Yeats. Macmillan wrote to Watt on 10 February 1922 that

> I think that we had better fall in with Mr. Yeats's latest suggestion, which I take to be (1.) that we should publish a volume of poems to contain all the poems hitherto published by Mr. Yeats which are not

> included in Fisher Unwin's volume; and (2) a volume of plays to contain what originally appeared under the title of 'Plays for an Irish Theatre' and such others of his plays as are at our disposal, which I take to be 'The Golden Helmet', 'Unicorn from the Stars' and 'Pot of Broth' (BL, 55576/875).

Thus both *Later Poems* and *Plays in Prose and Verse* were published by Macmillan on 3 November 1922.

Yeats persisted about additional volumes. On 4 January 1923, he asked Watt to propose to Macmillan "that they bring out two new volumes of their Collected Edition of my work," *The Irish Dramatic Movement* and *Stories and Early Poetry* (BL, 54898/217). Macmillan agreed to this plan in a letter of 9 January 1923 (BL, 55585/13).[28] *The Irish Dramatic Movement* was the first to go to press, ending up as part of *Plays and Controversies* (1923). In their letter of 27 June acknowledging receipt of copy for that edition, Macmillan noted, "There is no great hurry about the second volume. I think that on the whole it would be better to publish one volume at a time; but of course we will take the 'copy' for the second volume as soon as Mr. Yeats can send it" (BL, 55589/344).

Yeats's receipt of the Nobel Prize modified the schedule for the collected works. On 20 November 1923, Watt wrote to Macmillan, quoting a letter from Yeats "just received":

> I think it very important to make as much use as I can of this new wave of interest in my work. It will probably affect the American reading public more than the English for the American reading public has less confidence in its own judgment. We might perhaps urge the Macmillan Co. in New York to bring out LATER POEMS, PLAYS IN PROSE AND VERSE, and PLAYS AND CONTROVERSIES, as soon as possible. I think it will be better for the London House to follow PLAYS AND CONTROVERSIES with a volume containing all my Critical Essays, instead of the book containing early Poems and Stories which I had suggested. If they will agree to this I will send them the material as soon as I return from Stockholm at latest. I go to Stockholm on December 3rd. and wont return till near Christmas. I may however be able to send the material next week. It should be hurried on as quickly as possible both in England and America (BL, 54898/280).

On 26 November 1923, Macmillan agreed to Yeats's proposal. Yeats managed to submit copy before leaving for Stockholm; Macmillan acknowledged its receipt from Watt on 10 December 1923, promising that "the printing . . . shall be put in hand at once" (BL, 55594/575). Yeats read proofs carefully from late January through the end of March, going through the volume twice: once in slips or galley proofs and again in page proofs. Surviving letters from his agent Watt to Macmillan attest to the return of corrected slips on 11, 14, and 23 February 1924. Another series of letters indicates the return of corrected page proofs on 6, 13, and 18 March, with further corrections to three pages of "Art and Ideas" following on 1 April.[29] *Essays* was published by Macmillan on 6 May 1924 in an edition of 2,240 copies. An American edition followed on 14 October 1924, with a signed limited edition on 26 October 1924.[30]

Like previous volumes of the collected edition published 1922–26, *Essays* carried a largely geometric design (though with a bird in each corner) by Charles Ricketts stamped blind on the front cover and spine, with gold lettering on the spine. White endpapers featured a unicorn, hawk, fountain, moon, and stars in black inside the front and back covers (see figs. 4 and 5). The designs delighted Yeats, who wrote enthusiastically to Ricketts from Merrion Square on November 1922 after receiving the uniformly designed *Later Poems* and *Plays in Prose and Verse*:

> Yesterday my wife brought the books up to my study, and not being able to restrain her excitement I heard her cry out before she reached the door "You have perfect books at last." Perfect they are—serviceable and perfect. The little design of the unicorn is a masterpiece in that difficult kind. You have given my work a decoration of which one will never tire and all I have done will gradually be put into this form. It is a pleasure to me to think that many young men here and elsewhere will never know my work except in this form. My own memory proves to me that at 17 there is an identity between an author's imagination and paper and bookcover one does not find in later life. I still do not quite separate Shelley from the green covers, or Blake from the blue covers and brown reproductions of pictures, of the books in which I first read them. I do not separate Rossetti at all from his covers (*L*, 691).

Cover of *Essays* (1924) by Charles Ricketts

Endpaper of *Essays* (1924) by Charles Ricketts

The volume garnered more than a dozen reviews, mostly respectful but sometimes mixed, with few as enthusiastic as Yeats's response to Ricketts's designs. At the most positive end, his old friend George Russell boomed the essays as "the only contribution of any importance made by an Irish writer to an Irish philosophy of literature and drama" and declared, "Hardly any literary critic excites us more than Yeats." Other reviewers showed respect but caution, often associating Yeats with the nineties, with Ireland, and with mysticism, and disagreeing about its permanent value. George Sampson writing in *The Bookman*, for example, declared, "I think his best criticism is as sure of perpetuity as Shelley's, for it is the finest of all criticism, a poet's criticism." In contrast, Norreys Jephson O'Conor, writing in *The Saturday Review of Literature,* judged that the essays "belong definitely to a period, rather than to permanent literature."[31] *The Times Literary Supplement* combined both positions. "This ideal of passive contemplation, of self-forgetfulness in self-absorption, which Mr. Yeats shares with the fakir, is not without its dangers to the artist . . . ," intoned the reviewer. "But as an interpreter of pure aesthetic values, of mystical or metaphysical art, or of the Celtic element in literature, he has made a contribution to his time in prose which we believe to be as sure of permanence as much of his poetry." That balanced assessment was doubtless more welcome than the jaunty boosterism of *The New York Evening Post Literary Review*, which proclaimed *Essays* "a book for the happy dabbler."[32]

## VI. THE EDITION DE LUXE AND THE SCRIBNER EDITION

By February 1930, Macmillan had become interested in publishing a limited edition of Yeats's major works. The project was discussed during the year, with Yeats writing Olivia Shakespear on 27 December 1930 that "Macmillan are going to bring out an Edition de Luxe of all my work published and unpublished. . . . I am to be ready next autumn at latest. Months of re-writing. What happiness!" (*L,* 780). The formal contract, dated 17 April 1931, was sent by Macmillan to Watt on 20 April 1931 (BL, 55715/241) and returned signed by Yeats on 4 May 1931 (BL, 54901/160).[33] Macmillan undertook to publish the edition no "later than the 30th day of September 1932"; but as it turned out, the marginal addenda "unless prevented by circumstances over which they had no control" proved prophetic.

Yeats submitted copy for six of the seven planned volumes when he met with Harold Macmillan on 1 June 1931 (BL, 54901/171). As he explained to an interviewer shortly thereafter, he had yet to submit any material for volume seven, which would be "entirely philosophical, with a small amount of fantastic romance."[34] Since *Essays*, the fifth volume, was identical in content to the 1924 edition (*Ideas of Good and Evil, The Cutting of an Agate*, and *Per Amica Silentia Lunae*), Yeats presumably submitted a copy of the volume, possibly with corrections.

On 13 April 1932, Yeats and Harold Macmillan met for a discussion of the project. Macmillan summarized the results of that meeting in a letter to Yeats two days later, noting of *Essays,* "You intend to let us have three or four additional essays for this volume" (BL, 55727/271–73). By the time of Yeats's letter to Macmillan on 27 September 1932, he planned to increase the number of additional pieces to five (BL, 55003/137). Around this time it is possible, though unlikely, that Yeats may have been sent a proof of *Essays*.[35]

Over the next few years Macmillan continued to postpone publication of the Edition de Luxe. In November 1935, Yeats received an offer from Charles Scribner's Sons in New York to publish a similar edition in America. By May 1936, Yeats was "favorably inclined" toward the proposal.[36] By early October 1936, the arrangements had been completed.

Yeats thus met with Watt on 23 October 1936, and asked him to obtain from Macmillan "a note of the contents of the De Luxe edition of his works which you are proposing to publish when the proper time comes" (BL, 54903/133), presumably so that Yeats could ensure that the contents of the two editions were essentially identical. Macmillan prepared two copies of a nine-page typed document headed "W. B. YEATS / DE LUXE EDITION" and forwarded them to Watt on 27 October 1936 (BL, 55786/497), asking Yeats to annotate and return one copy and retain the other. Watt was able to send the copy with Yeats's comments to Macmillan on 10 November 1936 (BL, 54903/148), Macmillan receiving it on 12 November 1936 (BL, 55787/362).

This list indicates that Yeats had expanded *Essays* by four items:

"Bishop Berkeley," "My Friend's Book," "Prometheus Unbound," and "Introduction to 'An Indian Monk'" (NLI, 30,202).[37] The new works are prefaced by a query: "A group of reviews for which we have no title. Should this section be called 'Reviews' and the title of the volume altered to 'Essays and Reviews'?" Yeats's response was "No there are far more 'Introductions' to books than reviews." He then listed a number of additional items to be included, even though Macmillan had indicated that "The present extent of this volume is about 476 pages."

In January 1937, Yeats prepared tables of contents for the Scribner edition and sent them to Watt, who forwarded them to New York on 28 January 1937 (Princeton). The list for volume V indicates that *Essays* had been even further expanded.[38] Yeats also noted that the *Ideas of Good and Evil*, *The Cutting of an Agate*, and *Per Amica Silentia Lunae* were "to be printed from 'Essays' Macmillan & Co London." Scribner's thus proceeded to acquire a photostatic copy of the 1924 edition (HRC). However, the publishers were unable to proceed with the project because they lacked various other materials, and a series of letters and cables ensued to both Watt and their agent in London, Charles Kingsley. Yeats may well have been at last spurred to action by a letter from Macmillan, which he would have received on 7 June 1937, asking about additional poems for the Edition de Luxe (BL, 55795/298), as well as by his scheduled departure for London the next day. He took out his copy of the 1936 Edition de Luxe list and made further annotations. After his departure, his wife prepared new tables of contents for the Scribner edition, which she sent in segments to Watt, along with copy, from 11 to 22 June 1937.[39]

The list for volume 5 is dated 22 June 1937. Scribner's was likely less than delighted with its content: "This will be delayed owing to final proofs of new essays not yet ready," a reference to *Essays: 1931–1936*, not to be published by the Cuala Press until 14 December 1937. In early October 1937, Yeats asked Macmillan to delay printing of volume IV (*Plays II*) until he could supply proofs from Scribner's. The publishers replied on 13 October 1937:

> We were not thinking of proceeding with the printing of Volumes IV [*Plays II*] and V [*Essays*] of the Edition de Luxe, but were about to

> obtain clean revises containing the new material which is to be included. It will be quite convenient for us to wait, as you kindly suggest, until you can let us have the proofs of the Scribner edition now in preparation. (BL, 55800/447)

They would wait in vain, as would Yeats's readers, for the publication of either the Edition de Luxe or the Scribner edition. Nor was Macmillan particularly enthusiastic about the idea of a "Collected Essays" that had been discussed in a meeting with Yeats on 22 June 1937, explaining that given the slow sales of *Essays* (1924), they preferred to "let the question of the possible Collected Essays stand over for the time being" (BL, 55796/224–26).[40]

Yeats's continuing involvement with the Edition de Luxe clarifies the vexed issue of "Explorations" and "Discoveries" as volume titles. The record establishes that he planned to use "Explorations" rather than "Discoveries" as the title for that section of *The Cutting of an Agate*. A draft of a letter from Macmillan to Mrs. Yeats circa 1960 recalls the revision:

> As regards the use of 'Explorations' ~~instead~~ in place of 'Discoveries['], T. M. [Thomas Mark] remembers that the instruction was given by WBY on material that was presumably returned to him with the first proofs. 'Discoveries' was to be ~~used as~~ the title of the volume containing *A Vision* and its associated essays in the Coole Edition. ~~'Explorations' was used as the title of that section part of The Cutting of an Agate in the first proofs of that edition.~~

A marginal comment adds "~~Those pro~~ 'Explorations' was actually used on those proofs (1932)" (BL, 55896).[41]

In contrast, *Discoveries* as a volume title is attested by a letter from Macmillan to Yeats on 15 April 1932 (BL, 55727/271–73). It also appears on a 27 October 1936 Macmillan list of contents for the Edition de Luxe and the January 1937 Scribner list. However, on the latter Yeats cancelled *Discoveries* and offered only *A Vision*, noting, "This must be taken from the new edition now in the press. It will be published by Macmillan & Co." *A Vision* is also the title on the June 1937 Scribner list and for the published volume of 19 October 1937. It is not clear whether Yeats intended *A Vision* to be used for the Edition de Luxe as well. If so, he must have changed his mind by the time he met with his publishers in the autumn of 1938.[42]

*Discoveries* as a volume title—which would preclude its use for a section of *The Cutting of an Agate*—was Yeats's final choice for the volume containing *A Vision,* at least for the Edition de Luxe. It is found on the materials for the prospectus for the Edition de Luxe prepared shortly after Yeats's death. Proofs of *Discoveries* (as well as of *Essays* and *Mythologies*) were sent to Mrs. Yeats on 26 June 1939 (BL, 55826/50). Accordingly, "Explorations" was used as a section title on both the 1949 and 1959 proofs of *The Cutting of an Agate.* In the event, though, Yeats's decision about that title was to be ignored. The circa 1960 draft letter to Mrs. Yeats quoted above continues:

> In view of a suggestion Mark has made, we think it would be a good idea to restore 'Discoveries' to the *Essays and Introductions* vol. It would only affect twenty page headings and would allow 'Explorations' to be used as the title of another possible collection of the remaining prose works. (BL, 55896)

Mrs. Yeats was agreed, as suggested by her letter sending a copy of *Mythologies* (1959) to Thomas MacGreevy on 17 August 1959:

> Herewith 'Mythologies'. The title was chosen by WBY in 1938—I do not like title, but even less do I like a change he made from 'Discoveries' to 'Explorations' which occurs in the forthcoming 'Essays' (TCD MS, 8104/91).[43]

Accordingly, the 22 September 1959 page proofs of *Essays and Introductions* (1961) include the instruction "Explorations to be called Discoveries" with the notation "Done" (BL, 55895). The title *Explorations* thus became available for a second collection of Yeats's prose, published in 1962, although that procedure contradicted Yeats's own intentions.

## VII. THE COOLE EDITION

Yeats's death precipitated a flurry of activity on the Edition de Luxe, renamed the Coole Edition by Mrs. Yeats on 15 April 1939 (NLI,

30,248). A printed prospectus was prepared and probably sent to Mrs. Yeats on 28 February 1939 (BL, 55820/203–5). The edition had been expanded to eleven volumes. *Essays* was divided into volumes 10 and 11, both entitled *Essays and Reviews* by Macmillan but revised by Mrs. Yeats to *Essays* (10) and *Essays and Introductions* (11). Moreover, *Per Amica Silentia Lunae* had replaced *The Irish Dramatic Movement* in *Mythologies,* volume 8. Volume 10 thus contained *Ideas of Good and Evil* and *The Irish Dramatic Movement,* volume 11 *The Cutting of an Agate* and what one version of the prospectus called "Miscellaneous later and unpublished papers" (Princeton). Although the editors of *The Secret Rose* claim that these changes "had been instigated by Thomas Mark at the time of drawing up the 'Preliminary Notice'" for the edition, it is clear that most if not all of the revisions were made at the autumn 1938 meeting noted above.[44]

On 14 April 1939, Thomas Mark wrote to Mrs. Yeats:

> There were some queries I was going to submit to Mr Yeats when I went through the revised proofs, and I should be glad to have your advice on some points if it would not be troubling you too much. The most important problem relates to some quotations from Blake. I was interested in the subject, and looked them up in what seemed to be the authoritative edition, but I found that the text differed considerably from that quoted by Mr Yeats. It seemed, as a matter of fact, to be a much better text, and I wonder if [you] would like the alterations made as marked on the pages of proofs enclosed herewith. Please let me know if you would rather let questions like these be decided here (BL, 55882/342–44).

Mrs. Yeats addressed the matter of quotations on 15 April 1939 (NLI, 30,248) and again on 7 June 1939, indicating in the latter that

> I think that the Blake quotations should, on the whole, be left as they are; for one reason, WBY repeats passages or one or two words often in other work, (he makes many of these quotations from his and Ellis' three volume Blake which was written at a time when there was no authoritative text; indeed, he copied such things as "Ahania" and "Vala" etc from manuscripts in various libraries. These copies made

> by him I have.) There are, however, a few obvious misprints, such as "owl from the beast" instead of "oak from the beech", which have obviously arisen from a printer not being able to read his writing. One can easily see how this particular misprint arose![45]

Mark acknowledged that letter on 12 June 1939:

> If you do not mind, I will let you see these passages again with the proofs of the whole book to make sure that I have understood your instructions. The other corrections you have supplied will all be inserted. I think that many of them have already been made, but it is most useful to have them confirmed in this way. . . .
> I should feel more at ease if you would let me send you any marked proofs of all the volumes before they go to press, as there are always one or two points on which I should like your advice (BL, 55825/171).

Finally, on 26 June 1939, Mark told Mrs. Yeats, "I am sending you to-day the marked proofs of Volumes VIII, IX and X, 'Mythologies', 'Discoveries', and 'Essays', with the marked proofs of Volume VIII. The other two volumes were not read by Mr. Yeats" (BL, 55826/50). Mark received the corrected proofs of what was now *Discoveries* on 14 July 1939 (BL, 55827/53). But there is no record of Mrs. Yeats returning the proofs of *Essays*. If she had not corrected *Essays* prior to receiving Mark's query about *Samhain*, which would have reached her on 6 or 7 July 1939, she likely would have waited for the arrival of the revised set of proofs.

When Mark finally received the corrected proofs of *Last Poems & Plays* on 19 October 1939, he had to inform Mrs. Yeats that the Coole Edition "has to wait for better times" (BL, 55830/334).[46] Even so, Mark asked her in that letter and again on 3 January 1940 if he could send her the proofs of volume 11, *Essays and Introductions,* but she does not seem to have replied (BL, 55830/334, 55833/223).[47] It is thus nearly certain that Mrs. Yeats's work at this time on the two volumes of *Essays* was, at most, a review of the proofs of the first volume.

## VIII. THE ABANDONED *ESSAYS* (1949)

In 1949 Macmillan planned an extensive collection of Yeats's prose—all of the material from volumes 10 and 11 of the Coole Edition except *The Irish Dramatic Movement.* Since *Ideas of Good and Evil* had been in volume 10 and *The Cutting of an Agate* in volume 11, on 14 June 1949 a new set of page proofs of those two works was prepared (BL, 55894). The "Other Essays" and the "Introductions" on the "Fourth Proof" of volume 11, with date stamps of 19 July 1939, were renumbered to follow *The Cutting of the Agate* on the new proofs.[48] The result would have been a volume of 625 pages of text. Macmillan was likely planning to issue this version of *Essays* in conjunction with the two-volume limited edition of *The Poems of W. B. Yeats,* which was published on 25 November 1949. In the event, however, the work was abandoned, and it would be over a decade before any of the projected volume was published.

Although both sets of proofs are corrected only by Mark, it is clear that Mrs. Yeats reviewed them, though whether in 1939, 1949, and/or a decade later is uncertain. For instance, next to the quotation from *Vala* which concludes "William Blake and the Imagination," Mark has noted "Mrs. Yeats says this is incorrect and asks if it should be referred to a Blake scholar or left as it is." Again, Mark has noted in pencil next to Yeats's reference to "Athene helmed 'in silver or electron,'" "Isn't it the spear that is 'of silver or electron.'" Although the passage from Robert Bridges just quoted indeed referred to "a spear / Of silver or electron," Mark later added in ink "Mrs. Yeats says stet" (BL, 55894).

## IX. ESSAYS AND INTRODUCTIONS (1961)

A decade after the 1949 volume failed to achieve publication, Macmillan again decided to produce an edition of Yeats's critical prose, *Essays and Introductions.* The contents were essentially identical to the expanded version of *Essays* planned for the Scribner edition in 1937. Page proofs were printed starting 22 September 1959 (BL, 55882).[49] A second proof of the 1949 page proofs provided the copy for *Ideas of Good and Evil* and *The Cutting of an Agate.* The first page of the 1959 proofs is headed "Essays and Introductions / Marked proofs for / Mrs. Yeats." Proof correction was a collaboration between Mrs. Yeats and Lovat Dickson, who had replaced the retired Thomas Mark at Macmillan, London. Dickson sent the proofs to Mrs. Yeats on 5 May 1960, and she returned them in two segments, later that month and on 23 July 1960 (NLI, 30,775; BL, 55895). As William H. O'Donnell has noted, Mrs. Yeats "replied to queries and paid much attention to improving the accuracy of Yeats's quotations" (*LE,* 472). While well intentioned, this "improving" did contradict Yeats's own intentions expressed through a variety of printings over many years, sometimes involved texts that he did not use, and occasionally introduced new problems of its own.

*Essays and Introductions* was published by Macmillan in London on 16 February 1961 and in New York on 31 May 1961. *Ideas of Good and Evil* and *The Cutting of an Agate* were at last back in print. Forty-six years later, we offer the present annotated edition. As with other volumes in the series, we have honored Yeats's final intentions as expressed by the written record. We thus use as copy-text the final versions of the essays as contained in *Essays* (London, 1924), with conservative emendations involving primarily obvious errors or misprints. At the same time, we gesture toward other states of those texts by including major dropped sections in appendices and incorporating shorter but interesting revisions into the notes (though of course we do not aim at a variorum edition). We also annotate direct references in the text and include facsimile reproductions of lost material features of earlier texts, such as book covers or Blake illustrations. *Early Essays* thus alerts readers to other forms of these texts even while offering them this particular one.

## Notes to Introduction

1. The unpublished poem "The Watch-Fire" may have been intended as an epigraph for this collection. See *Under the Moon: The Unpublished Early Poetry,* ed. George Bornstein (New York: Scribner, 1995), 93.
2. Presumably the new material included "The Galway Plains," first published in *The New Liberal Review* for March 1903, and "Emotion of Multitude," first published in *The All Ireland Review* for 11 April 1903.

3. Besides the green boards and spine, *Ideas of Good and Evil* carried a white label printed in black. Cords, which would have added to the expense of the binding, were not used.
4. Nevertheless, at least three Irish reviews were published: *The Irish Times* for 22 May 1903; by John Eglinton in *The United Irishman* for 27 June 1903; and by "Imaal" (J. J. O'Toole) in *The Leader* for 26 September 1903. As indicated below, none was favorable.
5. Despite the 2,580 copies of the 1903 editions of *Ideas of Good and Evil,* Foster notes that "By June 1904 the total income made by *The Celtic Twilight* and *Ideas of Good and Evil* was less than £100, swallowed by advances . . ." (I: 314).
6. The acknowledgment was printed opposite the beginning of "What is 'Popular Poetry'?" The essay on "Symbolism in Painting" originally formed part of an Introduction to *A Book of Images drawn by W. T. Horton* (London: Unicorn Press, 1898).
7. Presumably Horton never discovered that the acknowledgment disappeared in the third edition!
8. *"Ideas of Good and Evil," The Athenaeum,* 27 June 1903, 807; "On the Line," *The Monthly Review,* October 1903, 96.
9. "The Essays of a Symbolist," *The Times Literary Supplement,* 12 June 1903, 184–85; "Ideas of Mr. Yeats," *The New York Times, Saturday Review of Books and Art,* 11 July 1903, 477–78.
10. "Ideas of Good and Evil," *The Irish Times,* 22 May 1903, 7; "A Rather Complex Personality," *The Leader,* 26 September 1903, 71.
11. The review was presumably that in the *British Weekly* for 14 May 1903, which noted that "to many of us it will seem the most important book of criticism that has been published in a long time . . ." (*CL*3, 369n1).
12. Almost thirty years later, in a letter of 24 December 1932 to Horace Reynolds about *Letters to the New Island* (1934), Yeats noted, "It seems to me that I remember almost the day and hour when revising for some reprint my essay upon the Celtic movement (in 'Ideas of Good and Evil') I saw clearly the unrealities and half-truths propaganda had involved me in, and the way out. All one's life one struggles towards reality, finding always but new veils" (*LNI,* xviii).
13. See Foster 1:371. Bullen requested a surety of £1,500 (1: 599n64). Foster's statement that "Since January 1907 discussion had been under way" about the collected edition (1: 371) apparently overlooks the 1905 letter to Lady Gregory.
14. The volume offered "Discoveries," "Edmund Spenser," "Poetry and Tradition," "Modern Irish Poetry," "Note [on *Stories of Red Hanrahan*]," "Lady Gregory's 'Cuchulain of Muirthemne,'" "Lady Gregory's 'Gods and Fighting Men,'" "Mr. Synge and his Plays," "Lionel Johnson," and "The Pathway," followed by bibliographical items by Allan Wade and John Quinn. The essays carried over to the 1912 *The*

*Cutting of an Agate* would be "Discoveries"; "Edmund Spenser"; the two items on Lady Gregory's work, retitled "Thoughts on Lady Gregory's Translations"; and "Mr. Synge and his Plays," retitled "Preface to the First Edition of the *Well of the Saints*."

Volume 3 of the *Collected Works* also published for the first time what would become parts 4 and 5 of "Speaking to the Psaltery": "Music for Lyrics" and "Note by Florence Farr."

15. *The Saturday Review of Politics, Literature, Science, and Art,* 27 February 1909, 280; *The Month,* April 1909, 148–52; James Huneker, *The Pathos of Distance: A Book of a Thousand and One Moments* (New York: Charles Scribner's Sons, 1913), 226.
16. *Synge and the Ireland of his Time* had been published by the Cuala Press just two days before Yeats's letter. "Literature and Tradition" is an error for "Poetry and Tradition," first published as "Poetry and Patriotism" in *Poetry and Ireland: Essays by W. B. Yeats and Lionel Johnson* (Dundrum: Cuala Press, 1908) and included as "Poetry and Tradition" in volume eight of the *Collected Works in Verse and Prose* (1908). The fourth item is "The Tragic Theatre," first published in *The Mask* (October 1910), revised and used as the preface to *Plays for an Irish Theatre* (London and Stratford-upon-Avon: A. H. Bullen, 1911), and revised again for *The Cutting of an Agate.*

    Foster twice notes that Yeats was also concerned about protecting the copyright of the Cuala volume in America (1: 421, 445).
17. For the dates of the Abbey tours, see Robert Hogan, Richard Burnham, and Daniel P. Poteet, *The Modern Irish Drama: A Documentary History, The Rise of the Realists, 1910–1915,* vol. 4, (Dublin: Dolmen Press, 1979), 134, 206.
18. Despite Yeats's date, it was only on 31 December 1902 that he was able to tell Lady Gregory, "I have finished the essay on Spenser" (*CL3,* 290); the edition itself was not published until October 1906. Yeats's preface to *The Cutting of an Agate,* dated "August, 1912" and composed with the order of the galley proofs in mind, begins with an extended comment on "Edmund Spenser" and then moves forward more or less chronologically.
19. The identity of this supposed writer remains elusive. In "The Stirring of the Bones," Yeats ascribed the remark to an 1896 comment by a member of the Order of the Golden Dawn: "One of my fellow-students quoted a Greek saying, 'Myths are the activities of the Daimons'" (*Au,* 281).
20. "John Synge," *The Nation,* 26 December 1912, 608–11; "J. M. Synge and his Work," *The Dial,* 16 March 1913, 233–35.
21. *Complete Poetical Works of Amy Lowell* (Boston: Houghton Mifflin, 1955), 591. The sonnet was first published in *Poetry and Drama* 2 (September 1914): 291.
22. See *P&I,* 119–34, 224–26, and 325–27. For *The Cutting of an Agate*

(1912), Yeats omitted the opening sections of what had been first published as the preface to Lady Gregory's *Cuchulain of Muirthemne* (1902) and included as "Lady Gregory's 'Cuchulain of Muirthemne'" in the 1908 *Collected Works in Verse and Prose.* Thus no longer present was the comment on *Cuchulain of Muirthemne* recalled by James Joyce in *Ulysses* (1922): "I think this book is the best that has come out of Ireland in my time. Perhaps I should say that it is the best book that has ever come out of Ireland . . ." (*P&I,* 224).

As William H. O'Donnell has noted, the text in *Explorations* (1962) derives from the 1902 and 1904 prefaces and thus overlooks Yeats's revisions (*P&I,* 237).

23. "Mr. Yeats's Odyssey," *The Bookman,* August 1919, 174; "Mr. Yeats in Prose," *The Nation,* 28 June 1919, 395.
24. "A Lapidary," *TLS,* 1 May 1919, 235; "A Foreign Mind," *The Athenaeum,* 4 July 1919, 552. Both reviews may also be found in *W. B. Yeats: The Critical Heritage,* ed. A. Norman Jeffares (London: Routledge and Kegan Paul, 1977), 226–32.
25. The others were *Later Poems* (1922), *Plays in Prose and Verse* (1922), *Plays and Controversies* (1923), *Early Poems and Stories* (1925), and *Autobiographies* (1926).
26. In a letter of 18 January 1922, Macmillan had indicated that they were "prepared to publish a Definitive Edition of the Poems and Plays in three volumes" and that "we should also propose to issue an edition limited to 250 copies on large paper to be sold only in sets at a higher price" (BL, 55576/243–44).
27. Macmillan is referring to an alternate proposal that Yeats had made in a letter of 23 December [1920]: "Another scheme would be to bring out 'Collected Poetical Works of W B Yeats' in 3 vols (1 of lyrical & narrative work & 2 vols of plays) and to leave the prose works till later. The objection to this is you will hardly want to include contents of 'Four Plays for Dancers' (this however might be added in a fourth volume some years later or as a new section at end of vol 3 when the present edition is exhausted" (BL, 55003/65).
28. Macmillan was no doubt motivated by the fact that "We have sold over 1,200 copies of Later Poems and over 900 of Plays in Prose and Verse" (BL, 55585/13).
29. *The Collected Letters of W. B. Yeats,* accession numbers 4476, 4478, 4484, 4495, 4496, 4498, and 4506 (*InteLex*).
30. On 22 April 1924, Watt passed on a request by Macmillan, New York, that Yeats sign sheets for 250 copies each for limited editions of the four volumes of the collected works. Yeats responded to Watt on 27 April 1914, "We should have notice of this matter some time ago. . . . If they are really going to bring out a very fine edition (American ideas of fine are seldom mine) I don't want to thwart them, though being a very lazy man an extra royalty of £12: 10: 0: ~~on each volume of~~ on each

new book of the collected edition, considering the price Macmillan will get & all the procrastination I shall go through, does not seem to me generous for signing my name 250 times" (Berg). Watt may have been able to negotiate better terms: on 19 May 1924 Yeats replied to a letter from Watt on 12 May 1924, indicating "I now accept Macmillan Companys terms & will send them the signed sheets as soon as possible" (Berg). Macmillan published limited editions of the first three volumes of the collected works on 16 September 1924.

31. "Literature and Life," *The Irish Statesman,* 7 June 1924, 397; "Two Ways of Criticism," *The Bookman,* July 1924, 201; and "A Pioneer in Retrospect," *The Saturday Review of Literature,* 9 May 1925, 738.
32. "Mr. Yeats's Prose," *The Times Literary Supplement,* 22 May 1924, 318; "In Quest of Poesy," *The New York Evening Post Literary Review,* 6 December 1924, 4.
33. We are grateful to Linda Shaughnessy of A P Watt Ltd for a copy of the contract.
34. See Louise Morgan, *Writers at Work* (London: Chatto and Windus, 1931), 8–9. The missing volume, then called *Discoveries,* would have included the first version of *A Vision* and other items.
35. A set of proofs for *Essays* was produced in June 1931 (Lanham, 94). Yeats met with Macmillan to discuss the Edition de Luxe on 13 April 1932 (BL, 55727/271–73). The publishers then began sending proofs in volume order, beginning with *Poems* (vol. 1) on 7 June 1932 (BL, 55729/477), followed by *Mythologies* (vol. 2) on 22 June 1932 (BL, 55729/605), *Plays I* (vol. 3) on 25 July 1932 (BL, 55731/85), and *Autobiographies* (vol. 6) on 23 August 1932 (BL, 55731/569). On 7 July 1932 Macmillan had promised to send the remaining proofs of the Edition de Luxe "before you leave Ireland early in October" (BL, 55730/301). However, there is no record in the Macmillan letter books of the dispatch (or receipt) of the proofs for *Plays II* (vol. 4) or *Essays* (vol. 5). The publishers may have decided it was not useful to send those proofs at the time, since at the 13 April 1932 meeting Yeats had indicated that he would supply additional material for both volumes (as of 27 September 1932, Yeats had yet to submit any new essays [BL, 55003/137]). On the other hand, a circa 1960 draft letter from Macmillan to Mrs. Yeats, quoted below, indicates that the first proofs were returned to Yeats, dating the event to 1932 (BL, 55896). If so, Yeats apparently failed to correct them. Sending proofs of *Essays* to Mrs. Yeats on 26 June 1939, Thomas Mark noted that the volume was "not read by Mr. Yeats" (BL, 55826/50).

    By 19 July 1939, *Essays* had reached the stage of a "Fourth Proof" (BL, 55895). However, on 14 June 1949 the publishers prepared a new set of proofs for *Ideas of Good and Evil* and *The Cutting of an Agate* (BL, 55894). The 1939 proofs were still extant, as Thomas Mark consulted them in the process of proofreading. Unfortunately, only the

"Other Essays" and "Introductions" sections of the 1939 proofs are now known to be extant (BL, 55895). The 1931 proofs do not survive.

36. Letter from John Hall Wheelock of Scribner's to Yeats, 26 May 1936 (Princeton). Wheelock is quoting what he heard from "my friends, the Colums" (the Irish writer Padraic Colum and his wife).
37. *Per Amica Silentia Lunae* remained in volume 5, as it would on the 1937 lists for the Scribner edition.
38. For the history of these additions, see *LE,* 461*ff.*
39. Two copies of this list are in National Library of Ireland MS 30,202. A copy of the list sent to Watt, made by Kingsley, is in the Princeton University Library. The materials sent to Scribner's are in the Harry Ransom Humanities Research Center, University of Texas at Austin.
40. Yeats's understanding of the discussion was rather different. He wrote Mrs. Yeats on [23 June 1937] that Macmillan "will bring out a large volume of my 'collected essays' & will add to this from time to time. . . ." (*InteLex*).
41. The title had also been queried on the 1949 proofs of *Ideas of Good and Evil* and *The Cutting of an Agate* (BL, 55894). Mark noted that "Mr Yeats altered this title [to "Explorations"] as he was thinking of using *Discoveries* as a title for Vol IX." Another comment reads "Can we say when Discoveries was altered to Explorations?" It is uncertain whether these remarks date from 1949 or 1959.
42. The date of this meeting is established by a comment on a slip of paper filed in BL, 55896, the 1961 galley proofs of *Explorations* (1962): "Please put a note to say that Yeats changed the title *Discoveries* for Explorations. Mr Mark will remember the date. I think it was when Yeats was passing through London 1938 before his last visit to France." Yeats was in England from 26 October 1938 until 26 November 1938. Ann Saddlemyer, who has graciously supplied those dates, has suggested that the meeting with Macmillan would have occurred on either 26 October, 15 November, or 25 November 1938, with the last the most likely.
43. "Mythologies, etc." had been the title of volume 2 of the Edition de Luxe at least as early as 15 April 1932 (BL, 55727/271–73). On the January 1937 Scribner list, *Mythologies and The Irish Dramatic Movement* had been revised to *Mythical Stories and The Irish Dramatic Movement,* but the June 1937 Scribner list reverts to *Mythologies and The Irish Dramatic Movement.* Since Mrs. Yeats typed both lists, her dating the title *Mythologies* to 1938 must refer to the shortened form (and possibly also to the replacement of *The Irish Dramatic Movement* by *Per Amica Silentia Lunae*).
44. *SR,* xxxviii. The rearrangement and expansion first appears not on the printed prospectus with the indication of "Preliminary Notice," which is headed "The Collected Edition of the Works of W. B. Yeats" (Princeton), but rather on an earlier state of the same headed "The [blank

space] Edition of the works of W. B. Yeats" (BL, 55890). The "Preliminary Notice" version was in print no later than 25 March 1939, when a copy was sent to Scribner's; it was doubtless approved at the meeting between Mrs. Yeats and Macmillan in London on 17 March 1939. The earlier version, which has "Mrs Yeats" in orange crayon on the top, was almost surely sent to her on 28 February 1939, although Macmillan's letter refers only to a "list" and a "second list" (BL, 55820/203–5). It is clear, however, that an expanded edition was projected as of that date, Macmillan writing that "We have now planned it as eleven volumes, provisionally arranged as shown on the list I enclose."

By the time of the autumn 1938 meeting, it would have been self-evident that the materials which Macmillan recently had published or were aware of had made a seven-volume Edition de Luxe all but impossible, and a discussion of how to proceed would have been an important item on the publisher's agenda. They would have been delighted to get Yeats's agreement for a revised and expanded project, as this would have greatly increased the "divergence" between their edition and the Scribner edition that they had always desired. As far as they knew, the Scribner edition (still in seven volumes) was in active preparation, so their more expansive project would trump the Americans when the time came. Indeed, when Charles Kingsley (Scribner's representative in London) discovered a notice of an eleven-volume edition in *The Bookseller* (30 March 1939), he wrote to John Hall Wheelock in New York on 4 April 1939, "It rather looks to me as if they [Macmillan] had put a fast one over on us" (Princeton). To their rather belated credit, Macmillan—of course aware of the forthcoming printed announcement—had in fact informed Scribner's of the extent of their edition a few days previously, in a letter of 27 March 1939 (Princeton).

45. Letters from Mrs. Yeats to Thomas Mark are in the British Library (uncatalogued), except for her letter of 15 April 1939, which is in the National Library of Ireland (NLI, 30,248).

46. There is no record in the Macmillan letter books of the period of the dispatch or receipt of the 24–29 August 1939 proofs of *The Irish Dramatic Movement*. Moreover, had Mark received corrected proofs from Mrs. Yeats, his usual practice would have called for the production of a revised set, which is not known to exist.

47. It is clear that around this time Mrs. Yeats began to be less responsive to Mark's letters. On 31 August 1939, for instance, he sent a set of page proofs of *Last Poems & Plays* to Yeats's agent, complaining that "The press proofs were sent to Mrs. Yeats for approval on August 4th, and we have not had any reply from her" (BL, 55828/511). When he finally received the proofs from Mrs. Yeats on 19 October 1939, he informed her rather curtly that they "were just in time, as the book was

about to go to press" (BL, 55830/334). On 12 February 1940 Mark again complained to Yeats's agent about Mrs. Yeats: not only had she failed to return the signed contract for the American edition of *Last Poems & Plays,* but also "I have written to her several times about some outstanding proofs of the big edition of her husband's works, but have had no reply" (BL, 55834/522–23). The state of things during the rest of the decade can be reconstructed from a letter to Yeats's agent from Macmillan on 12 May 1949: "Mrs. Yeats has written from time to time about certain details to Mr. Mark, who has been preparing the book [*Poems,* 1949]. It is so satisfactory for her to write and answer letters that I have rather encouraged her without bothering you; you will remember how difficult we found it to get a reply from her." Ann Saddlemyer's *Becoming George: The Life of Mrs. W. B. Yeats* (Oxford: Oxford University Press, 2002) details the myriad responsibilities of Mrs. Yeats during these years.

48. The 1939 proofs are found in British Library Additional Manuscript 55895. On the 1949 proofs, "Printed by R. & R. Clark, Ltd., Edinburgh" at the bottom of page [383] is cancelled in ink; the new numbering in pencil of the 1939 proofs begins with page 385. The works in the projected 1949 collection were eventually divided between *Essays and Introductions* (1961) and *Explorations* (1962). See *LE,* 464–66.

49. The first section of the proofs, through the cancelled dedication to Lennox Robinson, is filed with BL, 55895.

# THE COLLECTED WORKS OF W. B. YEATS

## VOLUME IV

# Early Essays

# IDEAS OF GOOD AND EVIL

(1896 – 1903)

# WHAT IS 'POPULAR POETRY'?

I think it was a Young Ireland Society that set my mind running on 'popular poetry.'[1] We used to discuss everything that was known to us about Ireland, and especially Irish literature and Irish history. We had no Gaelic, but paid great honour to the Irish poets who wrote in English, and quoted them in our speeches. I could have told you at that time the dates of the birth and death, and quoted the chief poems, of men whose names you have not heard, and perhaps of some whose names I have forgotten. I knew in my heart that the most of them wrote badly, and yet such romance clung about them, such a desire for Irish poetry was in all our minds, that I kept on saying, not only to others but to myself, that most of them wrote well, or all but well. I had read Shelley and Spenser and had tried to mix their styles together in a pastoral play which I have not come to dislike much, and yet I do not think Shelley or Spenser ever moved me as did these poets.[2] I thought one day—I can remember the very day when I thought it—'If somebody could make a style which would not be an English style and yet would be musical and full of colour, many others would catch fire from him, and we would have a really great school of ballad poetry in Ireland. If these poets, who have never ceased to fill the newspapers and the ballad-books with their verses, had a good tradition they would write beautifully and move everybody as they move me.'[3] Then a little later on I thought, 'If they had something else to write about besides political opinions, if more of them would write about the beliefs of the people like Allingham, or about old legends like Ferguson, they would find it easier to get a style.'[4] Then with a deliberateness that still surprises me, for in my heart of hearts I have never been quite certain that one should be more than an artist, that even patriotism is more than an impure desire in an artist, I set to work to find a style and things to write about that the ballad writers might be the better.

They are no better, I think, and my desire to make them so was, it may be, one of the illusions Nature holds before one, because she knows that the gifts she has to give are not worth troubling about. It is for her sake that we must stir ourselves, but we would not trouble to get out of bed in the morning, or to leave our chairs once we are in them, if she had not her conjuring bag. She wanted a few verses from me, and because it would not have seemed worth while taking so much trouble to see my books lie on a few drawing-room tables, she filled my head with thoughts of making a whole literature, and plucked me out of the Dublin art schools where I should have stayed drawing from the round, and sent me into a library to read bad translations from the Irish, and at last down into Connacht to sit by turf fires.[5] I wanted to write 'popular poetry' like those Irish poets, for I believed that all good literatures were popular, and even cherished the fancy that the Adelphi melodrama, which I had never seen, might be good literature, and I hated what I called the coteries.[6] I thought that one must write without care, for that was of the coteries, but with a gusty energy that would put all straight if it came out of the right heart. I had a conviction, which indeed I have still, that one's verses should hold, as in a mirror, the colours of one's own climate and scenery in their right proportion; and, when I found my verses too full of the reds and yellows Shelley gathered in Italy, I thought for two days of setting things right, not as I should now by making my rhythms faint and nervous and filling my images with a certain coldness, a certain wintry wildness, but by eating little and sleeping upon a board.[7] I felt indignant with Matthew Arnold because he complained that somebody, who had translated Homer into a ballad measure, had tried to write epic to the tune of 'Yankee Doodle.'[8] It seemed to me that it did not matter what tune one wrote to, so long as that gusty energy came often enough and strongly enough. And I delighted in Victor Hugo's book upon Shakespeare, because he abused critics and coteries and thought that Shakespeare wrote without care or premeditation and to please everybody.[9] I would indeed have had every illusion had I believed in that straightforward logic, as of newspaper articles, which so tickles an ignorant ear; but I always knew that the line of Nature is crooked, that, though we dig the canal beds as straight as we can, the rivers run hither and thither in their wildness.

From that day to this I have been busy among the verses and stories that the people make for themselves, but I had been busy a very little while before I knew that what we call popular poetry never came from the people at all. Longfellow, and Campbell, and Mrs. Hemans, and Macaulay in his *Lays,* and Scott in his longer poems are the poets of a predominant portion of the middle class, of people who have unlearned the unwritten tradition which binds the unlettered, so long as they are masters of themselves, to the beginning of time and to the foundation of the world, and who have not learned the written tradition which has been established upon the unwritten.[10] I became certain that Burns, whose greatness has been used to justify the littleness of others, was in part a poet of this portion of the middle class, because though the farmers he sprang from and lived among had been able to create a little tradition of their own, less a tradition of ideas than of speech, they had been divided by religious and political changes from the images and emotions which had once carried their memories backward thousands of years.[11] Despite his expressive speech which sets him above all other popular poets, he has the triviality of emotion, the poverty of ideas, the imperfect sense of beauty of a poetry whose most typical expression is in Longfellow. Longfellow has his popularity, in the main, because he tells his story or his idea so that one needs nothing but his verses to understand it. No words of his borrow their beauty from those that used them before, and one can get all that there is in story and idea without seeing them, as if moving before a half-faded curtain embroidered with kings and queens, their loves and battles and their days out hunting, or else with holy letters and images of so great antiquity that nobody can tell the god or goddess they would commend to an unfading memory. Poetry that is not popular poetry presupposes, indeed, more than it says, though we, who cannot know what it is to be disinherited, only understand how much more, when we read it in its most typical expressions, in the *Epipsychidion* of Shelley, or in Spenser's description of the gardens of Adonis, or when we meet the misunderstandings of others.[12] Go down into the street and read to your baker or your candlestick-maker any poem which is not popular poetry. I have heard a baker, who was clever enough with his oven, deny that Tennyson could have known what he was writing when he wrote 'Warming his five wits, the white owl in the belfry sits,' and once when I read out Omar Khayyám to one of the best of candlestick-makers, he said, 'What is the meaning of "we come like water and like wind we go"?'[13] Or go down into the street with some thought whose bare meaning must be plain to everybody; take with you Ben Jonson's 'Beauty like sorrow dwelleth everywhere,' and find out how utterly its enchantment depends on an association of beauty with sorrow which written tradition has from the unwritten, which had it in its turn from ancient religion; or take with you these lines in whose bare meaning also there is nothing to stumble over, and find out what men lose who are not in love with Helen:

Brightness falls from the air,
Queens have died young and fair,
Dust hath closed Helen's eye.[14]

I pick my examples at random, for I am writing where I have no books to turn the pages of, but one need not go east of the sun or west of the moon in so simple a matter.[15]

On the other hand, when Walt Whitman writes in seeming defiance of tradition, he needs tradition for protection, for the butcher and the baker and the candlestick-maker grow merry over him when they meet his work by chance.[16] Nature, being unable to endure emptiness, has made them gather conventions which cannot hide that they are low-born things though copies, as from far off, of the dress and manners of the well-bred and the well-born. The gatherers mock all expression that is wholly unlike their own, just as little boys in the street mock at strangely-dressed people and at old men who talk to themselves.

There is only one kind of good poetry, for the poetry of the coteries, which presupposes the written tradition, does not differ in kind from the true poetry of the people, which presupposes the unwritten tradition. Both are alike strange and obscure, and unreal to all who have not understanding, and both, instead of that manifest logic, that clear rhetoric of the 'popular poetry,' glimmer with thoughts and images whose 'ancestors were stout and wise,' 'anigh to Paradise' 'ere yet men knew the gift of corn.' It may be that we know as little of their descent as men knew of 'the man born to be a king' when they found him in that cradle marked with the red lion crest, and yet we know somewhere in the heart that they have been sung in temples, in ladies' chambers, and quiver with a recognition our nerves have been shaped to by a thousand emotions.[17] If men did not remember or half remember impossible things, and, it may be, if the worship of sun and moon had not left a faint reverence behind it, what Aran fisher-girl would sing—[†]

> 'It is late last night the dog was speaking of you; the snipe was speaking of you in her deep marsh. It is you are the lonely bird throughout the woods; and that you may be without a mate until you find me.
>
> 'You promised me and you said a lie to me, that you would be before me where the sheep are flocked. I gave a whistle and three hundred cries to you; and I found nothing there but a bleating lamb.
>
> 'You promised me a thing that was hard for you, a ship of gold under a silver mast; twelve towns and a market in all of them, and a fine white court by the side of the sea.
>
> 'You promised me a thing that is not possible; that you would give me gloves of the skin of a fish; that you would give me shoes of the skin of a bird, and a suit of the dearest silk in Ireland.
>
> 'My mother said to me not to be talking with you, to-day or to-morrow or on Sunday. It was a bad time she took for telling me that, it was shutting the door after the house was robbed. . . .
>
> 'You have taken the east from me, you have taken the west from me, you have taken what is before me and what is behind me; you have taken the moon, you have taken the sun from me, and my fear is great you have taken God from me'?[†18]

The Gael of the Scottish islands could not sing his beautiful song over a bride, had he not a memory of the belief that Christ was the only man who measured six feet and not a little more or less, and was perfectly shaped in all other ways, and if he did not remember old symbolical observances—

> I bathe thy palms
> In showers of wine,

In the cleansing fire,
In the juice of raspberries,
In the milk of honey.
. . . . . . . . . . .
Thou art the joy of all joyous things,
Thou art the light of the beam of the sun,
Thou art the door of the chief of hospitality,
Thou art the surpassing pilot star,
Thou art the step of the deer of the hill,
Thou art the step of the horse of the plain,
Thou art the grace of the sun rising,
Thou art the loveliness of all lovely desires.

The lovely likeness of the Lord
Is in thy pure face,
The loveliest likeness that was upon earth.[19]

I soon learned to cast away one other illusion of 'popular poetry.' I learned from the people themselves, before I learned it from any book, that they cannot separate the idea of an art or a craft from the idea of a cult with ancient technicalities and mysteries. They can hardly separate mere learning from witchcraft, and are fond of words and verses that keep half their secret to themselves. Indeed, it is certain that before the counting-house had created a new class and a new art without breeding and without ancestry, and set this art and this class between the hut and the castle, and between the hut and the cloister, the art of the people was as closely mingled with the art of the coteries as was the speech of the people that delighted in rhythmical animation, in idiom, in images, in words full of far-off suggestion, with the unchanging speech of the poets.

Now I see a new generation in Ireland which discusses Irish literature and history in Young Ireland societies, and societies with newer names, and there are far more than when I was a boy who would make verses for the people.[20] They have the help, too, of a vigorous journalism, and this journalism sometimes urges them to desire the direct logic, the clear rhetoric of 'popular poetry.' It sees that Ireland has no cultivated minority, and it does not see, though it would cast out all English things, that its literary ideal belongs more to England than to other countries. I have hope that the new writers will not fall into its illusion, for they write in Irish, and for a people the counting-house has not made forgetful. Among the seven or eight hundred thousand who have had Irish from the cradle, there is, perhaps, nobody who has not enough of the unwritten tradition to know good verses from bad ones, if he have enough mother-wit. Among all that speak English in Australia, in America, in Great Britain, are there many more than the ten thousand the prophet saw, who have enough of the written tradition education has set in room of the unwritten to know good verses from bad ones, even though their mother-wit has made them Ministers of the Crown or what you will?[21] Nor can things be better till that ten thousand have gone hither and thither to preach their faith that 'the imagination is the man himself,' and that the world as imagination sees it is the durable world, and have won men as did the disciples of Him who—

> His seventy disciples sent
> Against religion and government.[22]

1901.

# SPEAKING TO THE PSALTERY

## I

I have always known that there was something I disliked about singing, and I naturally dislike print and paper, but now at last I understand why, for I have found something better. I have just heard a poem spoken with so delicate a sense of its rhythm, with so perfect a respect for its meaning, that if I were a wise man and could persuade a few people to learn the art I would never open a book of verses again. A friend, who was here a few minutes ago, has sat with a beautiful stringed instrument upon her knee, her fingers passing over the strings, and has spoken to me some verses from Shelley's 'Skylark' and Sir Ector's lamentations over the dead Launcelot out of the *Morte d'Arthur* and some of my own poems.[1] Wherever the rhythm was most delicate, and wherever the emotion was most ecstatic, her art was most beautiful, and yet, although she sometimes spoke to a little tune, it was never singing, as we sing to-day, never anything but speech. A singing note, a word chanted as they chant in churches, would have spoiled everything; nor was it reciting, for she spoke to a notation as definite as that of song, using the instrument, which murmured sweetly and faintly, under the spoken sounds, to give her the changing notes. Another speaker could have repeated all her effects, except those which came from her own beautiful voice, a voice that would have given her fame if the only art that offers the speaking voice its perfect opportunity were as well known among us as it was known in the ancient world.

## II

Since I was a boy I have always longed to hear poems spoken to a harp, as I imagined Homer to have spoken his, for it is not natural to enjoy an art only when one is by oneself.[2] Whenever one finds a fine verse one wants to read it to somebody, and it would be much less trouble and much pleasanter if we could all listen, friend by friend, lover by beloved. Images used to rise up before me, as I am sure they have arisen before nearly everybody else who cares for poetry, of wild-eyed men speaking harmoniously to murmuring wires while audiences in many-coloured robes listened, hushed and excited. Whenever I spoke of my desire to anybody they said I should write for music, but when I heard anything sung I did not hear the words, or if I did their natural pronunciation was altered and their natural music was altered, or it was drowned in another music which I did not understand. What was the good of writing a love-song if the singer pronounced love, 'lo-o-o-o-o-ve,' or even if he said 'love,' but did not give it its exact place and weight in the rhythm? Like every other poet, I spoke verses in a kind of chant when I was making them; and sometimes, when I was alone on a country road, I would speak them in a loud chanting voice, and feel that if I dared I would speak them in that way to other people.[3] One day I was walking through a Dublin street with Mr. George Russell ('A.E.'), and he began speaking his verses out aloud with the confidence of those who have the inner light.[4] He did not mind that people stopped and looked after him even on the far side of the road, but went on through poem after poem. Like myself, he knew nothing of music, but was certain that he had written them to a manner of music, and he had once asked somebody who played on a wind instrument of some kind, and then a violinist, to write out the music and play it. The violinist had played it, or something like it, but had not written it down; but the man with the wind instrument said it could not be played because it contained quarter-tones and would be out of tune. We were not at all convinced by this, and one day, when we were staying with a Galway friend who is a learned musician, I asked him to listen to our verses, and to the way we spoke them.[5] Mr. Russell found to his surprise that he did not make every poem to a different tune, and to the surprise of the musician that he did make them all to two quite definite tunes, which are, it seems, like very simple Arabic music. It was, perhaps, to some such music, I thought, that Blake sang his *Songs of Innocence* in Mrs. Williams' drawing-room, and perhaps he, too, spoke rather than sang.[6] I, on the other hand, did not often compose to a tune, though I sometimes did, yet always to notes that could be written down and played on my friend's organ, or turned into something like a Gregorian hymn if one sang them in the ordinary way.[7] I varied more than Mr. Russell, who never forgot his two tunes, one for long and one for short lines, and[†] could not always speak a poem in the same way.[8] When I got to London I gave the notation, as it had been played on the organ, to the friend who has just gone out, Miss Florence Farr, and she spoke it to me, giving my words a new quality by the beauty of her voice.

## III

But she and I soon wandered into the wood of error; we tried speaking through music in the ordinary way under I know not whose evil influence, until we got to hate the two competing tunes and rhythms that were so often at discord with one another, the tune and rhythm of the verse and the tune and rhythm of the music. Then we tried, persuaded by somebody who thought quarter-tones and less intervals the especial mark of speech as distinct from singing, to write out what we did in wavy lines.[9] On finding something like these lines in Tibetan music, we became so confident that we covered a large piece of pasteboard, which now blows up my fire in the morning, with a notation in wavy lines as a demonstration for a lecture; but at last Mr. Dolmetsch put us back to our first thought. He made us a beautiful instrument, half psaltery, half lyre, which contains, I understand, all the chromatic intervals within the range of the speaking voice; and he taught us to regulate our speech by the ordinary musical notes.

Some of the notations he taught us—those in which there is no lilt, no recurring pattern of sounds—are like this notation for a song out of the first Act of *The Countess Cathleen.*

It is written in the old C clef, which is, I am told, the most reasonable way to write it, for it would be 'below the stave on the treble clef or above it on the bass clef.' The central line of the stave 'corresponds to the middle C of the piano; the first note of the poem is therefore D.' The marks of long and short over the syllables are not marks of scansion, but show the syllables one makes the voice hurry or linger over.[10]

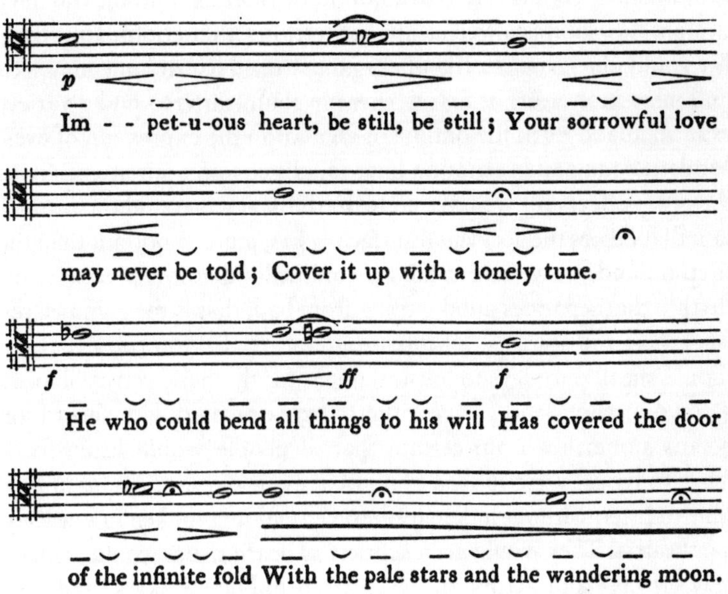


One needs, of course, a far less complicated notation than a singer, and one is even permitted slight modifications of the fixed note when dramatic expression demands it and the instrument is not sounding. The notation, which regulates the general form of the sound, leaves it free to add a complexity of dramatic expression from its own incommunicable genius which compensates the lover of speech for the lack of complex musical expression. Ordinary speech is formless, and its variety is like the variety which separates bad prose from the regulated speech of Milton, or anything that is formless and void from anything that has form and beauty. The orator, the speaker who has some little of the great tradition of his craft, differs from the debater very largely because he understands how to assume that subtle monotony of voice which runs through the nerves like fire.

Even when one is speaking to a single note sounded faintly on the psaltery, if one is sufficiently practised to speak on it without thinking about it one can get an endless variety of expression. All art is, indeed, a monotony in external things for the sake of an interior variety, a sacrifice of gross effects to subtle effects, an asceticism of the imagination.[11] But this new art, new in modern life I mean, will have to train its hearers as well as its speakers, for it takes time to surrender gladly the gross effects[†] one is accustomed to, and one may well find mere monotony at first where one soon learns to find a variety as incalculable as in the outline of faces or in the expression of eyes. Modern acting and recitation have taught us to fix our attention on the gross effects till we have come to think gesture, and the intonation that copies the accidental surface of life, more important than the rhythm; and yet we understand theoretically that it is precisely this rhythm that separates good writing from bad, that is the glimmer, the fragrance, the spirit of all intense literature. I do not say that we should speak our plays to musical notes, for dramatic verse will need its own method, and I have hitherto experimented with short lyric poems alone; but I am certain that, if people would listen for a while to lyrical verse spoken to notes, they would soon find it impossible to listen without indignation to verse as it is spoken in our leading theatres. They would get a subtlety of hearing that would demand new effects from actors and even from public speakers, and they might, it may be, begin even to notice one another's voices till poetry and rhythm had come nearer to common life.

I cannot tell what changes this new art is to go through, or to what greatness or littleness of fortune; but I can imagine little stories in prose with their dialogues in metre going pleasantly to the strings. I am not certain that I shall not see some Order naming itself from the Golden Violet of the Troubadours or the like, and having among its members none but well-taught and well-mannered speakers who will keep the new art from disrepute.[12] They will know how to keep from singing notes and from prosaic lifeless intonations, and they will always understand, however far they push their experiments, that poetry and not music is their object; and they will have by heart, like the Irish *File,* so many poems and notations that they will never have to bend their heads over the book, to the ruin of dramatic expression and of that wild air the bard had always about him in my boyish imagination.[13] They will go here and there speaking their verses and their little stories wherever they can find a score or two of poetical-minded people in a big room, or a couple of poetical-minded friends sitting by the hearth, and poets will write them poems and little stories to the confounding of print and paper. I, at any rate, from this out mean to write all my longer poems for the stage, and all my shorter ones for the psaltery, if only some strong angel keep me to my good resolutions.

1902.

## IV. POEMS FOR THE PSALTERY[14]

The relation between formal music and speech will yet become the subject of science, not less than the occasion of artistic discovery. I suggest that we will discover in this relation a very early stage in the development of music, with its own great beauty, and that those who love lyric poetry but cannot tell one tune from another repeat a state of mind which created music and yet was incapable of the emotional abstraction which delights in patterns of sound separated from words. To it the music was an unconscious creation, the words a conscious, for no beginnings are in the intellect, and no living thing remembers its own birth.

Three of the following settings are by Miss Farr, and she accompanies the words upon her psaltery for the most part. I give after Miss Farr's three settings two taken down by Mr. Arnold Dolmetsch from myself, and one from Mr. A. H. Bullen, a fine scholar in poetry, who hates all music but that of poetry, and knows of no instrument that does not fill him with rage and misery.[15] I do not mean that there is only one way of reciting a poem that is correct, for different tunes will fit different speakers or different moods of the same speaker, but as a rule the more the music of the verse becomes a movement of the stanza as a whole, at the same time detaching itself from the sense as in much of Mr. Swinburne's poetry, the less does the poet vary in his recitation.[16] I mean in the way he recites when alone, or unconscious of an audience, for before an audience he will remember the imperfection of his ear in note and tune, and cling to daily speech, or something like it.

Sometimes one composes to a remembered air. I wrote and I still speak the verses that begin 'Autumn is over the long leaves that love us' to some traditional air, though I could not tell that air or any other on another's lips, and 'The Ballad of Father Gilligan' to a modification of the air 'A Fine Old English Gentleman.'[17] When, however, the rhythm is more personal than it is in these simple verses, the tune will always be original and personal, alike in the poet and in the reader who has the right ear; and these tunes will now and again have great beauty.

1907.

## V. NOTE BY FLORENCE FARR UPON HER SETTINGS

I made an interesting discovery after I had been elaborating the art of speaking to the psaltery for some time. I had tried to make it more beautiful than the speaking by priests at High Mass, the singing of recitative in opera and the speaking through music of actors in melodrama. My discovery was that those who had invented these arts had all said about them exactly what Mr. Arnold Dolmetsch and Mr. W. B. Yeats said about my art. Any one can prove this for himself who will go to a library and read the authorities that describe how early liturgical chant, plain-song and jubilations or melismata were adapted from the ancient traditional music; or if they read the history of the beginning of opera and the 'nuove musiche' by Caccini, or study the music of Monteverdi and Carissimi, who flourished at the beginning of the seventeenth century, they will find these masters speak of doing all they can to give an added beauty to the words of the poet, often using simple vowel sounds when a purely vocal effect was to be made whether of joy or sorrow.[18] There is no more beautiful sound than the alternation of carolling or keening and a voice speaking in regulated declamation. The very act of alternation has a peculiar charm.

Now to read these records of music of the eighth and seventeenth centuries one would think that the Church and the opera were united in the desire to make beautiful speech more beautiful, but I need not say if we put such a hope to the test we discover it is groundless. There is no ecstasy in the delivery of ritual, and recitative is certainly not treated by opera-singers in a way that makes us wish to imitate them.

When beginners attempt to speak to musical notes they fall naturally into the intoning as heard throughout our lands in our various religious rituals. It is not until they have been forced to use their imaginations and express the inmost meaning of the words, not until their thought imposes itself upon all listeners and each word invokes a special mode of beauty, that the method rises once more from the dead and becomes a living art.

It is the belief in the power of words and the delight in the purity of sound that will make the arts of plain-chant and recitative the great arts they are described as being by those who first practised them.[19–24]

F. F., 1907.

# THE WIND BLOWS OUT OF THE GATES OF THE DAY[1]

FLORENCE FARR.

The wind blows out of the gates of the day, The wind blows
over the lonely of heart, And the lonely of heart is withered
away, While the fairies dance in a place apart, Shaking their
milkwhite feet in a ring, Tossing their milkwhite arms in the
air. For they hear the wind laugh and murmur and sing Of
a land where even the old are fair, And even the wise are
merry of tongue. But I heard a reed of Coolaney say,
When the wind has laughed and murmured and sung, The
lonely of heart must wither away.

[1] The music as written suits my speaking voice if played an octave lower than the notation.—F. F.

## THE HAPPY TOWNLAND [1]

FLORENCE FARR.

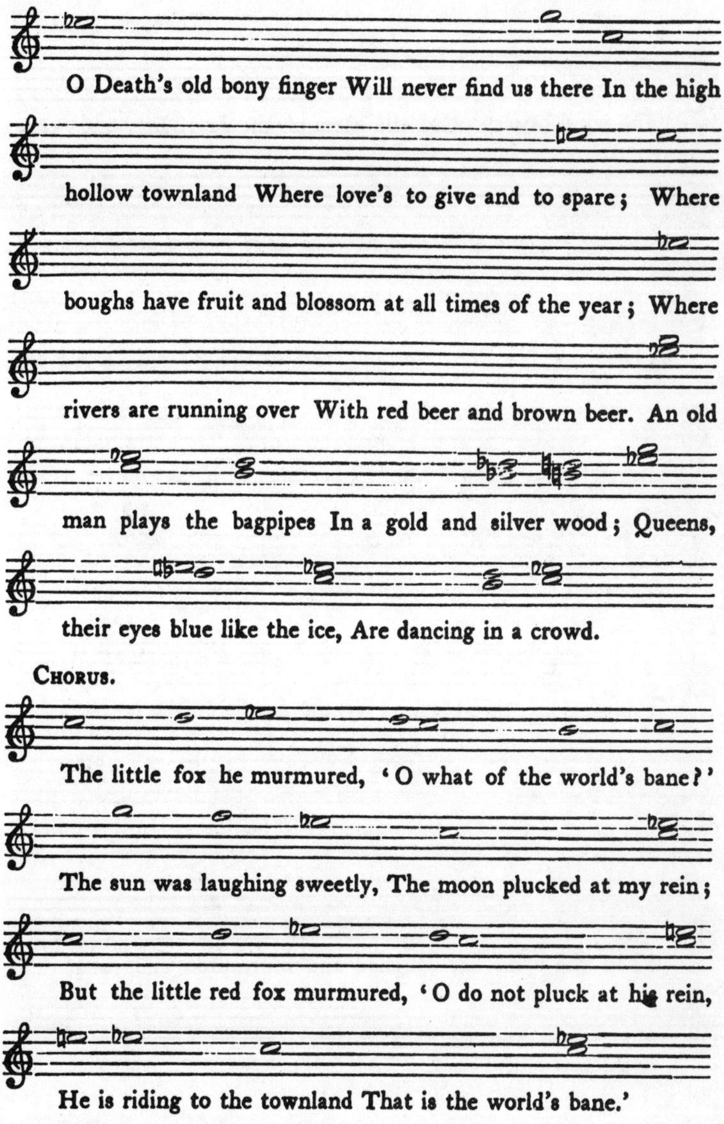

O Death's old bony finger Will never find us there In the high

hollow townland Where love's to give and to spare; Where

boughs have fruit and blossom at all times of the year; Where

rivers are running over With red beer and brown beer. An old

man plays the bagpipes In a gold and silver wood; Queens,

their eyes blue like the ice, Are dancing in a crowd.

CHORUS.

The little fox he murmured, 'O what of the world's bane?'

The sun was laughing sweetly, The moon plucked at my rein;

But the little red fox murmured, 'O do not pluck at his rein,

He is riding to the townland That is the world's bane.'

[1] The music as written suits my speaking voice if played an octave lower than the notation.—F. F.

# I HAVE DRUNK ALE FROM THE COUNTRY OF THE YOUNG[1]

FLORENCE FARR.

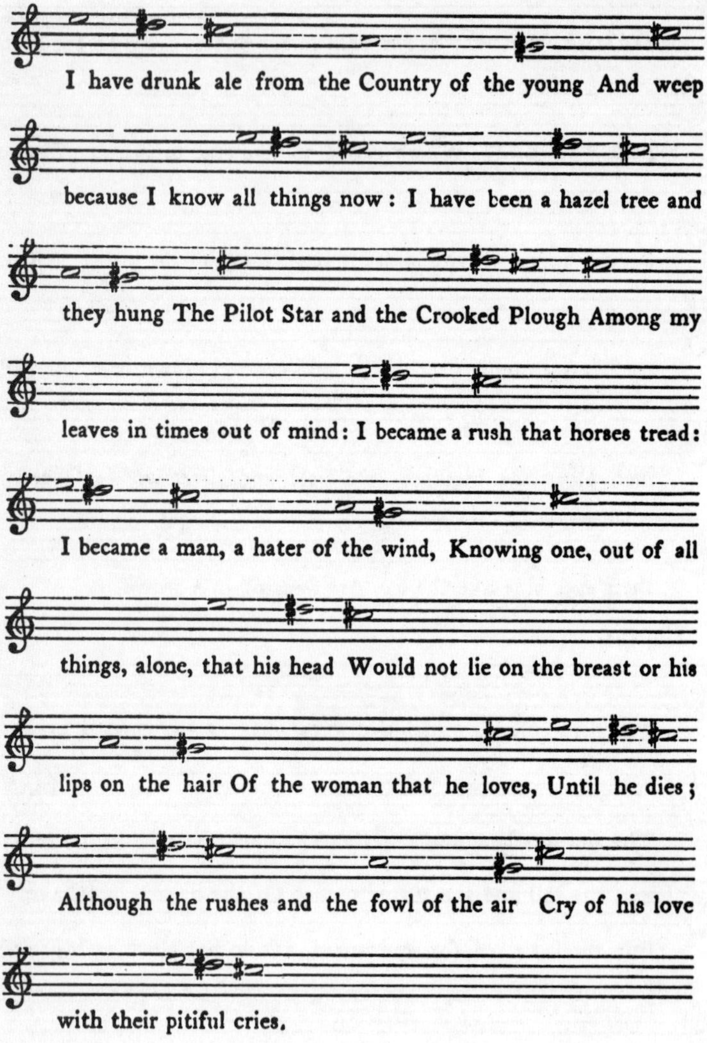

I have drunk ale from the Country of the young And weep

because I know all things now: I have been a hazel tree and

they hung The Pilot Star and the Crooked Plough Among my

leaves in times out of mind: I became a rush that horses tread:

I became a man, a hater of the wind, Knowing one, out of all

things, alone, that his head Would not lie on the breast or his

lips on the hair Of the woman that he loves, Until he dies;

Although the rushes and the fowl of the air Cry of his love

with their pitiful cries.

[1] To be spoken an octave lower than it would be sung.—F. F.

## THE SONG OF WANDERING AENGUS

W. B. Y.

I went out to the hazel wood, Be-cause a fire was in my head,

And cut and peeled a hazel wand, And hooked a berry to a thread;

And when white moths were on the wing, And moth-like stars were flickering out,

I dropped the berry in a stream, and caught a little silver trout.

## THE HOST OF THE AIR

A. H. B.

O'Driscoll drove with a song, The wild duck and the drake,

From the tall and the tufted reeds Of the drear Hart Lake.

## THE SONG OF THE OLD MOTHER

W. B. Y.

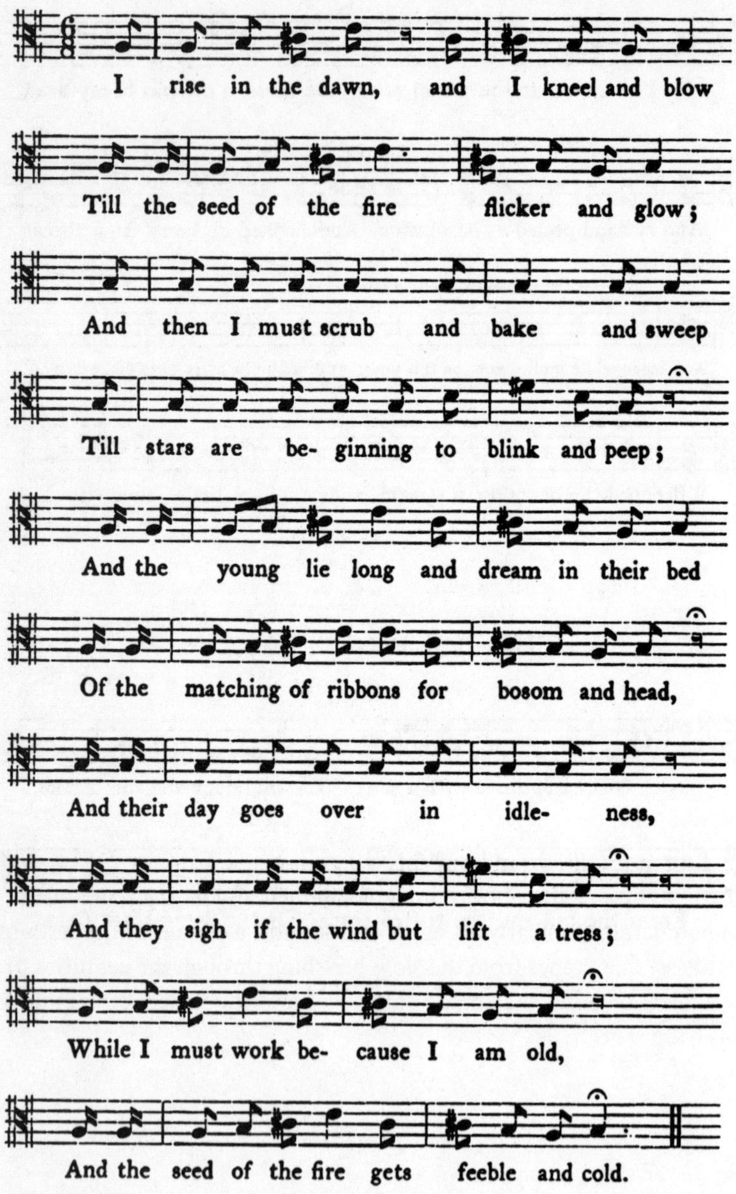

# MAGIC

## I

I believe in the practice and philosophy of what we have agreed to call magic, in what I must call the evocation of spirits, though I do not know what they are, in the power of creating magical illusions, in the visions of truth in the depths of the mind when the eyes are closed; and I believe in three doctrines, which have, as I think, been handed down from early times, and been the foundations of nearly all magical practices. These doctrines are—

> (1) That the borders of our mind are ever shifting, and that many minds can flow into one another, as it were, and create or reveal a single mind, a single energy.
>
> (2) That the borders of our memories are as shifting, and that our memories are a part of one great memory, the memory of Nature herself.
>
> (3) That this great mind and great memory can be evoked by symbols.[1]

I often think I would put this belief in magic from me if I could, for I have come to see or to imagine, in men and women, in houses, in handicrafts, in nearly all sights and sounds, a certain evil, a certain ugliness, that comes from the slow perishing through the centuries of a quality of mind that made this belief and its evidences common over the world.

## II

Some ten or twelve years ago, a man with whom I have since quarrelled for sound reasons, a very singular man who had given his life to studies other men despised, asked me and an acquaintance, who is now dead, to witness a magical work.[2] He lived a little way from London, and on the way my acquaintance told me that he did not believe in magic, but that a novel of Bulwer Lytton's had taken such a hold upon his imagination that he was going to give much of his time and all his thought to magic.[3] He longed to believe in it, and had studied, though not learnedly, geomancy, astrology, chiromancy, and much cabalistic symbolism, and yet doubted if the soul outlived the body. He awaited the magical work full of scepticism. He expected nothing more than an air of romance, an illusion as of the stage, that might capture the consenting imagination for an hour. The evoker of spirits and his beautiful wife received us in a little house, on the edge of some kind of garden or park belonging to an eccentric rich man, whose curiosities he arranged and dusted, and he made his evocation in a long room that had a raised place on the floor at one end, a kind of dais, but was furnished meagrely and cheaply.[4] I sat with my acquaintance in the middle of the room, and the evoker of spirits on the dais, and his wife between us and him. He held a wooden mace in his hand, and turning to a tablet of many-coloured squares, with a number on each of the squares, that stood near him on a chair, he repeated a form of words.[5] Almost at once my imagination began to move of itself and to bring before me vivid images that, though never too vivid to be imagination, as I had always understood it, had yet a motion of their own, a life I could not change or shape. I remember seeing a number of white figures, and wondering whether their mitred heads had been suggested by the mitred head of the mace, and then, of a sudden, the image of my acquaintance in the midst of them. I told what I had seen, and the evoker of spirits cried in a deep voice, 'Let him be blotted out,' and as he said it the image of my acquaintance vanished, and the evoker of spirits or his wife saw a man dressed in black with a curious square cap standing among the white figures.[6] It was my acquaintance, the seeress said, as he had been in a past life, the life that had moulded his present, and that life would now unfold before us. I too seemed to see the man with a strange vividness. The story unfolded itself chiefly before the mind's eye of the seeress, but sometimes I saw what she described before I heard her description. She thought the man in black was perhaps a Fleming of the sixteenth century, and I could see him pass along narrow streets till he came to a narrow door with some rusty iron-work above it. He went in, and wishing to find out how far we had one vision among us, I kept silent when I saw a dead body lying upon the table within the door. The seeress described him going down a long hall and up into what she called a pulpit, and beginning to speak. She said, 'He is a clergyman, I can hear his words. They sound like Low Dutch.' Then after a little silence, 'No, I am wrong. I can see the listeners; he is a doctor lecturing among his pupils.' I said, 'Do you see anything near the door?' and she said, 'Yes, I see a subject for dissection.' Then we saw him go out again into the narrow streets, I following the story of the seeress, sometimes merely following her words, but sometimes seeing for myself. My acquaintance saw nothing; I think he was forbidden to see, it being his own life, and I think could not in any case. His imagination had no will of its own.[7] Presently the man in black went into a house with two gables facing the road, and up some stairs into a room where a hump-backed woman gave him a key; and then along a corridor, and down some stairs into a large cellar full of retorts and strange vessels of all kinds. Here he seemed to stay a long while, and one saw him eating bread that he took down from a shelf. The evoker of spirits and the seeress began to speculate about the man's character and habits, and decided, from a visionary impression, that his mind was absorbed in naturalism, but that his imagination had been excited by stories of the marvels wrought by magic in past times, and that he was trying to copy them by naturalistic means. Presently one of them saw him go to a vessel that stood over a slow fire, and take out of the vessel a thing wrapped up in numberless cloths, which he partly unwrapped, showing at length what looked like the image of a man made by somebody who could not model. The evoker of spirits said that the man in black was trying to make flesh by chemical means, and though he had not succeeded, his brooding had drawn so many evil spirits about him that the image was partly alive. He could see it moving a little where it lay upon a table. At that moment I heard something like little squeals, but kept silent, as when I saw the dead body. In a moment more the seeress said, 'I hear little squeals.' Then the evoker of spirits heard them, but said, 'They are not squeals; he is pouring a red liquid out of a retort through a slit in the cloth; the slit is over the mouth of the image and the liquid is gurgling in rather a curious way.' Weeks seemed to pass by hurriedly, and somebody saw the man still busy in his cellar. Then more weeks seemed to pass, and now we saw him lying sick in a room upstairs, and a man in a conical cap standing beside him. We could see the image too. It was in the cellar, but now it could move feebly about the floor. I saw fainter images of the image passing continually from where it crawled to the man in his bed, and I asked the evoker of spirits what they were. He said, 'They are the images of his terror.' Presently the man in the conical cap began to speak, but who heard him I cannot remember. He made the sick man get out of bed and walk, leaning upon him, and in much terror till they came to the cellar. There the man in the conical cap made some symbol over the image, which fell back as if asleep, and putting a knife into the other's hand he said, 'I have taken from it the magical life, but you must take from it the life you gave.' Somebody saw the sick man stoop and sever the head of the image from its body, and then fall as if he had given himself a mortal wound, for he had filled it with his own life. And then the vision changed and fluttered, and he was lying sick again in the room upstairs. He seemed to lie there a long time with the man in the conical cap watching beside him, then, I cannot remember how, the evoker of spirits discovered that though he would in part recover, he would never be well, and that the story had got abroad in the town and shattered his good name. His pupils had left him and men avoided him. He was accursed. He was a magician.

The story was finished, and I looked at my acquaintance. He was white and awestruck. He said, as nearly as I can remember, 'All my life I have seen myself in dreams making a man by some means like that. When I was a child I was always thinking out contrivances for galvanising a corpse into life.' Presently he said, 'Perhaps my bad health in this life comes from that experiment.' I asked if he had read *Frankenstein,* and he answered that he had. He was the only one of us who had, and he had taken no part in the vision.[8]

## III

Then I asked to have some past life of mine revealed, and a new evocation was made before the tablet full of little squares. I cannot remember so well who saw this or that detail, for now I was interested in little but the vision itself. I had come to a conclusion about the method. I knew that the vision may be in part common to several people.

A man in chain armour passed through a castle door, and the seeress noticed with surprise the bareness and rudeness of castle rooms. There was nothing of the magnificence or the pageantry she had expected. The man came to a large hall and to a little chapel opening out of it, where a ceremony was taking place. There were six girls dressed in white, who took from the altar some yellow object—I thought it was gold, for though, like my acquaintance, I was told not to see, I could not help seeing. Somebody else thought that it was yellow flowers, and I think the girls, though I cannot remember clearly, laid it between the man's hands. He went out for a time, and as he passed through the great hall one of us, I forget whom, noticed that he passed over two gravestones. Then the vision became broken, but presently he stood in a monk's habit among men-at-arms in the middle of a village reading from a parchment. He was calling villagers about him, and presently he and they and the men-at-arms took ship for some long voyage. The vision became broken again, and when we could see clearly they had come to what seemed the Holy Land. They had begun some kind of sacred labour among palm-trees. The common men among them stood idle, but the gentlemen carried large stones, bringing them from certain directions, from the cardinal points I think, with a ceremonious formality. The evoker of spirits said they must be making some masonic house. His mind, like the minds of so many students of these hidden things, was always running on masonry and discovering it in strange places.[9]

We broke the vision that we might have supper, breaking it with some form of words which I forget. When supper had ended the seeress cried out that while we had been eating they had been building, and that they had built not a masonic house but a great stone cross. And now they had all gone away but the man who had been in chain armour and two monks we had not noticed before. He was standing against the cross, his feet upon two stone rests a little above the ground, and his arms spread out. He seemed to stand there all day, but when night came he went to a little cell, that was beside two other cells. I think they were like the cells I have seen in the Aran Islands, but I cannot be certain.[10] Many days seemed to pass, and all day every day he stood upon the cross, and we never saw anybody there but him and the two monks. Many years seemed to pass, making the vision flutter like a drift of leaves before our eyes, and he grew old and white-haired, and we saw the two monks, old and white-haired, holding him upon the cross. I asked the evoker of spirits why the man stood there, and before he had time to answer I saw two people, a man and a woman, rising like a dream within a dream, before the eyes of the man upon the cross. The evoker of spirits saw them too, and said that one of them held up his arms and they were without hands. I thought of the two gravestones the man in chain mail had passed over in the great hall when he came out of the chapel, and asked the evoker of spirits if the knight was undergoing a penance for violence, and while I was asking him, and he was saying that it might be so but he did not know, the vision, having completed its circle, vanished.

It had not, so far as I could see, the personal significance of the other vision, but it was certainly strange and beautiful, though I alone seemed to see its beauty. Who was it that made the story, if it were but a story? I did not, and the seeress did not, and the evoker of spirits did not and could not. It arose in three minds, for I cannot remember my acquaintance taking any part, and it rose without confusion, and without labour, except the labour of keeping the mind's eye awake, and more swiftly than any pen could have written it out. It may be, as Blake said of one of his poems, that the author was in eternity.[11] In coming years I was to see and hear of many such visions, and though I was not to be convinced, though half convinced once or twice, that they were old lives, in an ordinary sense of the word life, I was to learn that they have almost always some quite definite relation to dominant moods and moulding events in this life. They are, perhaps, in most cases, though the vision I have but just described was not, it seems, among the cases, symbolical histories of these moods and events, or rather symbolical shadows of the impulses that have made them, messages as it were out of the ancestral being of the questioner.

At the time these two visions meant little more to me, if I can remember my feeling at the time, than a proof of the supremacy of imagination, of the power of many minds to become one, overpowering one another by spoken words and by unspoken thought till they have become a single intense, unhesitating energy. One mind was doubtless the master, I thought, but all the minds gave a little, creating or revealing for a moment what I must call a supernatural artist.

## IV

Some years afterwards I was staying with some friends in Paris.[12] I had got up before breakfast and gone out to buy a newspaper. I had noticed the servant, a girl who had come from the country some years before, laying the table for breakfast. As I had passed her I had been telling myself one of those long foolish tales which one tells only to oneself. If something had happened that had not happened, I would have hurt my arm, I thought. I saw myself with my arm in a sling in the middle of some childish adventures. I returned with the newspaper and met my host and hostess in the door. The moment they saw me they cried out, 'Why, the *bonne* has just told us you had your arm in a sling. We thought something must have happened to you last night, that you had been run over maybe'—or some such words. I had been dining out at the other end of Paris, and had come in after everybody had gone to bed. I had cast my imagination so strongly upon the servant that she had seen it, and with what had appeared to be more than the mind's eye.

One afternoon, about the same time, I was thinking very intently of a certain fellow-student for whom I had a message, which I hesitated about writing.[13] In a couple of days I got a letter from a place some hundreds of miles away where that student was. On the afternoon when I had been thinking so intently I had suddenly appeared there amid a crowd of people in a hotel and as seeming solid as if in the flesh. My fellow-student had seen me, but no one else, and had asked me to come again when the people had gone. I had vanished, but had come again in the middle of the night and given the message. I myself had no knowledge of either apparition.

I could tell of stranger images, of stranger enchantments, of stranger imaginations, cast consciously or unconsciously over as great distances by friends or by myself, were it not that the greater energies of the mind seldom break forth but when the deeps are loosened. They break forth amid events too private or too sacred for public speech, or seem themselves, I know not why, to belong to hidden things. I have written of these breakings forth, these loosenings of the deep, with some care and some detail, but I shall keep my record shut. After all, one can but bear witness less to convince him who won't believe than to protect him who does, as Blake puts it, enduring unbelief and misbelief and ridicule as best one may.[14] I shall be content to show that past times have believed as I do, by quoting Joseph Glanvil's description of the Scholar-Gipsy. Joseph Glanvil is dead, and will not mind unbelief and misbelief and ridicule.

The Scholar-Gipsy, too, is dead, unless indeed perfectly wise magicians can live till it please them to die, and he is wandering somewhere, even if one cannot see him, as Arnold imagined, 'at some lone ale-house in the Berkshire moors, on the warm ingle-bench,' or 'crossing the stripling Thames at Bablock Hithe,' or 'trailing his fingers in the cool stream,' or 'giving store of flowers—the frail-leaf'd white anemone, dark hare-bells drenched with dew of summer eves,' to the girls 'who from the distant hamlets come to dance around the Fyfield elm in May,' or 'sitting upon the river bank o'ergrown,' living on through time 'with a free onward impulse.'[15] This is Joseph Glanvil's story—

> There was very lately a lad in the University of Oxford who, being of very pregnant and ready parts and yet wanting the encouragement of preferment, was by his poverty forced to leave his studies there, and to cast himself upon the wide world for a livelihood. Now his necessities growing daily on him, and wanting the help of friends to relieve him, he was at last forced to join himself to a company of vagabond gipsies, whom occasionally he met with, and to follow their trade for a maintenance. . . . After he had been a pretty while exercised in the trade, there chanced to ride by a couple of scholars, who had formerly been of his acquaintance. The scholar had quickly spied out these old friends among the gipsies, and their amazement to see him among such society had well-nigh discovered him; but by a sign he prevented them owning him before that crew, and taking one of them aside privately, desired him with his friend to go to an inn, not far distant, promising there to come to them. They accordingly went thither and he follows: after their first salutation his friends inquire how he came to lead so odd a life as that was, and so joined himself into such a beggarly company. The scholar gipsy having given them an account of the necessity which drove him to that kind of life, told them that

> the people he went with were not such impostors as they were taken for, but that they had a traditional kind of learning among them and could do wonders by the power of imagination, and that himself had learned much of their art and improved it further than themselves could. And to evince the truth of what he told them, he said he'd remove into another room, leaving them to discourse together; and upon his return tell them the sense of what they had talked of; which accordingly he performed, giving them a full account of what had passed between them in his absence. The scholars being amazed at so unexpected a discovery, earnestly desired him to unriddle the mystery. In which he gave them satisfaction, by telling them that what he did was by the power of imagination, his phantasy leading theirs; and that himself had dictated to them the discourse they had held together while he was from them; that there were warrantable ways of heightening the imagination to that pitch as to bend another's, and that when he had compassed the whole secret, some parts of which he was yet ignorant of, he intended to leave their company and give the whole world an account of what he had learned.[16]

If all who have described events like this have not dreamed, we should rewrite our histories, for all men, certainly all imaginative men, must be for ever casting forth enchantments, glamours, illusions; and all men, especially tranquil men who have no powerful egotistic life, must be continually passing under their power. Our most elaborate thoughts, elaborate purposes, precise emotions, are often, as I think, not really ours, but have on a sudden come up, as it were, out of hell or down out of heaven. The historian should remember, should he not? angels and devils not less than kings and soldiers, and plotters and thinkers. What matter if the angel or devil, as indeed certain old writers believed, first wrapped itself with an organized shape in some man's imagination? what matter 'if God himself only acts or is in existing beings or men,' as Blake believed? we must none the less admit that invisible beings, far wandering influences, shapes that may have floated from a hermit of the wilderness, brood over council-chambers and studies and battle-fields.[17] We should never be certain that it was not some woman treading in the wine-press who began that subtle change in men's minds, that powerful movement of thought and imagination about which so many Germans have written; or that the passion, because of which so many countries were given to the sword, did not begin in the mind of some shepherd boy, lighting up his eyes for a moment before it ran upon its way.

## V

We cannot doubt that barbaric people receive such influences more visibly and obviously, and in all likelihood more easily and fully than we do, for our life in cities, which deafens or kills the passive meditative life, and our education that enlarges the separated, self-moving mind, have made our souls less sensitive. Our souls that were once naked to the winds of heaven are now thickly clad, and have learned to build a house and light a fire upon its hearth, and shut-to the doors and windows. The winds can, indeed, make us draw near to the fire, or can even lift the carpet and whistle under the door, but they could do worse out on the plains long ago. A certain learned man, quoted by Mr. Lang in his *Making of Religion,* contends that the memories of primitive man and his thoughts of distant places must have had the intensity of hallucination, because there was nothing in his mind to draw his attention away from them—an explanation that does not seem to me complete—and Mr. Lang goes on to quote certain travellers to prove that savages live always on the edges of vision.[18] One Laplander who wished to become a Christian, and thought visions but heathenish, confessed to a traveller, to whom he had given a minute account of many distant events, read doubtless in that traveller's mind, 'that he knew not how to make use of his eyes, since things altogether distant were present to them.'[19] I myself could find in one district in Galway but one man who had not seen what I can but call spirits, and he was in his dotage. 'There is no man mowing a meadow but sees them at one time or another,' said a man in a different district.[20]

If I can unintentionally cast a glamour, an enchantment, over persons of our own time who have lived for years in great cities, there is no reason to doubt that men could cast intentionally a far stronger enchantment, a far stronger glamour, over the more sensitive people of ancient times, or that men can still do so where the old order of life remains unbroken. Why should not the Scholar-Gipsy cast his spell over his friends? Why should not St. Patrick, or he of whom the story was first told, pass his enemies, he and all his clerics, as a herd of deer?[21] Why should not enchanters like him in the *Morte d'Arthur* make troops of horse seem but grey stones?[22] Why should not the Roman soldiers, though they came of a civilisation which was ceasing to be sensitive to these things, have trembled for a moment before the enchantments of the Druids of Mona?[23] Why should not the Jesuit father, or the Count Saint-Germain, or whoever the tale was first told of, have really seemed to leave the city in a coach and four and by all the Twelve Gates at once?[24] Why should not Moses and the enchanters of Pharaoh have made their staffs as the medicine men of many primitive peoples make their pieces of old rope seem like devouring serpents?[25] Why should not that mediæval enchanter have made summer and all its blossoms seem to break forth in middle winter?

May we not learn some day to rewrite our histories, when they touch upon these things?

Men who are imaginative writers to-day may well have preferred to influence the imagination of others more directly in past times. Instead of learning their craft with paper and a pen they may have sat for hours imagining themselves to be stocks and stones and beasts of the wood, till the images were so vivid that the passers-by became but a part of the imagination of the dreamer, and wept or laughed or ran away as he would have them. Have not poetry and music arisen, as it seems, out of the sounds the enchanters made to help their imagination to enchant, to charm, to bind with a spell themselves and the passers-by? These very words, a chief part of all praises of music or poetry, still cry to us their origin. And just as the musician or the poet enchants and charms and binds with a spell his own mind when he would enchant the mind of others, so did the enchanter create or reveal for himself as well as for others the supernatural artist or genius, the seeming transitory mind made out of many minds, whose work I saw, or thought I saw, in that suburban house. He kept the doors too, as it seems, of those less transitory minds, the genius of the family, the genius of the tribe, or it may be, when he was mighty-souled enough, the genius of the world. Our history speaks of opinions and discoveries, but in ancient times when, as I think, men had their eyes ever upon those doors, history spoke of commandments and revelations. They looked as carefully and as patiently towards

Sinai and its thunders as we look towards parliaments and laboratories. We are always praising men in whom the individual life has come to perfection, but they were always praising the one mind, their foundation of all perfection.

## VI

I once saw a young Irish woman, fresh from a convent school, cast into a profound trance, though not by a method known to any hypnotist. In her waking state she thought the apple of Eve was the kind of apple you can buy at the greengrocer's, but in her trance she saw the Tree of Life with ever-sighing souls moving in its branches instead of sap, and among its leaves all the fowl of the air, and on its highest bough one white fowl wearing a crown.[26] When I went home I took from the shelf a translation of *The Book of Concealed Mystery,** an old Jewish book, and cutting the pages came upon this passage, which I cannot think I had ever read: 'The Tree, . . . is the Tree of the Knowledge of Good and Evil . . . in its branches the birds lodge and build their nests, the souls and the angels have their place.'[27]

I once saw a young Church of Ireland man, a bank clerk in the west of Ireland, thrown in a like trance.[28] I have no doubt that he, too, was quite certain that the apple of Eve was a greengrocer's apple, and yet he saw the tree and heard the souls sighing through its branches, and saw apples with human faces, and laying his ear to an apple heard a sound as of fighting hosts within. Presently he strayed from the tree and came to the edge of Eden, and there he found himself not by the wilderness he had learned of at the Sunday-school, but upon the summit of a great mountain, of a mountain 'two miles high.'[29] The whole summit, in contradiction to all that would have seemed probable to his waking mind, was a great walled garden. Some years afterwards I found a mediæval diagram, which pictured Eden as a walled garden upon a high mountain.

Where did these intricate symbols come from? Neither I nor the one or two people present or the seers had ever seen, I am convinced, the description in *The Book of Concealed Mystery,* or the mediæval

*Translated by Mathers in *The Kabbalah Unveiled* [1924].

diagram. Remember that the images appeared in a moment perfect in all their complexity. If one can imagine that the seers or that I myself or another had indeed read of these images and forgotten it, that the supernatural artist's knowledge of what was in our buried memories accounted for these visions, there are numberless other visions to account for. One cannot go on believing in improbable knowledge for ever. For instance, I find in my diary that on December 27, 1897, a seer, to whom I had given a certain old Irish symbol, saw Brigid, the goddess, holding out 'a glittering and wriggling serpent,' and yet I feel certain that neither I nor he knew anything of her association with the serpent until *Carmina Gadelica* was published a few months ago.[30] And an old Irish woman who can neither read nor write has described to me a woman dressed like Dian, with helmet, and short skirt and sandals, and what seemed to be buskins.[31] Why, too, among all the countless stories of visions that I have gathered in Ireland, or that a friend has gathered for me, are there none that mix the dress of different periods?[32] The seers when they are but speaking from tradition will mix everything together, and speak of Finn mac Cumhal going to the Assizes at Cork.[33] Almost every one who has ever busied himself with such matters has come, in trance or dream, upon some new and strange symbol or event, which he has afterwards found in some work he had never read or heard of. Examples like this are as yet too little classified, too little analysed, to convince the stranger, but some of them are proof enough for those they have happened to, proof that there is a memory of nature that reveals events and symbols of distant centuries. Mystics of many countries and many centuries have spoken of this memory; and the honest men and charlatans, who keep the magical traditions which will some day be studied as a part of folk-lore, base most that is of importance in their claims upon this memory. I have read of it in *Paracelsus* and in some Indian book that describes the people of past days as still living within it, 'thinking the thought and doing the deed.'[34] And I have found it in the prophetic books of William Blake, who calls its images 'the bright sculptures of Los's Hall'; and says that all events, 'all love stories,' renew themselves from those images.[35] It is perhaps well that so few believe in it, for if many did many would go out of parliaments and universities and libraries and run into the wilderness to so waste the body, and to so hush the unquiet mind that, still living, they might pass the doors the dead pass daily; for who among the wise would trouble himself with making laws or in writing history or in weighing the earth if the things of eternity seemed ready to hand?

## VII

I find in my diary of magical events for 1899 that I awoke at 3 A.M. out of a nightmare, and imagined one symbol to prevent its recurrence, and imagined another, a simple geometrical form, which calls up dreams of luxuriant vegetable life, that I might have pleasant dreams.[36] I imagined it faintly, being very sleepy, and went to sleep. I had confused dreams which seemed to have no relation with the symbol. I awoke about eight, having for the time forgotten both nightmare and symbol. Presently I dozed off again and began half to dream and half to see, as one does between sleep and waking, enormous flowers and grapes. I awoke and recognised that what I had dreamed or seen was the kind of thing appropriate to the symbol before I remembered having used it. I find another record, though made some time after the event, of having imagined over the head of a person, who was a little of a seer, a combined symbol of elemental air and elemental water. This person, who did not know what symbol I was using, saw a pigeon flying with a lobster in his bill. I find that on December 13, 1898, I used a certain star-shaped symbol with a seeress, getting her to look at it intently before she began seeing. She saw a rough stone house, and in the middle of the house the skull of a horse. I find that I had used the same symbol a few days before with a seer, and that he had seen a rough stone house, and in the middle of the house something under a cloth marked with the Hammer of Thor.[37] He had lifted the cloth and discovered a skeleton of gold with teeth of diamonds, and eyes of some unknown dim precious stones. I had made a note to this last vision, pointing out that we had been using a Solar symbol a little earlier. Solar symbols often call up visions of gold and precious stones. I do not give these examples to prove my arguments, but to illustrate them. I know that my examples will awaken in all who have not met the like, or who are not on other grounds inclined towards my arguments, a most natural incredulity.[38] It was long before I myself would admit an inherent power in symbols, for it long seemed to me that one could account for everything by the power of one imagination over another, or by telepathy, as 'The Society for Psychical Research' would say.[39] The symbol seemed powerful, I thought, merely because we thought it powerful, and we would do just as well without it. In those days I used symbols made with some ingenuity instead of merely imagining them. I used to give them to the person I was experimenting with, and tell him to hold them to his forehead without looking at them; and sometimes I made a mistake. I learned from these mistakes that if I did not myself imagine the symbol, in which case he would have a mixed vision, it was the symbol I gave by mistake* that produced the vision. Then I met with a seer who could say to me, 'I have a vision of a square pond, but I can see your thought, and you expect me to see an oblong pond,' or, 'The symbol you are imagining has made me see a woman holding a crystal, but it was a moonlight sea I should have seen.'[40] I discovered that the symbol hardly ever failed to call up its typical scene, its typical event, its typical person, but that I could practically never call up, no matter how vividly I imagined it, the particular scene, the particular event, the particular person I had in my own mind, and that when I could, the two visions rose side by side.

I cannot now think symbols less than the greatest of all powers whether they are used consciously by the masters of magic, or half unconsciously by their successors, the poet, the musician and the artist.[41] At first I tried to distinguish between symbols and symbols, between what I called inherent symbols and arbitrary symbols, but the distinction has come to mean little or nothing. Whether their power has arisen out of themselves, or whether it has an arbitrary origin, matters little, for they act, as I believe, because the great memory associates them with certain events and moods and persons. Whatever the passions of man have gathered about, becomes a symbol in the great memory, and in the hands of him who has the secret it is a worker of wonders, a caller-up of angels or of devils. The symbols are of all kinds, for everything in heaven or earth has its association, momentous or trivial, in the great memory, and one never knows

*I forgot that my 'subconsciousness' would know clairvoyantly what symbol I had really given and would respond to the associations of that symbol. I am, however, certain that the main symbols (symbolic roots, as it were) draw upon associations which are beyond the reach of the individual 'subconsciousness'. 1924.

what forgotten events may have plunged it, like the toadstool and the ragweed, into the great passions. Knowledgeable men and women in Ireland sometimes distinguish between the simples that work cures by some medical property in the herb, and those that do their work by magic.[42] Such magical simples as the husk of the flax, water out of the fork of an elm-tree, do their work, as I think, by awaking in the depths of the mind where it mingles with the great mind, and is enlarged by the great memory, some curative energy, some hypnotic command. They are not what we call faith cures, for they have been much used and successfully, the traditions of all lands affirm, over children and over animals, and to me they seem the only medicine that could have been committed safely to ancient hands. To pluck the wrong leaf would have been to go uncured, but, if one had eaten it, one might have been poisoned.

## VIII

I have now described that belief in magic which has set me all but unwilling among those lean and fierce minds who are at war with their time, who cannot accept the days as they pass, simply and gladly; and I look at what I have written with some alarm, for I have told more of the ancient secret than many among my fellow-students think it right to tell.[43] I have come to believe so many strange things because of experience, that I see little reason to doubt the truth of many things that are beyond my experience; and it may be that there are beings who watch over that ancient secret, as all tradition affirms, and resent, and perhaps avenge, too fluent speech. They say in the Aran Islands that if you speak overmuch of the things of Faery your tongue becomes like a stone, and it seems to me, though doubtless naturalistic reason would call it Auto-suggestion or the like, that I have often felt my tongue become just so heavy and clumsy.[44] More than once, too, as I wrote this very essay I have become uneasy, and have torn up some paragraph, not for any literary reason, but because some incident or some symbol that would perhaps have meant nothing to the reader, seemed, I know not why, to belong to hidden things. Yet I must write or be of no account to any cause, good or evil; I must commit what merchandise of wisdom I have to this ship of written speech, and after all, I have many a time watched it put out to sea with not less alarm when all the speech was rhyme. We who write, we who bear witness, must often hear our hearts cry out against us, complaining because of their hidden things, and I know not but he who speaks of wisdom may not sometimes, in the change that is coming upon the world, have to fear the anger of the people of Faery, whose country is the heart of the world—'The Land of the Living Heart.' Who can keep always to the little pathway between speech and silence, where one meets none but discreet revelations? And surely, at whatever risk, we must cry out that imagination is always seeking to remake the world according to the impulses and the patterns in that great Mind, and that great Memory? Can there be anything so important as to cry out that what we call romance, poetry, intellectual beauty, is the only signal that the supreme Enchanter, or some one in His councils, is speaking of what has been, and shall be again, in the consummation of time?

1901.

# THE HAPPIEST OF THE POETS

## I

Rossetti in one of his letters numbers his favourite colours in the order of his favour, and throughout his work one feels that he loved form and colour for themselves and apart from what they represent.[1] One feels sometimes that he desired a world of essences, of unmixed powers, of impossible purities. It is as though the Last Judgement had already begun in his mind and that the essences and powers, which the Divine Hand had mixed into one another to make the loam of life, fell asunder at his touch.[2] If he painted a flame or a blue distance, he painted as though he had seen the flame out of whose heart all flames had been taken, or the blue of the abyss that was before all life; and if he painted a woman's face he painted it in some moment of intensity when the ecstasy of the lover and of the saint are alike, and desire becomes wisdom without ceasing to be desire. He listens to the cry of the flesh till it becomes proud and passes beyond the world where some immense desire that the intellect cannot understand mixes with the desire for a body's warmth and softness. His genius like Shelley's can hardly stir but to the rejection of nature, whose delight is profusion, but never intensity, and like Shelley's it follows the Star of the Magi, the Morning and Evening Star, the mother of impossible hope, although it follows through deep woods, where the Star glimmers among dew-drenched boughs, and not through 'a wind-swept valley of the Apennine.'[3] Men like him cannot be happy as we understand happiness, for to be happy one must delight like nature in mere profusion, in mere abundance, in making and doing things, and if one sets an image of the perfect before one it must be the image that draws her perpetually, the image of a perfect fullness of natural life, of an Earthly Paradise.[4] That is to say, one must not be among those that would have prayed in old times in some chapel of the Star, but among those who would have prayed under the shadow of the Green Tree, and on the wet stones of the Well, among the worshippers of natural abundance.[5]

## II

I do not think it was accident, so subtle are the threads that lead the soul, that made William Morris, who seems to me the one perfectly happy and fortunate poet of modern times, celebrate the Green Tree and the goddess Habundia, and wells and enchanted waters in so many books.[6] In *The Well at the World's End* green trees and enchanted waters are shown to us, as they were understood by old writers, who thought that the generation of all things was through water; for when the water that gives a long and a fortunate life and that can be found by none but such a one as all women love is found at last, the Dry Tree, the image of the ruined land, becomes green. To him indeed as to older writers Well and Tree are all but images of the one thing, of an 'energy' that is not the less 'eternal delight' because it is half of the body.[7] He never wrote, and could not have written, of a man or woman who was not of the kin of Well or Tree. Long before he had named either he had made his 'Wanderers' follow a dream indeed, but a dream of natural happiness, and all the people of all his poems and stories from the confused beginning of his art in *The Hollow Land* to its end in *The Sundering Flood,* are full of the heavy sweetness of this dream.[8] He wrote indeed of nothing but of the quest of the Grail, but it was the Heathen Grail that gave every man his chosen food, and not the Grail of Malory or Wagner; and he came at last to praise, as other men have praised the martyrs of religion or of passion, men with lucky eyes and men whom all women love.[9]

We know so little of man and of the world that we cannot be certain that the same invisible hands, that gave him an imagination preoccupied with good fortune, gave him also health and wealth, and the power to create beautiful things without labour, that he might honour the Green Tree. It pleases me to imagine the copper mine which brought, as Mr. Mackail has told, so much unforeseen wealth and in so astonishing a way, as no less miraculous than the three arrows in

*The Sundering Flood.*[10] No mighty poet in his misery dead could have himself delighted or made us delight in men 'who knew no vain desire of foolish fame,' but who thought the dance upon 'the stubble field' and 'the battle with the earth' better than 'the bitter war' 'where right and wrong are mixed together.'[11] 'Oh the trees, the trees!' he wrote in one of his early letters, and it was his work to make us, who had been taught to sympathise with the unhappy till we had grown morbid, to sympathise with men and women who turned everything into happiness because they had in them something of the abundance of the beechen boughs or of the bursting wheat-ear.[12] He alone, I think, has told the story of Alcestis with perfect sympathy for Admetus, with so perfect a sympathy that he cannot persuade himself that one so happy died at all; and he, unlike all other poets, has delighted to tell us that the men after his own heart, the men of his *News from Nowhere,* sorrowed but a little while over unhappy love.[13] He cannot even think of nobility and happiness apart, for all his people are like his men of Burg Dale who lived 'in much plenty and ease of life, though not delicately or desiring things out of measure. They wrought with their hands and wearied themselves; and they rested from their toil and feasted and were merry; to-morrow was not a burden to them, nor yesterday a thing which they would fain forget; life shamed them not nor did death make them afraid. As for the Dale wherein they dwelt, it was indeed most fair and lovely and they deemed it the Blessing of the earth, and they trod the flowery grass beside its rippled stream amidst the green tree-boughs proudly and joyfully with goodly bodies and merry hearts.'[14]

## III

I think of his men as with broad brows and golden beards and mild eyes and tranquil speech, and of his good women as like 'The Bride' in whose face Rossetti saw and painted for once the abundance of earth and not the half-hidden light of his star.[15] They are not in love with love for its own sake, with a love that is apart from the world or at enmity with it, as Swinburne imagines Mary Stuart and as all men have imagined Helen.[16] They do not seek in love that ecstasy, which Shelley's nightingale called death, that extremity of life in which life seems to pass away like the Phœnix in flame of its own lighting, but rather a gentle self-surrender that would lose more than half its sweetness if it lost the savour of coming days.[17] They are good housewives; they sit often at the embroidery frame, and they have wisdom in flocks and herds and they are before all fruitful mothers. It seems at times as if their love was less a passion for one man out of the world than submission to the hazard of destiny, and the hope of motherhood and the innocent desire of the body. They accept changes and chances of life as gladly as they accept spring and summer and autumn and winter, and because they have sat under the shadow of the Green Tree and drunk the Waters of Abundance out of their hollow hands, the barren blossoms do not seem to them the most beautiful. When Habundia takes the shape of Birdalone she comes first as a young naked girl standing among great trees, and then as an old carline, Birdalone in stately old age. And when she praises Birdalone's naked body, and speaks of the desire it shall awaken, praise and desire are innocent because they would not break the links that chain the days to one another. The desire seems not other than the desire of the bird for its mate in the heart of the wood, and we listen to that joyous praise as though a bird watching its plumage in still water had begun to sing in its joy, or as if we heard hawk praising hawk in the middle air, and because it is the praise of one made for all noble life and not for pleasure only, it seems, though it is the praise of the body, that it is the noblest praise.

Birdalone has never seen her image but in 'a broad latten-dish,' so the wood woman must tell her of her body and praise it.

'Thus it is with thee; thou standest before me a tall and slim maiden, somewhat thin as befitteth thy seventeen summers; where thy flesh is bare of wont, as thy throat and thine arms and thy legs from the middle down, it is tanned a beauteous colour, but otherwhere it is even as fair a white, wholesome and clean as if the golden sunlight which fulfilleth the promise of the earth were playing therein. . . . Delicate and clean-made is the little trench that goeth from thy mouth to thy lips, and sweet it is, and there is more might in it than in sweet words spoken. Thy lips they are of the finest fashion, yet rather thin than full; and some would not have it so; but I would, whereas I see therein a sign of thy valiancy and friendliness. Surely he who did thy carven chin had a mind to a master work and did no less. Great was the deftness of thine imaginer, and he would have all folk who see thee wonder at thy deep thinking and thy carefulness and thy kindness. Ah, maiden! is it so that thy thoughts are ever deep and solemn? Yet at least I know it of thee that they be hale and true and sweet.

'My friend, when thou hast a mirror, some of all this thou shalt see, but not all; and when thou hast a lover some deal wilt thou hear, but not all. But now thy she-friend may tell it thee all, if she have eyes to see it, as have I; whereas no man could say so much of thee before the mere love should overtake him, and turn his speech into the folly of love and the madness of desire.'[18]

All his good women, whether it is Danaë in her tower, or that woman in *The Wood beyond the World* who can make the withered flowers in her girdle grow young again by the touch of her hand, are of the kin of the wood woman.[19] All his bad women too and his half-bad women are of her kin. The evils their enchantments make are a disordered abundance like that of weedy places, and they are cruel as wild creatures are cruel and they have unbridled desires. One finds these evils in their typical shape in that isle of the Wondrous Isles, where the wicked witch has her pleasure-house and her prison, and in that 'isle of the old and the young,' where until her enchantment is broken second childhood watches over children who never grow old and who seem to the bystander who knows their story 'like images' or like 'the rabbits on the grass.'[20] It is as though Nature spoke through him at all times in the mood that is upon her when she is opening the apple-blossom or reddening the apple or thickening the shadow of the boughs, and that the men and women of his verse and of his stories are all the ministers of her mood.

## IV

When I was a child I often heard my elders talking of an old turreted house where an old great-uncle of mine lived, and of its gardens and its long pond where there was an island with tame eagles; and one day somebody read me some verses and said they made him think of that old house where he had been very happy.[21] The verses ran in my head for years and became to me the best description of happiness in the world, and I am not certain that I know a better even now. They were those first dozen verses of 'Golden Wings' that begin:

Midways of a walled garden
  In the happy poplar land
  Did an ancient castle stand,
With an old knight for a warden.

Many scarlet bricks there were
  In its walls, and old grey stone;
  Over which red apples shone
At the right time of the year.

On the bricks the green moss grew,
  Yellow lichen on the stone,
  Over which red apples shone;
Little war that castle knew.[22]

When William Morris describes a house of any kind, and makes his description poetical, it is always, I think, some house that he would have liked to have lived in, and I remember him saying about the time when he was writing of that great house of the Wolfings, 'I decorate modern houses for people, but the house that would please me would be some great room where one talked to one's friends in one corner and ate[†] in another and slept in another and worked in another.'[23] Indeed all he writes seems to me like the make-believe of a child who is remaking the world, not always in the same way, but always after its own heart; and so, unlike all other modern writers, he makes his poetry out of unending pictures of a happiness that is often what a child might imagine, and always a happiness that sets mind and body at ease. Now it is a picture of some great room full of merriment, now of the wine-press, now of the golden threshing-floor, now of an old mill among apple-trees, now of cool water after the heat of the sun, now of some well-sheltered, well-tilled place among woods or mountains, where men and women live happily, knowing of nothing that is too far off or too great for the affections. He has but one story to tell us, how some man or woman lost and found again the happiness that is always half of the body; and even when they are wandering from it, leaves must fall over them, and flowers make fragrances about them, and warm winds fan them, and birds sing to them, for being of Habundia's kin they must not forget the shadow of her Green Tree even for a moment, and the waters of her Well must be always wet upon their sandals. His poetry often wearies us as the unbroken green of July wearies us, for there is something in us, some bitterness because of the Fall it may be, that takes a little from the sweetness of Eve's apple after the first mouthful; but he who did all things gladly and easily, who never knew the curse of labour, found it always as sweet as it was in Eve's mouth. All kinds of associations have gathered about the pleasant things of the world and half taken the pleasure out of them for the greater number of men, but he saw them as when they came from the Divine Hand. I often see him in my mind as I saw him once at Hammersmith holding up a glass of claret towards the light and saying, 'Why do people say it is prosaic to get inspiration out of wine? Is it not the sunlight and the sap in the leaves? Are not grapes made by the sunlight and the sap?'[24]

## V

In one of his little Socialist pamphlets he tells how he sat under an elm-tree and watched the starlings and thought of an old horse and an old labourer that had passed him by, and of the men and women he had seen in towns; and he wondered how all these had come to be as they were.[25] He saw that the starlings were beautiful and merry, and that men and the old horse they had subdued to their service were ugly and miserable, and yet the starlings, he thought, were of one kind whether there or in the South of England, and the ugly men and women were of one kind with those whose nobility and beauty had moved the ancient sculptors and poets to imagine the gods and the heroes after the images of men. Then he began, he tells us, to meditate how this great difference might be ended and a new life, which would permit men to have beauty in common among them as the starlings have, be built on the wrecks of the old life. In other words, his mind was illuminated from within and lifted into prophecy in the full right sense of the word, and he saw the natural things he was alone gifted to see in their perfect form; and having that faith which is alone worth having, for it includes all others, a sure knowledge established in the constitution of his mind that perfect things are final things, he announced that all he had seen would come to pass.

I do not think he troubled to understand books of economics, and Mr. Mackail says, I think, that they vexed him and wearied him.[26] He found it enough to hold up, as it were, life as it is to-day beside his visions, and to show how faded its colours were and how sapless it was. And if we had not enough artistic feeling, enough feeling for the perfect that is, to admit the authority of the vision; or enough faith to understand that all that is imperfect passes away, he would not, as I think, have argued with us in a serious spirit. Though I think that he never used the kinds of words I use in writing of him, though I think he would even have disliked a word like faith with its theological associations, I am certain that he understood thoroughly, as all artists understand a little, that the important things, the things we must believe in or perish, are beyond argument. We can no more reason about them than can the pigeon, come but lately from the egg, about the hawk whose shadow makes it cower among the grass. His vision is true because it is poetical, because we are a little happier when we are looking at it; and he knew as Shelley knew by an act of faith that the economists should take their measurements not from life as it is, but from the vision of men like him, from the vision of the world made perfect that is buried under all minds.[27] The early Christians were of the kin of the Wilderness and of the Dry Tree, and they saw an unearthly Paradise, but he was of the kin of the Well and of the Green Tree and he saw an Earthly Paradise.

He obeyed his vision when he tried to make first his own house, for he was in this matter also like a child playing with the world, and then houses of other people, places where one could live happily; and he obeyed it when he wrote essays about the nature of happy work, and when he spoke at street corners about the coming changes.

He knew clearly what he was doing towards the end, for he lived at a time when poets and artists have begun again to carry the burdens that priests and theologians took from them angrily some few hundred years ago. His art was not more essentially religious than Rossetti's art, but it was different, for Rossetti, drunken with natural beauty, saw the supernatural beauty, the impossible beauty, in his frenzy, while he being less intense and more tranquil would show us a beauty that would wither if it did not set us at peace with natural things, and if we did not believe that it existed always a little, and would some day exist in its fullness. He may not have been, indeed he was not, among the very greatest of the poets, but he was among the greatest of those who prepare the last reconciliation when the Cross shall blossom with roses.[28]

1902.

# THE PHILOSOPHY OF SHELLEY'S POETRY

## I. HIS RULING IDEAS

When I was a boy in Dublin I was one of a group who rented a room in a mean street to discuss philosophy.[1] My fellow-students got more and more interested in certain modern schools of mystical belief, and I never found anybody to share my one unshakable belief. I thought that whatever of philosophy has been made poetry is alone permanent, and that one should begin to arrange it in some regular order, rejecting nothing as the make-believe of the poets. I thought, so far as I can recollect my thoughts after so many years, that if a powerful and benevolent spirit has shaped the destiny of this world, we can better discover that destiny from the words that have gathered up the heart's desire of the world, than from historical records, or from speculation, wherein the heart withers. Since then I have observed dreams and visions very carefully, and am now certain that the imagination has some way of lighting on the truth that the reason has not, and that its commandments, delivered when the body is still and the reason silent, are the most binding we can ever know. I have re-read *Prometheus Unbound,* which I had hoped my fellow-students would have studied as a sacred book, and it seems to me to have an even more certain place than I had thought, among the sacred books of the world. I remember going to a learned scholar to ask about its deep meanings, which I felt more than understood, and his telling me that it was Godwin's *Political Justice* put into rhyme, and that Shelley was a crude revolutionist, and believed that the overturning of kings and priests would regenerate mankind.[2] I quoted the lines which tell how the halcyons ceased to prey on fish, and how poisonous leaves became good for food, to show that he foresaw more than any political regeneration, but was too timid to push the argument.[3] I still believe that one cannot help believing him, as this scholar I know believes him, a vague thinker, who mixed occasional great poetry with a phantastic rhetoric, unless one compares such passages, and above all such passages as describe the liberty he praised, till one has discovered the system of belief that lay behind them. It should seem natural to find his thought full of subtlety, for Mrs. Shelley has told how he hesitated whether he should be a metaphysician or a poet, and has spoken of his 'huntings after the obscure' with regret,[4] and said of that *Prometheus Unbound*, which so many for three generations have thought *Political Justice* put into rhyme, 'It requires a mind as subtle and penetrating as his own to understand the mystic meanings scattered throughout the poem. They elude the ordinary reader by their abstraction and delicacy of distinction, but they are far from vague. It was his design to write prose metaphysical essays on the Nature of Man, which would have served to explain much of what is obscure in his poetry; a few scattered fragments of observation and remarks alone remain. He considered these philosophical views of mind and nature to be instinct with the intensest spirit of poetry.'[5] From these scattered fragments and observations, and from many passages read in their light, one soon comes to understand that his liberty was so much more than the liberty of *Political Justice* that it was one with Intellectual Beauty, and that the regeneration he foresaw was so much more than the regeneration many political dreamers have foreseen, that it could not come in its perfection till the Hours bore 'Time to his grave in eternity.'[6] In *A Defence of Poetry*, he will have it that the poet and the lawgiver hold their station by the right of the same faculty, the one uttering in words and the other in the forms of society, his vision of the divine order, the Intellectual Beauty. 'Poets, according to the circumstances of the age and nation in which they appeared, were called in the earliest epoch of the world legislators or prophets, and a poet essentially comprises and unites both these characters. For he not only beholds intensely the present as it is, and discovers those laws according to which present things are to be ordained, but he beholds the future in the present, and his thoughts are the germs of the flowers and the fruit of latest time.' 'Language, colour, form, and religious and civil habits of action are all the instruments and materials of poetry.' Poetry is 'the creation of actions according to the unchangeable process of human nature as existing in the mind of the creator, which is itself the image of all other minds.' 'Poets have been challenged to resign the civic crown to reasoners and merchants. . . . It is admitted that the exercise of the imagination is the most delightful, but it is alleged that that of reason is the more useful. . . . Whilst the mechanist abridges and the political economist combines labour, let them be sure that their speculations, for want of correspondence with those first principles which belong to the imagination, do not tend, as they have in modern England, to exasperate at once the extremes of luxury and want. . . . The rich have become richer, the poor have become poorer, . . . such are the effects which must ever flow from an unmitigated exercise of the calculating faculty.'[7] The speaker of these things might almost be Blake, who held that the Reason not only created Ugliness, but all other evils.[8] The books of all wisdom are hidden in the cave of the Witch of Atlas, who is one of his personifications of beauty, and when she moves over the enchanted river that is an image of all life, the priests cast aside their deceits, and the king crowns an ape to mock his own sovereignty, and the soldiers gather about the anvils to beat their swords to ploughshares, and lovers cast away their timidity, and friends are united;[9] while the power, which in *Laon and Cythna,* awakens the mind of the reformer to contend, and itself contends, against the tyrannies of the world, is first seen, as the star of love or beauty.[10] And at the end of the 'Ode to Naples,' he cries out to 'the spirit of beauty' to overturn the tyrannies of the world, or to fill them with its 'harmonising ardours.'[11] He calls the spirit of beauty liberty, because despotism, and perhaps, as 'the man of virtuous soul commands not nor obeys,' all authority, pluck virtue from her path towards beauty, and because it leads us by that love whose service is perfect freedom.[12] It leads all things by love, for he cries again and again that love is the perception of beauty in thought and things, and it orders all things by love, for it is love that impels the soul to its expressions in thought and in action, by making us 'seek to awaken in all things that are, a community with what we experience within ourselves.' 'We are born into the world, and there is something within us which, from the instant that we live, more and more thirsts after its likeness.' We have 'a soul within our soul that describes a circle around its proper paradise which pain and sorrow and evil dare not overleap,' and we labour to see this soul in many mirrors, that we may possess it the more abundantly.[13] He would hardly seek the progress of the world by any less gentle labour, and would hardly have us resist evil itself. He bids the reformers in *The Philosophical Review of Reform* receive 'the onset of the cavalry,' if it be sent to disperse their meetings, 'with folded arms,' and 'not because active resistance is not justifiable, but because temperance and courage would produce greater advantages than the most decisive victory'[14] and he gives them like advice in *The Masque of Anarchy,* for liberty, the poem cries, 'is love,' and can make the rich man kiss its feet, and, like those who followed Christ, give away his goods and follow it throughout the world.[15]

He does not believe that the reformation of society can bring this beauty, this divine order, among men without the regeneration of the hearts of men. Even in *Queen Mab,* which was written before he had found his deepest thought, or rather perhaps before he had found words to utter it, for I do not think men change much in their deepest thought, he is less anxious to change men's beliefs, as I think, than to cry out against that serpent more subtle than any beast of the field, 'the cause and the effect of tyranny.'[16] He affirms again and again that the virtuous, those who have 'pure desire and universal love,' are happy in the midst of tyranny, and he foresees a day when 'the spirit of nature,' the spirit of beauty of his later poems, who has her 'throne of power unappealable in every human heart,' shall have made men so virtuous that 'kingly glare will lose its power to dazzle and silently pass by,' and as it seems commerce, 'the venal interchange of all that human art or nature yields, which wealth should purchase not,' come as silently to an end.[17]

He was always, indeed in chief, a witness for that 'power unappealable.' Maddalo, in *Julian and Maddalo,* says that the soul is powerless, and can only, like a 'dreary bell hung in a heaven-illumined tower, toll our thoughts and our desires to meet round the rent heart and pray'; but Julian, who is Shelley himself, replies, as the makers of all religions have replied—

> Where is the love, beauty and truth we seek
> But in our mind? And if we were not weak,
> Should we be less in deed than in desire?[18]

while 'Mont Blanc' is an intricate analogy to affirm that the soul has its sources in 'the secret strength of things,' 'which governs thought and to the infinite heavens is a law.'[19] He even thought that men might be immortal were they sinless, and his Cythna bids the sailors be without remorse, for all that live are stained as they are. It is thus, she says, that time marks men and their thoughts for the tomb.[20] And the 'Red Comet,' the image of evil in *Laon and Cythna,* when it began its war with the star of beauty, brought not only 'Fear, Hatred, Fraud and Tyranny,' but 'Death, Decay, Earthquake, and Blight and Madness pale.'

When the Red Comet is conquered, when Jupiter is overthrown by Demogorgon, when the prophecy of Queen Mab is fulfilled, visible nature will put on perfection again.[21] He declares, in one of the notes to *Queen Mab,* that 'there is no great extravagance in presuming . . . that there should be a perfect identity between the moral and physical improvement of the human species,' and thinks it 'certain that wisdom is not compatible with disease, and that, in the present state of the climates of the earth, health in the true and comprehensive sense of the word is out of the reach of civilised man.'[22] In *Prometheus Unbound* he sees, as in the ecstasy of a saint, the ships moving among the seas of the world without fear of danger

by the light
Of wave-reflected flowers, and floating odours,
And music soft,

and poison dying out of the green things, and cruelty out of all living things, and even the toads and efts becoming beautiful, and at last Time being borne 'to his tomb in eternity.'[23]

This beauty, this divine order, whereof all things shall become a part in a kind of resurrection of the body, is already visible to the dead and to souls in ecstasy, for ecstasy is a kind of death. The dying Lionel hears the song of the nightingale, and cries—

Heardst thou not sweet words among
That heaven-resounding minstrelsy?
Heardst thou not that those who die
Awake in a world of ecstasy?

That love, when limbs are interwoven,
And sleep, when the night of life is cloven,
And thought, to the world's dim boundaries clinging,
And music when one beloved is singing,
Is death? Let us drain right joyously
The cup which the sweet bird fills for me.[24]

And in the most famous passage in all his poetry he sings of Death as of a mistress. 'Life, like a dome of many-coloured glass, stains the white radiance of eternity.' 'Die, if thou wouldst be with that which thou dost seek'; and he sees his own soon-coming death in a rapture of prophecy, for 'the fire for which all thirst' beams upon him, 'consuming the last clouds of cold mortality.'[25] When he is dead he will still influence the living, for though Adonais has fled 'to the burning fountains whence he came,' and 'is a portion of the eternal which must glow through time and change unquenchably the same,' and has 'awaked from the dream of life,' he has not gone from 'the young dawn,' or the 'caverns in the forests,' or 'the faint flowers and fountains.' He has been 'made one with nature,' and his voice is 'heard in all her music,' and his presence is felt wherever 'that power may move which has withdrawn his being to its own,' and he bears 'his part' when it is compelling mortal things to their appointed forms, and he overshadows men's minds at their supreme moments, for

when lofty thought
Lifts a young heart above its mortal lair,
And love and life contend in it for what
Shall be its earthly doom, the dead live there,
And move like winds of light on dark and stormy air.[26]

'Of his speculations as to what will befall this inestimable spirit when we appear to die,' Mrs. Shelley has written, 'a mystic ideality tinged these speculations in Shelley's mind; certain stanzas in the poem of *The Sensitive Plant* express, in some degree, the almost inexpressible idea, not that we die into another state, when this state is no longer, from some reason, unapparent as well as apparent, accordant with our being—but that those who rise above the ordinary nature of man, fade from before our imperfect organs; they remain in their "love, beauty, and delight," in a world congenial to them, and we, clogged by "error, ignorance, and strife," see them not till we are fitted by purification and improvement to their higher state.'[27] Not merely happy souls, but all beautiful places and movements and gestures and events, when we think they have ceased to be, have become portions of the eternal.

In this life
Of error, ignorance, and strife,
Where nothing is, but all things seem,
And we the shadow of the dream,

It is a modest creed, and yet
Pleasant, if one considers it,
To own that death itself must be,
Like all the rest, a mockery.

That garden sweet, that lady fair,
And all sweet shapes and odours there,
In truth have never passed away;
'Tis we, 'tis ours are changed, not they.

For love and beauty and delight
There is no death, nor change; their might
Exceeds our organs, which endure
No light, being themselves obscure.[28]

He seems in his speculations to have lit on that memory of nature the visionaries claim for the foundation of their knowledge; but I do not know whether he thought, as they do, that all things good and evil remain for ever, 'thinking the thought and doing the deed,' though not, it may be, self-conscious; or only thought that 'love and beauty and delight' remain for ever. The passage where Queen Mab awakes 'all knowledge of the past,' and the good and evil 'events of old and wondrous times,' was no more doubtless than a part of the machinery of the poem, but all the machineries of poetry are parts of the convictions of antiquity, and readily become again convictions in minds that brood over them with visionary intensity.[29]

Intellectual Beauty has not only the happy dead to do her will, but ministering spirits who correspond to the Devas of the East, and the Elemental Spirits of mediæval Europe, and the Sidhe of ancient Ireland, and whose too constant presence, and perhaps Shelley's ignorance of their more traditional forms, give some of his poetry an air of rootless phantasy.[30] They change continually in his poetry, as they do in the visions of the mystics everywhere and of the common people in Ireland, and the forms of these changes display, in an especial sense, the flowing forms of his mind when freed from all impulse not out of itself or out of super-sensual power. These are 'gleams of a remoter world which visit us in sleep,' spiritual essences whose shadows are the delights of all the senses, sounds 'folded in cells of crystal silence,' 'visions swift and sweet and quaint,' which lie waiting their moment 'each in his thin sheath like a chrysalis,' 'odours' among 'ever-blooming eden trees,' 'liquors' that can give 'happy sleep,' or can make tears 'all wonder and delight';[31] 'the golden genii who spoke to the poets of Greece in dreams'; 'the phantoms' which become the forms of the arts when 'the mind, arising bright from the embrace of beauty,' 'casts on them the gathered rays which are reality'; 'the guardians' who move in 'the atmosphere of human thought,' as 'the birds within the wind, or the fish within the wave,' or man's thought itself through all things; and who join the throng of the happy Hours when Time is passing away—

As the flying fish leap
From the Indian deep,
And mix with the seabirds half asleep.[32]

It is these powers which lead Asia and Panthea, as they would lead all the affections of humanity, by words written upon leaves, by faint songs, by eddies of echoes that draw 'all spirits on that secret way,' by the 'dying odours' of flowers and by 'the sunlight of the sphered dew,' beyond the gates of birth and death to awake Demogorgon, eternity, that 'the painted veil called life' may be 'torn aside.'[33]

There are also ministers of ugliness and all evil, like those that came to Prometheus—

> As from the rose which the pale priestess kneels
> To gather for her festal crown of flowers,
> The aërial crimson falls, flushing her cheek,
> So from our victim's destined agony
> The shade which is our form invests us round;
> Else we are shapeless as our mother Night.[34]

Or like those whose shapes the poet sees in *The Triumph of Life,* coming from the procession that follows the car of life, as 'hope' changes to 'desire,' shadows 'numerous as the dead leaves blown in autumn evening from a poplar tree'; and resembling those they come from, until, if I understand an obscure phrase aright, they are 'wrapt' round 'all the busy phantoms that live there as the sun shapes the clouds.'[35] Some to sit 'chattering like apes,' and some like 'old anatomies' 'hatching their bare broods under the shade of dæmons' wings,' laughing 'to reassume the delegated powers' they had given to the tyrants of the earth, and some 'like small gnats and flies' to throng 'about the brow of lawyers, statesmen, priest and theorist,' and some 'like discoloured shapes of snow' to fall 'on fairest bosoms and the sunniest hair,' to be 'melted by the youthful glow which they extinguish,' and many to 'fling shadows of shadows yet unlike themselves,' shadows that are shaped into new forms by that 'creative ray' in which all move like motes.[36]

These ministers of beauty and ugliness were certainly more than metaphors or picturesque phrases to one who believed the 'thoughts which are called real or external objects' differed but in regularity of recurrence from 'hallucinations, dreams, and the ideas of madness,' and lessened this difference by telling how he had dreamed 'three several times, between intervals of two or more years, the same precise dream,' and who had seen images with the mind's eye that left his nerves shaken for days together.[37] Shadows that were as when there

> hovers
> A flock of vampire bats before the glare

Of the tropic sun, bringing, ere evening,
Strange night upon some Indian isle,[38]

could not but have had more than a metaphorical and picturesque being to one who had spoken in terror with an image of himself, and who had fainted at the apparition of a woman with eyes in her breasts, and who had tried to burn down a wood, if we can trust Mrs. Williams' account, because he believed a devil, who had first tried to kill him, had sought refuge there.[39]

It seems to me, indeed, that Shelley had reawakened in himself the age of faith, though there were times when he would doubt, as even the saints have doubted, and that he was a revolutionist, because he had heard the commandment, 'If ye know these things, happy are ye if ye do them.'[40] I have re-read his *Prometheus Unbound* for the first time for many years, in the woods of Drim-na-Rod, among the Echtge hills, and sometimes I have looked towards Slieve-nan-Orr where the country people say the last battle of the world shall be fought till the third day, when a priest shall lift a chalice, and the thousand years of peace begin.[41] And I think this mysterious song utters a faith as simple and as ancient as the faith of those country people, in a form suited to a new age, that will understand with Blake that the Holy Spirit is 'an intellectual fountain,' and that the kinds and degrees of beauty are the images of its authority.[42]

## II. HIS RULING SYMBOLS

At a comparatively early time Shelley made his imprisoned Cythna become wise in all human wisdom through the contemplation of her own mind, and write out this wisdom upon the sands in 'signs' that were 'clear elemental shapes whose smallest change' made 'a subtler language within language,' and were 'the key of truths, which once were dimly taught in old Crotona.'[43] His early romances and much throughout his poetry show how strong a fascination the traditions of magic and of the magical philosophy had cast over his mind, and one can hardly suppose that he had not brooded over their doctrine of symbols or signatures, though I do not find anything to show that he gave it any deep study. One finds in his poetry, besides innumerable images that have not the definiteness of symbols, many images that are certainly symbols, and as the years went by he began to use these with a more and more deliberately symbolic purpose. I imagine that, when he wrote his earlier poems he allowed the subconscious life to lay its hands so firmly upon the rudder of his imagination, that he was little conscious of the abstract meaning of the images that rose in what seemed the idleness of his mind. Any one who has any experience of any mystical state of the soul knows how there float up in the mind profound symbols,* whose meaning, if indeed they do not delude one into the dream that they are meaningless, one does not perhaps understand for years. Nor I think has any one, who has known that experience with any constancy, failed to find some day, in some old book or on some old monument, a strange or intricate image, that had floated up before him, and to grow perhaps dizzy with the sudden conviction that our little memories are but a part of some great memory that renews the world and men's thoughts age after age, and that our thoughts are not, as we suppose, the deep but a little foam upon the deep. Shelley understood this as is proved by what he says of the eternity of beautiful things and of the influence of the dead, but whether he understood that the great memory is also a dwelling-house of symbols, of images that are living souls, I cannot tell. He had certainly experience of all but the most profound of the mystical states, and known that union with created things which assuredly must precede the soul's union with the uncreated spirit. He says, in his fragment of an essay 'On Life,' mistaking a unique experience for the common experience of all: 'Let us recollect our sensations as children . . . we less habitually distinguished all that we saw and felt from ourselves. They seemed as it were to constitute one mass. There are some persons who in this respect are always children. Those who are subject to the state called reverie, feel as if their nature were resolved into the surrounding universe or as if the surrounding universe were resolved into their being,' and he must have expected to receive thoughts and images from beyond his own mind, just in so far as that mind transcended its preoccupation with particular time and place, for he believed inspiration a kind of death;[45] and he could hardly have helped perceiving that an image that has tran-

*'Marianne's Dream' was certainly copied from a real dream of somebody's, but like images come to the mystic in his waking state.[44] [1903]

scended particular time and place becomes a symbol, passes beyond death, as it were, and becomes a living soul.

When Shelley went to the Continent with Godwin's daughter in 1814 they sailed down certain great rivers in an open boat, and when he summed up in his preface to *Laon and Cythna* the things that helped to make him a poet, he spoke of these voyages: 'I have sailed down mighty rivers and seen the sun rise and set and the stars come forth whilst I sailed night and day down a rapid stream among mountains.'[46]

He may have seen some cave that was the bed of a rivulet by some river side, or have followed some mountain stream to its source in a cave, for from his return to England rivers and streams and wells, flowing through caves or rising in them, came into every poem of his that was of any length, and always with the precision of symbols. Alastor passed in his boat along a river in a cave; and when for the last time he felt the presence of the spirit he loved and followed, it was when he watched his image in a silent well; and when he died it was where a river fell into 'an abysmal chasm'; and the Witch of Atlas in her gladness, as he in his sadness, passed in her boat along a river in a cave, and it was where it bubbled out of a cave that she was born; and when Rousseau, the typical poet of *The Triumph of Life,* awoke to the vision that was life, it was where a rivulet bubbled out of a cave; and the poet of *Epipsychidion* met the evil beauty 'by a well under blue nightshade bowers';[47] and Cythna bore her child imprisoned in a great cave beside 'a fountain round and vast, in which the wave imprisoned leaped and boiled perpetually'; and her lover Laon was brought to his prison in a high column through a cave where there was 'a putrid pool,' and when he went to see the conquered city he dismounted beside a polluted fountain in the market-place, foreshadowing thereby that spirit who at the end of *Prometheus Unbound* gazes at a regenerated city from 'within a fountain in the public square'; and when Laon and Cythna are dead they awake beside a fountain and drift into Paradise along a river;[48] and at the end of things Prometheus and Asia are to live amid a happy world in a cave where a fountain 'leaps with an awakening sound';[49] and it was by a fountain, the meeting-place of certain unhappy lovers, that Rosalind and Helen told their unhappiness to one another; and it was under a willow by a fountain that the enchantress and her lover began their unhappy love;[50] while his lesser poems and his prose fragments use caves and rivers and wells and fountains continually as metaphors. It may be that his subconscious life seized upon some passing scene, and moulded it into an ancient symbol without help from anything but that great memory; but so good a Platonist as Shelley could hardly have thought of any cave as a symbol, without thinking of Plato's cave that was the world; and so good a scholar may well have had Porphyry on 'the Cave of the Nymphs' in his mind.[51] When I compare Porphyry's description of the cave where the Phæacian boat left Odysseus, with Shelley's description of the cave of the Witch of Atlas, to name but one of many, I find it hard to think otherwise. I quote Taylor's translation, only putting Mr. Lang's prose for Taylor's bad verse.[52] 'What does Homer obscurely signify by the cave in Ithaca which he describes in the following verses? "Now at the harbour's head is a long-leaved olive tree, and hard by is a pleasant cave and shadowy, sacred to the nymphs, that are called Naiads. And therein are mixing bowls and jars of stone, and there moreover do bees hive. And there are great looms of stone, whereon the nymphs weave raiment of purple stain, a marvel to behold; and there are waters welling evermore. Two gates there are to the cave, the one set towards the North wind, whereby men may go down, but the portals towards the South pertain rather to the gods, whereby men may not enter: it is the way of the immortals."' He goes on to argue that the cave was a temple before Homer wrote, and that 'the ancients did not establish temples without fabulous symbols,' and then begins to interpret Homer's description in all its detail. The ancients, he says, 'consecrated a cave to the world' and held 'the flowing waters' and the 'obscurity of the cavern' 'apt symbols of what the world contains,' and he calls to witness Zoroaster's cave with fountains; and often caves are, he says, symbols of 'all invisible power; because as caves are obscure and dark, so the essence of all these powers is occult,' and quotes a lost hymn to Apollo to prove that nymphs living in caves fed men 'from intellectual fountains'; and he contends that fountains and rivers symbolise generation, and that the word nymph 'is commonly applied to all souls descending into generation,' and that the two gates of Homer's cave are the gate of generation and the gate of ascent through death to the gods, the gate of cold and moisture, and the gate of heat and fire. Cold, he says, causes life in the world, and heat causes life among the gods, and the constellation of the Cup is set in the heavens near the sign Cancer, because it is there that the souls descending from the Milky Way receive their draught of the intoxicating cold drink of generation. 'The mixing bowls and jars of stone' are consecrated to the Naiads, and are also, as it seems, symbolical of Bacchus, and are of stone because of the rocky beds of the rivers. And 'the looms of stone' are the symbols of the 'souls that descend into generation.' 'For the formation of the flesh is on or about the bones, which in the bodies of animals resemble stones,' and also because 'the body is a garment' not only about the soul, but about all essences that become visible, for 'the heavens are called by the ancients a veil, in consequence of being as it were the vestments of the celestial gods.' The bees hive in the mixing bowls and jars of stone, for so Porphyry understands the passage, because honey was the symbol adopted by the ancients for 'pleasure arising from generation.'[53] The ancients, he says, called souls not only Naiads but bees, 'as the efficient cause of sweetness'; but not all souls 'proceeding into generation' are called bees, 'but those who will live in it justly and who after having performed such things as are acceptable to the gods will again return (to their kindred stars). For this insect loves to return to the place from whence it came and is eminently just and sober.' I find all these details in the cave of the Witch of Atlas, the most elaborately described of Shelley's caves, except the two gates, and these have a far-off echo in her summer journeys on her cavern river and in her winter sleep in 'an inextinguishable well of crimson fire.' We have for the mixing bowls, and jars of stone full of honey, those delights of the senses, 'sounds of air' 'folded in cells of crystal silences,' 'liquors clear and sweet' 'in crystal vials,' and for the bees, visions 'each in his thin sheath like a chrysalis,' and for 'the looms of stone' and 'raiment of purple stain' the Witch's spinning and embroidering; and the Witch herself is a Naiad, and was born from one of the Atlantides, who lay in 'a chamber of grey rock' until she was changed by the sun's embrace into a cloud.[54]

When one turns to Shelley for an explanation of the cave and fountain one finds how close his thought was to Porphyry's. He looked upon thought as a condition of life in generation and believed that the reality beyond was something other than thought. He wrote in his fragment 'On Life,' 'That the basis of all things cannot be, as the popular philosophy alleges, mind, is sufficiently evident. Mind, as far as we have any experience of its properties, and beyond that experience how vain is argument, cannot create, it can only perceive'; and in another passage he defines mind as existence.[55] Water is his great symbol of existence, and he continually meditates over its mysterious source. In his prose he tells how 'thought can with difficulty visit the intricate and winding chambers which it inhabits. It is like a river, whose rapid and perpetual stream flows outward. . . . The caverns of the mind are obscure and shadowy; or pervaded with a lustre, beautiful and bright indeed, but shining not beyond their portals.'[56] When the Witch has passed in her boat from the caverned river, that is doubtless her own destiny, she passes along the Nile 'by Moeris and the Mareotid lakes,' and sees all human life shadowed upon its waters in shadows that 'never are erased but tremble ever'; and in many a dark and subterranean street under the Nile—new caverns—and along the bank of the Nile; and as she bends over the unhappy, she compares unhappiness to the strife that 'stirs the liquid surface of man's life'; and because she can see the reality of things she is described as journeying 'in the calm depths' of 'the wide lake' we journey over unpiloted.[57] Alastor calls the river that he follows an image of his mind, and thinks that it will be as hard to say where his thought will be when he is dead as where its waters will be in ocean or cloud in a little while.[58] In 'Mont Blanc,' a poem so overladen with descriptions in parentheses that one loses sight of its logic, Shelley compares the flowing through our mind of 'the universe of things,' which are, he has explained elsewhere, but thoughts, to the flowing of the Arve through the ravine, and compares the unknown sources of our thoughts, in some 'remoter world' whose 'gleams' 'visit the soul in sleep,' to Arve's sources among the glaciers on the mountain heights.[59] Cythna, in the passage where she speaks of making signs 'a subtle language within language' on the sand by the 'fountain' of sea water in the cave where she is imprisoned, speaks of the 'cave' of her mind which gave its secrets to her, and of 'one mind the type of all' which is a 'moveless wave' reflecting 'all moveless things that are';[60] and then passing more completely under the power of the symbol, she speaks of growing wise through contemplation of the images that rise out of the fountain at the call of her will. Again and again one finds some passing allusion to the cave of man's mind, or to the caves of his youth, or to the cave of mysteries we enter at death, for to Shelley as to Porphyry it is more than an image of life in the world. It may mean any enclosed life, as when it is the dwelling-place of Asia and Prometheus, or when it is 'the still cave of poetry,' and it may have all meanings at once, or it may have as little meaning as some ancient religious symbol enwoven from the habit of centuries with the patterns of a carpet or a tapestry.[61]

As Shelley sailed along those great rivers and saw or imagined the cave that associated itself with rivers in his mind, he saw half-ruined towers upon the hilltops, and once at any rate a tower is used to symbolise a meaning that is the contrary to the meaning symbolised by caves.[62] Cythna's lover is brought through the cave where there is a polluted fountain to a high tower, for being man's far-seeing mind, when the world has cast him out he must to the 'towers of thought's crowned powers'; nor is it possible for Shelley to have forgotten this first imprisonment when he made men imprison Lionel in a tower for a like offence;[63] and because I know how hard it is to forget a symbolical meaning, once one has found it, I believe Shelley had more than a romantic scene in his mind when he made Prince Athanase follow his mysterious studies in a lighted tower above the sea, and when he made the old hermit watch over Laon in his sickness in a half-ruined tower, wherein the sea, here doubtless as to Cythna, 'the one mind,' threw 'spangled sands' and 'rarest sea shells.'[64] The tower, important in Maeterlinck, as in Shelley, is, like the sea, and rivers, and caves with fountains, a very ancient symbol, and would perhaps, as years went by, have grown more important in his poetry.[65] The contrast between it and the cave in *Laon and Cythna* suggests a contrast between the mind looking outward upon men and things and the mind looking inward upon itself, which may or may not have been in Shelley's mind, but certainly helps, with one knows not how many other dim meanings, to give the poem mystery and shadow. It is only by ancient symbols, by symbols that have numberless meanings beside the one or two the writer lays an emphasis upon, or the half-score he knows of, that any highly subjective art can escape from the barrenness and shallowness of a too conscious arrangement, into the abundance and depth of nature. The poet of essences and pure ideas must seek in the half-lights that glimmer from symbol to symbol as if to the ends of the earth, all that the epic and dramatic poet finds of mystery and shadow in the accidental circumstances of life.

The most important, the most precise of all Shelley's symbols, the one he uses with the fullest knowledge of its meaning, is the Morning and Evening Star. It rises and sets for ever over the towers and rivers, and is the throne of his genius. Personified as a woman it leads Rousseau, the typical poet of *The Triumph of Life,* under the power of the destroying hunger of life, under the power of the sun that we shall find presently as a symbol of life, and it is the Morning Star that wars against the principle of evil in *Laon and Cythna,* at first as a star with a red comet, here a symbol of all evil as it is of disorder in *Epipsychidion,* and then as a serpent with an eagle—symbols in Blake too and in the Alchemists;[66] and it is the Morning Star that appears as a winged youth to a woman, who typifies humanity amid its sorrows, in the first canto of *Laon and Cythna;* and it is invoked by the wailing women of *Hellas,* who call it 'lamp of the free' and 'beacon of love' and would go where it hides flying from the deepening night among those 'kingless continents sinless as Eden,' and 'mountains and islands' 'prankt on the sapphire sea' that are but the opposing hemispheres to the senses, but, as I think, the ideal world, the world of the dead, to the imagination; and in the 'Ode to Liberty,' Liberty is bid lead wisdom out of the inmost cave of man's mind as the Morning Star leads the sun out of the waves.[67] We know too that had *Prince Athanase* been finished it would have described the finding of Pandemos, the stars' lower genius, and the growing weary of her, and the coming to its true genius Urania at the coming of death, as the day finds the Star at evening.[68] There is hardly indeed a poem of any length in which one does not find it as a symbol of love, or liberty, or wisdom, or beauty, or of some other expression of that Intellectual Beauty, which was to Shelley's mind the central power of the world;[69] and to its faint and fleeting light he offers up all desires, that are as

The desire of the moth for the star,
  Of the night for the morrow,
The devotion to something afar
  From the sphere of our sorrow.[70]

When its genius comes to Rousseau, shedding dew with one hand, and treading out the stars with her feet, for she is also the genius of the dawn, she brings him a cup full of oblivion and love. He drinks and his mind becomes like sand 'on desert Labrador' marked by the feet of deer and a wolf. And then the new vision, life, the cold light of day moves before him, and the first vision becomes an invisible presence.[71] The same image was in his mind too when he wrote

> Hesperus flies from awakening night
> And pants in its beauty and speed with light,
> Fast fleeting, soft and bright.[72]

Though I do not think that Shelley needed to go to Porphyry's account of the cold intoxicating cup, given to the souls in the constellation of the Cup near the constellation Cancer, for so obvious a symbol as the cup, or that he could not have found the wolf and the deer and the continual flight of his Star in his own mind, his poetry becomes the richer, the more emotional, and loses something of its appearance of idle phantasy when I remember that these are ancient symbols, and still come to visionaries in their dreams.[73] Because the wolf is but a more violent symbol of longing and desire than the hound, his wolf and deer remind me of the hound and deer that Oisin saw in the Gaelic poem chasing one another on the water before he saw the young man following the woman with the golden apple; and of a Galway tale that tells how Niamh, whose name means brightness or beauty, came to Oisin as a deer; and of a vision that a friend of mine saw when gazing at a dark-blue curtain.[74] I was with a number of Hermetists, and one of them said to another, 'Do you see something in the curtain?' The other gazed at the curtain for a while and saw presently a man led through a wood by a black hound, and then the hound lay dead at a place the seer knew was called, without knowing why, 'the Meeting of the Suns,' and the man followed a red hound, and then the red hound was pierced by a spear. A white fawn watched the man out of the wood, but he did not look at it, for a white hound came and he followed it trembling, but the seer knew that he would follow the fawn at last, and that it would lead him among the gods. The most learned of the Hermetists said, 'I cannot tell the meaning of the hounds or where the Meeting of the Suns is, but I think the fawn is the Morning and Evening Star.' I have little doubt that when the man saw the white fawn he was coming out of the darkness and passion of the world into some day of partial regeneration, and that it was the Morning Star and would be the Evening Star at its second coming. I have little doubt that it was but the story of Prince Athanase and what may have been the story of Rousseau in *The Triumph of Life,* thrown outward once again from that great memory, which is still the mother of the Muses, though men no longer believe in it.

It may have been this memory, or it may have been some impulse of his nature too subtle for his mind to follow, that made Keats, with his love of embodied things, of precision of form and colouring, of emotions made sleepy by the flesh, see Intellectual Beauty in the Moon; and Blake, who lived in that energy he called eternal delight, see it in the Sun, where his personification of poetic genius labours at a furnace.[75] I think there was certainly some reason why these men took so deep a pleasure in lights that Shelley thought of with weariness and trouble. The Moon is the most changeable of symbols, and not merely because it is the symbol of change. As mistress of the waters she governs the life of instinct and the generation of things, for, as Porphyry says, even 'the apparition of images' in the 'imagination' is through 'an excess of moisture';[76] and, as a cold and changeable fire set in the bare heavens, she governs alike chastity and the joyless idle drifting hither and thither of generated things. She may give God a body and have Gabriel to bear her messages, or she may come to men in their happy moments as she came to Endymion, or she may deny life and shoot her arrows; but because she only becomes beautiful in giving herself, and is no flying ideal, she is not loved by the children of desire.

Shelley could not help but see her with unfriendly eyes. He is believed to have described Mary Shelley at a time when she had come to seem cold in his eyes, in that passage of *Epipsychidion* which tells how a woman like the Moon led him to her cave and made 'frost' creep over the sea of his mind, and so bewitched Life and Death with 'her silver voice' that they ran from him crying, 'Away, he is not of our crew.'[77] When he describes the Moon as part of some beautiful scene he can call her beautiful, but when he personifies, when his words come under the influence of that great memory or of some mysterious tide in the depth of our being, he grows unfriendly or not truly friendly or at the most pitiful. The Moon's lips 'are pale and waning,' it is 'the cold Moon,' or 'the frozen and inconstant Moon,' or it is 'forgotten' and 'waning,' or it 'wanders' and is 'weary,' or it is 'pale and grey,' or it is 'pale for weariness,' and 'wandering companionless' and 'ever changing,' and finding 'no object worth' its 'constancy,' or it is like a 'dying lady' who 'totters' 'out of her chamber led by the insane and feeble wanderings of her fading brain,' and even when it is no more than a star, it casts an evil influence that makes the lips of lovers 'lurid' or pale.[78] It only becomes a thing of delight when Time is being borne to his tomb in eternity, for then the spirit of the Earth, man's procreant mind, fills it with his own joyousness. He describes the spirit of the Earth and of the Moon, moving above the rivulet of their lives, in a passage which reads like a half-understood vision. Man has become 'one harmonious soul of many a soul' and 'all things flow to all' and 'familiar acts are beautiful through love,' and an 'animation of delight' at this change flows from spirit to spirit till the snow 'is loosened from the Moon's lifeless mountains.'[79]

Some old magical writer, I forget who, says if you wish to be melancholy hold in your left hand an image of the Moon made out of silver, and if you wish to be happy hold in your right hand an image of the Sun made out of gold.* The Sun is the symbol of sensitive life, and of belief and joy and pride and energy, of indeed the whole life of the will, and of that beauty which neither lures from far off, nor becomes beautiful in giving itself, but makes all glad because it is beauty. Taylor quotes Proclus as calling it 'the Demiurgos of everything sensible.'[81] It was therefore natural that Blake, who was always praising energy, and all exalted overflowing of oneself, and who thought art an impassioned labour to keep men from doubt and despondency, and woman's love an evil, when it would trammel man's will, should see the poetic genius not in a woman star but in the Sun, and should rejoice throughout his poetry in 'the Sun in his strength.'[82] Shelley, however, except when he uses it to describe the peculiar beauty of Emilia Viviani, who was 'like an incarnation of the Sun when light is changed to love,' saw it with less friendly eyes.[83] He

*Wilde told me that he had read this somewhere. He had suggested it to Burne-Jones as a subject for a picture.[80] 1924.

seems to have seen it with perfect happiness only when veiled in mist, or glimmering upon water, or when faint enough to do no more than veil the brightness of his own Star; and in *The Triumph of Life,* the one poem in which it is part of the avowed symbolism, its power is the being and the source of all tyrannies. When the woman personifying the Morning Star has faded from before his eyes, Rousseau sees a 'new vision' in 'a cold bright car' with a rainbow hovering over her, and as she comes the shadow passes from 'leaf and stone' and the souls she has enslaved seem in 'that light like atomies to dance within a sunbeam,' or they dance among the flowers that grow up newly 'in the grassy verdure of the desert,' unmindful of the misery that is to come upon them. 'These are the great, the unforgotten,' all who have worn 'mitres and helms and crowns or wreaths of light,' and yet have not known themselves. Even 'great Plato' is there, because he knew joy and sorrow, because life that could not subdue him by gold or pain, by 'age or sloth or slavery,' subdued him by love. All who have ever lived are there except Christ and Socrates and the 'sacred few' who put away all life could give, being doubtless followers throughout their lives of the forms borne by the flying ideal, or who, 'as soon as they had touched the world with living flame, flew back like eagles to their native noon.'[84]

In ancient times, it seems to me that Blake, who for all his protest was glad to be alive, and ever spoke of his gladness, would have worshipped in some chapel of the Sun, but that Shelley, who hated life because he sought 'more in life than any understood,' would have wandered, lost in a ceaseless reverie, in some chapel of the Star of infinite desire.[85]

I think too that as he knelt before an altar, where a thin flame burnt in a lamp made of green agate, a single vision would have come to him again and again, a vision of a boat drifting down a broad river between high hills where there were caves and towers, and following the light of one Star; and that voices would have told him how there is for every man some one scene, some one adventure, some one picture that is the image of his secret life, for wisdom first speaks in images, and that this one image, if he would but brood over it his life long, would lead his soul, disentangled from unmeaning circumstance and the ebb and flow of the world, into that far household, where the undying gods await all whose souls have become simple as flame, whose bodies have become quiet as an agate lamp.[86]

But he was born in a day when the old wisdom had vanished and was content merely to write verses, and often with little thought of more than verses.[87]

1900.

# AT STRATFORD-ON-AVON

## I

I have been hearing Shakespeare, as the traveller in *News from Nowhere* might have heard him, had he not been hurried back into our noisy time.[1] One passes through quiet streets, where gabled and red-tiled houses remember the Middle Age, to a theatre that has been made not to make money, but for the pleasure of making it, like the market houses that set the traveller chuckling; nor does one find it among hurrying cabs and ringing pavements, but in a green garden by a river side. Inside I have to be content for a while with a chair, for I am unexpected, and there is not an empty seat but this; and yet there is no one who has come merely because one must go somewhere after dinner. All day, too, one does not hear or see an incongruous or noisy thing, but spends the hours reading the plays, and the wise and foolish things men have said of them, in the library of the theatre, with its oak-panelled walls and leaded windows of tinted glass; or one rows by reedy banks and by old farm-houses, and by old churches among great trees. It is certainly one's fault if one opens a newspaper, for Mr. Benson offers a new play every night, and there is no need to talk of anything but the play in the inn-parlour, under oak beams blackened by time, showing the mark of the adze that shaped them.[2] I have seen this week *King John, Richard II.*, the second part of *Henry IV., Henry V.*, the second part of *Henry VI.*, and *Richard III.* played in their right order, with all the links that bind play to play unbroken; and partly because of a spirit in the place, and partly because of the way play supports play, the theatre has moved me as it has never done before.[3] That strange procession of kings and queens, of warring nobles, of insurgent crowds, of courtiers, and of people of the gutter, has been to me almost too visible, too audible, too full of an unearthly energy. I have felt as I have sometimes felt on grey days on the Galway shore, when a faint mist has hung over the grey sea and the grey stones, as if the world might suddenly vanish and leave nothing behind, not even a little dust under one's feet. The people my mind's eye has seen have too much of the extravagance of dreams, like all the inventions of art before our crowded life had brought moderation and compromise, to seem more than a dream, and yet all else has grown dim before them.

In London the first man you meet puts any high dream out of your head, for he will talk of something at once vapid and exciting, the moment's choice among those subjects of discourse that build up our social unity. But here he gives back one's dream like a mirror. If we do not talk of the plays, we talk of the theatre, and how many more people may be got to come, and our isolation from common things makes the future become grandiose and important. One man tells how the theatre and the library were at their foundation but part of a scheme the future is to fulfil.[4] To them will be added a school where speech, and gesture, and fencing, and all else that an actor needs will be taught, and the council, which will have enlarged its Festivals to some six weeks, will engage all the chief players of Shakespeare, and perhaps of other great dramatists in this and other countries. These chief players will need to bring but few of their supporters, for the school will be able to fill all the lesser parts with players who are slowly recovering the lost tradition of musical speech. Another man is certain that the Festival, even without the school, which would require a new endowment, will grow in importance year by year, and that it may become with favouring chance the supreme dramatic event of the world; and when I suggest that it may help to break the evil prestige of London he becomes enthusiastic.

Surely a bitter hatred of London is becoming a mark of those that love the arts, and all that have this hatred should help anything that looks like a beginning of a centre of art elsewhere.[5] The easiness of travel, which is always growing, began by emptying the country, but it may end by filling it: for adventures like this of Stratford-on-Avon show that people are ready to journey from all parts of England and Scotland and Ireland, and even from America, to live with their favourite art as shut away from the world as though they were in 'retreat,' as Catholics say. Nobody but an impressionist painter, who hides it in light and mist, even pretends to love a street for its own sake; and could we meet our friends and hear music and poetry in the country, none of us that are not captive would ever leave the thrushes. In London, we hear something that we like some twice or thrice in a winter, and among people who are thinking the while of a music-hall singer or of a member of parliament, but there we would hear it and see it among people who liked it well enough to have travelled some few hours to find it; and because those who care for the arts have few near friendships among those that do not, we would hear and see it among near friends. We would escape, too, from those artificial tastes and interests we cultivate, that we may have something to talk about among people we meet for a few minutes and not again, and the arts would grow serious as the Ten Commandments.

## II

I do not think there is anything I disliked in Stratford, besides certain new houses, but the shape of the theatre; and as a larger theatre must be built sooner or later, that would be no great matter if one would put a wiser shape into somebody's head.[6] I cannot think there is any excuse for a half-round theatre, where land is not expensive, or no very great audience to be seated within earshot of the stage; or that it was adopted for a better reason than because it has come down to us, though from a time when the art of the stage was a different art. The Elizabethan theatre was a half-round, because the players were content to speak their lines on a platform, as if they were speakers at a public meeting, and we go on building in the same shape, although our art of the stage is the art of making a succession of pictures. Were our theatres of the shape of a half-closed fan, like Wagner's theatre, where the audience sit on seats that rise towards the broad end while the play is played at the narrow end, their pictures could be composed for eyes at a small number of points of view, instead of for eyes at many points of view, above and below and at the sides, and what is no better than a trade might become an art.[7] With the eyes watching from the sides of a half-round, on the floor and in the boxes and galleries, would go the solid-built houses and the flat trees that shake with every breath of air; and we could make our pictures with robes that contrasted with great masses of colour in the back cloth[†] and such severe or decorative forms of hills and trees and houses as would not overwhelm, as our naturalistic scenery does, the idealistic art of the poet, and all at a little price. Naturalistic scene-painting is not an art, but a trade, because it is, at best, an attempt to copy the more obvious effects of nature by the methods of the ordinary landscape-painter, and by his methods made coarse and summary. It is but flashy landscape-painting and lowers the taste it appeals to, for the taste it appeals to has been formed by a more delicate art. Decorative scene-painting would be, on the other hand, as inseparable from the movements as from the robes of the players and from the falling of the light; and being in itself a grave and quiet thing it would mingle with the tones of the voices and with the sentiment of the play, without overwhelming them under an alien interest. It would be a new and legitimate art appealing to a taste formed by itself and copying but itself. Mr. Gordon Craig used scenery of this kind at the Purcell Society performance the other day, and despite some marring of his effects by the half-round shape of the theatre, it was the first beautiful scenery our stage has seen.[8] He created an ideal country where everything was possible, even speaking in verse, or speaking in music, or the expression of the whole of life in a dance, and I would like to see Stratford-on-Avon decorate its Shakespeare with like scenery. As we cannot, it seems, go back to the platform and the curtain, and the argument for doing so is not without weight, we can only get rid of the sense of unreality, which most of us feel when we listen to the conventional speech of Shakespeare, by making scenery as conventional. Time after time his people use at some moment of deep emotion an elaborate or deliberate metaphor, or do some improbable thing which breaks an emotion of reality we have imposed upon him by an art that is not his, nor in the spirit of his. It also is an essential part of his method to give slight or obscure motives of many actions that our attention may dwell on what is of chief importance, and we set these cloudy actions among solid-looking houses, and what we hope are solid-looking trees, and illusion comes to an end, slain by our desire to increase it. In his art, as in all the older art of the world, there was much make-believe, and our scenery, too, should remember the time when, as my nurse used to tell me, herons built their nests in old men's beards! Mr. Benson did not venture to play the scene in *Richard III.* where the ghosts walk, as Shakespeare wrote it, but had his scenery been as simple as Mr. Gordon Craig's purple back cloth that made Dido and Æneas seem wandering on the edge of eternity, he would have found nothing absurd in pitching the tents of Richard and Richmond side by side. Goethe has said, 'Art is art, because it is not nature!'[9] It brings us near to the archetypal ideas themselves, and away from nature, which is but their looking-glass.

## III

In *La Peau de Chagrin* Balzac spends many pages in describing a coquette, who seems the image of heartlessness, and then invents an improbable incident that her chief victim may discover how beautifully she can sing. Nobody had ever heard her sing, and yet in her singing, and in her chatter with her maid, Balzac tells us, was her true self. He would have us understand that behind the momentary self, which acts and lives in the world, and is subject to the judgement of the world, there is that which cannot be called before any mortal Judgement seat, even though a great poet, or novelist, or philosopher be sitting upon it.[10] Great literature has always been written in a like spirit, and is, indeed, the Forgiveness of Sin, and when we find it becoming the Accusation of Sin, as in George Eliot, who plucks her Tito in pieces with as much assurance as if he had been clockwork, literature has begun to change into something else.[11] George Eliot had a fierceness hardly to be found but in a woman turned argumentative, but the habit of mind her fierceness gave its life to was characteristic of her century, and is the habit of mind of the Shakespearian critics. They and she grew up in a century of utilitarianism, when nothing about a man seemed important except his utility to the State, and nothing so useful to the State as the actions whose effect can be weighed by reason. The deeds of Coriolanus, Hamlet, Timon, Richard II. had no obvious use, were, indeed, no more than the expression of their personalities, and so it was thought Shakespeare was accusing them, and telling us to be careful lest we deserve the like accusations. It did not occur to the critics that you cannot know a man from his actions because you cannot watch him in every kind of circumstance, and that men are made useless to the State as often by abundance as by emptiness, and that a man's business may at times be revelation, and not reformation. Fortinbras was, it is likely enough, a better King than Hamlet would have been, Aufidius was a more reasonable man than Coriolanus, Henry V. was a better man-at-arms than Richard II., but, after all, were not those others who changed nothing for the better and many things for the worse greater in the Divine Hierarchies? Blake has said that 'the roaring of lions, the howling of wolves, the raging of the stormy sea, and the destructive sword are portions of Eternity, too great for the eye of man,' but Blake belonged by right to the ages of Faith, and thought the State of less moment than the Divine Hierarchies.[12] Because reason can only discover completely the use of those obvious actions which everybody admires, and because every character was to be judged by efficiency in action, Shakespearian criticism became a vulgar worshipper of success. I have turned over many books in the library at Stratford-on-Avon, and I have found in nearly all an antithesis, which grew in clearness and violence as the century grew older, between two types, whose representatives were Richard II., 'sentimental,' 'weak,' 'selfish,' 'insincere,' and Henry V., 'Shakespeare's only hero.' These books took the same delight in abasing Richard II. that school-boys do in persecuting some boy of fine temperament, who has weak muscles and a distaste for school games. And they had the admiration for Henry V. that school-boys have for the sailor or soldier hero of a romance in some boys' paper. I cannot claim any minute knowledge of these books, but I think that these emotions began among the German critics, who perhaps saw something French and Latin in Richard II., and I know that Professor Dowden, whose book I once read carefully, first made these emotions eloquent and plausible.[13] He lived in Ireland, where everything has failed, and he meditated frequently upon the perfection of character which had, he thought, made England successful, for, as we say, 'cows beyond the water have long horns.'[14] He forgot that England, as Gordon has said, was made by her adventurers, by her people of wildness and imagination and eccentricity; and thought that Henry V., who only seemed to be these things because he had some commonplace vices, was not only the typical Anglo-Saxon, but the model Shakespeare held up before England; and he even thought it worth while pointing out that Shakespeare himself was making a large fortune while he was writing about Henry's victories. In Professor Dowden's successors this apotheosis went further; and it reached its height at a moment of imperialistic enthusiasm, of ever-deepening conviction that the commonplace shall inherit the earth, when somebody of reputation, whose name I cannot remember, wrote that Shakespeare admired this one character alone out of all his characters.[15] The Accusation of Sin produced its necessary fruit, hatred of all that was abundant, extravagant, exuberant, of all that sets a sail for shipwreck, and flattery of the commonplace emotions and conventional ideals of the mob, the chief Paymaster of accusation.

## IV

I cannot believe that Shakespeare looked on his Richard II. with any but sympathetic eyes, understanding indeed how ill-fitted he was to be King, at a certain moment of history, but understanding that he was lovable and full of capricious fancy, 'a wild creature' as Pater has called him.[16] The man on whom Shakespeare modelled him had been full of French elegancies, as he knew from Holinshed, and had given life a new luxury, a new splendour, and been 'too friendly' to his friends, 'too favourable' to his enemies.[17] And certainly Shakespeare had these things in his head when he made his King fail, a little because he lacked some qualities that were doubtless common among his scullions, but more because he had certain qualities that are uncommon in all ages. To suppose that Shakespeare preferred the men who deposed his King is to suppose that Shakespeare judged men with the eyes of a Municipal Councillor weighing the merits of a Town Clerk; and that had he been by when Verlaine cried out from his bed, 'Sir, you have been made by the stroke of a pen, but I have been made by the breath of God,' he would have thought the Hospital Superintendent the better man.[18] He saw indeed, as I think, in Richard II. the defeat that awaits all, whether they be Artist or Saint, who find themselves where men ask of them a rough energy and have nothing to give but some contemplative virtue, whether lyrical phantasy, or sweetness of temper, or dreamy dignity, or love of God, or love of His creatures. He saw that such a man through sheer bewilderment and impatience can become as unjust or as violent as any common man, any Bolingbroke or Prince John, and yet remain 'that sweet lovely rose.'[19] The courtly and saintly ideals of the Middle Ages were fading, and the practical ideals of the modern age had begun to threaten the unuseful dome of the sky; Merry England was fading, and yet it was not so faded that the poets could not watch the procession of the world with that untroubled sympathy for men as they are, as apart from all they do and seem, which is the substance of tragic irony.

Shakespeare cared little for the State, the source of all our judgements, apart from its shows and splendours, its turmoils and battles, its flamings out of the uncivilised heart. He did indeed think it wrong to overturn a King, and thereby to swamp peace in civil war, and the historical plays from *Henry IV.* to *Richard III.,* that monstrous birth and last sign of the wrath of Heaven, are a fulfilment of the prophecy of the Bishop of Carlisle, who was 'raised up by God' to make it; but he had no nice sense of utilities, no ready balance to measure deeds, like that fine instrument, with all the latest improvements, Gervinus and Professor Dowden handle so skilfully.[20] He meditated as Solomon, not as Bentham meditated, upon blind ambitions, untoward accidents, and capricious passions, and the world was almost as empty in his eyes as it must be in the eyes of God.[21]

> Tired with all these, for restful death I cry;—
>   As, to behold desert a beggar born,
> And needy nothing trimm'd in jollity,
>   And purest faith unhappily forsworn,
> And gilded honour shamefully misplaced,
>   And maiden virtue rudely strumpeted,
> And right perfection wrongfully disgraced,
>   And strength by limping sway disabled,
> And Art made tongue-tied by authority,
>   And folly, doctor-like, controlling skill,
> And simple truth miscall'd simplicity,
>   And captive good attending captain ill:
> Tired with all these, from these would I be gone,
> Save that, to die, I leave my love alone.[22]

## V

The Greeks, a certain scholar has told me, considered that myths are the activities of the Dæmons, and that the Dæmons shape our characters and our lives.[23] I have often had the fancy that there is some one Myth for every man, which, if we but knew it, would make us understand all he did and thought. Shakespeare's Myth, it may be, describes a wise man who was blind from very wisdom, and an empty man who thrust him from his place, and saw all that could be seen from very emptiness. It is in the story of Hamlet, who saw too great issues everywhere to play the trivial game of life, and of Fortinbras, who came from fighting battles about 'a little patch of ground' so poor that one of his captains would not give 'six ducats' to 'farm it,' and who was yet acclaimed by Hamlet and by all as the only befitting King.[24] And it is in the story of Richard II., that unripened Hamlet, and of Henry V., that ripened Fortinbras. To pose character against character was an element in Shakespeare's art, and scarcely a play is lacking in characters that are the complement of one another, and so, having made the vessel of porcelain Richard II., he had to make the vessel of clay Henry V. He makes him the reverse of all that Richard was. He has the gross vices, the coarse nerves, of one who is to rule among violent people, and he is so little 'too friendly' to his friends that he bundles them out of doors when their time is over. He is as remorseless and undistinguished as some natural force, and the finest thing in his play is the way his old companions fall out of it broken-hearted or on their way to the gallows; and instead of that lyricism which rose out of Richard's mind like the jet of a fountain to fall again where it had risen, instead of that phantasy too enfolded in its own sincerity to make any thought the hour had need of, Shakespeare has given him a resounding rhetoric that moves men, as a leading article does to-day.[25] His purposes are so intelligible to everybody that everybody talks of him as if he succeeded, although he fails in the end, as all men great and little fail in Shakespeare. His conquests abroad are made nothing by a woman turned warrior. That boy he and Katharine were to 'compound,' 'half French, half English,' 'that' was to 'go to Constantinople and take the Turk by the beard,' turns out a Saint and loses all his father had built up at home and his own life.[26]

Shakespeare watched Henry V. not indeed as he watched the greater souls in the visionary procession, but cheerfully, as one watches some handsome spirited horse, and he spoke his tale, as he spoke all tales, with tragic irony.

## VI

The five plays, that are but one play, have, when played one after another, something extravagant and superhuman, something almost mythological.[27] These nobles with their indifference to death and their immense energy seem at times no nearer the common stature of men than do the Gods and the heroes of Greek plays. Had there been no Renaissance and no Italian influence to bring in the stories of other lands, English history would, it may be, have become as important to the English imagination as the Greek Myths to the Greek imagination; and many plays by many poets would have woven it into a single story whose contours, vast as those of Greek myth, would have made living men and women seem like swallows building their nests under the architrave of some Temple of the Giants. English literature, because it would have grown out of itself, might have had the simplicity and unity of Greek literature, for I can never get out of my head that no man, even though he be Shakespeare, can write perfectly when his web is woven of threads that have been spun in many lands. And yet, could those foreign tales have come in if the great famine, the sinking down of popular imagination, the dying out of traditional phantasy, the ebbing out of the energy of race, had not made them necessary? The metaphors and language of Euphuism, compounded of the natural history and mythology of the classics, were doubtless a necessity also that something might be poured into the emptiness. Yet how they injured the simplicity and unity of the speech! Shakespeare wrote at a time when solitary great men were gathering to themselves the fire that had once flowed hither and thither among all men, when individualism in work and thought and emotion was breaking up the old rhythms of life, when the common people, sustained no longer by the myths of Christianity and of still older faiths, were sinking into the earth.

The people of Stratford-on-Avon have remembered little about him, and invented no legend to his glory. They have remembered a drinking-bout of his, and invented some bad verses for him, and that is about all.[28] Had he been some hard-drinking, hard-living, hard-riding, loud-blaspheming Squire they would have enlarged his fame by a legend of his dealings with the devil; but in his day the glory of a

Poet, like that of all other imaginative powers, had ceased, or almost ceased, outside a narrow class. The poor Gaelic rhymer leaves a nobler memory among his neighbours, who will talk of Angels standing like flames about his death-bed, and of voices speaking out of bramble-bushes that he may have the wisdom of the world.[29] The Puritanism that drove the theatres into Surrey was but part of an inexplicable movement that was trampling out the minds of all but some few thousands born to cultivated ease.[30]

MAY, 1901.

# WILLIAM BLAKE AND THE IMAGINATION

There have been men who loved the future like a mistress, and the future mixed her breath into their breath and shook her hair about them, and hid them from the understanding of their times. William Blake was one of these men, and if he spoke confusedly and obscurely it was because he spoke of things for whose speaking he could find no models in the world he knew. He announced the religion of art, of which no man dreamed in the world he knew; and he understood it more perfectly than the thousands of subtle spirits who have received its baptism in the world we know, because, in the beginning of important things—in the beginning of love, in the beginning of the day, in the beginning of any work—there is a moment when we understand more perfectly than we understand again until all is finished. In his time educated people believed that they amused themselves with books of imagination, but that they 'made their souls' by listening to sermons and by doing or by not doing certain things. When they had to explain why serious people like themselves honoured the great poets greatly they were hard put to it for lack of good reasons. In our time we are agreed that we 'make our souls' out of some one of the great poets of ancient times, or out of Shelley or Wordsworth, or Goethe or Balzac, or Flaubert, or Count Tolstoy, in the books he wrote before he became a prophet and fell into a lesser order, or out of Mr. Whistler's pictures, while we amuse ourselves, or, at best, make a poorer sort of soul, by listening to sermons or by doing or by not doing certain things.[1] We write of great writers, even of writers whose beauty would once have seemed an unholy beauty, with rapt sentences like those our fathers kept for the beatitudes and mysteries of the Church; and no matter what we believe with our lips, we believe with our hearts that beautiful things, as Browning said in his one prose essay that was not in verse, have 'lain burningly on the Divine hand,' and that when time has begun to wither, the Divine hand will fall heavily on bad taste and vulgarity.[2] When no man believed these things William Blake believed them, and began that preaching against the Philistines, which is as the preaching of the Middle Ages against the Saracen.[3]

He had learned from Jacob Boehme and from old alchemist writers that imagination was the first emanation of divinity, 'the body of God,' 'the Divine members,' and he drew the deduction, which they did not draw, that the imaginative arts were therefore the greatest of Divine revelations, and that the sympathy with all living things, sinful and righteous alike, which the imaginative arts awaken, is that forgiveness of sins commanded by Christ.[4] The reason, and by the reason he meant deductions from the observations of the senses, binds us to mortality because it binds us to the senses, and divides us from each other by showing us our clashing interests; but imagination divides us from mortality by the immortality of beauty, and binds us to each other by opening the secret doors of all hearts.[5] He cried again and again that every thing that lives is holy, and that nothing is unholy except things that do not live—lethargies, and cruelties, and timidities, and that denial of imagination which is the root they grew from in old times.[6] Passions, because most living, are most holy—and this was a scandalous paradox in his time—and man shall enter eternity borne upon their wings.[7]

And he understood this so literally that certain drawings to *Vala,* had he carried them beyond the first faint pencillings, the first faint washes of colour, would have been a pretty scandal to his time and to our time. The sensations of this 'foolish body,' this 'phantom of the earth and water,' were in themselves but half-living things, 'vegetative' things, but passion that 'eternal glory' made them a part of the body of God.[8]

This philosophy kept him more simply a poet than any poet of his time, for it made him content to express every beautiful feeling that came into his head without troubling about its utility or chaining it to any utility. Sometimes one feels, even when one is reading poets of a better time—Tennyson or Wordsworth, let us say—that they have troubled the energy and simplicity of their imaginative passions by asking whether they were for the helping or for the hindrance of the world, instead of believing that all beautiful things have 'lain burningly on the Divine hand.'[9] But when one reads Blake, it is as though the spray of an inexhaustible fountain of beauty was blown into our faces, and not merely when one reads the *Songs of Innocence,* or the lyrics he wished to call 'The Ideas of Good and Evil,' but when one reads those 'Prophetic Works' in which he spoke confusedly and obscurely because he spoke of things for whose speaking he could find no models in the world about him.[10] He was a symbolist who had to invent his symbols; and his counties of England, with their correspondence to tribes of Israel, and his mountains and rivers, with their correspondence to parts of a man's body, are arbitrary as some of the symbolism in the *Axël* of the symbolist Villiers de L'Isle-Adam is arbitrary, while they mix incongruous things as *Axël* does not.[11] He was a man crying out for a mythology, and trying to make one because he could not find one to his hand. Had he been a Catholic of Dante's time he would have been well content with Mary and the angels; or had he been a scholar of our time he would have taken his symbols where Wagner took his, from Norse mythology; or have followed, with the help of Professor Rhys, that pathway into Welsh mythology which he found in *Jerusalem;*[12] or have gone to Ireland and chosen for his symbols the sacred mountains, along whose sides the peasant still sees enchanted fires, and the divinities which have not faded from the belief, if they have faded from the prayers of simple hearts;[13] and have spoken without mixing incongruous things because he spoke of things that had been long steeped in emotion; and have been less obscure because a traditional mythology stood on the threshold of his meaning and on the margin of his sacred darkness. If 'Enitharmon' had been named Freia, or Gwydeon, or Danu, and made live in Ancient Norway, or Ancient Wales, or Ancient Ireland, we would have forgotten that her maker was a mystic;[14] and the hymn of her harping, that is in *Vala,* would but have reminded us of many ancient hymns.

The joy of woman in the death of her most beloved,
Who dies for love of her,
In torments of fierce jealousy and pangs of adoration.
The lover's night bears on my song,
And the nine spheres rejoice beneath my powerful control.

They sing unwearied to the notes of my immortal hand.
The solemn, silent moon
Reverberates the long harmony sounding upon my limbs.
The birds and beasts rejoice and play,
And every one seeks for his mate to prove his inmost joy.
Furious and terrible they sport and rend the nether deep.
The deep lifts up his rugged head,
And lost in infinite hovering wings vanishes with a cry.
The fading cry is ever dying,
The living voice is ever living in its inmost joy.[15]

1897.

# WILLIAM BLAKE AND HIS ILLUSTRATIONS TO *THE DIVINE COMEDY*

## I. HIS OPINIONS UPON ART

William Blake was the first writer of modern times to preach the indissoluble marriage of all great art with symbol. There had been allegorists and teachers of allegory in plenty, but the symbolic imagination, or, as Blake preferred to call it, 'vision,' is not allegory, being 'a representation of what actually exists really and unchangeably.'[1] A symbol is indeed the only possible expression of some invisible essence, a transparent lamp about a spiritual flame; while allegory is one of many possible representations of an embodied thing, or familiar principle, and belongs to fancy and not to imagination: the one is a revelation, the other an amusement. It is happily no part of my purpose to expound in detail the relations he believed to exist between symbol and mind, for in doing so I should come upon not a few doctrines which, though they have not been difficult to many simple persons, ascetics wrapped in skins, women who had cast away all common knowledge, peasants dreaming by their sheepfolds upon the hills, are full of obscurity to the man of modern culture; but it is necessary to just touch upon these relations, because in them was the fountain of much of the practice and of all the precept of his artistic life.

If a man would enter into 'Noah's rainbow,' he has written, and 'make a friend' of one of 'the images of wonder' which dwell there, and which always entreat him 'to leave mortal things,' 'then would he arise from the grave and meet the Lord in the air'; and by this rainbow, this sign of a covenant granted to him who is with Shem and

Japhet, 'painting, poetry and music,' 'the three powers in man of conversing with Paradise which the flood "of time and space" did not sweep away,'[2] Blake represented the shapes of beauty haunting our moments of inspiration: shapes held by most for the frailest of ephemera, but by him for a people older than the world, citizens of eternity, appearing and reappearing in the minds of artists and of poets, creating all we touch and see by casting distorted images of themselves upon 'the vegetable glass of nature';[3] and because beings, none the less symbols, blossoms, as it were, growing from invisible immortal roots, hands, as it were, pointing the way into some divine labyrinth. If 'the world of imagination' was 'the world of eternity,' as this doctrine implied, it was of less importance to know men and nature than to distinguish the beings and substances of imagination from those of a more perishable kind, created by the phantasy, in uninspired moments, out of memory and whim;[4] and this could best be done by purifying one's mind, as with a flame, in study of the works of the great masters, who were great because they had been granted by divine favour a vision of the unfallen world from which others are kept apart by the flaming sword that turns every way; and by flying from the painters who studied 'the vegetable glass' for its own sake, and not to discover there the shadows of imperishable beings and substances, and who entered into their own minds, not to make the unfallen world a test of all they heard and saw and felt with the senses, but to cover the naked spirit with 'the rotten rags of memory' of older sensations.[5] The struggle of the first part of his life had been to distinguish between these two schools, and to cleave always to the Florentine, and so to escape the fascination of those who seemed to him to offer the sleep of nature to a spirit weary with the labours of inspiration; but it was only after his return to London from Felpham in 1804 that he finally escaped from 'temptations and perturbations' which sought to destroy 'the imaginative power' at 'the hands of Venetian and Flemish Demons.'[6] 'The spirit of Titian'—and one must always remember that he had only seen poor engravings, and what his disciple, Palmer, has called 'picture-dealers' Titians'[7]—'was particularly active in raising doubts concerning the possibility of executing without a model; and when once he had raised the doubt it became easy for him to snatch away the vision time after time'; and Blake's imagination 'weakened' and 'darkened' until a 'memory of nature and of the pictures of various schools possessed his mind, instead of appropriate execution' flowing from the vision itself.[8] But now he wrote, 'O glory, and O delight! I have entirely reduced that spectrous fiend to his station'—he had overcome the merely reasoning and sensual portion of the mind—'whose annoyance has been the ruin of my labours for the last twenty years of my life. . . . I speak with perfect confidence and certainty of the fact which has passed upon me. Nebuchadnezzar had seven times passed over him, I have had twenty; thank God I was not altogether a beast as he was. . . . Suddenly, on the day after visiting the Truchsessian Gallery of pictures'—this was a gallery containing pictures by Albert Dürer and by the great Florentines—'I was again enlightened with the light I enjoyed in my youth, and which had for exactly twenty years been closed from me, as by a door and window shutters. . . . Excuse my enthusiasm, or rather madness, for I am really drunk with intellectual vision whenever I take a pencil or graver in my hand, as I used to be in my youth.'[9]

This letter may have been the expression of a moment's enthusiasm, but was more probably rooted in one of those intuitions of coming technical power which every creator feels, and learns to rely upon; for all his greatest work was done, and the principles of his art were formulated, after this date. Except a word here and there, his writings hitherto had not dealt with the principles of art except remotely and by implication; but now he wrote much upon them, and not in obscure symbolic verse, but in emphatic prose, and explicit if not very poetical rhyme. He explained spiritual art, and praised the painters of Florence and their influence, and cursed all that has come of Venice and Holland in his *Descriptive Catalogue,* in *The Address to the Public,* in the notes on Sir Joshua Reynolds, in *The Book of Moonlight*—of which some not very dignified rhymes alone remain—in beautiful detached passages of his *MS. Book.*[10] The limitation of his view was from the very intensity of his vision; he was a too literal realist of imagination, as others are of nature; and because he believed that the figures seen by the mind's eye, when exalted by inspiration, were 'eternal existences,' symbols of divine essences, he hated every grace of style that might obscure their lineaments.[11] To wrap them about in reflected lights was to do this, and to dwell overfondly upon any softness of hair or flesh was to dwell upon that which was least permanent and least characteristic, for 'The great and golden rule of art, as of life, is this: that the more distinct, sharp and wiry the boundary-line, the more perfect the work of art; and the less keen and sharp, the greater is the evidence of weak imitation, plagiarism and bungling.'[12] Inspiration was to see the permanent and characteristic in all forms, and if you had it not, you must needs imitate with a languid mind the things you saw or remembered, and so sink into the sleep of nature where all is soft and melting. 'Great inventors in all ages knew this. Protogenes and Apelles knew each other by their line. Raphael and Michael Angelo and Albert Dürer are known by this and this alone. How do we distinguish the owl from the beast, the horse from the ox, but by the bounding outline? How do we distinguish one face or countenance from another but by the bounding-line and its infinite inflections and movements? What is it that builds a house and plants a garden but the definite and determinate? What is it that distinguishes honesty from knavery but the hard and wiry line of rectitude and certainty in the actions and intentions? Leave out this line and you leave out life itself; and all is chaos again, and the line of the Almighty must be drawn out upon it before man or beast can exist.'[13] He even insisted that 'colouring does not depend upon where the colours are put, but upon where the light and dark are put, and all depends upon the form or outline'—meaning, I suppose, that a colour gets its brilliance or its depth from being in light or in shadow.[14] He does not mean by outline the bounding-line dividing a form from its background, as one of his commentators has thought, but the line that divides it from surrounding space, and unless you have an overmastering sense of this you cannot draw true beauty at all, but only 'the beauty that is appended to folly,' a beauty of mere voluptuous softness, 'a lamentable accident of the mortal and perishing life,' for 'the beauty proper for sublime art is lineaments, or forms and features capable of being the receptacles of intellect,' and 'the face or limbs that alter least from youth to old age are the face and limbs of the greatest beauty and perfection.'[15] His praise of a severe art had been beyond price had his age rested a moment to listen, in the midst of its enthusiasm for Correggio and the later Renaissance, for Bartolozzi and for Stothard.[16] What matter if in his visionary realism, in his enthusiasm for what, after all, is perhaps the greatest art, he refused to admit that he who wraps the vision in lights and shadows, in iridescent or glowing colour, until form be half lost in pattern, may, as did Titian in his Bacchus and Ariadne, create a talisman as powerfully charged with intellectual virtue as though it were a jewel-studded door of the city seen on Patmos?[17]

To cover the imperishable lineaments of beauty with shadows and reflected lights was to fall into the power of his *Vala,* the indolent fascination of nature, the woman divinity who is so often described in 'the prophetic books' as 'sweet pestilence,' and whose children weave webs to take the souls of men; but there was a yet more lamentable chance, for nature has also a 'masculine portion' or 'spectre' which kills instead of taking prisoners, and is continually at war with inspiration.[18] To 'generalise' forms and shadows, to 'smooth out' spaces and lines in obedience to 'laws of composition,' and of painting; founded not upon imagination, which always thirsts for variety and delights in freedom, but upon reasoning from sensation, which is always seeking to reduce everything to a lifeless and slavish uniformity; as the popular art of Blake's day had done, and as he understood Sir Joshua Reynolds to advise, was to fall into 'Entuthon Benithon,' or 'the Lake of Udan Adan,' or some other of those regions where the imagination and the flesh are alike dead, that he names by so many resonant phantastical names.[19] 'General knowledge is remote knowledge,' he wrote; 'it is in particulars that wisdom consists, and happiness too. Both in art and life general masses are as much art as a pasteboard man is human. Every man has eyes, nose and mouth; this every idiot knows. But he who enters into and discriminates most minutely the manners and intentions, the characters in all their branches, is the alone wise or sensible man, and on this discrimination all art is founded. . . . As poetry admits not a letter that is insignificant, so painting admits not a grain of sand or a blade of grass insignificant, much less an insignificant blot or blur.'[20]

Against another desire of his time, derivative also from what he has called 'corporeal reason,' the desire for 'a tepid moderation,' for a lifeless 'sanity in both art and life,' he had protested years before with a paradoxical violence.[21] 'The roadway of excess leads to the palace of wisdom,' and we must only 'bring out weight and measure in time of dearth.'[22] This protest, carried, in the notes on Sir Joshua Reynolds, to the point of dwelling with pleasure on the thought that 'The *Lives of the Painters* say that Raphael died of dissipation,' because dissipation is better than emotional penury, seemed as important to his old age as to his youth.[23] He taught it to his disciples, and one finds it in its purely artistic shape in a diary written by Samuel Palmer, in 1824: 'Excess is the essential vivifying spirit, vital spark, embalming spice of the finest art. There are many mediums in the *means*—none, oh, not a jot, not a shadow of a jot, in the *end* of great art. In a picture whose merit is to be excessively brilliant, it can't be too brilliant, but individual tints may be too brilliant. . . . We must not begin with medium, but think always on excess and only use medium to make excess more abundantly excessive.'[24]

These three primary commands, to seek a determinate outline, to avoid a generalised treatment, and to desire always abundance and exuberance, were insisted upon with vehement anger, and their opponents called again and again 'demons' and 'villains,' 'hired' by the wealthy and the idle; but in private, Palmer has told us, he could find 'sources of delight throughout the whole range of art,' and was ever ready to praise excellence in any school, finding, doubtless, among friends, no need for the emphasis of exaggeration.[25] There is a beautiful passage in *Jerusalem* in which the merely mortal part of the mind, 'the spectre,' creates 'pyramids of pride,' and 'pillars in the deepest hell to reach the heavenly arches,' and seeks to discover wisdom in 'the spaces between the stars,' not 'in the stars,' where it is, but the immortal part makes all his labours vain, and turns his pyramids to 'grains of sand,' his 'pillars' to 'dust on the fly's wing,' and makes of 'his starry heavens a moth of gold and silver mocking his anxious grasp.'[26] So when man's desire to rest from spiritual labour, and his thirst to fill his art with mere sensation and memory, seem upon the point of triumph, some miracle transforms them to a new inspiration; and here and there among the pictures born of sensation and memory is the murmuring of a new ritual, the glimmering of new talismans and symbols.

It was during and after the writing of these opinions that Blake did the various series of pictures which have brought him the bulk of his fame. He had already completed the illustrations to Young's *Night Thoughts*—in which the great sprawling figures, a little wearisome even with the luminous colours of the original water-colour, became nearly intolerable in plain black and white—and almost all the illustrations to 'the prophetic books,' which have an energy like that of the elements, but are rather rapid sketches taken while some phantasmic procession swept over him, than elaborate compositions, and in whose shadowy adventures one finds not merely, as did Dr. Garth Wilkinson, 'the hells of the ancient people, the Anakim, the Nephalim, and the Rephaim . . . gigantic petrifactions from which the fires of lust and intense selfish passion have long dissipated what was animal and vital'; not merely the shadows cast by the powers who had closed the light from him as 'with a door and window shutters,' but the shadows of those who gave them battle.[27] He did now, however, the many designs to Milton, of which I have only seen those to *Paradise Regained;* the reproductions of those to *Comus,* published, I think, by Mr. Quaritch; and the three or four to *Paradise Lost,* engraved by Bell Scott—a series of designs which one good judge considers his greatest work;[28] the illustrations to Blair's *Grave,* whose gravity and passion struggled with the mechanical softness and trivial smoothness of Schiavonetti's engraving; the illustrations to Thornton's *Virgil,* whose influence is manifest in the work of the little group of landscape-painters who gathered about him in his old age and delighted to call him master.[29] The member of the group, whom I have already so often quoted, has alone praised worthily these illustrations to the first *eclogue:* 'There is in all such a misty and dreamy glimmer as penetrates and kindles the inmost soul and gives complete and unreserved delight, unlike the gaudy daylight of this world. They are like all this wonderful artist's work, the drawing aside of the fleshly curtain, and the glimpse which all the most holy, studious saints and sages have enjoyed, of the rest which remains to the people of God.'[30] Now, too, he did the great series, the crowning work of his life, the illustrations to *The Book of Job* and the illustrations to *The Divine Comedy.*[31] Hitherto he had protested against the mechanical 'dots and lozenges' and 'blots and blurs' of Woollett and Strange,* but had himself used both 'dot and lozenge,' 'blot and blur,' though always in subordination 'to a firm and determinate outline'; but in Marc Antonio, certain of whose engravings he was shown by Linnell, he found a style

*Woollett and Strange had established names when Blake began to draw, and must have seemed to Blake in certain moods the types of all triumphant iniquity. Woollett used to fire a cannon from the roof of his house whenever he finished an important plate.[32] [1924]

full of delicate lines, a style where all was living and energetic, strong and subtle.[33] And almost his last words, a letter written upon his death-bed, attack the 'dots and lozenges' with even more than usually quaint symbolism, and praise expressive lines. 'I know that the majority of Englishmen are bound by the indefinite . . . a line is a line in its minutest particulars, straight or crooked. It is itself not intermeasurable by anything else . . . but since the French Revolution'—since the reign of reason began, that is—'Englishmen are all intermeasurable with one another, certainly a happy state of agreement in which I do not agree.'[34] The Dante series occupied the last years of his life; even when too weak to get out of bed he worked on, propped up with the great drawing-book before him. He sketched a hundred designs, but left nearly all incomplete, some greatly so, and partly engraved seven plates, of which the 'Francesca and Paolo' is the most finished. It is not, I think, inferior to any but the finest in Job, if indeed to them, and shows in its perfection Blake's mastery over elemental things, the swirl in which the lost spirits are hurried, 'a watery flame' he would have called it, the haunted waters and the huddling shapes.[35] In the illustrations of Purgatory there is a serene beauty, and one finds his Dante and Virgil climbing among the rough rocks under a cloudy sun, and in their sleep upon the smooth steps towards the summit, a placid, marmoreal, tender, starry rapture.[36]

All in this great series are in some measure powerful and moving, and not, as it is customary to say of the work of Blake, because a flaming imagination pierces through a cloudy and indecisive technique, but because they have the only excellence possible in any art, a mastery over artistic expression. The technique of Blake was imperfect, incomplete, as is the technique of well-nigh all artists who have striven to bring fires from remote summits; but where his imagination is perfect and complete, his technique has a like perfection, a like completeness. He strove to embody more subtle raptures, more elaborate intuitions than any before him; his imagination and technique are more broken and strained under a great burden than the imagination and technique of any other master. 'I am,' wrote Blake, 'like others, just equal in invention and execution.'[37] And again, 'No man can improve an original invention; nor can an original invention exist without execution, organised, delineated and articulated either by God or man . . . I have heard people say, "Give me the ideas; it is no matter what words you put them into"; and others say, "Give me the designs; it is no matter for the execution." . . . Ideas cannot be given but in their minutely appropriate words, nor can a design be made without its minutely appropriate execution.'[38] Living in a time when technique and imagination are continually perfect and complete, because they no longer strive to bring fire from heaven, we forget how imperfect and incomplete they were in even the greatest masters, in Botticelli, in Orcagna, and in Giotto.[39]

The errors in the handiwork of exalted spirits are as the more phantastical errors in their lives; as Coleridge's opium cloud; as Villiers de L'Isle-Adam's candidature for the throne of Greece; as Blake's anger against causes and purposes he but half understood; as that veritable madness an Eastern scripture thinks permissible among the saints; for he who half lives in eternity endures a rending of the structures of the mind, a crucifixion of the intellectual body.[40]

## II. HIS OPINIONS ON DANTE

As Blake sat bent over the great drawing-book, in which he made his designs to *The Divine Comedy,* he was very certain that he and Dante represented spiritual states which face one another in an eternal enmity. Dante, because a great poet, was 'inspired by the Holy Ghost'; but his inspiration was mingled with a certain philosophy, blown up out of his age, which Blake held for mortal and the enemy of immortal things, and which from the earliest times has sat in high places and ruled the world.[41] This philosophy was the philosophy of soldiers, of men of the world, of priests busy with government, of all who, because of the absorption in active life, have been persuaded to judge and to punish, and partly also, he admitted, the philosophy of Christ, who in descending into the world had to take on the world; who, in being born of Mary, a symbol of the law in Blake's symbolic language, had to 'take after his mother,' and drive the money-changers out of the Temple.[42] Opposed to this was another philosophy, not made by men of action, drudges of time and space, but by Christ when wrapped in the divine essence, and by artists and poets, who are taught by the nature of their craft to sympathise with all living things, and who, the more pure and fragrant is their lamp, pass the further from all limitations, to come at last to forget good and evil in an absorbing vision of the happy and the unhappy. The one philosophy was worldly, and established for the ordering of the body and the fallen will, and so long as it did not call its 'laws of prudence' 'the laws of God,' was a necessity, because 'you cannot have liberty in this world without what you call moral virtue';[43] the other was divine, and established for the peace of the imagination and the unfallen will, and, even when obeyed with a too literal reverence, could make men sin against no higher principality than prudence. He called the followers of the first philosophy pagans, no matter by what name they knew themselves, because the pagans, as he understood the word pagan, believed more in the outward life, and in what he called 'war, princedom, and victory,' than in the secret life of the spirit;[44] and the followers of the second philosophy Christians, because only those whose sympathies had been enlarged and instructed by art and poetry could obey the Christian command of unlimited forgiveness. Blake had already found this 'pagan' philosophy in Swedenborg, in Milton, in Wordsworth, in Sir Joshua Reynolds, in many persons, and it had roused him so constantly and to such angry paradox that its overthrow became the signal passion of his life, and filled all he did and thought with the excitement of a supreme issue.[45] Its kingdom was bound to grow weaker so soon as life began to lose a little in crude passion and naïve tumult, but Blake was the first to announce its successor, and he did this, as must needs be with revolutionists who have 'the law' for 'mother,' with a firm conviction that the things his opponents held white were indeed black, and the things they held black, white; with a strong persuasion that all busy with government are men of darkness and 'something other than human life.'[46] One is reminded of Shelley, who was the next to take up the cry, though with a less abundant philosophic faculty, but still more of Nietzsche, whose thought flows always, though with an even more violent current, in the bed Blake's thought has worn.[47]

The kingdom that was passing was, he held, the kingdom of the Tree of Knowledge; the kingdom that was coming was the kingdom of the Tree of Life: men who ate from the Tree of Knowledge wasted their days in anger against one another, and in taking one another captive in great nets; men who sought their food among the green leaves of the Tree of Life condemned none but the unimaginative and the idle, and those who forget that even love and death and old age are an imaginative art.

In these opposing kingdoms is the explanation of the petulant sayings he wrote on the margins of the great sketch-book, and of those others, still more petulant, which Crabb Robinson has recorded in his diary. The sayings about the forgiveness of sins have no need for further explanation, and are in contrast with the attitude of that excellent commentator, Herr Hettinger, who, though Dante swooned from pity at the tale of Francesca, will only 'sympathise' with her 'to a certain extent,' being taken in a theological net.[48] 'It seems as if Dante,' Blake wrote, 'supposes God was something superior to the Father of Jesus; for if He gives rain to the evil and the good, and His sun to the just and the unjust, He can never have builded Dante's Hell, nor the Hell of the Bible, as our parsons explain it. It must have been framed by the dark spirit itself, and so I understand it.' And again, 'Whatever task is of vengeance and whatever is against forgiveness of sin is not of the Father but of Satan, the accuser, the father of Hell.'[49] And again, and this time to Crabb Robinson, 'Dante saw devils where I saw none. I see good only.' 'I have never known a very bad man who had not something very good about him.'[50] This forgiveness was not the forgiveness of the theologian who has received a commandment from afar off, but of the poet and artist, who believes he has been taught, in a mystical vision, 'that the imagination is the man himself,' and believes he has discovered in the practice of his art that without a perfect sympathy there is no perfect imagination, and therefore no perfect life.[51] At another moment he called Dante 'an atheist, a mere politician busied about this world, as Milton was, till, in his old age, he returned to God whom he had had in his childhood.' 'Everything is atheism,' he had already explained, 'which assumes the reality of the natural and unspiritual world.'[52] Dante, he held, assumed its reality when he made obedience to its laws a condition of man's happiness hereafter, and he set Swedenborg beside Dante in misbelief for calling Nature 'the ultimate of Heaven,' a lowest rung, as it were, of Jacob's ladder, instead of a net woven by Satan to entangle our wandering joys and bring our hearts into captivity.[53] There are certain curious unfinished diagrams scattered here and there among the now separated pages of the sketch-book, and of these there is one which, had it had all its concentric rings filled with names, would have been a systematic exposition of his animosities and of their various intensity. It represents Paradise, and in the midst, where Dante emerges from the earthly Paradise, is written 'Homer,' and in the next circle 'Swedenborg,' and on the margin these words: 'Everything in Dante's Paradise shows that he has made the earth the foundation of all, and its goddess Nature, memory,' memory of sensations, 'not the Holy Ghost. . . . Round Purgatory is Paradise, and round Paradise vacuum. Homer is the centre of all, I mean the poetry of the heathen.'[54] The statement that round Paradise is vacuum is a proof of the persistence of his ideas, and of his curiously literal understanding of his own symbols; for it is but another form of the charge made against Milton many years before in *The Marriage of Heaven and Hell.* 'In Milton the Father is destiny, the Son a ratio of the five senses,' Blake's definition of the reason which is the enemy of the imagination, 'and the Holy Ghost vacuum.'[55] Dante, like other mediæval mystics, symbolised the highest order of created beings by the fixed stars, and God by the darkness beyond them, the *Primum Mobile.* Blake, absorbed in his very different vision, in which God took always a human shape, believed that to think of God under a symbol drawn from the outer world was in itself idolatry, but that to imagine Him as an unpeopled immensity was to think of Him under the one symbol furthest from His essence—it being a creation of the ruining reason, 'generalising' away 'the minute particulars of life.'[56] Instead of seeking God in the deserts of time and space, in exterior immensities, in what he called 'the abstract void,' he believed that the further he dropped behind him memory of time and space, reason builded upon sensation, morality founded for the ordering of the world; and the more he was absorbed in emotion; and, above all, in emotion escaped from the impulse of bodily longing and the restraints of bodily reason, in artistic emotion; the nearer did he come to Eden's 'breathing garden,' to use his beautiful phrase, and to the unveiled face of God. No worthy symbol of God existed but the inner world, the true humanity, to whose various aspects he gave many names, 'Jerusalem,' 'Liberty,' 'Eden,' 'The Divine Vision,' 'The Body of God,' 'The Human Form Divine,' 'The Divine Members,' and whose most intimate expression was art and poetry.[57] He always sang of God under this symbol:

For Mercy, Pity, Peace, and Love
  Is God our Father dear;
And Mercy, Pity, Peace, and Love
  Is man, His child and care.
For Mercy has a human heart;
  Pity a human face;
And Love the human form divine;
  And Peace, the human dress.

Then every man of every clime,
  That prays in his distress,
Prays to the human form divine—
  Love, Mercy, Pity, Peace.[58]

Whenever he gave this symbol a habitation in space he set it in the sun, the father of light and life; and set in the darkness beyond the stars, where light and life die away, Og and Anak and the giants that were of old, and the iron throne of Satan.[59]

By thus contrasting Blake and Dante by the light of Blake's paradoxical wisdom, and as though there was no important truth hung from Dante's beam of the balance, I but seek to interpret a little-understood philosophy rather than one incorporate in the thought and habits of Christendom. Every philosophy has half its truth from times and generations; and to us one-half of the philosophy of Dante is less living than his poetry, while the truth Blake preached and sang and painted is the root of the cultivated life, of the fragile perfect blossom of the world born in ages of leisure and peace, and never yet to last more than a little season; the life those Phæacians, who told Odysseus that they had set their hearts in nothing but in 'the dance and changes of raiment, and love and sleep,' lived before Poseidon heaped a mountain above them;[60] the lives of all who, having eaten of the Tree of Life, love, more than did the barbarous ages when none had time to live, 'the minute particulars of life,' the little fragments of space and time, which are wholly flooded by beautiful emotion because they are so little they are hardly of time and space at all. 'Every space smaller than a globule of man's blood,' he wrote, 'opens into eternity of which this vegetable earth is but a shadow.'[61] And again, 'Every time less than a pulsation of the artery is equal' in its tenor and value 'to six thousand years, for in this period the poet's work is done, and all the great events of time start forth, and are conceived: in such a period within a moment, a pulsation of the artery.'[62] Dante, indeed, taught, in the *Purgatorio,* that sin and virtue are alike from love, and that love is from God; but this love he would restrain by a complex external law, a complex external Church. Blake upon the other hand cried scorn upon the whole spectacle of external things, a vision to pass away in a moment, and preached the cultivated life, the internal Church which has no laws but beauty, rapture and labour. 'I know of no other Christianity, and of no other gospel, than the liberty, both of body and mind, to exercise the divine arts of imagination, the real and eternal world of which this vegetable universe is but a faint shadow, and in which we shall live in our eternal or imaginative bodies when these vegetable mortal bodies are no more. The Apostles knew of no other gospel. What are all their spiritual gifts? What is the divine spirit? Is the Holy Ghost any other than an intellectual fountain? What is the harvest of the gospel and its labours? What is the talent which it is a curse to hide? What are the treasures of heaven which we are to lay up for ourselves? Are they any other than mental studies and performances? What are all the gifts of the gospel, are they not all mental gifts? Is God a spirit who must be worshipped in spirit and truth? Are not the gifts of the spirit everything to man? O ye religious! discountenance every one among you who shall pretend to despise art and science. I call upon you in the name of Jesus! What is the life of man but art and science? Is it meat and drink? Is not the body more than raiment? What is mortality but the things relating to the body which dies? What is immortality but the things relating to the spirit which lives immortally? What is the joy of Heaven but improvement in the things of the spirit? What are the pains of Hell but ignorance, idleness, bodily lust, and the devastation of the things of the spirit? Answer this for yourselves, and expel from amongst you those who pretend to despise the labours of art and science, which alone are the labours of the gospel. Is not this plain and manifest to the thought? Can you think at all, and not pronounce heartily that to labour in knowledge is to build Jerusalem, and to despise knowledge is to despise Jerusalem and her builders? And remember, he who despises and mocks a mental gift in another, calling it pride, and selfishness, and sin, mocks Jesus, the giver of every mental gift, which always appear to the ignorance-loving hypocrites as sins. But that which is sin in the sight of cruel man is not sin in the sight of our kind God. Let every Christian as much as in him lies engage himself openly and publicly before all the world in some mental pursuit for the building of Jerusalem.'[63] I have given the whole of this long passage because, though the very keystone of his thought, it is little known, being sunk, like nearly all of his most profound thoughts, in the mysterious prophetic books. Obscure about much else, they are always lucid on this one point, and return to it again and again. 'I care not whether a man is good or bad,' are the words they put into the mouth of God, 'all I care is whether he is a wise man or a fool. Go put off holiness and put on intellect.'[64] This cultivated life, which seems to us so artificial a thing, is really, according to them, the laborious rediscovery of the golden age, of the primeval simplicity, of the simple world in which Christ taught and lived, and its lawlessness is the lawlessness of Him 'who being all virtue, acted from impulse and not from rules,'[65]

> And His seventy disciples sent
> Against religion and government.[66]

The historical Christ was indeed no more than the supreme symbol of the artistic imagination, in which, with every passion wrought to perfect beauty by art and poetry, we shall live, when the body has passed away for the last time; but before that hour man must labour through many lives and many deaths. 'Men are admitted into heaven not because they have curbed and governed their passions, but because they have cultivated their understandings. The treasures of heaven are not negations of passion but realities of intellect from which the passions emanate uncurbed in their eternal glory. The fool shall not enter into heaven, let him be ever so holy. Holiness is not the price of entering into heaven. Those who are cast out are all those who, having no passions of their own, because no intellect, have spent their lives in curbing and governing other people's lives by the various arts of poverty and cruelty of all kinds. The modern Church crucifies Christ with the head downwards. Woe, woe, woe to you hypocrites.'[67] After a time man has 'to return to the dark valley whence he came and begin his labours anew,' but before that return he dwells in the freedom of imagination, in the peace of the 'divine image,' 'the divine vision,' in the peace that passes understanding and is the peace of art.[68] 'I have been very near the gates of death,' Blake wrote in his last letter, 'and have returned very weak and an old man, feeble and tottering but not in spirit and life, not in the real man, the imagination which liveth for ever. In that I grow stronger and stronger as this foolish body decays. . . . Flaxman is gone, and we must all soon follow, every one to his eternal home, leaving the delusions of goddess Nature and her laws, to get into freedom from all the laws of the numbers,' the multiplicity of nature, 'into the mind in which every one is king and priest in his own house.'[69] The phrase about the king and priest is a memory of the crown and mitre set upon Dante's head before he entered Paradise. Our imaginations are but fragments of the universal imagination, portions of the universal body of God, and as we enlarge our imagination by imaginative sympathy, and transform with the beauty and peace of art the sorrows and joys of the world, we put off the limited mortal man more and more and put on the unlimited 'immortal man.'[70] 'As the seed waits eagerly watching for its flower and fruit, anxious its little soul looks out into the clear expanse to see if hungry winds are abroad with their invisible array, so man looks out in tree, and herb, and fish, and bird, and beast, collecting up the fragments of his immortal body into the elemental forms of everything that grows. . . . In pain he sighs, in pain he labours in his universe, sorrowing in birds over the deep, or howling in the wolf over the slain, and moaning in the cattle, and in the winds.'[71] Mere sympathy for living things is not enough, because we must learn to separate their 'infected' from their eternal, their satanic from their divine part; and this can only be done by desiring always beauty, the one mask through which can be seen the unveiled eyes of eternity. We must then be artists in all things, and understand that love and old age and death are first among the arts. In this sense he insists that 'Christ's apostles were artists,' that 'Christianity is Art,' and that 'the whole business of man is the arts.'[72] Dante, who deified law, selected its antagonist, passion, as the most important of sins, and made the regions where it was punished the largest. Blake, who deified imaginative freedom, held 'corporeal reason' for the most accursed of things, because it makes the imagination revolt from the sovereignty of beauty and pass under the sovereignty of corporeal law, and this is 'the captivity in Egypt.'[73] True art is expressive and symbolic, and makes every form, every sound, every colour, every gesture, a signature of some unanalysable imaginative essence. False art is not expressive, but mimetic, not from experience but from observation, and is the mother of all evil, persuading us to save our bodies alive at no matter what cost of rapine and fraud. True art is the flame of the last day, which begins for every man, when he is first moved by beauty, and which seeks to burn all things until they become 'infinite and holy.'[74]

## III. THE ILLUSTRATIONS OF DANTE

The late Mr. John Addington Symonds wrote—in a preface to certain Dante illustrations by Stradanus, a sixteenth-century artist of no great excellence, published in phototype by Mr. Unwin in 1892—that the illustrations of Gustave Doré, 'in spite of glaring artistic defects, must, I think, be reckoned first among numerous attempts to translate Dante's conceptions into terms of plastic art.'[75] One can only account for this praise of a noisy and demagogic art by supposing that a temperament, strong enough to explore with unfailing alertness the countless schools and influences of the Renaissance in Italy, is of necessity a little lacking in delicacy of judgement and in the finer substances of emotion. It is more difficult to account for so admirable a scholar not only preferring these illustrations to the work of what he called 'the graceful and affected Botticelli,'—although 'Doré was fitted for his task, not by dramatic vigour, by feeling for beauty, or by anything sterling in sympathy with the supreme poet's soul, but by a very effective sense of luminosity and gloom'—but preferring them because 'he created a fanciful world, which makes the movement of Dante's *dramatis personæ* conceivable, introducing the ordinary intelligence into those vast regions thronged with destinies of souls and creeds and empires.'[76] When the ordinary student finds this intelligence in an illustrator, he thinks, because it is his own intelligence, that it is an accurate interpretation of the text, while work of the extraordinary intelligences is merely an expression of their own ideas and feelings. Doré and Stradanus, he will tell you, have given us something of the world of Dante, but Blake and Botticelli have builded worlds of their own and called them Dante's—as if Dante's world were more than a mass of symbols of colour and form and sound which put on humanity, when they arouse some mind to an intense and romantic life that is not theirs; as if it was not one's own sorrows and angers and regrets and terrors and hopes that awaken to condemnation or repentance while Dante treads his eternal pilgrimage; as if any poet or painter or musician could be other than an enchanter calling with a persuasive or compelling ritual, creatures, noble or ignoble, divine or dæmonic, covered with scales or in shining raiment, that he never imagined, out of the bottomless deeps of imaginations he never foresaw; as if the noblest achievement of art was not when the artist enfolds himself in darkness, while he casts over his readers a light as of a wild and terrible dawn.

Let us therefore put away the designs to *The Divine Comedy* in which there is 'an ordinary intelligence,' and consider only the designs in which the magical ritual has called up extraordinary shapes, the magical light glimmered upon a world, different from the Dantesque world of our own intelligence in its ordinary and daily moods, upon a difficult and distinguished world. Most of the series of designs to Dante, and there are a good number, need not busy any one for a moment. Genelli has done a copious series, which is very able in the 'formal' 'generalised' way which Blake hated, and which is spiritually ridiculous.[77] Pinelli has transformed the *Inferno* into a vulgar Walpurgis night, and a certain Schuler, whom I do not find in the biographical dictionaries, but who was apparently a German, has prefaced certain flaccid designs with some excellent charts, while Stradanus has made a series for the *Inferno,* which has so many of the more material and unessential powers of art, and is so extremely undistinguished in conception, that one supposes him to have touched in the sixteenth century the same public Doré has touched in the nineteenth.[78]

Though with many doubts, I am tempted to value Flaxman's designs to the *Inferno,* the *Purgatorio,* and the *Paradiso,* only a little above the best of these, because he does not seem to have ever been really moved by Dante, and so to have sunk into a formal manner, which is a reflection of the vital manner of his Homer and Hesiod.[79] His designs to *The Divine Comedy* will be laid, one imagines, with some ceremony in that immortal wastepaper-basket in which Time carries with many sighs the failures of great men. I am perhaps wrong, however, because Flaxman even at his best has not yet touched me very deeply, and I hardly ever hope to escape this limitation of my ruling stars. That Signorelli does not seem greatly more interesting except here and there, as in the drawing of 'The Angel,' full of innocence and energy, coming from the boat which has carried so many souls to the foot of the mountain of purgation, can only be because one knows him through poor reproductions from frescoes half mouldered away with damp.[80] A little-known series, drawn by Adolph Stürler, an artist of German extraction, who was settled in Florence in the first half of this century, are very poor in drawing, very pathetic and powerful in invention, and full of most interesting Pre-Raphaelitic detail.[81] There are admirable and moving figures, who, having set love above reason, listen in the last abandonment of despair to the judgement of Minos, or walk with a poignant melancholy to the foot of his throne through a land where owls and strange beasts move hither and thither with the sterile content of the evil that neither loves nor hates, and a Cerberus full of patient cruelty. All Stürler's designs have, however, the languor of a mind that does its work by a succession of laborious critical perceptions rather than the decision and energy of true creation, and are more a curious contribution to artistic methods than an imaginative force.

The only designs that compete with Blake's are those of Botticelli and Giulio Clovio, and these contrast rather than compete;[82] for Blake did not live to carry his *Paradiso* beyond the first faint pencillings, the first thin washes of colour, while Botticelli only, as I think, became supremely imaginative in his *Paradiso* and Clovio never attempted the *Inferno* and *Purgatorio* at all. The imaginations of Botticelli and Clovio were overshadowed by the cloister, and it was only when they passed beyond the world or into some noble peace, which is not the world's peace, that they won a perfect freedom. Blake had not such mastery over figure and drapery as had Botticelli, but he could sympathise with the persons and delight in the scenery of the *Inferno* and the *Purgatorio* as Botticelli could not, and could fill them with a mysterious and spiritual significance born perhaps of mystical pantheism. The flames of Botticelli give[†] one no emotion, and his car of Beatrice is no symbolic chariot of the Church led by the gryphon, half eagle, half lion, of Christ's dual nature, but is a fragment of some mediæval pageant pictured with a merely technical inspiration.

Clovio, the illuminator of missals, has tried to create with that too easy hand of his a Paradise of serene air reflected in a little mirror, a heaven of sociability and humility and prettiness, a heaven of women and of monks; but one cannot imagine him deeply moved, as the modern world is moved, by the symbolism of bird and beast, of tree and mountain, of flame and darkness. It was a profound understanding of all creatures and things, a profound sympathy with passionate and lost souls, made possible in their extreme intensity by his revolt against corporeal law, and corporeal reason, which made Blake the one perfectly fit illustrator for the *Inferno* and the *Purgatorio;* in the serene and rapturous emptiness of Dante's Paradise he would find no symbols but a few abstract emblems, and he had no love for the abstract, while with the drapery and the gestures of Beatrice and Virgil, he would have prospered less than Botticelli or even Clovio.

1897.

*P.S.*—Some seven or eight years ago I asked my friend Mr. Ezra Pound to point out everything in the language of my poems that he thought an abstraction, and I learned from him how much further the movement against abstraction had gone than my generation had thought possible.[83] Now, in reading these essays I am ashamed when I come upon such words as 'corporeal reason,' 'corporeal law,' and think how I must have wasted the keenness of my youthful senses. I would like to believe that there was no help for it, that we were compelled to protect ourselves by such means against people and things we should never have heard of.

1924.

# SYMBOLISM IN PAINTING

In England, which has made great Symbolic Art, most people dislike an art if they are told it is symbolic, for they confuse symbol and allegory. Even Johnson's Dictionary sees no great difference, for it calls a Symbol 'That which comprehends in its figure a representation of something else'; and an Allegory, 'A figurative discourse, in which something other is intended than is contained in the words literally taken.'[1] It is only a very modern Dictionary that calls a Symbol 'the sign or representation of any moral thing by the images or properties of natural things,' which, though an imperfect definition, is not unlike 'The things below are as the things above' of the Emerald Tablet of Hermes![2] *The Faerie Queene* and *The Pilgrim's Progress* have been so important in England that Allegory has overtopped Symbolism, and for a time has overwhelmed it in its own downfall.[3] William Blake was perhaps the first modern to insist on a difference; and the other day, when I sat for my portrait to a German Symbolist in Paris, whose talk was all of his love for Symbolism and his hatred for Allegory, his definitions were the same as William Blake's, of whom he knew nothing.[4] William Blake has written, 'Vision or imagination'—meaning symbolism by these words—'is a representation of what actually exists, really or unchangeably. Fable or Allegory is formed by the daughters of Memory.'[5] The German insisted with many determined gestures that Symbolism said things which could not be said so perfectly in any other way, and needed but a right instinct for its understanding; while Allegory said things which could be said as well, or better, in another way, and needed a right knowledge for its understanding. The one thing gave dumb things voices, and bodiless things bodies; while the other read a meaning—which had never lacked its voice or its body—into something heard or seen, and loved less for the meaning than for its own sake. The only symbols he cared for were the shapes and motions of the body; ears hidden by the hair, to make one think of a mind busy with inner voices; and a head so bent that back and neck made the one curve, as in Blake's *Vision of Bloodthirstiness,* to call up an emotion of bodily strength; and he would not put even a lily, or a rose, or a poppy into a picture to express purity, or love, or sleep, because he thought such emblems were allegorical, and had their meaning by a traditional and not by a natural right.[6] I said that the rose, and the lily, and the poppy were so married, by their colour and their odour and their use, to love and purity and sleep, or to other symbols of love and purity and sleep, and had been so long a part of the imagination of the world, that a symbolist might use them to help out his meaning without becoming an allegorist. I think I quoted the lily in the hand of the angel in Rossetti's *Annunciation,* and the lily in the jar in his *Childhood of Mary Virgin,* and thought they made the more important symbols, the women's bodies, and the angels' bodies, and the clear morning light, take that place, in the great procession of Christian symbols, where they can alone have all their meaning and all their beauty.[7]

It is hard to say where Allegory and Symbolism melt into one another, but it is not hard to say where either comes to its perfection; and though one may doubt whether Allegory or Symbolism is the greater in the horns of Michael Angelo's *Moses,* one need not doubt that its symbolism has helped to awaken the modern imagination; while Tintoretto's *Origin of the Milky Way,* which is Allegory without any Symbolism, is, apart from its fine painting, but a moment's amusement for our fancy.[8] A hundred generations might write out what seemed the meaning of the one, and they would write different meanings, for no symbol tells all its meaning to any generation; but when you have said, 'That woman there is Juno, and the milk out of her breast is making the Milky Way,' you have told the meaning of the other, and the fine painting, which has added so much irrelevant beauty, has not told it better.

All Art that is not mere story-telling, or mere portraiture, is symbolic, and has the purpose of those symbolic talismans which mediæval magicians made with complex colours and forms, and bade their patients ponder over daily, and guard with holy secrecy; for it entangles, in complex colours and forms, a part of the Divine Essence. A person or a landscape that is a part of a story or a portrait, evokes but so much emotion as the story or the portrait can permit without loosening the bonds that make it a story or a portrait; but if you liberate a person or a landscape from the bonds of motives and their actions, causes and their effects, and from all bonds but the bonds of your love, it will change under your eyes, and become a symbol of an infinite emotion, a perfected emotion, a part of the Divine Essence; for we love nothing but the perfect, and our dreams make all things perfect, that we may love them. Religious and visionary people, monks and nuns, and medicine-men and opium-eaters, see symbols in their trances; for religious and visionary thought is thought about perfection and the way to perfection; and symbols are the only things free enough from all bonds to speak of perfection.

Wagner's dramas, Keats' odes, Blake's pictures and poems, Calvert's pictures, Rossetti's pictures, Villiers de L'Isle-Adam's plays, and the black-and-white art of Mr. Beardsley and Mr. Ricketts, and the lithographs of Mr. Shannon, and the pictures of Mr. Whistler, and the plays of M. Maeterlinck, and the poetry of Verlaine, in our own day, but differ from the religious art of Giotto and his disciples in having accepted all symbolisms, the symbolism of the ancient shepherds and star-gazers, that symbolism of bodily beauty which seemed a wicked thing to Fra Angelico, the symbolism in day and night, and winter and summer, spring and autumn, once so great a part of an older religion than Christianity; and in having accepted all the Divine Intellect, its anger and its pity, its waking and its sleep, its love and its lust, for the substance of their art.[9] A Keats or a Calvert is as much a symbolist as a Blake or a Wagner; but he is a fragmentary symbolist, for while he evokes in his persons and his landscapes an infinite emotion, a perfected emotion, a part of the Divine Essence, he does not set his symbols in the great procession as Blake would have him, 'in a certain order, suited' to his 'imaginative energy.'[10] If you paint a beautiful woman and fill her face, as Rossetti filled so many faces, with an infinite love, a perfected love, 'one's eyes meet no mortal thing when they meet the light of her peaceful eyes,' as Michael Angelo said of Vittoria Colonna; but one's thoughts stray to mortal things, and ask, maybe, 'Has her lover gone from her, or is he coming?' or 'What predestinated unhappiness has made the shadow in her eyes?'[11] If you paint the same face, and set a winged rose or a rose of gold somewhere about her, one's thoughts are of her immortal sisters, Piety and

Jealousy, and of her mother, Ancestral Beauty, and of her high kinsmen, the Holy Orders, whose swords make a continual music before her face.[12] The systematic mystic is not the greatest of artists, because his imagination is too great to be bounded by a picture or a song, and because only imperfection in a mirror of perfection, or perfection in a mirror of imperfection, delights our frailty. There is indeed a systematic mystic in every poet or painter who, like Rossetti, delights in a traditional Symbolism, or, like Wagner, delights in a personal Symbolism; and such men often fall into trances, or have waking dreams. Their thought wanders from the woman who is Love herself, to her sisters and her forebears, and to all the great procession; and so august a beauty moves before the mind that they forget the things which move before the eyes. William Blake, who was the chanticleer of the new dawn, has written: 'If the spectator could enter into one of these images of his imagination, approaching them on the fiery chariot of his contemplative thought, if . . . he could make a friend and companion of one of these images of wonder, which always entreat him to leave mortal things (as he must know), then would he arise from the grave, then would he meet the Lord in the air, and then he would be happy.' And again, 'The world of imagination is the world of Eternity. It is the Divine bosom into which we shall all go after the death of the vegetated body. The world of imagination is infinite and eternal, whereas the world of generation or vegetation is finite and temporal. There exist in that eternal world the eternal realities of everything which we see reflected in the vegetable glass of nature.'[13]

Every visionary knows that the mind's eye soon comes to see a capricious and variable world, which the will cannot shape or change, though it can call it up and banish it again. I closed my eyes a moment ago, and a company of people in blue robes swept by me in a blinding light, and had gone before I had done more than see little roses embroidered on the hems of their robes, and confused, blossoming apple-boughs somewhere beyond them, and recognised one of the company by his square, black, curling beard.* I have often

*I did not mean that this particular vision had the intensity either of a dream or of those pictures that pass before us between sleep and waking. I had learned, and my fellow-students had learned, as described in *The Trembling of the Veil,* to set free imagination when we would, that it might follow its own law and impulse. 1924.[14]

seen him; and one night a year ago I asked him questions which he answered by showing me flowers and precious stones, of whose meaning I had no knowledge, and he seemed too perfected a soul for any knowledge that cannot be spoken in symbol or metaphor.

Are he and his blue-robed companions, and their like, 'the Eternal realities' of which we are the reflection 'in the vegetable glass of nature,' or a momentary dream? To answer is to take sides in the only controversy in which it is greatly worth taking sides, and in the only controversy which may never be decided.

1898.

# THE SYMBOLISM OF POETRY

## I

'Symbolism, as seen in the writers of our day, would have no value if it were not seen also, under one disguise or another, in every great imaginative writer,' writes Mr. Arthur Symons in *The Symbolist Movement in Literature,* a subtle book which I cannot praise as I would, because it has been dedicated to me; and he goes on to show how many profound writers have in the last few years sought for a philosophy of poetry in the doctrine of symbolism, and how even in countries where it is almost scandalous to seek for any philosophy of poetry, new writers are following them in their search.[1] We do not know what the writers of ancient times talked of among themselves, and one bull is all that remains of Shakespeare's talk, who was on the edge of modern times; and the journalist is convinced, it seems, that they talked of wine and women and politics, but never about their art, or never quite seriously about their art.[2] He is certain that no one, who had a philosophy of his art or a theory of how he should write, has ever made a work of art, that people have no imagination who do not write without forethought and afterthought as he writes his own articles. He says this with enthusiasm, because he has heard it at so many comfortable dinner-tables, where some one had mentioned through carelessness, or foolish zeal, a book whose difficulty had offended indolence, or a man who had not forgotten that beauty is an accusation. Those formulas and generalisations, in which a hidden sergeant has drilled the ideas of journalists and through them the ideas of all but all the modern world, have created in their turn a forgetfulness like that of soldiers in battle, so that journalists and their readers have forgotten, among many like events, that Wagner spent seven years arranging and explaining his ideas before he began his most characteristic music; that opera, and with it modern music, arose from certain talks at the house of one Giovanni Bardi of Florence; and that the Pléiade laid the foundations of modern French literature with a pamphlet.[3] Goethe has said, 'a poet needs all philosophy, but he must keep it out of his work,' though that is not always necessary; and almost certainly no great art, outside England, where journalists are more powerful and ideas less plentiful than elsewhere, has arisen without a great criticism, for its herald or its interpreter and protector, and it may be for this reason that great art, now that vulgarity has armed itself and multiplied itself, is perhaps dead in England.[4]

All writers, all artists of any kind, in so far as they have had any philosophical or critical power, perhaps just in so far as they have been deliberate artists at all, have had some philosophy, some criticism of their art; and it has often been this philosophy, or this criticism, that has evoked their most startling inspiration, calling into outer life some portion of the divine life, or of the buried reality, which could alone extinguish in the emotions what their philosophy or their criticism would extinguish in the intellect. They have sought for no new thing, it may be, but only to understand and to copy the pure inspiration of early times, but because the divine life wars upon our outer life, and must needs change its weapons and its movements as we change ours, inspiration has come to them in beautiful startling shapes. The scientific movement brought with it a literature, which was always tending to lose itself in externalities of all kinds, in opinion, in declamation, in picturesque writing, in word-painting, or in what Mr. Symons has called an attempt 'to build in brick and mortar inside the covers of a book'; and now writers have begun to dwell upon the element of evocation, of suggestion, upon what we call the symbolism in great writers.[5]

## II

In 'Symbolism in Painting,' I tried to describe the element of symbolism that is in pictures and sculpture, and described a little the symbolism in poetry, but did not describe at all the continuous indefinable symbolism which is the substance of all style.

There are no lines with more melancholy beauty than these by Burns—

The white moon is setting behind the white wave,
And Time is setting with me, O!

and these lines are perfectly symbolical.[6] Take from them the whiteness of the moon and of the wave, whose relation to the setting of Time is too subtle for the intellect, and you take from them their beauty. But, when all are together, moon and wave and whiteness and setting Time and the last melancholy cry, they evoke an emotion which cannot be evoked by any other arrangement of colours and sounds and forms. We may call this metaphorical writing, but it is better to call it symbolical writing, because metaphors are not profound enough to be moving, when they are not symbols, and when they are symbols they are the most perfect of all, because the most subtle, outside of pure sound, and through them one can the best find out what symbols are. If one begins the reverie with any beautiful lines that one can remember, one finds they are like those by Burns. Begin with this line by Blake—

The gay fishes on the wave when the moon sucks up the dew;

or these lines by Nash—

Brightness falls from the air,
Queens have died young and fair,
Dust hath closed Helen's eye;

or these lines by Shakespeare—

Timon hath made his everlasting mansion
Upon the beached verge of the salt flood;
Who once a day with his embossed froth
The turbulent surge shall cover;

or take some line that is quite simple, that gets its beauty from its place in a story, and see how it flickers with the light of the many symbols that have given the story its beauty, as a sword-blade may flicker with the light of burning towers.[7]

All sounds, all colours, all forms, either because of their preordained energies or because of long association, evoke indefinable and yet precise emotions, or, as I prefer to think, call down among us certain disembodied powers, whose footsteps over our hearts we call emotions; and when sound, and colour, and form are in a musical relation, a beautiful relation to one another, they become as it were one sound, one colour, one form, and evoke an emotion that is made out of their distinct evocations and yet is one emotion. The same relation exists between all portions of every work of art, whether it be an epic or a song, and the more perfect it is, and the more various and numerous the elements that have flowed into its perfection, the more powerful will be the emotion, the power, the god it calls among us. Because an emotion does not exist, or does not become perceptible and active among us, till it has found its expression, in colour or in sound or in form, or in all of these, and because no two modulations or arrangements of these evoke the same emotion, poets and painters and musicians, and in a less degree because their effects are momentary, day and night and cloud and shadow, are continually making and un-making mankind. It is indeed only those things which seem useless or very feeble that have any power, and all those things that seem useful or strong, armies, moving wheels, modes of architecture, modes of government, speculations of the reason, would have been a little different if some mind long ago had not given itself to some emotion, as a woman gives herself to her lover, and shaped sounds or colours or forms, or all of these, into a musical relation, that their emotion might live in other minds. A little lyric evokes an emotion, and this emotion gathers others about it and melts into their being in the making of some great epic; and at last, needing an always less delicate body, or symbol, as it grows more powerful, it flows out, with all it has gathered, among the blind instincts of daily life, where it moves a power within powers, as one sees ring within ring in the stem of an old tree. This is maybe what Arthur O'Shaughnessy meant when he made his poets say they had built Nineveh with their sighing; and I am certainly never certain, when I hear of some war, or of some religious excitement or of some new manufacture, or of anything else that fills the ear of the world, that it has not all happened because of something that a boy piped in Thessaly.[8] I remember once telling a seer to ask one among the gods who, as she believed, were standing about her in their symbolic bodies, what would come of a charming but seeming trivial labour of a friend, and the form answering, 'the devastation of peoples and the overwhelming of cities.'[9] I doubt indeed if the crude circumstance of the world, which seems to create all our emotions, does more than reflect, as in multiplying mirrors, the emotions that have come to solitary men in moments of poetical contemplation; or that love itself would be more than an animal hunger but for the poet and his shadow the priest, for unless we believe that outer things are the reality, we must believe that the gross is the shadow of the subtle, that things are wise before they become foolish, and secret before they cry out in the market-place. Solitary men in moments of contemplation receive, as I think, the creative impulse from the lowest of the Nine Hierarchies, and so make and unmake mankind, and even the world itself, for does not 'the eye altering alter all'?[10]

> Our towns are copied fragments from our breast;
> And all man's Babylons strive but to impart
> The grandeurs of his Babylonian heart.[11]

## III

The purpose of rhythm, it has always seemed to me, is to prolong the moment of contemplation, the moment when we are both asleep and awake, which is the one moment of creation, by hushing us with an alluring monotony, while it holds us waking by variety, to keep us in that state of perhaps real trance, in which the mind liberated from the pressure of the will is unfolded in symbols. If certain sensitive persons listen persistently to the ticking of a watch, or gaze persistently on the monotonous flashing of a light, they fall into the hypnotic trance; and rhythm is but the ticking of a watch made softer, that one must needs listen, and various, that one may not be swept beyond memory or grow weary of listening; while the patterns of the artist are but the monotonous flash woven to take the eyes in a subtler enchantment. I have heard in meditation voices that were forgotten the moment they had spoken; and I have been swept, when in more profound meditation, beyond all memory but of those things that came from beyond the threshold of waking life. I was writing once at a very symbolical and abstract poem, when my pen fell on the ground; and as

I stooped to pick it up, I remembered some phantastic adventure that yet did not seem phantastic, and then another like adventure, and when I asked myself when these things had happened, I found that I was remembering my dreams for many nights.[12] I tried to remember what I had done the day before, and then what I had done that morning; but all my waking life had perished from me, and it was only after a struggle that I came to remember it again, and as I did so that more powerful and startling life perished in its turn. Had my pen not fallen on the ground and so made me turn from the images that I was weaving into verse, I would never have known that meditation had become trance, for I would have been like one who does not know that he is passing through a wood because his eyes are on the pathway. So I think that in the making and in the understanding of a work of art, and the more easily if it is full of patterns and symbols and music, we are lured to the threshold of sleep, and it may be far beyond it, without knowing that we have ever set our feet upon the steps of horn or of ivory.[13]

## IV

Besides emotional symbols, symbols that evoke emotions alone,—and in this sense all alluring or hateful things are symbols, although their relations with one another are too subtle to delight us fully, away from rhythm and pattern,—there are intellectual symbols, symbols that evoke ideas alone, or ideas mingled with emotions; and outside the very definite traditions of mysticism and the less definite criticism of certain modern poets, these alone are called symbols. Most things belong to one or another kind, according to the way we speak of them and the companions we give them, for symbols, associated with ideas that are more than fragments of the shadows thrown upon the intellect by the emotions they evoke, are the playthings of the allegorist or the pedant, and soon pass away. If I say 'white' or 'purple' in an ordinary line of poetry, they evoke emotions so exclusively that I cannot say why they move me; but if I bring them into the same sentence with such obvious intellectual symbols as a cross or a crown of thorns, I think of purity and sovereignty. Furthermore, innumerable meanings, which are held to 'white' or to 'purple' by bonds of subtle suggestion, and alike in the emotions and in the intellect, move visibly through my mind, and move invisibly beyond the threshold of sleep, casting lights and shadows of an indefinable wisdom on what had seemed before, it may be, but sterility and noisy violence. It is the intellect that decides where the reader shall ponder over the procession of the symbols, and if the symbols are merely emotional, he gazes from amid the accidents and destinies of the world; but if the symbols are intellectual too, he becomes himself a part of pure intellect, and he is himself mingled with the procession. If I watch a rushy pool in the moonlight, my emotion at its beauty is mixed with memories of the man that I have seen ploughing by its margin, or of the lovers I saw there a night ago; but if I look at the moon herself and remember any of her ancient names and meanings, I move among divine people, and things that have shaken off our mortality, the tower of ivory, the queen of waters, the shining stag among enchanted woods, the white hare sitting upon the hilltop, the fool of faery with his shining cup full of dreams, and it may be 'make a friend of one of these images of wonder,' and 'meet the Lord in the air.'[14] So, too, if one is moved by Shakespeare, who is content with emotional symbols that he may come the nearer to our sympathy, one is mixed with the whole spectacle of the world; while if one is moved by Dante, or by the myth of Demeter, one is mixed into the shadow of God or of a goddess.[15] So too one is furthest from symbols when one is busy doing this or that, but the soul moves among symbols and unfolds in symbols when trance, or madness, or deep meditation has withdrawn it from every impulse but its own. 'I then saw,' wrote Gérard de Nerval of his madness, 'vaguely drifting into form, plastic images of antiquity, which outlined themselves, became definite, and seemed to represent symbols of which I only seized the idea with difficulty.'[16] In an earlier time he would have been of that multitude, whose souls austerity withdrew, even more perfectly than madness could withdraw his soul, from hope and memory, from desire and regret, that they might reveal those processions of symbols that men bow to before altars, and woo with incense and offerings. But being of our time, he has been like Maeterlinck, like Villiers de L'Isle-Adam in *Axël,* like all who are preoccupied with intellectual symbols in our time, a foreshadower of the new sacred book, of which all the arts, as somebody has said, are begging to dream.[17] How can the arts overcome the slow dying of men's hearts that we call the progress of the world, and lay their hands upon men's heart-strings again, without becoming the garment of religion as in old times?

## V

If people were to accept the theory that poetry moves us because of its symbolism, what change should one look for in the manner of our poetry? A return to the way of our fathers, a casting out of descriptions of nature for the sake of nature, of the moral law for the sake of the moral law, a casting out of all anecdotes and of that brooding over scientific opinion that so often extinguished the central flame in Tennyson, and of that vehemence that would make us do or not do certain things; or, in other words, we should come to understand that the beryl stone was enchanted by our fathers that it might unfold the pictures in its heart, and not to mirror our own excited faces, or the boughs waving outside the window.[18] With this change of substance, this return to imagination, this understanding that the laws of art, which are the hidden laws of the world, can alone bind the imagination, would come a change of style, and we would cast out of serious poetry those energetic rhythms, as of a man running, which are the invention of the will with its eyes always on something to be done or undone; and we would seek out those wavering, meditative, organic rhythms, which are the embodiment of the imagination, that neither desires nor hates, because it has done with time, and only wishes to gaze upon some reality, some beauty; nor would it be any longer possible for anybody to deny the importance of form, in all its kinds, for although you can expound an opinion, or describe a thing when your words are not quite well chosen, you cannot give a body to something that moves beyond the senses, unless your words are as subtle, as complex, as full of mysterious life, as the body of a flower or of a woman. The form of sincere poetry, unlike the form of the popular poetry, may indeed be sometimes obscure, or ungrammatical as in some of the best of the *Songs of Innocence and Experience,* but it must have the perfections that escape analysis, the subtleties that have a new meaning every day, and it must have all this whether it be but a little song made out of a moment of dreamy indolence, or some great epic made out of the dreams of one poet and of a hundred generations whose hands were never weary of the sword.[19]

1900.

# THE THEATRE

## I

I remember, some years ago, advising a distinguished, though too little recognised, writer of poetical plays to write a play as unlike ordinary plays as possible, that it might be judged with a fresh mind, and to put it on the stage in some little suburban hall, where a little audience would pay its expenses.[1] I said that he should follow it the year after, at the same time of the year, with another play, and so on from year to year; and that the people who read books, and do not go to the theatre, would gradually find out about him. I suggested that he should begin with a pastoral play, because nobody would expect from a pastoral play the succession of nervous tremors which the plays of commerce, like the novels of commerce, have substituted for the purification that comes with pity and terror to the imagination and intellect. He followed my advice in part, and had a small but perfect success, filling his small theatre for twice the number of performances he had announced; but instead of being content with the praise of his equals, and waiting to win their praise another year, he hired immediately a well-known London theatre, and put his pastoral play and a new play before a meagre and unintelligent audience.[2] I still remember his pastoral play with delight, because, if not always of a high excellence, it was always poetical; but I remember it at the small theatre, where my pleasure was magnified by the pleasure of those about me, and not at the big theatre, where it made me uncomfortable, as an unwelcome guest always makes one uncomfortable.

Why should we thrust our works, which we have written with imaginative sincerity and filled with spiritual desire, before those quite excellent people who think that Rossetti's women are 'guys,' that

Rodin's women are 'ugly,' and that Ibsen is 'immoral,' and who only want to be left at peace to enjoy the works so many clever men have made especially to suit them?[3] We must make a theatre for ourselves and our friends, and for a few simple people who understand from sheer simplicity what we understand from scholarship and thought. We have planned the Irish Literary Theatre with this hospitable emotion, and that the right people may find out about us, we hope to act a play or two in the spring of every year; and that the right people may escape the stupefying memory of the theatre of commerce which clings even to them, our plays will be for the most part remote, spiritual, and ideal.

A common opinion is that the poetic drama has come to an end, because modern poets have no dramatic power; and Mr. Binyon seems to accept this opinion when he says: 'It has been too often assumed that it is the manager who bars the way to poetic plays. But it is much more probable that the poets have failed the managers. If poets mean to serve the stage, their dramas must be dramatic.'[4] I find it easier to believe that audiences, who have learned, as I think, from the life of crowded cities to live upon the surface of life, and actors and managers, who study to please them, have changed, than that imagination, which is the voice of what is eternal in man, has changed. The arts are but one Art; and why should all intense painting and all intense poetry have become not merely unintelligible but hateful to the greater number of men and women, and intense drama move them to pleasure? The audiences of Sophocles and of Shakespeare and of Calderón were not unlike the audiences I have heard listening in Irish cabins to songs in Gaelic about 'an old poet telling his sins,' and about 'the five young men who were drowned last year,' and about 'the lovers that were drowned going to America,' or to some tale of Oisin and his three hundred years in *Tir na nÓg*.[5] Mr. Bridges' *Return of Ulysses,* one of the most beautiful and, as I think, dramatic of modern plays, might have some success in the Aran Islands, if the Gaelic League would translate it into Gaelic, but I am quite certain that it would have no success in the Strand.[6]

Blake has said that all art is a labour to bring again the Golden Age, and all culture is certainly a labour to bring again the simplicity of the first ages, with knowledge of good and evil added to it.[7] The drama has need of cities that it may find men in sufficient numbers, and cities destroy the emotions to which it appeals, and therefore the days of the drama are brief and come but seldom. It has one day when the emotions of cities still remember the emotions of sailors and husbandmen and shepherds and users of the spear and the bow; as the houses and furniture and earthen vessels of cities, before the coming of machinery, remember the rocks and the woods and the hillside; and it has another day, now beginning, when thought and scholarship discover their desire. In the first day, it is the art of the people; and in the second day, like the dramas acted of old times in the hidden places of temples, it is the preparation of a Priesthood. It may be, though the world is not old enough to show us any example, that this Priesthood will spread their Religion everywhere, and make their Art the Art of the people.

When the first day of the drama had passed by, actors found that an always larger number of people were more easily moved through the eyes than through the ears. The emotion that comes with the music of words is exhausting, like all intellectual emotions, and few people like exhausting emotions; and therefore actors began to speak as if they were reading something out of the newspapers. They forgot the noble art of oratory, and gave all their thought to the poor art of acting, that is content with the sympathy of our nerves; until at last those who love poetry found it better to read alone in their rooms what they had once delighted to hear sitting friend by friend, lover by beloved. I once asked Mr. William Morris if he had thought of writing a play, and he answered that he had, but would not write one, because actors did not know how to speak poetry with the half-chant men spoke it with in old times. Mr. Swinburne's *Locrine* was acted a month ago, and it was not badly acted, but nobody could tell whether it was fit for the stage or not, for not one rhythm, not one cry of passion, was spoken with a musical emphasis, and verse spoken without a musical emphasis seems but an artificial and cumbersome way of saying what might be said naturally and simply in prose.[8]

As audiences and actors changed, managers learned to substitute meretricious landscapes, painted upon wood and canvas, for the descriptions of poetry, until the painted scenery, which had in Greece been a charming explanation of what was least important in the story, became as important as the story. It needed some imagination, some gift for day-dreams, to see the horses and the fields and flowers of Colonus as one listened to the elders gathered about Œdipus, or to see 'the pendent bed and procreant cradle' of the 'martlet' as one listened to Duncan before the castle of Macbeth; but it needs no imagination to admire a painting of one of the more obvious effects of nature painted by somebody who understands how to show everything to the most hurried glance.[9] At the same time the managers made the costumes of the actors more and more magnificent, that the mind might sleep in peace, while the eye took pleasure in the magnificence of velvet and silk and in the physical beauty of women. These changes gradually perfected the theatre of commerce, the masterpiece of that movement towards externality in life and thought and Art, against which the criticism of our day is learning to protest.

Even if poetry were spoken as poetry, it would still seem out of place in many of its highest moments upon a stage, where the superficial appearances of nature are so closely copied; for poetry is founded upon convention, and becomes incredible the moment painting or gesture reminds us that people do not speak verse when they meet upon the highway. The theatre of Art, when it comes to exist, must therefore discover grave and decorative gestures, such as delighted Rossetti and Madox Brown, and grave and decorative scenery that will be forgotten the moment an actor has said 'It is dawn,' or 'It is raining,' or 'The wind is shaking the trees'; and dresses of so little irrelevant magnificence that the mortal actors and actresses may change without much labour into the immortal people of romance.[10] The theatre began in ritual, and it cannot come to its greatness again without recalling words to their ancient sovereignty.

It will take a generation, and perhaps generations, to restore the theatre of Art; for one must get one's actors, and perhaps one's scenery, from the theatre of commerce, until new actors and new painters have come to help one; and until many failures and imperfect successes have made a new tradition, and perfected in detail the ideal that is beginning to float before our eyes. If one could call one's painters and one's actors from where one would, how easy it would be! I know some painters,* who have never painted scenery, who could paint the scenery I want, but they have their own work to do;

*I had Charles Ricketts in mind. 1924.[11]

and in Ireland I have heard a red-haired orator* repeat some bad political verses with a voice that went through one like flame, and made them seem the most beautiful verses in the world; but he has no practical knowledge of the stage, and probably despises it.

May 1899.

## II

Dionysius, the Areopagite, wrote that 'He has set the borders of the nations according to His angels.'[13] It is these angels, each one the genius of some race about to be unfolded, that are the founders of intellectual traditions; and as lovers understand in their first glance all that is to befall them, and as poets and musicians see the whole work in its first impulse, so races prophesy at their awakening whatever the generations that are to prolong their traditions shall accomplish in detail. It is only at the awakening—as in ancient Greece, or in Elizabethan England, or in contemporary Scandinavia—that great numbers of men understand that a right understanding of life and of destiny is more important than amusement. In London, where all the intellectual traditions gather to die, men hate a play if they are told it is literature, for they will not endure a spiritual superiority; but in Athens, where so many intellectual traditions were born, Euripides once changed hostility to enthusiasm by asking his playgoers whether it was his business to teach them, or their business to teach him.[14] New races understand instinctively, because the future cries in their ears, that the old revelations are insufficient, and that all life is revelation beginning in miracle and enthusiasm, and dying out as it unfolds itself in what we have mistaken for progress. It is one of our illusions, as I think, that education, the softening of manners, the perfecting of law—countless images of a fading light—can create nobleness and beauty, and that life moves slowly and evenly towards some perfection. Progress is miracle, and it is sudden, because miracles are the work of an all-powerful energy, and nature in herself has no power except to die and to forget. If one studies one's own mind, one comes to think with Blake that 'every time less than a pulsation

*J. F. Taylor. [1924][12]

of the artery is equal to six thousand years, for in this period the poet's work is done, and all the great events of time start forth and are conceived in such a period, within a pulsation of the artery.'[15]

FEBRUARY 1900.

# THE CELTIC ELEMENT IN LITERATURE

## I

Ernest Renan described what he held to be Celtic characteristics in *The Poetry of the Celtic Races.*[1] I must repeat the well-known sentences: 'No race communed so intimately as the Celtic race with the lower creation, or believed it to have so big a share of moral life.' The Celtic race had 'a realistic naturalism,' 'a love of nature for herself, a vivid feeling for her magic, commingled with the melancholy a man knows when he is face to face with her, and thinks he hears her communing with him about his origin and his destiny.' 'It has worn itself out in mistaking dreams for realities,' and 'compared with the classical imagination the Celtic imagination is indeed the infinite contrasted with the finite.' 'Its history is one long lament, it still recalls its exiles, its flights across the seas.' 'If at times it seems to be cheerful, its tear is not slow to glisten behind the smile. Its songs of joy end as elegies; there is nothing to equal the delightful sadness of its national melodies.'[2] Matthew Arnold, in *The Study of Celtic Literature,* has accepted this passion for nature, this imaginativeness, this melancholy, as Celtic characteristics, but has described them more elaborately.[3] The Celtic passion for nature comes almost more from a sense of her 'mystery' than of her 'beauty,' and it adds 'charm and magic' to nature, and the Celtic imaginativeness and melancholy are alike 'a passionate, turbulent, indomitable reaction against the despotism of fact.'[4] The Celt is not melancholy, as Faust or Werther are melancholy, from 'a perfectly definite motive,' but because of something about him 'unaccountable, defiant and titanic.'[5] How well one knows these sentences, better even than Renan's, and how well one knows the passages of prose and verse which he uses to prove that wherever

English literature has the qualities these sentences describe, it has them from a Celtic source. Though I do not think any of us who write about Ireland have built any argument upon them, it is well to consider them a little, and see where they are helpful and where they are hurtful. If we do not, we may go mad some day, and the enemy root up our rose-garden and plant a cabbage-garden instead. Perhaps we must restate a little, Renan's and Arnold's argument.[6]

## II

Once every people in the world believed that trees were divine, and could take a human or grotesque shape and dance among the shadows; and that deer, and ravens and foxes, and wolves and bears, and clouds and pools, almost all things under the sun and moon, and the sun and moon, were not less divine and changeable. They saw in the rainbow the still bent bow of a god thrown down in his negligence; they heard in the thunder the sound of his beaten water-jar, or the tumult of his chariot wheels; and when a sudden flight of wild ducks, or of crows, passed over their heads, they thought they were gazing at the dead hastening to their rest; while they dreamed of so great a mystery in little things that they believed the waving of a hand, or of a sacred bough, enough to trouble far-off hearts, or hood the moon with darkness. All old literatures are full of these or of like imaginations, and all the poets of races, who have not lost this way of looking at things, could have said of themselves, as the poet of the *Kalevala* said of himself, 'I have learned my songs from the music of many birds, and from the music of many waters.'[7] When a mother in the *Kalevala* weeps for a daughter, who was drowned flying from an old suitor, she weeps so greatly that her tears become three rivers, and cast up three rocks, on which grow three birch-trees, where three cuckoos sit and sing, the one 'love, love,' the one 'suitor, suitor,' the one 'consolation, consolation.'[8] And the makers of the Sagas made the squirrel run up and down the sacred ash-tree carrying words of hatred from the eagle to the worm, and from the worm to the eagle; although they had less of the old way than the makers of the *Kalevala,* for they lived in a more crowded and complicated world, and were learning the abstract meditation which lures men from visible beauty, and were unlearning, it may be, the impassioned meditation which brings men beyond the edge of trance and makes trees, and beasts, and dead things talk with human voices.[9]

The old Irish and the old Welsh, though they had less of the old way than the makers of the *Kalevala,* had more of it than the makers of the Sagas, and it is this that distinguishes the examples Matthew Arnold quotes of their 'natural magic,' of their sense of 'the mystery' more than of 'the beauty' of nature. When Matthew Arnold wrote it was not easy to know as much as we know now of folk song and folk belief, and I do not think he understood that our 'natural magic' is but the ancient religion of the world, the ancient worship of nature and that troubled ecstasy before her, that certainty of all beautiful places being haunted, which it brought into men's minds. The ancient religion is in that passage of the *Mabinogion* about the making of 'Flower Aspect.'[10] Gwydion and Math made her 'by charms and illusions' 'out of flowers.' 'They took the blossoms of the oak, and the blossoms of the broom, and the blossoms of the meadow-sweet, and produced from them a maiden the fairest and most graceful that man ever saw; and they baptized her, and called her Flower Aspect'; and one finds it in the not less beautiful passage about the burning Tree, that has half its beauty from calling up a fancy of leaves so living and beautiful, they can be of no less living and beautiful a thing than flame: 'They saw a tall tree by the side of the river, one half of which was in flames from the root to the top, and the other half was green and in full leaf.'[11] And one finds it very certainly in the quotations he makes from English poets to prove a Celtic influence in English poetry; in Keats's 'magic casements opening on the foam of perilous seas in faery lands forlorn'; in his 'moving waters at their priest-like task of pure ablution round earth's human shore'; in Shakespeare's 'floor of heaven,' 'inlaid with patens of bright gold'; and in his Dido standing 'on the wild sea banks,' 'a willow in her hand,' and waving it in the ritual of the old worship of nature and the spirits of nature, to wave 'her love to come again to Carthage.'[12] And his other examples have the delight and wonder of devout worshippers among the haunts of their divinities. Is there not such delight and wonder in the description of Olwen in the *Mabinogion*—'More yellow was her hair than the flower of the broom, and her skin was whiter than the foam of the wave, and fairer were her hands and her fingers than the blossoms of the wood-anemone amidst the spray of the meadow fountains'?[13] And is there not such delight and wonder in—

> Meet we on hill, in dale, forest, or mead,
> By paved fountain or by rushy brook,
> Or on the beached margent of the sea?[14]

If men had never dreamed that fair women could be made out of flowers, or rise up out of meadow fountains and paved fountains, neither passage could have been written. Certainly the descriptions of nature made in what Matthew Arnold calls 'the faithful way,' or in what he calls 'the Greek way,' would have lost nothing if all the meadow fountains or paved fountains were but what they seemed.[15] When Keats wrote, in the Greek way, which adds lightness and brightness to nature—

> What little town by river or sea-shore
> Or mountain built with quiet citadel,
> Is emptied of its folk, this pious morn;

when Shakespeare wrote in the Greek way—

> I know a bank where the wild thyme blows,
> Where oxlips and the nodding violet grows;

when Virgil wrote in the Greek way—

> Muscosi fontes et somno mollior herba,

and

> Pallentes violas et summa papavera carpens
> Narcissum et florem jungit bene olentis anethi;

they looked at nature without ecstasy, but with the affection a man feels for the garden where he has walked daily and thought pleasant thoughts.[16] They looked at nature in the modern way, the way of people who are poetical, but are more interested in one another than in a nature which has faded to be but friendly and pleasant, the way of people who have forgotten the ancient religion.

## III

Men who lived in a world where anything might flow and change, and become any other thing; and among great gods whose passions were in the flaming sunset, and in the thunder and the thunder-shower, had not our thoughts of weight and measure.[17] They worshipped nature and the abundance of nature, and had always, as it seems, for a supreme ritual that tumultuous dance among the hills or in the depths of the woods, where unearthly ecstasy fell upon the dancers, until they seemed the gods or the godlike beasts, and felt their souls overtopping the moon; and, as some think, imagined for the first time in the world the blessed country of the gods and of the happy dead. They had imaginative passions because they did not live within our own strait limits, and were nearer to ancient chaos, every man's desire, and had immortal models about them.[18] The hare that ran by among the dew might have sat up on his haunches when the first man was made, and the poor bunch of rushes under their feet might have been a goddess laughing among the stars; and with but a little magic, a little waving of the hands, a little murmuring of the lips, they too could become a hare or a bunch of rushes, and know immortal love and immortal hatred.

All folk literature, and all literature that keeps the folk tradition, delights in unbounded and immortal things. The *Kalevala* delights in the seven hundred years that Luonnotar wanders in the depths of the sea with Wäinämöinen in her womb, and the Mahomedan king in the Song of Roland, pondering upon the greatness of Charlemagne, repeats over and over, 'He is three hundred years old, when will he be weary of war?'[19] Cuchulain in the Irish folk tale had the passion of victory, and he overcame all men, and died warring upon the waves, because they alone had the strength to overcome him.[20] The lover in the Irish folk song bids his beloved come with him into the woods, and see the salmon leap in the rivers, and hear the cuckoo sing, because death will never find them in the heart of the woods.[21] Oisin, new come from his three hundred years of faeryland, and of the love that is in faeryland, bids Saint Patrick cease his prayers a while and listen to the blackbird, because it is the blackbird of Derrycarn that Finn brought from Norway, three hundred years before, and set its nest upon the oak-tree with his own hands.[22] Surely if one goes far enough into the woods, one will find there all that one is seeking? Who knows how many centuries the birds of the woods have been singing?

All folk literature has indeed a passion whose like is not in modern literature and music and art, except where it has come by some straight or crooked way out of ancient times. Love was held to be a fatal sickness in ancient Ireland, and there is a love-poem in the *The Songs of Connacht* that is like a death cry: 'My love, O she is my love, the woman who is most for destroying me, dearer is she for making me ill than the woman who would be for making me well. She is my treasure, O she is my treasure, the woman of the grey eyes . . . a woman who would not lay a hand under my head. . . . She is my love, O she is my love, the woman who left no strength in me; a woman who would not breathe a sigh after me, a woman who would not raise a stone at my tomb. . . . She is my secret love, O she is my secret love. A woman who tells me nothing, . . . a woman who does not remember me to be out. . . . She is my choice, O she is my choice, the woman who would not look back at me, the woman who would not make peace with me. . . . She is my desire, O she is my desire: a woman dearest to me under the sun, a woman who would not pay me heed, if I were to sit by her side. It is she ruined my heart and left a sigh for ever in me.'[23] There is another song that ends, 'The Erne shall be in strong flood, the hills shall be torn down, and the sea shall have red waves, and blood shall be spilled, and every mountain valley and every moor shall be on high, before you shall perish, my little black rose.'[24] Nor do the old Irish weigh and measure their hatred. The nurse of O'Sullivan Bere in the folk song prays that the bed of his betrayer may be the red hearth-stone of hell for ever.[25] And an Elizabethan Irish poet cries: 'Three things are waiting for my death. The devil, who is waiting for my soul and cares nothing for my body or my wealth; the worms, who are waiting for my body but care nothing for my soul or my wealth; my children, who are waiting for my wealth and care nothing for my body or my soul. O Christ, hang all three in the one noose.'[26] Such love and hatred seek no mortal thing but their own infinity, and such love and hatred soon become love and hatred of the idea. The lover who loves so passionately can soon sing to his beloved like the lover in the poem by 'A.E.,' 'A vast desire awakes and grows into forgetfulness of thee.'[27]

When an early Irish poet calls the Irishman famous for much loving, and a proverb, a friend* has heard in the Highlands of Scotland, talks of the lovelessness of the Irishman, they may say but the same thing, for if your passion is but great enough it leads you to a country where there are many cloisters.[29] The hater who hates with too good a heart soon comes also to hate the idea only; and from this idealism in love and hatred comes, as I think, a certain power of saying and forgetting things, especially a power of saying and forgetting things in politics, which others do not say and forget. The ancient farmers and herdsmen were full of love and hatred, and made their friends gods, and their enemies the enemies of gods, and those who keep their tradition are not less mythological. From this 'mistaking dreams,' which are perhaps essences, for 'realities,' which are perhaps accidents, from this 'passionate, turbulent reaction against the despotism of fact,' comes, it may be, that melancholy which made all ancient peoples delight in tales that end in death and parting, as modern peoples delight in tales that end in marriage bells; and made all ancient peoples, who, like the old Irish, had a nature more lyrical than dramatic, delight in wild and beautiful lamentations.[30] Life was so weighed down by the emptiness of the great forests and by the mystery of all things, and by the greatness of its own desires, and, as I think, by the loneliness of much beauty; and seemed so little and so fragile and so brief, that nothing could be more sweet in the memory than a tale that ended in death and parting, and than a wild and beautiful lamentation. Men did not mourn merely because their beloved was married to another, or because learning was bitter in the mouth, for such mourning believes that life might be happy were it different, and is therefore the less mourning; but because they had been born and must die with their great thirst unslaked. And so it is that all the august sorrowful persons of literature, Cassandra and Helen and Deirdre, and Lear and Tristan, have come out of legends and are indeed but the images of the primitive imagination mirrored in the lit-

*William Sharp, who probably invented the proverb, but invented or not, it remains true. 1924.[28]

tle looking-glass of the modern and classic imagination.[31] This is that 'melancholy a man knows when he is face to face' with nature, and thinks 'he hears her communing with him about' the mournfulness of being born and of dying; and how can it do otherwise than call into his mind 'its exiles, its flights across the seas,' that it may stir the ever-smouldering ashes?[32] No Gaelic poetry is so popular in Gaelic-speaking places as the lamentations of Oisin, old and miserable, remembering the companions and the loves of his youth, and his three hundred years in faeryland, and his faery love: all dreams withering in the winds of time lament in his lamentations: 'The clouds are long above me this night; last night was a long night to me; although I find this day long, yesterday was still longer. Every day that comes to me is long. . . . No one in this great world is like me—a poor old man dragging stones. The clouds are long above me this night. I am the last man of the Fianna, the great Oisin, the son of Finn, listening to the sound of bells. The clouds are long above me this night.'[33] Matthew Arnold quotes the lamentation of Llywarch Hen as a type of the Celtic melancholy, but I prefer to quote it as a type of the primitive melancholy: 'O my crutch, is it not autumn when the fern is red and the water flag yellow? Have I not hated that which I love? . . . Behold, old age, which makes sport of me, from the hair of my head and my teeth, to my eyes which women loved. The four things I have all my life most hated fall upon me together—coughing and old age, sickness and sorrow. I am old, I am alone, shapeliness and warmth are gone from me, the couch of honour shall be no more mine; I am miserable, I am bent on my crutch. How evil was the lot allotted to Llywarch, the night he was brought forth! Sorrows without end and no deliverance from his burden.'[34] An Elizabethan writer describes extravagant sorrow by calling it 'to weep Irish'; and Oisin and Llywarch Hen are, I think, a little nearer even to us modern Irish than they are to most people.[35] That is why our poetry and much of our thought is melancholy. 'The same man,' writes Dr. Hyde in the beautiful prose which he first writes in Gaelic, 'who will to-day be dancing, sporting, drinking, and shouting, will be soliloquising by himself to-morrow, heavy and sick and sad in his own lonely little hut, making a croon over departed hopes, lost life, the vanity of this world, and the coming of death.'[36]

## IV

Matthew Arnold asks how much of the Celt must one imagine in the ideal man of genius.[37] I prefer to say, how much of the ancient hunters and fishers and of the ecstatic dancers among hills and woods must one imagine in the ideal man of genius? Certainly a thirst for unbounded emotion and a wild melancholy are troublesome things in the world, and do not make its life more easy or orderly, but it may be the arts are founded on the life beyond the world, and that they must cry in the ears of our penury until the world has been consumed and become a vision. Certainly, as Samuel Palmer wrote, 'Excess is the vivifying spirit of the finest art, and we must always seek to make excess more abundantly excessive.'[38] Matthew Arnold has said that if he were asked 'where English got its turn for melancholy and its turn for natural magic,' he 'would answer with little doubt that it got much of its melancholy from a Celtic source, with no doubt at all that from a Celtic source is got nearly all its natural magic.'[39]

I will put this differently and say that literature dwindles to a mere chronicle of circumstance, or passionless phantasies, and passionless meditations, unless it is constantly flooded with the passions and beliefs of ancient times,* and that of all the fountains of the passions and beliefs of ancient times in Europe, the Slavonic, the Finnish, the Scandinavian, and the Celtic, the Celtic alone has been for centuries close to the main river of European literature. It has again and again brought 'the vivifying spirit' 'of excess' into the arts of Europe. Ernest Renan has told how the visions of purgatory seen by pilgrims to Lough Derg—once visions of the pagan underworld, as the boat made out of a hollow tree that bore the pilgrim to the holy island were alone enough to prove—gave European thought new symbols of a more abundant penitence; and had so great an influence that he has written, 'It cannot be doubted for a moment that to the number of poetical themes Europe owes to the genius of the Celt is to be added the framework of *The Divine Comedy*.'[40]

*I should have added as an alternative that the supernatural may at any moment create new myths, but I was timid. 1924.

A little later the legends of Arthur and his table, and of the Holy Grail, once it seems the cauldron of an Irish god, changed the literature of Europe, and it maybe, changed, as it were, the very roots of man's emotions by their influence on the spirit of chivalry and on the spirit of romance; and later still Shakespeare found his Mab, and probably his Puck, and one knows not how much else of his faery kingdom, in Celtic legend; while at the beginning of our own day Sir Walter Scott gave Highland legends and Highland excitability so great a mastery over all romance that they seem romance itself.[41]

In our own time Scandinavian tradition, because of the imagination of Richard Wagner and of William Morris and of the earlier and, as I think, greater Henrik Ibsen, has created a new romance, and, through the imagination of Richard Wagner, become all but the most passionate element in the arts of the modern world.[42] There is indeed but one other element as passionate, the still unfaded legends of Arthur and of the Holy Grail; and now a new fountain of legends, and, as I think, a more abundant fountain than any in Europe, is being opened, the fountain of Gaelic legends: the tale of Deirdre, who alone among women who have set men mad had equal loveliness and wisdom; the tale of the Sons of Tuireann, with its unintelligible mysteries, an old Grail Quest as I think; the tale of the four children changed into four swans, and lamenting over many waters; the tale of the love of Cuchulain for an immortal goddess, and his coming home to a mortal woman in the end; the tale of his many battles at the ford with that dear friend he kissed before the battles, and over whose dead body he wept when he had killed him; the tale of his death and of the lamentations of Emer; the tale of the flight of Grania with Diarmuid, strangest of all tales of the fickleness of woman, and the tale of the coming of Oisin out of faeryland, and of his memories and lamentations.[43] 'The Celtic movement,' as I understand it, is principally the opening of this fountain, and none can measure of how great importance it may be to coming times, for every new fountain of legends is a new intoxication for the imagination of the world. It comes at a time when the imagination of the world is as ready as it was at the coming of the tales of Arthur and of the Grail for a new intoxication. The reaction against the rationalism of the eighteenth century has mingled with a reaction against the materialism of the nineteenth century, and the symbolical movement, which has come to perfection in

Germany in Wagner, in England in the Pre-Raphaelites, and in France in Villiers de L'Isle-Adam, and Mallarmé, and Maeterlinck, and has stirred the imagination of Ibsen and D'Annunzio, is certainly the only movement that is saying new things.[44] The arts by brooding upon their own intensity have become religious, and are seeking, as I think Verhaeren has said, to create a sacred book.[45] They must, as religious thought has always done, utter themselves through legends; and the Slavonic and Finnish legends tell of strange woods and seas, and the Scandinavian legends are held by a great master, and tell also of strange woods and seas, and the Welsh legends are held by almost as many great masters as the Greek legends, while the Irish legends move among known woods and seas, and have so much of a new beauty that they may well give the opening century its most memorable symbols.

1897.

I could have written this essay with much more precision and have much better illustrated my meaning if I had waited until Lady Gregory had finished her book of legends, *Cuchulain of Muirthemne,* a book to set beside the *Morte d' Arthur* and the *Mabinogion.*[46]

1902.

# THE AUTUMN OF THE BODY

Our thoughts and emotions are often but spray flung up from hidden tides that follow a moon no eye can see. I remember that when I first began to write I desired to describe outward things as vividly as possible, and took pleasure, in which there was, perhaps, a little discontent, in picturesque and declamatory books. And then quite suddenly I lost the desire of describing outward things, and found that I took little pleasure in a book unless it was spiritual and unemphatic. I did not then understand that the change was from beyond my own mind, but I understand now that writers are struggling all over Europe, though not often with a philosophic understanding of their struggle, against that picturesque and declamatory way of writing, against that 'externality' which a time of scientific and political thought has brought into literature.[1] This struggle has been going on for some years, but it has only just become strong enough to draw within itself the little inner world which alone seeks more than amusement in the arts. In France, where movements are more marked, because the people are pre-eminently logical, *The Temptation of S. Anthony,* the last great dramatic invention of the old romanticism, contrasts very plainly with *Axël,* the first great dramatic invention of the new; and Maeterlinck has followed Count Villiers de L'Isle-Adam.[2] Flaubert wrote unforgettable descriptions of grotesque, bizarre, and beautiful scenes and persons, as they show to the ear and to the eye, and crowded them with historic and ethnographical details; but Count Villiers de L'Isle-Adam swept together, by what seemed a sudden energy, words behind which glimmered a spiritual and passionate mood, as the flame glimmers behind the dusky blue and red glass in an Eastern lamp; and created persons from whom has fallen all even of personal characteristic except a thirst for that hour when all things shall pass away like a cloud, and a pride like that of the Magi following their star over many mountains; while Maeterlinck has plucked away even this thirst and this pride and set before us faint souls, naked and pathetic shadows already half vapour and sighing to one another upon the border of the last abyss.[3] There has been, as I think, a like change in French painting, for one sees everywhere, instead of the dramatic stories and picturesque moments of an older school, frail and tremulous bodies unfitted for the labour of life, and landscape where subtle rhythms of colour and of form have overcome the clear outline of things as we see them in the labour of life.

There has been a like change in England, but it has come more gradually and is more mixed with lesser changes than in France. The poetry which found its expression in the poems of writers like Browning and of Tennyson, and even of writers, who are seldom classed with them, like Swinburne, and like Shelley in his earlier years, pushed its limits as far as possible, and tried to absorb into itself the science and politics, the philosophy and morality of its time; but a new poetry, which is always contracting its limits, has grown up under the shadow of the old.[4] Rossetti began it, but was too much of a painter in his poetry to follow it with a perfect devotion; and it became a movement when Mr. Lang and Mr. Gosse and Mr. Dobson devoted themselves to the most condensed of lyric poems, and when Mr. Bridges, a more considerable poet, elaborated a rhythm too delicate for any but an almost bodiless emotion, and repeated over and over the most ancient notes of poetry, and none but these.[5] The poets who followed have either, like Mr. Kipling, turned from serious poetry altogether, and so passed out of the processional order, or speak out of some personal or spiritual passion in words and types and metaphors that draw one's imagination as far as possible from the complexities of modern life and thought.[6] The change has been more marked in English painting, which, when intense enough to belong to the procession order, began to cast out things, as they are seen by minds plunged in the labour of life, so much before French painting that ideal art is sometimes called English art upon the Continent.

I see, indeed, in the arts of every country those faint lights and faint colours and faint outlines and faint energies which many call 'the decadence,' and which I, because I believe that the arts lie dreaming of things to come, prefer to call the autumn of the body.[7] An Irish poet whose rhythms are like the cry of a sea-bird in autumn twilight has told its meaning in the line, 'The very sunlight's weary, and it's time to quit the plough.'[8] Its importance is the greater because it comes to us at the moment when we are beginning to be interested in many things which positive science, the interpreter of exterior law, has always denied: communion of mind with mind in thought and without words, foreknowledge in dreams and in visions, and the coming among us of the dead, and of much else. We are, it may be, at a crowning crisis of the world, at the moment when man is about to ascend, with the wealth, he has been so long gathering, upon his shoulders, the stairway he has been descending from the first days. The first poets, if one may find their images in the *Kalevala,* had not Homer's preoccupation with things, and he was not so full of their excitement as Virgil.[9] Dante added to poetry a dialectic which, although he made it serve his laborious ecstasy, was the invention of minds trained by the labour of life, by a traffic among many things, and not a spontaneous expression of an interior life; while Shakespeare shattered the symmetry of verse and of drama that he might fill them with things and their accidental relations to one another.[10]

Each of these writers had come further down the stairway than those who had lived before him, but it was only with the modern poets, with Goethe and Wordsworth and Browning, that poetry gave up the right to consider all things in the world as a dictionary of types and symbols and began to call itself a critic of life and an interpreter of things as they are.[11] Painting, music, science, politics, and even religion, because they have felt a growing belief that we know nothing but the fading and flowering of the world, have changed in numberless elaborate ways. Man has wooed and won the world, and has fallen weary, and not, I think, for a time, but with a weariness that will not end until the last autumn, when the stars shall be blown away like withered leaves. He grew weary when he said, 'These things that I touch and see and hear are alone real,' for he saw them without illusion at last, and found them but air and dust and moisture.[12] And now he must be philosophical above everything, even about the arts, for he can only return the way he came, and so escape from weariness, by philosophy. The arts are, I believe, about to take upon their shoulders the burdens that have fallen from the shoulders of priests, and to lead us back upon our journey by filling our thoughts with the essences of things, and not with things. We are about to substitute once more the distillation of alchemy for the analyses of chemistry and for some other sciences; and certain of us are looking everywhere for the perfect alembic that no silver or golden drop may escape. Mr. Symons has written lately on M. Mallarmé's method, and has quoted him as saying that we should 'abolish the pretension, æsthetically an error, despite its dominion over almost all the masterpieces, to enclose within the subtle pages other than—for example—the horror of the forest or the silent thunder in the leaves, not the intense dense wood of the trees,' and as desiring to substitute for 'the old lyric afflatus or the enthusiastic personal direction of the phrase' words 'that take light from mutual reflection, like an actual trail of fire over precious stones,' and 'to make an entire word hitherto unknown to the language' 'out of many vocables.'[13] Mr. Symons understands these and other sentences to mean that poetry will henceforth be a poetry of essences, separated one from another in little and intense poems.[14] I think there will be much poetry of this kind, because of an ever more arduous search for an almost disembodied ecstasy, but I think we will not cease to write long poems, but rather that we will write them more and more as our new belief makes the world plastic under our hands again. I think that we will learn again how to describe at great length an old man wandering among enchanted islands, his return home at last, his slow-gathering vengeance, a flitting shape of a goddess, and a flight of arrows, and yet to make all of these so different things 'take light by mutual reflection, like an actual trail of fire over precious stones,' and become 'an entire word,' the signature or symbol of a mood of the divine imagination as imponderable as 'the horror of the forest or the silent thunder in the leaves.'[15]

1898.

# THE MOODS

Literature differs from explanatory and scientific writing in being wrought about a mood, or a community of moods, as the body is wrought about an invisible soul; and if it uses argument, theory, erudition, observation, and seems to grow hot in assertion or denial, it does so merely to make us partakers at the banquet of the moods. It seems to me that these moods are the labourers and messengers of the Ruler of All, the gods of ancient days still dwelling on their secret Olympus, the angels of more modern days ascending and descending upon their shining ladder; and that argument, theory, erudition, observation, are merely what Blake called 'little devils who fight for themselves,' illusions of our visible passing life, who must be made serve the moods, or we have no part in eternity.[1] Everything that can be seen, touched, measured, explained, understood, argued over, is to the imaginative artist nothing more than a means, for he belongs to the invisible life, and delivers its ever new and ever ancient revelation. We hear much of his need for the restraints of reason, but the only restraint he can obey is the mysterious instinct that has made him an artist, and that teaches him to discover immortal moods in mortal desires, an undecaying hope in our trivial ambitions, a divine love in sexual passion.

1895.

# THE BODY OF THE FATHER CHRISTIAN ROSENCRUX

The followers of the Father Christian Rosencrux, says the old tradition, wrapped his imperishable body in noble raiment and laid it under the house of their order, in a tomb containing the symbols of all things in heaven and earth, and in the waters under the earth, and set about him inextinguishable magical lamps, which burnt on generation after generation, until other students of the order came upon the tomb by chance.[1] It seems to me that the imagination has had no very different history during the last two hundred years, but has been laid in a great tomb of criticism, and had set over it inextinguishable magical lamps of wisdom and romance, and has been altogether so nobly housed and apparelled that we have forgotten that its wizard lips are closed, or but opened for the complaining of some melancholy and ghostly voice. The ancients and the Elizabethans abandoned themselves to imagination as a woman abandons herself to love, and created beings who made the people of this world seem but shadows, and great passions which made our loves and hatreds appear but ephemeral and trivial phantasies; but now it is not the great persons or the great passions we imagine which absorb us, for the persons and passions in our poems are mainly reflections our mirror has caught from older poems or from the life about us, but the wise comments we make upon them, the criticism of life we wring from their fortunes. Arthur and his Court are nothing, but the many-coloured lights that play about them are as beautiful as the lights from cathedral windows; Pompilia and Guido are but little, while the ever-recurring meditations and expositions which climax in the mouth of the Pope are among the wisest of the Christian age.[2] I cannot get it out of my mind that this age of criticism is about to pass, and an age of imagination, of emotion, of moods, of revelation, about to come in its place; for certainly belief in a supersensual world is at hand again; and when the notion that we are 'phantoms of the earth and water' has gone down the wind, we will trust our own being and all it desires to invent; and when the external world is no more the standard of reality, we will learn again that the great Passions are angels of God, and that to embody them 'uncurbed in their eternal glory,' even in their labour for the ending of man's peace and prosperity, is more than to comment, however wisely, upon the tendencies of our time, or to express the socialistic, or humanitarian, or other forces of our time, or even 'to sum up' our time, as the phrase is; for art is a revelation, and not a criticism, and the life of the artist is in the old saying, 'The wind bloweth where it listeth, and thou hearest the sound thereof, but canst not tell whence it cometh and whither it goeth; so is every one that is born of the spirit.'[3]

1895.

# *THE RETURN OF ULYSSES*

## I

M. Maeterlinck, in his beautiful *Treasure of the Humble,* compares the dramas of our stage to the paintings of an obsolete taste; and the dramas of the stage for which he hopes, to the paintings of a taste that cannot become obsolete.[1] 'The true artist,' he says, 'no longer chooses Marius triumphing over the Cimbrians, or the assassination of the Duke of Guise, as fit subjects for his art; for he is well aware that the psychology of victory or murder is but elementary and exceptional, and that the solemn voice of men and things, the voice that issues forth so timidly and hesitatingly, cannot be heard amidst the idle uproar of acts of violence. And therefore will he place on his canvas a house lost in the heart of the country, a door open at the end of a passage, a face or hands at rest.'[2] I do not understand him to mean that our dramas should have no victories or murders, for he quotes for our example plays that have both, but only that their victories and murders shall not be to excite our nerves, but to illustrate the reveries of a wisdom which shall be as much a part of the daily life of the wise as a face or hands at rest. And certainly the greater plays of the past ages have been built after such a fashion. If this fashion is about to become our fashion also, and there are signs that it is, plays like some of Mr. Robert Bridges will come out of that obscurity into which all poetry that is not lyrical poetry has fallen, and even popular criticism will begin to know something about them.[3] Some day the few among us who care for poetry more than any temporal thing, and who believe that its delights cannot be perfect when we read it alone in our rooms and long for one to share its delights, but that they might be perfect in the theatre, when we share them friend with friend, lover with beloved, will persuade a few idealists to seek out the lost art of speaking, and seek out ourselves the lost art, that is perhaps nearest of all arts to eternity, the subtle art of listening. When that day comes we will talk much of Mr. Bridges; for did he not write scrupulous, passionate poetry to be sung and to be spoken, when there were few to sing and as yet none to speak?[4] There is one play especially, *The Return of Ulysses,* which we will praise for perfect after its kind, the kind of our new drama of wisdom, for it moulds into dramatic shape, and with as much as possible of literal translation, those closing books of the *Odyssey* which are perhaps the most perfect poetry of the world, and compels that great tide of song to flow through delicate dramatic verse, with little abatement of its own leaping and clamorous speed.[5] As I read, the gathering passion overwhelms me, as it did when Homer himself was the singer, and when I read at last the lines in which the maid describes to Penelope the battle with the suitors, at which she looks through the open door, I tremble with excitement.

*Penelope:* Alas! what cries! Say, is the prince still safe?
*The Maid:* He shieldeth himself well, and striketh surely;
His foes fall down before him. Ah! now what can I see?
Who cometh? Lo! a dazzling helm, a spear
Of silver or electron; sharp and swift
The piercings. How they fall! Ha! shields are raised
In vain. I am blinded, or the beggar-man
Hath waxed in strength. He is changed, he is young. O strange!
He is all in golden armour. These are gods
That slay the suitors. (*Runs to Penelope*) O lady, forgive me.
'Tis Ares' self. I saw his crispèd beard;
I saw beneath his helm his curlèd locks.[6]

The coming of Athene helmed 'in silver or electron' and her transformation of Ulysses are not, as the way is with the only modern dramas that popular criticism holds to be dramatic, the climax of an excitement of the nerves, but of that unearthly excitement which has wisdom for fruit, and is of like kind with the ecstasy of the seers, an altar flame, unshaken by the winds of the world, and burning every moment with whiter and purer brilliance.[7]

Mr. Bridges has written it in what is practically the classical manner, as he has done in *Achilles in Scyros*—a placid and charming setting for many placid and charming lyrics—

> And ever we keep a feast of delight,
> The betrothal of hearts, when spirits unite,
> Creating an offspring of joy, a treasure
>     Unknown to the bad, for whom
>     The gods foredoom
>     The glitter of pleasure
>     And a dark tomb.[8]

The poet who writes best in the Shakespearian manner is a poet with a circumstantial and instinctive mind, who delights to speak with strange voices and to see his mind in the mirror of Nature; while Mr. Bridges, like most of us to-day, has a lyrical and meditative mind, and delights to speak with his own voice and to see Nature in the mirror of his mind. In reading his plays in a Shakespearian manner, I find that he is constantly arranging his story in such and such a way because he has read that the persons he is writing of did such and such things, and not because his soul has passed into the soul of their world and understood its unchangeable destinies. His *Return of Ulysses* is admirable in beauty, because its classical gravity of speech, which does not, like Shakespeare's verse, desire the vivacity of common life, purifies and subdues all passion into lyrical and meditative ecstasies, and because the unity of place and time in the late acts compels a logical rather than instinctive procession of incidents; and if the Shakespearian *Nero: Second Part* approaches it in beauty and in dramatic power, it is because it eddies about Nero and Seneca, who had both, to a great extent, lyrical and meditative minds.[9] Had Mr. Bridges been a true Shakespearian, the pomp and glory of the world would have drowned that subtle voice that speaks amid our heterogeneous lives of a life lived in obedience to a lonely and distinguished ideal.

## II

The more a poet rids his verses of heterogeneous knowledge and irrelevant analysis, and purifies his mind with elaborate art, the more does the little ritual of his verse resemble the great ritual of Nature, and become mysterious and inscrutable. He becomes, as all the great mystics have believed, a vessel of the creative power of God; and whether he be a great poet or a small poet, we can praise the poems, which but seem to be his, with the extremity of praise that we give this great ritual which is but copied from the same eternal model. There is poetry that is like the white light of noon, and poetry that has the heaviness of woods, and poetry that has the golden light of dawn or of sunset; and I find in the poetry of Mr. Bridges in the plays, but still more in the lyrics, the pale colours, the delicate silence, the low murmurs of cloudy country days, when the plough is in the earth, and the clouds darkening towards sunset; and had I the great gift of praising, I would praise it as I would praise these things.[10]

1896.[11]

# IRELAND AND THE ARTS

The arts have failed; fewer people are interested in them every generation. The mere business of living, of making money, of amusing oneself, occupies people more and more, and makes them less and less capable of the difficult art of appreciation. When they buy a picture it generally shows a long-current idea, or some conventional form that can be admired in that lax mood one admires a fine carriage in or fine horses in; and when they buy a book it is so much in the manner of the picture that it is forgotten, when its moment is over, as a glass of wine is forgotten. We who care deeply about the arts find ourselves the priesthood of an almost forgotten faith, and we must, I think, if we would win the people again, take upon ourselves the method and the fervour of a priesthood. We must be half humble and half proud. We see the perfect more than others, it may be, but we must find the passions among the people. We must baptize as well as preach.

The makers of religions have established their ceremonies, their form of art, upon fear of death, on the hope of the father in his child, upon the love of man and woman. They have even gathered into their ceremonies the ceremonies of more ancient faiths, for fear a grain of the dust turned into crystal in some past fire, a passion that had mingled with the religious idea, might perish if the ancient ceremony perished. They have renamed wells and images and given new meanings to ceremonies of spring and midsummer and harvest. In very early days the arts were so possessed by this method that they were almost inseparable from religion, going side by side with it into all life. But, to-day, they have grown, as I think, too proud, too anxious to live alone with the perfect, and so one sees them, as I think, like charioteers standing by deserted chariots and holding broken reins in their hands, or seeking to go upon their way drawn by that sexual passion which alone remains to them out of the passions of the world.[1] We should not blame them, but rather a mysterious tendency in things which will have its end some day. In England, men like William Morris, seeing about them passions so long separated from the perfect that it seemed as if they could not be changed until society had been changed, tried to unite the arts once more to life by uniting them to use.[2] They advised painters to paint fewer pictures upon canvas, and to burn more of them on plates; and they tried to persuade sculptors that a candlestick might be as beautiful as a statue. But here in Ireland, when the arts have grown humble, they will find two passions ready to their hands, love of the Unseen Life and love of country. I would have a devout writer or painter often content himself with subjects taken from his religious beliefs; and if his religious beliefs are those of the majority, he may at last move hearts in every cottage. While even if his religious beliefs are those of some minority, he will have a better welcome than if he wrote of the rape of Persephone, or painted the burning of Shelley's body.[3] He will have founded his work on a passion which will bring him to many besides those who have been trained to care for beautiful things by a special education. If he is a painter or a sculptor he will find churches awaiting his hand everywhere, and if he follows the masters of his craft our other passion will come into his work also, for he will show his Holy Family winding among hills like those of Ireland, and his Bearer of the Cross among faces copied from the faces of his own town. Our art teachers should urge their pupils into this work, for I can remember, when I was myself a Dublin art student, how I used to despond, when youthful ardour burned low, at the general indifference of the town.[4]

But I would rather speak to those who, while moved in other things than the arts by love of country, are beginning to write, as I was some sixteen years ago, without any decided impulse to one thing more than another, and especially to those who are convinced, as I was convinced, that art is tribeless, nationless, a blossom gathered in No Man's Land. The Greeks looked within their borders, and we, like them, have a history fuller than any modern history of imaginative events; and legends which surpass, as I think, all legends but theirs in wild beauty, and in our land, as in theirs, there is no river or mountain that is not associated in the memory with some event or legend; while political reasons have made love of country, as I think, even greater among us than among them. I would have our writers and craftsmen of many kinds master this history and these legends, and fix upon their memory the appearance of mountains and rivers and make it all visible again in their arts, so that Irishmen, even though they had gone thousands of miles away, would still be in their own country. Whether they chose for the subject the carrying off of the Brown Bull or the coming of Patrick, or the political struggle of later times, the other world comes so much into it all that their love of it would move in their hands also, and as much, it may be, as in the hands of the Greek craftsmen.[5] In other words, I would have Ireland recreate the ancient arts, the arts as they were understood in Judæa, in India, in Scandinavia, in Greece and Rome, in every ancient land; as they were understood when they moved a whole people and not a few people who have grown up in a leisured class and made this understanding their business.

I think that my reader* will have agreed with most that I have said up till now, for we all hope for arts like these. I think indeed I first learned to hope for them myself in Young Ireland Societies, or in reading the essays of Davis.[6] An Englishman, with his belief in progress, with his instinctive preference for the cosmopolitan literature of the last century, may think arts like these parochial, but they are the arts we have begun the making of.

I will not, however, have all my readers with me when I say that no writer, no artist, even though he choose Brian Borúmha or Saint Patrick for his subject, should try to make his work popular.[7] Once he has chosen a subject he must think of nothing but giving it such an expression as will please himself. As Walt Whitman has written—

> The oration is to the orator, the acting is to the actor and
> actress, not to the audience:
> And no man understands any greatness or goodness, but his
> own or the indication of his own.[8]

He must make his work a part of his own journey towards beauty and truth. He must picture saint or hero, or hillside, as he sees them, not as he is expected to see them, and he must comfort himself, when

*This essay was first published in the *United Irishman.* [1903]

others cry out against what he has seen, by remembering that no two men are alike, and that there is no 'excellent beauty without strangeness.'[9] In this matter he must be without humility. He may, indeed, doubt the reality of his vision if men do not quarrel with him as they did with the Apostles, for there is only one perfection and only one search for perfection, and it sometimes has the form of the religious life and sometimes of the artistic life; and I do not think these lives differ in their wages, for 'The end of art is peace,' and out of the one as out of the other comes the cry: *Sero te amavi, Pulchritudo tam antiqua et tam nova! Sero te amavi!*[10]

The Catholic Church is not the less the Church of the people because the Mass is spoken in Latin, and art is not less the art of the people because it does not always speak in the language they are used to. I once heard my friend Mr. Ellis say, speaking at a celebration in honour of a writer whose fame had not come till long after his death, 'It is not the business of a poet to make himself understood, but it is the business of the people to understand him. That they are at last compelled to do so is the proof of his authority.'[11] And certainly if you take from art its martyrdom, you will take from it its glory. It might still reflect the passing modes of mankind, but it would cease to reflect the face of God.

If our craftsmen were to choose their subjects under what we may call, if we understand faith to mean that belief in a spiritual life which is not confined to one Church, the persuasion of their faith and their country, they would soon discover that although their choice seemed arbitrary at first, it had obeyed what was deepest in them. I could not now write of any other country but Ireland, for my style has been shaped by the subjects I have worked on, but there was a time when my imagination seemed unwilling, when I found myself writing of some Irish event in words that would have better fitted some Italian or Eastern event, for my style had been shaped in that general stream of European literature which has come from so many watersheds, and it was slowly, very slowly, that I made a new style. It was years before I could rid myself of Shelley's Italian light, but now I think my style is myself. I might have found more of Ireland if I had written in Irish, but I have found a little, and I have found all myself.[12] I am persuaded that if the Irishmen who are painting conventional pictures or writing conventional books on alien subjects, which have been worn away like pebbles on the shore, would do the same, they, too, might find themselves. Even the landscape-painter, who paints a place that he loves, and that no other man has painted, soon discovers that no style learned in the studios is wholly fitted to his purpose. And I cannot but believe that if our painters of Highland cattle and moss-covered barns were to care enough for their country to care for what makes it different from other countries, they would discover, when struggling, it may be, to paint the exact grey of the bare Burren Hills,* and of a sudden it may be, a new style, their very selves. And I admit, though in this I am moved by some touch of fanaticism, that even when I see an old subject written of or painted in a new way, I am yet jealous for Cuchulain, and for Baile, and Aillinn, and for those grey mountains that still are lacking their celebration.[14] I sometimes reproach myself because I cannot admire Mr. Hughes' beautiful, piteous *Orpheus and Eurydice* with an unquestioning mind.[15] I say with my lips, 'The Spirit made it, for it is beautiful, and the Spirit bloweth where it listeth,' but I say in my heart, 'Aengus and Etain would have served his turn'; but one cannot, perhaps, love or believe at all if one does not love or believe a little too much.[16]

And I do not think with unbroken pleasure of our scholars who write about German writers or about periods of Greek history. I always remember that they could give us a number of little books which would tell, each book for some one county, or some one parish, the verses, or the stories, or the events that would make every lake or mountain a man can see from his own door an excitement in his imagination. I would have some of them leave that work of theirs which will never lack hands, and begin to dig in Ireland the garden of the future, understanding that here in Ireland the spirit of man may be about to wed the soil of the world.

Art and scholarship like these I have described would give Ireland more than they received from her, for they would make love of the unseen more unshakable, more ready to plunge deep into the abyss,

*Robert Gregory painted the Burren Hills and thereby found what promised to grow into a great style, but he had hardly found it before he was killed. His few finished pictures, so full of austerity and sweetness, should find their way into Irish public galleries. 1924.[13]

and they would make love of country more fruitful in the mind, more a part of daily life. One would know an Irishman into whose life they had come—and in a few generations they would come into the life of all, rich and poor—by something that set him apart among men. He himself would understand that more was expected of him than of others because he had greater possessions. The Irish race would have become a chosen race, one of the pillars that uphold the world.

1901.

# THE GALWAY PLAINS

Lady Gregory has just given me her beautiful *Poets and Dreamers*, and it has brought to mind a day two or three years ago when I stood on the side of Slieve Echtge, looking out over Galway.[1] The Burren Hills were to my left, and though I forget whether I could see the cairn over Bald Conan of the Fianna, I could certainly see many places there that are in poems and stories.[2] In front of me, over many miles of level Galway plains, I saw a low blue hill flooded with evening light. I asked a countryman who was with me what hill that was, and he told me it was Cruachmaa of the Sidhe.[3] I had often heard of Cruachmaa of the Sidhe even as far north as Sligo, for the country people have told me a great many stories of the great host of the Sidhe who live there, still fighting and holding festivals.

I asked the old countryman about it, and he told me of strange women who had come from it, and who would come into a house having the appearance of countrywomen, but would know all that happened in that house; and how they would always pay back with increase, though not by their own hands, whatever was given to them. And he had heard, too, of people who had been carried away into the hill, and how one man went to look for his wife there, and dug into the hill and all but got his wife again, but at the very moment she was coming out to him, the pick he was digging with struck her upon the head and killed her. I asked him if he had himself seen any of its enchantments, and he said, 'Sometimes when I look over to the hill, I see a mist lying on the top of it, that goes away after a while.'

A great part of the poems and stories in Lady Gregory's book were made or gathered between Burren and Cruachmaa. It was here that Raftery, the wandering country poet of ninety years ago, praised and blamed, chanting fine verses, and playing badly on his fiddle.[4] It is here the ballads of meeting and parting have been sung, and some whose lamentations for defeat are still remembered may have passed through this plain flying from the battle of Aughrim.[5]

'I will go up on the mountain alone; and I will come hither from it again. It is there I saw the camp of the Gael, the poor troop thinned, not keeping with one another; Och Ochone!'[6] And here, if one can believe many devout people whose stories are in the book, Christ has walked upon the roads, bringing the needy to some warm fireside, and sending one of His saints to anoint the dying.[7]

I do not think these country imaginations have changed much for centuries, for they are still busy with those two themes of the ancient Irish poets, the sternness of battle and the sadness of parting and death. The emotion that in other countries has made many love songs has here been given, in a long wooing, to danger, that ghostly bride. It is not a difference in the substance of things that the lamentations that were sung after battles are now sung for men who have died upon the gallows.[8]

The emotion has become not less, but more noble, by the change, for the man who goes to death with the thought—

> It is with the people I was,
> It is not with the law I was,

has behind him generations of poetry and poetical life.[9]

The poets of to-day speak with the voice of the unknown priest who wrote, some two hundred years ago, that *Sorrowful Lament for Ireland* Lady Gregory has put into passionate and rhythmical prose—

> I do not know of anything under the sky
> That is friendly or favourable to the Gael,
> But only the sea that our need brings us to,
> Or the wind that blows to the harbour
> The ship that is bearing us away from Ireland;
> And there is reason that these are reconciled with us,
> For we increase the sea with our tears,
> And the wandering wind with our sighs.[10]

There is still in truth upon these great level plains a people, a community bound together by imaginative possessions, by stories and poems which have grown out of its own life, and by a past of great passions which can still waken the heart to imaginative action. One could still, if one had the genius, and had been born to Irish, write for these people plays and poems like those of Greece. Does not the greatest poetry always require a people to listen to it? England or any other country which takes its tunes from the great cities and gets its taste from schools and not from old custom, may have a mob, but it cannot have a people. In England there are a few groups of men and women who have good taste, whether in cookery or in books; and the great multitudes but copy them or their copiers. The poet must always prefer the community where the perfected minds express the people, to a community that is vainly seeking to copy the perfected minds. To have even perfectly the thoughts that can be weighed, the knowledge that can be got from books, the precision that can be learned at school, to belong to any aristocracy, is to be a little pool that will soon dry up. A people alone are a great river; and that is why I am persuaded that where a people has died, a nation is about to die.

1903.

# EMOTION OF MULTITUDE

I have been thinking a good deal about plays lately, and I have been wondering why I dislike the clear and logical construction which seems necessary if one is to succeed on the Modern Stage. It came into my head the other day that this construction, which all the world has learnt from France, has everything of high literature except the emotion of multitude. The Greek drama has got the emotion of multitude from its chorus, which called up famous sorrows, even all the gods and all heroes to witness, as it were, some well-ordered fable, some action separated but for this from all but itself. The French play delights in the well-ordered fable, but by leaving out the chorus it has created an art where poetry and imagination, always the children of far-off multitudinous things, must of necessity grow less important than the mere will. This is why, I said to myself, French dramatic poetry is so often rhetorical, for what is rhetoric but the will trying to do the work of the imagination? The Shakespearian Drama gets the emotion of multitude out of the sub-plot which copies the main plot, much as a shadow upon the wall copies one's body in the firelight.[1] We think of King Lear less as the history of one man and his sorrows than as the history of a whole evil time. Lear's shadow is in Gloucester, who also has ungrateful children, and the mind goes on imagining other shadows, shadow beyond shadow till it has pictured the world. In *Hamlet,* one hardly notices, so subtly is the web woven, that the murder of Hamlet's father and the sorrow of Hamlet are shadowed in the lives of Fortinbras and Ophelia and Laertes, whose fathers, too, have been killed. It is so in all the plays, or in all but all, and very commonly the sub-plot is the main plot working itself out in more ordinary men and women, and so doubly calling up before us the image of multitude. Ibsen and Maeterlinck have on the other hand created a new form, for they get multitude from the wild duck in the attic, or from the crown at the bottom of the fountain, vague symbols that set the mind wandering from idea to idea, emotion to emotion.[2] Indeed all the great Masters have understood, that there cannot be great art without the little limited life of the fable, which is always the better the simpler it is, and the rich, far-wandering, many-imaged life of the half-seen world beyond it. There are some who understand that the simple unmysterious things living as in a clear noonlight[†] are of the nature of the sun, and that vague, many-imaged things have in them the strength of the moon. Did not the Egyptian carve it on emerald that all living things have the sun for father and the moon for mother, and has it not been said that a man of genius takes the most after his mother?[3]

1903.

# THE CUTTING OF AN AGATE

(1903 – 1915)

# CERTAIN NOBLE PLAYS OF JAPAN

## I

I am writing with my imagination stirred by a visit to the studio of Mr. Dulac, the distinguished illustrator of the *Arabian Nights*.[1] I saw there the mask and head-dress to be worn in a play of mine by the player who will speak the part of Cuchulain, and who, wearing this noble, half-Greek, half-Asiatic face, will appear perhaps like an image seen in reverie by some Orphic worshipper.[2] I hope to have attained the distance from life which can make credible strange events, elaborate words. I have written a little play that can be played in a room for so little money that forty or fifty readers of poetry can pay the price. There will be no scenery, for three musicians, whose seeming sunburned faces will, I hope, suggest that they have wandered from village to village in some country of our dreams, can describe place and weather, and at moments action, and accompany it all by drum and gong or flute and dulcimer. Instead of the players working themselves into a violence of passion indecorous in our sitting-room, the music, the beauty of form and voice all come to climax in pantomimic dance.

In fact, with the help of Japanese plays 'translated by Ernest Fenollosa and finished by Ezra Pound,' I have invented a form of drama, distinguished, indirect, and symbolic, and having no need of mob or press to pay its way—an aristocratic form.[3] When this play and its performance run as smoothly as my skill can make them, I shall hope to write another of the same sort and so complete a dramatic celebration of the life of Cuchulain planned long ago.[4] Then having given enough performances for, I hope, the pleasure of personal friends and a few score people of good taste, I shall record all discoveries of method and turn to something else. It is an advantage of this noble form that it need absorb no one's life, that its few properties can be packed up in a box or hung upon the walls where they will be fine ornaments.

## II

And yet this simplification is not mere economy. For nearly three centuries invention has been making the human voice and the movements of the body seem always less expressive. I have long been puzzled why passages, that are moving when read out or spoken during rehearsal, seem muffled or dulled during performance. I have simplified scenery, having *The Hour Glass,* for instance, played now before green curtains, now among those admirable ivory-coloured screens invented by Gordon Craig.[5] With every simplification the voice has recovered something of its importance, and yet when verse has approached in temper to let us say 'Kubla Khan,' or the 'Ode to the West Wind,' the most typical modern verse, I have still felt as if the sound came to me from behind a veil.[6] The stage-opening, the powerful light and shade, the number of feet between myself and the players have destroyed intimacy. I have found myself thinking of players who needed perhaps but to unroll a mat in some Eastern garden. Nor have I felt this only when I listened to speech, but even more when I have watched the movement of a player or heard singing in a play. I love all the arts that can still remind me of their origin among the common people, and my ears are only comfortable when the singer sings as if mere speech had taken fire, when he appears to have passed into song almost imperceptibly. I am bored and wretched, a limitation I greatly regret, when he seems no longer a human being but an invention of science. To explain him to myself I say that he has become a wind instrument and sings no longer like active men, sailor or camel driver, because he has had to compete with an orchestra, where the loudest instrument has always survived. The human voice can only become louder by becoming less articulate, by discovering some new musical sort of roar or scream. As poetry can do neither, the voice must be freed from this competition and find itself among little instruments, only heard at their best perhaps when we are close about them. It should be again possible for a few poets to write as all did once, not for the printed page but to be sung. But movement also has grown less expressive, more declamatory, less intimate. When I called the other day upon a friend I found myself among some dozen people who were watching a group of Spanish boys and girls, professional dancers, dancing some national dance in the midst of a drawing-room.[7] Doubtless their training had been long, laborious, and wearisome; but now one could not be deceived, their movement was full of joy. They were among friends, and it all seemed but the play of children; how powerful it seemed, how passionate, while an even more miraculous art, separated from us by the footlights, appeared in the comparison laborious and professional. It is well to be close enough to an artist to feel for him a personal liking, close enough perhaps to feel that our liking is returned.

My play is made possible by a Japanese dancer whom I have seen dance in a studio and in a drawing-room and on a very small stage lit by an excellent stage-light.[8] In the studio and in the drawing-room alone, where the lighting was the light we are most accustomed to, did I see him as the tragic image that has stirred my imagination. There, where no studied lighting, no stage-picture made an artificial world, he was able, as he rose from the floor, where he had been sitting crossed-legged, or as he threw out an arm, to recede from us into some more powerful life. Because that separation was achieved by human means alone, he receded, but to inhabit as it were the deeps of the mind. One realised anew, at every separating strangeness, that the measure of all arts' greatness can be but in their intimacy.

## III

All imaginative art remains at a distance and this distance once chosen must be firmly held against a pushing world. Verse, ritual, music, and dance in association with action require that gesture, costume, facial expression, stage arrangement must help in keeping the door. Our unimaginative arts are content to set a piece of the world as we know it in a place by itself, to put their photographs as it were in a plush or a plain frame, but the arts which interest me, while seeming to separate from the world and us a group of figures, images, symbols, enable us to pass for a few moments into a deep of the mind that had hitherto been too subtle for our habitation. As a deep of the mind can only be approached through what is most human, most delicate, we should distrust bodily distance, mechanism, and loud noise.

It may be well if we go to school in Asia, for the distance from life in European art has come from little but difficulty with material. In half-Asiatic Greece Kallimachos could still return to a stylistic management of the falling folds of drapery, after the naturalistic drapery of Phidias, and in Egypt the same age that saw the village Head-man carved in wood, for burial in some tomb, with so complete a naturalism saw, set up in public places, statues full of an august formality that implies traditional measurements, a philosophic defence.[9] The spiritual painting of the fourteenth century passed on into Tintoretto and that of Velasquez into modern painting with no sense of loss to weigh against the gain, while the painting of Japan, not having our European Moon to churn the wits, has understood that no styles that ever delighted noble imaginations have lost their importance, and chooses the style according to the subject.[10] In literature also we have had the illusion of change and progress, the art of Shakespeare passing into that of Dryden, and so into the prose drama, by what has seemed when studied in its details unbroken progress.[11] Had we been Greeks, and so but half-European, an honourable mob would have martyred though in vain the first man who set up a painted scene, or who complained that soliloquies were unnatural, instead of repeating with a sigh, 'we cannot return to the arts of childhood however beautiful.' Only our lyric poetry has kept its Asiatic habit and renewed itself at its own youth, putting off perpetually what has been called its progress in a series of violent revolutions.

Therefore it is natural that I go to Asia for a stage-convention, for more formal faces, for a chorus that has no part in the action, and perhaps for those movements of the body copied from the marionette shows of the fourteenth century.[12] A mask will enable me to substitute for the face of some commonplace player, or for that face repainted to suit his own vulgar fancy, the fine invention of a sculptor, and to bring the audience close enough to the play to hear every inflection of the voice. A mask never seems but a dirty face, and no matter how close you go is yet a work of art; nor shall we lose by stilling the movement of the features, for deep feeling is expressed by a movement of the whole body. In poetical painting and in sculpture the face seems the nobler for lacking curiosity, alert attention, all that we sum up under the famous word of the realists 'vitality.' It is even possible that being is only possessed completely by the dead, and that it is some knowledge of this that makes us gaze with so much emotion upon the face of the Sphinx or of Buddha. Who can forget the face of Chaliapin as the Mogul King in Prince Igor, when a mask covering its upper portion made him seem like a Phœnix at the end of its thousand wise years, awaiting in condescension the burning nest, and what did it not gain from that immobility in dignity and in power?[13]

## IV

Realism is created for the common people and was always their peculiar delight, and it is the delight to-day of all those whose minds, educated alone by schoolmasters and newspapers, are without the memory of beauty and emotional subtlety. The occasional humorous realism that so much heightened the emotional effect of Elizabethan Tragedy—Cleopatra's old man with an asp, let us say—carrying the tragic crisis by its contrast above the tide-mark of Corneille's courtly theatre, was made at the outset to please the common citizen standing on the rushes of the floor; but the great speeches were written by poets who remembered their patrons in the covered galleries.[14] The fanatic Savonarola was but dead a century, and his lamentation, in the frenzy of his rhetoric, that every prince of the Church or State throughout Europe was wholly occupied with the fine arts, had still its moiety of truth.[15] A poetical passage cannot be understood without a rich memory, and like the older school of painting appeals to a tradition, and that not merely when it speaks of 'Lethe's Wharf' or 'Dido on the wild sea-banks' but in rhythm, in vocabulary; for the ear must notice slight variations upon old cadences and customary words, all that high breeding of poetical style where there is nothing ostentatious, nothing crude, no breath of parvenu or journalist.[16]

Let us press the popular arts on to a more complete realism—that would be their honesty—for the commercial arts demoralise by their compromise, their incompleteness, their idealism without sincerity or elegance, their pretence that ignorance can understand beauty. In the studio and in the drawing-room we can found a true theatre of beauty.[17] Poets from the time of Keats and Blake have derived their descent only through what is least declamatory, least popular in the art of Shakespeare, and in such a theatre they will find their habitual audience and keep their freedom. Europe is very old and has seen many arts run through the circle and has learned the fruit of every flower and known what this fruit sends up, and it is now time to copy the East and live deliberately.

## V

Ye shall not, while ye tarry with me, taste
From unrinsed barrel the diluted wine
Of a low vineyard or a plant ill-pruned,
But such as anciently the Ægean Isles
Poured in libation at their solemn feasts:
And the same goblets shall ye grasp embost
With no vile figures of loose languid boors,
But such as Gods have lived with and have led.[18]

The Noh theatre of Japan became popular at the close of the fourteenth century, gathering into itself dances performed at Shinto shrines in honour of spirits and gods, or by young nobles at the court, and much old lyric poetry, and receiving its philosophy and its final shape perhaps from priests of a contemplative school of Buddhism. A small daimio or feudal lord of the ancient capital Nara, a contemporary of Chaucer's, was the author, or perhaps only the stage-manager, of many plays. He brought them to the court of the Shogun at Kioto. From that on the Shogun and his court were as busy with dramatic poetry as the Mikado and his with lyric.[19] When for the first time *Hamlet* was being played in London, Noh was made a necessary part of official ceremonies at Kioto, and young nobles and princes, forbidden to attend the popular theatre, in Japan as elsewhere a place of mimicry and naturalism, were encouraged to witness and to perform in spectacles where speech, music, song, and dance created an image of nobility and strange beauty.[20] When the modern revolution came, Noh after a brief unpopularity was played for the first time in certain ceremonious public theatres, and in 1897 a battleship was named *Takasago,* after one of its most famous plays.[21] Some of the old noble families are to-day very poor, their men it may be but servants and labourers, but they still frequent these theatres. 'Accomplishment' the word Noh means, and it is their accomplishment and that of a few cultivated people who understand the literary and mythological allusions and the ancient lyrics quoted in speech or chorus, their discipline, a part of their breeding. The players themselves, unlike the despised players of the popular theatre, have passed on proudly from father to son an elaborate art, and even now a player will publish his family tree to prove his skill. One player wrote in 1906 in a business circular—I am quoting from Mr. Pound's redaction of the Notes of Fenollosa—that after thirty generations of nobles a woman of his house dreamed that a mask was carried to her from heaven, and soon after she bore a son who became a player and the father of players. His family, he declared, still possessed a letter from a fifteenth-century Mikado conferring upon them a theatre-curtain, white below and purple above.[22]

There were five families of these players and, forbidden before the Revolution to perform in public, they had received grants of land or salaries from the State.[23] The white and purple curtain was no doubt to hang upon a wall behind the players or over their entrance door, for the Noh stage is a platform surrounded upon three sides by the audience. No 'naturalistic' effect is sought. The players wear masks and found their movements upon those of puppets: the most famous of all Japanese dramatists composed entirely for puppets.[24] A swift or a slow movement and a long or a short stillness, and then another movement.[25] They sing as much as they speak, and there is a chorus which describes the scene and interprets their thought and never becomes as in the Greek theatre a part of the action. At the climax, instead of the disordered passion of nature there is a dance, a series of positions and movements which may represent a battle, or a marriage, or the pain of a ghost in the Buddhist purgatory. I have lately studied certain of these dances, with Japanese players, and I notice that their ideal of beauty, unlike that of Greece and like that of pictures from Japan and China, makes them pause at moments of muscular tension. The interest is not in the human form but in the rhythm to which it moves, and the triumph of their art is to express the rhythm in its intensity. There are few swaying movements of arms or body such as make the beauty of our dancing. They move from the hip, keeping constantly the upper part of their body still, and seem to associate with every gesture or pose some definite thought. They cross the stage with a sliding movement, and one gets the impression not of undulation but of continuous straight lines.

The Print Room of the British Museum is now closed as a war-economy, so I can only write from memory of theatrical colour-prints, where a ship is represented by a mere skeleton of willows or osiers painted green, or a fruit tree by a bush in a pot, and where actors have tied on their masks with ribbons that are gathered into a bunch behind the head.[26] It is a child's game become the most noble poetry, and there is no observation of life, because the poet would set before us all those things which we feel and imagine in silence.

Mr. Ezra Pound has found among the Fenollosa manuscripts a story traditional among Japanese players. A young man was following a stately old woman through the streets of a Japanese town, and presently she turned to him and spoke: 'Why do you follow me?' 'Because you are so interesting.' 'That is not so, I am too old to be interesting.' But he wished, he told her, to become a player of old women on the Noh stage. 'If he would become famous as a Noh player,' she said, 'he must not observe life, nor put on an old face and stint the music of his voice. He must know how to suggest an old woman and yet find it all in the heart.'[27]

## VI

In the plays themselves I discover a beauty or a subtlety that I can trace perhaps to their threefold origin. The love-sorrows—the love of father and daughter, of mother and son, of boy and girl—may owe their nobility to a courtly life, but he to whom the adventures happen, a traveller commonly from some distant place, is most often a Buddhist priest; and the occasional intellectual subtlety is perhaps Buddhist. The adventure itself is often the meeting with ghost, god, or goddess at some holy place or much-legended tomb; and god, goddess, or ghost reminds me at times of our own Irish legends and beliefs, which once, it may be, differed little from those of the Shinto worshipper.

The feather-mantle, for whose lack the moon goddess (or should we call her fairy?) cannot return to the sky, is the red cap whose theft can keep our fairies of the sea upon dry land; and the ghost-lovers in *Nishikigi* remind me of the Aran boy and girl who in Lady Gregory's story come to the priest after death to be married.[28] These Japanese poets, too, feel for tomb and wood the emotion, the sense of awe that our Gaelic-speaking country people will sometimes show when you speak to them of Castle Hackett or of some Holy Well; and that is why perhaps it pleases them to begin so many plays by a traveller asking his way with many questions, a convention agreeable to me, for when I first began to write poetical plays for an Irish theatre I had to put away an ambition of helping to bring again to certain places their old sanctity or their romance.[29] I could lay the scene of a play on Baile's Strand, but I found no pause in the hurried action for descriptions of strand or sea or the great yew tree that once stood there; and I could not in *The King's Threshold* find room, before I began the ancient story, to call up the shallow river and the few trees and rocky fields of modern Gort.[30] But in the *Nishikigi* the tale of the lovers would lose its pathos if we did not see that forgotten tomb where 'the hiding fox' lives among 'the orchids and the chrysanthemum flowers.'[31] The men who created this convention were more like ourselves than were the Greeks and Romans, more like us even than are Shakespeare and Corneille. Their emotion was self-conscious and reminiscent, always associating itself with pictures and poems. They measured all that time had taken or would take away and found their delight in remembering celebrated lovers in the scenery pale passion loves. They travelled seeking for the strange and for the picturesque: 'I go about with my heart set upon no particular place, no more than a cloud. I wonder now would the sea be that way, or the little place Kefu that they say is stuck down against it.'[32] When a traveller asks his way of girls upon the roadside he is directed to find it by certain pine trees, which he will recognise because many people have drawn them.

I wonder am I fanciful in discovering in the plays themselves (few examples have as yet been translated and I may be misled by accident or the idiosyncrasy of some poet) a playing upon a single metaphor, as deliberate as the echoing rhythm of line in Chinese and Japanese painting. In the *Nishikigi* the ghost of the girl-lover carries the cloth she went on weaving out of grass when she should have opened the chamber door to her lover, and woven grass returns again and again in metaphor and incident. The lovers, now that in an aëry body they must sorrow for unconsummated love, are 'tangled up as the grass patterns are tangled.'[33] Again they are like an unfinished cloth: 'these bodies, having no weft, even now are not come together, truly a shameful story, a tale to bring shame on the gods.'[34] Before they can bring the priest to the tomb they spend the day 'pushing aside the grass from the over-grown ways in Kefu,' and the countryman who directs them is 'cutting grass on the hill'; and when at last the prayer of the priest unites them in marriage the bride says that he has made 'a dream-bridge over wild grass, over the grass I dwell in'; and in the end bride and bridegroom show themselves for a moment 'from under the shadow of the love-grass.'[35]

In *Hagoromo* the feather-mantle of the fairy woman creates also its rhythm of metaphor. In the beautiful day of opening spring 'the plumage of Heaven drops neither feather nor flame,' 'nor is the rock of earth over-much worn by the brushing of the feathery skirt of the stars.'[36] One half remembers a thousand Japanese paintings, or whichever comes first into the memory: that screen painted by Korin, let us say, shown lately at the British Museum, where the same form is echoing in wave and in cloud and in rock.[37] In European poetry I remember Shelley's continually repeated fountain and cave, his broad stream and solitary star.[38] In neglecting character which seems to us essential in drama, as do their artists in neglecting relief and depth, whether in their paintings or in arranging flowers in a vase in a thin row, they have made possible a hundred lovely intricacies.

## VII

These plays arose in an age of continual war and became a part of the education of soldiers. These soldiers, whose natures had as much of Walter Pater as of Achilles, combined with Buddhist priests and women to elaborate life in a ceremony, the playing of football, the drinking of tea, and all great events of State, becoming a ritual.[39] In the painting that decorated their walls and in the poetry they recited one discovers the only sign of a great age that cannot deceive us, the most vivid and subtle discrimination of sense and the invention of images more powerful than sense; the continual presence of reality. It is still true that the Deity gives us, according to His promise, not His thoughts or His convictions but His flesh and blood, and I believe that the elaborate technique of the arts, seeming to create out of itself a superhuman life, has taught more men to die than oratory or the Prayer Book. We only believe in those thoughts which have been conceived not in the brain but in the whole body. The Minoan soldier who bore upon his arm the shield ornamented with the dove in the Museum at Crete, or had upon his head the helmet with the winged horse, knew his rôle in life.[40] When Nobuzane painted the child Saint Kobo, Daishi kneeling full of sweet austerity upon the flower of the lotus, he set up before our eyes exquisite life and the acceptance of death.[41]

I cannot imagine those young soldiers and the women they loved pleased with the ill-breeding and theatricality of Carlyle, nor, I think, with the magniloquence of Hugo.[42] These things belong to an industrial age, a mechanical sequence of ideas; but when I remember that curious game which the Japanese called, with a confusion of the senses that had seemed typical of our own age, 'listening to incense,' I know that some among them would have understood the prose of Walter Pater, the painting of Puvis de Chavannes, the poetry of Mallarmé and Verlaine.[43] When heroism returned to our age it bore with it as its first gift technical sincerity.

## VIII

For some weeks now I have been elaborating my play in London where alone I can find the help I need, Mr. Dulac's mastery of design and Mr. Ito's genius of movement; yet it pleases me to think that I am working for my own country. Perhaps some day a play in the form I am adapting for European purposes may excite once more, whether in Gaelic or in English, under the slope of Slieve-na-mon or Croagh Patrick, ancient memories; for this form has no need of scenery that runs away with money nor of a theatre-building.[44] Yet I know that I only amuse myself with a fancy; for my writings if they be seaworthy will put to sea, and I cannot tell where they may be carried by the wind. Are not the fairy-stories of Oscar Wilde, which were written for Mr. Ricketts and Mr. Shannon and for a few ladies, very popular in Arabia?[45]

April 1916.

# THE TRAGIC THEATRE

I did not find a word in the printed criticism of Synge's *Deirdre of the Sorrows* about the qualities that made certain moments seem to me the noblest tragedy, and the play was judged by what seemed to me but wheels and pulleys necessary to the effect, but in themselves nothing.[1]

Upon the other hand, those who spoke to me of the play never spoke of these wheels and pulleys, but if they cared at all for the play, cared for the things I cared for. One's own world of painters, of poets, of good talkers, of ladies who delight in Ricard's portraits or Debussy's music, all those whose senses feel instantly every change in our mother the moon, saw the stage in one way; and those others who look at plays every night, who tell the general playgoer whether this play or that play is to his taste, saw it in a way so different that there is certainly some body of dogma—whether in the instincts or in the memory—pushing the ways apart.[2] A printed criticism, for instance, found but one dramatic moment, that when Deirdre in the second act overhears her lover say that he may grow weary of her; and not one—if I remember rightly—chose for praise or explanation the third act which alone had satisfied the author, or contained in any abundance those sentences that were quoted at the fall of the curtain and for days after.[3]

Deirdre and her lover, as Synge tells the tale, returned to Ireland, though it was nearly certain they would die there, because death was better than broken love, and at the side of the open grave that had been dug for one and would serve for both, quarrelled, losing all they had given their life to keep. 'Is it not a hard thing that we should miss the safety of the grave and we trampling its edge?'[4] That is Deirdre's cry at the outset of a reverie of passion that mounts and mounts till grief itself has carried her beyond grief into pure contemplation. Up to this the play had been a Master's unfinished work, monotonous and melancholy, ill-arranged, little more than a sketch of what it would have grown to, but now I listened breathless to sentences that may never pass away, and as they filled or dwindled in their civility of sorrow, the player, whose art had seemed clumsy and incomplete, like the writing itself, ascended into that tragic ecstasy which is the best that art—perhaps that life—can give.[5] And at last when Deirdre, in the paroxysm before she took her life, touched with compassionate fingers him that had killed her lover, we knew that the player had become, if but for a moment, the creature of that noble mind which had gathered its art in waste islands, and we too were carried beyond time and persons to where passion, living through its thousand purgatorial years, as in the wink of an eye, becomes wisdom; and it was as though we too had touched and felt and seen a disembodied thing.[6]

One dogma of the printed criticism is that if a play does not contain definite character, its constitution is not strong enough for the stage, and that the dramatic moment is always the contest of character with character.

In poetical drama there is, it is held, an antithesis between character and lyric poetry, for lyric poetry—however much it move you when read out of a book—can, as these critics think, but encumber the action. Yet when we go back a few centuries and enter the great periods of drama, character grows less and sometimes disappears, and there is much lyric feeling, and at times a lyric measure will be wrought into the dialogue, a flowing measure that had well-befitted music, or that more lumbering one of the sonnet. Suddenly it strikes us that character is continuously present in comedy alone, and that there is much tragedy, that of Corneille, that of Racine, that of Greece and Rome, where its place is taken by passions and motives, one person being jealous, another full of love or remorse or pride or anger.[7] In writers of tragi-comedy (and Shakespeare is always a writer of tragi-comedy) there is indeed character, but we notice that it is in the moments of comedy that character is defined, in Hamlet's gaiety let us say; while amid the great moments, when Timon orders his tomb, when Hamlet cries to Horatio 'absent thee from felicity awhile,' when Antony names 'Of many thousand kisses the poor last,' all is lyricism, unmixed passion, 'the integrity of fire.'[8] Nor does character ever attain to complete definition in these lamps ready for the taper, no matter how circumstantial and gradual the opening of events, as it does in Falstaff who has no passionate purpose to fulfil, or as it does in Henry the Fifth whose poetry, never touched by lyric heat, is oratorical; nor when the tragic reverie is at its height do we say, 'How well that man is realised, I should know him were I to meet him in the street,' for it is always ourselves that we see upon the stage, and should it be a tragedy of love we renew, it may be, some loyalty of our youth, and go from the theatre with our eyes dim for an old love's sake.[9]

I think it was while rehearsing a translation of *Les Fourberies de Scapin* in Dublin, and noticing how passionless it all was, that I saw what should have been plain from the first line I had written, that tragedy must always be a drowning and breaking of the dykes that separate man from man, and that it is upon these dykes comedy keeps house.[10] But I was not certain of the site of that house (one always hesitates when there is no testimony but one's own)[†] till somebody told me of a certain letter of Congreve's. He describes the external and superficial expressions of 'humour' on which farce is founded and then defines 'humour' itself—the foundation of comedy—as a 'singular and unavoidable way of doing anything peculiar to one man only, by which his speech and actions are distinguished from all other men,' and adds to it that 'passions are too powerful in the sex to let humour have its course,' or as I would rather put it, that you can find but little of what we call character in unspoiled youth, whatever be the sex, for as he indeed shows in another sentence, it grows with time like the ash of a burning stick, and strengthens towards middle life till there is little else at seventy years.[11]

Since then I have discovered an antagonism between all the old art and our new art of comedy and understand why I hated at nineteen years Thackeray's novels and the new French painting.[12] A big picture of cocottes sitting at little tables outside a café, by some follower of Manet's, was exhibited at the Royal Hibernian Academy while I was a student at a life class there, and I was miserable for days.[13] I found no desirable place, no man I could have wished to be, no woman I could have loved, no Golden Age, no lure for secret hope, no adventure with myself for theme out of that endless tale I told myself all day long. Years after I saw the *Olympia* of Manet at the Luxembourg and watched it without hostility indeed, but as I might some incomparable talker whose precision of gesture gave me pleasure, though I did not understand his language.[14] I returned to it again and again at intervals of years, saying to myself, 'some day I will understand'; and yet, it was not until Sir Hugh Lane brought the *Eva Gonzales* to Dublin, and I had said to myself, 'How perfectly that woman is realised as distinct from all other women that have lived or shall live,' that I understood I was carrying on in my own mind that quarrel between a tragedian and a comedian which the Devil on Two Sticks in Le Sage showed to the young man who had climbed through the window.[15]

There is an art of the flood, the art of Titian when his *Ariosto,* and his *Bacchus and Ariadne,* give new images to the dreams of youth, and of Shakespeare when he shows us Hamlet broken away from life by the passionate hesitations of his reverie.[16] And we call this art poetical, because we must bring more to it than our daily mood if we would take our pleasure; and because it takes delight in the moment of exaltation, of excitement, of dreaming (or in the capacity for it, as in that still face of Ariosto's[†] that is like some vessel soon to be full of wine). And there is an art that we call real, because character can only express itself perfectly in a real world, being that world's creature, and because we understand it best through a delicate discrimination of the senses which is but entire wakefulness, the daily mood grown cold and crystalline.

We may not find either mood in its purity, but in mainly tragic art one distinguishes devices to exclude or lessen character, to diminish the power of that daily mood, to cheat or blind its too clear perception. If the real world is not altogether rejected, it is but touched here and there, and into the places we have left empty we summon rhythm, balance, pattern, images that remind us of vast passions, the vagueness of past times, all the chimeras that haunt the edge of trance; and if we are painters, we shall express personal emotion through ideal form, a symbolism handled by the generations, a mask from whose eyes the disembodied looks, a style that remembers many masters that it may escape contemporary suggestion; or we shall leave out some element of reality as in Byzantine painting, where there is no mass, nothing in relief; and so it is that in the supreme moment of tragic art there comes upon one that strange sensation as though the hair of one's head stood up. And when we love, if it be in the excitement of youth, do we not also, that the flood may find no stone to convulse, no wall to narrow it, exclude character or the signs of it by choosing that beauty which seems unearthly because the individual woman is lost amid the labyrinth of its lines as though life were trembling into stillness and silence, or at last folding itself away? Some little irrelevance of line, some promise of character to come, may indeed put us at our ease, 'give more interest' as the humour of the old man with the basket does to Cleopatra's dying; but should it come as we had dreamed in love's frenzy to our dying for that woman's sake, we would find that the discord had its value from the tune.[17] Nor have we chosen illusion in choosing the outward sign of that moral genius that lives among the subtlety of the passions, and can for her moment make her of the one mind with great artists and poets. In the studio we may indeed say to one another 'character is the only beauty,' but when we choose a wife, as when we go to the gymnasium to be shaped for woman's eyes, we remember academic form, even though we enlarge a little the point of interest and choose 'a painter's beauty,' finding it the more easy to believe in the fire because it has made ashes.[18]

When we look at the faces of the old tragic paintings, whether it is in Titian or in some painter of mediæval China, we find there sadness and gravity, a certain emptiness even, as of a mind that waited the supreme crisis (and indeed it seems at times as if the graphic art, unlike poetry which sings the crisis itself, were the celebration of waiting). Whereas in modern art, whether in Japan or Europe, 'vitality' (is not that the great word of the studios?), the energy, that is to say, which is under the command of our common moments, sings, laughs, chatters or looks its busy thoughts.

Certainly we have here the Tree of Life and that of the† Knowledge of Good and Evil which is rooted in our interests, and if we have forgotten their differing virtues it is surely because we have taken delight in a confusion of crossing branches.[19] Tragic art, passionate art, the drowner of dykes, the confounder of understanding, moves us by setting us to reverie, by alluring us almost to the intensity of trance. The persons upon the stage, let us say, greaten till they are humanity itself. We feel our minds expand convulsively or spread out slowly like some moon-brightened image-crowded sea. That which is before our eyes perpetually vanishes and returns again in the midst of the excitement it creates, and the more enthralling it is, the more do we forget it.

AUGUST 1910.

# POETRY AND TRADITION

## I

When O'Leary died I could not bring myself to go to his funeral, though I had been once his close fellow-worker, for I shrank from seeing about his grave so many whose Nationalism was different from anything he had taught or that I could share.[1] He belonged, as did his friend John F. Taylor, to the romantic conception of Irish Nationality on which Lionel Johnson and myself founded, so far as it was founded on anything but literature, our Art and our Irish criticism.[2] Perhaps his spirit, if it can care for or can see old friends now, will accept this apology for an absence that has troubled me. I learned much from him and much from Taylor, who will always seem to me the greatest orator I have heard; and that ideal Ireland, perhaps from this out an imaginary Ireland, in whose service I labour, will always be in many essentials their Ireland. They were the last to speak an understanding of life and Nationality, built up by the generation of Grattan, which read Homer and Virgil, and by the generation of Davis, which had been pierced through by the idealism of Mazzini,* and of the European revolutionists of the mid-century.[4]

O'Leary had joined the Fenian movement with no hope of success, as we know, but because he believed such a movement good for the moral character of the people; and had taken his long imprisonment without complaining. Even to the very end, while often speaking of his prison life, he would have thought it took from his Roman courage to describe its hardship. The worth of a man's acts in the

*Rose Kavanagh, the poet, wrote to her religious adviser from, I think, Leitrim, where she lived, and asked him to get her the works of Mazzini. He replied, 'You must mean Manzone.'[3] [1908]

moral memory, a continual height of mind in the doing of them, seemed more to him than their immediate result, if, indeed, the sight of many failures had not taken away the thought of success. A man was not to lie, or even to give up his dignity, on any patriotic plea, and I have heard him say, 'I have but one religion, the old Persian: to bend the bow and tell the truth,' and again, 'There are things a man must not do to save a nation,' and again, 'A man must not cry in public to save a nation,' and that we might not forget justice in the passion of controversy, 'There was never cause so bad that it has not been defended by good men for what seemed to them good reasons.' His friend had a burning and brooding imagination that divided men not according to their achievement but by their degrees of sincerity, and by their mastery over a straight and, to my thought, too obvious logic that seemed to him essential to sincerity. Neither man had an understanding of style or of literature in the right sense of the word, though both were great readers, but because their imagination could come to rest no place short of greatness, they hoped, John O'Leary especially, for an Irish literature of the greatest kind.[5] When Lionel Johnson and Katharine Tynan (as she was then), and I, myself, began to reform Irish poetry, we thought to keep unbroken the thread running up to Grattan which John O'Leary had put into our hands, though it might be our business to explore new paths of the labyrinth.[6] We sought to make a more subtle rhythm, a more organic form, than that of the older Irish poets who wrote in English, but always to remember certain ardent ideas and high attitudes of mind which were the nation itself, to our belief, so far as a nation can be summarised in the intellect. If you had asked an ancient Spartan what made Sparta Sparta, he would have answered, the Laws of Lycurgus, and many Englishmen look back to Bunyan and to Milton as we did to Grattan and to Mitchel.[7] Lionel Johnson was able to take up into his Art one portion of this tradition that I could not, for he had a gift of speaking political thought in fine verse that I have always lacked. I, on the other hand, was more preoccupied with Ireland (for he had other interests), and took from Allingham and Walsh their passion for country spiritism, and from Ferguson his pleasure in heroic legend, and while seeing all in the light of European literature found my symbols of expression in Ireland.[8] One thought often possessed me very strongly. New from the influence, mainly the personal influence, of

William Morris, I dreamed of enlarging Irish hate, till we had come to hate with a passion of patriotism what Morris and Ruskin hated.[9] Mitchel had already all but poured some of that hate drawn from Carlyle, who had it of an earlier and, as I think, cruder sort, into the blood of Ireland, and were we not a poor nation with ancient courage, unblackened fields and a barbarous gift of self-sacrifice?[10] Ruskin and Morris had spent themselves in vain because they had found no passion to harness to their thought, but here were unwasted passion and precedents in the popular memory for every needed thought and action. Perhaps, too, it would be possible to find in that new philosophy of spiritism coming to a seeming climax in the work of Frederic Myers, and in the investigations of uncounted obscure persons, what could change the country spiritism into a reasoned belief that would put its might into all the rest.[11] A new belief seemed coming that could be so simple and demonstrable and above all so mixed into the common scenery of the world, that it would set the whole man on fire and liberate him from a thousand obediences and complexities. We were to forge in Ireland a new sword on our old traditional anvil for that great battle that must in the end re-establish the old, confident, joyous world. All the while I worked with this idea, founding societies that became quickly or slowly everything I despised, one part of me looked on, mischievous and mocking, and the other part spoke words which were more and more unreal, as the attitude of mind became more and more strained and difficult. Miss Maud Gonne could still gather great crowds out of the slums by her beauty and sincerity, and speak to them of 'Mother Ireland with the crown of stars about her head'; but gradually the political movement she was associated with, finding it hard to build up any fine lasting thing, became content to attack little persons and little things.[12] All movements are held together more by what they hate than by what they love, for love separates and individualises and quiets, but the nobler movements, the only movements on which literature can found itself, hate great and lasting things. All who have any old traditions have something of aristocracy, but we had opposing us from the first, though not strongly from the first, a type of mind which had been without influence in the generation of Grattan, and almost without it in that of Davis, and which has made a new nation out of Ireland, that was once old and full of memories.

I remember, when I was twenty years old, arguing, on my way home from a Young Ireland Society, that Ireland, with its hieratic Church, its readiness to accept leadership in intellectual things,—and John O'Leary spoke much of this readiness,*—its Latin hatred of middle paths and uncompleted arguments, could never create a democratic poet of the type of Burns, although it had tried to do so more than once, but that its genius would in the long run be distinguished and lonely.[14] Whenever I had known some old countryman, I had heard stories and sayings that arose out of an imagination that would have understood Homer better than 'The Cotter's Saturday Night' or 'Highland Mary,' because it was an ancient imagination, where the sediment had found the time to settle, and I believe that the makers of deliberate literature could still take passion and theme, though but little thought, from such as he. On some such old and broken stem, I thought, have all the most beautiful roses been grafted.

## II

> Him who trembles before the flame and the flood,
> And the winds that blow through the starry ways;
> Let the starry winds and the flame and the flood
> Cover over and hide, for he has no part
> With the proud, majestical multitude.[15]

Three types of men have made all beautiful things. Aristocracies have made beautiful manners, because their place in the world puts them above the fear of life, and the countrymen have made beautiful stories and beliefs, because they have nothing to lose and so do not fear, and the artists have made all the rest, because Providence has filled them with recklessness. All these look backward to a long tradition, for, being without fear, they have held to whatever pleased them. The others being always anxious have come to possess little that is good in itself, and are always changing from thing to thing, for whatever they do or have must be a means to something else, and they

*I have heard him say more than once, 'I will not say our people know good from bad, but I will say that they don't hate the good when it is pointed out to them, as a great many people do in England.'[13] [1908]

have so little belief that anything can be an end in itself, that they cannot understand you if you say, 'All the most valuable things are useless.' They prefer the stalk to the flower, and believe that painting and poetry exist that there may be instruction, and love that there may be children, and theatres that busy men may rest, and holidays that busy men may go on being busy. At all times they fear and even hate the things that have worth in themselves, for that worth may suddenly, as it were a fire, consume their book of Life, where the world is represented by cyphers and symbols; and before all else, they fear irreverent joy and unserviceable sorrow. It seems to them, that those who have been freed by position, by poverty, or by the traditions of Art, have something terrible about them, a light that is unendurable to eyesight. They complain much of that commandment that we can do almost what we will, if we do it gaily, and think that freedom is but a trifling with the world.

If we would find a company of our own way of thinking, we must go backward to turreted walls, to courts, to high rocky places, to little walled towns, to jesters like that jester of Charles the Fifth who made mirth out of his own death; to the Duke Guidobaldo in his sickness, or Duke Frederick in his strength, to all those who understood that life is not lived, if not lived for contemplation or excitement.[16]

Certainly we could not delight in that so courtly thing, the poetry of light love, if it were sad; for only when we are gay over a thing, and can play with it, do we show ourselves its master, and have minds clear enough for strength. The raging fire and the destructive sword are portions of eternity, too great for the eye of man, wrote Blake, and it is only before such things, before a love like that of Tristan and Iseult, before noble or ennobled death, that the free mind permits itself aught but brief sorrow.[17] That we may be free from all the rest, sullen anger, solemn virtue, calculating anxiety, gloomy suspicion, prevaricating hope, we should be reborn in gaiety. Because there is submission in a pure sorrow, we should sorrow alone over what is greater than ourselves, nor too soon admit that greatness, but all that is less than we are should stir us to some joy, for pure joy masters and impregnates; and so to world end, strength shall laugh and wisdom mourn.

## III

In life courtesy and self-possession, and in the arts style, are the sensible impressions of the free mind, for both arise out of a deliberate shaping of all things, and from never being swept away, whatever the emotion, into confusion or dullness. The Japanese have numbered with heroic things courtesy at all times whatsoever, and though a writer, who has to withdraw so much of his thought out of his life that he may learn his craft, may find many his betters in daily courtesy, he should never be without style, which is but high breeding in words and in argument. He is indeed the Creator of the standards of manners in their subtlety, for he alone can know the ancient records and be like some mystic courtier who has stolen the keys from the girdle of time, and can wander where it please him amid the splendours of ancient courts.

Sometimes, it may be, he is permitted the licence of cap and bell, or even the madman's bunch of straws, but he never forgets or leaves at home the seal and the signature. He has at all times the freedom of the well-bred, and being bred to the tact of words can take what theme he pleases, unlike the linen drapers, who are rightly compelled to be very strict in their conversation. Who should be free if he were not? for none other has a continual deliberate self-delighting happiness—style, 'the only thing that is immortal in literature,' as Sainte-Beuve has said, a still unexpended energy, after all that the argument or the story needs, a still unbroken pleasure after the immediate end has been accomplished—and builds this up into a most personal and wilful fire, transfiguring words and sounds and events.[18] It is the playing of strength when the day's work is done, a secret between a craftsman and his craft, and is so inseparate in his nature, that he has it most of all amid overwhelming emotion, and in the face of death. Shakespeare's persons, when the last darkness has gathered about them, speak out of an ecstasy that is one half the self-surrender of sorrow, and one half the last playing and mockery of the victorious sword, before the defeated world.

It is in the arrangement of events as in the words, and in that touch of extravagance, of irony, of surprise, which is set there after the desire of logic has been satisfied and all that is merely necessary established, and that leaves one, not in the circling necessity, but caught up into the freedom of self-delight: it is, as it were, the foam upon the cup, the long pheasant's feather on the horse's head, the spread peacock over the pasty. If it be very conscious, very deliberate, as it may be in comedy, for comedy is more personal than tragedy, we call it fantasy, perhaps even mischievous fantasy, recognising how disturbing it is to all that drag a ball at the ankle. This joy, because it must be always making and mastering, remains in the hands and in the tongue of the artist, but with his eyes he enters upon a submissive, sorrowful contemplation of the great irremediable things, and he is known from other men by making all he handles like himself, and yet by the unlikeness to himself of all that comes before him in a pure contemplation. It may have been his enemy or his love or his cause that set him dreaming, and certainly the phœnix can but open her young wings in a flaming nest; but all hate and hope vanishes in the dream, and if his mistress brag of the song or his enemy fear it, it is not that either has its praise or blame, but that the twigs of the holy nest are not easily set afire. The verses may make his mistress famous as Helen or give a victory to his cause, not because he has been either's servant, but because men delight to honour and to remember all that have served contemplation.[19] It had been easier to fight, to die even, for Charles's house with Marvell's poem in the memory, but there is no zeal of service that had not been an impurity in the pure soil where the marvel grew.[20] Timon of Athens contemplates his own end, and orders his tomb by the beachy margent of the flood, and Cleopatra sets the asp to her bosom, and their words move us because their sorrow is not their own at tomb or asp, but for all men's fate.[21] That shaping joy has kept the sorrow pure, as it had kept it were the emotion love or hate, for the nobleness of the Arts is in the mingling of contraries, the extremity of sorrow, the extremity of joy, perfection of personality, the perfection of its surrender, overflowing turbulent energy, and marmorean stillness; and its red rose opens at the meeting of the two beams of the cross, and at the trysting-place of mortal and immortal, time and eternity. No new man has ever plucked that rose, or found that trysting-place, for he could but come to the understanding of himself, to the mastery of unlocking words after long frequenting of the great Masters, hardly without ancestral memory of the like. Even knowledge is not enough, for the 'recklessness' Castiglione thought necessary in good manners is necessary in this likewise, and if a man has it not he will be gloomy, and had better to his marketing again.[22]

## IV

When I saw John O'Leary first, every young Catholic man who had intellectual ambition fed his imagination with the poetry of Young Ireland; and the verses of even the least known of its poets were expounded with a devout ardour at Young Ireland Societies and the like, and their birthdays celebrated. The school of writers I belonged to tried to found itself on much of the subject-matter of this poetry, and, what was almost more in our thoughts, to begin a more imaginative tradition in Irish literature, by a criticism at once remorseless and enthusiastic. It was our criticism, I think, that set Clarence Mangan at the head of the Young Ireland poets in the place of Davis, and put Sir Samuel Ferguson, who had died with but little fame as a poet, next in the succession.[23] Our attacks, mine especially, on verse which owed its position to its moral or political worth, roused a resentment which even I find it hard to imagine to-day, and our verse was attacked in return, and not for anything peculiar to ourselves, but for all that it had in common with the accepted poetry of the world, and most of all for its lack of rhetoric, its refusal to preach a doctrine or to consider the seeming necessities of a cause. Now, after so many years, I can see how natural, how poetical, even, an opposition was, that shows what large numbers could not call up certain high feelings without accustomed verses, or believe we had not wronged the feeling when we did but attack the verses. I have just read in a newspaper that Sir Charles Gavan Duffy recited upon his death-bed his favourite poem, one of the worst of the patriotic poems of Young Ireland, and it has brought all this to mind, for the opposition to our School claimed him as its leader.[24] When I was at Siena, I noticed that the Byzantine style persisted in faces of Madonnas for several generations after it had given way to a more natural style, in the less loved faces of saints and martyrs.[25] Passion had grown accustomed to those narrow eyes, which are almost Japanese, and to those gaunt cheeks, and would have thought it sacrilege to change. We would not, it is likely, have found listeners if John O'Leary, the irreproachable patriot, had not supported us. It was as clear to him that a writer must not write badly, or ignore the examples of the great Masters in the fancied or real service of a cause, as it was that he must not lie for it or grow hysterical. I believed in those days that a new intellectual life would begin, like that of Young Ireland, but more profound and personal, and that could we but get a few plain principles accepted, new poets and writers of prose would make an immortal music. I think I was more blind than Johnson, though I judge this from his poems rather than anything I remember of his talk, for he never talked ideas, but, as was common with his generation in Oxford, facts and immediate impressions from life. With others this renunciation was but a pose, a superficial reaction from the disordered abundance of the middle century, but with him it was the radical life. He was in all a traditionalist, gathering out of the past phrases, moods, attitudes, and disliking ideas less for their uncertainty than because they made the mind itself changing and restless. He measured the Irish tradition by another greater than itself, and was quick to feel any falling asunder of the two, yet at many moments they seemed but one in his imagination. Ireland, all through his poem of that name, speaks to him with the voice of the great poets, and in 'Ireland's Dead' she is still mother of perfect heroism, but there doubt comes too.

Can it be they do repent
That they went, thy chivalry,
Those sad ways magnificent?[26]

And in 'Ways of War,' dedicated to John O'Leary, he dismissed the belief in an heroic Ireland as but a dream.

A dream! a dream! an ancient dream!
Yet ere peace come to Innisfail,
Some weapons on some field must gleam,
Some burning glory fire the Gael.

That field may lie beneath the sun,
Fair for the treading of an host:

That field in realms of thought be won,
And armed hands do their uttermost:

Some way, to faithful Innisfail,
Shall come the majesty and awe
Of martial truth, that must prevail
To lay on all the eternal law.[27]

I do not think either of us saw that, as belief in the possibility of armed insurrection withered, the old romantic nationalism would wither too, and that the young would become less ready to find pleasure in whatever they believed to be literature. Poetical tragedy, and indeed all the more intense forms of literature, had lost their hold on the general mass of men in other countries as life grew safe, and the sense of comedy which is the social bond in times of peace as tragic feeling is in times of war, had become the inspiration of popular art. I always knew this, but I believed that the memory of danger, and the reality of it seemed near enough sometimes, would last long enough to give Ireland her imaginative opportunity. I could not foresee that a new class, which had begun to rise into power under the shadow of Parnell, would change the nature of the Irish movement, which, needing no longer great sacrifices, nor bringing any great risk to individuals, could do without exceptional men, and those activities of the mind that are founded on the exceptional moment.*[29] John O'Leary had spent much of his thought in an unavailing war with the agrarian party, believing it the root of change, but the fox that crept into the badger's hole did not come from there.[30] Power passed to small shopkeepers, to clerks, to that very class who had seemed to John O'Leary so ready to bend to the power of others, to men who had risen above the traditions of the countryman, without learning those of cultivated life or even educating themselves, and who because of their poverty, their ignorance, their superstitious piety, are much

*A small political organiser told me once that he and a certain friend got together somewhere in Tipperary a great meeting of farmers for O'Leary on his coming out of prison, and O'Leary had said at it: 'The landlords gave us some few leaders, and I like them for that, and the artisans have given us great numbers of good patriots, and so I like them best: but you I do not like at all, for you have never given us any one.'[28] [1908]

subject to all kinds of fear. Immediate victory, immediate utility, became everything, and the conviction, which is in all who have run great risks for a cause's sake, in the O'Learys and Mazzinis as in all rich natures, that life is greater than the cause, withered, and we artists, who are the servants not of any cause but of mere naked life, and above all of that life in its nobler forms, where joy and sorrow are one, Artificers of the Great Moment, became as elsewhere in Europe protesting individual voices.[31] Ireland's great moment had passed, and she had filled no roomy vessels with strong sweet wine, where we have filled our porcelain jars against the coming winter.

AUGUST 1907.

# DISCOVERIES

## PROPHET, PRIEST AND KING

The little theatrical company I write my plays for had come to a West of Ireland town, and was to give a performance in an old ball-room, for there was no other room big enough.[1] I went there from a neighbouring country-house, and, arriving a little before the players, tried to open a window.[2] My hands were black with dirt in a moment, and presently a pane of glass and a part of the window-frame came out in my hands. Everything in this room was half in ruins, the rotten boards cracked under my feet, and our new proscenium and the new boards of the platform looked out of place, and yet the room was not really old, in spite of the musicians' gallery over the stage. It had been built by some romantic or philanthropic landlord some three or four generations ago, and was a memory of we knew not what unfinished scheme.

From there I went to look for the players, and called for information on a young priest, who had invited them and taken upon himself the finding of an audience.[3] He lived in a high house with other priests, and as I went in I noticed with a whimsical pleasure a broken pane of glass in the fanlight over the door, for he had once told me the story of an old woman who a good many years ago quarrelled with the bishop, got drunk and hurled a stone through the painted glass. He was a clever man who read Meredith and Ibsen, but some of his books had been packed in the fire-grate by his housekeeper, instead of the customary view of an Italian lake or the coloured tissue-paper.[4] The players, who had been giving a performance in a neighbouring town, had not yet come, or were unpacking their costumes and properties at the hotel he had recommended them.[5] We should have time, he said, to go through the half-ruined town and to visit the convent schools and the cathedral, where, owing to his influence, two of our young Irish sculptors had been set to carve an altar and the heads of pillars. I had only heard of this work, and I found its strangeness and simplicity—one of them had been Rodin's pupil—could not make me forget the meretriciousness of the architecture and the commercial commonplace of the inlaid pavement.[6] The new movement had seized on the cathedral midway in its growth, and the worst of the old and the best of the new were side by side without any sign of transition. The convent school was, as other like places have been to me,—a long room in a workhouse hospital at Portumna, in particular,—a delight to the imagination and the eyes.[7] A new floor had been put into some ecclesiastical building, and the light from a great mullioned window, cut off at the middle, fell aslant upon rows of clean and seemingly happy children. The nuns, who show in their own convents, where they can put what they like, a love of what is mean and pretty, make beautiful rooms where the regulations compel them to do all with a few colours and a few flowers. I think it was that day, but am not sure, that I had lunch at a convent and told fairy stories to a couple of nuns, and I hope it was not mere politeness that made them seem to have a child's interest in such things.

A good many of our audience, when the curtain went up in the old ball-room, were drunk, but all were attentive, for they had a great deal of respect for my friend, and there were other priests there. Presently the man at the door opposite to the stage strayed off somewhere and I took his place, and when boys came up offering two or three pence and asking to be let into the sixpenny seats, I let them join the melancholy crowd. The play professed to tell of the heroic life of ancient Ireland, but was really full of sedentary refinement and the spirituality of cities.[8] Every emotion was made as dainty-footed and dainty-fingered as might be, and a love and pathos where passion had faded into sentiment, emotions of pensive and harmless people, drove shadowy young men through the shadows of death and battle. I watched it with growing rage. It was not my own work, but I have sometimes watched my own work with a rage made all the more salt in the mouth from being half despair. Why should we make so much noise about ourselves and yet have nothing to say that was not better said in that workhouse dormitory, where a few flowers and a few coloured counterpanes and the coloured walls had made a severe appropriate beauty? Presently the play was changed and our comedian began to act a little farce, and when I saw him struggle to wake into laughter an audience out of whom the life had run as if it were water, I rejoiced, as I had over that broken window-pane.[9] Here was something secular, abounding, even a little vulgar, for he was gagging horribly, condescending to his audience, though not without contempt.

We had supper in the priest's house, and a Government official who had come down from Dublin, partly out of interest in this attempt 'to educate the people,' and partly because it was his holiday and it was necessary to go somewhere, entertained us with little jokes. Somebody, not, I think, a priest, talked of the spiritual destiny of our race and praised the night's work, for the play was refined and the people really very attentive, and he could not understand my discontent; but presently he was silenced by the patter of jokes.

I had my breakfast by myself the next morning, for the players had got up in the middle of the night and driven some ten miles to catch an early train to Dublin, and were already on their way to their shops and offices. I had brought the visitors' book of the hotel, to turn over its pages while waiting for my bacon and eggs, and found several pages full of obscenities, scrawled there some two or three weeks before, by Dublin visitors, it seemed, for a notorious Dublin street was mentioned. Nobody had thought it worth his while to tear out the page or blacken out the lines, and as I put the book away impressions that had been drifting through my mind for months rushed up into a single thought. 'If we poets are to move the people, we must reintegrate the human spirit in our imagination. The English have driven away the kings, and turned the prophets into demagogues, and you cannot have health among a people if you have not prophet, priest and king.'

## PERSONALITY AND THE INTELLECTUAL ESSENCES

My work in Ireland has continually set this thought before me: 'How can I make my work mean something to vigorous and simple men whose attention is not given to art but to a shop, or teaching in a National School, or dispensing medicine?'[1] I had not wanted to 'elevate them' or 'educate them,' as these words are understood, but to make them understand my vision, and I had not wanted a large audience, certainly not what is called a national audience, but enough people for what is accidental and temporary to lose itself in the lump. In England, where there have been so many changing activities and so much systematic education, one only escapes from crudities and temporary interests among students, but here there is the right audience, could one but get its ears. I have always come to this certainty: what moves natural men in the arts is what moves them in life, and that is, intensity of personal life, intonations that show them in a book or a play, the strength, the essential moment of a man who would be exciting in the market or at the dispensary door. They must go out of the theatre with the strength they live by strengthened from looking upon some passion that could, whatever its chosen way of life, strike down an enemy, fill a long stocking with money or move a girl's heart. They have not much to do with the speculations of science, though they have a little, or with the speculations of metaphysics, though they have a little. Their legs will tire on the road if there is nothing in their hearts but vague sentiment, and though it is charming to have an affectionate feeling about flowers, that will not pull the cart out of the ditch. An exciting person, whether the hero of a play or the maker of poems, will display the greatest volume of personal energy, and this energy must seem to come out of the body as out of the mind. We must say to ourselves continually when we imagine a character: 'Have I given him the roots, as it were, of all faculties necessary for life?' And only when one is certain of that may one give him the one faculty that fills the imagination with joy. I even doubt if any play had ever a great popularity that did not use, or seem to use, the bodily energies of its principal actor to the full. Villon the robber could have delighted these Irishmen with plays and songs, if he and they had been born to the same traditions of word and symbol, but Shelley could not; and as men came to live in towns and to read printed books and to have many specialised activities, it has become more possible to produce Shelleys and less and less possible to produce Villons.[2] The last Villon dwindled into Robert Burns because the highest faculties had faded, taking the sense of beauty with them, into some sort of vague heaven and left the lower to lumber where they best could.[3] In literature, partly from the lack of that spoken word which knits us to normal man, we have lost in personality, in our delight in the whole man—blood, imagination, intellect, running together—but have found a new delight, in essences, in states of mind, in pure imagination, in all that comes to us most easily in elaborate music. There are two ways before literature—upward into ever-growing subtlety, with Verhaeren, with Mallarmé, with Maeterlinck, until at last, it may be, a new agreement among refined and studious men gives birth to a new passion, and what seems literature becomes religion; or downward, taking the soul with us until all is simplified and solidified again.[4] That is the choice of choices—the way of the bird until common eyes have lost us, or to the market carts; but we must see to it that the soul goes with us, for the bird's song is beautiful, and the traditions of modern imagination, growing always more musical, more lyrical, more melancholy, casting up now a Shelley, now a Swinburne, now a Wagner, are, it may be, the frenzy of those that are about to see what the magic hymn printed by the Abbé de Villiers has called the Crown of Living and Melodious Diamonds.[5] If the carts have hit our fancy we must have the soul tight within our bodies, for it has grown so fond of a beauty accumulated by subtle generations that it will for a long time be impatient with our thirst for mere force, mere personality, for the tumult of the blood. If it begin to slip away we must go after it, for Shelley's Chapel of the Morning Star is better than Burns's beer-house—surely it was beer, not barleycorn—except at the day's weary end; and it is always better than that uncomfortable place where there is no beer, the machine shop of the realists.[6]

## THE MUSICIAN AND THE ORATOR

Walter Pater says music is the type of all the Arts, but somebody else, I forget now who, that oratory is their type.[1] You will side with the one or the other according to the nature of your energy, and I in my present mood am all for the man who, with an average audience before him, uses all means of persuasion—stories, laughter, tears, and but so much music as he can discover on the wings of words. I would even avoid the conversation of the lovers of music, who would draw us into the impersonal land of sound and colour, and I would have no one write with a sonata in his memory. We may even speak a little evil of musicians, having admitted that they will see before we do that melodious crown.[2] We may remind them that the housemaid does not respect the piano-tuner as she does the plumber, and of the enmity that they have aroused among all poets. Music is the most impersonal of things, and words the most personal, and that is why musicians do not like words. They masticate them for a long time, being afraid they would not be able to digest them, and when the words are so broken and softened and mixed with spittle that they are not words any longer, they swallow them.

## A GUITAR PLAYER

A girl has been playing on the guitar.[1] She is pretty, and if I had not listened to her I could have watched her, and if I had not watched her I could have listened. Her voice, the movements of her body, the expression of her face, all said the same thing. A player of a different temper and body would have made all different, and might have been delightful in some other way. A movement not of music only but of life came to its perfection. I was delighted and I did not know why until I thought, 'That is the way my people, the people I see in the mind's eye, play music, and I like it because it is all personal, as personal as Villon's poetry.'[2] The little instrument is quite light, and the player can move freely and express a joy that is not of the fingers and the mind only but of the whole being; and all the while her movements call up into the mind, so erect and natural she is, whatever is most beautiful in her daily life. Nearly all the old instruments were like that, even the organ was once a little instrument, and when it grew big our wise forefathers gave it to God in the cathedrals, where it befits Him to be everything.[3] But if you sit at the piano, it is the piano, the mechanism, that is the important thing, and nothing of you means anything but your fingers and your intellect.

## THE LOOKING-GLASS

I have just been talking to a girl with a shrill monotonous voice and an abrupt way of moving.[1] She is fresh from school, where they have taught her history and geography 'whereby a soul can be discerned,' but what is the value of an education, or even in the long run of a science, that does not begin with the personality, the habitual self, and illustrate all by that?[2] Somebody should have taught her to speak for the most part on whatever note of her voice is most musical, and soften those harsh notes by speaking, not singing, to some stringed instrument, taking note after note and, as it were, caressing her words a little as if she loved the sound of them, and have taught her after this some beautiful pantomimic dance, till it had grown a habit to live for eye and ear. A wise theatre might make a training in strong and beautiful life the fashion, teaching before all else the heroic discipline of the looking-glass, for is not beauty, even as lasting love, one of the most difficult of the arts?

## THE TREE OF LIFE

We artists have taken over-much to heart that old commandment about seeking after the Kingdom of Heaven.[1] Verlaine told me that he had tried to translate *In Memoriam*, but could not because Tennyson was 'too noble, too anglais, and, when he should have been broken-hearted, had many reminiscences.'[2] About that time I found in some English review an essay of his on Shakespeare. 'I had once a fine Shakespeare,' he wrote, or some such words, 'but I have it no longer. I write from memory.'[3] One wondered in what vicissitude he had sold it, and for what money; and an image of the man rose in the imagination. To be his ordinary self as much as possible, not a scholar or even a reader, that was certainly his pose; and in the lecture he gave at Oxford he insisted 'that the poet should hide nothing of himself,' though he must speak it all with 'a care of that dignity which should manifest itself, if not in the perfection of form, at all events with an invisible, insensible, but effectual endeavour after this lofty and severe quality, I was about to say this virtue.'[4] It was this feeling for his own personality, his delight in singing his own life, even more than that life itself, which made the generation I belong to compare him to Villon.[5] It was not till after his death that I understood the meaning his words should have had for me, for while he lived I was interested in nothing but states of mind, lyrical moments, intellectual essences. I would not then have been as delighted as I am now by that guitar player, or as shocked as I am now by that girl whose movements have grown abrupt, and whose voice has grown harsh by the neglect of all but external activities.[6] I had not learned what sweetness, what rhythmic movement, there is in those who have become the joy that is themselves. Without knowing it, I had come to care for nothing but impersonal beauty. I had set out on life with the thought of putting my very self into poetry, and had understood this as a representation of my own visions and an attempt to cut away the non-essential, but as I imagined the visions outside myself my imagination became full of decorative landscape and of still life. I thought of myself as something unmoving and silent living in the middle of my own mind and body, a grain of sand in Bloomsbury or in Connacht that Satan's watch fiends cannot find.[7] Then one day I understood quite suddenly, as the way is, that I was seeking something unchanging and unmixed and always outside myself, a Stone or an Elixir that was always out of reach, and that I myself was the fleeting thing that held out its hand. The more I tried to make my art deliberately beautiful, the more did I follow the opposite of myself, for deliberate beauty is like a woman always desiring man's desire.[8] Presently I found that I entered into myself and pictured myself and not some essence when I was not seeking beauty at all, but merely to lighten the mind of some burden of love or bitterness thrown upon it by the events of life. We are only permitted to desire life, and all the rest should be our complaints or our praise of that exacting mistress who can awake our lips into song with her kisses. But we must not give her all, we must deceive her a little at times, for, as Le Sage says in *Diable Boiteux,* the false lovers who do not become melancholy or jealous with honest passion have the happiest mistresses and are rewarded the soonest and by the most beautiful.[9] Our deceit will give us style, mastery, that dignity, that lofty and severe quality Verlaine spoke of. To put it otherwise, we should ascend out of common interests, the thoughts of the newspapers, of the market-place, of men of science, but only so far as we can carry the normal, passionate, reasoning self, the personality as a whole. We must find some place upon the Tree of Life for the Phœnix nest, for the passion that is exaltation and the negation of the will, for the wings that are always upon fire, set high that the forked branches may keep it safe, yet low enough to be out of the little wind-tossed boughs, the quivering of the twigs.[10]

## THE PRAISE OF OLD WIVES' TALES

An art may become impersonal because it has too much circumstance or too little, because the world is too little or too much with it, because it is too near the ground or too far up among the branches. I met an old man out fishing a year ago, who said to me, 'Don Quixote and Odysseus are always near to me'; that is true for me also, for even Hamlet and Lear and Œdipus are more cloudy.[1] No playwright ever has made or ever will make a character that will follow us out of the theatre as Don Quixote follows us out of the book,* for no playwright can be wholly episodical, and when one constructs, bringing one's characters into complicated relations with one another, something impersonal comes into the story. Society, fate, 'tendency,' something not quite human, begins to arrange the characters and to excite into action only so much of their humanity as they find it necessary to show to one another. The common heart will always love better the tales that have something of an old wives' tale and that look upon their hero from every side as if he alone were wonderful, as a child does with a new penny. In plays of a comedy too extravagant to photograph life, or written in verse, the construction is of a necessity woven out of naked motives and passions, but when an atmosphere of modern reality has to be built up as well, and the tendency, or fate, or society has to be shown as it is about ourselves, the characters grow fainter, and we have to read the book many times or see the play many times before we can remember them. Even then they are only possible in a certain drawing-

*I had forgotten Falstaff, who is an episode in a chronicle play.[2] [1912]

room and among such-and-such people, and we must carry all that lumber in our heads. I thought Tolstoy's *War and Peace* the greatest story I had ever read, and yet it has gone from me; even Launcelot, ever a shadow, is more visible in my memory than all its substance.[3]

## THE PLAY OF MODERN MANNERS

Of all artistic forms that have had a large share of the world's attention, the worst is the play about modern educated people. Except where it is superficial or deliberately argumentative it fills one's soul with a sense of commonness as with dust. It has one mortal ailment. It cannot become impassioned, that is to say, vital, without making somebody gushing and sentimental. Educated and well-bred people do not wear their hearts upon their sleeves, and they have no artistic and charming language except light persiflage and no powerful language at all, and when they are deeply moved they look silently into the fireplace. Again and again I have watched some play of this sort with growing curiosity through the opening scene. The minor people argue, chaff one another, hint sometimes at some deeper stream of life just as we do in our houses, and I am content. But all the time I have been wondering why the chief character, the man who is to bear the burden of fate, is gushing, sentimental and quite without ideas. Then the great scene comes and I understand that he cannot be well-bred or self-possessed or intellectual, for if he were he would draw a chair to the fire and there would be no duologue at the end of the third act. Ibsen understood the difficulty and made all his characters a little provincial that they might not put each other out of countenance, and made a leading-article sort of poetry—phrases about vine leaves and harps in the air—it was possible to believe them using in their moments of excitement, and if the play needed more than that, they could always do something stupid.[1] They could go out and hoist a flag as they do at the end of *Little Eyolf*.[2] One only understands that this manner, deliberately adopted one doubts not, had gone into his soul and filled it with dust, when one has noticed that he could no longer create a man of genius. The happiest writers are those that, knowing this form of play to be slight and passing, keep to the surface, never showing anything but the arguments and the persiflage of daily observation, or now and then, instead of the expression of passion, a stage picture, a man holding a woman's hand or sitting with his head in his hands in dim light by the red glow of a fire. It was certainly an understanding of the slightness of the form, of its incapacity for the expression of the deeper sorts of passion, that made the French invent the play with a thesis, for where there is a thesis people can grow hot in argument, almost the only kind of passion that displays itself in our daily life.[3] The novel of contemporary educated life is upon the other hand a permanent form because, having the power of psychological description, it can follow the thought of a man who is looking into the grate.

## HAS THE DRAMA OF CONTEMPORARY LIFE A ROOT OF ITS OWN?

In watching a play about modern educated people, with its meagre language and its action crushed into the narrow limits of possibility, I have found myself constantly saying: 'Maybe it has its power to move, slight as that is, from being able to suggest fundamental contrasts and passions which romantic and poetical literature have shown to be beautiful.' A man facing his enemies alone in a quarrel over the purity of the water in a Norwegian Spa and using no language but that of the newspapers can call up into our minds, let us say, the passion of Coriolanus.[1] The lovers and fighters of old imaginative literature are more vivid experiences in the soul than anything but one's own ruling passion that is itself riddled by their thought as by lightning, and even two dumb figures on the roads can call up all that glory. Put the man who has no knowledge of literature before a play of this kind and he will say, as he has said in some form or other in every age at the first shock of naturalism, 'Why should I leave my home to hear but the words I have used there when talking of the rates?' And he will prefer to it any play where there is visible beauty or mirth, where life is exciting, at high tide as it were. It is not his fault that he will prefer in all likelihood a worse play although its kind may be greater, for we have been following the lure of science for generations and forgotten him and his. I come always back to this thought. There is something of an old wives' tale in fine literature. The makers of it are like an old peasant telling stories of the great famine or the hangings of '98 or from his own memories.[2] He has felt something in the depth of his mind and he wants to make it as visible and powerful to our senses as possible. He will use the most extravagant words or illustrations if they suit his purpose. Or he will invent a wild parable, and the more his mind is on fire or the more creative it is, the less will he look at the outer world or value it for its own sake. It gives him metaphors and examples, and that is all. He is even a little scornful of it, for it seems to him while the fit is on that the fire has gone out of it and left it but white ashes. I cannot explain it, but I am certain that every high thing was invented in this way, between sleeping and waking, as it were, and that peering and peeping persons are but hawkers of stolen goods. How else could their noses have grown so ravenous or their eyes so sharp?

## WHY THE BLIND MAN IN ANCIENT TIMES WAS MADE A POET

A description in the *Iliad* or the *Odyssey,* unlike one in the *Æneid* or in most modern writers, is the swift and natural observation of a man as he is shaped by life.[1] It is a refinement of the primary hungers and has the least possible of what is merely scholarly or exceptional. It is, above all, never too observant, too professional, and when the book is closed we have had our energies enriched, for we have been in the mid-current. We have never seen anything Odysseus could not have seen while his thought was of the Cyclops, or Achilles when Briseis moved him to desire.[2] In the art of the greatest periods there is something careless and sudden in all habitual moods though not in their expression, because these moods are a conflagration of all the energies of active life. In primitive times the blind man became a poet, as he became a fiddler in our villages, because he had to be driven out of activities all his nature cried for, before he could be contented with the praise of life. And often it is Villon or Verlaine with impediments plain to all, who sings of life with the ancient simplicity.[3] Poets of coming days, when once more it will be possible to write as in the great epochs, will recognise that their sacrifice shall be to refuse what blindness and evil name, or imprisonment at the outsetting, denied to men who missed thereby the sting of a deliberate refusal. The poets of the ages of silver need no refusal of life, the dome of many-coloured glass is already shattered while they live.[4] They look at life deliberately and as if from beyond life, and the greatest of them need suffer nothing but the sadness that the saints have known. This is their aim, and their temptation is not a passionate activity, but the approval of their fellows, which comes to them in full abundance only when they delight in the general thoughts that hold together a cultivated middle-class, where irresponsibilities of position and poverty are lacking; the things that are more excellent among educated men who have political preoccupations, Augustus Cæsar's affability, all that impersonal fecundity which muddies the intellectual passions.[5] Ben Jonson says in the *Poetaster,* that even the best of men without Promethean fire is but a hollow statue, and a studious man will commonly forget after some forty winters that of a certainty Promethean fire will burn somebody's fingers.[6] It may happen that poets will be made more often by their sins than by their virtues, for general praise is unlucky, as the villages know, and not merely as I imagine—for I am superstitious about these things—because the praise of all but an equal enslaves and adds a pound to the ball at the ankle with every compliment.

All energy that comes from the whole man is as irregular as the lightning, for the communicable and forecastable and discoverable is a part only, a hungry chicken under the breast of the pelican, and the test of poetry is not in reason but in a delight not different from the delight that comes to a man at the first coming of love into the heart. I knew an old man who had spent his whole life cutting hazel and privet from the paths, and in some seventy years he had observed little but had many imaginations. He had never seen like a naturalist, never seen things as they are, for his habitual mood had been that of a man stirred in his affairs; and Shakespeare, Tintoretto, though the times were running out when Tintoretto painted, nearly all the great men of the Renaissance, looked at the world with eyes like his.[7] Their minds were never quiescent, never as it were in a mood for scientific observations, always in exaltation, never—to use known words—founded upon an elimination of the personal factor; and their attention and the attention of those they worked for dwelt constantly with what is present to the mind in exaltation. I am too modern fully to enjoy Tintoretto's *Creation of the Milky Way,* I cannot fix my thoughts upon that glowing and palpitating flesh intently enough to forget, as I can the make-believe of a fairy tale, that heavy drapery hanging from a cloud, though I find my pleasure in *King Lear* heightened by the make-believe that comes upon it all when the Fool says: 'This prophecy Merlin shall make, for I live before his time';—and I always find it quite natural, so little does logic in the mere circumstance matter in the finest art, that Richard's and Richmond's tents should be side by side.[8] I saw with delight *The Knight of the Burning Pestle* when Mr. Carr revived it, and found it none the worse because the apprentice acted a whole play upon the spur of the moment and without committing a line to heart.[9] When *The Silent Woman* rammed a century of laughter into the two hours' traffic, I found with amazement that almost every journalist had put logic on the seat, where our lady imagination should pronounce that unjust and favouring sentence her woman's heart is ever plotting, and had felt bound to cherish none but reasonable sympathies and to resent the baiting of that grotesque old man.[10] I have been looking over a book of engravings made in the eighteenth century from those wall-pictures of Herculaneum and Pompeii that were, it seems, the work of journeymen copying from finer paintings, for the composition is always too good for the execution.[11] I find in great numbers an indifference to obvious logic, to all that the eye sees at common moments. Perseus shows Andromeda the death she lived by in a pool, and though the lovers are carefully drawn the reflection is shown reversed that the forms it reflects may be seen the right side up and our eyes be the more content.[12] There is hardly an old master who has not made known to us in some like way how little he cares for what every fool can see and every knave can praise. The men who imagined the arts were not less superstitious in religion, understanding the spiritual relations, but not the mechanical, and finding nothing that need strain the throat in those gnats the floods of Noah and Deucalion.[13]

## CONCERNING SAINTS AND ARTISTS

I took the Indian hemp with certain followers of Saint-Martin on the ground floor of a house in the Latin Quarter.[1] I had never taken it before, and was instructed by a boisterous young poet, whose English was no better than my French.[2] He gave me a little pellet, if I am not forgetting, an hour before dinner, and another after we had dined together at some restaurant. As we were going through the streets to the meeting-place of the Martinists, I felt suddenly that a cloud I was looking at floated in an immense space, and for an instant my being rushed out, as it seemed, into that space with ecstasy. I was myself again immediately, but the poet was wholly above himself, and presently he pointed to one of the street lamps now brightening in the fading twilight, and cried at the top of his voice, 'Why do you look at me with your great eye?' There were perhaps a dozen people already much excited when we arrived; and after I had drunk some cups of coffee and eaten a pellet or two more, I grew very anxious to dance, but did not, as I could not remember any steps. I sat down and closed my eyes; but no, I had no visions, nothing but a sensation of some dark shadow which seemed to be telling me that some day I would go into a trance and so out of my body for a while, but not yet. I opened my eyes and looked at some red ornament on the mantelpiece, and at once the room was full of harmonies of red, but when a blue china figure caught my eye the harmonies became blue upon the instant. I was puzzled, for the reds were all there, nothing had changed, but they were no longer important or harmonious; and why had the blues so unimportant but a moment ago become exciting and delightful? Thereupon it struck me that I was seeing like a painter, and that in the course of the evening every one there would change through every kind of artistic perception.

After a while a Martinist ran towards me with a piece of paper on which he had drawn a circle with a dot in it, and pointing at it with his finger he cried out, 'God, God!' Some immeasurable mystery had been revealed, and his eyes shone; and at some time or other a lean and shabby man, with rather a distinguished face, showed me his horoscope and pointed with an ecstasy of melancholy at its evil aspects. The boisterous poet, who was an old eater of the Indian hemp, had told me that it took one three months growing used to it, three months more enjoying it, and three months being cured of it. These men were in their second period; but I never forgot myself, never really rose above myself for more than a moment, and was even able to feel the absurdity of that gaiety, an Herr Nordau among the men of genius, but one that was abashed at his own sobriety.[3] The sky outside was beginning to grey when there came a knocking at the window shutters. Somebody opened the window, and a woman and two young girls in evening dress, who were not a little bewildered to find so many people, were helped down into the room. She and her husband's two sisters had been at a students' ball unknown to her husband, who was asleep overhead, and had thought to have crept home unobserved, but for a confederate at the window. All those talking or dancing men laughed in a dreamy way; and she, understanding that there was no judgement in the laughter of men that had no thought but of the spectacle of the world, blushed, laughed, and darted through the room and so upstairs. Alas that the hangman's rope should be own brother to that Indian happiness that keeps alone, were it not for some stray cactus, mother of as many dreams, immemorial impartiality.

## THE SUBJECT MATTER OF DRAMA

I read this sentence a few days ago, or one like it, in an obituary of Ibsen: 'Let nobody again go back to the old ballad material of Shakespeare, to murders, and ghosts, for what interests us on the stage is modern experience and the discussion of our interests'; and in another part of the article Ibsen was blamed because he had written of suicides and in other ways made use of 'the morbid terror of death.'[1] Dramatic literature has for a long time been left to the criticism of journalists, and all these, the old stupid ones and the new clever ones, have tried to impress upon it their absorption in the life of the moment, their delight in obvious originality and in obvious logic, their shrinking from the ancient and insoluble. The writer I have quoted is much more than a journalist, but he has lived their hurried life, and instinctively turns to them for judgement. He is not thinking of the great poets and painters, of the cloud of witnesses, who are there that we may become, through our understanding of their minds, spectators of the ages, but of this age. Drama is a means of expression, not a special subject matter, and the dramatist is as free to choose where he has a mind to, as the poet of *Endymion,* or as the painter of Mary Magdalene at the door of Simon the Pharisee.[2] So far from the discussion of our interests and the immediate circumstance of our life being the most moving to the imagination, it is what is old and far off that stirs us the most deeply.

There is a sentence in *The Marriage of Heaven and Hell* that is meaningless until we understand Blake's system of correspondences. 'The best wine is the oldest, the best water the newest.'[3] Water is experience, immediate sensation, and wine is emotion, and it is with the intellect, as distinguished from imagination, that we enlarge the bounds of experience and separate it from all but itself, from illusion, from memory, and create among other things science and good journalism. Emotion, on the other hand, grows intoxicating and delightful after it has been enriched with the memory of old emotions, with all the uncounted flavours of old experience; and it is necessarily some antiquity of thought, emotions that have been deepened by the experiences of many men of genius, that distinguishes the cultivated man. The subject matter of his meditation and invention is old, and he will disdain a too conscious originality in the arts as in those matters of daily life where, is it not Balzac who says, 'we are all conservatives'?[4] He is above all things well-bred, and whether he write or paint will not desire a technique that denies or obtrudes his long and noble descent. Corneille and Racine did not deny their masters, and when Dante spoke of his master Virgil there was no crowing of the cock.[5] In their day imitation was conscious or all but conscious, and because originality was but so much the more a part of the man himself, so much the deeper because unconscious, no quick analysis could unravel their miracle, that needed generations, it may be, for its understanding; but it is our imitation that is unconscious and that waits the certainties of time. The more religious the subject matter of an art, the more will it be as it were stationary, and the more ancient will be the emotion that it arouses and the circumstance that it calls up before our eyes. When in the Middle Ages the pilgrim to St. Patrick's Purgatory found himself on the lake side, he found a boat made out of a hollow tree to ferry him to the cave of vision.[6] In religious painting and poetry, crowns and swords of an ancient pattern take upon themselves new meanings, and it is impossible to separate our idea of what is noble from a mystic stair, where not men and women, but robes, jewels, incidents, ancient utilities float upward slowly over the all but sleeping mind, putting on emotional and spiritual life as they ascend until they are swallowed up by some far glory that they even were too modern and momentary to endure. All art is dream, and what the day is done with is dreaming ripe, and what art has moulded religion accepts, and in the end all is in the wine cup, all is in the drunken fantasy, and the grapes begin to stammer.

## THE TWO KINDS OF ASCETICISM

It is not possible to separate an emotion or a spiritual state from the image that calls it up and gives it expression. Michael Angelo's *Moses,* Velasquez' *Philip the Second,* the colour purple, a crucifix, call into life an emotion or state that vanishes with them because they are its only possible expression, and that is why no mind is more valuable than the images it contains.[1] The imaginative writer differs from the saint in that he identifies himself—to the neglect of his own soul, alas!—with the soul of the world, and frees himself from all that is impermanent in that soul, an ascetic not of women and wine, but of the newspapers. Those things that are permanent in the soul of the world, the great passions that trouble all and have but a brief recurring life of flower and seed in any man, are indeed renounced by the saint who seeks not an eternal art, but his own eternity. The artist stands between the saint and the world of impermanent things, and just in so far as his mind dwells on what is impermanent in his sense, on all that 'modern experience and the discussion of our interests,'[2] that is to say, on what never recurs, as desire and hope, terror and weariness, spring and autumn, recur, will his mind losing rhythm grow critical, as distinguished from creative, and his emotions wither. He will think less of what he sees and more of his own attitude towards it, and will express this attitude by an essentially critical selection and emphasis. I am not quite sure of my memory, but I think that Mr. Ricketts has said somewhere that he feels the critic in Velasquez for the first time in painting, and we all feel the critic in Whistler and Degas, in Browning, even in Mr. Swinburne, in much great art that is not the greatest of all.[3] The end of art is the ecstasy awakened by the presence before an ever-changing mind of what is permanent in the world, or by the arousing of that mind itself into the very delicate and fastidious mood habitual with it when it is seeking those permanent and recurring things. There is a little of both ecstasies at all times, but at this time we have a small measure of the creative impulse itself, of the divine vision, a great measure of 'the lost traveller's dream under the hill,' perhaps because all the old simple things have been painted or written, and they will only have meaning for us again when a new race or a new civilisation has made us look upon all with new eyesight.[4]

## IN THE SERPENT'S MOUTH

If it be true that God is a circle whose centre is everywhere, the saint goes to the centre, the poet and artist to the ring where everything comes round again.[1] The poet must not seek for what is still and fixed, for that has no life for him; and if he did, his style would become cold and monotonous, and his sense of beauty faint and sickly, as are both style and beauty to my imagination in the prose and poetry of Newman, but be content to find his pleasure in all that is for ever passing away that it may come again, in the beauty of woman, in the fragile flowers of spring, in momentary heroic passion, in whatever is most fleeting, most impassioned, as it were, for its own perfection, most eager to return in its glory.[2] Yet perhaps he must endure the impermanent a little, for these things return, but not wholly, for no two faces are alike, and, it may be, had we more learned eyes, no two flowers. Is it that all things are made by the struggle of the individual and the world, of the unchanging and the returning, and that the saint and the poet are over all, and that the poet has made his home in the Serpent's mouth?[3]

## THE BLACK AND THE WHITE ARROWS

Instinct creates the recurring and the beautiful, all the winding of the serpent; but reason, the most ugly man, as Blake called it, is a drawer of the straight line, the maker of the arbitrary and the impermanent, for no recurring spring will ever bring again yesterday's clock.[1] Sanctity has its straight line also, darting from the centre, and with these arrows the many-coloured serpent, theme of all our poetry, is maimed and hunted. He that finds the white arrow shall have wisdom older than the Serpent, but what of the black arrow? How much knowledge, how heavy a quiver of the crow-feathered ebony rods, can the soul endure?

## HIS MISTRESS'S EYEBROWS

The preoccupation of our Art and Literature with knowledge, with the surface of life, with the arbitrary, with mechanism, has arisen out of the root. A careful but not necessarily very subtle man could foretell the history of any religion if he knew its first principle, and that it would live long enough to fulfil itself. The mind can never do the same thing twice over, and having exhausted simple beauty and meaning, it passes to the strange and hidden, and at last must find its delight—having outrun its harmonies—in the emphatic and discordant. When I was a boy at the art school I watched an older student late returned from Paris, with a wonder that had no understanding in it.[1] He was very amorous, and every new love was the occasion of a new picture, and every new picture was uglier than its forerunner. He was excited about his mistress's eyebrows, as was fitting, but the interest of beauty had been exhausted by the logical energies of Art, which destroys where it has rummaged, and can but discover, whether it will or no. We cannot discover our subject matter by deliberate intellect, for when a subject matter ceases to move us we must go elsewhere, and when it moves us, even though it be 'that old ballad material of Shakespeare' or even 'the morbid terror of death,' we can laugh at reason.[2] We must not ask is the world interested in this or that, for nothing is in question but our own interest, and we can understand no other. Our place in the Hierarchy is settled for us by our choice of a subject matter, and all good criticism is hieratic, delighting in setting things above one another, Epic and Drama above Lyric and so on, and not merely side by side. But it is our instinct and not our intellect that chooses. We can deliberately refashion our characters, but not our painting or our poetry. If our characters also were not unconsciously refashioned so completely by the unfolding of the logical energies of Art, that even simple things have in the end a new aspect in our eyes, the Arts would not be among those things that return for ever. The ballads that Bishop Percy gathered returned in the 'Ancient Mariner,' and the delight in the world of old Greek sculptors sprang into a more delicate loveliness in that archaistic head of the young athlete down the long corridor to your left hand as you go into the British Museum.[3]

Civilisation too, will not that also destroy where it has loved, until it shall bring the simple and natural things again and a new Argo with all the gilding on her bows sail out to find another Fleece?[4]

## THE TRESSES OF THE HAIR

Hafiz cried to his beloved, 'I made a bargain with that brown hair before the beginning of time, and it shall not be broken through unending time,' and it may be that Mistress Nature knows that we have lived many times, and that whatsoever changes and winds into itself belongs to us.[1] She covers her eyes away from us, but she lets us play with the tresses of her hair.

## A TOWER ON THE APENNINES

The other day I was walking towards Urbino, where I was to spend the night, having crossed the Apennines from San Sepolcro, and had come to a level place on the mountain-top near the journey's end.[1] My friends were in a carriage somewhere behind, on a road which was still ascending in great loops, and I was alone amid a visionary, fantastic, impossible scenery. It was sunset and the stormy clouds hung upon mountain after mountain, and far off on one great summit a cloud darker than the rest glimmered with lightning. Away south upon another mountain a mediæval tower, with no building near nor any sign of life, rose into the clouds. I saw suddenly in the mind's eye an old man, erect and a little gaunt, standing in the door of the tower, while about him broke a windy light. He was the poet who had at last, because he had done so much for the word's sake, come to share in the dignity of the saint. He had hidden nothing of himself, but he had taken care of 'that dignity . . . the perfection of form . . . this lofty and severe quality . . . this virtue.'[2] And though he had but sought it for the word's sake, or for a woman's praise, it had come at last into his body and his mind. Certainly as he stood there he knew how from behind that laborious mood, that pose, that genius, no flower of himself but all himself, looked out as from behind a mask that other Who alone of all men, the country-people say, is not a hair's-breadth more nor less than six feet high.[3] He has in his ears well-instructed voices and seeming solid sights are before his eyes, and not, as we say of many a one, speaking in metaphor, but as this were Delphi or Eleusis, and the substance and the voice come to him among his memories which are of women's faces; for was it Columbanus or another that wrote, 'There is one among the birds that is perfect, and one perfect among the fish'?[4]

## THE THINKING OF THE BODY

Those learned men who are a terror to children and an ignominious sight in lovers' eyes, all those butts of a traditional humour where there is something of the wisdom of peasants, are mathematicians, theologians, lawyers, men of science of various kinds. They have followed some abstract reverie, which stirs the brain only and needs that only, and have therefore stood before the looking-glass without pleasure and never known those thoughts that shape the lines of the body for beauty or animation, and wake a desire for praise or for display.

There are two pictures of Venice side by side in the house where I am writing this, a Canaletto that has little but careful drawing, and a not very emotional pleasure in clean bright air, and a Frans Francken (the younger), where the blue water, that in the other stirs one so little, can make one long to plunge into the green depth where a cloud shadow falls.[1] Neither painting could move us at all, if our thought did not rush out to the edges of our flesh, and it is so with all good art, whether the Victory of Samothrace which reminds the soles of our feet of swiftness, or the Odyssey that would send us out under the salt wind, or the young horsemen on the Parthenon, that seem happier than our boyhood ever was, and in our boyhood's way.[2] Art bids us touch and taste and hear and see the world, and shrinks from what Blake calls mathematic form, from every abstract thing, from all that is of the brain only, from all that is not a fountain jetting from the entire hopes, memories, and sensations of the body.[3] Its morality is personal, knows little of any general law, has no blame for Little Musgrave, no care for Lord Barnard's house, seems lighter than a breath and yet is hard and heavy, for if a man is not ready to face toil and risk, and in all gaiety of heart, his body will grow unshapely and his heart lack the wild will that stirs desire.[4] It approved before all men those that talked or wrestled or tilted under the walls of Urbino, or sat in those great window-seats discussing all things, with love ever in their thought, when the wise Duchess ordered all, and the Lady Emilia gave the theme.[5]

## RELIGIOUS BELIEF NECESSARY TO RELIGIOUS ART

All art is sensuous, but when a man puts only his contemplative nature and his more vague desires into his art, the sensuous images through which it speaks become broken, fleeting, uncertain, or are chosen for their distance from general experience, and all grows unsubstantial and fantastic. When imagination moves in a dim world like the country of sleep in *Love's Nocturne* and 'Siren there winds her dizzy hair and sings,' we go to it for delight indeed but in our weariness.[1] If we are to sojourn there that world must grow consistent with itself, emotion must be related to emotion by a system of ordered images, as in *The Divine Comedy.*[2] It must grow to be symbolic, that is, for the soul can only achieve a distinct separated life where many related objects at once distinguish and arouse its energies in their fullness. All visionaries have entered into such a world in trances, and all ideal art has trance for warranty. Shelley seemed to Matthew Arnold to beat his ineffectual wings in the void, and I only made my pleasure in him contented pleasure by massing in my imagination his recurring images of towers and rivers, and caves with fountains in them, and that one Star of his, till his world had grown solid underfoot and consistent enough for the soul's habitation.[3]

But even then I lacked something to compensate my imagination for geographical and historical reality, for the testimony of our ordinary senses, and found myself wishing for and trying to imagine, as I had also when reading Keats's *Endymion,* a crowd of believers who could put into all those strange sights the strength of their belief and the rare testimony of their visions.[4] A little crowd had been sufficient, and I would have had Shelley a sectary that his revelation might display the only sufficient evidence of religion, miracle. All symbolic art should arise out of a real belief, and that it cannot do so in this age proves that this age is a road and not a resting-place for the imaginative arts. I can only understand others by myself, and I am certain that there are many who are not moved as they would be by that solitary light burning in the tower of Prince Athanase, because it has not entered into men's prayers nor lighted any through the sacred dark of religious contemplation.[5]

Lyrical poems, when they but speak of emotions common to all, require not indeed a religious belief like the spiritual arts, but a life that has leisure for itself, and a society that is quickly stirred that our emotion may be strengthened by the emotion of others. All circumstance that makes emotion at once dignified and visible increases the poet's power, and I think that is why I have always longed for some stringed instrument, and a listening audience, not drawn out of the hurried streets, but from a life where it would be natural to murmur over again the singer's thought. When I heard Yvette Guilbert the other day, who has the lyre or as good, I was not content, for she sang among people whose life had nothing it could share with an exquisite art, that should rise out of life as the blade out of the spear-shaft, a song out of the mood, the fountain from its pool, all art out of the body, laughter from a happy company.[6] I longed to make all things over again, that she might sing in some great hall, where there was no one that did not love life and speak of it continually.

## THE HOLY PLACES

When all art was struck out of personality, whether as in our daily business or in the adventure of religion, there was little separation between holy and common things, and just as the arts themselves passed quickly from passion to divine contemplation, from the conversation of peasants to that of princes, the one song remembering the drunken miller and but half forgetting Cambuscan bold; so did a man feel himself near sacred presences when he turned his plough from the slope of Cruachmaa or of Olympus.[1] The occupations and the places known to Homer or to Hesiod, those pure first artists, might, as it were, if but the fashioners' hands had loosened, have changed before the poem's end to symbols and vanished, caught up as in a golden cloud into the unchanging worlds where religion alone can discover life as well as peace.[2] A man of that unbroken day could have all the subtlety of Shelley, and yet use no image unknown among the common people, and speak no thought that was not a deduction from the common thought. Unless the discovery of legendary knowledge and the returning belief in miracle, or what we must needs call so, can bring once more a new belief in the sanctity of common ploughland, and new wonders that reward no difficult ecclesiastical routine but the common, wayward, spirited man, we may never see again a Shelley and a Dickens in the one body, but be broken to the end.[3] We have grown jealous of the body, and we dress it in dull unshapely clothes, that we may cherish aspiration alone. Molière being but the master of common sense lived ever in the common daylight, but Shakespeare could not, and Shakespeare seems to bring us to the very market-place, when we remember Shelley's dizzy and Landor's calm disdain of usual daily things.[4] And at last we have Villiers de L'Isle-Adam crying in the ecstasy of a supreme culture, of a supreme refusal, 'as for living, our servants will do that for us.'[5] One of the means of loftiness, of marmorean stillness, has been the choice of strange and far-away places for the scenery of art, but this choice has grown bitter to me, and there are moments when I cannot believe in the reality of imaginations that are not inset with the minute life of long familiar things and symbols and places. I have come to think of even Shakespeare's journeys to Rome or to Verona as the outflowing of an unrest, a dissatisfaction with natural interests, an unstable equilibrium of the whole European mind that would not have come had John Palæologus cherished, despite that high and heady look, copied by Burne-Jones for his Cophetua, a hearty disposition to fight the Turk.[6] I am orthodox and pray for a resurrection of the body, and am certain that a man should find his Holy Land where he first crept upon the floor, and that familiar woods and rivers should fade into symbol with so gradual a change that he may never discover, no, not even in ecstasy itself, that he is beyond space, and that time alone keeps him from Primum Mobile, Supernal Eden, Yellow Rose over all.[7]

1906.

# PREFACE TO THE FIRST EDITION OF *THE WELL OF THE SAINTS*

Six years ago I was staying in a students' hotel in the Latin Quarter, and somebody, whose name I cannot recollect, introduced me to an Irishman, who, even poorer than myself, had taken a room at the top of the house.[1] It was J. M. Synge, and I, who thought I knew the name of every Irishman who was working at literature, had never heard of him. He was a graduate of Trinity College, Dublin, too, and Trinity College does not, as a rule, produce artistic minds. He told me that he had been living in France and Germany, reading French and German literature, and that he wished to become a writer. He had, however, nothing to show but one or two poems and impressionistic essays, full of that kind of morbidity that has its root in too much brooding over methods of expression, and ways of looking upon life, which come, not out of life, but out of literature, images reflected from mirror to mirror. He had wandered among people whose life is as picturesque as the Middle Ages, playing his fiddle to Italian sailors, and listening to stories in Bavarian woods, but life had cast no light into his writings. He had learned Irish years ago, but had begun to forget it, for the only language that interested him was that conventional language of modern poetry which has begun to make us all weary. I was very weary of it, for I had finished *The Secret Rose*, and felt how it had separated my imagination from life, sending my Red Hanrahan, who should have trodden the same roads with myself, into some undiscoverable country.*[2] I said: 'Give up Paris. You will never create anything by reading Racine, and

*Since writing this I have with Lady Gregory's help put 'Red Hanrahan' into the common speech.—W. B. Y.[3] [1919]

Arthur Symons will always be a better critic of French literature. Go to the Aran Islands. Live there as if you were one of the people themselves; express a life that has never found expression.' I had just come from Aran, and my imagination was full of those grey islands where men must reap with knives because of the stones.[4]

He went to Aran and became a part of its life, living upon salt fish and eggs, talking Irish for the most part, but listening also to the beautiful English which has grown up in Irish-speaking districts, and takes its vocabulary from the time of Malory and of the translators of the Bible, but its idiom and its vivid metaphor from Irish.[5] When Mr. Synge began to write in this language, Lady Gregory had already used it finely in her translations of Dr. Hyde's lyrics and plays, or of old Irish literature, but she had listened with different ears.[6] He made his own selection of word and phrase, choosing what would express his own personality. Above all, he made word and phrase dance to a very strange rhythm, which will always, till his plays have created their own tradition, be difficult to actors who have not learned it from his lips. It is essential, for it perfectly fits the drifting emotion, the dreaminess, the vague yet measureless desire, for which he would create a dramatic form. It blurs definition, clear edges, everything that comes from the will, it turns imagination from all that is of the present, like a gold background in a religious picture, and it strengthens in every emotion whatever comes to it from far off, from brooding memory and dangerous hope. When he brought *The Shadow of the Glen,* his first play, to the Irish National Theatre Society, the players were puzzled by the rhythm, but gradually they became certain that his woman of the glens, as melancholy as a curlew, driven to distraction by her own sensitiveness, her own fineness, could not speak with any other tongue, that all his people would change their life if the rhythm changed.[7] Perhaps no Irish countryman had ever that exact rhythm in his voice, but certainly if Mr. Synge had been born a countryman, he would have spoken like that. It makes the people of his imagination a little disembodied; it gives them a kind of innocence even in their anger and their cursing. It is part of its maker's attitude towards the world, for while it makes the clash of wills among his persons indirect and dreamy, it helps him to see the subject matter of his art with wise, clear-seeing, unreflecting eyes; to preserve the integrity of art in an age of reasons and purposes. Whether he write of old beggars by the roadside, lamenting over the misery and ugliness of life, or of an old Aran woman mourning her drowned sons, or of a young wife married to an old husband, he has no wish to change anything, to reform anything; all these people pass by as before an open window, murmuring strange, exciting words.[8]

If one has not fine construction, one has not drama, but if one has not beautiful or powerful and individual speech, one has not literature, or, at any rate, one has not great literature. Rabelais, Villon, Shakespeare, William Blake, would have known one another by their speech. Some of them knew how to construct a story, but all of them had abundant, resonant, beautiful, laughing, living speech. It is only the writers of our modern dramatic movement, our scientific dramatists, our naturalists of the stage, who have thought it possible to be like the greatest, and yet to cast aside even the poor persiflage of the comedians, and to write in the impersonal language that has come, not out of individual life, nor out of life at all, but out of necessities of commerce, of parliament, of Board schools, of hurried journeys by rail.[9]

If there are such things as decaying art and decaying institutions, their decay must begin when the element they receive into their care from the life of every man in the world, begins to rot. Literature decays when it no longer makes more beautiful, or more vivid, the language which unites it to all life, and when one finds the criticism of the student, and the purpose of the reformer, and the logic of the man of science, where there should have been the reveries of the common heart, ennobled into some raving Lear or unabashed Don Quixote.[10] One must not forget that the death of language, the substitution of phrases as nearly impersonal as algebra for words and rhythms varying from man to man, is but a part of the tyranny of impersonal things. I have been reading through a bundle of German plays, and have found everywhere a desire not to express hopes and alarms common to every man that ever came into the world, but politics or social passion, a veiled or open propaganda. Now it is duelling that has need of reproof; now it is the ideas of an actress, returning from the free life of the stage, that must be contrasted with the prejudice of an old-fashioned town; now it is the hostility of Christianity and Paganism in our own day that is to find an obscure symbol in a bell thrown from its tower by spirits of the wood.[11] I compare the work of these dramatists with the greater plays of their Scandinavian master, and remember that even he, who has made so many clear-drawn characters, has made us no abundant character, no man of genius in whom we could believe, and that in him also, even when it is Emperor and Galilean that are face to face, even the most momentous figures are subordinate to some tendency, to some movement, to some inanimate energy, or to some process of thought whose very logic has changed it into mechanism—always to 'something other than human life.'[12]

We must not measure a young talent, whether we praise or blame, with that of men who are among the greatest of our time, but we may say of any talent, following out a definition, that it takes up the tradition of great drama as it came from the hands of the masters who are acknowledged by all time, and turns away from a dramatic movement, which, though it has been served by fine talent, has been imposed upon us by science, by artificial life, by a passing order.

When the individual life no longer delights in its own energy, when the body is not made strong and beautiful by the activities of daily life, when men have no delight in decorating the body, one may be certain that one lives in a passing order, amid the inventions of a fading vitality. If Homer were alive to-day, he would only resist, after a deliberate struggle, the temptation to find his subject not in Helen's beauty, that every man has desired, nor in the wisdom and endurance of Odysseus that has been the desire of every woman that has come into the world, but in what somebody would describe, perhaps, as 'the inevitable contest,' arising out of economic causes, between the country-places and small towns on the one hand, and, upon the other, the great city of Troy, representing one knows not what 'tendency to centralisation.'[13]

Mr. Synge has in common with the great theatre of the world, with that of Greece and that of India, with the creator of Falstaff, with Racine, a delight in language, a preoccupation with individual life.[14] He resembles them also by a preoccupation with what is lasting and noble, that came to him, not as I think from books, but while he listened to old stories in the cottages, and contrasted what they remembered with reality. The only literature of the Irish country-people is their songs, full often of extravagant love, and their stories of kings and of kings' children. 'I will cry my fill, but not for God, but because Finn and the Fianna are not living,' says Oisin in the story.[15] Every writer, even every small writer, who has belonged to the great tradition, has had his dream of an impossibly noble life, and the greater he is, the more does it seem to plunge him into some beautiful or bitter reverie. Some, and of these are all the earliest poets of the world, gave it direct expression; others mingle it so subtly with reality, that it is a day's work to disentangle it; others bring it near by showing us whatever is most its contrary. Mr. Synge, indeed, sets before us ugly, deformed or sinful people, but his people, moved by no practical ambition, are driven by a dream of that impossible life. That we may feel how intensely his woman of the glen dreams of days that shall be entirely alive, she that is 'a hard woman to please' must spend her days between a sour-faced old husband, a man who goes mad upon the hills, a craven lad and a drunken tramp; and those two blind people of *The Well of the Saints* are so transformed by the dream, that they choose blindness rather than reality.[16] He tells us of realities, but he knows that art has never taken more than its symbols from anything that the eye can see or the hand measure.

It is the preoccupation of his characters with their dream that gives his plays their drifting movement, their emotional subtlety. In most of the dramatic writing of our time, and this is one of the reasons why our dramatists do not find the need for a better speech, one finds a simple motive lifted, as it were, into the full light of the stage. The ordinary student of drama will not find anywhere in *The Well of the Saints* that excitement of the will in the presence of attainable advantages, which he is accustomed to think the natural stuff of drama, and if he see it played he will wonder why Act is knitted to Act so loosely, why it is all like a decoration on a flat surface, why there is so much leisure in the dialogue, even in the midst of passion. If he see *The Shadow of the Glen,* he will ask, Why does this woman go out of her house? Is it because she cannot help herself, or is she content to go? Why is it not all made clearer?[17] And yet, like everybody when caught up into great events, she does many things without being quite certain why she does them. She hardly understands at moments why her action has a certain form, more clearly than why her body is tall or short, fair or brown. She feels an emotion that she does not understand. She is driven by desires that need for their expression, not

'I admire this man,' or 'I must go, whether I will or no,' but words full of suggestion, rhythms of voice, movements that escape analysis. In addition to all this, she has something that she shares with none but the children of one man's imagination. She is intoxicated by a dream which is hardly understood by herself, but possesses her like something half remembered on a sudden wakening.

While I write, we are rehearsing *The Well of the Saints,* and are painting for it decorative scenery, mountains in one or two flat colours and without detail, ash trees and red salleys with something of recurring pattern in their woven boughs.[18] For though the people of the play use no phrase they could not use in daily life, we know that we are seeking to express what no eye has ever seen.

ABBEY THEATRE,
JANUARY 27, 1905.

# PREFACE TO THE FIRST EDITION OF JOHN M. SYNGE'S *POEMS AND TRANSLATIONS*

'The Lonely returns to the Lonely, the Divine to the Divinity.'—Proclus.[1]

## I

While this work was passing through the press Mr. J. M. Synge died.[2] Upon the morning of his death one friend of his and mine, though away in the country, felt the burden of some heavy event, without understanding where or for whom it was to happen; but upon the same morning one of my sisters said, 'I think Mr. Synge will recover, for last night I dreamed of an ancient galley labouring in a storm and he was in the galley, and suddenly I saw it run into bright sunlight and smooth sea, and I heard the keel grate upon the sand.'[3] The misfortune was for the living certainly, that must work on, perhaps in vain, to magnify the minds and hearts of our young men, and not for the dead that, having cast off the ailing body, is now, as I believe, all passionate and fiery, an heroical thing. Our Daimon is as dumb as was that of Socrates, when they brought in the hemlock; and if we speak among ourselves, it is of the thoughts that have no savour because we cannot hear his laughter, of the work more difficult because of the strength he has taken with him, of the astringent joy and hardness that was in all he did, and of his fame in the world.[4]

## II

In his Preface he speaks of these poems as having been written during the last sixteen or seventeen years, though the greater number were written very recently, and many during his last illness.[5] 'An Epitaph' and 'On an Anniversary' show how early the expectation of death came to him, for they were made long ago.[6] But the book as a whole is a farewell, written when life began to slip from him. He was a reserved man, and wished no doubt by a vague date to hide, while still living, what he felt and thought, from those about him. I asked one of the nurses in the hospital where he died if he knew he was dying, and she said, 'He may have known it for months, but he would not have spoken of it to any one.' Even the translations of poems that he has made his own by putting them into that melancholy dialect of his, seem to express his emotion at the memory of poverty and the approach of death. The whole book is of a kind almost unknown in a time when lyricism has become abstract and impersonal.

## III

Now and then in history some man will speak a few simple sentences which never die, because his life gives them energy and meaning. They affect us as do the last words of Shakespeare's people, that gather up into themselves the energy of elaborate events and they put strange meaning into half-forgotten things and accidents, like cries that reveal the combatants in some dim battle. Often a score of words will be enough, as when we repeat to ourselves, 'I am a servant of the Lord God of War and I understand the lovely art of the Muses,' all that remains of a once famous Greek poet and sea rover.[7] And is not that epitaph Swift made in Latin for his own tomb more immortal than his pamphlets, perhaps than his great allegory? 'He has gone where fierce indignation can lacerate his heart no more.'[8] I think this book too has certain sentences, fierce or beautiful or melancholy, that will be remembered in our history, having behind their passion his quarrel with ignorance, and those passionate events, his books.

But for the violent nature that strikes brief fire in 'A Question,' hidden though it was under much courtesy and silence, his genius had never borne those lion cubs of his.[9] He could not have loved had he not hated, nor honoured had he not scorned; though his hatred and his scorn moved him but seldom, as I think, for his whole nature was lifted up into a vision of the world, where hatred played with the grotesque and love became an ecstatic contemplation of noble life.

He once said to me, 'We must unite asceticism, stoicism, ecstasy; two of these have often come together, but not all three': and the strength that made him delight in setting the hard virtues by the soft, the bitter by the sweet, salt by mercury, the stone by the elixir, gave him a hunger for harsh facts, for ugly surprising things, for all that defies our hope.[10] In 'The Passing of the Shee' he is repelled by the contemplation of a beauty too far from life to appease his mood; and in his own work, benign images, ever present to his soul, must have beside them malignant reality, and the greater the brightness, the greater must the darkness be.[11] Though like 'Usheen after the Fenians' he remembers his[†] master and his friends, he cannot put from his mind coughing and old age and the sound of the bells.[12] The old woman in *The Riders to the Sea,* in mourning for her six fine sons, mourns for the passing of all beauty and strength, while the drunken woman of *The Tinker's Wedding* is but the more drunken and the more thieving because she can remember great queens. And what is it but desire of ardent life, like that of Oisin for his 'golden salmon of the sea, clean hawk of the air,' that makes the young girls of *The Playboy of the Western World* prefer to any peaceful man their eyes have looked upon, a seeming murderer?[13] Person after person in these laughing, sorrowful, heroic plays is, 'the like of the little children do be listening to the stories of an old woman, and do be dreaming after in the dark night it's in grand houses of gold they are, with speckled horses to ride, and do be waking again in a short while and they destroyed with the cold, and the thatch dripping, maybe, and the starved ass braying in the yard.'[14]

## IV

It was only at the last in his unfinished *Deirdre of the Sorrows* that his mood changed. He knew some twelve months ago that he was dying, though he told no one about it but his betrothed, and he gave all his thought to this play, that he might finish it.[15] Sometimes he would despond and say that he could not; and then his betrothed would act it for him in his sick-room, and give him heart to write again. And now by a strange chance, for he began the play before the last failing of his health, his persons awake to no disillusionment but to death only, and as if his soul already thirsted for the fiery fountains there is nothing grotesque, but beauty only.

## V

He was a solitary, undemonstrative man, never asking pity, nor complaining, nor seeking sympathy but in this book's momentary cries: all folded up in brooding intellect, knowing nothing of new books and newspapers, reading the great masters alone; and he was but the more hated because he gave his country what it needed, an unmoved mind where there is a perpetual last day, a trumpeting, and coming up to judgement.

APRIL 4, 1909.

# J. M. SYNGE AND THE IRELAND OF HIS TIME

## I

On Saturday, January 26, 1907, I was lecturing in Aberdeen, and when my lecture was over I was given a telegram which said, 'Play great success.'[1] It had been sent from Dublin after the Second Act of *The Playboy of the Western World,* then being performed for the first time. After one in the morning, my host brought to my bedroom this second telegram, 'Audience broke up in disorder at the word shift.' I knew no more until I got the Dublin papers on my way from Belfast to Dublin on Tuesday morning. On the Monday night no word of the play had been heard. About forty young men had sat on the front seats of the pit, and stamped and shouted and blown trumpets from the rise to the fall of the curtain. On the Tuesday night also the forty young men were there. They wished to silence what they considered a slander upon Ireland's womanhood. Irish women would never sleep under the same roof with a young man without a chaperon, nor admire a murderer, nor use a word like 'shift'; nor could any one recognise the countrymen and women of Davis and Kickham in these poetical, violent, grotesque persons, who used the name of God so freely, and spoke of all things that hit their fancy.[2]

A patriotic journalism which had seen in Synge's capricious imagination the enemy of all it would have young men believe, had for years prepared for this hour, by that which is at once the greatest and most ignoble power of journalism, the art of repeating a name again and again with some ridiculous or evil association. The preparation had begun after the first performance of *The Shadow of the Glen,* Synge's first play, with an assertion made in ignorance but repeated in dishonesty, that he had taken his fable and his characters, not from his own mind nor that profound knowledge of cot and curragh he was admitted to possess, but 'from a writer of the Roman decadence.'[3] Some spontaneous dislike had been but natural, for genius like his can but slowly, amid what it has of harsh and strange, set forth the nobility of its beauty, and the depth of its compassion; but the frenzy that would have silenced his master-work was, like most violent things artificial, that defence of virtue by those who have but little, which is the pomp and gallantry of journalism and its right to govern the world.

As I stood there watching, knowing well that I saw the dissolution of a school of patriotism that held sway over my youth, Synge came and stood beside me, and said, 'A young doctor has just told me that he can hardly keep himself from jumping on to a seat, and pointing out in that howling mob those whom he is treating for venereal disease.'

## II

Thomas Davis, whose life had the moral simplicity which can give to actions the lasting influence that style alone can give to words, had understood that a country which has no national institutions must show its young men images for the affections, although they be but diagrams of what should be or may be. He and his school imagined the Soldier, the Orator, the Patriot, the Poet, the Chieftain, and above all the Peasant; and these, as celebrated in essay and songs and stories, possessed so many virtues that no matter how England, who, as Mitchel said, 'had the ear of the world,' might slander us, Ireland, even though she could not come at the world's other ear, might go her way unabashed.[4] But ideas and images which have to be understood and loved by large numbers of people, must appeal to no rich personal experience, no patience of study, no delicacy of sense; and if at rare moments some 'Memory of the Dead' can take its strength from one, at all other moments manner and matter will be rhetorical, conventional, sentimental; and language, because it is carried beyond life perpetually, will be worn and cold like the thought, with unmeaning pedantries and silences, and a dread of all that has salt and savour.[5] After a while, in a land that has given itself to agitation over-much, abstract thoughts are raised up between men's minds and Nature, who never does the same thing twice, or makes one man like another, till minds, whose patriotism is perhaps great enough to carry them to the scaffold, cry down natural impulse with the morbid persistence of minds unsettled by some fixed idea. They are preoccupied with the nation's future, with heroes, poets, soldiers, painters, armies, fleets, but only as these things are understood by a child in a National school, while a secret feeling that what is so unreal needs continual defence makes them bitter and restless.[6] They are like some State which has only paper money, and seeks by punishments to make it buy whatever gold can buy. They no longer love, for only life is loved, and at last, a generation is like an hysterical woman who will make unmeasured accusations and believe impossible things, because of some logical deduction from a solitary thought which has turned a portion of her mind to stone.

## III

Even if what one defends be true, an attitude of defence, a continual apology, whatever the cause, makes the mind barren because it kills intellectual innocence; that delight in what is unforeseen, and in the mere spectacle of the world, the mere drifting hither and thither that must come before all true thought and emotion. A zealous Irishman, especially if he lives much out of Ireland, spends his time in a never-ending argument about Oliver Cromwell, the Danes, the penal laws, the rebellion of 1798, the famine, the Irish peasant, and ends by substituting a traditional casuistry for a country; and if he be a Catholic, yet another casuistry that has professors, schoolmasters, letter-writing priests and the authors of manuals to make the meshes fine, comes between him and English literature, substituting arguments and hesitations for the excitement at the first reading of the great poets which should be a sort of violent imaginative puberty.[7] His hesitations and arguments may have been right, the Catholic philosophy may be more profound than Milton's morality, or Shelley's vehement vision; but none the less do we lose life by losing that recklessness Castiglione thought necessary even in good manners, and offend our Lady Truth, who would never, had she desired a courtship so anxious and elaborate, have digged a well to be her parlour.[8]

I admired, though we were always quarrelling, J. F. Taylor, the orator, who died just before the first controversy over these plays.[9] It often seemed to me that when he spoke Ireland herself had spoken; one got that sense of surprise that comes when a man has said what is unforeseen because it is far from the common thought, and yet obvious because when it has been spoken, the gate of the mind seems suddenly to roll back and reveal forgotten sights and let loose lost passions. I have never heard him speak except in some Irish literary or political society, but there at any rate, as in conversation, I found a man whose life was a ceaseless reverie over the religious and political history of Ireland. He saw himself pleading for his country before an invisible jury, perhaps of the great dead, against traitors at home and enemies abroad, and a sort of frenzy in his voice and the moral elevation of his thoughts gave him for the moment style and music. One asked oneself again and again, 'Why is not this man an artist, a man of genius, a creator of some kind?' The other day under the influence of memory, I read through his one book, a Life of Owen Roe O'Neill, and found there no sentence detachable from its context because of wisdom or beauty.[10] Everything was argued from a premise; and wisdom and style, whether in life or letters, come from the presence of what is self-evident, from that which requires but statement, from what Blake called 'naked beauty displayed.'[11] The sense of what was unforeseen and obvious, the rolling backward of the gates, had gone with the living voice, with the nobility of will that made one understand what he saw and felt in what was now but argument and logic. I found myself in the presence of a mind like some noisy and powerful machine, of thought that was no part of wisdom but the apologetic of a moment, a woven thing, no intricacy of leaf and twig, of words with no more of salt and of savour than those of a Jesuit professor of literature, or of any other who does not know that there is no lasting writing which does not define the quality, or carry the substance of some pleasure. How can one, if one's mind be full of abstractions and images created not for their own sake but for the sake of party, even if there were still the need, make pictures for the mind's eye and sounds that delight the ear, or discover thoughts that tighten the muscles, or quiver and tingle in the flesh, and so stand like St. Michael with the trumpet that calls the body to resurrection?[12]

## IV

Young Ireland had taught a study of our history with the glory of Ireland for event; and this for lack, when less than Taylor studied, of comparison with that of other countries wrecked the historical instinct. The man who doubted, let us say, our fabulous ancient kings running up to Adam, or found but mythology in some old tale, was as hated as if he had doubted the authority of Scripture.[13] Above all no man was so ignorant, that he had not by rote familiar arguments and statistics to drive away amid familiar applause all those that had found strange truth in the world or in their mind, and all whose knowledge has passed out of memory and become an instinct of hand or eye. There was no literature, for literature is a child of experience always, of knowledge never; and the nation itself, instead of being a dumb struggling thought seeking a mouth to utter it or hand to show it, a teeming delight that would re-create the world, had become, at best, a subject of knowledge.

## V

Taylor always spoke with confidence, though he was no determined man, being easily flattered or jostled from his way; and this, putting as it were his fiery heart into his mouth, made him formidable. And I have noticed that all those who speak the thoughts of many, speak confidently, while those who speak their own thoughts are hesitating and timid, as though they spoke out of a mind and body grown sensitive to the edge of bewilderment among many impressions. They speak to us that we may give them certainty, by seeing what they have seen; and so it is, that enlargement of experience does not come from those oratorical thinkers, or from those decisive rhythms that move large numbers of men, but from writers that seem by contrast as feminine as the soul when it explores in Blake's picture the recesses of the grave, carrying its faint lamp trembling and astonished; or as the Muses who are never pictured as one-breasted Amazons, but as women needing protection.[14] Indeed, all art which appeals to individual man and awaits the confirmation of his senses and his reveries, seems when arrayed against the moral zeal, the confident logic, the ordered proof of journalism, a trifling, impertinent, vexatious thing, a tumbler who has unrolled his carpet in the way of a marching army.

## VI

I attack things that are as dear to many as some holy image carried hither and thither by some broken clan, and can but say that I have felt in my body the affections I disturb, and believed that if I could raise them into contemplation I would make possible a literature, that, finding its subject matter all ready in men's minds, would be, not as ours is, an interest for scholars, but the possession of a people. I have founded societies with this aim, and was indeed founding one in Paris when I first met with J. M. Synge, and I have known what it is to be changed by that I would have changed, till I became argumentative and unmannerly, hating men even in daily life for their opinions.[15] And though I was never convinced that the anatomies of last year's leaves are a living forest, nor thought a continual apologetic could do other than make the soul a vapour and the body a stone; nor believed that literature can be made by anything but by what is still blind and dumb within ourselves, I have had to learn how hard, in one who lives where forms of expression and habits of thought have been born, not for the pleasure of begetting but for the public good, is that purification from insincerity, vanity, malignity, arrogance, which is the discovery of style. But life became sweet again when I had learnt all I had not learnt in shaping words, in defending Synge against his enemies, and knew that rich energies, fine, turbulent or gracious thoughts, whether in life or letters, are but love-children.

Synge seemed by nature unfitted to think a political thought, and with the exception of one sentence, spoken when I first met him in Paris, that implied some sort of Nationalist conviction, I cannot remember that he spoke of politics or showed any interest in men in the mass, or in any subject that is studied through abstractions and statistics. Often for months together he and I and Lady Gregory would see no one outside the Abbey Theatre, and that life, lived as it were in a ship at sea, suited him, for unlike those whose habit of mind fits them to judge of men in the mass, he was wise in judging individual men, and as wise in dealing with them as the faint energies of ill-health would permit; but of their political thoughts he long understood nothing. One night when we were still producing plays in a little hall, certain members of the Company told him that a play on the Rebellion of '98 would be a great success. After a fortnight he brought them a scenario which read like a chapter out of Rabelais.[16] Two women, a Protestant and a Catholic, take refuge in a cave, and there quarrel about religion, abusing the Pope or Queen Elizabeth and Henry VIII., but in low voices, for the one fears to be ravished by the soldiers, the other by the rebels.[17] At last one woman goes out because she would sooner any fate than such wicked company. Yet, I doubt if he would have written at all if he did not write of Ireland, and for it, and I know that he thought creative art could only come from such preoccupation. Once, when in later years, anxious about the educational effect of our movement, I proposed adding to the Abbey Company a second Company to play international drama, Synge, who had not hitherto opposed me, thought the matter so important that he did so in a formal letter.

I had spoken of a German municipal theatre as my model, and he said that the municipal theatres all over Europe gave fine performances of old classics, but did not create (he disliked modern drama for its sterility of speech, and perhaps ignored it), and that we would create nothing if we did not give all our thoughts to Ireland.[18] Yet in Ireland he loved only what was wild in its people, and in 'the grey and wintry sides of many glens.'[19] All the rest, all that one reasoned over, fought for, read of in leading articles, all that came from education, all that came down from Young Ireland—though for this he had not lacked a little sympathy—first wakened in him perhaps that irony which runs through all he wrote; but once awakened, he made it turn its face upon the whole of life. The women quarrelling in the cave would not have amused him, if something in his nature had not looked out on most disputes, even those wherein he himself took sides, with a mischievous wisdom. He told me once that when he lived in some peasant's house, he tried to make those about him forget that he was there, and it is certain that he was silent in any crowded room. It is possible that low vitality helped him to be observant and contemplative, and made him dislike, even in solitude, those thoughts which unite us to others, much as we all dislike, when fatigue or illness has sharpened the nerves, hoardings covered with advertisements, the fronts of big theatres, big London hotels, and all architecture which has been made to impress the crowd. What blindness did for Homer, lameness for Hephaestus, asceticism for any saint you will, bad health did for him by making him ask no more of life than that it should keep him living, and above all perhaps by concentrating his imagination upon one thought, health itself.[20] I think that all noble things are the result of warfare; great nations and classes, of warfare in the visible world, great poetry and philosophy, of invisible warfare, the division of a mind within itself, a victory, the sacrifice of a man to himself. I am certain that my friend's noble art, so full of passion and heroic beauty, is the victory of a man who in poverty and sickness created from the delight of expression, and in the contemplation that is born of the minute and delicate arrangement of images, happiness, and health of mind. Some early poems have a morbid melancholy, and he himself spoke of early work he had destroyed as morbid, for as yet the craftsmanship was not fine enough to bring the artist's joy which is of one substance with that of sanctity.[21] In one poem he waits at some street-corner for a friend, a woman perhaps, and while he waits and gradually understands that nobody is coming, he sees two funerals and shivers at the future; and in another written on his twenty-fifth birthday, he wonders if the twenty-five years to come shall be as evil as those gone by.[22] Later on, he can see himself as but a part of the spectacle of the world and mix into all he sees that flavour of extravagance, or of humour, or of philosophy, that makes one understand that he contemplates even his own death as if it were another's and finds in his own destiny but as it were a projection through a burning-glass of that general to men. There is in the creative joy an acceptance of what life brings, because we have understood the beauty of what it brings, or a hatred of death for what it takes away, which arouses within us, through some sympathy perhaps with all other men, an energy so noble, so powerful, that we laugh aloud and mock, in the terror or the sweetness of our exaltation, at death and oblivion.

In no modern writer that has written of Irish life before him, except it may be Miss Edgeworth in *Castle Rackrent,* was there anything to change a man's thought about the world or stir his moral nature, for they but play with pictures, persons and events, that whether well or ill observed are but an amusement for the mind where it escapes from meditation, a child's show that makes the fables of his art as significant by contrast as some procession painted on an Egyptian wall; for in these fables, an intelligence, on which the tragedy of the world had been thrust in so few years, that Life had no time to brew her sleepy drug, has spoken of the moods that are the expression of its wisdom.[23] All minds that have a wisdom come of tragic reality seem morbid to those that are accustomed to writers who have not faced reality at all; just as the saints, with that Obscure Night of the Soul, which fell so certainly that they numbered it among spiritual states, one among other ascending steps, seem morbid to the rationalist and the old-fashioned Protestant controversialist. The thoughts of journalists, like the thoughts of the Irish novelists, are neither healthy nor unhealthy, not having risen to that state where either is possible, nor should we call them happy; for who, if happiness were not the supreme attainment of man, would have sought it in heroic toils, in the cell of the ascetic, or imagined it above the cheerful newspapers, above the clouds?

## VII

Not that Synge brought out of the struggle with himself any definite philosophy, for philosophy in the common meaning of the word is created out of an anxiety for sympathy or obedience, and he was that rare, that distinguished, that most noble thing, which of all things still of the world is nearest to being sufficient to itself, the pure artist. Sir Philip Sidney complains of those who could hear 'sweet tunes' (by which he understands could look upon his lady) and not be stirred to 'ravishing delight.'

Or if they do delight therein, yet are so closed with wit,
As with sententious lips to set a title vain on it;
Oh let them hear these sacred tunes, and learn in Wonder's schools
To be, in things past bonds of wit, fools if they be not fools![24]

Ireland for three generations has been like those churlish logicians. Everything is argued over, everything has to take its trial before the dull sense and the hasty judgement, and the character of the nation has so changed that it hardly keeps but among country-people, or where some family tradition is still stubborn, those lineaments that made Borrow cry out as he came from among the Irish monks—his friends and entertainers for all his Spanish Bible scattering—'Oh, Ireland, mother of the bravest soldiers and of the most beautiful women!'[25] It was, as I believe, to seek that old Ireland which took its mould from the duellists and scholars of the eighteenth century and from generations older still, that Synge returned again and again to Aran, to Kerry, and to the wild Blaskets.[26]

## VIII

'When I got up this morning,' he writes, after he had been a long time in Inishmaan, 'I found that the people had gone to Mass and latched the kitchen door from the outside, so that I could not open it to give myself light.

'I sat for nearly an hour beside the fire with a curious feeling that I should be quite alone in this little cottage. I am so used to sitting here with the people that I have never felt the room before as a place where any man might live and work by himself. After a while as I waited, with just light enough from the chimney to let me see the rafters and the greyness of the walls, I became indescribably mournful, for I felt that this little corner on the face of the world, and the people who live in it, have a peace and dignity from which we are shut for ever.'[27]

This life, which he describes elsewhere as the most primitive left in Europe, satisfied some necessity of his nature. Before I met him in Paris he had wandered over much of Europe, listening to stories in the Black Forest, making friends with servants and with poor people, and this from an æsthetic interest, for he had gathered no statistics, had no money to give, and cared nothing for the wrongs of the poor, being content to pay for the pleasure of eye and ear with a tune upon the fiddle.[28] He did not love them the better because they were poor and miserable, and it was only when he found Inishmaan and the Blaskets, where there is neither riches nor poverty, neither what he calls 'the nullity of the rich' nor 'the squalor of the poor,' that his writing lost its old morbid brooding, that he found his genius and his peace.[29] Here were men and women who under the weight of their necessity lived, as the artist lives, in the presence of death and childhood, and the great affections and the orgiastic moment when life outleaps its limits, and who, as it is always with those who have refused or escaped the trivial and the temporary, had dignity and good manners where manners mattered. Here above all was silence from all our great orator took delight in, from formidable men, from moral indignation, from the 'sciolist' who 'is never sad,' from all in modern life that would destroy the arts; and here, to take a thought from another playwright of our school, he could love Time as only women and great artists do and need never sell it.[30]

## IX

As I read *The Aran Islands* right through for the first time since he showed it me in manuscript, I come to understand how much knowledge of the real life of Ireland went to the creation of a world which is yet as fantastic as the Spain of Cervantes. Here is the story of *The Playboy,* of *The Shadow of the Glen;* here is the ghost on horseback and the finding of the young man's body of *Riders to the Sea,* numberless ways of speech and vehement pictures that had seemed to owe nothing to observation, and all to some overflowing of himself, or to some mere necessity of dramatic construction.[31] I had thought the violent quarrels of *The Well of the Saints* came from his love of bitter condiments, but here is a couple that quarrel all day long amid neighbours who gather as for a play.[32] I had defended the burning of Christy Mahon's leg on the ground that an artist need but make his characters self-consistent, and yet, that too was observation, for 'although these people are kindly towards each other and their children, they have no sympathy for the suffering of animals, and little sympathy for pain when the person who feels it is not in danger.' I had thought it was in the wantonness of fancy Martin Doul accused the smith of plucking his living ducks, but a few lines farther on, in this book where moral indignation is unknown, I read, 'Sometimes when I go into a cottage, I find all the women of the place down on their knees plucking the feathers from live ducks and geese.'[33]

He loves all that has edge, all that is salt in the mouth, all that is rough to the hand, all that heightens the emotions by contest, all that stings into life the sense of tragedy; and in this book, unlike the plays where nearness to his audience moves him to mischief, he shows it without thought of other taste than his. It is so constant, it is all set out so simply, so naturally, that it suggests a correspondence between a lasting mood of the soul and this life that shares the harshness of rocks and wind. The food of the spiritual-minded is sweet, an Indian scripture says, but passionate minds love bitter food.[34] Yet he is no indifferent observer, but is certainly kind and sympathetic to all about him. When an old and ailing man, dreading the coming winter, cries at his leaving, not thinking to see him again, and he notices that the old man's mitten has a hole in it where the palm is accustomed to the stick, one knows that it is with eyes full of interested affection as befits a simple man and not in the curiosity of study.[35] When he had left the Blaskets for the last time, he travelled with a lame pensioner who had drifted there, why Heaven knows, and one morning having missed him from the inn where they were staying, he believed he had gone back to the island, and searched everywhere and questioned everybody, till he understood of a sudden that he was jealous as though the island were a woman.[36]

The book seems dull if you read much at a time, as the later Kerry essays do not, but nothing that he has written recalls so completely to my senses the man as he was in daily life; and as I read, there are moments when every line of his face, every inflection of his voice, grows so clear in memory that I cannot realise that he is dead. He was no nearer when we walked and talked than now while I read these unarranged, unspeculating pages, wherein the only life he loved with his whole heart reflects itself as in the still water of a pool. Thought comes to him slowly, and only after long seemingly unmeditative watching, and when it comes (and he had the same character in matters of business), it is spoken without hesitation and never changed. His conversation was not an experimental thing, an instrument of research, and this made him silent; while his essays recall events, on which one feels that he pronounces no judgement even in the depth of his own mind, because the labour of Life itself had not yet brought the philosophic generalisation, which was almost as much his object as the emotional generalisation of beauty. A mind that generalises rapidly, continually prevents the experience that would have made it feel and see deeply, just as a man whose character is too complete in youth seldom grows into any energy of moral beauty. Synge had indeed no obvious ideals, as these are understood by young men, and even as I think disliked them, for he once complained to me that our modern poetry was but the poetry 'of the lyrical boy,' and this lack makes his art have a strange wildness and coldness, as of a man born in some far-off spacious land and time.[37]

## X

There are artists like Byron, like Goethe, like Shelley, who have impressive personalities, active wills and all their faculties at the service of the will; but he belonged to those who, like Wordsworth, like Coleridge, like Goldsmith, like Keats, have little personality, so far as the casual eye can see, little personal will, but fiery and brooding imagination. I cannot imagine him anxious to impress, or convince in any company, or saying more than was sufficient to keep the talk circling. Such men have the advantage that all they write is a part of knowledge, but they are powerless before events and have often but one visible strength, the strength to reject from life and thought all that would mar their work, or deafen them in the doing of it; and only this so long as it is a passive act. If Synge had married young or taken some profession, I doubt if he would have written books or been greatly interested in a movement like ours; but he refused various opportunities of making money in what must have been an almost unconscious preparation. He had no life outside his imagination, little interest in anything that was not its chosen subject. He hardly seemed aware of the existence of other writers. I never knew if he cared for work of mine, and do not remember that I had from him even a conventional compliment, and yet he had the most perfect modesty and simplicity in daily intercourse, self-assertion was impossible to him. On the other hand, he was useless amidst sudden events. He was much shaken by the *Playboy* riot; on the first night confused and excited, knowing not what to do, and ill before many days, but it made no difference in his work. He neither exaggerated out of defiance nor softened out of timidity. He wrote on as if nothing had happened, altering *The Tinker's Wedding* to a more unpopular form, but writing a beautiful serene *Deirdre,* with, for the first time since his *Riders to the Sea,* no touch of sarcasm or defiance.[38] Misfortune shook his physical nature while it left his intellect and his moral nature untroubled. The external self, the mask, the *persona,* was a shadow, character was all.

## XI

He was a drifting silent man full of hidden passion, and loved wild islands, because there, set out in the light of day, he saw what lay hidden in himself. There is passage after passage in which he dwells upon some moment of excitement. He describes the shipping of pigs at Kilronan on the North Island for the English market:

'When the steamer was getting near, the whole drove was moved down upon the slip and the curraghs were carried out close to the sea. Then each beast was caught in its turn and thrown on its side, while its legs were hitched together in a single knot, with a tag of rope remaining, by which it could be carried.

'Probably the pain inflicted was not great, yet the animals shut their eyes and shrieked with almost human intonations, till the suggestion of the noise became so intense that the men and women who were merely looking on grew wild with excitement, and the pigs waiting their turn foamed at the mouth and tore each other with their teeth.

'After a while there was a pause. The whole slip was covered with a mass of sobbing animals, with here and there a terrified woman crouching among the bodies and patting some special favourite, to keep it quiet while the curraghs were being launched. Then the screaming began again while the pigs were carried out and laid in their places, with a waistcoat tied round their feet to keep them from damaging the canvas. They seemed to know where they were going, and looked up at me over the gunnel with an ignoble desperation that made me shudder to think that I had eaten this whimpering flesh. When the last curragh went out, I was left on the slip with a band of women and children, and one old boar who sat looking out over the sea.

'The women were over-excited, and when I tried to talk to them they crowded round me and began jeering and shrieking at me because I am not married. A dozen screamed at a time, and so rapidly that I could not understand all they were saying, yet I was able to make out that they were taking advantage of the absence of their husbands to give me the full volume of their contempt. Some little boys who were listening threw themselves down, writhing with laughter among the seaweed, and the young girls grew red and embarrassed and stared down in the surf.'[39]

The book is full of such scenes. Now it is a crowd going by train to the Parnell celebration, now it is a woman cursing her son who made himself a spy for the police, now it is an old woman keening at a funeral.[40] Kindred to his delight in the harsh grey stones, in the hardship of the life there, in the wind and in the mist, there is always delight in every moment of excitement, whether it is but the hysterical excitement of the women over the pigs, or some primary passion. Once indeed, the hidden passion instead of finding expression by its choice among the passions of others shows itself in the most direct way of all, that of dream. 'Last night,' he writes, at Inishmaan, 'after walking in a dream among buildings with strangely intense light on them, I heard a faint rhythm of music beginning far away on some stringed instrument.

'It came closer to me, gradually increasing in quickness and volume with an irresistibly definite progression. When it was quite near the sound began to move in my nerves and blood, to urge me to dance with them.

'I knew that if I yielded I would be carried away into some moment of terrible agony, so I struggled to remain quiet, holding my knees together with my hands.

'The music increased continually, sounding like the strings of harps tuned to a forgotten scale, and having a resonance as searching as the strings of the 'cello.

'Then the luring excitement became more powerful than my will, and my limbs moved in spite of me.

'In a moment I swept away in a whirlwind of notes. My breath and my thoughts and every impulse of my body became a form of the dance, till I could not distinguish between the instrument or the rhythm and my own person or consciousness.

'For a while it seemed an excitement that was filled with joy; then it grew into an ecstasy where all existence was lost in the vortex of movement. I could not think that there had been a life beyond the whirling of the dance.

'Then with a shock, the ecstasy turned to agony and rage. I struggled to free myself but seemed only to increase the passion of the steps I moved to. When I shrieked I could only echo the notes of the rhythm.

'At last, with a movement of uncontrollable frenzy I broke back to consciousness and awoke.

'I dragged myself trembling to the window of the cottage and looked out. The moon was glittering across the bay and there was no sound anywhere on the island.'[41]

## XII

In all drama which would give direct expression to reverie, to the speech of the soul with itself, there is some device that checks the rapidity of dialogue. When Œdipus speaks out of the most vehement passions, he is conscious of the presence of the Chorus, men before whom he must keep up appearances, 'children latest born of Cadmus' line' who do not share his passion.[42] Nobody is hurried or breathless. We listen to reports and discuss them, taking part as it were in a council of State. Nothing happens before our eyes. The dignity of Greek drama, and in a lesser degree of that of Corneille and Racine, depends, as contrasted with the troubled life of Shakespearian drama, on an almost even speed of dialogue, and on a so continuous exclusion of the animation of common life, that thought remains lofty and language rich. Shakespeare, upon whose stage everything may happen, even the blinding of Gloucester, and who has no formal check except what is implied in the slow, elaborate structure of blank verse, obtains time for reverie by an often encumbering Euphuism, and by such a loosening of his plot as will give his characters the leisure to look at life from without.[43] Maeterlinck—to name the first modern of the old way who comes to mind—reaches the same end, by choosing instead of human beings persons who are as faint as a breath upon a looking-glass, symbols who can speak a language slow and heavy with dreams because their own life is but a dream.[44] Modern drama, on the other hand, which accepts the tightness of the classic plot, while expressing life directly, has been driven to make indirect its expression of the mind, which it leaves to be inferred from some commonplace sentence or gesture as we infer it in ordinary life; and this is, I believe, the cause of the perpetual disappointment of the hope imagined this hundred years that France or Spain or Germany or Scandinavia would at last produce the master we await.

The divisions in the arts are almost all in the first instance technical, and the great schools of drama have been divided from one another by the form or the metal of their mirror, by the check chosen for the rapidity of dialogue. Synge found the check that suited his temperament in an elaboration of the dialects of Kerry and Aran. The cadence is long and meditative, as befits the thought of men who are much alone, and who when they meet in one another's houses—as their way is at the day's end—listen patiently, each man speaking in turn and for some little time, and taking pleasure in the vaguer meaning of the words and in their sound. Their thought, when not merely practical, is as full of traditional wisdom and extravagant pictures as that of some Æschylean chorus, and no matter what the topic is, it is as though the present were held at arm's length. It is the reverse of rhetoric, for the speaker serves his own delight, though doubtless he would tell you that like Raftery's whiskey-drinking it was but for the company's sake.[45] A medicinal manner of speech too, for it could not even express, so little abstract it is and so rammed with life, those worn generalisations of national propaganda. 'I'll be telling you the finest story you'd hear any place from Dundalk to Ballinacree with great queens in it, making themselves matches from the start to the end, and they with shiny silks on them. . . . I've a grand story of the great queens of Ireland, with white necks on them the like of Sarah Casey, and fine arms would hit you a slap. . . . What good am I this night, God help me? What good are the grand stories I have when it's few would listen to an old woman, few but a girl maybe would be in great fear the time her hour was come, or little child wouldn't be sleeping with the hunger on a cold night.'[46] That has the flavour of Homer, of the Bible, of Villon, while Cervantes would have thought it sweet in the mouth though not his food.[47] This use of Irish dialect for noble purpose by Synge, and by Lady Gregory, who had it already in her *Cuchulain of Muirthemne,* and by Dr. Hyde in those first translations he has not equalled since, has done much for National dignity.[48] When I was a boy I was often troubled and sorrowful because Scottish dialect was capable of noble use, but the Irish of obvious roystering humour only; and this error fixed on my imagination by so many novelists and rhymers made me listen badly. Synge wrote down words and phrases wherever he went, and with that knowledge of Irish which made all our country idioms easy to his hand, found it so rich a thing, that he had begun translating into it fragments of the great literatures of the world, and had planned a complete version of *The Imitation of Christ.*[49] It gave him imaginative richness and yet left to him the sting and tang of reality. How vivid in his translation from Villon are those 'eyes with a big gay look out of them would bring folly from a great scholar'![50] More vivid surely than anything in Swinburne's version, and how noble those words which are yet simple country speech, in which his Petrarch mourns that death came upon Laura just as time was making chastity easy, and the day come when 'lovers may sit together and say out all things are in their hearts,' and 'my sweet enemy was making a start, little by little, to give over her great wariness, the way she was wringing a sweet thing out of my sharp sorrow.'[51]

## XIII

I remember saying once to Synge that though it seemed to me that a conventional descriptive passage encumbered the action at the moment of crisis, I liked *The Shadow of the Glen* better than *Riders to the Sea,* that seemed for all the nobility of its end, its mood of Greek tragedy, too passive in suffering, and had quoted from Matthew Arnold's introduction to *Empedocles on Etna* to prove my point.[52] Synge answered: 'It is a curious thing that *Riders to the Sea* succeeds with an English but not with an Irish audience, and *The Shadow of the Glen,* which is not liked by an English audience, is always liked in Ireland, though it is disliked there in theory.' Since then *Riders to the Sea* has grown into great popularity in Dublin, partly because with the tactical instinct of an Irish mob, the demonstrators against *The Playboy* both in the press and in the theatre, where it began the evening, selected it for applause. It is now what Shelley's 'Cloud' was for many years, a comfort to those who do not like to deny altogether the genius they cannot understand.[53] Yet I am certain that, in the long run, his grotesque plays with their lyric beauty, their violent laughter, *The Playboy of the Western World* most of all, will be loved for holding so much of the mind of Ireland. Synge has written of *The Playboy:* 'Any one who has lived in real intimacy with the Irish peasantry will know that the wildest sayings in this play are tame indeed compared with the fancies one may hear at any little hillside cottage of Geesala, or Carraroe, or Dingle Bay.'[54] It is the strangest, the most beautiful expression in drama of that Irish fantasy which overflowing through all Irish literature that has come out of Ireland itself (compare the fantastic Irish account of the Battle of Clontarf with the sober Norse account) is the unbroken character of Irish genius.[55] In modern days this genius has delighted in mischievous extravagance, like that of the Gaelic poet's curse upon his children: 'There are three things that I hate: the Devil that is waiting for my soul; the worms that are waiting for my body; my children, who are waiting for my wealth and care neither for my body nor my soul: Oh, Christ, hang all in the same noose!'[56] I think those words were spoken with a delight in their vehemence that took out of anger half the bitterness with all the gloom. An old man on the Aran Islands told me the very tale on which *The Playboy* is founded, beginning with the words: 'If any gentleman has done a crime we'll hide him. There was a gentleman that killed his father, and I had him in my own house six months till he got away to America.'[57] Despite the solemnity of his slow speech his eyes shone as the eyes must have shone in that Trinity College branch of the Gaelic League which began every meeting with prayers for the death of an old Fellow of College who disliked their movement, or as they certainly do when patriots are telling how short a time the prayers took to the killing of him.[58] I have seen a crowd, when certain Dublin papers had wrought themselves into an imaginary loyalty, so possessed by what seemed the very genius of satiric fantasy, that one all but looked to find some feathered heel among the cobble stones.[59] Part of the delight of crowd or individual is always that somebody will be angry, somebody take the sport for gloomy earnest. We are mocking at his solemnity, let us therefore so hide our malice that he may be more solemn still, and the laugh run higher yet. Why should we speak his language and so wake him from a dream of all those emotions which men feel because they should, and not because they must? Our minds, being sufficient to themselves, do not wish for victory but are content to elaborate our extravagance, if fortune aid, into wit or lyric beauty, and as for the rest, 'There are nights when a king like Conchobar would spit upon his arm-ring and queens will stick out their tongues at the rising moon.'[60] This habit of the mind has made Oscar Wilde and Mr. Bernard Shaw the most celebrated makers of comedy to our time, and if it has sounded plainer still in the conversation of the one, and in some few speeches of the other, that is but because they have not been able to turn out of their plays an alien trick of zeal picked up in struggling youth. Yet, in Synge's plays also, fantasy gives the form and not the thought, for the core is always as in all great art, an overpowering vision of certain virtues, and our capacity for sharing in that vision is the measure of our delight. Great art chills us at first by its coldness or its strangeness, by what seems capricious, and yet it is from these qualities it has authority, as though it had fed on locust and wild honey. The imaginative writer shows us the world as a painter does his picture, reversed in a looking-glass that we may see it, not as it seems to eyes habit has made dull, but as we were Adam and this the first morning; and when the new image becomes as little strange as the old we shall stay with him, because he has, besides the strangeness, not strange to him, that made us share his vision, sincerity that makes us share his feeling.[61]

To speak of one's emotions without fear or moral ambition, to come out from under the shadow of other men's minds, to forget their needs, to be utterly oneself, that is all the Muses care for. Villon, pander, thief and man-slayer, is as immortal in their eyes, and illustrates in the cry of his ruin as great a truth as Dante in abstract ecstasy, and touches our compassion more.[62] All art is the disengaging of a soul from place and history, its suspension in a beautiful or terrible light to await the Judgement, though it must be, seeing that all its days were a Last Day, judged already. It may show the crimes of Italy as Dante did, or Greek mythology like Keats, or Kerry and Galway villages, and so vividly that ever after I shall look at all with like eyes, and yet I know that Cino da Pistoia thought Dante unjust, that Keats knew no Greek, that those country men and women are neither so lovable nor so lawless as 'mine author sung it me'; that I have added to my being, not my knowledge.[63]

## XIV

I wrote the most of these thoughts in my diary on the coast of Normandy, and as I finished came upon Mont Saint Michel, and thereupon doubted for a day the foundation of my school.[64] Here I saw the places of assembly, those cloisters on the rock's summit, the church, the great halls where monks, or knights, or men-at-arms sat at meals, beautiful from ornament or proportion. I remembered ordinances of the Popes forbidding drinking-cups with stems of gold to these monks who had but a bare dormitory to sleep in.[65] The individual, even in imagining, had taken more from his fellows and his fathers than he gave; one man finishing what another had begun; and all that majestic fantasy, seeming more of Egypt than of Christendom, spoke nothing to the solitary soul, but seemed to announce whether past or yet to come an heroic temper of social men, a bondage of adventure and of wisdom. Then I thought more patiently and I saw that what had made these but as one and given them for a thousand years the miracles of their shrine and temporal rule by land and sea, was not a condescension to knave or dolt, an impoverishment of the common thought to make it serviceable and easy, but a dead language and a communion in whatever, even to the greatest saint, is of incredible difficulty.[66] Only by the substantiation of the soul I thought, whether in literature or in sanctity, can we come upon those agreements, those separations from all else, that fasten men together lastingly; for while a popular and picturesque Burns and Scott can but create a province, and our Irish cries and grammars serve some passing need, Homer, Shakespeare, Dante, Goethe and all who travel in their road define races and create everlasting loyalties.

Synge, like all of the great kin, sought for the race, not through the eyes or in history, or even in the future, but where those monks found God, in the depths of the mind, and in all art like his, although it does not command—indeed because it does not—may lie the roots of far-branching events. Only that which does not teach, which does not cry out, which does not persuade, which does not condescend, which does not explain, is irresistible. It is made by men who expressed themselves to the full, and it works through the best minds; whereas the external and picturesque and declamatory writers, that they may create kilts and bagpipes and newspapers and guide-books, leave the best minds empty, and in Ireland and Scotland, England runs into the hole. It has no array of arguments and maxims, because the great and the simple (and the Muses have never known which of the two most pleases them) need their deliberate thought for the day's work, and yet will do it worse if they have not grown into or found about them, most perhaps in the minds of women, the nobleness of emotion associated with the scenery and events of their country by those great poets who have dreamed it in solitude, and who to this day in Europe are creating indestructible spiritual races, like those religion has created in the East.

SEPTEMBER 14, 1910.

# JOHN SHAWE-TAYLOR

There is a portrait of John Shawe-Taylor by a celebrated painter in the Dublin Municipal Gallery, but painted in the midst of a movement of the arts that exalts characteristics above the more typical qualities, it does not show us that beautiful and gracious nature.[1] There is an exaggeration of the hollows of the cheeks and of the form of the bones which empties the face of the balance and delicacy of its lines. He was a very handsome man, as women who have imagination and tradition understand those words, and had he not been so, mind and character had been different. There are certain men, certain famous commanders of antiquity, for instance, of whose good looks the historian always speaks, and whose good looks are the image of their faculty; and these men copying hawk or leopard have an energy of swift decision, a power of sudden action, as if their whole body were their brain.

A few years ago he was returning from America, and the liner reached Queenstown in a storm so great that the tender that came out to it for passengers returned with only one man. It was John Shawe-Taylor, who had leaped as it was swept away from the ship.[2]

The achievement that has made his name historic and changed the history of Ireland came from the same faculty of calculation and daring, from that instant decision of the hawk, between the movement of whose wings and the perception of whose eye no time passes capable of division. A proposal for a Land Conference had been made, and cleverer men than he were but talking the life out of it. Every argument for and against had been debated over and over, and it was plain that nothing but argument would come of it. One day we found a letter in the daily papers, signed with his name, saying that a conference would be held on a certain date, and that certain leaders of the landlords and of the tenants were invited.[3] He had made his swift calculation, probably he could not have told the reason for it: a decision had arisen out of his instinct. He was then almost an unknown man. Had the letter failed, he would have seemed a crack-brained fool to his life's end; but the calculation of his genius was justified. He had, as men of his type have often, given an expression to the hidden popular desires; and the expression of the hidden is the daring of the mind. When he had spoken, so many others spoke that the thing was taken out of the mouths of the leaders, it was as though some power deeper than our daily thought had spoken, and men recognised that common instinct, that common sense which is genius. Men like him live near this power because of something simple and impersonal within them which is, as I believe, imaged in the fire of their minds, as in the shape of their bodies and their faces.

I do not think I have known another man whose motives were so entirely pure, so entirely unmixed with any personal calculation, whether of ambition, of prudence or of vanity. He caught up into his imagination the public gain as other men their private gain. For much of his life he had seemed, though a good soldier and a good shot, and a good rider to hounds, to care deeply for nothing but religion, and this religion, so curiously lacking in denominational limits, concerned itself alone with the communion of the soul with God. Such men, before some great decision, will sometimes give to the analysis of their own motive the energy that other men give to the examination of the circumstances wherein they act, and it is often those who attain in this way to purity of motive who act most wisely at moments of great crisis. It is as though they sank a well through the soil where our habits have been built, and where our hopes take root or lie uprooted, to the lasting rock and to the living stream. They are those for whom Tennyson claimed the strength of ten, and the common and clever wonder at their simplicity and at a triumph that has always an air of miracle.[4]

Some two years ago Ireland lost a great æsthetic genius, and it may be it should mourn, as it must mourn John Synge always, that which is gone from it in this young man's moral genius.[5] And yet it may be that the sudden flash of his mind was of those things that come but seldom in a lifetime, and that his work is as fully accomplished as though he had lived through many laborious years.

July 1, 1911.

# ART AND IDEAS

## I

Two days ago I was at the Tate Galleries to see the early Millais's, and before his *Ophelia* as before the *Mary Magdalene* and *Mary of Galilee* of Rossetti that hung near, I recovered an old emotion. I saw these pictures as I had seen pictures in my childhood.[1] I forgot the art criticism of friends and saw wonderful, sad, happy people, moving through the scenery of my dreams. The painting of the hair, the way it was smoothed from its central parting, something in the oval of the peaceful faces, called up memories of sketches of my father's on the margins of the first Shelley I had read, while the strong colours made me half remember studio conversations, words of Wilson, or of Potter perhaps, praise of the primary colours, heard, it may be, as I sat over my toys or a child's story-book.[2] One picture looked familiar, and suddenly I remembered it had hung in our house for years. It was Potter's *Field Mouse*.[3] I had learned to think in the midst of the last phase of Pre-Raphaelitism and now I had come to Pre-Raphaelitism again and rediscovered my earliest thought.[4] I murmured to myself, 'The only painting of modern England that could give pleasure to a child, the only painting that would seem as moving as the *Pilgrim's Progress* or Hans[†] Andersen.'[5] 'Am I growing old,' I thought, 'like the woman in Balzac, the rich bourgeois' ambitious wife, who could not keep, when old age came upon her, from repeating the jokes of the concierge's lodge, where she had been born and bred; or is it because of some change in the weather that I find beauty everywhere, even in Burne-Jones's *King Cophetua,* one of his later pictures, and find it without shame?'[6] I have had like admiration many times in the last twenty years, for I have always loved these pictures where I meet persons associated with the poems or the religious ideas that have most moved me; but never since my boyhood have I had it without shame, without the certainty that I would hear the cock crow presently. I remembered that as a young man I had read in Schopenhauer that no man—so unworthy a thing is life seen with unbesotted eyes—would live another's life, and had thought I would be content to paint like Burne-Jones and Morris under Rossetti's rule the Union at Oxford, to set up there the traditional images most moving to young men while the adventure of uncommitted life can still change all to romance, even though I should know that what I painted must fade from the walls.[7]

II

Thereon I ask myself if my conception of my own art is altering, if there, too, I praise what I once derided. When I began to write I avowed for my principles those of Arthur Hallam in his essay upon Tennyson.[8] Tennyson, who had written but his early poems when Hallam wrote, was an example of the school of Keats and Shelley, and Keats and Shelley, unlike Wordsworth, intermixed into their poetry no elements from the general thought, but wrote out of the impression made by the world upon their delicate senses. They were of the æsthetic school—was he the inventor of the name?—and could not be popular because their readers could not understand them without attaining to a like delicacy of sensation and so must needs turn from them to Wordsworth or another, who condescended to moral maxims, or some received philosophy, a multitude of things that even common sense could understand. Wordsworth had not less genius than the others—even Hallam allowed his genius—we are not told that Mary of Galilee was more beautiful than the more popular Mary; but certainly we might consider Wordsworth a little disreputable.[9]

I developed these principles to the rejection of all detailed description, that I might not steal the painter's business, and indeed I was always discovering some art or science that I might be rid of: and I found encouragement by noticing all round me painters* who were

*This thought, which seemed a discovery, was old enough. Balzac derides in a story a certain Pierre Grassou who attained an immense popularity by painting a Chouan rebel going to his death. 1924.[10]

ridding their pictures, and indeed their minds, of literature. Yet those delighted senses, when I had got from them all that I could, left me discontented. Impressions that needed so elaborate a record did not seem like the handiwork of those careless old writers one imagines squabbling over a mistress, or riding on a journey, or drinking round a tavern fire, brisk and active men. Crashaw could hymn St. Teresa in the most impersonal of ecstasies and seem no sedentary man out of reach of common sympathy, no disembodied mind, and yet in his day the life that appeared most rich and stirring was already half-forgotten with Villon and Dante.[11]

This difficulty was often in my mind, but I put it aside, for the new formula was a good switch while the roads were beset with geese; it set us free from politics, theology, science, all that zeal and eloquence Swinburne and Tennyson found so intoxicating after the passion of their youth had sunk, free from the conventional nobility borne hither from ancient Rome in the galley that carried academic form to vex the painters.[12] Among the little group of poets that met at the Cheshire Cheese I alone loved criticism of Arthur Hallam's sort, with a shamefaced love—criticism founded upon general ideas was itself an impurity—and perhaps I alone knew Hallam's essay, but all silently obeyed a canon that had become powerful for all the arts since Whistler, in the confidence of his American *naïveté,* had told everybody that Japanese painting had no literary ideas.[13] Yet all the while envious of the centuries before the Renaissance, before the coming of our intellectual class with its separate interests, I filled my imagination with the popular beliefs of Ireland, gathering them up among forgotten novelists in the British Museum or in Sligo cottages. I sought some symbolic language reaching far into the past and associated with familiar names and conspicuous hills that I might not be alone amid the obscure impressions of the senses, and I wrote essays recommending my friends to paint on chapel walls the Mother of God flying with St. Joseph into Egypt along some Connacht road, a Connemara shawl about her head, or mourned the richness or reality lost to Shelley's *Prometheus Unbound* because he had not discovered in England or in Ireland his Caucasus.[14]

I notice like contradictions among my friends who are still convinced that art should not be 'complicated by ideas' while picturing St. Brandon in stained glass for a Connemara chapel, and even among those exuberant young men who make designs for a Phallic Temple, but consider Augustus John lost amid literature.[15]

## III

But after all could we clear the matter up we might save some hours from sterile discussion. The arts are very conservative and have a great respect for those wanderers who still stitch into their carpets among the Mongolian plains religious symbols so old they have not even a meaning. It cannot be they would lessen an association with one another and with religion that gave them authority among ancient peoples. They are not radicals, and if they deny themselves to any it can only be to the *nouveau riche,* and if they have grown rebellious it can only be against something that is modern, something that is not simple.

I think that before the religious change that followed on the Renaissance men were greatly preoccupied with their sins, and that to-day they are troubled by other men's sins, and that this trouble has created a moral enthusiasm so full of illusion that art, knowing itself for sanctity's scapegrace brother, cannot be of the party. We have but held to our ancient Church, where there is an altar and no pulpit, and founded, the guide-book tells us, upon the ruins of the temple of Jupiter Ammon, and turned away from the too great vigour of those, who, living for mutual improvement, have a pulpit and no altar.[16] We fear that a novel enthusiasm might make us forget the little round of poetical duties and imitations—humble genuflexions and circumambulations as it were—that does not unseat the mind's natural impulse, and seems always but half-conscious, almost bodily.

Painting had to free itself from a Classicalism that denied the senses, a domesticity that denied the passions, and poetry from a demagogic system of morals which destroyed the humility, the daily dying of the imagination in the presence of beauty. A soul shaken by the spectacle of its sins, or discovered by the Divine Vision in tragic delight, must offer to the love that cannot love but to infinity a goal, unique and unshared; while a soul busied with others' sins is soon melted to some shape of vulgar pride. What can I offer to God but the ghost that must return undisfeatured to the hands that have not made the same thing twice, but what would I have of others but that they do some expected thing, reverence my plans, be in some way demure and reliable. The turning of Rossetti to religious themes, his dislike of Wordsworth were but the one impulse, for he more than any other was in reaction against the period of philanthropy and reform that created the pedantic composure of Wordsworth, the rhetoric of Swinburne, the passionless sentiment of Tennyson.[17] The saint does not claim to be a good example, hardly even to tell men what to do, for is he not the chief of sinners, and of how little can he be certain whether in the night of the soul or lost in the sweetness coming after? Nor can that composure of the moralists be dear to one who has heard the commandment, that is for the saint and his brother the poet alike, 'Make excess ever more abundantly excessive' even were it possible to one shaken and trembling from his daily struggle.[18]

## IV

We knew that system of popular instruction was incompatible with our hopes, but we did not know how to refute it and so turned away from all ideas. We would not even permit ideas, so greatly had we come to distrust them, to leave their impressions upon our senses. Yet works of art are always begotten by previous works of art, and every masterpiece becomes the Abraham of a chosen people.[19] When we delight in a spring day there mixes, perhaps, with our personal emotion an emotion Chaucer found in Guillaume de Lorris, who had it from the poetry of Provence; we celebrate our draughty May with an enthusiasm made ripe by more meridian suns; and all our art has its image in the Mass that would lack authority were it not descended from savage ceremonies taught amid what perils and by what spirits to naked savages.[20] The old images, the old emotions, awakened again to overwhelming life, like the Gods Heine tells of, by the belief and passion of some new soul are the only masterpieces.[21] The resolution to stand alone, to owe nothing to the past, when it is not mere sense of property, the greed and pride of the counting-house, is the result of that individualism of the Renaissance which had done its work when it gave us personal freedom. The soul which may not obscure or change its form can yet receive those passions and symbols of antiquity, certain they are too old to be bullies, too well mannered not to respect the rights of others.

Nor had we better warrant to separate one art from another, for there has been no age before our own wherein the arts have been other than a single authority, a Holy Church of Romance, the might of all lying behind all, a circle of cliffs, a wilderness where every cry has its echoes. Why should a man cease to be a scholar, a believer, a ritualist before he begin to paint or rhyme or to compose music, or why if he have a strong head should he put away any means of power?

## V

Yet it is plain that the casting out of ideas was the more natural, misunderstanding though it was, because it had come to matter very little. The manner of painting had changed, and we were interested in the fall of drapery and the play of light without concerning ourselves with the meaning, the emotion of the figure itself. How many successful portrait painters gave their sitters the same attention, the same interest they might have given to a ginger-beer bottle and an apple? and in our poems an absorption in fragmentary sensuous beauty or detachable ideas, had deprived us of the power to mould vast material into a single image. What long modern poem equals the old poems in architectural unity, in symbolic importance? *The Revolt of Islam, The Excursion, Gebir, The Idylls of the King,* even perhaps *The Ring and the Book,* which fills me with so much admiring astonishment that my judgement sleeps, are remembered for some occasional passage, some moment which gains little from the context.[22] Until very lately even the short poems which contained as clearly as an Elizabethan Lyric the impression of a single idea seemed accidental, so much the rule were the 'Faustines' and 'Dolores' where the verses might be arranged in any order, like shot poured out of a bag.[23] Arnold when he withdrew his *Empedocles on Etna,* though one had been sorry to lose so much lyrical beauty for ever, showed himself a great critic by his reasons, but his *Sohrab and Rustum* proved that the unity he imagined was a classical imitation and not an organic thing, not the flow of flesh under the impulse of passionate thought.[24]

Those poets with whom I feel myself in sympathy have tried to give to little poems the spontaneity of a gesture or of some casual emotional phrase. Meanwhile it remains for some greater time, living once more in passionate reverie, to create a *King Lear*, a *Divine Comedy*, vast worlds moulded by their own weight like drops of water.[25]

In the visual arts, indeed, 'the fall of man into his own circumference' seems at an end, and when I look at the photograph of a picture by Gauguin, which hangs over my breakfast table, the spectacle of tranquil Polynesian girls crowned with lilies gives me, I do not know why, religious ideas.[26] Our appreciations of the older schools are changing too, becoming simpler, and when we take pleasure in some Chinese painting of an old man, meditating upon a mountain path, we share his meditation, without forgetting the beautiful intricate pattern of the lines like those we have seen under our eyelids as we fell asleep; nor do the Bride and Bridegroom of Rajput painting, sleeping upon a house-top, or wakening when out of the still water the swans fly upward at the dawn, seem the less well painted because they remind us of many poems.[27] We are becoming interested in expression in its first phase of energy, when all the arts play like children about the one chimney and turbulent innocence can yet amuse those brisk and active men who have paid us so little attention of recent years. Shall we be rid of the pride of intellect, of sedentary meditation, of emotion that leaves us when the book is closed or the picture seen no more; and live amid the thoughts that can go with us by steam-boat and railway as once upon horse-back,[†] or camel-back, rediscovering, by our re-integration of the mind, our more profound Pre-Raphaelitism, the old abounding, nonchalant reverie?

1913.

# EDMUND SPENSER

## I

We know little of Spenser's childhood and nothing of his parents, except that his father was probably an Edmund Spenser of north-east Lancashire, a man of good blood and 'belonging to a house of ancient fame.'[1] He was born in London in 1552, nineteen years after the death of Ariosto, and when Tasso was about eight years old.[2] Full of the spirit of the Renaissance, at once passionate and artificial, looking out upon the world now as craftsman, now as connoisseur, he was to found his art upon theirs rather than upon the more humane, the more noble, the less intellectual art of Malory and the Minstrels.[3] Deafened and blinded by their influence, as so many of us were in boyhood by that art of Hugo, that made the old simple writers seem but as brown bread and water, he was always to love the journey more than its end, the landscape more than the man, and reason more than life, and the tale less than its telling.[4] He entered Pembroke College, Cambridge, in 1569, and translated allegorical poems out of Petrarch and Du Bellay.[5] To-day a young man translates out of Verlaine and Verhaeren; but at that day Ronsard and Du Bellay were the living poets, who promised revolutionary and unheard-of things to a poetry moving towards elaboration and intellect, as ours—the serpent's tooth in his own tail again—moves towards simplicity and instinct.[6] At Cambridge he met with Hobbinol of *The Shepheards Calender,* a certain Gabriel Harvey, son of a rope-maker at Saffron Walden, but now a Fellow of Pembroke College, a notable man, some five or six years his elder.[7] It is usual to think ill of Harvey because of his dislike of rhyme and his advocacy of classical metres, and because he complained that Spenser preferred his *Faerie Queene* to the *Nine Muses,* and encouraged Hobgoblin to 'run off with the Garland of Apollo.'[8] But at that crossroad, where so many crowds mingled talking of so many lands, no one could foretell in what bed he would sleep after nightfall. Milton was in the end to dislike rhyme as much, and it is certain that rhyme is one of the secondary causes of that disintegration of the personal instincts which has given to modern poetry its deep colour for colour's sake, its overflowing pattern, its background of decorative landscape, and its insubordination of detail.[9] At the opening of a movement we are busy with first principles, and can find out everything but the road we are to go, everything but the weight and measure of the impulse, that has come to us out of life itself, for that is always in defiance of reason, always without a justification but by faith and works. Harvey set Spenser to the making of verses in classical metre, and certain lines have come down to us written in what Spenser called 'Iambicum trimetrum.'[10] His biographers agree that they are very bad, but, though I cannot scan them,* I find in them the charm of what seems a sincere personal emotion. The man himself, liberated from the minute felicities of phrase and sound, that are the temptation and the delight of rhyme, speaks of his Mistress some thought that came to him not for the sake of poetry, but for love's sake, and the emotion instead of dissolving into detached colours, into 'the spangly gloom' that Keats saw 'froth and boil' when he put his eyes into 'the pillowy cleft,' speaks to her in poignant words as if out of a tear-stained love-letter:[11]

> Unhappie verse, the witnesse of my unhappie state,
> Make thy selfe fluttring winge for thy fast flying
> Thought, and fly forth to my love wheresoever she be.
> Whether lying restlesse in heavy bedde, or else
> Sitting so cheerlesse at the cheerful boorde, or else
> Playing alone carelesse on her heavenlie virginals.
> If in bed, tell her that my eyes can take no rest;
> If at boorde tell her that my mouth can eat no meate;
> If at her virginals, tell her that I can heare no mirth.[12]

*I could not scan them because I accentuated them unconsciously. Spoken without accent they are musical. 1924.

## II

He left College in his twenty-fourth year, and stayed for a while in Lancashire, where he had relations, and there fell in love with one he has written of in *The Shepheards Calender* as 'Rosalind, the widdowes daughter of the Glenn,' though she was, for all her shepherding, as one learns from a College friend, 'a gentle-woman of no mean house.'[13] She married Menalcas of the *Calender* and Spenser lamented her for years, in verses so full of disguise that one cannot say if his lamentations come out of a broken heart or are but a useful movement in the elaborate ritual of his poetry, a well-ordered incident in the mythology of his imagination.[14] To no English poet, perhaps to no European poet before his day, had the natural expression of personal feeling been so impossible, the clear vision of the lineaments of human character so difficult; no other's head and eyes had sunk so far into the pillowy cleft. After a year of this life he went to London, and by Harvey's advice and introduction entered the service of the Earl of Leicester, staying for a while in his house on the banks of the Thames; and it was there in all likelihood that he met with the Earl's nephew, Sir Philip Sidney, still little more than a boy, but with his head full of affairs of State.[15] One can imagine that it was the great Earl or Sir Philip Sidney that gave his imagination its moral and practical turn, and one imagines him seeking from philosophical men, who distrust instinct because it disturbs contemplation, and from practical men who distrust everything they cannot use in the routine of immediate events, that impulse and method of creation that can only be learned with surety from the technical criticism of poets, and from the excitement of some movement in the artistic life. Marlowe and Shakespeare were still at school, and Ben Jonson was but five years old.[16] Sidney was doubtless the greatest personal influence that came into Spenser's life, and it was one that exalted moral zeal above every faculty. The great Earl impressed his imagination very deeply also, for the lamentation over the Earl of Leicester's death is more than a conventional Ode to a dead patron. Spenser's verses about men, nearly always indeed, seem to express more of personal joy and sorrow than those about women, perhaps because he was less deliberately a poet when he spoke of men. At the end of a long beautiful passage he laments that unworthy men should be in the dead Earl's place, and compares them to the fox—an unclean feeder—hiding in the lair 'the badger swept.'[17] The imaginer of the festivals of Kenilworth was indeed the fit patron for him, and alike, because of the strength and weakness of Spenser's art, one regrets that he could not have lived always in that elaborate life, a master of ceremony to the world, instead of being plunged into a life that but stirred him to bitterness, as the way is with theoretical minds in the tumults of events they cannot understand.[18] In the winter of 1579–80 he published *The Shepheards Calender,* a book of twelve eclogues, one for every month of the year, and dedicated it to Sir Philip Sidney. It was full of pastoral beauty and allegorical images of current events, revealing too that conflict between the æsthetic and moral interests that was to run through well-nigh all his works, and it became immediately famous. He was rewarded with a place as private secretary to the Lord-Lieutenant, Lord Grey de Wilton, and sent to Ireland, where he spent nearly all the rest of his life.[19] After a few years there he bought Kilcolman Castle, which had belonged to the rebel Earl of Desmond, and the rivers and hills about this castle came much into his poetry.[20] Our Irish Aubeg is 'Mulla mine, whose waves I taught to weep,' and the Ballyvaughan Hills it has its rise among, 'old Father Mole.' He never pictured the true countenance of Irish scenery, for his mind turned constantly to the courts of Elizabeth and to the umbrageous level lands, where his own race was already seeding like a great poppy:

> Both heaven and heavenly graces do much more
> (Quoth he), abound in that same land then this:
> For there all happie peace and plenteous store
> Conspire in one to make contented blisse.
> No wayling there nor wretchednesse is heard,
> No bloodie issues nor no leprosies,
> No griesly famine, nor no raging sweard,
> No nightly bordrags, nor no hue and cries;
> The shepheards there abroad may safely lie
> On hills and downes, withouten dread or daunger,
> No ravenous wolves the good mans hope destroy,
> Nor outlawes fell affray the forest raunger,

The learned arts do florish in great honor,
And Poets wits are had in peerlesse price.[21]

Nor did he ever understand the people he lived among or the historical events that were changing all things about him. Lord Grey de Wilton had been recalled almost immediately, but it was his policy, brought over ready-made in his ship, that Spenser advocated throughout all his life, equally in his long prose book *The Present State of Ireland* as in the *Faerie Queene,* where Lord Grey was Artegall and the Iron Man the soldiers and executioners by whose hands he worked.[22] Like an hysterical patient he drew a complicated web of inhuman logic out of the bowels of an insufficient premise—there was no right, no law, but that of Elizabeth, and all that opposed her opposed themselves to God, to civilisation, and to all inherited wisdom and courtesy, and should be put to death. He made two visits to England, celebrating one of them in *Colin Clouts come Home againe,* to publish the first three books and the second three books of the *Faerie Queene* respectively, and to try for some English office or pension.[23] By the help of Raleigh, now his neighbour at Kilcolman, he had been promised a pension, but was kept out of it by Lord Burleigh, who said, 'All that for a song!'[24] From that day Lord Burleigh became that 'rugged forehead' of the poems, whose censure of this or that is complained of. During the last three or four years of his life in Ireland he married a fair woman of his neighbourhood, and about her wrote many intolerable artificial sonnets and that most beautiful passage in the sixth book of the *Faerie Queene,* which tells of Colin Clout piping to the Graces and to her; and he celebrated his marriage in the most beautiful of all his poems, the *Epithalamium.*[25] His genius was pictorial, and these pictures of happiness were more natural to it than any personal pride, or joy, or sorrow. His new happiness was very brief, and just as he was rising to something of Milton's grandeur in the fragment that has been called *Mutabilitie,* 'the wandering companies that keep the wood,' as he called the Irish armies, drove him to his death.[26] Ireland, where he saw nothing but work for the Iron Man, was in the midst of the last struggle of the old Celtic order with England, itself about to turn bottom upward, of the passion of the Middle Ages with the craft of the Renaissance. Seven years after Spenser's arrival in Ireland a large merchant ship had carried off from

Lough Swilly, by a very crafty device common in those days, certain persons of importance. Red Hugh, a boy of fifteen, and the coming head of Tir Conaill, and various heads of clans had been enticed on board the merchant ship to drink of a fine vintage, and there made prisoners.[27] All but Red Hugh were released, on finding substitutes among the boys of their kindred, and the captives were hurried to Dublin and imprisoned in the Birmingham Tower. After four years of captivity and one attempt that failed, Red Hugh and certain of his companions escaped into the Dublin mountains, one dying there of cold and privation, and from that to their own country-side. Red Hugh allied himself to Hugh O'Neill, the most powerful of the Irish leaders, an Oxford man too, a man of the Renaissance, in Camden's words 'a profound dissembling heart so as many deemed him born either for the great good or ill of his country,' and for a few years defeated English armies and shook the power of England.[28] The Irish, stirred by these events, and with it maybe some rumours of *The Present State of Ireland* sticking in their stomachs, drove Spenser out of doors and burnt his house, one of his children, as tradition has it, dying in the fire. He fled to England, and died some three months later in January 1599, as Ben Jonson says, 'of lack of bread.'[29]

During the last four or five years of his life he had seen, without knowing that he saw it, the beginning of the great Elizabethan poetical movement. In 1598 he had pictured the Nine Muses lamenting each one over the evil state in England, of the things that she had in charge, but, like William Blake's more beautiful 'Whether on Ida's shady brow,' their lamentations should have been a cradle-song.[30] When he died *Romeo and Juliet, Richard III.*, and *Richard II.*, and the plays of Marlowe had all been acted, and in stately houses were sung madrigals and love songs whose like has not been in the world since.[31] Italian influence had strengthened the old French joy that had never died out among the upper classes, and an art was being created for the last time in England which had half its beauty from continually suggesting a life hardly less beautiful than itself.

## III

When Spenser was buried at Westminster Abbey many poets read verses in his praise, and then threw their verses and the pens that had written them into his tomb.[32] Like him they belonged, for all the moral zeal that was gathering like a London fog, to that indolent, demonstrative Merry England that was about to pass away. Men still wept when they were moved, still dressed themselves in joyous colours, and spoke with many gestures. Thoughts and qualities sometimes come to their perfect expression when they are about to pass away, and Merry England was dying in plays, and in poems, and in strange adventurous men. If one of those poets who threw his copy of verses into the earth that was about to close over his master were to come alive again, he would find some shadow of the life he knew, though not the art he knew, among young men in Paris, and would think that his true country. If he came to England he would find nothing there but the triumph of the Puritan and the merchant—those enemies he had feared and hated—and he would weep perhaps, in that womanish way of his, to think that so much greatness had been, not as he had hoped, the dawn, but the sunset of a people. He had lived in the last days of what we may call the Anglo-French nation, the old feudal nation that had been established when the Norman and the Angevin made French the language of court and market.[33] In the time of Chaucer English poets still wrote much in French, and even English labourers lilted French songs over their work; and I cannot read any Elizabethan poem or romance without feeling the pressure of habits of emotion, and of an order of life which were conscious, for all their Latin gaiety, of a quarrel to the death with that new Anglo-Saxon nation that was arising amid Puritan sermons and Marprelate pamphlets.[34] This nation had driven out the language of its conquerors, and now it was to overthrow their beautiful haughty imagination and their manners, full of abandon and wilfulness, and to set in their stead earnestness and logic and the timidity and reserve of a counting-house. It had been coming for a long while, for it had made the Lollards; and when Anglo-French Chaucer was at Westminster its poet, Langland, sang the office at St. Paul's.[35] Shakespeare, with his delight in great persons, with his indifference to the State, with his scorn of the crowd, with his feudal passion, was of the old nation, and Spenser, though a joyless earnestness had cast shadows upon him, and darkened his intellect wholly at times, was of the old nation too. His *Faerie Queene* was written in Merry England, but when Bunyan wrote in prison the other great English allegory, Modern England had been born.[36] Bunyan's men would do right that they might come some day to the Delectable Mountains, and not at all that they might live happily in a world whose beauty was but an entanglement about their feet. Religion had denied the sacredness of an earth that commerce was about to corrupt and ravish, but when Spenser lived the earth had still its sheltering sacredness. His religion, where the paganism that is natural to proud and happy people had been strengthened by the platonism of the Renaissance, cherished the beauty of the soul and the beauty of the body with, as it seemed, an equal affection.[37] He would have had men live well, not merely that they might win eternal happiness but that they might live splendidly among men and be celebrated in many songs. How could one live well if one had not the joy of the Creator and of the Giver of gifts? He says in his 'Hymne in Honour of Beautie' that a beautiful soul, unless for some stubbornness in the ground, makes for itself a beautiful body, and he even denies that beautiful persons ever lived who had not souls as beautiful.[38] They may have been tempted until they seemed evil, but that was the fault of others. And in his 'Hymne of Heavenly Beautie' he sets a woman little known to theology, one that he names Wisdom or Beauty, above Seraphim and Cherubim and in the very bosom of God, and in the *Faerie Queene* it is pagan Venus and her lover Adonis who create the forms of all living things and send them out into the world, calling them back again to the gardens of Adonis at their lives' end to rest there, as it seems, two thousand years between life and life.[39] He began in English poetry, despite a temperament that delighted in sensuous beauty alone with perfect delight, that worship of Intellectual Beauty which Shelley carried to a greater subtlety and applied to the whole of life.[40]

The qualities, to each of whom he had planned to give a Knight, he had borrowed from Aristotle and partly Christianised, but not to the forgetting of their heathen birth. The chief of the Knights, who would have combined in himself the qualities of all the others, had Spenser lived to finish the *Faerie Queene,* was King Arthur, the representative of an ancient quality, Magnificence.[41] Born at the moment of change, Spenser had indeed many Puritan thoughts. It has been recorded that he cut his hair short and half regretted his hymns to Love and Beauty. But he has himself told us that the many-headed beast overthrown and bound by Calidor, Knight of Courtesy, was

Puritanism itself.[42] Puritanism, its zeal and its narrowness, and the angry suspicion that it had in common with all movements of the ill-educated, seemed no other to him than a slanderer of all fine things. One doubts, indeed, if he could have persuaded himself that there could be any virtue at all without courtesy, perhaps without something of pageant and eloquence. He was, I think, by nature altogether a man of that old Catholic feudal nation, but, like Sidney, he wanted to justify himself to his new masters. He wrote of knights and ladies, wild creatures imagined by the aristocratic poets of the twelfth century, and perhaps chiefly by English poets who had still the French tongue; but he fastened them with allegorical nails to a big barn-door of common sense, of merely practical virtue. Allegory itself had risen into general importance with the rise of the merchant class in the thirteenth and fourteenth centuries; and it was natural when that class was about for the first time to shape an age in its image, that the last epic poet of the old order should mix its art with his own long-descended, irresponsible, happy art.

## IV

Allegory and, to a much greater degree, symbolism are a natural language by which the soul when entranced, or even in ordinary sleep, communes with God and with angels. They can speak of things which cannot be spoken of in any other language, but one will always, I think, feel some sense of unreality when they are used to describe things which can be described as well in ordinary words. Dante used allegory to describe visionary things, and the first maker of *The Romance of the Rose,* for all his lighter spirits, pretends that his adventures came to him in a vision one May morning; while Bunyan, by his preoccupation with heaven and the soul, gives his simple story a visionary strangeness and intensity: he believes so little in the world, that he takes us away from all ordinary standards of probability and makes us believe even in allegory for a while.[43] Spenser, on the other hand, to whom allegory was not, as I think, natural at all, makes us feel again and again that it disappoints and interrupts our preoccupation with the beautiful and sensuous life he has called up before our eyes. It interrupts us most when he copies Langland, and writes in what he believes to be a mood of edification, and the least when he is not quite serious, when he sets before us some procession like a court pageant made to celebrate a wedding or a crowning. One cannot think that he should have occupied himself with moral and religious questions at all. He should have been content to be, as Emerson thought Shakespeare was, a Master of the Revels to mankind.[44] I am certain that he never gets that visionary air which can alone make allegory real, except when he writes out of a feeling for glory and passion. He had no deep moral or religious life. He has never a line like Dante's 'Thy Will is our Peace,' or like Thomas à Kempis's 'The Holy Spirit has liberated me from a multitude of opinions,' or even like Hamlet's objection to the bare bodkin.[45] He had been made a poet by what he had almost learnt to call his sins. If he had not felt it necessary to justify his art to some serious friend, or perhaps even to 'that rugged forehead,' he would have written all his life long, one thinks, of the loves of shepherdesses and shepherds, among whom there would have been perhaps the morals of the dovecot. One is persuaded that his morality is official and impersonal—a system of life which it was his duty to support—and it is perhaps a half understanding of this that has made so many generations believe that he was the first poet laureate, the first salaried moralist among the poets.[46] His processions of deadly sins, and his houses, where the very cornices are arbitrary images of virtue, are an unconscious hypocrisy, an undelighted obedience to the 'rugged forehead,' for all the while he is thinking of nothing but lovers whose bodies are quivering with the memory or the hope of long embraces. When they are not together, he will indeed embroider emblems and images much as those great ladies of the courts of love embroidered them in their castles; and when these are imagined out of a thirst for magnificence and not thought out in a mood of edification, they are beautiful enough; but they are always tapestries for corridors that lead to lovers' meetings or for the walls of marriage chambers. He was not passionate, for the passionate feed their flame in wanderings and absences, when the whole being of the beloved, every little charm of body and of soul, is always present to the mind, filling it with heroical subtleties of desire. He is a poet of the delighted senses, and his song becomes most beautiful when he writes of those islands of Phædria and Acrasia, which angered 'that rugged forehead,' as it seems, but gave to Keats his 'Belle Dame sans

Merci' and his 'perilous seas in faery lands forlorn,' and to William Morris his 'Water of the Wondrous Isles.'[47]

## V

The dramatists lived in a disorderly world, reproached by many, persecuted even, but following their imagination wherever it led them. Their imagination, driven hither and thither by beauty and sympathy, put on something of the nature of eternity. Their subject was always the soul, the whimsical, self-awakening, self-exciting, self-appeasing soul. They celebrated its heroical, passionate will going by its own path to immortal and invisible things. Spenser, on the other hand, except among those smooth pastoral scenes and lovely effeminate islands that have made him a great poet, tried to be of his time, or rather of the time that was all but at hand. Like Sidney, whose charm it may be led many into slavery, he persuaded himself that we enjoy Virgil because of the virtues of Æneas, and so planned out his immense poem that it would set before the imagination of citizens, in whom there would soon be no great energy, innumerable blameless Æneases.[48] He had learned to put the State, which desires all the abundance for itself, in the place of the Church, and he found it possible to be moved by expedient emotions, merely because they were expedient, and to think serviceable thoughts with no self-contempt. He loved his Queen a little because she was the protectress of poets and an image of that old Anglo-French nation that lay a-dying, but a great deal because she was the image of the State which had taken possession of his conscience. She was over sixty years old, ugly and historians will have it selfish, but in his poetry she is 'fair Cynthia,' 'a crown of lilies,' 'the image of the heavens,' 'without mortal blemish,' and has 'an angelic face,' where 'the red rose' has 'meddled with the white'; 'Phœbus thrusts out his golden head' but to look upon her, and blushes to find himself outshone. She is 'a fourth Grace,' 'a queen of love,' 'a sacred saint,' and 'above all her sex that ever yet has been.'[49] In the midst of his praise of his own sweetheart he stops to remember that Elizabeth is more beautiful, and an old man in 'Daphnaida,' although he has been brought to death's door by the death of a beautiful daughter, remembers that though his daughter 'seemed of angelic race,' she was yet but the primrose to the rose beside Elizabeth.[50] Spenser had learned to look to the State not only as the rewarded of virtue but as the maker of right and wrong, and had begun to love and hate as it bid him. The thoughts that we find for ourselves are timid and a little secret, but those modern thoughts that we share with large numbers are confident and very insolent. We have little else to-day, and when we read our newspaper and take up its cry, above all its cry of hatred, we will not think very carefully, for we hear the marching feet. When Spenser wrote of Ireland he wrote as an official, and out of thoughts and emotions that had been organised by the State. He was the first of many Englishmen to see nothing but what he was desired to see. Could he have gone there as a poet merely, he might have found among its poets more wonderful imaginations than even those islands of Phædria and Acrasia. He would have found among wandering story-tellers, not indeed his own power of rich, sustained description, for that belongs to lettered ease, but certainly all the kingdom of Faerie, still unfaded, of which his own poetry was often but a troubled image. He would have found men doing by swift strokes of the imagination much that he was doing with painful intellect, with that imaginative reason that soon was to drive out imagination altogether and for a long time. He would have met with, at his own door, story-tellers among whom the perfection of Greek art was indeed as unknown as his own power of sustained description, but who, none the less, imagined or remembered beautiful incidents and strange, pathetic outcrying that made them of Homer's lineage. Flaubert says somewhere: 'There are things in Hugo, as in Rabelais, that I could have mended, things badly built, but then what thrusts of power beyond the reach of conscious art!'[51] Is not all history but the coming of that conscious art which first makes articulate and then destroys the old wild energy? Spenser, the first poet struck with remorse, the first poet who gave his heart to the State, saw nothing but disorder, where the mouths that have spoken all the fables of the poets had not yet become silent. All about him were shepherds and shepherdesses still living the life that made Theocritus and Virgil think of shepherd and poet as the one thing; but though he dreamed of Virgil's shepherds he wrote a book to advise, among many like things, the harrying of all that followed flocks upon the hills, and of all 'the wandering companies that keep the wood.'[52] His *View of the Present State of Ireland* commends indeed the beauty of the hills and woods where they did their shepherding, in that powerful and subtle language of his which I sometimes think more full of youthful energy than even the language of the great playwrights. He is 'sure it is yet a most beautiful and sweet country as any under heaven,' and that all would prosper but for those agitators, 'those wandering companies that keep the wood,' and he would rid it of them by a certain expeditious way. There should be four great garrisons. 'And those fowre garrisons issuing foorthe, at such convenient times as they shall have intelligence or espiall upon the enemye, will so drive him from one side to another and tennis him amongst them, that he shall finde nowhere safe to keepe his creete, or hide himselfe, but flying from the fire shall fall into the water, and out of one daunger into another, that in short space his creete, which is his moste sustenence, shall be wasted in preying, or killed in driving, or starved for wante of pasture in the woodes, and he himselfe brought soe lowe, that he shall have no harte nor abilitye to indure his wretchednesse, the which will surely come to passe in very short space; for one winters well following of him will so plucke him on his knees that he will never be able to stand up agayne.'

He could commend this expeditious way from personal knowledge, and could assure the Queen that the people of the country would soon 'consume themselves and devoure one another. The proofs whereof I saw sufficiently ensampled in these late warres of Mounster; for notwithstanding that the same was a most rich and plentifull countrey, full of corne and cattell, that you would have thought they would have bene able to stand long, yet ere one yeare and a halfe they were brought to such wretchednesse, as that any stonye harte would have rued the same. Out of every corner of the woodes and glynnes they came creeping forth upon theyr hands, for theyr legges could not beare them; they looked like anatomyes of death, they spake like ghosts crying out of their graves; they did eate of the dead carrions, happy were they if they could finde them, yea, and one another soone after, insomuch as the very carcasses they spared not to scrape out of theyr graves; and if they found a plot of watercresses or shamrokes, there they flocked as to a feast for the time, yet not able long to continue therewithall; that in short space there were none allmost left, and a most populous and plentifull countrey suddaynely left voyde of man or beast; yet sure in all that warre, there perished not many by the sword, but all by the extremitye of famine.'[53]

## VI

In a few years the Four Masters were to write the history of that time, and they were to record the goodness or the badness of Irishman and Englishman with entire impartiality.[54] They had seen friends and relatives persecuted, but they would write of that man's poisoning and this man's charities and of the fall of great houses, and hardly with any other emotion than a thought of the pitiableness of all life. Friend and enemy would be for them a part of the spectacle of the world. They remembered indeed those Anglo-French invaders who conquered for the sake of their own strong hand, and when they had conquered became a part of the life about them, singing its songs, when they grew weary of their own Iseult and Guinevere.[55] But famines and exterminations had not made them understand, as I think, that new invaders were among them, who fought for an alien State, for an alien religion. Such ideas were difficult to them, for they belonged to the old individual, poetical life, and spoke a language even, in which it was all but impossible to think an abstract thought. They understood Spain, possibly, which persecuted in the interests of religion, but I doubt if anybody in Ireland could have understood as yet that the Anglo-Saxon nation was beginning to persecute in the service of ideas it believed to be the foundation of the State. I doubt if anybody in Ireland saw that with certainty, till the Great Demagogue had come and turned the old house of the noble into 'the house of the Poor, the lonely house, the accursed house of Cromwell.'[56] He came, another Cairbry Cathead, with that great rabble, who had overthrown the pageantry of Church and Court, but who turned towards him faces full of the sadness and docility of their long servitude, and the old individual, poetical life went down, as it seems, for ever.[57] He had studied Spenser's book and approved of it, as we know, finding, doubtless, his own head there, for Spenser, a king of the old race, carried a mirror which showed kings yet to come though but kings of the mob. Those Bohemian poets of the theatres were wiser, for the States that touched them nearly were the States where Helen and Dido had sorrowed, and so their mirrors showed none but beautiful heroical heads.[58] They wandered in the places that pale passion loves, and were happy, as one thinks, and troubled little about those marching and hoarse-throated thoughts that the State has in its pay. They knew that those marchers, with the dust of so many roads upon them, are very robust and have great and well-paid generals to write expedient despatches in sound prose; and they could hear mother earth singing among her cornfields:

> Weep not, my wanton! smile upon my knee;
> When thou art old there's grief enough for thee.[59]

## VII

There are moments when one can read neither Milton nor Spenser, moments when one recollects nothing but that their flesh had partly been changed to stone, but there are other moments when one recollects nothing but those habits of emotion that made the lesser poet especially a man of an older, more imaginative time. One remembers that he delighted in smooth pastoral places, because men could be busy there or gather together there, after their work, that he could love handiwork and the hum of voices. One remembers that he could still rejoice in the trees, not because they were images of loneliness and meditation, but because of their serviceableness. He could praise 'the builder oake,' 'the aspine, good for staves,' 'the cypresse funerall,' 'the eugh, obedient to the bender's will,' 'the birch for shaftes,' 'the sallow for the mill,' 'the mirrhe sweete-bleeding in the bitter wound,' 'the fruitful olive,' and 'the carver holme.'[60] He was of a time before undelighted labour had made the business of men a desecration. He carries one's memory back to Virgil's and Chaucer's praise of trees, and to the sweet-sounding song made by the old Irish poet in their praise.

I got up from reading the *Faerie Queene* the other day and wandered into another room. It was in a friend's house, and I came of a sudden to the ancient poetry and to our poetry side by side—an engraving of Claude's *Mill* hung under an engraving of Turner's *Temple of Jupiter*.[61] Those dancing country-people, those cowherds, resting after the day's work, and that quiet mill-race made one think of Merry England with its glad Latin heart, of a time when men in every land found poetry and imagination in one another's company and in the day's labour. Those stately goddesses, moving in slow procession towards that marble architrave among mysterious trees, belong to Shelley's thought, and to the religion of the wilderness—the only religion possible to poetry to-day. Certainly Colin Clout, the companionable shepherd, and Calidore, the courtly man-at-arms, are gone, and Alastor is wandering from lonely river to river finding happiness in nothing but in that star where Spenser too had imagined the fountain of perfect things.[62] This new beauty, in losing so much, has indeed found a new loftiness, a something of religious exaltation that the old had not. It may be that those goddesses, moving with a majesty like a procession of the stars, mean something to the soul of man that those kindly women of the old poets did not mean, for all the fullness of their breasts and the joyous gravity of their eyes. Has not the wilderness been at all times a place of prophecy?

## VIII

Our poetry, though it has been a deliberate bringing back of the Latin joy and the Latin love of beauty, has had to put off the old marching rhythms, that once could give delight to more than expedient hearts, in separating itself from a life where servile hands have become powerful. It has ceased to have any burden for marching shoulders, since it learned ecstasy from Smart in his mad cell, and from Blake, who made joyous little songs out of almost unintelligible visions, and from Keats, who sang of a beauty so wholly preoccupied with itself that its contemplation is a kind of lingering trance.[63] The poet, if he would not carry burdens that are not his and obey the orders of servile lips, must sit apart in contemplative indolence playing with fragile things.

If one chooses at hazard a Spenserian stanza out of Shelley and compares it with any stanza by Spenser, one sees the change, though it would be still more clear if one had chosen a lyrical passage. I will take a stanza out of *Laon and Cythna,* for that is story-telling and runs nearer to Spenser than the meditative *Adonais:*

> The meteor to its far morass returned:
> The beating of our veins one interval

Made still; and then I felt the blood that burned
Within her frame, mingle with mine, and fall
Around my heart like fire; and over all
A mist was spread, the sickness of a deep
And speechless swoon of joy, as might befall
Two disunited spirits when they leap
In union from this earth's obscure and fading sleep.[64]

The rhythm is varied and troubled, and the lines, which are in Spenser like bars of gold thrown ringing one upon another, are broken capriciously. Nor is the meaning the less an inspiration of indolent muses, for it wanders hither and thither at the beckoning of fancy. It is now busy with a meteor and now with throbbing blood that is fire, and with a mist that is a swoon and a sleep that is life. It is bound together by the vaguest suggestion, while Spenser's verse is always rushing on to some preordained thought. 'A popular poet' can still indeed write poetry of the will, just as factory girls wear the fashion of hat or dress the moneyed classes wore a year ago, but 'popular poetry' does not belong to the living imagination of the world. Old writers gave men four temperaments, and they gave the sanguineous temperament to men of active life, and it is precisely the sanguineous temperament that is fading out of poetry and most obviously out of what is most subtle and living in poetry—its pulse and breath, its rhythm. Because poetry belongs to that element in every race which is most strong, and therefore most individual, the poet is not stirred to imaginative activity by a life which is surrendering its freedom to ever new elaboration, organisation, mechanism. He has no longer a poetical will, and must be content to write out of those parts of himself which are too delicate and fiery for any deadening exercise. Every generation has more and more loosened the rhythm, more and more broken up and disorganised, for the sake of subtlety of detail, those great rhythms which move, as it were, in masses of sound. Poetry has become more spiritual, for the soul is of all things the most delicately organised, but it has lost in weight and measure and in its power of telling long stories and of dealing with great and complicated events. *Laon and Cythna,* though I think it rises sometimes into loftier air than the *Faerie Queene;* and *Endymion,* though its shepherds and wandering divinities have a stranger and more intense beauty than

Spenser's, have need of too watchful and minute attention for such lengthy poems.[65] In William Morris, indeed, one finds a music smooth and unexacting like that of the old story-tellers, but not their energetic pleasure, their rhythmical wills. One too often misses in his *Earthly Paradise* the minute ecstasy of modern song without finding that old happy-go-lucky tune that had kept the story marching.[66]

Spenser's contemporaries, writing lyrics or plays full of lyrical moments, write a verse more delicately organised than his and crowd more meaning into a phrase than he, but they could not have kept one's attention through so long a poem. A friend who has a fine ear told me the other day that she had read all Spenser with delight and yet could remember only four lines. When she repeated them they were from the poem by Matthew Roydon, which is bound up with Spenser because it is a commendation of Sir Philip Sidney:

A sweet, attractive kind of grace,
A full assurance given by looks,
Continual comfort in a face,
The lineaments of Gospel books.[67]

Yet if one were to put even these lines beside a fine modern song one would notice that they had a stronger and rougher energy, a featherweight more, if eye and ear were fine enough to notice it, of the active will, of the happiness that comes out of life itself.

## IX

I have put into this book* only those passages from Spenser that I want to remember and carry about with me. I have not tried to select what people call characteristic passages, for that is, I think, the way to make a dull book. One never really knows anybody's taste but one's own, and if one likes anything sincerely one may be certain that there are other people made out of the same earth to like it too. I have taken out of *The Shepheards Calender* only those parts which are about love or about old age, and I have taken out of the *Faerie*

***Poems of Spenser; Selected and with an Introduction by W. B. Yeats*. (T. C. and E. C. Jack, Edinburgh, n.d.) [1908]

*Queene* passages about shepherds and lovers, and fauns and satyrs, and a few allegorical processions. I find that though I love symbolism, which is often the only fitting speech for some mystery of disembodied life, I am for the most part bored by allegory, which is made, as Blake says, 'by the daughters of memory,' and coldly, with no wizard frenzy.[68] The processions I have chosen are either those, like the House of Mammon, that have enough ancient mythology, always an implicit symbolism, or, like the Cave of Despair, enough sheer passion to make one forget or forgive their allegory, or else they are, like that vision of Scudamour, so visionary, so full of a sort of ghostly midnight animation, that one is persuaded that they had some strange purpose and did truly appear in just that way to some mind worn out with war and trouble.[69] The vision of Scudamour is, I sometimes think, the finest invention in Spenser. Until quite lately I knew nothing of Spenser but the parts I had read as a boy. I did not know that I had read so far as that vision, but year after year this thought would rise up before me coming from I knew not where. I would be alone perhaps in some old building, and I would think suddenly 'out of that door might come a procession of strange people doing mysterious things with tumult. They would walk over the stone floor, then suddenly vanish, and everything would become silent again.' Once I saw what is called, I think, a Board School continuation class play *Hamlet*.[70] There was no stage, but they walked in procession into the midst of a large room full of visitors and of their friends. While they were walking in, that thought came to me again from I knew not where. I was alone in a great church watching ghostly kings and queens setting out upon their unearthly business.

It was only last summer, when I read the Fourth Book of the *Faerie Queene*, that I found I had been imagining over and over the enchanted persecution of Amoret.[71]

I give too, in a section which I call 'Gardens of Delight,' the good gardens of Adonis and the bad gardens of Phædria and Acrasia, which are mythological and symbolical, but not allegorical, and show, more particularly those bad islands, his power of describing bodily happiness and bodily beauty at its greatest.[72] He seemed always to feel through the eyes, imagining everything in pictures. Marlowe's *Hero and Leander* is more energetic in its sensuality, more complicated in its intellectual energy than this languid story, which pictures always a happiness that would perish if the desire to which it offers so many roses lost its indolence and its softness.[73] There is no passion in the pleasure he has set amid perilous seas, for he would have us understand that there alone could the war-worn and the sea-worn man find dateless leisure and unrepining peace.[74]

October 1902.

# Yeats's Prefaces and Dedication

# PREFACE TO *THE CUTTING OF AN AGATE* (1912)

When I wrote the essay on Edmund Spenser the company of Irish players who have now their stage at the Abbey Theatre in Dublin had been founded, but gave as yet few performances in a twelvemonth.[1] I could let my thought stray where it would, and even give a couple of summers to *The Faerie Queene*; while for some ten years now I have written little verse and no prose that did not arise out of some need of those players or some thought suggested by their work, or was written in the defence of some friend whose life has been a part of the movement of events which is creating a new Ireland unintelligible to an old Ireland that watches with anger or indifference. The detailed defence of plays and players, published originally in *Samhain,* the occasional periodical of the theatre, and now making some three hundred pages of Mr. Bullen's collected edition of my writings, is not here, but for the most part an exposition of principles, whether suggested by my own work or by the death of friend or fellow-worker, that, intended for no great public, has been printed and published from a Hand Press which my sisters manage at Dundrum with the help of the village girls.[2] I have been busy with a single art, that of the theatre, of a small, unpopular theatre; and this art may well seem to practical men, busy with some programme of industrial or political regeneration, of no more account than the shaping of an agate; and yet in the shaping of an agate, whether in the cutting or the making of the design, one discovers, if one have a speculative mind, thoughts that seem important and principles that may be applied to life itself, and certainly if one does not believe so, one is but a poor cutter of so hard a stone.

W. B. YEATS
AUGUST, 1912

# PREFACE TO *THE CUTTING OF AN AGATE* (1919, 1924)

I wrote the greater number of these essays during the ten years after 1902. During those years I wrote little verse and no prose that did not arise out of some need of the Irish players, or from some thought suggested by their work, or in the defence of some friend connected with that work, or with the movement of events that made it possible. I was busy with a single art, that of a small, unpopular theatre; and this art may well seem to practical men busy with some programme of industrial or political regeneration—and in Ireland we have many excellent programmes—of no more account than the shaping of an agate; and yet in the shaping of an agate, whether in the cutting, or in the making of the design, one discovers, if one have a speculative mind, thoughts that seem important and principles that may be applied to life itself. Certainly if one does not believe so, one is but a poor cutter of so hard a stone.

W. B. YEATS.
DECEMBER 1918.

*P.S.*—I have to thank Mr. T. C. and Mr. E. C. Jack of Edinburgh for leave to reprint the essay I wrote in their selection from Edmund Spenser before the ten years began, and while I had still time to give a couple of summers to *The Faerie Queene*.[1]

# DEDICATION OF *ESSAYS* (1924)

TO
LENNOX ROBINSON

I dedicate this book to you because I have seen your admirable little play *Crabbed Youth and Age,* and would greet the future. My friends and I loved symbols, popular beliefs, and old scraps of verse that made Ireland romantic to herself, but the new Ireland, overwhelmed by responsibility, begins to long for psychological truth. You have been set free from your work at our Abbey Theatre, which you have managed so skilfully for many years, that you may create another satirical masterpiece.[1]

W. B. YEATS
DUBLIN,
NOVEMBER 26, 1923.

# Appendices

# APPENDIX A

## A Chronological List of Essays by Date of First Publication

The dates in brackets are those provided in *Essays* (1924). The half-title pages from 1924 onward include the dates 1896–1903 for *Ideas of Good and Evil* and 1903–1915 for *The Cutting of an Agate*, creating an impression of seamless publication. As the table below indicates, correct dates of first publication of the essays would be 1895–1903 for the first volume and 1905–1916 for the second (excluding the deleted essay on Lady Gregory's translations).

### Ideas of Good and Evil

| | |
|---|---|
| August 1895 | "The Moods" (in *The Bookman* as the first paragraph of "Irish National Literature: [II]") [1895] |
| September 1895 | "The Body of the Father Christian Rosencrux" (in *The Bookman* as the first paragraph of "Irish National Literature: III") [1895] |
| July–September 1896 | "William Blake and His Illustrations to *The Divine Comedy*" (in *The Savoy*) [1897] |
| June 1897 | *"The Return of Ulysses"* (in *The Bookman* under the title "Living Poets. IV—Mr. Robert Bridges") [1896] |
| June 19, 1897 | "William Blake and the Imagination" (in *The Academy*) [1897] |
| March 1898 | "Symbolism in Painting" (as the introduction to *A Book of Images*) [1898] |
| June 1898 | "The Celtic Element in Literature" (in *Cosmopolis*) [1897] |
| December 3, 1898 | "The Autumn of the Body" (in the Dublin *Daily Express*) [1898] |
| April 1899 | "The Theatre" (Part 1 only appears in *The Dome*) [May 1899] |

| | |
|---|---|
| January 1900 | "The Theatre" (Part 2 appears in *The Dome* as part of "The Irish Literary Theatre, 1900") [February 1900] |
| April 1900 | "The Symbolism of Poetry" (in *The Dome*) [1900] |
| May–July 1900 | "The Philosophy of Shelley's Poetry" (Part 1 only published in *The Dome*) [1900] |
| May 11 and 18, 1901 | "At Stratford-on-Avon" (in *The Speaker*) [May 1901] |
| August 31, 1901 | "Ireland and the Arts" (in *The United Irishman*) [1901] |
| September 1901 | "Magic" (in *The Monthly Review*) [1901] |
| March 1902 | "What is 'Popular Poetry'?" (in *The Cornhill Magazine*) [1901] |
| May 1902 | "Speaking to the Psaltery" (in *The Monthly Review*) [sections 1–3 dated 1902; sections 4–5 dated 1907] |
| March 1903 | "The Happiest of the Poets" (in *The Fortnightly Review*) [1902] |
| | "The Galway Plains" (in *The New Liberal Review* under the title "Poets and Dreamers") [1903] |
| April 11, 1903 | "Emotion of Multitude" (in *The All Ireland Review*) [1903] |

## The Cutting of an Agate

| | |
|---|---|
| April 1902 | "Thoughts on Lady Gregory's Translations" ("I. Cuchulain and his Cycle" appeared as the preface to *Cuchulain of Muirthemne*) [not in *Essays* (1924); dated 1903 in the 1912 *The Cutting of an Agate*] |
| February 1904 | "Thoughts on Lady Gregory's Translations" ("II. Fion and his Cycle" appeared as the preface to *Gods and Fighting Men*) [not in *Essays* (1924); dated 1903 in the 1912 *The Cutting of an Agate*] |
| Early December 1905 | "Preface to the First Edition of *The Well of the Saints*" (under the title "Mr. Synge and His Plays," in *The Well of the Saints. By J. M. Synge. With An Introduction by W. B. Yeats. Being Volume Four of Plays for an Irish Theatre* [1905]) [Abbey Theatre, January 27, 1905] |

| | |
|---|---|
| Late September 1906 | "Edmund Spenser" (as the introduction to *Poems of Spenser*) [October 1902] |
| September–November 1906 | "Discoveries" (first seventeen sections printed in three installments in *The Gentleman's Magazine* as "My Thoughts and my Second Thoughts") [1906] |
| October 1907 | "Discoveries" (final four sections printed in *The Shanachie*) [1906] |
| December 1908 | "Poetry and Tradition" (in the 1908 *Collected Works in Verse and Prose*) [August 1907] |
| July 5, 1909 | "Preface to the First Edition of John M. Synge's *Poems and Translations*" (as the preface to the Cuala Press *Poems and Translations by John M. Synge*) [April 4, 1909] |
| October 1910 | "The Tragic Theatre" (in *The Mask*) [August 1910] |
| July 2, 1911 | "John Shawe-Taylor" (in *The Observer*) [July 1, 1911] |
| July 26, 1911 | "J. M. Synge and the Ireland of his Time" (in the Cuala Press *Synge and the Ireland of His Time*) [September 14, 1910] |
| June 20 and 27, 1914 | "Art and Ideas" (in *The New Weekly*) [1913] |
| September 16, 1916 | "Certain Noble Plays of Japan" (as the introduction to the Cuala Press *Certain Noble Plays of Japan*) [April 1916] |

"The Pathway" (see appendix B) first appeared in *The Speaker* for 14 April 1900 as "The Way of Wisdom." It was included under the revised title in the 1908 *Collected Works in Verse and Prose* and dated 1900–1908 there. It was not reprinted later.

# APPENDIX B

## "The Pathway" (1900, 1908)

Most of us who are writing books in Ireland to-day have some kind of a spiritual philosophy; and some among us when we look backward upon our lives see that the coming of a young Brahmin into Ireland helped to give our vague thoughts a shape.[1] When we were schoolboys we used to discuss whatever we could find to read of mystical philosophy and to pass crystals over each others' hands and eyes and to fancy that we could feel a breath flowing from them as people did in a certain German book; and one day somebody told us he had met a Brahmin in London who knew more of these things than any book.[2] With a courage which I still admire, we wrote and asked him to come and teach us, and he came with a little bag in his hand and *Marius the Epicurean* in his pocket, and stayed with one of us, who gave him a plate of rice and an apple every day at two o'clock; and for a week and all day long he unfolded what seemed to be all wisdom.[3] He sat there beautiful, as only an Eastern is beautiful, making little gestures with his delicate hands, and to him alone among all the talkers I have heard, the delight of ordered words seemed nothing, and all thought a flight into the heart of truth.

We brought him, on the evening of his coming, to a certain club which still discusses everything with that leisure which is the compensation of unsuccessful countries; and there he overthrew or awed into silence whatever metaphysics the town had.[4] And next day, when we would have complimented him, he was remorseful and melancholy, for was it not 'intellectual lust'? And sometimes he would go back over something he had said and explain to us that his argument had been a fallacy, and apologise as though he had offended against good manners. And once, when we questioned him of some event, he told us what he seemed to remember, but asked us not to give much weight to his memory, for he had found that he observed carelessly. He said, 'We Easterns are taught to state a principle carefully, but we are not taught to observe and to remember and to describe a fact. Our sense of what truthfulness is is quite different from yours.'[5] His principles were a part of his being, while our facts, though he was too polite to say it, were doubtless a part of that bodily life, which is, as he believed, an error. He certainly did hold that we lived too much to understand the truth or to live long, for he remembered that his father, who had been the first of his family for two thousand years to leave his native village, had repeated over and over upon his deathbed, 'The West is dying because of its restlessness.' Once when he had spoken of some Englishman who had gone down the crater of Vesuvius, some listener adventured: 'We like men who do that kind of thing, because a man should not think too much of his life,' but was answered solidly, 'You do not think little of your lives, but you think so much of your lives that you would enjoy them everywhere, even in the crater of Vesuvius.'[6] Somebody asked him if we should pray, but even prayer was too full of hope, of desire, of life, to have any part in that acquiescence that was his beginning of wisdom, and he answered that one should say, before sleeping: 'I have lived many lives. I have been a slave and a prince. Many a beloved has sat upon my knees, and I have sat upon the knees of many a beloved. Everything that has been shall be again.' Beautiful words, that I spoilt once by turning them into clumsy verse.[7]

Nearly all that we call education was to him but a means to bring us under the despotism of life; and I remember the bewilderment of a schoolmaster who asked about the education of children and was told to 'teach them fairy tales, and that they did not possess even their own bodies.'[8] I think he would not have taught anybody anything that had to be written in prose, for he said, very seriously, 'I have thought much about it, and I have never been able to discover any reason why prose should exist.'[9] I think he would not have trained anybody in anything but in the arts and in philosophy, which sweeps the pathway before them, for he certainly thought, as William Blake did, that the 'imagination is the man himself,' and can, if it be strong enough, work every miracle.[10] A man had come to him in London, and had said, 'My wife believes that you have the wisdom of the East and can cure her neuralgia, from which she has suffered for years.'[11] He had answered: 'Are you certain that she believes that? because, if you are, I can cure her.' He had gone to her and made a circle round her and recited a poem in Sanscrit, and she had never had neuralgia since. He recited the poem to us, and was very disappointed because we did not know by the sound that it was a description of the spring. Not only did he think that the imaginative arts were the only things that were quite sinless, but he spent more than half a day proving, by many subtle and elaborate arguments, that 'art for art's sake' was the only sinless doctrine, for any other would hide the shadow of the world as it exists in the mind of God by shadows of the accidents and illusions of life, and was but Sadducean blasphemy.[12] Religion existed also for its own sake; and every soul quivered between two emotions, the desire to possess things, to make them a portion of its egotism, and a delight in just and beautiful things for their own sake—and all religions were a doctrinal or symbolical crying aloud of this delight. He would not give his own belief a name for fear he might seem to admit that there could be religion that expressed another delight, and if one urged him too impetuously, he would look embarrassed and say, 'This body is a Brahmin.'[13] All other parts of religion were unimportant, for even our desire of immortality was no better than our other desires. Before I understood him, I asked what he would answer to one who began the discussion by denying the immortality of the soul, for the accident of a discussion with religious people had set him grafting upon this stock, and he said, 'I would say to him, What has that to do with you?'

I remember these phrases and these little fragments of argument quite clearly, for their charm and their unexpectedness has made them cling to the memory; but when I try to remember his philosophy as a whole, I cannot part it from what I myself have built about it, or have gathered in the great ruined house of 'the prophetic books' of William Blake; but I am certain that he taught us by what seemed an invincible logic that those who die, in so far as they have imagined beauty or justice, are made a part of beauty or justice, and move through the minds of living men, as Shelley believed; and that mind overshadows mind even among the living, and by pathways that lie beyond the senses; and that he measured labour by this measure, and put the hermit above all other labourers, because, being the most silent and the most hidden, he lived nearer to the Eternal Powers, and showed their mastery of the world.[14] Alcibiades fled from Socrates lest he might do nothing but listen to him all life long, and I am certain that we, seeking as youth will for some unknown deed and thought, all dreamed that but to listen to this man who threw the enchantment of power about silent and gentle things, and at last to think as he did, was the one thing worth doing and thinking; and that all action and all words that lead to action were a little vulgar, a little trivial.[15] Ah, how many years it has taken me to awake out of that dream!

1900–1908.

## Notes

This essay is a revised version of "The Way of Wisdom," *The Speaker* (14 April 1900). As of 27 June 1902, Yeats intended to include it in *Ideas of Good and Evil* (1903), informing the publisher that "I have written to the *Speaker* to send you the copy containing 'The Way of Wisdom' a short essay. I daresay it will reach you at the same time with the copy I send. There are a few misprints which I will correct in proof' (*CL3*, 210–11). It is unknown why the work was not included in the published volume. Yeats revised and retitled "The Way of Wisdom" for volume eight of the 1908 *Collected Works,* where it became the final item of "Other Essays." Yeats did not select the essay for *The Cutting of an Agate* (1912), and it was not republished thereafter.

The revisions for the 1908 printing begin with the deletion of the epigraph, Yeats's favorite quotation from *Axël* (first published as a volume in 1890) by the French writer Jean-Marie-Mathias-Philippe-Auguste, comte de Villiers de L'Isle-Adam (1838–89): "As for living, our servants will do that for us." He also deleted the second and third sentences of the opening paragraph: "I had thought to write of one whom I, at any rate, owe more than to any book years hence, when our little school had done something worthy of remembrance, or had faded in the impersonal past; but it is better to give my words time to come to his ears, perhaps, by some long and unlikely road. Even if it were no better than prudence it were well to praise the wise voices that none among them might grow weary of wisdom and not to keep silent because one's praise might have little of their wisdom." Yeats also revised the conclusion of the essay, which in 1900 read " . . . listen to him all his life, and certainly there were few among us who did not think that to listen to this man who threw the enchantment of power about silent and gentle things, and at last to think as he did, was the one thing worth doing; and that all action and all words that lead to action were a little vulgar, a little trivial; nor am I quite certain that any among us has quite awoke out of the dreams he brought among us." There were other minor revisions as well.

1. Mohini Chatterjee (1858–1936), an Indian Brahmin and an emissary of Madame Blavatsky's Theosophical Society, lectured in Dublin in April 1886. In *Reveries over Childhood and Youth,* Yeats described him as "a handsome young man with the typical face of Christ" and noted, "Consciousness, he taught, does not merely spread out its surface but has, in vision and in contemplation, another motion and can change in height and in depth" (*Au,* 98). On 29 September 1935 Yeats wrote to Chatterjee:

> I have often wondered where you were. Somebody sent me a book of yours a couple of years ago which interested me, and now I have been able to get your address through a friend. I write merely to tell you that you are vivid in my memory after all these years. That week of talk when you were in Dublin did much for my intellect, gave me indeed my first philosophical exposition of life. When I knew you, you were a very beautiful young man; I think you were twenty-seven years old, and astonished us all, learned and simple, by your dialectical power. My wife tells me that I often quote you.

2. The German book was probably *Physikalisch-physiologische Untersuchungen über die Dynamide des Magnetismus, der Elektricität, der Wärme, des Lichtes, der Kristallisation, des Chemismus in ihren Beziehungen zur Lebenskraft* (1845) by the German scientist Karl, Baron von Reichenbach (1788–1869). Two translations of the second edition (1849) were published in London: *Researches on Magnetism, Electricity, Heat, Light, Crystallization, and Chemical Attraction, in their Relations to the Vital Force* (1850), and *Physico-*

*physiological Researches on the Dynamics of Magnetism, Electricity, Heat, Light, Crystallization, and Chemism in their Relations to the Vital Force* (1850–51). Reichenbach argued that "there resides in matter a peculiar force, hitherto overlooked. . . ." Yeats noted that after reading Reichenbach, he and Charles Johnston (1867–1931), a schoolmate at the high school in Dublin who shared his interest in the occult (probably the "somebody" of this sentence), "spent a good deal of time in the Kildare Street Museum passing our hands over the glass cases, feeling or believing we felt the Odic Force flowing from big crystals" (*Au,* 97).

3. Walter Pater's *Marius the Epicurean* was published in 1885. Chatterjee's host is unidentified.
4. The Dublin Theosophical Society, formed from the Dublin Hermetic Society in April 1886.
5. In a 1909 entry in his journal, Yeats commented, "Something brings to mind that I forgot out of 'The Pathway' this saying of Mohini's. 'When I was young I was very happy. I thought that truth was something that could be conveyed from one man's mind to another's. I now know that it is a state of mind'" (*Mem,* 145).
6. Vesuvius is an active volcano near Naples in Italy.
7. In "Kanva on Himself" (*P,* 527), published only in *The Wanderings of Oisin and Other Poems* (1889). Yeats eventually rewrote the poem as "Mohini Chatterjee" (*P,* 251–52), first published in *A Packet for Ezra Pound* (1929).
8. The schoolmaster is unidentified.
9. Nevertheless, Chatterjee's "The Common Sense of Theosophy" was published in *The Dublin University Review* for May 1886. In a journal entry of October 1889, Yeats complained that although Chatterjee had made "the one adequate appeal that has been made to educated people," "he could not write decently" (*Mem,* 282).
10. Many passages in Blake suggest that "the imagination is the man himself" though not with that exact phraseology. Compare his reference to "The Real Man The Imagination which Liveth for Ever" (letter to George Cumberland, 12 April 1827) and "The Imagination is not a State: it is the Human Existence itself" (*Milton* 32.32) in Erdman, 783 and 132, respectively. Ellis-Yeats prints the letter in the "Memoir" of volume 1, page 162; plate 32 of *Milton* is missing from some copies and from editions based on them, apparently including Ellis-Yeats.
11. The couple is unidentified.
12. The Sadducees, a sect of Jews of the time of Jesus, rejected any concept not found in the first five books of the Bible. They thus denied the existence of demons and angels as well as immortality and the resurrection.
13. Presumably an error for "Brahman," god or the supreme spirit. The essential self of every individual is identical with the ultimate reality of the universe.

14. Blake's "prophetic books" include such works as *The Four Zoas, Milton,* and *Jerusalem: The Emanation of the Giant Albion.*
15. In his early years Alcibiades (ca. 450–404 BC), an Athenian statesman and general, was a pupil and intimate friend of the Greek philosopher Socrates (469–399 BC).

# APPENDIX C

## Omitted Section from "At Stratford-on-Avon"

The passage below appeared as a separate concluding section III in the original version of "At Stratford-on-Avon," published in *The Speaker: A Liberal Review* for Saturday, 11 May 1901: 159. It concerns the oral delivery of the Shakespearean plays that Yeats discussed in the previous two sections of the essay and that were staged by Sir Frank Robert Benson during the "Week of Kings" in April 1901. The actors mentioned were all part of Benson's company. Oscar Asche (1871–1936), whose name Yeats misspells, was an Australian actor, manager, and writer who toured with Benson for eight years beginning in 1893. Gertrude Constance Benson (1864–1946) met Benson in 1884 and married him in 1886; she ran an acting school in London whose most memorable alumnus was John Gielgud. Frank Rodney (1859–1902) also played Finn MacCool in the 1901 production of *Diarmuid and Grania*. E. Lyall Swete (1865–1930), whose name Yeats misspells, was a former schoolmaster who joined the Benson troupe after the summer of 1891, spoke with a lisp, and designed props and costumes. George R. Weir (1853–1909) was a comedian and close friend of Benson; he was born in Glasgow and raised in Belfast. Further information on the plays and productions is contained in the main essay and in the notes to it, above.

### III

Of Mr. Benson and his players one need say little, for they have been in London till a few weeks ago, but one or two things one must say. They speak their verse not indeed, perfectly, but less imperfectly than any other players upon our stage, and the stage management is more imaginative than that of other companies. Richard II. beating time to the music at the end of the abdication scene and his leaning on Bolinbroke for his protection at the end of scene before Flint Castle are dramatic in the highest sense. Of Mr. Benson's playing as Richard II. one need not speak, for most people who are likely to read this have seen it, but only those who have been to Stratford have seen Mr. Weir's admirable, though too benevolent and cleanly, Falstaff, or Mr. Ash's Jack Cade, and Mrs. Benson's Doll Tearsheet, which had the extravagance and energy one desires and seldom finds in the representations of the most extravagant of poets. Mr. Rodney and Mr. Sweet played Falconbridge and King John with a barbaric simplicity that was entirely admirable, and helped with a certain bareness and simplicity in the costumes to contrast meaningly with the playing and costuming in *Richard II.*, which describes a time when, as Shakespeare knew from Holinshed, life became more splendid and luxurious than it had been before in England. I thought Mr. Benson's Henry V. nearly as good as his Richard II., and admired how he kept that somewhat crude king, as Mr. Waller did not, from becoming vulgar in the love scene at the end, when the language of passion has to become the instrument of policy; but I will speak of Henry V., when I speak of the cycle as a whole, as I believe his character, when contrasted with that of Richard II., lets out a little of Shakespeare's secret, and all but all the secret of his critics.

# APPENDIX D

## Illustrations to Dante included in Periodical Version of "William Blake and His Illustrations to The Divine Comedy"

The original publication of this essay in three successive numbers of *The Savoy* magazine for July, August, and September 1896, included eleven illustrations, ten from Blake and one from Botticelli. They are reproduced here together with Yeats's comments on them in each of the three parts of his essay, except for the illustration showing Paolo and Francesca, which is the frontispiece to the present volume. *The Savoy* included separate tables of contents for literary work and for art work. The captions used here are those from the "Art Contents" pages of the magazine, with the section of *The Divine Comedy* and canto numbers added in square brackets; in the case of the last two illustrations to parts 1 and 2, the plural "Drawings" applied to both illustrations by a brace has been changed to singular.

In place of the last sentence of the penultimate paragraph in part 1, *The Savoy* version contained this passage:

> The luminous globe, a symbol used again in the Purgatory, is Francesca's and Paolo's dream of happiness, their 'Heaven in Hell's despite.' The other three drawings have never been published before, and appear here, as will those which will follow them, through the courtesy of the Linnell family. The passing of Dante and Virgil through the portico of Hell is the most unfinished and loses most in reproduction, for the flames, rising from the half-seen circles, are in the original full of intense and various colour; while the angry spirits fighting on the waters of the Styx above the sluggish bodies of the melancholy, loses the least, its daemonic energy being in the contour of the bodies and faces. Both this and the Antaeus setting down Virgil and Dante upon the verge of Cocytus, a wonderful piece of colour in the original, resemble the illustrations to his 'prophetic books' in exuberant strength and lavish motion, and are in contrast with the illustrations to the Purgatory, which are placid, marmoreal, tender, starry, rapturous.

Yeats's phrase "Heaven in Hell's despite" conflates two slightly different phrases from Blake's lyric "The Clod and the Pebble": "a Heaven in Hells despair," line 4, and "a Hell in Heavens despite," line 12 (Ellis-Yeats 3: 49; Erdman, 19).

*THE PASSING OF DANTE AND VIRGIL THROUGH THE PORTICO OF HELL*. After an unpublished Water-Colour Drawing by WILLIAM BLAKE (*Inferno* III)

*ANGRY SPIRITS FIGHTING IN THE WATERS OF THE STYX*. After unpublished Water-Colour Drawing by WILLIAM BLAKE (*Inferno* VII)

*ANTAEUS SETTING VIRGIL AND DANTE UPON THE VERGE OF COCYTUS*. After unpublished Water-Colour Drawing by WILLIAM BLAKE (*Inferno* XXXI)

The *Savoy* version of part 2 of this essay concluded with the following two paragraphs of commentary on the accompanying illustrations:

> Blake's distaste for Dante's philosophy did not make him a less sympathetic illustrator, any more than did his distaste for the philosophy of Milton mar the beauty of his illustrations to 'Paradise Lost.' The illustrations which accompany the present article are, I think, among the finest he ever did, and are certainly faithful to the text of 'The Divine Comedy.' That of Dante talking with Uberti, and that of Dante in the circle of the thieves, are notable for the flames which, as always in Blake, live with a more vehement life than any mere mortal thing: fire was to him no unruly offspring of human hearths, but the Kabalistic element, one fourth of creation, flowing and leaping from world to world, from hell to hell, from heaven to heaven; no accidental existence, but the only fit signature, because the only pure substance, for the consuming breath of God. In the man, about to become a serpent, and in the serpent, about to become a man, in the second design, he has created, I think, very curious and accurate symbols of

an evil that is not violent, but is subtle, finished, plausible. The sea and clouded sun in the drawing of Dante and Virgil climbing among the rough rocks at the foot of the Purgatorial mountain, and the night sea and spare vegetation in the drawing of the sleep of Virgil, Dante and Statius near to its summit, are symbols of divine acceptance, and foreshadow the landscapes of his disciples Calvert, Palmer, and Linnell, famous interpreters of peace.

The faint unfinished figures in the globe of light in the drawing of the sleepers are the Leah and Rachel of Dante's dream, the active and the contemplative life of the spirit, the one gathering flowers, the other gazing at her face in the glass. It is curious that Blake has made no attempt, in these drawings, to make Dante resemble any of his portraits, especially as he had, years before, painted Dante in a series of portraits of poets, of which many certainly tried to be accurate portraits. I have not yet seen this picture, but if it has Dante's face, it will convince me that he intended to draw, in the present case, the soul rather than the body of Dante, and read 'The Divine Comedy' as a vision seen not in the body but out of the body. Both the figures of Dante and Virgil have the slightly feminine look which he gave to representations of the soul.

*DANTE AND UBERTI.* After an unpublished Water-Colour Drawing by WILLIAM BLAKE (*Inferno* X)

*THE CIRCLE OF THE THIEVES.* After the rare Engraving by WILLIAM BLAKE (*Inferno* XXV)

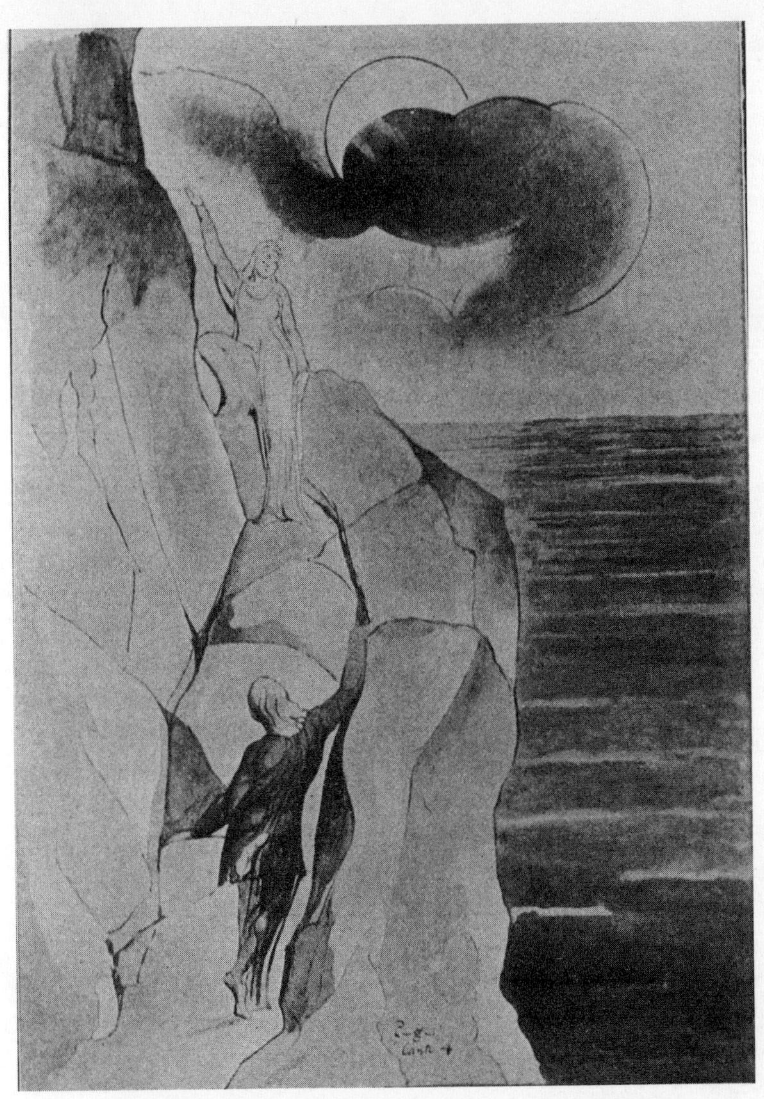

*DANTE AND VIRGIL CLIMBING THE FOOT OF THE MOUNTAIN OF PURGATORY.* After unpublished Water-Colour Drawing by WILLIAM BLAKE (*Purgatorio* IV)

*DANTE, VIRGIL, AND STATIUS.* After unpublished Water-Colour Drawing by WILLIAM BLAKE (*Purgatorio* XXVII)

*The Savoy* version of part 3 of this essay concluded with the following paragraph on the designs accompanying it:

> The drawing of the car of Beatrice, following the seven candlesticks in slow procession along the borders of Lethe, is from a tracing made many years ago by the late John Linnell and his son, John Linnell also, from a drawing which is too faint for reproduction. The Botticelli is reproduced with the permission of Messrs. Lawrence and Bullen from their admirable edition of his designs to 'The Divine Comedy.'

*THE CAR OF BEATRICE.* After an unpublished Water-Colour Drawing by WILLIAM BLAKE (*Purgatorio* XXX)

*THE CAR OF BEATRICE.* After the Drawing
by BOTTICELLI (*Purgatorio* XXX)

*THE CAR FOLLOWING THE SEVEN CANDLESTICKS.*
After a Tracing by JOHN LINNELL from an unpublished
Drawing by WILLIAM BLAKE (*Purgatorio* XXIX)

# APPENDIX E

## Omitted Passage from "Symbolism in Painting"

When "Symbolism in Painting" was first published as the 'introduction' to *A Book of Images, Drawn by W. T. Horton and Introduced by W. B. Yeats* (London: Unicorn Press, 1898), it contained a third section that Yeats deleted for *IGE*. That section is reproduced below. For more information on Yeats's relation to Horton, see Richard J. Finneran and George Mills Harper, "'He loved strange thought': W. B. Yeats and William Thomas Horton," in *W. B. Yeats and the Occult*, ed. George Mills Harper (Toronto: Macmillan of Canada, 1975), 190–203. Thomas Lake Harris (1823–1906) founded the 'Brotherhood of the New Life' referred to in the first sentence of the section below; many members of the Golden Dawn were familiar with his writings. Notes are not supplied here for references glossed in "Symbolism in Painting" or for titles of works by Horton reproduced in *A Book of Images* itself. The "old drawing in *The Savoy*" was an illustration to Matthew 7:14 in *The Savoy* 2 (April 1896): 77.

3. Mr. Horton, who is a disciple of "The Brotherhood of the New Life," which finds the way to God in waking dreams, has his waking dreams, but more detailed and vivid than mine; and copies them in his drawings as if they were models posed for him by some unearthly master. A disciple of perhaps the most mediæval movement in modern mysticism, he has delighted in picturing the streets of mediæval German towns, and the castles of mediæval romances; and, at moments, as in *All Thy waves are gone over me,* the images of a kind of humorous piety like that of the mediæval miracle-plays and moralities. Always interesting when he pictures the principal symbols of his faith, the woman of *Rosa Mystica* and *Ascending into Heaven,* who is the Divine womanhood, the man-at-arms of *St. George* and *Be Strong,* who is the Divine manhood, he is at his best in picturing the Magi, who are the wisdom of the world, uplifting their thuribles before the Christ, who is the union of the Divine manhood and the Divine womanhood. The rays of the halo, the great beams of the manger, the rich ornament of the thuribles and of the cloaks, make up a pattern where the homeliness come of his pity mixes with an elaborateness come of his adoration. Even the phantastic landscapes, the entangled chimneys against a white sky, the dark valley with its little points of light,

the cloudy and fragile towns and churches, are part of the history of a soul; for Mr. Horton tells me that he has made them spectral, to make himself feel all things but a waking dream; and whenever spiritual purpose mixes with artistic purpose, and not to its injury, it gives it a new sincerity, a new simplicity. He tried at first to copy his models in colour, and with little mastery over colour when even great mastery would not have helped him, and very literally: but soon found that you could only represent a world where nothing is still for a moment, and where colours have odours and odours musical notes, by formal and conventional images, midway between the scenery and persons of common life, and the geometrical emblems on mediæval talismans. His images are still few, though they are becoming more plentiful, and will probably be always but few; for he who is content to copy common life need never repeat an image, because his eyes show him always changing scenes, and none that cannot be copied; but there must always be a certain monotony in the work of the Symbolist, who can only make symbols out of the things that he loves. Rossetti and Botticelli have put the same face into a number of pictures; M. Maeterlinck has put a mysterious corner, and a lighthouse, and a well in a wood into several plays; and Mr. Horton has repeated again and again the woman of *Rosa Mystica,* and the man-at-arms of *Be Strong;* and has put the crooked way of *The Path to the Moon,* "the straight and narrow way" into *St. George,* and an old drawing in *The Savoy;* the abyss of *The Gap,* the abyss which is always under all things, into drawings that are not in this book; and the wave of *The Wave,* which is God's overshadowing love, into *All Thy waves are gone over me.*

These formal and conventional images were at first but parts of his waking dreams, taken away from the parts that could not be drawn; for he forgot, as Blake often forgot, that you should no more draw the things the mind has seen than the things the eyes have seen, without considering what your scheme of colour and line, or your shape and kind of paper can best say: but his later drawings, *Sancta Dei Genitrix* and *Ascending into Heaven* for instance, show that he is beginning to see his waking dreams over again in the magical mirror of his art. He is beginning, too, to draw more accurately, and will doubtless draw as accurately as the greater number of the more visionary Symbolists, who have never, from the days when visionary Symbolists carved formal and conventional images of stone in Assyria and Egypt, drawn as accurately as men who are interested in things and not in the meaning of things. His art is immature, but it is more interesting than the mature art of our magazines, for it is the reverie of a lonely and profound temperament.

W. B. YEATS

# APPENDIX F

## Omitted Passages from "The Return of Ulysses"

For *IGE* Yeats deleted the following two long passages from the June 1897 version of his essay "The Return of Ulysses" in *The Bookman.* The first extract follows the current second paragraph of the article (ending "purer brilliance"), and the second extract follows the current fourth paragraph (ending "distinguished ideal," immediately before part 2). All of the verse plays mentioned by Yeats are in *Eight Plays* (London: George Bell and Sons, and Edward Bumpus, 1885–94) except for *Prometheus the Firegiver* (not "Fire Bringer"), which was published separately by George Bell and Sons in 1884. The verse at the end of the first extract is from "Spring. Ode II. Reply," *The Shorter Poems* (London: George Bell and Sons, 1894; revised from 1890; O'Shea #280), 38. Of the three indented poetry quotations in the second passage, the first is from "January," *Eros and Psyche* (London: George Bell and Sons, 1894; O'Shea #276), 144; the second from "The storm is over," *Shorter Poems,* 81 (which reads "in grassy" rather than "In the grassy"); and the third from "I heard a linnet courting," *The Shorter Poems* (London: George Bell and Sons, 1894, revised from 1890), 9.

### FIRST DELETED PASSAGE

The other eight plays have not this gathering passion, but they have much beauty, and much beauty even that might be a delight upon the stage if we had but possessed our lost arts for a little while and grown easy in their use. *Prometheus, the Fire Bringer, Nero: The First Part,* and *Palicio* are early work, and, with the exception of the first, which is vigorous and simple, though a little slow in its motion, they appear to me rather loose in their hold on character and incident, and, with the exception of *Prometheus, the Fire Bringer,* do not move me greatly. *The Christian Captives,* which followed *The Return of Ulysses,* and *The Humours of the Court,* and *Nero: the Second Part* are, like *Nero: the First Part* and *Palicio,* in a more or less Shakespearean manner; and though excellent critics consider *Nero: the Second Part* Mr. Bridges' best play, and though I find much beauty in all and great beauty in it, I prefer Mr. Bridges when he follows a more or less classical model, as he does in *The Feast of Bacchus,* which is, however, less a poem than an admirable farce condensed from Terence.†

Or some Terentian play
Renew, whose excellent
Adjusted folds betray
How once Meander went.

## SECOND DELETED PASSAGE

*The Return of Ulysses* and *Achilles in Scyros* move me most of Mr. Bridges' longer poems, and after them, and I think before the *Nero: Second Part,* I number *Eros and Psyche,* in which the part that comes closest to folk lore, the description of the tasks that Aphrodite sets to Psyche, is particularly moving:

Then Psyche said: "This is the biting flood
Of black Cocytus, silvered with the gleam
Of souls, that guilty of another's blood
Are pent therein, and as they swim they scream."

I cannot judge properly of *Eden: an Oratorio,* and of the *Purcell Commemoration Ode,* and of the little I have seen of *The Yattingdon Hymnal,* for they must be judged with the music, and I have no knowledge of music. I find the little I have seen of the Hymnal full of intellectual passion; and *Eden,* which does not, and I know not well why, greatly move me when I read it as a poem, has, when I imagine it as sung, a curious dramatic ecstasy, particularly in such things as the repeated "And what is man?" at the opening. These poems, except possibly the Hymnal, of which I cannot yet judge, however, seem to me of a less accomplished rhythm and easy beauty than the poems in the *Shorter Poems* which are written to be read only. Mr. Bridges has a more assured mastery over the theory and practice of a various and subtle rhythm of words than any living poet, and though his poems for music are honourable deeds, his poems are at their best when free from the bondage of any rhythm but the rhythm of words. Had he to remember the rhythm of a tune he could not, it is probable, have written.

But, ah! the leaves of summer that lie on the ground!
What havoc! The laughing timbrels of June,
That curtained the birds' cradles, and screened their song,
That sheltered the cooing birds at noon,
Of airy fans the delicate throng,—
Torn and scattered around!
Far out afield they lie,
In the watery furrows die,

In the grassy pools of the flood they sink and drown,
Green-golden, orange, vermillion, golden and brown,
The high year's flaunting crown,
Shattered and trampled down.

The day is done; the tired land looks for night;
She prays to the night to keep
In peace her nerves of delight:
While silver mist upstealeth silently,
And the broad cloud-driving moon in the clear sky
Lifts o'er the firs her shining shield
And in her tranquil light
Sleep falls on forest and field.
See! sleep hath fallen; the trees are asleep;
The night is come. The land is wrapt in sleep.

I know of no poet of our time, and few of our century, who can so perfectly knead thought and rhythm into the one mystical body of faint flame. Who can say whether the charm of these verses, the first three in one of his early lyrics, is in their thought or in their rhythm?

I heard a linnet courting
 His lady in the spring;
His mates were idly sporting,
 Nor stayed to hear him sing
  His song of love.
I fear my speech distorting
  His tender love.

The phrases of his pleading
 Were full of young delight;
And she that gave him heeding
 Interpreted aright
  His gay—sweet notes—
So sadly marred in the reading—
  His tender notes.

And when he ceased, the hearer
 Awaited the refrain,
Till swiftly perching nearer
 He sang his song again,
  His pretty song:—
Would that my verse spake fitter
  His tender song.

# APPENDIX G

## Conclusion to "The Tragic Theatre" in Plays for an Irish Theatre (1911)

. . . do we forget it.] When I am watching my own *Deirdre* I am content with the players and myself, if I am moved for a while not by the contrasted sorrows of Deirdre and Naisi, but because the words have called up before me the image of the sea-born woman so distinctly that Deirdre seems by contrast to those unshaken eyelids that had but the sea's cold blood what I had wished her to seem, a wild bird in a cage.[1]

It was only by watching my own plays that I came to understand that this reverie, this twilight between sleep and waking, this bout of fencing, alike on the stage and in the mind, between man and phantom, this perilous path as on the edge of a sword, is the condition of tragic pleasure, and to understand why it is so rare and so brief. If an actor becomes over emphatic, picking out what he believes to be the important words with violence, and running up and down the scale, or if he stresses his lines in the wrong places, or even if an electric lamp that should have cast but a reflected light from sky or sea, shows from behind the post of a door, I discover at once the proud fragility of dreams.

At first I was driven into teaching too statuesque a pose, too monotonous a delivery, that I might not put 'vitality' in the place of the sleep walking of passion, and for the rest became a little deaf and blind.

But alas! it is often my own words that break the dream. Then I take the play from the stage and write it over again, perhaps many times. As first I always believed it must be something in the management of events, in all that is the same in prose or verse, that was wrong, but after I had reconstructed a scene with the messenger in *Deirdre* in many ways, I discovered that my language must keep at all times a certain even richness. I had used 'traitor', 'sword', 'suborned,' words of a too traditional usage, without plunging them into personal thought and metaphor, and I had forgotten in a moment of melodrama that tragic drama must be carved out of speech as a statue is out of stone.[2]

But train our players and our mechanists as we will and if we have not thought out the art of stage decoration afresh every brush stroke of our scene painter will mix into the reveries the meretricious or the irrelevant. We shall have hired some journeyman to accompany the poet's description with a painted landscape which, because it must give all to the first glance and yet copy nature, will alone copy what is obvious, and which even if it could keep the attention and give it pleasure could but keep it to the poet's loss:—

> 'A vapour, sometime, like a bear, or lion,
> A tower'd citadel, a pendant rock,
> A forked mountain, or blue promontory
> With trees upon't that nod unto the world
> And mock our eyes with air.'[3]

I have heard Antony speak those lines before a painted cloth that, though it could not make them nothing, left in the memory the sensation of something childish, theatrical as we say. Words as solemn, and having more for the mind's eye than those of the Book of Common Prayer are spoken where no reformer has cast out the idolatrous mummery and no tradition sanctified.[4]

In no art can we do well unless we keep to those effects that are peculiar to it or it can show better than the other arts. We no longer paint wood with a grain that is not its own, but are content that it should display itself or be covered with paint that pretends to be but paint, and if we make a design for a vase or a plate, we are careful not to attempt something that can be better done in an easel picture. But in the art of the theatre we imitate an easel picture even though we ignore or mar for its sake the elements we should have worked in, the characteristics of the stage, light and shadow, the movement of the players. Our tree-wings . . . let us say . . . can only be given mass and detail by painted light and shadow and these will contradict, or be in no relation to the real light, and this real light will be so cut up and cut off by wings and borders arranged for effects of painting that we shall be content to use it in but a few obvious ways. Then too our background will be full of forms and colours, instead of showing an even or almost even surface whereon the players are outlined clearly that we may see their movements and feel their importance; and all the while the background, even if it were fine painting and had no false light and shadow and did not reduce the players to a picturesque group in the foreground of a water colour painting by my grandmother, could but insist on the unreality we are anxious to forget, for every time a player stood too close to that garden scene we would but feel over again on how flat a surface they had painted that long garden walk dwindling away into the distance.

If we would give our theatre the dignity of a church, of a Greek open air theatre, of an Elizabethan platform stage, and cannot be content with any of these, we must have a scene where there is no painted light and shade, and that is but another way of saying, no realism, no objects represented in mass (unless they can be copied exactly as we can sometimes copy an interior), and the mechanism of this scene must as little as possible prevent the free and delicate use of light and shadow.

When we have made this change in obedience to a logic which has been displayed in the historical development of all the other arts, we shall have created a theatre that will please the poet and the player and the painter. An old quarrel will be ended, the stage will be beautifully decorated, every change will be full of meaning and yet never create a competing interest, or set bounds to the suggestions of speech and motion. At last liberated from the necessity of an always complete realization, the producer, recovering caprice, will be as free as a modern painter, as Signor Mancini let us say, to give himself up to an elliptical imagination.[5] Gloucester will be able to fall but from his own height and think he has fallen from Dover cliff, and Richard's and Richmond's tents can face one another again.[6] We shall have made possible once more a noble, capricious, extravagant, resonant, fantastic art.

All summer I have been playing with a little model where there is a scene capable of endless transformation, of the expression of every mood that does not require a photographic reality. Mr. Craig—who has invented all this—has permitted me to set up upon the stage of the Abbey another scene that corresponds to this, in the scale of a foot for an inch, and henceforth I shall be able, by means so simple that one laughs, to lay the events of my plays amid a grandeur like that of Babylon; and where there is neither complexity nor compromise nothing need go wrong, no lamps become suddenly unmasked, no ill-painted corner come suddenly into sight. Henceforth I can all but 'produce' my play while I write it, moving hither and thither little figures of cardboard through gay or solemn light and shade, allowing the scene to give the words and the words the scene. I am very grateful for he has banished a whole world that wearied me and was undignified and given me forms and lights upon which I can play as upon some stringed instrument.[7]

*P.S.* Two of Mr. Craig's designs, 'The Heroic Age—Morning', and 'The Heroic Age—Evening', are impressions worked out in Mr. Craig's scene, of the world my people move in, rather than exact pictures of any moment of a play. The one, however, suggests to me *On Baile's Strand*, and the other *Deirdre*. The design for *The Hour-Glass* shows the scene as it was used in Dublin, and 'The Fool'—who belongs to *The Hour-Glass* and *On Baile's Strand*—is as he was in Dublin in the first play, except that we have found no one who can make us a mask of leather, and we do not yet know how to make it ourselves.[8]

## Notes

For *The Cutting of an Agate* (1912), Yeats omitted the conclusion to the essay as found in *The Mask* (October 1910) and *Plays for an Irish Theatre* (1911). The postscript was included only in the latter, the source of this text.

1. In *Deirdre,* Naoise tells the story of Lugaid Redstripe and his wife, Dervorgilla, playing chess while awaiting their deaths. Deirdre eventually comments, "I cannot go on playing like that woman / That had but the cold blood of the sea in her veins" (*Plays,* 191).
2. Yeats refers to the following passage of the play as found in *Deirdre* (London: A. H. Bullen, 1907) and in volume two of *The Collected Works in Verse and Prose* (Stratford-on-Avon: Shakespeare Head Press, 1908). *Naoise*: "Tell Conchubar to meet me in some place / Where none can come between us, but swords." *Messenger.* "I take no message from a traitor's lips." *Fergus:* "He has been suborned." See *VPl,* 370–71.

   At this point the text in *The Mask* offered the following paragraph, deleted in *Plays for an Irish Theatre:*

   > It is certain therefore that should suggestion run thin, should some one move violently[,] should there be a sudden noise, any one out of a thousand accidents that would hardly trouble the robust pleasure of comedy, the climbing shoulders will come from under the stone. Perhaps there is in tragic art something womanish come from the continual presence of the Muses who have given Comedy a later and a slighter love, and we know that men can have their day[']s work amid the abrupt, the common, the foolish even without utter loss, but that women cannot keep their fineness lacking a fine company.

3. From Shakespeare's *Antony and Cleopatra,* 4.15.3–7 (Shakespeare, p. 2689).
4. The Book of Common Prayer evolved in the sixteenth century and reached its final form in 1662.
5. The Italian artist Antonio Mancini (1852–1930) had painted Yeats's portrait in 1907.
6. Episodes in Shakespeare's *King Lear,* 4.6.1–79 and *Richard III,* 5.3.
7. The English actor, producer, and stage designer Edward Gordon Craig (1872–1966) provided Yeats with a model theater on 1 February 1910. Yeats used it to experiment with the staging of *The Hour-Glass,* plotting the results in a small notebook. Craig's screens were first used at the Abbey Theatre on 12 January 1911, for productions of both *The Hour-Glass* and Lady Gregory's *The Deliverer.* See Liam Miller, *The Noble Drama of W. B. Yeats* (Dublin: Dolmen Press, 1977), 153–69.
8. *Plays for an Irish Theatre* included four drawings by Craig, one of which was used as the frontispiece.

# APPENDIX H

## Omitted Passage from "Preface to the First Edition of John M. Synge's Poems and Translations" (1909)

II

Last September he wrote to me as follows.[1]

Dear Yeats,

Roberts wants me to give him the enclosed verses for publication. I read them to him the other day and he seemed taken with them, and I would be very grateful if you would let me know what you think about it.[2] I do not feel very sure of them; yet enough of myself has gone into them to make me sorry to destroy them and I feel at times it would be better to print them while I am alive than to leave them after me to go God knows where.

If I bring them out I would possibly write a short preface to say that as there has been a false 'poetic diction' so there has been and is a false 'poetic material;' and that if verse is to remain a living thing it must be occupied, when it likes, with the whole of a poet's life and experience as it was with Villon and Herrick and Burns; for though exalted verse may be the highest, it cannot keep its power unless there is more essentially vital verse—not necessarily written by the same man—at the side of it.[3]

You will gather that I am most interested now in my grimmer verses, and the ballads (which are from actual life.) There is a funny coincidence about 'The Curse' you will find among them. . . . [4]

Excuse this disjointed production; I cannot write letters with a type-writer: and please let me know your opinion as soon as you can. If I print them I might put some of my Petrarch translations into the book also, to make it a little less thin.[5]

Yours ever
J.M. Synge.

The full title of 'The Curse' is 'To a sister of an enemy of the author who disapproved of The Playboy.'

Lord, confound this surly sister,
Blight her brow with blotch and blister,
Cramp her larynx, lung, and liver,
In her guts a galling give her.
Let her learn to eat her dinners
In Mountjoy with seedy sinners.
Lord, this judgment quickly bring,
And I'm your servant, J. M. Synge.[6]

He was persuaded to leave these lines out of this edition of his poem, but what he says about the rough poems that give weight to the more ecstatic, justifies me in restoring it. [In his Preface . . .

Notes

1. The letter was dated 7 September 1908 (*Letters* 2: 195).
2. George Roberts (1873–1953) was a Dublin publisher and a member of the Irish National Theatre Society.
3. Synge's preface repeats the arguments of the first two paragraphs of this letter (see *Poems,* xxxvi). Robert Herrick (1591–1674) was an English lyric poet.
4. The passage omitted by Yeats reads "the lady in question has since been overtaken with unnamable disasters. That is between ourselves." The lady was Molly Allgood's oldest sister, Mrs. Tom Callender (1879–1959). In his journal, Yeats recorded Synge telling him that since he had written the poem "her husband had got drunk, gone with a harlot, got syphilis, and given it to his wife" (*Mem,* 202).
5. The volume included eight translations from the Italian poet Petrarch (Francesco Petrarca) (1304–74).
6. *Poems,* 49. Synge sent a copy of the poem to Molly Allgood on 25 March 1907. Mountjoy is a Dublin prison.

# APPENDIX I

## Preface to J. M. Synge and the Ireland of His Time (1911)

At times during Synge's last illness, Lady Gregory and I would speak of his work and always find some pleasure in the thought that unlike ourselves, who have made our experiments in public, he would leave nothing to the world to be wished away—nothing that was not beautiful or powerful in itself, or necessary as an expression of his life and thought. When he died we were in much anxiety, for a letter written before his last illness, and printed in the selection of his poems published at the Cuala Press, had shown that he was anxious about the fate of his manuscripts and scattered writings.[1] On the evening of the night he died he had asked that I might come to him the next day; and my diary of the days following his death shows how great was our anxiety.[2] Presently however, all seemed to have come right, for the Executors sent me the following letter that had been found among his papers, and promised to carry out his wishes.[3]

May 4th, 1908

*Dear Yeats,*

This is only to go to you if anything should go wrong with me under the operation or after it. I am a little bothered about my 'papers.' I have a certain amount of verse that I think would be worth preserving, possibly also the 1st and 3rd acts of 'Deirdre,' and then I have a lot of Kerry and Wicklow articles that would go together in a book. The other early stuff I wrote I have kept as a sort of curiosity, but I am anxious that it should not get into print. I wonder could you get someone—say. . . . . who is now in Dublin to go through them for you and do whatever you and Lady Gregory think desirable.[4] It is rather a hard thing to ask you but I do not want my good things destroyed or my bad things printed rashly—especially a morbid thing about a mad fiddler in Paris which I hate.[5] Do what you can—Good Luck.

J. M. Synge

In the summer of 1909, the Executors sent me a large bundle of papers, cuttings from newspapers and magazines, manuscript and typewritten prose and verse, put together and annotated by Synge himself before his last illness. I spent a portion of each day for weeks reading and re-reading early dramatic writing, poems, essays, and so forth, and with the exception of ninety pages which have been published without my consent, made consulting Lady Gregory from time to time the Selection of his work published by Messrs. Maunsel. It is because of these ninety pages, that neither Lady Gregory's name nor mine appears in any of the books, and that the Introduction which I now publish, was withdrawn by me after it has been advertised by the publishers. Before the publication of the books the Executors discovered a piece of paper with a sentence by J. M. Synge saying that Selections might be taken from his Essays on the Congested Districts. I do not know if this was written before his letter to me, which made no mention of them, or contained his final directions. The matter is unimportant, for the publishers decided to reject my offer to select as well as my original decision to reject, and for this act of theirs they have given me no reasons except reasons of convenience, which neither Lady Gregory nor I could accept.[6]

## Notes

Yeats did not reprint this preface from the 1911 publication.

1. See page 317 of this edition for Synge's letter.
2. For example, see the journal entry for 17 April 1909 (*Mem*, 217–18).
3. Synge's executors were his brother Edward Synge (1859–1939) and his nephew Frank (Francis Edmund) Stephens (1884–1948). Yeats received the letter on 13 May 1909.
4. Yeats omitted "MacKenna"—Stephen MacKenna (1872–1934), journalist and translator of Plotinus and one of Synge's closest friends.
5. "Étude Morbide" (*Prose*, 25–26).
6. Because of the decision to include the essays on the Congested Districts, Yeats withdrew his support of the *Collected Works* published by Maunsel in 1910.

# Textual Matters and Notes

# A NOTE ON THE TEXT

The base-text for this edition is *Essays* (London: Macmillan, 1924), the last published edition of *Ideas of Good and Evil* and *The Cutting of an Agate* prepared by Yeats in his lifetime. As a part of the ongoing Collected Works series published by Macmillan 1922–26, the volume received Yeats's careful attention. He submitted copy just before leaving for Stockholm to accept the Nobel Prize, and he read proofs twice upon his return in early 1924, once in galleys and again in pages. The volume thus represents his most advanced and realized intentions for the collections that it contains. It appeared from Macmillan, London, on 6 May 1924, in an edition of 2,240 copies. An American edition was published by Macmillan, New York, on 14 October 1924, with a signed limited edition on 26 October 1924. Other than signing the sheets, there is no evidence that Yeats was involved in the production of the American edition: minor variants, such as the "correction" of "Penelli" to "Genelli," were presumably the work of the copy editor in New York. When Yeats prepared the table of contents for the never published Scribner edition in January 1937, he specified that *Essays* should follow the London edition, a clear indication that he considered it the most authoritative text. No proofs of *Essays* were produced during Yeats's lifetime for the Scribner edition. As noted in the introduction, a set of proofs for *Essays* in the never published Macmillan (London) Edition de Luxe was produced in June 1931, but there is no evidence that they were reviewed by Yeats and they are not known to survive. *Essays* (1924) thus remains the last text that can be established as having Yeats's authority.

Given the care with which Yeats prepared the *Essays* (1924) London edition, we have emended it only in a very conservative manner, limited largely to the correction of misprints or other obvious errors. We have also regularized names, titles, and the like that are referred to in different essays. The following lists of "Corrections and Regularizations" and of "Specific Emendations" set forth the changes specifically. We have not followed the minor emendations marked in two corrected copies of *Essays* in the National Library of Ireland because none of the changes can be ascribed with confidence to Yeats. Many of the corrections are clearly in the hand of George Yeats (Mrs. W. B. Yeats) and others (such as occasional punctuation marks) presumably come from her but cannot be ascribed with confidence. The London edition has on the flyleaf "George Yeats. Her copy / not to be taken by me / W B Yeats." An American edition has on the flyleaf "George Yeats/~~corrected copy.~~" The London edition was apparently intended for the

Scribner edition; however, it was not submitted to them in June 1937 along with the materials for the other volumes, and if it was later sent to Scribner, it must have been returned. Many of the corrections are identical in the two copies; most correct quotations, especially from Blake, and proper or place names. The only substantive change is found in the London edition: "not come to dislike" to "now come to dislike" in the opening paragraph of "What is 'Popular Poetry'?" Whether Yeats approved that revision, or any of the other changes in either copy, is unknown. We have correlated our edition against the posthumous changes introduced into *Essays and Introductions* (1961) by George Yeats and Lovat Dickson, and earlier Thomas Mark, but have not followed their readings as they lack Yeats's own authority and occasionally introduce new errors of their own. We have not accepted the weak argument of posthumous delegated authority.

A particular issue in both these and other Yeats texts concerns punctuation. Yeats's grasp on punctuation was never strong and on at least one occasion he professed not to understand it. Yet he did punctuate his texts and did carefully review proofs and the like before publication. In common with numerous scholars since at least Curtis Bradford, we believe that Yeats often followed "rhetorical as opposed to grammatical punctuation" designed to indicate pauses for rhetorical effect rather than merely to denote grammatical syntax.[1] Yeats's punctuation in *Essays* (1924) may occasionally seem surprising if read according to syntactic expectations but comes across clearly if read according to rhetorical ones. We believe that readers would rather see what Yeats did and approved than what "improvements" later editors can make, and accordingly have followed the carefully proofread 1924 base-text.

Similar thinking governs our policy on quotations. When quoting from memory Yeats often made small slips; and when he did consult specific texts they sometimes were not the "standard" ones. In other cases (such as Shelley) he used multiple editions that sometimes make it difficult to determine what specific one he might be (mis-)quoting. Again, rather than silently correct such quotations either according to works he might have consulted or according to current standard editions, we have preserved his quotations as given in 1924 both as clues to what editions he was using (often cited in our notes) and as instances of his imaginative misremembering of a given passage. In many cases we have consulted and cited the same editions

1. Curtis Bradford, *Yeats at Work* (Carbondale: Southern Illinois University Press, 1965), 14. Richard J. Finneran makes a similar argument in his essay "Text and Interpretation in the Poems of W. B. Yeats," in *Representing Modernist Texts: Editing as Interpretation,* ed. George Bornstein (Ann Arbor: University of Michigan Press, 1991), 25–27. For a broader historical argument, including several examples from modernist writers, see the chapter on punctuation in E. A. Levenston, *The Stuff of Literature: Physical Aspects of Texts and Their Relation to Literary Meaning* (Albany: State University of New York Press, 1992).

owned by Yeats. At the same time, our notes record substantive changes from either source editions or standard modern ones (and sometimes both, as with the Blake quotations) so that readers can decide for themselves what to make of Yeats's renderings.

While our edition follows the principle of final and expressed authorial intention common to the collected edition, we have gestured toward other ways of editing that allow the reader additional information and allow him or her to reach independent and informed judgments. For example, the notes to essays indicate important material dropped from earlier versions of the essays but still of interest, including whole paragraphs as well as shorter remarks. The appendices contain longer sections that once formed part of the essays. In an effort to acknowledge the increasing importance of material textuality to recent editorial theory and criticism, we have also restored the original illustrations to Yeats's essay on Blake's Dante. We reproduce, too, significant cover designs for *Ideas of Good and Evil, The Cutting of an Agate,* and *Essays* with which Yeats was involved to varying degrees and which add to the overall meaning of the text.

Besides the "Corrections and Regularizations" and the "Specific Emendations" in the lists below, we have followed standard policies of the collected edition of the works of W. B. Yeats:

1. We have preserved hyphenations within lines of the base-text and have adjudicated ambiguous line-end hyphenations by the form of the word used elsewhere in Yeats's canon and in earlier texts of *IGE* and *COA.*
2. Large initial letters, whether caps or small caps, at the beginning of some essays have not been reproduced.
3. The presentation of titles and headings is standardized. Section numbers are in roman capitals. Headings and section numbers are centered and have no concluding full point.
4. Quotations that are set off from the text and indented are not placed within quotation marks.
5. Except in headings, titles of stories and poems are placed within quotation marks; titles of books, plays, long poems, periodicals, operas, and works of art are set in italics.
6. Regardless of its length in the base-text, a dash is set as an unspaced em dash when used as punctuation.
7. An asterisk has been used in place of Yeats's superscript numbers to his own footnotes, in order to keep such notes separate from our own explanatory ones.
8. The dates in brackets have been placed after undated footnotes; dates without brackets are those included by Yeats himself.

# TEXTUAL EMENDATIONS AND CORRECTIONS

## Corrections and Regularizations

The following are corrections of obvious errors, misprints, and inconsistencies as well as regularizations to Yeats's preferred form of certain Irish names.

| *1924 Reading* | *Revised Reading* |
|---|---|
| Abbé de Villars | Abbé de Villiers |
| Anglais | anglais |
| Anthony | Antony |
| Artigall | Artegall |
| Athanais | Athanase |
| Boroihme | Borúmha |
| Brigit | Brigid |
| Cairbry Cat Head | Cairbry Cathead |
| Calidor | Calidore |
| Chaliapine | Chaliapin |
| cleen | clean |
| Conchobar | Conchubar |
| Connaught | Connacht |
| Cottar's | Cotter's |
| Darrycarn | Derrycarn |
| Dhoul | Doul |
| the divine comedy *or* the *Divine Comedy* | *The Divine Comedy* |
| Drim-da-rod | Drim-na-rod |
| Echte | Echtge |
| *Epithalamium* | *Epithalamion* |
| Finn mac Cool | Finn mac Cumhal |
| Franz Francken | Frans Francken |
| Gloster | Gloucester |
| Grainne | Grania |
| Heinrich Ibsen | Henrik Ibsen |
| Hettingen | Hettinger |

| *1924 Reading* | *Revised Reading* |
|---|---|
| Hollingshead | Holinshed |
| the hours | the Hours |
| *Hymn to Beauty* | 'Hymne in Honour of Beautie' |
| *Hymn to Heavenly Beauty* | 'Hymne of Heavenly Beautie' |
| Iron man | Iron Man |
| Kallimachos | Callimachus |
| Lancelot | Launcelot |
| The Last Judgement | the Last Judgement |
| Leyrach | Llywarch |
| Loch Swilly | Lough Swilly |
| Luonaton | Luonnotar |
| Manzone | Manzoni |
| Mar-Prelate | Marprelate |
| Martin Dhoul | Martin Doul |
| Menalchus | Menalcas |
| Mitchell | Mitchel |
| Monteverde | Monteverdi |
| Niam | Niamh |
| Omar Khayyam | Omar Khayyám |
| Pandemus | Pendemos |
| Penelli | Pinelli |
| Pleiade | Pléiade |
| pre-Raphaelitism, pre-Raphaelite | Pre-Raphaelitism, Pre-Raphaelite |
| Psaltery | psaltery |
| *The Riders to the Sea* | *Riders to the Sea* |
| Saint Germain | Saint-Germain |
| St. Martin | Saint-Martin |
| Scholar Gipsy | Scholar-Gipsy |
| Sclavonic | Slavonic |
| Shee | Sidhe |
| *The State of Ireland* | *The Present State of Ireland* |
| Tirconnell | Tir Conaill |
| *Tir nan Oge* | *Tir na nÓg* |
| Tolstoi's | Tolstoy's |
| Usheen | Oisin |
| Villiers de L'Isle Adam | Villiers de L'Isle-Adam |
| Yankee Doodle | 'Yankee Doodle' |

## Specific Emendations

Specific emendations in the text are indicated by a †. This table lists page and line number in this edition; the reading of the London edition of *Essays* (1924); the emended reading; and the authority, if any, for the emendation.

### *What is 'Popular Poetry'?*

| | | |
|---|---|---|
| 9.8 would sing?— | would sing— | no contemporary authority |
| 9.27 from me.' | from me'? | no contemporary authority |

### *Speaking to the Psaltery*

| | | |
|---|---|---|
| 14.10 and, could | and could | cf. earlier texts |
| 16.7 gross efforts | gross effects | previous sentence and 1908 |

### *The Happiest of the Poets*

| | | |
|---|---|---|
| 47.19 and eat | and ate | rest of sentence |

### *At Stratford-on-Avon*

| | | |
|---|---|---|
| 75.35 black cloth | back cloth | context and earlier readings |

### *William Blake and His Illustrations to* The Divine Comedy

| | | |
|---|---|---|
| 106.35 gave | give | rest of sentence and earlier readings |

### *Emotion of Multitude*

| | | |
|---|---|---|
| 160.8 moonlight | noonlight | rest of sentence and earlier readings |

### *The Tragic Theatre*

| | | |
|---|---|---|
| 176.17 own); till | own) till | rest of sentence |
| 177.19 'Ariosto's' | Ariosto's | all previous printings |
| 178.30 The Knowledge | the Knowledge | *Plays for an Irish Theatre* (1911) and parallelism to rest of sentence |

### *Preface to the First Edition of John M. Synge's* Poems and Translations

| | | |
|---|---|---|
| 225.16 is master | his master | typographical error |

### *Art and Ideas*

| | | |
|---|---|---|
| 251.19 or 'Hans | or Hans | *The New Weekly* |
| 257.26 horseback | horse-back | cf. "camel-back" |

### *Appendix F—Omitted Passages from* "The Return of Ulysses"

| | | |
|---|---|---|
| 312.2 'Terence' | Terence | not a title |

# BACKGROUND NOTES ON FREQUENTLY CITED WRITERS

**Arnold,** Matthew (1822–88). English poet and critic, and archetypal Victorian sage. Son of Thomas Arnold, the influential headmaster of Rugby School, Arnold became a central figure in Victorian culture and one against whom Yeats often reacted. Yeats studied Arnold's *On the Study of Celtic Literature* (1867) carefully and critiqued it several times, including in his own "The Celtic Element in Literature" from *IGE*. Arnold produced other volumes of widely influential criticism including *Essays in Criticism* (1st ser., 1865; 2nd ser., 1888) and *Culture and Anarchy* (1869). Yeats also knew Arnold's poetry and cited especially "The Scholar-Gypsy," which contrasted the life of imagination with that of British society in the nineteenth century.

**Blake,** William (1757–1827). Visionary artist and poet who championed imagination over nature and greatly influenced Yeats. Much of his major poetry appeared in "illuminated books," often with hand-colored illustrations from his own engravings. Works of particular importance to Yeats include *Songs of Innocence* (1789), which Blake combined with *Songs of Experience* (1794) as "Shewing the Two Contrary States of the Human Soul"; the psychological, religious, and political *Marriage of Heaven and Hell* (engraved 1790–93); and the illuminated "Prophetic Books," such as Blake's struggle with his precursor *Milton* (1804, but engraved 1804–8) and *Jerusalem: The Emanation of the Giant Albion* (1804–20). Blake also engraved illustrations for texts by others, including the biblical book of Job, several of Milton's works, and Dante's *The Divine Comedy.* Yeats knew and quoted Blake's letters and copious comments on his own work and on that of others, especially his *Descriptive Catalogue* for a failed exhibition in 1809.

Besides reading Blake, Yeats also edited him. The three-volume edition of *The Works of William Blake: Poetical, Symbolic, and Critical* (London: Bernard Quaritch, 1893) helped Blake's growing reputation and contained the first publication of the epic *Four Zoas* or *Vala.* It also featured a biographical memoir, extensive commentary on Blake's symbolical system, and numerous facsimile illustrations. In addition, Yeats edited the one-volume *Poems of William Blake* (London: Lawrence and Bullen, 1893) aimed at a more popular audience. Yeats wrote two essays on Blake for the present collection and referred to him repeatedly in his writings, including the late poems "Under Ben Bulben" (*P*, 335) and "An Acre of Grass," in which he called him "that William Blake / Who beat upon the wall / Till truth obeyed his call" (*P*, 308). Yeats borrowed the title *Ideas of Good and Evil* from Blake's "Rossetti Manuscript."

**Dante** Alighieri (1265–1321). Italian poet and political exile who wrote *La Vita Nuova* (The New Life) upon the death of his beloved Beatrice. His *Divine Comedy* is the supreme work of medieval poetic synthesis. A poem in a hundred cantos, it tells the story of Dante guided in part by Virgil making his way through hell, purgatory, and finally paradise. Dante's love for Beatrice, his exile, and his search for a cosmic synthesis all appealed to Yeats, who in *A Vision* put Dante into the same phase (seventeen) as himself and Shelley in terms of the struggle toward Unity of Being. In the poem "Ego Dominus Tuus," Yeats called Dante the "chief imagination of Christendom" (*P*, 162).

**Goethe,** Johann Wolfgang von (1749–1832). German writer of poetry, drama, and fiction as well as an accomplished scientist and a holder of various governmental positions. Yeats saw him as a type of all-around genius and particularly admired his most famous work, the two-part poetic drama *Faust* (first part 1808; second part 1832) about the struggle of the German magical philosopher Faust with Mephistopheles, whom he promises to serve should the devil bring him to say of any moment "Stay, thou art so fair." Yeats saw that work, which contained a famous encounter with Helen in part 2, as the only work of Goethe's to have moved "the imagination of the world" (*UP2*, 141). Goethe's other works include, among many others, the epistolary novel *Sorrows of the Young Werther* (1774), the Wilhelm Meister novels (1777–1829), the autobiography, *Poetry and Truth* (1811–32), and the remarks recorded in his secretary Johann Peter Eckermann's *Conversations with Goethe* (1836–48; translated 1850).

**Gregory,** Lady Isabella Augusta (1852–1932). Born into the Anglo-Irish ascendancy in the west of Ireland, Isabella Augusta Persse in 1880 married Sir William Gregory, former governor of Ceylon and inheritor of Coole Park. Yeats and Lady Gregory first met in 1894 and within a couple of years had become firm friends and collaborators in the movement for an Irish national theater. Yeats spent twenty summers at Coole Park. Lady Gregory was a prolific author, and besides numerous and popular plays on Irish subjects, she published various works on and translations of Irish folklore and legend. Yeats began his preface to her *Cuchulain of Muirthemne* (1902) with the bold assertion that "this book is the best that has come out of Ireland in my time" (*P&I*, 224), a phrase later parodied by James Joyce, and adapted some of its material in his plays and poems about the Irish hero Cuchulain.

The essay "The Galway Plains" in the present collection is a review of her *Poets and Dreamers* (1903). Yeats contributed two essays and the notes to Lady Gregory's *Visions and Beliefs in the West of Ireland* (1920) and mentioned her frequently in his poetry, including the moving tribute "Coole Park, 1929" (*P*, 246–47).

**Keats,** John (1795–1821). English Romantic poet who died young of tuberculosis and left behind a moving body of poetry and letters. Yeats admired him both for his own achievement and for his role in nineteenth-century poetics, for instance as an exemplar of subjective, sensitive poetry in Hallam's essay on Tennyson. Keats's adaptations of folklike or fairy themes such as "La Belle Dame Sans Merci" and his great odes, especially "Ode on a Grecian Urn," appealed to Yeats's imagination. He invoked Keats frequently in his prose and in passages of his poetry, of which the best known is the memorable if problematic portrait of Keats making "luxuriant song" in "Ego Dominus Tuus" (*P*, 163).

**Morris,** William (1834–96). Victorian poet, craftsman, painter, and socialist. A polymath, Morris joined forces with Dante Gabriel Rossetti, Edward Burne-Jones, and others to work on frescoes in the Oxford Union and was one of the founders of the *Oxford and Cambridge Magazine* (1856). He published *The Defence of Guenevere and Other Poems* in 1858 and became a prolific writer of poetry (*The Earthly Paradise,* 1868–70), of translations (*The Odyssey,* 1887), and of prose romances (*The House of the Wolfings,* 1889; *The Well at the World's End,* 1896; and *The Water of the Wondrous Isles,* 1897). His designs and workshops inspired the Arts and Crafts movement, and his work at Kelmscott Press affected English fine printing and Yeats's own ideas about material textuality. Yeats first met Morris in 1886 in Dublin but knew him better in England, when Yeats for a time became his disciple and attended small suppers at Kelmscott House after lectures. For a retrospective account of Yeats's relation with Morris in the late 1880s and early 1890s, see *Au,* 130–38. "The Happiest of the Poets" in *IGE* gives Yeats's views on Morris closer to the time.

**Pater,** Walter (1839–94). Victorian writer and critic, who was elected to a fellowship at Brasenose College, Oxford, in 1864. His most important books include *Studies in the History of the Renaissance* (1873), the novel *Marius the Epicurean* (1885), and *Appreciations* (1889). His work affected many of the writers associated with the doctrines of art for art's sake and of the Decadence of the 1890s, including Oscar Wilde. His emphasis on the cult of the moment, the purity of artistic expression, and the use of Italian art as touchstones all influenced Yeats, who began his edition of *The Oxford Book of Modern Verse* (1936) with a free-verse arrangement of Pater's "famous passage" about the *Mona Lisa* in the essay on Leonardo da Vinci from *Renaissance.*

**Rossetti,** Dante Gabriel (1828–82). Son of an Italian patriot, Rossetti became a leading painter, poet, and translator in Victorian England. With Holman Hunt and John Everett Millais he founded the Pre-Raphaelite Brotherhood, which looked to painters before Raphael for inspiration. Rossetti also formed close friendships with John Ruskin, Edward Burne-Jones, and William Morris, all of whom championed his work. He first established his literary reputation with such poems as "The Blessed Damozel" in the Pre-Raphaelite magazine *The Germ* (1850). *Poems* (1870) contained other fine work, including "Jenny" and the first part of the sonnet sequence *The House of Life.* The next year Robert Buchanan excoriated Rossetti and his associates in the famous attack "The Fleshly School of Poetry" on the grounds of impurity and obscenity, to which Rossetti responded with his own article, "The Stealthy School of Criticism." Rossetti's best-known paintings often combine religious themes with sensuous detail, as in *Beata Beatrix* (1864–70) and *Blessed Damozel* (1875–79). In the present volume, Yeats discusses him particularly in "The Happiest of the Poets" and in *The Bounty of Sweden* (1925) included him among "the great myth-makers and mask-makers" (*Au,* 403).

**Shakespeare,** William (1564–1616). Greatest English playwright. In *IGE,* Yeats most frequently mentions the history plays, especially the characters of Richard II, Richard III, and Henry V in the works treated in "At Stratford-on-Avon." Elsewhere, he especially invokes *The Merchant of Venice* (1596–97), *Hamlet* (1600–1601), *Othello* (1603–4), *King Lear* (1604–5), *Antony and Cleopatra* (1606), and *Timon of Athens* (1607–8). Yeats saw Shakespeare as coming at a turning point from medieval and Renaissance synthesis to modern fragmentation and subjectivity. In the late works, Yeats linked him to notions of tragic joy or gaiety. He invoked Shakespeare numerous times in his poetry and prose, including in the late poem "Lapis Lazuli" (*P,* 300).

**Shelley,** Percy Bysshe (1792–1822). English Romantic poet so important to Yeats that he wrote that Shelley "shaped my life" (*LE,* 122). Introduced to his precursor by John Butler Yeats when still a boy, Yeats absorbed and reacted to Shelley throughout his life, most positively in his youth and more critically later on. He studied *Prometheus Unbound* as a "sacred book" and knew most of it by heart. Yeats valued especially the solitary quest in *Alastor* and *Prince Athanase,* the political drama of the doomed lovers in *The Revolt of Islam* (*Laon and Cythna*), the witch as incarnation of poetry or imagination in *The Witch of Atlas,* the reunion of the individual with the One in *Adonais,* the visionary politics of *Hellas,* and the degeneration of Rousseau into nature in *The Triumph of Life.* Among the lyrics Yeats admired in particular were "Hymn to Intellectual Beauty," "Mont Blanc," "Ode to the West Wind," and "To a Skylark." Yeats knew Shelley's prose well, too, and praised especially the *Defence of Poetry* as a profound treatise.

Shelley pervades Yeats's work, from the first unpublished plays that he said imitated Shelley and Spenser through the Intellectual Beauty of the rose and other symbols of the 1890s, and on to the towers of the great mature works. He invoked Shelley by name in both "The Phases of the Moon" and "Blood and the Moon" (*P*, 165 and 241, respectively). His major prose treatments include the laudatory "The Philosophy of Shelley's Poetry" in *IGE* and the more critical and shorter late essay on *Prometheus Unbound* (*LE*, 118–22). Yeats assigned Shelley to Phase 17 of *A Vision* along with Dante and himself, though by that time he saw Shelley as attracted too much to the ideal and not enough to the actual. Yet he still invoked Shelley's Witch of Atlas as late as the testamentary "Under Ben Bulben" (*P*, 333).

**Spenser,** Edmund (ca. 1552–99). English poet and courtier, who served as secretary to the lord deputy of Ireland and was rewarded with Kilcolman Castle in County Cork. He affected Yeats's early verse dramas, the early epic *The Wanderings of Oisin*, and other works. Yeats particularly admired the pastorals of *The Shepherds Calendar*, the myth-making ability of parts of *The Faerie Queene*, and the lament for the Earl of Leicester in *The Ruines of Time*. Spenser's prose *View of the Present State of Ireland* (written 1596) both fascinated Yeats with its vividness and repelled him by its harshness. Besides studying and imitating Spenser, Yeats edited him too; the essay "Edmund Spenser" in *COA* was first published as the introduction to Yeats's *Poems of Spenser* (Edinburgh: T. C. and E. C. Jack, 1906), which he said contained "only those passages from Spenser that I want to remember and carry about with me" (xliv). Yeats invoked Spenser at the end of his late poem "The Municipal Gallery Re-visited," where he cited "An image out of Spenser and the common tongue" (*P*, 328).

**Synge,** John (1871–1909). Irish playwright, poet, and prose writer. The young Synge intended to study music as a career and was torn between that and literature. Yeats met him in Paris in 1896 and famously advised him to travel to the Aran Islands and use the Irish lore there as a basis for literary creation. Synge worked with Yeats and Lady Gregory in the movement for an Irish national theater and became codirector of the Abbey with them in 1905. His plays include the one-act dramas *In the Shadow of the Glen* (performed 1903) and *Riders to the Sea* (1904), which were followed by *The Well of the Saints* (1905), and his controversial masterpiece *The Playboy of the Western World* (1907). Synge also wrote such poems as "The Passing of the Shee" and prose works as *The Aran Islands* (1907). He was engaged to the Abbey actress Máire O'Neill (Molly Allgood) and died of Hodgkin's disease in 1909. In addition to the three essays in *COA*, Yeats mentioned Synge frequently in his work, including extended comments in the "Estrangement" and "The Death of Synge" sections of *Autobiographies*, stanza 4 of "In Memory of Major Robert Gregory," and stanzas 6 and 7 of "The Municipal Gallery Re-visited" (*P*, 133 and 328, respectively).

**Wordsworth,** William (1770–1850). English Romantic poet, whose collaborative volume *Lyrical Ballads* (1798) with Samuel Taylor Coleridge helped inaugurate the Romantic movement. Wordsworth's most famous poems include the lyrics "Lines Composed a Few Miles Above Tintern Abbey" and "Ode: Intimations of Immortality" and the autobiographical epic *The Prelude; or Growth of a Poet's Mind,* which he worked on most intensively from 1799 to 1805 but revised continually thereafter before its posthumous publication in 1850. Yeats lamented what he saw as Wordsworth's decline from imaginative rebel to poet laureate of the establishment. He mentions Wordsworth repeatedly in his other prose, including sections 6 and 13 of the "Anima Hominis" part of *Per Amica Silentia Lunae (LE,* 10 and 16, respectively).

# NOTES

## *What is 'Popular Poetry'?*

First published in *The Cornhill Magazine,* new series, 12 (March 1902). *The Cornhill* had originally been edited by William Makepeace Thackeray and remained a major outlet for literary work through Yeats's day. The agent A. P. Watt submitted the article to *The Cornhill* on 14 October 1901 under the title "The Hut, the Castle and Counting House" but indicated in a postscript that Yeats would accept a change to either "Popular Poetry" or "What is Popular Poetry?" instead (*InteLex*). Although Yeats made no major later revisions to the essay after its original publication, some later minor ones did mitigate some of his hostility toward the middle class as a whole. The phrase about "an ignorant ear" at the end of the second paragraph originally read "the ears of the shopkeepers," and near the start of the third paragraph "the poets of a predominant portion of the middle class" originally read "the poets of the middle class."

1. The Young Ireland societies were founded in the 1880s but looked back to the Young Irelanders of the 1840s, such as Thomas Davis. Yeats writes in his autobiography (*Au,* 103) that he belonged to a small branch that "met in the lecture hall of a workmen's club in York Street with O'Leary for president" and that included the orator John F. Taylor. O'Leary gave the inaugural address in January 1885, and Yeats joined the society the next year.
2. The pastoral play combining aspects of Shelley and Spenser was *The Island of Statues,* first published in *The Dublin University Review,* April–July 1885. Yeats later reprinted parts of it, including "The Cloak, the Boat, and the Shoes" and "The Song of the Happy Shepherd," in the *Crossways* section of his collected poems. See Bornstein, chapter 2 passim. In retaining "not" we have followed the documentary printed record, which was reviewed by Yeats, rather than the correction to "now" (likely by George Yeats) in the marked copies of *Essays* in NLI and the posthumous *E&I.*
3. The revival of the ballad tradition became a recurrent idea for Yeats. He had earlier published "Popular Ballad Poetry of Ireland" in *The Leisure Hour* for November 1889 (*EAR,* 93–108), a review article on James Duffy's Library of Ireland series, which reprinted nineteenth-century Irish ballad poets beginning with Edward Walsh and Jere-

miah Joseph Callanan (Yeats considered James Clarence Mangan the greatest of them). Yeats had written to his friend the poet Katharine Tynan in December 1888, "I do not mean that we should not go to the old ballads and poems for inspiration but we should sea[r]ch them for new methods of expressing our selves" (*CL1*, 119).

4. The nineteenth-century Irish poet William Allingham (1824–89) elicited two articles from Yeats, "The Poet of Ballyshannon" (1888; *LNI*, 71–78) and "A Poet We Have Neglected" (1891; *EAR*, 149–52). Yeats also edited *Sixteen Poems by William Allingham* for the Dun Emer Press (1905). Yeats preferred Allingham's shorter poems on fairy lore to his longer ones, though he respected *Laurence Bloomfield in Ireland*.

   Yeats's first two published articles were a memorial essay in two parts on Sir Samuel Ferguson (1810–86), who wrote numerous ballads as well as the "epics" *Congal* and *Deirdre* drawing on old Irish legends. Quoting liberally from Ferguson's work, Yeats argued against dismissive critics such as Edward Dowden that Ferguson was "the greatest poet Ireland has produced, because the most central and most Celtic" (*EAR*, 26). A founding member of the Protestant Repeal Association in 1848, Ferguson went on to a distinguished public career, for which he was knighted in 1878.

5. An erratic student, Yeats was unlikely to pass the entrance exam for Trinity College, Dublin, where his painter-father John Butler Yeats had studied, and instead from 1884 to 1886 attended the Metropolitan School of Art. Late June and July 1888 was spent in the area around Sligo collecting tales of fairies and the supernatural, for the anthology *Fairy and Folk Tales of the Irish Peasantry*.

6. The "Adelphi melodramas" were a series performed at the celebrated Adelphi Theatre in the London Strand beginning in the 1880s. They included *Harbour Lights* (1885) by George Sims (1847–1922) and Henry Pettitt (1848–93) and *The Union Jack* (1888) by Pettitt and Sydney Grundy (1848–1914).

7. In "The Stirring of the Bones" section of *Autobiographies,* Yeats writes of this thought: "When in my twenty-second year I had finished *The Wanderings of Oisin,* my style seemed too elaborate, too ornamental, and I thought for some weeks of sleeping upon a board. Had I been anywhere but at Sligo, where I was afraid of my grandfather and grandmother, I would have made the attempt" (*Au,* 279).

8. In his essay "On Translating Homer" (1861), Matthew Arnold refers to several recent translations of Homer into English, including Professor F. W. Newman's *The Iliad of Homer* (1856), which began: "Good people all with one accord / Give ear unto my story. . . ." In the course of his critique, Arnold paraphrases the remark of the American critic George P. Marsh in his *Lectures on the English Language* about Newman's translation provoking for Americans the effect of setting

Homer to the rhythm of "Yankee Doodle." Arnold continues, "Mr. Newman joins to a bad rhythm so bad a diction that it is difficult to distinguish exactly whether in any given passage it is his words or his measure which produces a total impression of such an unpleasant kind." See *The Complete Prose Works of Matthew Arnold,* ed. R. H. Super (Ann Arbor: University of Michigan Press 1960–77) 1: 132–33.

9. In his review article on William Watson entitled "A Scholar Poet" (*LNI*, 102–7), Yeats begins by quoting a sarcastic passage from *William Shakespeare* (1864) by the great French novelist and dramatist Victor Hugo (1802–85). Yeats admired Hugo enormously and even told Maud Gonne that he wanted to become an "Irish Victor Hugo" (*Mem,* 41).

10. Born in Maine, the New England poet Henry Wadsworth Longfellow (1807–82) served as professor of modern foreign languages first at Bowdoin and then at Harvard. His best-known works include "The Village Blacksmith," "The Wreck of the Hesperus," and "Paul Revere's Ride," in addition to the translation of Dante's *The Divine Comedy* and the adaptation of Native American folklore in *Hiawatha.*

    The Scots poet Thomas Campbell (1777–1844) was born and educated in Glasgow and best known for battle poetry such as "Ye Mariners of England." He also wrote *Gertrude of Wyoming* (1809), a long poem in Spenserian stanzas.

    Born in Wales, the Romantic poet Felicia Dorothea Hemans (1793–1835) combined rousing efforts like "The boy stood on the burning deck" with poems dealing particularly with the situation of women, as in her early volume *The Domestic Affections*. She also translated Camoens and other poets.

    Thomas Babington Macaulay (1800–1859) had distinguished careers as politician, historian, poet, and critic. A strong Whig in politics, in literature he turned especially to Sir Walter Scott. John Butler Yeats had read Macaulay's *Lays of Ancient Rome* and Scott's *The Lay of the Last Minstrel* to his son as a young boy.

    Born and educated in Edinburgh, Sir Walter Scott (1771–1832) became famous for his poetry and prose influenced by Scots Border tales and ballads; his works included *Minstrelsy of the Scottish Border* and *The Lay of the Last Minstrel,* as well as influential historical novels such as *Waverley, Kenilworth,* and *Ivanhoe.*

11. The popular Scots poet Robert Burns (1759–96) wrote with ease in both standard eighteenth-century English and in his native Scots dialect. His best-known poems on Scots rural life include "The Cotter's Saturday Night" and "To a Mouse." He also wrote more than two hundred songs, including "Auld Lang Syne" and "My Love Is Like a Red, Red Rose," and collected Scots folk songs. Yeats often contrasted him to Shelley.

12. Shelley's *Epipsychidion* is a partially autobiographical love poem treat-

ing the search for Eternal or Intellectual Beauty in earthly feminine form. Spenser's Garden of Adonis appears in his epic *The Faerie Queene,* book 3, canto 6, where in contrast to the Bower of Bliss in book 2, it represents a Golden Age or prelapsarian state of idealized nature. Yeats included its description in his own later edition of Spenser.

13. Alfred (later first Baron) Tennyson (1809–92) succeeded Wordsworth as poet laureate in 1850 and was perhaps the best-known poet of Victorian England. The passage that Yeats quotes, "Warming his five wits, the white owl in the belfry sits," comes from Tennyson's early poem "Song—The Owl" and should have a line break after "wits." *The Poems of Tennyson,* ed. Christopher Ricks (London: Longman; New York: Norton, 1972), 204.

    Edward Fitzgerald's translation of *The Rubáiyát of Omar Khayyám,* the twelfth-century Persian poet, appeared anonymously in 1859 and then in expanded editions later. After a slow start it became one of the most popular poetic works in English. The line "We come like water and like wind we go" concludes quatrain 28, where it reads "I came like Water and like Wind I go."

14. The quotation "Beauty like sorrow dwelleth everywhere" ascribed to Ben Jonson has not been identified and is likely not from Jonson. The lines beginning "Brightness falls from the air" are by Thomas Nashe (1567–1601), a versatile writer who, as one of the University Wits, moved to London and wrote in a variety of forms. The lines appear in his comedy *Summer's Last Will and Testament* (1600) but are more often printed separately as a lyric, often under the title "A Litany in Time of Plague" or "Adieu, farewell earth's bliss." Yeats took the line "Dust hath closed Helen's eye" as the title of a section in *The Celtic Twilight* in the revised and enlarged 1902 edition and quoted all three lines again in his "Note by W. B. Yeats on the Conversation of Cuchulain and Emer" in Lady Gregory's *Cuchulain of Muirthemne* (*P&I,* 227) and in the essay "The Symbolism of Poetry" in the present volume.

15. "The Land East of the Sun and West of the Moon" is the title of a lengthy section of the *The Earthly Paradise* by William Morris (1834–96), who is the subject of the later essay "The Happiest of the Poets."

16. The major American poet Walt Whitman (1819–92) rebelled against polite poetic tradition in *Leaves of Grass* (1855; expanded later) and other works. He often took his material from common life, even when writing on the great public themes of his day.

17. The phrases about ancestors "stout and wise" come from the section of Morris's *The Earthly Paradise* called "The Man Born to Be King." See *The Collected Works of William Morris,* ed. May Morris (London: Longman's Green, 1910–15; O'Shea #1389) 3:166; that edition is the

basis of subsequent collected editions of Morris, which are often identical with it in texts. The phrases that Yeats quotes all come from four consecutive lines, which should read: "Ages agone his line was born / Ere yet men knew the gift of corn; / And there, anigh to Paradise, / His ancestors grew stout and wise."

18. The long quotation comes from the concluding poem "The Grief of a Girl's Heart" in the chapter "West Irish Ballads" from Lady Gregory's *Poets and Dreamers: Studies & Translations from the Irish* (Dublin: Hodges, Figgis; New York: Charles Scribner's Sons, 1903; O'Shea #807), a volume that Yeats knew well. She dates the essay 1901 there; it was first published in *The Monthly Review* for October 1902, the same year that Yeats's essay was published in *The Cornhill Magazine.* Yeats omits several stanzas and also substitutes "towns and" for "towns with" in the third stanza and "on Sunday" for "on the Sunday" in the fifth stanza as well as introducing several variants in punctuation.

19. Yeats here refers to the traditional belief that as the perfect man Jesus measured exactly six feet tall. As the somewhat autobiographical Michael Hearne explains to Margaret in Yeats's novel *The Speckled Bird:* "He means that Christ, being the perfect man, had alone the perfect measurements. We are all imperfect. It is an idea the people have. They always seem to think that what we would call beauty [is] a mark of holiness or divinity" (*SB,* 75).

    The long verse quotation comes from the song "Ora Nam Buadh," which Alexander Carmichael (1832–1912) translates as "The Invocation of the Graces" in his *Carmina Gadelica: Hymns and Incantations* (1900; 2nd ed., Edinburgh: Oliver and Boyd, 1928) 1:7–11, and says "Probably it was compposed to a maiden on her marriage." Yeats's lines 3–5 render imperfectly lines 3–6 of Carmichael's translation: "In the lustral fire, / In the seven elements, / In the juice of the rasps, / In the milk of honey." Yeats's ellipsis indicates omission of thirty-five lines of Carmichael's text. In Carmichael, the fourth line after the ellipsis reads "star of guidance" rather than "pilot star"; the sixth line reads "steed of the plain" rather than "horse of the plain" and the seventh line reads "of the swan of swimming" rather than "of the sun rising."

20. In the early 1890s, Yeats put considerable effort into Irish cultural nationalist movements, seeking to revive the past as a way of influencing the present and future. Those included the Young Ireland societies, the Irish Literary Society, the National Literary Society, and the Irish theater movement.

21. The "ten thousand the prophet saw" probably refers to the Epistle of Jude 14 in the New Testament in which the prophet Enoch says "Behold, the Lord cometh with ten thousands of his saints . . ."

22. Many passages in Blake suggest that "the imagination is the man himself," though not with that exact phraseology. Compare his references

to "The Real Man The Imagination which Liveth for Ever" (letter to George Cumberland, 12 April 1827) and "The Imagination is not a State: it is the Human Existence itself" (*Milton,* 32:32) in Erdman, 783 and 132, respectively. Ellis-Yeats prints the letter in the "Memoir" (1: 162); plate 32 of *Milton* is missing from some copies and from editions based on them, apparently including Ellis-Yeats. The couplet about the seventy disciples comes from Blake's "The Everlasting Gospel," fragment d (Ellis-Yeats 2: 59; Erdman, 878). Yeats uses the phrase "the imagination is the man himself" again in "The Pathway" (see appendix B) and in the "By the Roadside" section of *The Celtic Twilight* (*Myth,* 139).

## Speaking to the Psaltery

The first three parts of this essay were published in *The Monthly Review,* edited by the poet and man of letters Henry Newbolt, for May 1902, partly to stimulate interest in a joint lecture and performance by Yeats and Florence Farr in Fleet Street, London, the next month. Yeats's part 4, then entitled "Music for Lyrics," and the note by Farr that comprises part 5 and was then entitled "Note by Florence Farr" were added in volume 3 of Yeats's *The Collected Works in Verse and Prose* (Stratford-on-Avon: Shakespeare Head Press, 1908). With significant revisions to part 4 (see note 14 below), they were incorporated into the text of "Speaking to the Psaltery" for *Essays* 1924.

1. A psaltery is an ancient stringed instrument similar to a dulcimer but played by plucking the strings.

   The actress Florence Farr (Mrs. Edward Emery, 1860–1917), was a close friend and soon-to-be mistress of Yeats. She performed several roles in his plays, including that of Aleel in the first performance of *The Countess Cathleen* (1899). She also shared Yeats's occult interests, becoming a *soror* of the Hermetic Order of the Golden Dawn in July 1890 and later a member of the Theosophical Society. Yeats dedicated the *In the Seven Woods* section of *Poems: 1899–1905* to her: "The only reciter of lyric poetry who is always a delight, because of the beauty of her voice and the rightness of her method" (*VP,* 850). Recalling the project of "Speaking to the Psaltery" in *Autobiographies,* he lamented the direction of her later stage career but still maintained that "her voice was among the most beautiful of her time, her elocution, her mastery of poetical rhythm incomparable" (*Au,* 303). One of the "New Women," Farr in 1912 suddenly changed careers and left for Ceylon, where she became the head of a girls' school. She died of breast cancer in Colombo in 1917.

   While Yeats was reputedly tone-deaf, he did exhibit a lifelong preoccupation with rhythm in poetry and often chanted or hummed his verses while composing. Ever since hearing Farr's voice in the 1890 Bedford Park Clubhouse production of John Todhunter's *A Sicilian Idyll,* Yeats collaborated with her off and on for more than twenty years. Shortly after the turn of the century, their project crystallized into the setting of verses to the psaltery, in which they were helped by the publisher and Elizabethan scholar A. H. Bullen (1857–1920) and the musician Arnold Dolmetsch (1858–1940). Following the publication of "Speaking to the Psaltery" in *The Monthly Review,* Yeats and Farr gave their first lecture-demonstration involving Yeats's essay on 10 June 1902; they had given an earlier joint performance in February 1901 and would give numerous others in both London and America during 1903 and continue doing so intermittently until February 1911. Bullen, of course, published several of Yeats's early books, including *Ideas of Good and Evil.*

Shelley's lyric "To a Skylark" is one of his best-known poems. Sir Ector's lamentations over the dead Launcelot may be found at the end of Sir Thomas Malory's (d. 1471) fifteenth-century *Le Morte d'Arthur,* book 21, chapter 13. Yeats owned a copy with designs by Aubrey Beardsley (O'Shea #1214, with very abbreviated title): *The Birth, Life and Acts of King Arthur, of His Noble Knights of the Round Table, Their Marvellous Enquests and Adventures, The Achieving of the San Greal and in the End Le Morte Darthur* (London: Dent, vol. 1, 1893; vol. 2, 1894).

2. Traditionally regarded as the author of the ancient Greek epics *The Iliad* (ca. 750 B.C.) and *The Odyssey* (ca. 725 B.C.), Homer is thus seen as the first Western poet.
3. Yeats may have been thinking in particular of Wordsworth here, both for his habit of composing aloud during walks and his contention in the "Preface" to the *Lyrical Ballads* that the poet should have the voice of a man speaking to men.
4. Yeats first met the Irish writer, mystic, and social reformer George William Russell ("AE") (1867–1935) at the Metropolitan School of Art in 1884 and despite occasional tensions they remained friends for life. In a letter to Dorothy Wellesley after Russell's death, Yeats recalled that "AE was my oldest friend—we began our work together" and also that George Yeats had remarked that "AE was the nearest to a saint you or I will ever meet. You are a better poet but no saint. I suppose one has to choose" (*L,* 838; 26 July 1935). Yeats devoted a section of the autobiographical *The Trembling of the Veil* to Russell (*Au,* 195–202) and dedicated both *The Secret Rose* and the *Crossways* section of his collected poems to him. Section 2 of "Speaking to the Psaltery" did not identify Russell by name from the first publication through 1914 but instead referred to him as "The Visionary." Despite years of intimacy, Yeats often referred to Russell as "A. E." rather than the correct "AE" (from the start of Russell's pen name, "Æon") in his works; the present

edition follows Yeats in his own texts but uses "AE" in explanatory notes.

5. The "Galway friend who is a learned musician" is likely Edward Martyn (1859–1923), whose family home, Tulira Castle, was in Ardrahan, Galway. A Catholic landowner, Martyn was heavily involved with Yeats and Lady Gregory in the Irish Literary Theatre and collaborated with Yeats and George Moore before falling out with them and launching his own Irish theatre movement. He also supported the Irish crafts movement, the Gaelic League, and Sinn Fein. Lanham notes a similar passage pertaining to the French-Swiss Arnold Dolmetsch, maker of harpsichords and clavichords, inventor of the modern recorder, and musical scholar of the seventeenth and eighteenth centuries, who lived in London: "I have been round at Dolmetsch's this evening and have found to my great surprise that I have made the poems of mine which have most 'folk' feeling, to actual little tunes, much like those A.E. writes to" (letter to William Archer, *CL3*, 204).
6. "Mrs. Williams" is an error for Mrs. Harriet Mathew, wife of Rev. A. S. Mathew, whose salon included John Flaxman, Hannah More, Laetitia Barbauld, and others along with Blake. According to Ellis-Yeats (1: 25, 27): 'They met at No. 28, Rathbone Place, home of the Rev. Mr. Mathews [error for Mathew] and his wife . . . Blake's original method of singing his poetry to music of his own, cannot have passed unappreciated . . . We would give him much now for a single note of those melodies."
7. A Gregorian hymn or chant is a monophonic system of Christian ritual music also known as plainsong or plainchant that uses free rhythm and a restricted scale. It is based on the *Antiphonarium* compiled by Gregory I (pope, 590–604).
8. Although there is some doubt about the accuracy of Yeats's contrast of himself and Russell here, according to the Irish poet F. R. Higgins (1896–1941) Yeats did read or chant particular poems to particular tunes. In a memorial tribute, Higgins stressed Yeats's interest in bringing poetry and song together and also invoked the experiments of speaking verse to the psaltery. "I remember him telling me some years back that most of his poems were composed to some vague tune, some lilt," recalled Higgins. "Indeed, when we were together, he sang in his own uncertain, shy way, some of these poems. Whenever these poems were repeated, at later dates, he always sang them to the same halting lilt." *Scattering Branches: Tributes to the Memory of W. B. Yeats,* ed. Stephen Gwynn (London: Macmillan, 1940), 150.
9. This distinction between the approach of Yeats and Farr on the one hand and Russell on the other also appears in *Samhain* for 1902: "I have been working with Miss Farr and Mr. Arnold Dolmetsch, who has made a psaltery for the purpose, to perfect a music of speech which can be recorded in something like ordinary musical notes; while

A. E. has got a musician to record little changes with intervals much smaller than those of modern music" (*IDM*, 14). Yeats did not identify Farr by name in the last sentence of section 2 until the 1924 revision for *Essays*.

10. The lyrics come from Yeats's play *The Countess Cathleen*, lines 672–77 (*Pl*, 52), in a song by Aleel, a role created by Farr onstage. The source may be *Poems* (1895) ("Impetuous heart be still, be still," *P*, 543), with three changes in accidentals.
11. Yeats may be remembering the first performance of his verse play *The Shadowy Waters* here, with green and blue scenery and costumes, and with Farr in the role of Dectora and playing a psaltery. He recalled, "The effect of this monotony of colour was to my eyes beautiful, and made the players seem like people in a dream" (*VP*, 815).
12. The practice of awarding a golden violet as a prize arose at the first floral games of the fourteenth-century troubadours, held at Toulouse in May 1324, and surviving until about 1500. Yeats and Farr were moving toward training young actresses to chant verse as a Golden Violet Order of Troubadours before their encounters with Dolmetsch took them in a different direction.
13. The File (or Filidh or Filí) were ancient Irish poets whose duties included praising patrons, preserving genealogies, and being learned in history and literature. They were both feared and honored.
14. This section was titled "Poems for the Psaltery" when it and the next one first appeared in volume 3 of *The Collected Works in Verse and Prose*. The following passages from 1908 were subsequently deleted or moved and rephrased: "She [Farr] has a beautiful speaking-voice, and, an almost rarer thing, a perfect ear for verse; and nothing but the attempting of it will show how far these things can be taught or developed where they exist but a little. I believe that they should be a part of the teaching of all children, for the beauty of the speaking-voice is more important to our lives than that of the singing, and the rhythm of words comes more into the structure of our daily being than any abstract pattern of notes. . . . for I am certain that all poets, even all delighted readers of poetry, speak certain kinds of poetry to distinct and simple tunes, though the speakers may be, perhaps generally are, deaf to ordinary music, even what we call tone-deaf. . . . Mr. Arnold Dolmetsch, when he took up the subject at my persuasion, wrote down the recitation of another lyric poet, who like myself knows nothing of music, and found little tunes that delighted him; and Mr. George Russell ("A.E.") writes all his lyrics, a musician tells me, to two little tunes which sound like old Arabic music" (234–35).
15. For the taking down of tunes, see *L*, 200: "Dolmetsch is now making little tunes for my Wandering Aengus and some of my other things to be spoken to" (to Lady Gregory, 13 June 1902).
16. The major Victorian poet and critic Algernon Charles Swinburne

(1837–1909) was an important early influence on Yeats, especially in rhythm and musicality. Conservative critics castigated his *Poems and Ballads* (1866) as too pagan and sensual, though others praised their technical skill and evocative imagery. Yeats later felt that Swinburne's political rhetoric and themes in other poetry had interfered with his lyricism.

17. "Autumn is over the long leaves that love us" is the first line of Yeats's early lyric "The Falling of the Leaves" from *The Wanderings of Oisin* (1889), *P,* 12.

"The Ballad of Father Gilligan" (*P,* 42–44) was first published in 1890. The author of the ballad "The Fine Old English Gentleman" is unknown though is sometimes said to be Henry Russell (1812–1900), who did an American adaptation. The first stanza reads "I'll sing you a good old song, / Made by a good old pate, / Of a fine old English gentleman / Who had an old estate, / And who kept up his old mansion / At a bountiful old rate; / With a good old porter to relieve / The old poor at his gate, / Like a fine old English gentleman / All of the olden time." *The Home Book of Verse,* ed. Burton Egbert Stevenson (New York: Henry Holt, 1945), 1:1721–22.

18. Giulio Caccini (ca. 1550–1618) was an Italian composer and singer who entered the service of the Florentine court and became a member of Giovanni Bardi's Florentine Camerata. One of the developers of modern secular opera, he evolved a new style of recitative singing that approached the naturalness of speech and often performed his own compositions, accompanied by the theorbo, or large lute.

The slightly later Claudio Monteverdi (1567–1643) composed eight books of madrigals and the opera *Orfeo* (1607). He contributed to the decline of the old polyphonic style and helped develop the new style of monody or accompanied melody.

Giacomo Carissimi (1605–74) popularized the chamber cantata and played an important role in the history of the oratorio. In his religious works he adapted the idiom of Monteverdi to sacred drama and preferred setting Latin text of Old Testament stories. He, too, was concerned with fusing words and music.

19. The words and music of the six settings at the end were added for *The Collected Works* of 1908, in which the lyrics were written by hand by one of Bullen's employees and hence not part of the valid chain of transmission.

"The Wind Blows out of the Gates of the Day" comes from *The Land of Heart's Desire,* lines 236–47 and 431–42 (*Pl,* 73 and 81; *P,* 542).

20. "The Happy Townland" (*P,* 83) was part of Yeats's *In the Seven Woods*. The direction "Chorus" does not appear there, but the lines beginning "The little fox he murmured" are italicized and do form a chorus for the poem.

21. "I have drunk ale from the Country of the Young" forms the opening of "He Thinks of his Past Greatness When a Part of the Constellations of Heaven" from *The Wind Among the Reeds* (1899), *P*, 70–71; the last two lines were later revised to "O beast of the wilderness, bird of the air, / Must I endure your amorous cries?"
22. The text is the first stanza of Yeats's "The Song of Wandering Aengus," from *The Wind Among the Reeds* (1899), *P*, 55–56.
23. The text is the first stanza of Yeats's "The Host of the Air," from *The Wind Among the Reeds* (1899), *P*, 52–54.
24. Yeats's "The Song of the Old Mother" comes from *The Wind Among the Reeds* (1899), *P*, 56.

## Magic

Yeats began the essay in October 1900, writing to Lady Gregory that while waiting for her to send him the manuscript of the second part of his essay on Shelley (see below in the present volume) "I shall start my essay on 'Magic' to fill the gap . . ." (*CL2*, 574). He had intended to send the essay to *The North American Review* but instead sent it to *The Monthly Review*, edited by the poet and man of letters Henry Newbolt (1862–1938), where it was first published in September 1900. After publication Yeats told Lady Gregory that Newbolt had called the essay "brilliantly successful" and wanted more of his work (*CL3*, 136). There were no significant changes, except that in 1903 Yeats deleted a sentence about Andrew Lang (see note 33 below); the two footnotes were added in 1924.

1. Yeats discusses the great mind and great memory in several places elsewhere. For an informative discussion, see *Per Amica Silentia Lunae:* "I came to believe in a great memory passing on from generation to generation. But that was not enough, for these images showed intention and choice. They had a relation to what one knew and yet were an extension of one's knowledge" (*LE*, 18). Yeats also cites Wordsworth's immortality ode and Henry More's *Anima Mundi.*
2. The man with whom Yeats quarreled was Samuel Liddell (later MacGregor) Mathers (1854–1918), whose ghost Yeats later invoked in "All Souls' Night," the epilogue to *A Vision* and the last poem of *The Tower* (1928): "I call MacGregor Mathers from his grave, / For in my first hard spring-time we were friends, / Although of late estranged. / I thought him half a lunatic, half knave, / And told him so, but friendship never ends" (*P*, 233). In 1888 Mathers was a founding member of the Isis-Urania Temple of the Hermetic Order of the Golden Dawn, which Mathers began to dominate from 1891 onward and into which he had inducted Yeats himself in 1890. The year before Yeats's present essay appeared, Mathers had been ousted from his increasingly dictatorial role in the London branch by a coup that involved Florence Farr

Emery and Yeats himself; it resulted in Yeats serving a temporary term as imperator of the order for almost a year. The "acquaintance, who is now dead" remains unidentified.

3. The novel of Bulwer-Lytton's was probably *Zanoni* (1842), though possibly *A Strange Story* (1861). Lord Lytton (1802–73) became Grand Patron of the Rosicrucian Society in 1871 and was one of Madame Blavatsky's sources for *Isis Unveiled.*
4. Mathers married Moina Bergson in June 1890. She was the sister of the philosopher Henri Bergson and dedicatee of Yeats's 1925 version of *A Vision* under her Golden Dawn name, *Vestigia Nulla Retrorsum.* Mathers and his wife lived in the "little house" as part of his position as curator at the Horniman Museum (established by F. J. Horniman in Forest Hill, London), one of Annie Horniman's many gestures of support before their quarrel. He lost that appointment in 1891 and moved to Paris with his wife the next year.
5. This is one of the Enochian Tablets, about which Golden Dawn members received instruction in order to evoke trance visions. Enochian magic derives from the work of the Elizabethan occultists Edward Kelley and Dr. John Dee. Enochian tablets included forty-nine-inch squares filled with letters of the alphabet, often with numbers on them; the magician would invoke a spirit who would communicate by pointing to various letters in turn.
6. Yeats's vision of a man dressed in black standing among white figures, and the following description of a doctor lecturing his pupils about dissection, may derive from a number of paintings, such as Rembrandt's *Anatomy Lesson of Dr. Nicholaes Tulp* (1632).
7. A document for prospective members of the Order of the Golden Dawn stated, "The Chiefs of the Order do not care to accept as Candidates any person accustomed to submit themselves as Mediums to the experiments of Hypnotism, Mesmerism; or who habitually allow themselves to fall into a complete Passive Condition of Will; also they disapprove of the methods made use of as a rule in such experiments." Ellic Howe, *The Magicians of the Golden Dawn: A Documentary History of a Magical Order, 1887–1923* (London: Routledge and Kegan Paul, 1972), 56.
8. Mary Shelley's *Frankenstein; or, the Modern Prometheus* was published in 1818. It recounts the story of Frankenstein's creation of a creature from inanimate matter.
9. Evolving from the guilds of medieval stonemasons, the secret fraternal order of Free and Accepted Masons is the largest worldwide secret society and requires of its members morality, charity, and obedience to the law of the land. It is especially strong in the British Isles and countries originally within the British empire. The Golden Dawn rituals derived partly from Masonry.
10. Yeats visited the Aran Islands, off the west coast of Ireland, 5–7 August

1896, together with Arthur Symons, Edward Martyn, and Martin Morris. Shortly thereafter Symons wrote of "Teampull Benen, the remains of an early oratory, surrounded by cloghans or stone dwellings made of heaped stones which, centuries ago, had been the cells of monks." "The Islands of Aran," dated summer 1896, in his *Cities and Sea-Coasts and Islands* (New York: Brentano, 1919), 312.

11. Blake said this not in one of his poems but in a letter about one of them, probably *Milton,* to Thomas Butts, 6 July 1803: "I may praise it, since I dare not pretend to be any other than the Secretary the Authors are in Eternity" (Ellis-Yeats 1: 87; Erdman, 730).
12. Yeats tells this anecdote again in "The Tragic Generation" section of his autobiographies (*Au,* 259). The friends were MacGregor Mathers and his wife, Moina, with whom Yeats stayed in Paris during late April and early May 1898.
13. Yeats's fellow-student was Maud Gonne, and the message pertained to his affair with "Diana Vernon" (Olivia Shakespear): "I had walked into the room in her hotel where she was sitting with friends. At first she thought I was really there, but presently on finding that no one else saw me knew that it was my ghost. She told me to return at twelve that night and I vanished. At twelve I had stood, dressed in some strange, priest-like costume, at her bedside and brought her soul away, and we had wandered round the cliffs [of] Howth where we had been together years before" (*Mem,* 87).
14. Blake wrote in the "Public Address" (Erdman, 578): "When I tell any Truth it is not for the sake of Convincing those who do not know it but for the sake of defending those who do." Ellis-Yeats slightly misquotes this passage, substituting: "When I tell a truth, it is not to convince those who do not know it, but to protect those who do" (1:20).
15. Yeats quotes here from the poem "The Scholar-Gipsy" by Matthew Arnold (1822–88), which itself is explicitly based on Joseph Glanvill's (1636–80) *The Vanity of Dogmatizing* (1661). Glanvill's treatise attacked the scholastic philosophy then dominant at Oxford; Glanvill himself became a divine and was influenced by the Cambridge Platonist Henry More (1614–87). For "trailing his fingers in the cool stream" read "Trailing in the cool steam thy fingers wet"; for "giving store . . . harebells" read "Oft thou hast given them store . . . bluebells"; and for "dew" read "dews."
16. Yeats quotes here from chapter 20 of *The Vanity of Dogmatizing* (1661) by Joseph Glanvill, Arnold's source for the story of "The Scholar-Gipsy." In 1853 Arnold published the poem with a note piecing together extracts from this passage in Glanvill, a wording retained in an edition of Arnold in Yeats's library (*Poetical Works* [London, Macmillan, 1892]; O'Shea #54). Here Yeats quotes instead from the full passage; although his exact source is unknown, the transcription here differs from other readings in small particulars.

17. Yeats quotes here from Blake's *The Marriage of Heaven and Hell,* plate 16. Both Erdman and Ellis-Yeats read "God only Acts & Is, in existing beings or Men" (Erdman, 40; Ellis-Yeats 3).
18. Andrew Lang in *The Making of Religion* (London: Longmans, Green, 1898), 60, quotes from Sir Edward Burnett Tylor, *Primitive Culture: Researches into the Development of Mythology, Philosophy, Religion, Art and Custom,* 2 vols. (London: J. Murray, 1871).
19. Yeats quotes here from Lang, *The Making of Religion,* 78; Lang's text reads "were presented" rather than "were present." Joseph Glanvill (see note 16 above) had also cited Laplanders in his *Saducismus Triumphatus* (2nd ed. [London: 1682]), section 18, "Some Considerations about Witchcraft": "most of the Laplanders, and some other Northern people, are Witches."
20. The man is called Fagan in Lady Gregory's *Visions and Beliefs in the West of Ireland* (New York: G. P. Putnam's Sons, 1920; O'Shea #811), 1:103–4. Yeats and Lady Gregory had hoped that he could improve Yeats's weak eyesight, but Fagan responded: "It's not from *them* [the Sidhe] the harm came to your eyes. I see them in all places—and there's no man mowing a meadow that doesn't see them at some time or other" (108). Yeats also used the quotation in "Irish Witch Doctors" (*LAR,* 30), where he ascribes it to the pseudonym "Kirwan" on the Galway coast, and also in his review of the County Galway schoolmaster Daniel Deeney's (Domhnall O'Duibhne's) *Peasant Lore from Gaelic Ireland* (*LAR,* 24).
21. In book 3 ("Blessed Patrick of the Bells") of *A Book of Saints and Wonders* (New York: Oxford University Press, 1971), 45–46, Lady Gregory writes that "Patrick made this hymn one time he was going to preach the Faith at Teamhuir, and his enemies lay in hiding to make an attack on him as he passed. But as he himself and Benen his servant went by, all they could see passing was a wild deer and a fawn. And the Deer's Cry is the name of the hymn to this day." Yeats's copy (London: John Murray, 1907) is O'Shea #792.
22. In *Le Morte d'Arthur,* the cycle of Arthurian legends by Sir Thomas Malory (ca. 1408–71), the enchantress Morgan le Fay evades the pursuing Arthur by changing herself and her soldiers to stone (bk. 4, chap. 14).
23. Tacitus (ca. A.D. 56–ca.120) tells this story in *Annals* 14:29–30; the Romans recovered and slaughtered the Druids. John Rhys transcribed the account in his *Celtic Britain* (London: SPCK, 1882), 82–83. Mona (modern Anglesey) is an island off the coast of England in the Irish Sea and was used as a refuge before the Romans subdued it.
24. The Count de Saint-Germain (ca. 1710–ca. 1782) had a mysterious background and was a founder of Freemasonry; he knew Eastern lore and was also reputed to have been a spy. Andrew Lang discussed "Saint-Germain the Deathless" in *Historical Mysteries* (1904), saying

that Saint-Germain was the original for Margrave in Bulwer-Lytton's *A Strange Story.*

25. The contest between Moses and Aaron on the one hand and Pharaoh's magicians on the other is told in Exodus 7 as part of Moses's efforts to persuade Pharaoh to allow the Hebrews to leave Egypt. Later in this section Yeats refers to Mount Sinai, where God spoke to Moses and gave him the Ten Commandments.
26. A similar vision appears in *The Speckled Bird:* " . . . she began to see forms and colours more distinctly than she had ever seen them with her ordinary eyes. She saw enormous multitudes of birds and in the midst of them was one very beautiful bird wearing a crown, a bird like a great white eagle. It had lit on a great tree, the others were perching among the branches" (*SB,* 77).
27. Yeats refers here not so much to the tree of knowledge of good and evil from the Garden of Eden in Genesis but rather to its elaboration in Jewish mystical tradition. *The Book of Concealed Mystery* is a book from *The Zohar* ('Book of Splendour'), the most important collection of texts from the Jewish Kabbalah tradition of mystical interpretation of the Hebrew scriptures begun in late medieval Spain. MacGregor Mathers translated this particular text from the Latin version by Knorr von Rosenroth in *Kabbala Denudata: The Kabbalah Unveiled* (1887). Yeats conflates the text itself with Rosenroth's parenthetical exegesis: "The tree which is mitigated (that is, the path of the kingdom or Schechinah, which is the tree of knowledge of good and evil, which in itself existeth from the judgments, but is mitigated by the bridegroom through the influx of mercies) resideth within (within the shells; because the kingdom hath its dominion over all things, and its feet descend into death). In its branches (in the inferior worlds) the birds lodge and build their nests (the souls and the angels have their place) . . ." (13th impression [London: Routledge and Kegan, 1975], 103–4). The term Shekhinah does not appear in the Bible but rather belongs to Talmudic tradition, where it refers to the presence of God, most often revealed as a light and sometimes anthropomorphized as a woman. Medieval Jewish philosophers viewed the Shekhinah as an entity separate from God though created by or emanating from him.
28. In *W. B. Yeats: 1865–1939,* 2nd ed. (London: Macmillan, 1962), 112, Joseph Hone says that a bank clerk sometimes came in for séances after dinner with Yeats's cousin Lucy Middleton, who was visiting her and Yeats's uncle George Pollexfen while Yeats was staying with him in Sligo (see *Au,* 209–10 for another version of the incident). Yeats recruited the astrologically inclined George Pollexfen to join the Golden Dawn. Yeats gives another version of the vision in a note to "The Poet Pleads with the Elemental Powers" in *The Wind Among the Reeds* (1899), *P,* 639–40.
29. According to Lanham, "This is the sacred Mountain of Abiegnus. In

the initiation ceremony for the Grade of Adeptus Minus, which Yeats underwent in June 1893, he would have seen a diagram accompanied by the words, 'This is the Symbolic Mountain of God in the centre of the Universe, the sacred Rosicrucian Mountain of Initiation, the Mystic Mountain of Abiegnus'" (217). Israel Regardie, *The Golden Dawn,* 2:237.

30. The *Carmina Gadelica* was a collection of Scottish Celtic prayers and blessings from the islands and highlands of Scotland collected and translated by Alexander Carmichael (1832–1912). Carmichael there records the association of the serpent with Saint Bride or Bridgid: "The serpent is supposed to emerge from its hollow among the hills on St. Bride's Day, and a propitiatory hymn was sung to it. . . . 'Early on Bride's morn / The serpent shall come from the hole, / I will not molest the serpent, / Nor will the serpent molest me.'" *Carmina Gadelica: Hymns and Incantations . . . Orally Collected in the Highlands and Islands of Scotland,* 2 vols. (1900; 2nd ed., Edinburgh and London: Oliver and Boyd, 1928), 1: 169.

31. The old Irishwoman was Mary Battle (Mrs. Mary Feeny, d. 1907 or 1908), the elderly housekeeper of George Pollexfen; she was credited with second sight and provided numerous stories to Yeats. See *Au,* 208–9, and "And Fair, Fierce Women" (*Myth,* 57–58) for other accounts of this incident.

32. The friend was Lady Gregory. Diana was the Roman goddess of the chase, the daughter of Zeus and Leto and the twin sister of Apollo. Buskins were the thick-soled boots worn by actors of tragedy in ancient Athens, in contrast to the sock or low shoe worn by actors of comedy there.

33. Finn mac Cumhal (often anglicized as Finn MacCool) is one of the most famous figures from Irish mythology. He led the Fianna in battle and magic, and was the father of Oisin. For a parallel passage to the present reference, see "Irish Witch Doctors" (*LAR,* 39).

    *The Monthly Review* version of the essay included an additional sentence after "the Assizes of Cork": "Mr. Lang, who is more preoccupied with scientific proofs than I am, tells of a crystal gazer of his acquaintance whose vision was corroborated by historical documents unknown at the time of the vision." Lang objected to that statement in the London *Morning Post* in September 1901, possibly prompting Yeats's later deletion of the offending remark.

34. Robert Browning's dramatic poem *Paracelsus* (1835) was one of his most popular early works and the first to appear under his own name. It uses the figure of the Renaissance doctor, alchemist, and hermeticist Paracelsus (Theophrastus Bombastus von Hohenheim, 1493–1541) as a type of the poet and seeker after knowledge.

    Yeats also uses the phrase "thinking the thought and doing the deed" in "The Philosophy of Shelley's Poetry" (below) and in the description of the term *"Record"* in *A Vision* (1937), 193. The "Indian book" remains unidentified.

35. The particular "Prophetic Book" of Blake is *Jerusalem,* chapter 1:

> All things acted on Earth are seen in the bright Sculptures of
> Los's Halls & every Age renews its powers from these Works
> With every pathetic story possible to happen from Hate or
> Wayward Love & every sorrow & distress is carved here. . . .
> Ellis-Yeats 3: *Jerusalem,* plate 16; Erdman, 161

36. Henry Newbolt, editor of *The Monthly Review*, describes a similar experiment of Yeats and Mrs. Robert Bridges in 1897: "Yeats produced a number of magic cards out of his pocket: they were each painted with a single symbol, enlarged from the tiny ornaments on the pages of Blake's handpainted books. The one which Mrs. Bridges selected was marked with a plain parallelogram in yellow. She was directed to press this card over her forehead and eyes and to describe what she saw. She reported almost immediately that she saw a green tree of unfamiliar shape—it was increasing rapidly in size, like a banyan tree, by sending down shoots on all sides which took root in the ground and sprang up in fresh stems, filling the whole field of vision. The yellow oblong was 'the symbol of vegetation': Yeats was triumphant. . . ." Sir Henry Newbolt, *My World as in My Time* (London: Faber, 1932), 192–93.
37. Norse mythology treated the hammer of the thunder god Thor as an anti-Christian symbol powerful in warding off the cross and the White Christ.
38. One exemplar of incredulity was Wilfrid Scawen Blunt (1840–1922), who described an effort that Yeats made on 1 April 1898 to have Blunt call up symbols: "Yeats experimented magically on me. He first took out a notebook and made what he called a pyramid in it which was a square of figures, then he bade me think of and see a square of yellow as it might be a door, and walk through it and tell him what I saw beyond. All that I could see at all clearly was that I seemed to be standing on a piece of green, rushy grass, in front of me a small pool from which issued two streams of very blue water to right and to left of me. He then bade me turn and go back through the door, and told me I should see either a man or woman who would give me something. I failed to see anything but darkness, but at last with some effort I made out the indistinct figure of a child, which offered me with its left hand some withered flowers. I could not see its face. Lastly he bade me thank the person to whose intervention the vision was due, and read from his notebook some vague sentences prefiguring this vision. The performance was very imperfect, not to say null." *My Diaries, Being a Personal Narrative of Events, 1888–1914* (New York: Alfred A. Knopf, 1923) 1:291.

39. Founded in 1882 by a group of Cambridge scholars and scientists, the Society for Psychical Research scientifically investigates paranormal or psychic phenomenon. In 1885 it pronounced Madame Blavatsky a fraudulent medium. From its first periodical publication through the 1914 edition of *IGE,* this sentence read: "It was long before I myself would admit an inherent power in symbols, for it long seemed to me that one could account for everything by the power of one imagination over another, telepathy as it is called with that separation of knowledge and life, of word and emotion, which is the sterility of scientific speech."
40. The "person I was experimenting with" and "a seer who could say" remain unidentified.
41. Yeats's triad of poet, artist, and musician here may derive from Blake's remark in *A Vision of the Last Judgment* about "Poetry Painting & Music the three Powers in Man of conversing with Paradise which the flood did not Sweep away" (Ellis-Yeats 2: 397; Erdman, 559). Yeats associated the three arts numerous times, including in the late poem "Lapis Lazuli" (*P,* 300–301). The French symbolist poet Mallarmé (1842–98) also associated magic and the arts in his own essay "Magie," which appeared in English in *The National Observer* for 28 January 1893.
42. Lady Gregory discussed "Herb-Healing" (first published in 1900) in *Poets and Dreamers: Studies and Translations from the Irish* (Dublin: Hodges, Figgis / New York: Scribner's, 1903; O'Shea #807), 111–20. Much of the same material also appears in her *Visions and Beliefs in the West of Ireland* (1920), especially in the chapter "Herbs, Charms, and Wise Women."
43. The fellow-students are likely those of the Hermetic Order of the Golden Dawn. In 1887 Yeats had joined a group of "Hermetic students" at the invitation of MacGregor Mathers (*Mem,* 26). This "study group," according to George Mills Harper (*Yeats's Golden Dawn* [London: Macmillan, 1974], 8), "probably included several prominent members of the Golden Dawn." Yeats did not join the Golden Dawn itself until 7 March 1890 and withdrew from active participation in the order on 26 or 27 February 1901. Ellic Howe, *Magicians of the Golden Dawn,* 69, 239; *CL3,* xvi.
44. Yeats describes one such occasion when he tried to relate a vision to Lady Gregory: "I felt a difficulty in articulation and became confused. I had wanted to tell her of some beautiful sight, and could see no reason for this. I remember then what I had read of mystics not being always [able] to speak, and remembered some tale of a lecturer on mysticism having to stop in the middle of a sentence. Even to this moment, though I can sometimes speak without difficulty, I am more often unable to. I am a little surprised that I can write what I please" (*Mem,* 128).

## The Happiest of the Poets

This essay was first published in *The Fortnightly Review* for March 1903. In a letter to Lady Gregory in December 1901, Yeats indicated that William Leonard Courtney (1850–1928), editor of *The Fortnightly* and also drama critic and literary editor of the *Daily Telegraph,* "has taken the 'Morris' at £3 a 1000 words" (*CL*3, 136); and in a letter to A. H. Bullen in late June 1902 he indicated that the manuscript of the essay was with Courtney (*CL*3, 210). In the event Courtney did not publish the essay until March 1903, thus delaying the appearance of *IGE* until May of that year. In writing to Sydney Cockerell for advice about the binding of *IGE,* Yeats called the essay "one of the best things of the sort I have done" (*CL*3, 331). There are no major changes in the published text of the essay, although the date at the end was first added for the second edition of 1903.

1. The poet and painter Dante Gabriel Rossetti (1828–82) was perhaps the key figure in the Pre-Raphaelite movement and one of the founders of the Pre-Raphaelite Brotherhood in 1848. Yeats slightly misremembers Rossetti's list here: it appeared not in a letter but in a passage from his notebooks:

   1866.—Thinking in what order I love colours, found the following:—
   1. Pure light warm green.
   2. Deep gold-colour.
   3. Certain tints of grey.
   4. Shadowy or steel blue.
   5. Brown, with crimson tinge.
   6. Scarlet.
   Other colours (comparatively) only loveable according to the relations in which they are placed.

   *Collected Works,* ed., William Michael Rossetti, 2 vols. (London: Ellis and Scrutton, 1886) 1:510. Yeats had a copy of the 1897 edition, published by Ellis and Elvey, in his library (O'Shea #1789).
2. Yeats alludes to one of his favorite tracts on poetry, Browning's "Essay on Shelley," originally the introductory essay to a collection of spurious Shelley letters published in 1852. Written in 1851, the essay distinguishes the "objective" from the "subjective" poet. Browning writes of the latter: "Not what man sees, but what God sees—the *Ideas* of Plato, seeds of creation lying burningly on the Divine Hand—it is toward these that he struggles." Robert Browning, *The Poems, Volume I,* ed. John Pettigrew and Thomas Collins (Harmondsworth and New York: Penguin Books, 1981), 1002.
3. The Star of the Magi is the one that led the wise men from the East to

the infant Jesus in the Bible. Yeats associates it with Shelley's important poetic symbol of Venus, the morning and evening star that is the brightest object in the sky after the sun and moon. Yeats slightly misquotes Percy Bysshe Shelley's phrase in "With a Guitar, to Jane": "On the wind-swept Apennine" (Hutchinson, 672). The Apennine mountains run from north to south in Italy along its eastern side.

4. Morris's long poem *The Earthly Paradise* (1868–70) established him as one of the most popular poets of Victorian England. It consists of a prologue and twenty-four tales in Chaucerian meters told by a company of Norsemen after their unsuccessful quest for a fabled land where none grow old. Before *Essays,* all book versions of the present essay included the sentence "One's emotion must never break the bonds of life, one's hands must never labour to loosen the silver cord, one's ears must never strain to catch the sound of Michael's trumpet." The periodical version of the sentence began with the phrase "That is to say" later transferred to the start of the following sentence.
5. In Morris's *The Well at the World's End* (1896), the well is located beyond the Dry Tree; its water gives various benefits, such as cleansing sorrow, curing wounds, and granting skill with words.
6. The benign enchantress Habundia rules the forest of Evilshaw in Morris's *The Water of the Wondrous Isles* (1897), where she helps the young Birdalone. Yeats may be remembering especially the verse in book 4, chapter 22:

   The Dry Tree shall be seen
   On the green earth, and green
   The Well-spring shall arise
   For the hope of the wise.
   They are one which were twain,
   The Tree bloometh again,
   And the Well-spring hath come
   From the waste to the home.
   *Collected Works* 19:196

7. Yeats quotes here from Blake's *The Marriage of Heaven and Hell:* "Energy is Eternal Delight" (Ellis-Yeats 3: plate 4; Erdman, 34).
8. Morris entitled the prologue to his *The Earthly Paradise* "The Wanderers"; they pursue their vision of the Earthly Paradise of eternal life. Morris contributed his early prose romance, *The Hollow Land,* to the *Oxford and Cambridge Magazine* in 1856; his late one, *The Sundering Flood,* appeared from Kelmscott in 1898.
9. In Arthurian legend, the Holy Grail is a symbol of perfection sought by the knights of the Round Table and is identified with the cup from the Last Supper in which Joseph of Arimathea caught blood from the crucified Jesus. Both Malory in *Le Morte D'Arthur* and Wagner in *Parsi-*

*fal* give Christian renderings of the legend. Before its Christianization, the story has roots in pagan fertility rituals and as a Celtic story. See R. S. Loomis, *The Grail from Celtic Myth to Christian Symbol* (New York: Columbia University Press, 1963).

10. J. W. Mackail (1859–1945), a distinguished classical scholar and later Professor of Poetry at Oxford, also wrote the first major biography of Morris. See his *The Life of William Morris,* 2 vols. (London: Longmans, Green, 1899), 1:13–14, for the story of the copper mine. The passage about the three arrows may be found in *The Sundering Flood* (1897): "here be three [shafts] which I will give thee; and if thou take heed, thou shalt not find them easy to lose, since ever they shall go home. But if ever thou lose two of them, then take the third and go into some waste place where there is neither meadow nor acre, and turn to the north-east and shoot upward toward the heavens, and say this rhyme. . . . And then shalt thou find the arrows lying at thy feet" (*Collected Works* 11:27).
11. Yeats here slightly misquotes from "The Love of Alcestis" section of *The Earthly Paradise* (*Collected Works* 4:114): in the first phrase, "who knew" should not be part of the quotation; in the second, "stubble" should read "stubbled"; and "where right and wrong are mixed together" should read "Wherein the right and wrong so mingled are."
12. The exclamation about the trees comes from Morris's letter to Cormell Price, 10 August 1855, from Avranches, Normandy, which Yeats probably read in Mackail, 1:76: "I think that valley was the most glorious of all we saw that day, there was not much grain there, it was nearly all grass land and the trees, O! the trees! it was all like the country in a beautiful poem, in a beautiful Romance. . . ."
13. "The Love of Alcestis" is a section of Morris's *The Earthly Paradise.* His *News from Nowhere* (1891) is a socialist prose romance.
14. The description of the people of Burg Dale comes from *The Roots of the Mountains* (1890). *Collected Works* 15:11. For "the flowery" read "its flowering"; for "stream" read "streams"; and for "the green-tree boughs" read "its green-tree boughs."
15. *The Bride* (1865–66), also known as *The Beloved,* is one of a series of luxurious half-length portraits of women produced by Rossetti during the 1860s; it is based on the Song of Solomon in the Bible.
16. The Victorian poet Algernon Charles Swinburne (1837–1909) wrote a trilogy on Mary, queen of Scots, that included *Chastelard* (1865), *Bothwell* (1874), and *Mary Stuart* (1881). Yeats might also be remembering Swinburne's 1882 poem "Adieux à Marie Stuart."
17. In part 1 of his essay "The Philosophy of Shelley's Poetry" (immediately following the present one), Yeats quotes ten lines of the passage from Shelley's *Rosalind and Helen: A Modern Eclogue,* in which the dying Lionel hears the nightingale's song and links it to ecstasy and death (Hutchinson, 185, lines 1121–30).

18. This passage and the events alluded to before it come from Morris's *The Water of the Wondrous Isles* (*Collected Works* 20:16–18); the three dots signal an ellipsis of twenty-six lines. For "clean as" read "clean, and as"; for "clean-made" read "clear-made"; for "thy mouth" read "thy nose"; for "folk who" read "folk that"; and for "thou shalt" read "shalt thou."
19. Danaë is the daughter of Acrisius in Morris's "The Doom of King Acrisius" chapter of *The Earthly Paradise* (*Collected Works* 3). The woman who makes the flowers in her girdle grow young again is known as the Maid in Morris's *The Wood Beyond the World* (*Collected Works* 17, chap. 25, p. 97).
20. Yeats has slightly garbled both title and quoted phrases here. The phrases come from a sentence in Morris's *The Water of the Wondrous Isles,* pt. 2, chap. 9, entitled "How Birdalone Came to the Isle of the Young and the Old" and should read in context "the children began to seem to her as images, or at the best not more to her than the rabbits or the goats" (*Collected Works* 20:90).
21. The house was Sandymount Castle in the Dublin suburbs, an eighteenth-century structure with extensive grounds and, later, Gothic battlements. It had belonged to Robert Corbet, Yeats's great-uncle on his father's side. Corbet lived the life of a prosperous Anglo-Irish gentleman but later lost his fortune and committed suicide by jumping off a ferry while crossing the Irish Sea in 1872.
22. Yeats quotes here the first three stanzas of Morris's "Golden Wings," from *The Defence of Guenevere and Other Poems* (1858) in *Collected Works* 1:116.
23. The great house of the Wolfings comes from Morris's prose romance *The House of the Wolfings* (1888), in which the Wolfings are descended from the gods and display a wolf on their banners.
24. This anecdote took place at Morris's home, Kelmscott House, in the borough of Hammersmith in Greater London. Yeats tells the anecdote again in his 1896 review of Morris's *The Well at the World's End* (*EAR,* 321). For a brief account of Yeats's Sunday evenings with the Socialist League in Kelmscott House, see part 12 of the "Four Years" section of *Autobiographies* (*Au,* 130–33). In an earlier version of the passage he wrote, "There were moments when I thought myself a Socialist and saw Morris more as a public man and social thinker" (*Mem,* 20).
25. The socialist pamphlet is "Under an Elm Tree; or, Thoughts in the Country-Side," first published in *The Commonweal* for July 1889, and as a separate pamphlet in 1891. For a reprint, see *William Morris: Artist, Writer, Socialist,* ed. May Morris (Oxford: Basil Blackwell, 1936), 2:507–12.
26. Mackail records that More's *Utopia* meant more to Morris "than the professedly Socialistic treatises—Marx's 'Capital,' Wallace's 'Land Nationalization,' and the like—which he had been rather dispiritedly

ploughing through" (*Life,* 2:89). In *Au,* 135, Yeats writes, "I did not read economics, having turned Socialist because of Morris's lectures and pamphlets, and I think it unlikely that Morris himself could read economics."

27. In "The Philosophy of Shelley's Poetry" (see pp. 51–72), Yeats cites several quotations from Shelley's *A Defence of Poetry* in support of this view.
28. The combination of Cross and Rose is an important Rosicrucian symbol often used by Yeats, as in the revised cover design by Althea Gyles for *Poems* (1899); the poems "To a Sister of the Cross and the Rose" (*Under the Moon: The Unpublished Early Poetry,* ed. George Bornstein [New York: Scribner, 1995], 94) and "A Song of the Rosy-Cross" (*P,* 538); and the essay "The Body of the Father Christian Rosencrux," later in the present collection.

## The Philosophy of Shelley's Poetry

Part 1 of this essay was published in *The Dome* for May–July 1900. *The Dome* ceased publication before publishing part 2, which first appeared in *IGE* together with part 1 in 1903. Yeats himself regarded part 2 as "not separable from the first essay" (*CL2,* 605). He probably began the essay in July 1899, when he wrote to his sister Susan (Lily) Yeats, "I am making notes for an article on the philosophical ideas in Shelleys [*sic*] poetry" (*CL2,* 433). *The Dome* was edited by Ernest J. Oldmeadow (1867–1949), with whose Unicorn Press Yeats had other dealings. The date 1900 was added for *IGE* (1903), and Yeats's footnote about Wilde and the Burne-Jones picture was added for *Essays* in 1924. There were numerous minor revisions after 1903 but only a few substantive ones, including dropping from the long first paragraph for the 1924 *Essays* the description of Shelley's *A Defence of Poetry* as "the profoundest essay on the foundation of poetry in English." A few other substantive alterations are noted below, in notes 29 and 83.

1. The group was the Dublin Hermetic Society, founded in June 1885. It included among others Charles Johnston, W. K. McGee, George Russell, Mir Alaud Ali (Professor of Persian, Arabic, and Hindustani at Trinity College), and Yeats himself as chairman; the next year it mutated into the Dublin Theosophical Society (Foster 1, 46–47). In his article "The Poetry of 'A.E.'" in the Dublin *Daily Express* of 3 September 1898, Yeats opened with the recollection: "A little body of young men hired a room in York Street, some dozen years ago, and began to read papers to one another on the Vedas, and the Upanishads, and the NeoPlatonists, and on modern mystics and spiritualists. They had no scholarship, and they spoke and wrote badly, but they discussed great problems ardently and simply and unconventionally as men, perhaps, discussed great problems in the mediæval Universities" (*UP1,* 121; for revised version, see *P&I,* 113).

2. The learned scholar was Edward Dowden (1843–1913), a friend of John Butler Yeats and the first Professor of English Literature in Trinity College. Yeats describes meeting him in *Au,* 94–96. Dowden published among other works a two-volume *Life of Percy Bysshe Shelley* (1886) in which he wrote: "Shelley, now as always, wrote as the disciple of William Godwin. All the glittering fallacies of 'Political Justice'—now sufficiently tarnished—together with all its encouraging and stimulating truths, may be found in the *caput mortuum* left when the critic has reduced the poetry of the 'Prometheus' to a series of doctrinaire statements" (2:264). William Godwin (1756–1836) was a rationalist philosopher whose *Enquiry Concerning Political Justice* first appeared in 1793. For more on the relations among Godwin, Shelley, and Yeats, see Bornstein, 43–48.
3. In *Prometheus Unbound* (1820), act 3, scene 4, lines 77–83, Shelley wrote:

   All things had put their evil nature off;
   I cannot tell my joy, when o'er a lake
   Upon a drooping bough with nightshade twined,
   I saw two azure halcyons clinging downward
   And thinning one bright bunch of amber berries,
   With quick long beaks, and in the deep there lay
   Those lovely forms imaged as in a sky; . . .
   (Hutchinson, 251)

4. For Mary Shelley's remark on her husband's hesitation between metaphysician and poet, see the first paragraph of her "Note on the *Revolt of Islam*" (Hutchinson, 156). For her remark about his "huntings after the obscure," see her "Preface to Second Collected Edition, 1839" (Hutchinson, xxiii).
5. For Mary Shelley's remark about her husband's subtlety of mind, see her "Note on *Prometheus Unbound*" (Hutchinson, 272).
6. Yeats quotes from the song of the Forms and Shadows in *Prometheus Unbound,* act 4, line 14 (Hutchinson, 254). For "grave" read "tomb."
7. This series of quotations comes from Shelley's *A Defence of Poetry* (Clark, 279, 281, 291–92). The ellipsis between "the more useful" and "Whilst the mechanist" is especially lengthy. For "earliest" read "earlier"; for "prophets, and a poet" read "prophets; a poet"; for "are to be ordained" read "ought to be ordered"; for "of the flowers" read "of the flower"; for "unchangeable process" read "unchangeable forms"; for "merchants" read "mechanists"; for "the most delightful" read "most delightful"; for "the more useful" read "more useful"; for "be sure that" read "beware that"; and for "richer, the poor" read "richer, and the poor."
8. Blake expresses such sentiments numerous times, as in *The Book of*

*Urizen* (1794). In *Jerusalem* he wrote, "I must create a system or be enslav'd by another Mans / I will not Reason & Compare: my business is to Create" (Ellis-Yeats 3: 1, plate 10; Erdman, 153).

9. These events happen in the final stanzas (72–78 lxxviii) of Shelley's poem *The Witch of Atlas* (Hutchinson, 386–88).
10. *Laon and Cythna* is the original title of the long poem in Spenserian stanzas that Shelley revised into *The Revolt of Islam* (1817–18). It tells the story of two lovers (originally brother and sister) who lead a revolt against the sultan of Turkey but then are defeated by the reactionary powers of Europe. The vision of the Morning Star comes from canto 1, stanzas 60–61 (Hutchinson, 49).
11. The quoted phrases come from the end of Shelley's "Ode to Naples" (written in 1820), lines 155 and 165 (Hutchinson, 620).
12. The quotation comes from Shelley's early radical poem *Queen Mab*, section 3, lines 174–75 (Hutchinson, 773).
13. Yeats here quotes three separate quotations from the last paragraph of Shelley's essay "On Love," probably written 1814–18, but first published posthumously (Clark, 170).
14. These phrases come from near the end of Shelley's treatise *A Philosophical View of Reform,* written 1819–20, and first published posthumously (Clark, 257).
15. Yeats cites here Shelley's poetic protest against the Peterloo Massacre, *The Mask of Anarchy,* written 1819, but only published posthumously; the correct phrasing is "art Love" (stanza 61; Hutchinson, 342).
16. The passage comes from *Queen Mab,* 5.31; at 5.22, the poem identifies the serpent as "Twin-sister of religion, selfishness" (Hutchinson, 779).
17. The quotations come from *Queen Mab,* 5.153, 3.214 and 218, 3.132–34, and 5.38–40 (Hutchinson, 781, 773, 772, and 779, respectively). For "throne of power unappealable in every human heart" read "in every human heart . . . Thy throne of power unappeasable"; for "dazzle and silently pass" read "dazzle; its authority / Will silently pass"; and for "nature yields" read "nature yield."
18. The quotations come from Shelley's poem *Julian and Maddalo: A Conversation,* composed 1818 and first published posthumously, lines 123–26 and 174–76 (Hutchinson, 192 and 193). For "dreary bell" read "dreary bell, the soul"; for "toll" read "must toll"; and for "meet round" read "meet below round."
19. Yeats cites Shelley's early major lyric "Mont Blanc" (composed 1816; published 1817), lines 139–41 (Hutchinson, 535). For "to the infinite heavens is a law" read "to the infinite dome / Of Heaven is as a law."
20. *The Revolt of Islam,* canto 8, stanza 19, and canto 1, stanza 29 (Hutchinson, 120 and 46).
21. The hero Prometheus overcomes the tyrant Jupiter in *Prometheus Unbound* by retracting his curse; Jupiter falls in act 3, scene 1 (Hutchinson, 242–44).

22. Yeats quotes from Shelley's own note to lines 45–46 of section 6 of *Queen Mab* (Hutchinson, 808).
23. Both quotations come from *Prometheus Unbound,* the first from Ocean's song in act 3, scene 2, lines 31–33, and the second from act 4, line 14; the description in between derives from act 3, scene 4, lines 64–77, immediately before the passage about the halcyons becoming vegetarians quoted by Yeats above (Hutchinson, 245, 254, and 250–51, respectively).
24. *Rosalind and Helen,* lines 1121–30 (Hutchinson, 185). *IGE* 1903 and *Essays* lack a comma after "music," but 1908 has one there and so do most editions of Shelley.
25. Yeats here quotes Shelley's elegy for the death of Keats, *Adonais* (1821), stanzas 52, lines 462–65, and 54, lines 485–86 (Hutchinson, 443).
26. The quotations come from *Adonais* (1821), stanzas 38–44 (Hutchinson, 440–43). For "fountains whence he came" read "fountain whence it came"; for "awaked" read "awakened"; for "the young" read "thou young"; for "caverns in the forests" read "ye caverns and ye forests"; for "the faint flowers" read "ye faint flowers"; and for "heard in all her music" read "heard / His voice in all her music."
27. Mary Shelley says this in her preface to the posthumous edition of Shelley's *Essays* (1840); for a modern redaction, see *The Novels and Selected Works of Mary Shelley,* ed. Nora Crook et al. (London: Pickering and Chatto, 1996), 2:337–38.
28. Yeats quotes the last four quatrains from the "Conclusion" of Shelley's *The Sensitive Plant* (1820) (Hutchinson, 596); for "shadow" read "shadows."
29. *Queen Mab* 2.246–47 (Hutchinson, 769). Until 1924, Yeats's paragraph ended "dwell upon them in a spirit of intense idealism" rather than "brood over them with visionary intensity."
30. In the Indian scriptures known as the Vedas, the Devas are divine spirits of good and are sometimes known as nature spirits; the name means "bright one." In Irish folk tradition, the Sidhe live in a hollow hill or fairy fort, or rath, and are identified with the Tuatha Dé Danaan; they appear in works from the Ulster Cycle such as the *Táin Bó Cuailnge* and throughout the Finn Cycle, among other places. In occult lore, as in the *Comte de Gabalis* of the Abbé de Villars (1635–ca. 1673), the "Elemental Spirits" are those of air, earth, fire, and water.
31. At the opening of section 3 of "Mont Blanc," lines 49–50, Shelley writes, "Some say that gleams of a remoter world / Visit the soul in sleep, . . ." (Hutchinson, 533). Yeats also quotes from stanzas 14, 15, 16, and 17 of *The Witch of Atlas* (Hutchinson, 375); for "his thin" read "its thin."
32. The "golden genii" come from *The Revolt of Islam,* canto 1, stanza 32, which Yeats is probably quoting from memory; the text reads "Then

Greece arose, and to its bards and sages, / In dream, the golden-pinioned Genii came" (Hutchinson, 47). The phantoms come from *Prometheus Unbound,* 3.3.50–53; the guardians come from *Prometheus Unbound,* 1.672–91; and the flying fish from *Prometheus Unbound,* 4.86–88 (Hutchinson, 246, 223, and 256, respectively); for "or the fish" read "as the fish."

33. The spirits lead Prometheus's love Asia and her sister Panthea along in *Prometheus Unbound,* 2.2.41–63, 86–87 (Hutchinson, 232–33). Demogorgon is a character often identified with necessity or eternity; the Spirit of the Hour speaks of tearing aside the painted veil in 3.4.190–92 (Hutchinson, 232–33 and 253). For "veil called life" read "veil, by those who were, called life."
34. The "ministers of ugliness" in *Prometheus Unbound* include the furies who come to torment him in act 1; the Second Fury speaks the lines quoted in 1.467–72 (Hutchinson, 218).
35. These phrases come from near the end of Shelley's last major poem, *The Triumph of Life,* lines 524–35 (Hutchinson, 520). Most modern editions read "wrought" rather than "wrapt." For "live there" read "were there."
36. *The Triumph of Life,* lines 487–514, 533 (Hutchinson, 519–20). For "like apes" read "like restless apes"; for "delegated powers" read "delegated power"; for "shapes of snow" read "flakes of snow"; and for "extinguish" read "extinguished."
37. Shelley says this in the fragment that Mary Shelley printed as "Speculations on Metaphysics" and Clark includes it as part of *A Treatise on Morals* (Clark, 183 and 193).
38. *The Triumph of Life,* lines 483–86, just before the passage containing the previous poetic quotations (Hutchinson, 519).
39. Dowden quotes accounts of Shelley's fearful dreams, including one of speaking in terror with an image of himself, in *The Life of Percy Bysshe Shelley,* 2.515–16, and another of a woman "who had eyes instead of nipples" in vol.2, p.34; he quotes the account of Jane Williams (1798–1884) about the apparition of the devil leaning against a tree in vol. 2, p. 355. Jane Williams had left her unsavoury first husband and was living with Shelley's friend the former Lieutenant Edward Williams as his "wife."
40. Jesus says this after washing the feet of the disciples in John 13:17.
41. Yeats's source for the lore of this battle was likely Lady Gregory, who, in the "Mountain Theology" chapter of *Poets and Dreamers* (Dublin and New York, 1903; O'Shea #807), 104, speaks of a Mary Glyn who "lives under Slieve-nan-Or, the Golden Mountain, where the last battle will be fought in the last great war of the world." She also writes in *A Book of Saints and Wonders* (New York: Oxford University Press, 1971), 51, that "the people of Slieve Echtge say there will be a great war yet in the whole world and in Ireland. . . . And there will be

great fighting on Slieve-nan-Or, the Golden Mountain, and in the Valley of the Black Pig." Lady Gregory's "Slieve-nan-Or" is Yeats's "Slieve-nan-Orr."

42. Blake says this in his address "To the Christians" in *Jerusalem* (Ellis-Yeats 3: *Jerusalem,* plate 77; Erdman, 231).
43. Cythna says this in *The Revolt of Islam,* 7.31–32 (Hutchinson, 113–14).
44. "Marianne's Dream" presents a vision of an anchor that is replaced by one of two mountain cities threatened by red volcano-like flames toward which a Lady floats on a plank. After her arrival at the city the marble forms of sculptures calm the scene until finally the mountains crack in an "earth-uplifiting" cataract that lifts the Lady from the stream and wakes her from her sleep. See Hutchinson, 536–39.
45. Essay "On Life" (Clark, 174). Yeats's ellipsis signals the omission of three sentences; for "resolved" read "absorbed."
46. Godwin's daughter is Mary Wollstonecraft Godwin Shelley (1797–1851), British writer and wife and editor of Percy Bysshe Shelley. The quotation comes from Shelley's preface to *The Revolt of Islam* (Hutchinson, 34); for "I sailed" read "I have sailed."
47. Yeats habitually referred to the anonymous poet-hero of *Alastor: or, The Spirit of Solitude* as "Alastor"; he falls into an "obscurest [not 'abysmal'] chasm" at line 637 (Hutchinson, 28). In *The Triumph of Life,* Rousseau wakes beside the rivulet and cave at lines 313–14 (Hutchinson, 515). The lover in *Epipsychidion* meets the evil beauty by a well under poisonous nightshade at lines 256–66 (Hutchinson, 417).
48. The passage about the "fountain round and vast" comes from *The Revolt of Islam,* 7.12; the polluted pool and fountain from 3.13 and 6.47; and the fountain by the river from 12.19–22 (Hutchinson, 109; 67 and 105; and 151). For "leaped and boiled" read "boiled and leaped."
49. The Spirit of the Earth hides in the fountain in a public square to watch ugly shapes float away in *Prometheus Unbound,* 3.4.62, and the fountain by which Prometheus and Asia awake "leaps in the midst with an awakening sound" at 3.3.14 (Hutchinson, 250 and 246).
50. The fountain by which Rosalind and Helen tell their unhappiness is in *Rosalind and Helen,* lines 112–13, and the willow and fountain by which the Indian enchantress and her lover sit comes from "Fragments of an Unfinished Drama," lines 63–64 (Hutchinson, 169 and 484).
51. The Greek philosopher Plato (ca. 427–ca. 348 B.C.) constructs his famous allegory of the mind progressing from ignorance to enlightenment being like someone in a cave learning to turn slowly toward the light in book 7 of his *Republic.* The Neoplatonic philosopher Porphyry (A.D. 233–ca. 301) was a student and editor of Plotinus and also wrote a life of Pythagoras. His *De Antro Nympharum* (On the Cave of the Nymphs) developed an elaborate allegorical reading of the Cave

of the Nymphs in Homer's *The Odyssey,* book 13, in terms of Neoplatonic mystical doctrine of the descent of the soul into the world of generation and its eventual return to the One.

52. For the cave of Shelley's Witch, see the opening stanzas of *The Witch of Atlas* with its "cavern, by a secret fountain" (Hutchinson, 372). The largely self-educated Thomas Taylor (1758–1835) became a leader in the Romantic revival of interest in Plato and the Neoplatonists and produced the first English translation of Plato's complete works (see Bornstein, 77ff.). He first published his essay on the Cave of the Nymphs in his *Select Works of Porphyry* (London: Thomas Rodd, 1823; hereafter cited as "Taylor"), of which Yeats may have read the reprint in *Theosophical Siftings* 7, 16–17 (1894–95); his following quotations all come from the first eleven paragraphs, which are numbered in Taylor. "Mr. Lang's prose" is *The Odyssey of Homer done into English Prose* (1879), which the Victorian man of letters Andrew Lang (1844–1912) did with the translator and scholar S. H. Butcher (1850–1910). Yeats makes several errors in transcription of the passage.
53. Yeats drew on Porphyry's association of honey with the pleasure of generation again for the fifth stanza of his poem "Among School Children," where he cited it in his own note to the phrase "honey of generation" (*P,* 606).
54. The "well / Of crimson fire" comes from stanza 29 of *The Witch of Atlas;* the sounds of air and cells of silence from stanza 14; the "liquors clear and sweet" from stanza 17; the thin sheath from stanza 15; the Witch's spinning from stanza 13; and the chamber of gray rock comes from stanza 2 (Hutchinson, 378, 375, and 372). For "silences" read "silence"; for "in crystal" read "in her crystal"; and for "in his thin" read "in its thin."
55. The quoted remark about mind comes from the essay "On Life" (Clark, 174). The passage alluded to is the last sentence of the same essay (Clark, 175).
56. "Speculations on Metaphysics" (Clark, 186); for "flows outward" read "flows outwards" and for "beautiful and bright" read "beautifully bright."
57. The quotations about Moeris, the Mareotid lakes, never erased shadows, and the Nile come from *The Witch of Atlas,* stanzas 58–60 (Hutchinson, 384); those about the liquid surface and calm depths come from stanzas 62–63 (Hutchinson, 384–85).
58. Yeats refers to the "O stream!" passage from *Alastor,* lines 502–13 (Hutchinson, 25–26).
59. The phrase "universe of things" appears in both line 1 and line 40 of Shelley's "Mont Blanc," and the phrase "gleams of a remoter world / Visit the soul in sleep" in lines 49–50 (Hutchinson, 532 and 533).
60. The passage about the subtler language comes from *The Revolt of Islam,* 7.31–32 (Hutchinson, 113–14), a passage that Yeats also cited

earlier in the present essay. For "subtle language" read "subtler language" and for "moveless things" read "moving things."

61. "The still cave of poetry" comes from "Mont Blanc," line 44 (Hutchinson, 533); Hutchinson reads "the still cave of the witch Poesy."
62. Yeats could have gotten information about the trip down a river from a number of places, including the Shelleys' own account, *History of a Six Weeks' Tour* (in the chapter "Germany") (London: Hookham, 1817; rept., Oxford: Woodstock, 1989), especially pp. 68–69 for "cliffs crowned by desolate towers."
63. The Chorus of Spirits sings of the "towers / Where Thought's crowned powers" watch in *Prometheus Unbound,* 4.102–3 (Hutchinson, 257); Yeats referred to that phrase again in his lyric "Blood and the Moon" (*P,* 241). The "ministers of misrule" carry Lionel off to a tower in *Rosalind and Helen,* lines 855–67 (Hutchinson, 181).
64. The title character of *Prince Athanase: A Fragment* studies philosophy in a tower; Yeats refers to him as "Shelley's visionary prince" in "The Phases of the Moon" (*P,* 165). Cythna mentions "One mind, the type of all" in *The Revolt of Islam,* 7.31; the "spangling [not "spangled"] sands" and "rarest sea-shells" come from 4.1 of the same poem (Hutchinson, 113 and 72).
65. The Belgian writer Maurice Maeterlinck (1862–1949) wrote symbolic dramas of the inner life. For Yeats's views on him, see "The Autumn of the Body" later in the present collection.
66. The French philosopher Jean-Jacques Rousseau (1712–78) appears as a major character brought to ruin in Shelley's unfinished visionary poem *The Triumph of Life.* The conflict between the Comet and the Morning Star takes place in canto 1, stanza 27 of Shelley's *The Revolt of Islam* (Hutchinson, 46); for the Comet as causing destruction in *Epipsychidion,* see, for example, lines 368–72 (Hutchinson, 419); and for the battle of the eagle and serpent, see *The Revolt of Islam,* 1.8–14 and 33 (Hutchinson, 42–43, and 47). Blake associates the eagle with genius and the serpent with nature; eagle and serpent occur in plate 15 of *The Marriage of Heaven and Hell,* to which the illustration shows an eagle holding a serpent in his talons (Ellis-Yeats 3: plate 15; Erdman, 40).
67. The youth associated with the Morning Star appears to the woman typifying humanity in *The Revolt of Islam,* 1.41–43. The chorus of women singing of Hesperus as the "lamp of the free" appears near the end of Shelley's verse drama *Hellas,* lines 1038–49, just before the closing chorus "The world's great age begins anew . . ." that was so important to Yeats. The figure of the Morning Star leading wisdom from the cave of man's spirit occurs in "Ode to Liberty," stanza 18 (Hutchinson, 49, 476, and 609).
68. Mary Shelley recorded this information about Shelley's design for the rest of the poem in her note to *Prince Athanase,* where she also indi-

cated that the original title was *Pandemos and Urania* (Hutchinson, 158–59).

69. Yeats saw Intellectual Beauty as central to all of Shelley's poetry, not only to the "Hymn to Intellectual Beauty" (Hutchinson, 529), and it was important to his own early poetry as well, particularly in the Rose poems. See Bornstein, 29–66.
70. These are the last four lines of the second stanza of "To——" ("One word is too often profaned") (Hutchinson, 645, where they end in a question mark).
71. The shape that Yeats calls "the genius of the dawn" appears to Rousseau in lines 344–99 of *The Triumph of Life;* the phrase "on desert Labrador" comes at line 407 (Hutchinson, 517).
72. These lines about Hesperus come from the passage near the end of *Hellas* that Yeats referred to earlier in the essay, in this case, lines 1038–40, which should read "fast-flashing" rather than "fast fleeting" (Hutchinson, 476).
73. The account of the intoxicating cup is by Macrobius rather than Porphyry. Thomas Taylor included it in a lengthy footnote to his translation of Porphyry's "On the Cave of the Nymphs" (Taylor, 186–89). The constellation of the Cup between Cancer and Lion is Crater.
74. The Gaelic poem is the *Lay of Oisin on the Land of Youth,* by Michael Comyn (1688–1760), text and translation by Bryan O'Looney in *Transactions of the Ossianic Society for the Year 1856* 4 (Dublin, 1859): "We saw also, by our sides / A hornless fawn leaping nimbly, / And a red-eared white dog, / Urging it boldly in the chase. // We beheld also, without fiction, / A young maid on a brown steed, / A golden apple in her right hand, / And she going on the top of the waves. // We saw after her, / A young rider on a white steed, / Under a purple, crimson mantle of satin, / And a gold-headed sword in his right hand" (249). Yeats used the passage himself in his only early narrative poem, *The Wanderings of Oisin,* lines 139–45 (*P,* 365). Niamh is the supernatural woman loved by Oisin in the poem. The vision seen while gazing at a blue curtain may have taken place in Yeats's rooms at Woburn Buildings, for which Lady Gregory had provided blue curtains.
75. Yeats may have been thinking of the role of the moon in Keats's *Endymion* here. The references to Blake are more precise, in that the voice of the devil in *The Marriage of Heaven and Hell* states that "Energy is Eternal Delight" (Ellis-Yeats 3: plate 4 of *The Marriage;* Erdman, 34). For an account of Blake's symbol of poetic genius, Los, laboring at his forge, see chapter 4, plate 88, of *Jerusalem* (Ellis-Yeats 3; Erdman, 246–47).
76. Taylor, 179.
77. *Epipsychidion,* lines 291–319 (Hutchinson, 418).
78. In this cento of passages about the moon, the pale lips and cold moon come from *Epipsychidion,* lines 309 and 281 (Hutchinson, 418 and

417); the "frozen and inconstant moon" from *Prometheus Unbound,* 3.4.87 (Hutchinson, 251); the forgotten moon that wanes from "Fragment: The False Laurel and the True" (Hutchinson, 661); the line "I wander and wane like the weary moon" from "Fragments of an Unfinished Drama," line 4 (Hutchinson, 482); the "pale and gray" moon from "The World's Wanderers," line 4 (Hutchinson, 624); the moon that is "pale for weariness," "wandering companionless," "ever changing," and finding "no object worth its constancy" from "To the Moon," stanza 1 (Hutchinson, 621); the moon like a dying lady tottering out of her chamber from "The Waning Moon" (Hutchinson, 721); the moon that makes lovers' lips "lurid" and "pale" from *The Revolt of Islam,* 6.38; and "Lines: The cold earth slept below" (Hutchinson, 103 and 527). For the quotation from *Epipsychidion,* for "are pale" read "whose pale" and for "cold moon" read "cold chaste moon."

79. These passages all come from the dialogue between the Earth and the Moon in *Prometheus Unbound,* 4.400–403, 322, and 356–57 (Hutchinson, 263, 261, and 262). For "till the snow 'is loosened from the Moon's lifeless mountains'" read that the moon says "The snow upon my lifeless mountains / Is loosened into living fountains."

80. The early Yeats had frequent conversations with the controversial writer and wit Oscar Wilde (1856–1900); for his retrospective account, see *Au,* 124–30. Sir Edward Burne-Jones (1833–98) was a Pre-Raphaelite painter who interacted with William Morris, Dante Gabriel Rossetti, and John Ruskin, among others.

81. Taylor, 179. Taylor is actually quoting Macrobius, who himself is quoting Proclus in this passage, an extended note.

82. For the first Blake quotation, see the letter to John Linnell, 25 April 1827: "Doubt & Fear that ruins Activity & are the greatest hurt to an Artist such as I am" (Erdman, 784, apparently not in Ellis-Yeats). For woman's will as trammeling man's in the fallen state of relationships, see for example *Jerusalem,* plate 88, lines 16–21 (Ellis-Yeats 3; Erdman, 247):

> . . . This is Womans World. . . .
> . . . . . . . . . . . . . . . . . .
> That he who loves Jesus may loathe terrified Female love
> Till God himself become a Male subservient to the Female.

The phrase "the Sun in his strength" seems not to be a direct quotation from Blake but rather a misremembering of the final lines of *Vala* (Ellis-Yeats 3: p. 138 of *Vala* transcription; Erdman, 407):

> The Sun arises from his dewy bed & the fresh airs
> Play in his smiling beams giving the seeds of life to grow
> And the fresh Earth beams forth ten thousand thousand springs of life

Urthona is arisen in his strength no longer now
Divided from Enitharmon no longer the Spectre Los.

83. Emilia (Teresa) Viviani (1801–36), the beautiful nineteen-year-old daughter of the governor of Pisa when Shelley met her, inspired Shelley's poem *Epipsychidion.* The quotation is from lines 335–36 (Hutchinson, 419). For "like an incarnation" read "soft as an Incarnation."
84. The quotations from the first sentence citing *The Triumph of Life* come from lines 434–49, those in the second sentence from lines 209–10, those in the third from lines 254–59, and those in the final sentence from lines 128–31 (Hutchinson, 517–18, 512, 513, and 510). For "verdure" read "vesture"; for "the great" read "the wise, the great"; and for "flew back" read "fled back."
85. Yeats may be slightly misquoting "The Zucca," line 4, "More in this world than any understand," or possibly "Unadopted Passage of Mont Blanc," line 1, "There is a voice, not understood by all" (Hutchinson, 664 and 535). An alternate source could be Arthur Hallam's essay "On Some of the Characteristics of Modern Poetry and on the Lyrical Poems of Alfred Tennyson," which Yeats also slightly misquoted in "A Bundle of Poets," his review of *The Poems of Arthur Henry Hallam* and other works: "How should they be popular whose senses told them a richer and ampler tale than most men could understand . . . ?" (*EAR*, 201). After the 1908 edition of *IGE,* Yeats dropped a clause between the passages on Blake and on Shelley that read "and that Keats, who accepted life gladly though 'with a delicious diligent indolence, would have worshipped in some chapel of the moon.'" The Keats phrase comes from Keats's letter to John Hamilton Reynolds, 19 February 1818.
86. In *Reveries over Childhood and Youth,* Yeats indicates that his own favorite myth derived from Shelley: "I soon chose Alastor for my chief of men and longed to share his melancholy, and maybe at last to disappear from everybody's sight as he disappeared drifting in a boat along some slow-moving river between great trees" (*Au,* 80).
87. Yeats often voiced this criticism of Shelley as cut off from living folk tradition, as in "The Message of the Folk-lorist" (1893), where he wrote: "Shakespeare and Keats had the folk-lore of their own day, while Shelley had but mythology; and a mythology which had been passing for long through literary minds without any new inflow from living tradition loses all the incalculable instinctive and convincing quality of the popular traditions" (*EAR,* 212).

## At Stratford-on-Avon

First published in *The Speaker: A Liberal Review* for May 11 and 18, 1901. The May 11 issue included a separate part 3 on Sir Frank Robert Benson and his productions of Shakespeare, reproduced in an appendix to the present volume (for information on Benson, see note 2 below). Yeats deleted that section for *Ideas of Good and Evil.* He told Lady Gregory on 13 April that writing on the Benson festival was "a chance that may never come again to see 'King John' & all the plays of the Wars of the Roses acted right through in consecutive order. . . . I have a lot of things to say about Shakespear & this seems the time to say them. It will go into the book of essays rather well" (*CL*3, 58–59).

1. Stratford-on-Avon is the birthplace of Shakespeare and home to the drama festival described in this essay. Yeats attended the "Week of Kings" in order to write the present essay as an extended review. "This is a beautiful place," he wrote to Lady Gregory (25 April 1901). "I am working very hard, reading all the chief criticisms of the plays & I think my essay will be one of the best things I have done" (*CL*3, 61). Yeats also refers to Morris's socialist prose romance *News from Nowhere* (1891) in his essay on Morris, "The Happiest of the Poets," earlier in the present volume.
2. The English actor, director, and producer Sir Frank Robert Benson (1858–1939) ran the annual festivals at Stratford from 1886 to 1919; in 1916 he was knighted onstage of the Drury Lane Theatre at the end of a tercentenary performance of *Julius Caesar.* George Moore, Yeats, and Lady Gregory all considered using the Benson Company for the Irish Literary Theatre and its successor, the Irish National Theatre Society, but in the end turned to Irish rather than English actors. Benson's company did perform *Diarmuid and Grania* in October 1901 on a bill that also included Douglas Hyde's *Casadh an tSúgáin.*
3. These six plays of Shakespeare constituted the "Week of Kings" in April 1901, which followed a week of comedies. By "their right order" Yeats means their order in the historical succession of the kings of England. The Plantagenet kings John and Richard II reigned 1199–1216 and 1377–99, respectively; the Lancastrian kings Henry IV, V, and VI reigned 1399–1413, 1413–22, and 1422–61, 1470–71, respectively; and the Yorkist king Richard III reigned 1483–85.
4. The theater, picture gallery, and library at Stratford resulted from the work of the Shakespeare Memorial Association, which was organized in 1874 and headed by Charles Edward Flower of the Stratford brewing dynasty.
5. Yeats had earlier identified hatred of London as the "motif" of his own novella *John Sherman and Dhoya,* writing to John O'Leary on 19 November 1888 of "my story—the *motif* of which is hatred of London" (*CL*1, 110). The Shakespeare Memorial Theatre was at first dismissed by the London press for locating itself outside London.
6. Completed in 1879, the theater at the time of Yeats's visit featured a proscenium stage. After it was gutted by fire in 1926, its replacement featured a fan-shaped auditorium.

7. Bayreuth, Germany, was and is the home of an annual festival dedicated to work by the German operatic composer Richard Wagner (1813–83).
8. [Edward] Gordon Craig (1872–1966) became one of Yeats's favorite set designers. His first set designs were for the production of Purcell's *Dido and Aeneas* for the Purcell Operatic Society in May 1900 and again in March 1901. "I thought your scenery to 'Aeneas and Dido' the only good scenery I ever saw," wrote Yeats to him. "You have created a new art" (*CL*1, 53). Craig pioneered a style of stretched colored backcloths for the stage and did a set of screens for the Abbey Theatre in 1911 that Yeats very much liked.
9. Although ascribed to Goethe by Yeats, the quotation about art and nature in fact comes from the American sculptor and author William Wetmore Story (1819–95). In *Conversations in a Studio* (Boston and New York: Houghton, Mifflin 1890), 2 vols., Story writes that "we must first clear our minds of the notion that the object of art is illusion. Art is art because it is not nature . . ." (2:328). Although the exact quote does not appear in English translations of Goethe (Yeats did not read German), it does accord with some of Goethe's sentiments. Perhaps the closest is a remark in (Johann Peter) Eckermann's *Conversations with Goethe,* trans. John Oxenford (London: J. M. Dent; New York: E. P. Dutton, 1951), 196: "art is not entirely subject to natural necessities, but has laws of its own." Heinrich Düntzer's *Life of Goethe* was translated by Yeats's acquaintance the librarian Thomas W. Lyster (London: Macmillan, 1883) and has a similar remark in Düntzer's paraphrase of Goethe's view of Kant's *Kritik der Urtheilskraft,* "that Nature and Art are two altogether distinct worlds" (88–89).
10. The French novelist Honoré de Balzac (1799–1850) achieved his first major success with the philosophical tale *La Peau de Chagrin* (1830). The coquette there is named Fœdora and the scene referred to takes place in part 2, "A Woman Without a Heart," in Balzac's *The Wild Ass's Skin* (*La Peau de Chagrin*), trans. Ellen Marriage, with preface by George Saintsbury (New York: Macmillan, 1901), 147–48 (O'Shea #111).
11. Tito Melema is the villain in George Eliot's novel *Romola* (1863), which is set in Florence at the end of the fifteenth century. After robbing and then abandoning to prison his childhood benefactor Baldassare, he marries Romola and then betrays her and his father.
12. Coriolanus, Hamlet, Timon, and Richard II are the title characters in Shakespearean plays; Fortinbras was Hamlet's rival and Aufidius that of Coriolanus. Henry V (Prince Hal in the *Henry IV* plays) is also a title character.

    The Blake quotation comes from plate 8 of *The Marriage of Heaven and Hell* (Ellis-Yeats 3; Erdman, 36, in both of which "eternity" is lowercase).

13. The book is *Shakspere: A Critical Study of His Mind and Art* (London: H. S. King, 1875) by John Butler Yeats's friend and W. B. Yeats's sometime antagonist Professor Edward Dowden (1843–1913) of Trinity College, Dublin. Dowden uses several of the terms that Yeats has just cited, including calling Richard II "sentimental" on page 168 and "weak" on page 193 and labeling Henry V "the hero, and central figure therefore of the historical plays" on page 210.
14. P. W. Joyce glosses the proverb "Cows beyond the water have long horns" in his *English As We Speak It in Ireland,* 2nd ed. (London: Longmans, Green, and Dublin: M. H. Gill, 1910) as meaning "We are inclined to magnify distant or only half known things" (118).
15. Of the many late Victorian critics besides Dowden who admired Henry V, Yeats most likely has in mind Sidney Lee in *A Life of William Shakespeare* (1898), who was particularly fulsome.
16. In his essay "Shakespeare's English Kings" in *Appreciations* (1889), Walter Pater (1839–94) saw in Richard II "the great meekness of the graceful, wild creature, tamed at last" (London: Macmillan, 1901), 200.
17. Raphael[l] Holinshed (d. 1580?) wrote several historical and descriptive works including his well-known *Chronicles of England, Scotland, and Ireland,* upon which Shakespeare drew for several of his plays. Holinshed makes the second half of the remark about not Richard II but rather King Sigiburt, who was murdered by two of his kinsmen because "he was too fauourable towards his enemies." See Raphaell Holinshed, *Holinshed's Chronicles of England, Scotland, and Ireland* (London: Printed for J. Johnson et al., 1807) vol. 1, book 5, chapter 31, p. 621.
18. This quotation is untraced and may not be by Verlaine.
19. Hotspur calls Richard II "that sweet lovely rose" in *Henry IV, Part I,* 1.3.173 (Shakespeare, 1168).
20. The bishop of Carlisle used the phrase "stirred [not "raised"] up by God" in delivering his prophecy of the bad effects of overthrowing the king in *Richard II,* 4.1.124 (Shakespeare, 995). The prolific German scholar Georg Gottfried Gervinus was the author of *Shakespeare Commentaries,* trans. F[anny]. E. Burnett, 2 vols. (London: Smith Elder, 1863 [for 1862]). In a letter to Lady Gregory on 25 April 1901, Yeats writes, "The boy has just brought me in a translation of Jervinus' [*sic*] 'Commentaries' & I must to work again. I do not even stop for Afternoon tea" (*CL*3, 62). For Dowden, see note 13 above.
21. Solomon is the tenth century BC king of Israel who built the First Temple and is renowned in the Bible for his wisdom, as in the famous dispute about the child in I Kings 3. In contrast, the English philosopher Jeremy Bentham (1748–1832) advocated judging all things by their utility, a standard that Yeats despised. In *Au,* 193, Yeats charges that Dowden "turned Shakespeare into a British Benthamite."

22. Yeats quotes here the entire text of Shakespeare's "Sonnet 66" (Shakespeare, 1945).
23. According to *Au,* 281, the unnamed scholar was a member of the Golden Dawn. In *LE,* 11, Yeats writes, "I think it was Heraclitus who said: the Dæmon is our destiny."
24. This exchange between Hamlet and the captain sent by Fortinbras occurs in *Hamlet* at the beginning of Act 4, scene 4, which gives the amount of the lease as "five ducats, five" rather than six.
25. The image of the jet of a fountain for positive acts of mind occurs repeatedly in Yeats, for instance in "The abounding glittering jet" of the "Ancestral Houses" section of the poem "Meditations in Time of Civil War" (*P,* 204) or repeatedly in "The Philosophy of Shelley's Poetry" above, in the current volume.
26. These phrases come from Henry V's wooing address to Katharine in *Henry V,* 5.2.194–96. The boy would become Henry VI.
27. Although the text reads "five plays" here, six were performed that week and Yeats has listed them by name earlier in the present essay. While it is possible that "five" is a slip for "six," more likely Yeats is thinking of the five plays other than *King John* as making "but one play." See note 3 above.
28. The notion of Shakespeare dying because of a drinking bout derives from the account of Stratford vicar John Ward (1629–81), who wrote that "Shakespear, Drayton, and Ben Jhohnson, had a merry meeting, and itt seems drank too hard, for Shakespear died of a feavour there contracted" [*sic*]; see Rupin W. Desai, *Yeats's Shakespeare* (Evanston: Northwestern University Press, 1971), 86n8. Yeats's allusion to the "bad verses" probably refers to what Desai calls "the well-known doggerel on Shakespeare's grave at Stratford ('Good friend, for Jesus' sake forbear / To dig the dust enclosed here. / Blest be the man that spares these stones / And curst be he that moves my bones.')"
29. The "poor Gaelic rhymer" was Yeats's favorite Gaelic poet Antoine Raftery (ca. 1784–1835), whom he refers to repeatedly in his poetry and prose. Yeats elaborates the account of Raftery's death in "Dust hath closed Helen's Eye," a section of *The Celtic Twilight* (*Myth,* 29–30).
30. During the Puritan interregnum of the mid-seventeenth century, Puritan hostility toward plays and playhouses (which, under Charles I, had become increasingly associated with the royalists) resulted in a Parliamentary Ordinance of 1642 that led to the closing of theaters and dispersal of acting companies. A few actors and companies tried to evade the ban, performing usually in smaller theaters, but the ordinance was largely successful.

## *William Blake and the Imagination*

This essay was first published in *The Academy* for 19 June 1897 under the title "Academy Portraits. / XXXII.—William Blake." *The Academy* also included a facsimile of a Blake portrait with the caption "William Blake" and the subcaption "From the Picture by T. Phillips, R. A., in the National Portrait Gallery." Other than omission of the portrait, the principal changes when the essay was collected for *IGE* were the omission of three lengthy quotations from Blake, two at the end of the present first paragraph and one at the end of the present second paragraph. They are reproduced in the notes below at the appropriate points.

1. This list includes several of Yeats's favorite nineteenth-century writers and the painter Whistler: the English poets Percy Bysshe Shelley (1792–1822) and William Wordsworth (1770–1850), the German Johann Wolfgang von Goethe (1749–1832), the French novelists Honoré de Balzac (1799–1850) and Gustave Flaubert (1821–80), the Russian novelist Count Leo Tolstoy (1828–1910), and the American-born but French-educated painter James Abbott McNeill Whistler (1834–1903), who lived mainly in England. "Make our souls" is an Irish expression meaning "prepare for death," as in the phrase "make my soul" from Yeats's poem "The Tower" (*P*, 203), but he also used it in a wider sense, as here (and see *P*, 661n. 205.181 for another example).
2. Yeats greatly admired the essay on Shelley by the Victorian poet Robert Browning (1812–89), which first appeared as an introduction to the problematic *Letters of Percy Bysshe Shelley* in 1852. There Browning distinguished between "objective" and "subjective" types of the poet and wrote of the subjective one that "Not what man sees, but what God sees—the Ideas of Plato, seeds of creation lying burningly on the Divine Hand—it is toward these that he struggles." Robert Browning, *The Poems*, 2 vols., ed. John Pettigrew and Thomas Collins (New Haven and London: Yale University Press, 1981), 1:1002.
3. The Saracens were the Muslim opponents of the Christian Crusaders during the Middle Ages. The original *Academy* publication of the essay included a long quotation from plate 77 and a short one from plate 91 of Blake's *Jerusalem* here:

   > "He wrote:
   > 'I know of no other Christianity, and of no other gospel, than the liberty both of body and mind to exercise the divine arts of imagination—imagination, the real and eternal world, of which this vegetable universe is but a faint shadow, and in which we shall live in our eternal or imaginative bodies when these veg-

> etable mortal bodies are no more. The Apostles knew of no other gospel. What are all their spiritual gifts? What is the Divine Spirit? Is the Holy Ghost other than an intellectual fountain? . . . What is the life of man but art and science? . . . Answer this for yourselves, and expel from among you those who pretend to despise the labours of art and science, which alone are the labours of the gospel.'
>
> And he wrote:
>
> 'I care not whether a man is good or bad, all that I care is, whether a man is a wise man or a fool. Go, put off holiness and put on intellect.'"

(Ellis-Yeats 3: plates 77 and 91 of *Jerusalem*; Erdman, 231–32 and 252). As often, Yeats slightly misquotes. Substantive errors include: "What are all" for "What were all"; deletion of "any" between "Is the Holy Ghost" and "other than"; after the ellipsis, "for yourselves" rather than "to yourselves"; there should be an additional ellipsis before "What is the life of man but art and science." In the second quotation Erdman reads "evil" for "bad" and "he" for the second "a man."

4. Jacob Boehme (1575–1624) was a Lutheran mystic theosopher admired by Newton, Goethe, and Hegel as well as by Yeats, who associated him with kabbalistic symbolism as well as with alchemy.

   The phrase "the body of God" probably derives from either a misreading of *Jerusalem,* plate 5, "the Bosom of God. The Human Imagination" or else from *Milton,* plate 3, "the Human Imagination / Which is the Divine Body of the Lord Jesus" (Ellis-Yeats 3: plate 20 of *Jerusalem* and plate 1 of *Milton;* Erdman, 147 and 96). "The Divine members" comes from *Milton,* plate 35, "Ideas themselves, (which are / The Divine Members)" (Ellis-Yeats 3; Erdman, 135).
5. For the reason as deductions from the observations of the senses, see Blake's "There is No Natural Religion" (Ellis-Yeats 3: unpaginated facsimile; Erdman, 2).
6. "For every thing that lives is Holy" is the last line of the "Song of Liberty" that concludes Blake's *The Marriage of Heaven and Hell* (plates 25–27: Ellis-Yeats 3; Erdman, 45). Blake repeats it on plate 8 of *America: A Prophecy* (Ellis-Yeats 3; Erdman, 54).
7. In *The Academy* version, this paragraph continues with a quotation from Blake: "Men are admitted into heaven not because they have curbed or governed their passions, or have no passions, but because they have cultivated their understandings. The treasures of heaven are not negations of passion but realities of intellect from which the passions emanate uncurbed in their eternal glory." The passage comes from "A Vision of the Last Judgment" (Ellis-Yeats 2: 401; Erdman, 564). Erdman reads: "<curbed &> . . . from which All the Passions Emanate <Uncurbed>."

8. The phrase about the "foolish body" comes from Blake's late letter to George Cumberland, 12 April 1827: "In that [the imagination] I am stronger & stronger as this Foolish Body decays" (Ellis-Yeats 3: 162, Erdman, 783). The phrase about the phantom comes from Blake's annotations to Lavatar: "man is either the ark of God or a phantom of the earth & of the water" (Erdman, 596). The allusion to "eternal glory" likely refers particularly to the passage from Blake that Yeats quoted in *The Academy* version but deleted for *IGE*: see note 7 above.
9. Yeats regularly deplored a utilitarian streak in poets such as William Wordsworth (1770–1850) and Alfred Tennyson (1809–92). The phrase about the "Divine hand" comes from Robert Browning's essay on Shelley; see note 2 above.
10. This refers to a passage in Blake's "Notebook," also known as the "Rossetti Manuscript," in which he entered the phrase "Ideas of Good and Evil" facing the first emblem drawing (Ellis-Yeats 1: 202; Erdman, 694); Ellis-Yeats states, "It had for title 'Ideas of Good and Evil,'" though modern scholars doubt that the title was intended for the whole book. In his introduction to the Muses Library edition of Blake, Yeats claims that the phrase "Ideas of Good and Evil" "was possibly a first and rejected attempt towards a title for the poems afterwards called 'The Songs of Innocence and Experience,' but probably a first thought for a title of 'The Songs of Experience' alone, 'experience' and eating the fruit of the Tree of the Knowledge of Good and Evil being one and the same in Blake's philosophy." *The Poems of William Blake,* ed. W. B. Yeats (London: Lawrence and Bullen, 1893), 241.
11. Blake associates the counties of England with the tribes of ancient Israel in *Jerusalem,* plate 16 (Ellis-Yeats 3; Erdman, 160–61). He compares mountains and rivers to parts of the body of Albion in plate 39 of *Milton* (Ellis-Yeats 3; Erdman, 140–41).

    Yeats often cited the French symbolist Villiers de L'Isle-Adam (1838–89), whose play *Axël* (1885; 1890) affected his own early poetic and dramatic work.
12. Yeats here refers to the Celtic scholar John Rhys (1840–1915), who was appointed the first Jesus Professor of Celtic in 1877, not Ernest Rhys, the publisher and cofounder of the Rhymers' Club. Yeats admired Rhys's *Lectures on the Origin and Growth of Religion as Illustrated by Celtic Heathendom* (London: Williams and Norgate, 1888), of which he owned the second edition of 1892 (O'Shea #1741).
13. In *The Academy* version of this essay the phrase read "or have gone to Ireland—and he was probably an Irishman—and . . ." Yeats often referred to an alleged Irish ancestry for Blake, perhaps most prominently in Ellis-Yeats 1: 2–3.
14. Enitharmon is a female character in Blake's poetry who is associated with spiritual beauty and is variously the twin, consort, and inspiration of the poet-figure Los; she appears most extensively throughout *The*

*Four Zoas*, which in Ellis-Yeats is called *Vala.* Yeats saw her as less anchored in folk tradition than the three powerful figures that he names: Freia, the goddess of beauty, in Norse mythology, drawn on by Wagner; Gwydeon, or Gwydion, a powerful magician from Welsh mythology, who appears in the *Mabinogian* and whom Yeats may have thought as female; and Danu, or Dana, the principal fertility goddess in Irish mythology and nourisher or mother of the Tuatha Dé Danann, the people or tribe of Dana.

15. The long quotation comes from the song of Enitharmon to Los in *The Four Zoas,* plate 34 (Ellis-Yeats 3: p. 29 of *Vala;* Erdman, 324); Erdman reads "is" for "in" and "most best beloved" rather than "most beloved" (line 1); "unceasing" for "unwearied" (line 6); "the living harmony upon my limbs" rather than "the long harmony sounding upon my limbs" (line 8); and "humming" for "hovering" (line 13).

## *William Blake and His Illustrations to* The Divine Comedy

The three parts of this essay first appeared in *The Savoy* magazine for July, August, and September 1896. The parts included eleven illustrations, ten from Blake and one from Botticelli, which are reproduced in an appendix (and one as frontispiece), together with Yeats's deleted comments on them. Additional deleted material, indicated at the appropriate place in the notes, included most of a long introductory paragraph to part I, the final two paragraphs of part II, and a short paragraph from part III. The "P.S." dated 1924 first appeared in *Essays* that year. A particularly interesting smaller revision is the change of the reference to "French mystics" near the end of the original first paragraph of part 2 to one to Shelley and Nietzsche from 1903 onward. Yeats published eight poems, three stories, and one other essay in *The Savoy* before its yearlong run came to an end, partly because the anatomical frankness of the reproduction of Blake's *Antaeus Setting Virgil and Dante upon the Verge of Cocytus* hurt railway station sales (see *Au,* 249 for Yeats's account of that episode).

1. In *The Savoy* the essay began with a long passage comparing Blake to the French symbolists that reads as follows:

> The recoil from scientific naturalism has created in our day the movement the French call *symboliste,* which, beginning with the memorable "Axel," by Villiers de l'Isle Adam, has added to drama a new kind of romance, at once ecstatic and picturesque, in the works of M. Maeterlinck; and beginning with certain pictures of the pre-Raphaelites, and of Mr. Watts and Mr. Burne-Jones, has brought into art a new and subtle inspiration. This movement, and in art more especially, has proved so consonant with a change in the times, in the desires of our

> hearts grown weary with material circumstance, that it has begun to touch even the great public; the ladies of fashion and men of the world who move so slowly; and has shown such copious signs of being a movement, perhaps the movement of the opening century, that one of the best known of French picture dealers will store none but the inventions of a passionate symbolism. It has no sufficient philosophy and criticism, unless indeed it has them hidden in the writings of M. Mallarmé, which I have not French enough to understand, but if it cared it might find enough of both philosophy and criticism in the writings of William Blake to protect it from its opponents, and what is perhaps of greater importance, from its own mistakes, for he was certainly the first great *symboliste* of modern times, and the first of any time to preach. . . .

The quotation about vision comes from Blake's "A Vision of the Last Judgment" (Ellis-Yeats 2: 393; Erdman, 554). Erdman reads "Vision or Imagination is a Representation of what Eternally Exists. Really & Unchangeably."

2. Both quotations come from "A Vision of the Last Judgment." In Erdman the first reads "if he could Enter into Noahs Rainbow or into his bosom or could make a Friend & Companion of one of these Images of wonder which always intreats him to leave mortal things as he must know then would he arise from his Grave then would he meet the Lord in the Air & then he would be happy" (Ellis-Yeats 2: 400; Erdman, 560); and the second reads "Poetry Painting & Music the three Powers <in Man> of conversing with Paradise which the flood did not Sweep away" (Ellis-Yeats 2: 397; Erdman, 559).
3. This phrase comes from "A Vision of the Last Judgment" (Ellis-Yeats 2: 394; Erdman, 555); Erdman reads "this Vegetable Glass of Nature."
4. The phrase comes from "A Vision of the Last Judgment" (Ellis-Yeats 2: 394; Erdman, 555); Erdman reads "This world of Imagination is the World of Eternity."
5. The flaming sword derives from Genesis 3:24 after Adam and Eve are expelled from Eden; Blake also uses it on plate 14 of *The Marriage of Heaven and Hell.* Ellis-Yeats notes that "The interpretation of the flaming sword in this passage is that same as that of the Jewish Kabalah" (1:298). It also played a part in the initiation ceremony for the Zelator grade of the Hermetic Order of the Golden Dawn. The "rotten rags of memory" come from *Milton,* plate 41, where Inspiration casts them off (Ellis-Yeats 3; Erdman, 142).
6. Felpham is the village on the coast of West Sussex where the Blakes lived for three years before returning to London in September 1803. The quoted phrases come from *A Descriptive Catalogue,* Number IX (Ellis-Yeats 2: 377; Erdman, 547).

7. Yeats takes this information from Alexander Gilchrist, *Life of William Blake with Selections from His Poems and Other Writings,* revised edition, 2 vols. (London: Macmillan, 1880), 1:312. The landscape painter Samuel Palmer (1805–81) as a young man became a disciple of the aged Blake. Yeats cited him in both "The Phases of the Moon" and "Under Ben Bulben" (*P,* 165 and 335).
8. *A Descriptive Catalogue,* Number IX (Ellis-Yeats 2: 378; Erdman, 547).
9. The cento of quotations comes from a letter to William Hayley, 23 October 1804 (Ellis-Yeats 1: 100–101; Erdman, 756–57). Erdman reads "has for" for "had for" and "even as" for "as."
10. These are well-known works of Blake except for *The Book of Moonlight,* a lost work known only through Blake's reference to it in the lines "Delicate Hands & Heads will never appear / While Titians &c as in the Book of Moonlight" (Ellis-Yeats 2: 389; Erdman, 514). By "the *MS. Book*" Yeats means the "Rossetti Manuscript."
11. Blake uses the phrase "Eternal Existence" (singular, not plural) in "On Virgil" (Ellis-Yeats 3; Erdman, 270): "Living Form is Eternal Existence." Yeats may have been thinking of the passage in "A Vision of the Last Judgment" alluded to above: "This world of Imagination is the World of Eternity . . . There Exist in that Eternal World the Permanent Realities of Every Thing which we see reflected in this Vegetable Glass of Nature" (Ellis-Yeats 2: 394; Erdman, 555).
12. *A Descriptive Catalogue,* Number XV (Ellis-Yeats 2: 380; Erdman, 550). Erdman reads "as well as of life" for "as of life" and "bounding-" for "boundary-."
13. This lengthy passage also comes from *A Descriptive Catalogue,* Number XV (Ellis-Yeats 2: 380; Erdman, 550). Substantive corrections include Protogenes and Apelles knowing each other "by this line" rather than "by their line" and insertion of "and" after the semicolon in the last quoted sentence. In addition, Yeats omits an entire sentence before "How do we distinguish the oak from the beech . . .": "The want of this determinate and bounding form evidences the want of idea in the artist's mind, and the pretence of the plagiary in all its branches." Perhaps the most glaring error is the printing of "the owl from the beast" instead of the correct "the oak from the beech"; both Ellis-Yeats and the periodical version give the correct reading, but the error was introduced in *IGE* (1903) and not corrected during Yeats's lifetime. For "light and dark" read "lights and darks."

    Protogenes was an ancient Greek painter and sculptor (fl. late fourth century BC), whose work was said to lack the grace of his rival and friend Apelles (also fl. late fourth century). Apelles was considered the foremost painter of his time and served as court painter to both Philip and Alexander of Macedon. Raphael Sanzio (1483–1520) and Michelangelo Buonarroti (1475–1564) are, of course, the great Italian

Renaissance artists, and Albrecht Dürer (1471–1528), the foremost German one.

14. "Preface" to *A Descriptive Catalogue* (Ellis-Yeats 2: 363; Erdman, 529–30); for "upon" read "on" both times.

15. *A Descriptive Catalogue,* Number V (Ellis-Yeats 2: 375; Erdman, 544). For "appended" read "annexed and appended"; for "accident" read "accident and error"; for "features capable" read "features that are capable"; for "youth" read "infancy"; for "the face or limbs that alter" read "the face and limbs that deviates or alters"; and for "are the face" read "is the face"; for "of the greatest" read "of greatest."

16. Blake criticizes the Italian Renaissance painter Correggio (ca. 1489–1534) in *A Descriptive Catalogue,* Number IX (Ellis-Yeats 2: 378; Erdman, 548) as a painter who "infuses a love of soft and even tints without boundaries, and of endless reflected lights, that confuse one another, and hinder all correct drawing . . ." The Florentine artist Francesco Bartolozzi (1727–1815) moved in 1764 to England, where he became engraver to King George III and a founding member of the Royal Academy. Blake saw his technique, too, as soft and blurring of outline. The prolific English painter and engraver Thomas Stothard (1755–1834) joined the Royal Academy in 1794 and became its librarian in 1814. He based his 1807 painting of *The Pilgrimage to Canterbury* on Blake by way of Cromek and thus earned Blake's vituperation.

17. This refers to the vision of the heavenly city of Jerusalem seen by John in Revelation 21:19–21: "And the foundations of the wall of the city were garnished with all manner of precious stones. . . . And the twelve gates were twelve pearls. . . ."

18. The phrase "sweet smiling pestilence" is applied to Leutha in *Europe, A Prophecy,* plate 14 (Ellis-Yeats 3; Erdman, 65). For the masculine portion of nature bringing death, see "A Vision of the Last Judgment" (Ellis-Yeats 2: 393; Erdman, 563): "Time & Space are Real Beings a Male & a Female Time is a Man Space is a Woman & her Masculine Portion is Death."

19. Blake inveighs against generalizing and smoothing out in obedience to the laws of composition in *A Descriptive Catalogue,* "Public Address," and "Annotations to *The Works of Sir Joshua Reynolds,*" among other places. Udan-Adan is the condition of formlessness or of the unborn in Blake's "Prophetic Books"; it is a lake, not of waters but of spaces. In plate 26 of *Milton,* Blake places it within the forest of the physical body, Entuthon Benython: "The Lake of Udan-Adan, in the Forests of Entuthon Benython" (Ellis-Yeats 3; Erdman, 123). For "blut or blur" read "Blur or Mark."

The English painter Sir Joshua Reynolds (1723–92) served as the first president of the Royal Academy and became one of Blake's principal targets, especially in Blake's annotations to Reynolds.

20. "A Vision of the Last Judgment" (Ellis-Yeats 2: 400; Erdman, 560). For "in art and life" read "in art and in life."
21. The terms "corporeal reason," the desire for "a tepid moderation," and for a lifeless "sanity in both art and life" are not actually in Blake but are in the spirit of Blake. Yeats comments upon the term "corporeal reason" in his 1924 postscript to this essay, below.
22. These are two of the "Proverbs of Hell" on plate 7 of *The Marriage of Heaven and Hell* (Ellis-Yeats 3; Erdman, 35–36); for "roadway" read "road"; for "weight" read "number weight"; and for "in time" read "in a year."
23. This remark is one of Blake's annotations to Joshua Reynolds's "First Discourse"; Blake omitted the "the" before "Painters" (Ellis-Yeats 2: 325; Erdman, 643).
24. Yeats took this remark from A. H. Palmer, *The Life and Letters of Samuel Palmer* (London: Seeley, & Co., 1892), 16, from which Yeats omits an additional sentence after the first "art": "Be ever saying to yourself 'Labour after the excess of excellence.'"
25. This remark of Palmer's is quoted in Alexander Gilchrist, *Life of William Blake,* 1:345.
26. The passage is on plate 91 of *Jerusalem:* "the Spectre reads the Voids / Between the Stars . . . erecting pillars in the deepest Hell, / To reach the heavenly arches . . . driving down the pyramids of pride . . . Then he sent forth the Spectre all his pyramids were grains / of sand & his pillars: dust on the flys wing: & his starry / Heavens: a moth of gold & silver mocking his anxious grasp . . ." (Ellis-Yeats 3; Erdman, 251–52).
27. *Night Thoughts* was the most celebrated work by the poet Edward Young (1683–1765). Blake engraved forty-three of his designs for the volume, which were published in 1797; a good modern edition is *William Blake's Designs for Edward Young's "Night Thoughts,"* ed. John E. Grant, Edward J. Rose, Michael J. Tolley (Oxford: Clarendon Press; New York: Oxford University Press, 1980). The quotation from Wilkinson comes from the preface to his edition of *Songs of Innocence and of Experience* (London: W. Pickering and W. Newbery, 1839), xviii, reprinted in G. E. Bentley, Jr., *William Blake: The Critical Heritage* (London: Routledge & Kegan Paul, 1975), 59. The phrase about the door and window shutters is from the letter to William Haley quoted previously in the essay (see note 9 above).
28. Blake illustrated many of the chief poems of the English poet John Milton (1608–74), including *Comus, Paradise Lost,* and *Paradise Regained* mentioned here. The *Comus* designs appeared in *Illustrations of Milton's Comus: Eight Drawings by William Blake* (London: Quaritch, 1890). The bookseller and publisher Bernard Quaritch (1819–99) brought out the three-volume Ellis-Yeats edition of Blake in 1893. Blake completed two sets of illustrations for *Paradise Lost,* a smaller

one for Rev. Joseph Thomas in 1807, and a larger one for Thomas Butts in 1808. In 1825 Blake sold his set of designs for *Paradise Regained* to John Linnell, which is probably how Yeats later came to see them. The poet, artist, and critic William Bell Scott (1811–90) was a friend of D. G. Rossetti. The "one good judge" may have been W. M. Rossetti, who wrote: "This is a marvelously fine series: Blake is here king of all his powers of design. . . . This series (belonging to Mr. J. C. Strange) would of itself suffice to rank Blake among the heroes of the art." As quoted in Gilchrist 2:219. For more information, see J. M. Q. Davies, *Blake's Milton Designs: The Dynamics of Meaning* (West Cornwall, CT: Locust Hill Press, 1993).

29. Robert Blair (1699–1746) was a member of the "graveyard school"; his best-known poem was the eight-hundred-line *The Grave* (1743). Blake's drawings for it were engraved by Luigi Schiavonetti (1765–1810), who emigrated from Italy to England and lived for a time with Francesco Bartolozzi (see above), who influenced him greatly. The drawings were first published in Robert Blair, *The Grave* (London: R. H. Cromek, 1808).

Dr. Robert Thornton (1768–1837) was primarily a botanical and medical writer and illustrator. He commissioned Blake to do a series of woodcuts for the 1821 edition of his *The Pastorals of Virgil, with a course of English reading adapted for the schools* (London: F. C. and J. Rivingtons, 1821). The illustrations are reproduced in *The Wood Engravings of William Blake: Seventeen Subjects Commissioned by Dr. Robert Thornton for his "Virgil" of 1821*, introduction by Andrew Wilton (London: British Museum Publications Ltd., 1977).

The group of landscape painters who gathered around Blake in old age was called "The Ancients" and included Edward Calvert (1799–1883), Samuel Palmer (1805–81), George Richmond (1809–96), and Frederick Tatham (1805–78).

30. The member of the group is Samuel Palmer. See A. H. Palmer, *The Life and Letters of Samuel Palmer,* cited above, pp. 15–16. Palmer has "mystic" for "misty"; "all that wonderful" for "all this wonderful"; "works" for "work"; and "remaineth" for "remains." Yeats used the phrase "people of God" again in "Under Ben Bulben" (*P,* 335).

31. Blake's *Illustrations of the Book of Job* was commissioned by his patron and disciple John Linnell in 1823 and published in 1825; it was Blake's last completed "Prophetic Book." He never finished his late project of illustrating the entire *Divine Comedy* of Dante, a project also commissioned by Linnell; Albert S. Roe's *Blake's Illustrations to the Divine Comedy* (Princeton: Princeton University Press, 1953) is a good modern edition and study.

32. Blake repeatedly deprecated the English engravers William Woollett (1735–85) and the even more successful Robert Strange (1721–92), especially in "Public Address," where he wrote, for example, "What

is Calld the English Style of Engraving such as proceeded from the Toilettes of Woolett & Strange . . . can never produce Character & Expression. I knew the Men intimately from their Intimacy with Basire my Master & knew them both to be heavy lumps of Cunning & Ignorance as their works Shew to all the Continent . . ." (Ellis-Yeats 2: 390–91; Erdman, 573). Yeats's own footnote about Woollett and Strange was first added in 1924.

33. Phrases about dots, blots, and blurs occur throughout the "Public Address." Blake saw Marcantonio Raimondi (ca. 1488–ca. 1534) as elevating Italian engraving to the standards of the German Albrecht Dürer. In "Public Address" he demands: "Ye English Engravers must come down from your high flights ye must condescend to study Marc Antonio & Albert Durer" (Ellis-Yeats 2: 391; Erdman, 573).

34. Yeats is quoting from Blake's letter to George Cumberland, 12 April 1827 (Ellis-Yeats 1: 162; Erdman, 783). The full passage reads: "I know too well that a great majority of Englishmen are fond of The Indefinite which they Measure by Newtons Doctrine of the Fluxions of an Atom. A Thing that does not Exist. These are Politicians & think that Republican Art is Inimical to their Atom. For a Line or Lineament is not formed by Chance a Line is a Line in its Minutest Subdivision Strait or Crooked It is Itself & Not Intermeasurable with or by any Thing Else Such is Job but since the French Revolution Englishmen are all Intermeasurable One by Another Certainly a happy state of Agreement to which I for One do not Agree."

35. The quotation comes from plate 14 of *Jerusalem* (Ellis-Yeats 3; Erdman, 158): "as a watry flame revolving every way." Yeats expresses a similarly high opinion of the illustrations to *Job* and Dante in his introduction to his one-volume Blake, reprinted in *P&I*, 98–99, where he labels Blake's designs to *Job* "perhaps his masterpiece" and praises *The Divine Comedy* illustrations, especially *Francesca and Paolo.* Francesca and Paolo are, of course, the doomed illicit lovers in the Second Circle of the *Inferno,* that of carnal lust.

36. *The Savoy* version of the essay included a longer passage in lieu of the last sentence of this paragraph; see appendix D for reproductions of the designs that originally accompanied the essay.

37. See "Public Address" (Ellis-Yeats 2: 388; Erdman, 582). Erdman reads "& in Execution" for "and execution."

38. "Public Address" (Ellis-Yeats 2: 383; Erdman, 576). Erdman reads "& minutely Delineated" for "delineated" and "many People" for "people" and "Design" for "designs."

39. Yeats's catalog of great Florentine painters of Dante's time and later includes Giotto di Bondone (ca. 1267–1337), Andrea Orcagna (ca. 1308–68), and Alessandro Botticelli (1445–1510).

40. The great English Romantic poet and critic Samuel Taylor Coleridge (1772–1834) became addicted to opium. In 1863 the Comte Villiers de

L'Isle-Adam (1838–89) was taken in by a planted newspaper column about candidacies for the Greek throne; he fell for the hoax and applied himself with comic results. For a turn-of-the-century account, see Vicomte Robert du Pontavice de Heussey, *Villiers de L'Isle Adam: His Life and Works* (London: Heinemann, 1894), trans. Lady Mary Loyd, 70–82.

41. Although the phrase "inspired by the Holy Ghost" is a common one, Yeats probably took its application to Dante from the diary of Henry Crabb Robinson (1775–1867), which provides helpful information about the writers and events of the Romantic period and later. See Henry Crabb Robinson, *Diary, Reminiscences, and Correspondence of Henry Crabb Robinson,* ed. Thomas Sadler (Boston: Fields, Osgood, 1870), 2 vols., 2:39: "Dante and Wordsworth, in spite of their Atheism, were inspired by the Holy Ghost." Blake says nearly the opposite on the design to *Hell,* canto 4 (Ellis-Yeats 1: 139; Erdman, 689): Erdman reads: "the Goddess Nature <Memory> <is his Inspirer> & not <Imagination> the Holy Ghost."

42. Yeats's source again appears to be Crabb Robinson's *Diary,* 2:69: "of the Old Testament he seemed to think not favourably. Christ, said he, took much after his mother, the Law. . . . On my asking for an explanation, he referred to the turning the money-changers out of the temple."

43. Yeats here brings together two quotations from Blake. The first comes from *The Book of Urizen,* plate 28 (Ellis-Yeats 3; Erdman, 83) and should read "the eternal laws of God" rather than "laws of God"; the second comes from "A Vision of the Last Judgment" (Ellis-Yeats 2: 402; Erdman, 564).

44. The phrase "war & princedom & victory" appears in both plate 4 of *Jerusalem* and plate 11 of *The Four Zoas* (Ellis-Yeats 3; Erdman, 147 and 306).

45. The Swedish philosopher and mystic Emanuel Swedenborg (1688–1772) was an important influence on Blake, who worked out his relationship to him in both *The Marriage of Heaven and Hell* and his annotations to various of Swedenborg's works. For the painter Sir Joshua Reynolds, see note 19 above.

46. "Public Address" (omitted from Ellis-Yeats 2: 386; Erdman, 580): "Princes appear to me to be Fools Houses of Commons & Houses of Lords appear to me to be fools they seem to me to be something Else besides Human Life." Yeats draws on this passage several other times, as in his note to "The Dolls" (*P,* 604 and note on 615).

47. Yeats associated the German philosopher Friedrich Nietzsche (1844–1900) with Blake several times, as in *CL3*, 284: "Nietzsche completes Blake and has the same roots."

48. Franz Hettinger, *Dante's Divina Commedia: Its Scope and Value,* trans. Henry Sebastian Bowden (London: Burns & Oates, 1887), 115:

"[Francesca's] simple avowal, in words so tender and delicate, such as only a woman could use, makes us sympathise to a certain extent with her bitter anguish." Hettinger (1819–90) was a German theologian and Dante scholar. Yeats owned the second edition of 1894 (O'Shea #891).

49. From the end of the inscription on design #101 for *The Divine Comedy* (Ellis-Yeats 1: 138–39; Erdman, 690). The full quotation in Erdman reads: "It seems as if Dantes supreme Good was something Superior to the Father or Jesus for if he gives his rain to the Evil & the Good & his Sun to the Just & the Unjust He could never have Builded Dantes Hell nor the Hell of the Bible neither in the way our Parsons explain it It must have been originally Formed by the Devil Him self & So I understand it to have been Whatever Book is for Vengeance for Sin & whatever Book is Against the Forgiveness of Sins is not of the Father but of Satan the Accuser & Father of Hell."
50. Crabb Robinson, *Diary*, 2: 27 and 69. In the first quotation, Robinson has "saw none" for "see none."
51. Many passages in Blake echo this thought, though not in these exact words. Yeats may have been thinking, for example, of the 12 April 1827 letter to George Cumberland that mentions "The Real Man The Imagination which Liveth for Ever" cited above (Ellis-Yeats 1: 162; Erdman, 783) or the annotation to Berkeley's *Siris* that "Jesus considered Imagination to be the Real Man" (Erdman, 663).
52. Crabb Robinson, *Diary*, 2: 28 and 27, respectively; Robinson reads "assumes" for "assumed."
53. On design no. 7 for *The Divine Comedy* (Ellis-Yeats 1: 139; Erdman, 689).
54. This also comes from the commentary on design no. 7 for *The Divine Comedy* (Ellis-Yeats 1: 139; Erdman, 689). Erdman reads: "Every thing in Dantes Comedia shews That for Tyrannical Purposes he has made This World the Foundation of All & the Goddess Nature Memory is his Inspirer & not Imagination the Holy Ghost as Poor Churchill said Nature thou art my Goddess Round Purgatory is Paradise is Vacuum or Limbo. so that Homer is the Center for All I mean the Poetry of the Heathen."
55. *The Marriage of Heaven and Hell*, plate 5 (Ellis-Yeats 3; Erdman, 35).
56. This quotation and the next two all come from *Jerusalem*, plates 88, 13, and 21 (Ellis-Yeats 3; Erdman, 247, 157, and 166, respectively). Erdman reads "voids" rather than "void" and "Gardens" rather than "garden."
57. The first five terms appear frequently in Blake. "The human form divine" comes from the description of God in "The Divine Image" (see next note); "The Divine Members" applies to "Ideas" in plate 35 of *Milton* (Ellis-Yeats 3; Erdman, 135).

58. These are the middle three stanzas of "The Divine Image" from *Songs of Innocence* (Ellis-Yeats 3: 42; Erdman, 12–13).
59. This refers to plate 20 of *Milton* (Ellis-Yeats 3; Erdman, 114).
60. Alcinous, king of the Phaecians, uses this phrase in *The Odyssey,* book 8, as translated by S. H. Butcher and Andrew Lang in *The Odyssey of Homer Done into English Prose* (London: Macmillan, 1879), 23. Yeats drops the phrase "and the warm bath" from the list.
61. The phrase "the minute particulars of life" comes from plate 88 of *Jerusalem* (Ellis-Yeats 3; Erdman, 247); the one about "a globule of man's blood" from plate 29 of *Milton* (Ellis-Yeats 3; Erdman, 127).
62. Plate 28 of *Milton* (Ellis-Yeats 3; Erdman, 127).
63. Plate 77 of *Jerusalem* (Ellis-Yeats 3; Erdman, 231–32). Erdman reads "what were" for "what are"; "that Talent" for "the talent"; "in Truth and are" for "and truth? Are"; "Lives Eternally" for "lives immortally"; "Bodily Lust, Idleness" for "idleness, bodily lust"; "Answer this to" rather than "Answer this for"; "among" for "amongst"; and "Build up Jerusalem" for "build Jerusalem."
64. Plate 91 of *Jerusalem* (Ellis-Yeats 3; Erdman, 252); Erdman reads "evil" for "bad."
65. Plates 23 and 24 of *The Marriage of Heaven and Hell* (Ellis-Yeats 3; Erdman, 43). The quotation should begin "Jesus was" rather than "who being."
66. The couplet about the seventy disciples comes from Blake's "The Everlasting Gospel," fragment d (Ellis-Yeats 2: 59; Erdman, 878). Yeats uses the phrase "the imagination is the man himself" again in "The Pathway" (see appendix B) and in "By the Roadside," a section of *The Celtic Twilight* (*Myth,* 139).
67. "A Vision of the Last Judgment" (Ellis-Yeats 2: 401; Erdman, 564). For "governed their passions" Erdman reads "governd their Passions or have No Passions"; for "from which the passions" Erdman reads "from which All the Passions"; and for "price of entering" Erdman reads "Price of Enterance."
68. The "dark valley" comes from *The Four Zoas* (Ellis-Yeats 3: p. 109 of *Vala;* Erdman, 385); Erdman reads "and return" and "to begin." The peace that passeth understanding comes from Philippians 4:7 in the New Testament.
69. The letter was to George Cumberland, 12 April 1827 (Ellis-Yeats 1: 162–63; Erdman, 783–84). Modern scholars, including Erdman, do not share Yeats's belief that this was Blake's last letter, though it was a very late one. Erdman reads "Delusive" for "delusions of" and "Members" rather than "numbers."
70. The phrase "the immortal man" appears at least twice in Blake. The one in "Night the Sixth" of *The Four Zoas* (Ellis-Yeats 3: p. 64 of *Vala;* Erdman, 351) fits the sense here better than that on plate 17 of *Milton.*
71. *The Four Zoas* (Ellis-Yeats 3: p. 109 of *Vala;* Erdman, 385); Erdman

reads "invisible army" for "invisible array"; "the scatterd [*sic*] portions of" for "fragments of"; "Screaming in birds" for "sorrowing in birds"; and "deep & howling" for "deep, or howling"; the ellipsis signals omission of twelve lines.

72. "The Laocoön" (Ellis-Yeats 3; Erdman, 273–74). For "Christ's apostles were all Artists" Erdman reads "Jesus & his apostles & Disciples were all Artists."

73. Although Blake uses the word "corporeal" frequently, neither "corporeal reason" nor "corporeal law" appears in his work, though he does use the phrase "corporeal understanding" in a letter to Thomas Butts, 6 July 1803: "Allegory addressd to the Intellectual powers while it is altogether hidden from the Corporeal Understanding is My Definition of the Most Sublime Poetry" (Erdman, 730).

The words "captivity" and "Egypt" both appear repeatedly in Blake, but "captivity in Egypt" does not; that biblical event is referred to, for example, in *Jerusalem,* plate 79 (Erdman, 234).

74. The phrase "infinite and holy" comes from plate 14 of *The Marriage of Heaven and Hell* (Ellis-Yeats 3; Erdman, 39). For two paragraphs that originally ended this section and that comment on the accompanying plates, see appendix D on illustrations to this essay.

75. The Victorian man of letters John Addington Symonds (1840–93) was a fellow of Magdalen College, Oxford, but spent much of his life in Italy and Switzerland, partly for health reasons and partly because of his attraction to the Italian Renaissance, about which he produced a series of studies collected in his *Renaissance in Italy* (1875–86). He also did volumes on Sidney, Shelley, Whitman, and Michelangelo, as well as several books of his own poetry and several translations. John (also Joannes or Jan) Stradanus (1523–1605) was a Flemish painter and printmaker who spent much of his career in Italy, where he did work for both Cosimo de' Medici and Giorgio Vasari. In 1587–88 he drew twenty-four designs to the *Inferno* and four to the *Purgatorio.* The quotation comes from *Illustrations to the 'Divine Comedy' of Dante.* Executed by the Flemish artist, John Stradanus, 1587, and reproduced in phototype from the originals existing in the Laurentian Library of Florence. Illuminations by Jan van der Straet. With an Introduction by Doct. Guido Biagi and a preface by John Addington Symonds (London: T. Fisher Unwin, 1892). Symonds's stance in the unpaginated preface does not differ from Yeats's own as much as the text suggests here. Symonds mentions "the few and rare designs which William Blake produced, with a penetrative imagination, and a spiritual sympathy far beyond the reach of any *improvisatore* like Doré"; Symonds also judges Flaxman's Dante designs a failure and calls Stradanus a "journey-man" of a "raw and facile Flemish nature."

Gustave Doré (1832–83) was the most popular French book illustrator of the Victorian period. He produced illustrations of Dante's

*Inferno,* Cervantes's *Don Quixote,* the Bible, and Bunyan's *The Pilgrim's Progress,* among other works.

76. Symonds, preface to *Illustrations to the 'Divine Comedy.'* Symonds reads: "for the task," "feeling for pure beauty," "sternly in sympathy," "but rather by a very effective sense of space and multitude, of luminosity and gloom."

The great Florentine painter Alessandro Botticelli (1445–1510) also did a series of drawings to illustrate Dante's *The Divine Comedy,* probably for Lorenzo de' Medici; he planned one hundred illustrations, of which ninety-two survive.

77. The German painter Giovanni Buonaventura Genelli (1798–1868) did a series of thirty-six designs for *The Divine Comedy* during the 1840s. Yeats's account may derive in part from Ludwig Volkmann, *Iconografia Dantesca: The Pictorial Representations to Dante's Divine Comedy* (London: H. Grevel, 1899), 146–47.

78. The Italian artist, designer, and engraver Bartolomeo Pinelli (1781–1835) did many once famous series of engravings, including a set of more than one hundred forty to *The Divine Comedy* (1825–26).

Yeats did not find the German Bernhard Schuler in biographical dictionaries because he was the editor and publisher rather than the artist in *La Divina Commedia di Dante Alighieri* (Munich: published by the author, 1893), which featured plates drawn by the Italian artists Luigi Ademollo (1764–1849) and Francesco Nenci (1782–1850) in 1817–19.

Walpurgis Night (April 30) is an old Nordic festival and revel marking the end of winter; in Goethe's *Faust* it is marked by the coming of witches.

79. Blake's friend John Flaxman (1755–1826) did a set of illustrations to *The Divine Comedy* in 1802 that appeared in several editions during the nineteenth century.

80. The Italian artist Luca Signorelli (ca. 1441–1523) did frescoes of eleven scenes from the *Purgatory* for the cathedral of Orvieto, 1499–1504. Yeats's remarks here follow those of Symonds in the book cited in note 74 above.

81. Franz Adolf von Stürler (1802–81) was a pupil of Ingres, who, with his friend Luigi Mussini (1813–1888), opened a small art school in Florence in 1844. His designs for the *Inferno, Purgatorio,* and *Paradiso* were published in *La Divine comédie de Dante Alighieri* (Paris: Firmin-Didot, 1884).

82. Giulio Clovio (1498–1578) was a painter and illuminator who was born in Croatia but spent most of his career in Italy. He often made use in his illuminations of motifs drawn from Michelangelo and Raphael. The miniatures of Dante's *Paradiso* that are attributed to him may have been done by Cesare Pollini (1560–1630) instead. For Botticelli, see above. For the short paragraph commenting on the illustrations that originally accompanied this section of the essay, see appendix D.

83. The American poet Ezra Pound (1885–1972) greatly admired Yeats and served as his secretary during the winters 1913–16 at Stone Cottage in Sussex. Yeats often asked the advice of the younger poet but was not always happy with the results.

## Symbolism in Painting

This essay first appeared as the introduction to *A Book of Images,* drawn by W. T. Horton and introduced by W. B. Yeats (London: Unicorn Press, 1898). William Thomas Horton (1864–1919) was an illustrator and visionary who was influenced by William Blake. Yeats and he became friends in the mid-1890s and Yeats sponsored him for membership in the Order of the Golden Dawn in 1896. Although Yeats and Horton remained friends until Horton's death, Yeats's omission of all references to Horton in the book version of the essay, including all of section 3 (reproduced in an appendix to the present volume), caused a temporary breach. Yeats tried to repair it in a letter of 17 July 1903, where he wrote in part: "I had a footnote stating where the essay was from but took it out of the last proof . . . because I had not acknowledged the sources of any of the essays. To do so always seems to weaken the unity of a book . . . When I wrote the essays originally I wrote it so that I could detach the general statement from the rest. In the same way I separated the statement of general principles as far as possible from the description of particular drawings, when reprinting my Blake essays" (*CL*3, 400). Reprinting the essay in *Ideas of Good and Evil* also caused a financial problem in that Yeats had neglected to obtain permission for reusing the material and the publisher Ernest James Oldmeadow demanded ten pounds in compensation, plus an acknowledgment in future editions (see introduction to the present volume and also *CL*3, 379–80). Yeats mentioned Horton prominently in the poem "All Souls' Night," where he devoted two stanzas to him that began "Horton's the first I call. He loved strange thought / And knew that sweet extremity of pride / That's called platonic love . . ." (*P*, 232).

1. The great eighteenth-century man of letters Samuel Johnson (1709–84) devoted nine years to his *Dictionary of the English Language,* the first major work of its kind in English. The dictionary was published in London in 1755 and established Johnson's reputation; five editions appeared during his lifetime.
2. That definition of "symbol" appeared in Noah Webster's *An American Dictionary of the English Language* in 1828, though Yeats presumably used a later edition of that or another work. Hermes Trismegistus, or Thrice-Great Hermes, was the name that the Greeks gave to the Egyptian god Thoth, the deity of wisdom and literature. From there the name became attached to both Neoplatonic and Christian or post-Christian mystical writings. A central icon was the Great Smaragdine (or Emerald) Tablet, which Yeats mentions in the late

poem "Ribh Denounces Patrick": "For things below are copies, the Great Smaragdine Tablet said" (*P*, 290). Hermetic writings influenced both theosophy and the Golden Dawn, and people whom Yeats knew well, like Madame Blavatsky and MacGregor Mathers, wrote about them.

3. *The Faerie Queene* is the major epic by the English Renaissance poet Edmund Spenser (1552–99). Yeats discusses both work and poet later in this collection, in his essay "Edmund Spenser."

   The English Puritan John Bunyan (1628–88) published the first part of his famous prose allegory *The Pilgrim's Progress* in 1678; it presented a dream journey of the pilgrim Christian through various obstacles to the Celestial City. The second part appeared in 1684 and presented the parallel journey of his wife and children. In 1899 Yeats urged his friend Horton to illustrate *The Pilgrim's Progress* (*CL2*, 447–48).
4. According to Giorgio Melchiori, the German Symbolist in Paris was probably Paul Hermann (b. 1864), who moved to Paris in 1895 and became a friend of Oscar Wilde, among others; see Melchiori, *The Whole Mystery of Art* (London: Routledge and Kegan Paul, 1960), 17n. Yeats may also be referring to the similarly named Hermann-Paul (Hermann Paul René Georges, 1864–1940), who was a printmaker, illustrator, and genre painter. In any case, three paragraphs later in the present essay, the paragraph beginning "Wagner's dramas, Keats' odes . . ." originally included "the black-and-white art of M. Herrmann" in the list.
5. "A Vision of the Last Judgment" (Ellis-Yeats 1: 307 and 2: 393; Erdman, 554). Erdman reads: "what Eternally Exists. Really & Unchangeably." Ellis-Yeats then explains, "A vision is, that is to say, a perception of the eternal symbols, about which the world is formed, while allegory is a memory of some natural event into which we read a spiritual meaning."
6. Yeats probably means Blake's tempera "Ghost of a Flea," circa. 1820. According to Gilchrist, John Varley reported that "During the time occupied in completing the drawing, the Flea told him that all fleas were inhabited by the souls of such men as were by nature bloodthirsty to excess . . ." Quoted in Alexander Gilchrist, *The Life of William Blake,* 2nd ed., 2 vols. (London: Macmillan, 1880) 1: 303–4. The only other use of the word "bloodthirsty" in Blake is in a discarded couplet of "Let the brothels of Paris be opened": "But the bloodthirsty people across the water / Will not submit to the gibbet & halter" (Erdman, 861).
7. Yeats here refers to two major paintings by the Pre-Raphaelite artist Dante Gabriel Rossetti (1828–82): *The Annunciation* and *The Girlhood* (not *Childhood*) *of Mary Virgin.*
8. The famous statue of Moses by Michelangelo Buonarroti (1475–1564)

is the most striking feature of the tomb of Pope Julius II in the church of San Pietro in Vinculi, Rome. Its distinctive horns derive from Saint Jerome's mistranslation in the Vulgate of the rays of light around Moses's head as horns after he met with God on Mount Sinai. The allegorical painting *Origin of the Milky Way* by Jacopo Tintoretto (ca. 1518–94) portrays Jupiter holding the infant Hercules to the breasts of the sleeping Juno, from which some milk spurted upward to form the Milky Way and some downward to form lilies.

9. Yeats's catalog of nineteenth-century creators here includes the German musician Richard Wagner (1813–83); the Romantic poets John Keats and William Blake; the English artists Edward Calvert (1799–1883), Aubrey Beardsley (1872–98), Charles Ricketts (1866–1931), Charles Hazelwood Shannon (1863–1937), and the American-born James Abbott McNeill Whistler (1834–1903); and the Continental symbolist writers Villiers de L'Isle-Adam (1838–89), Maurice Maeterlinck (1862–1949), and Paul Verlaine (1844–96). In contrast, Giotto di Bondone (ca. 1267–1337) and Fra Angelico (1387–1455) are leading artists of the early Italian Renaissance.

10. "A Vision of the Last Judgment" (Ellis-Yeats 2: 394; Erdman, 555). Erdman reads "the Images of Existences according to a certain order suited to my Imaginative Eye."

11. Yeats cites Michelangelo's sonnet "Non vider gli occhi" in an unidentified translation. Yeats had the third edition of John Addington Symonds's translation *The Sonnets of Michael Angelo Buonarroti* in his library (London: Smith, Elder: 1912; O'Shea #1313), which reads "I saw no mortal beauty with these eyes / When perfect peace in thy fair eyes I found" (57).

12. Yeats may refer to a specific work in the conditional clause that begins this sentence; Lanham suggests possibly *Un Masque Ivoire* by the Belgian Rosicrucian painter Fernand Khnopff (1858–1921) (Lanham, 405). That work has a rose in the middle of a band across the forehead of a winged bust, but his phraseology echoes the last lines of Arthur Symons's "Impression"; see Symons's *Silhouettes* (London: Leonard Smithers, 2nd edition, 1896), of which Yeats had an inscribed presentation copy in his library (O'Shea #2064): "Ah, what is this? what wings unfold / In this miraculous rose of gold?" (15). The swords making continual music before the occult face may be a kabbalistic reference to a Golden Dawn ritual; compare, too, the young Irishwoman of the essay "Magic" in the present volume (cf. *Au*, 209–10).

13. "A Vision of the Last Judgment" (Ellis-Yeats 2: 400; Erdman, 560). Erdman reads "Enter into these Images in," "intreats," and "arise from his." The following quotation comes from the same work (Ellis-Yeats 3: 394; Erdman, 555). Erdman reads "This" for "the" world of Imagination" (both times); "Permanent" for "external" realities; and "this Vegetable" for "the vegetable."

14. Yeats refers to the "Hodos Chameliontos" section of *Trembling of the Veil* (especially *Au,* 205–15). See also *Memoirs,* 27–28.

## The Symbolism of Poetry

This essay first appeared in *The Dome* for April 1900, the same journal that would publish the first part of Yeats's essay on Shelley the following year. There were no major revisions but numerous small ones, of which the dropping of an extended clause from the first paragraph (recorded in the note to the appropriate place) was the most significant. Yeats wrote to Lady Gregory on 30 March 1900: "My essay on Symbolism has grown to be a rather elaborate thing—about four times as long as I expected. It is in four parts of which I have one still to write. It is I think good . . . . Now that I have had to read Symons [*sic*] book very carefully I have found it curiously vague in its philosophy" (*CL2,* 506). When eventually published, the essay had five rather than four parts.

1. A leading spirit in the Decadent movement and editor of *The Savoy,* Arthur William Symons (1865–1945) attended the meetings of the Rhymers' Club and shared rooms with Yeats for a time. The two-page dedication to Yeats in Symons's influential book *The Symbolist Movement in Literature* (London: William Heinemann, 1899; O'Shea #2068) began: "May I dedicate to you this book on the Symbolist movement in literature, both as an expression of a deep personal friendship and because you, more than anyone else, will sympathise with what I say in it, being yourself the chief representative of that movement in our country?" (v).
2. In *Yeats's Shakespeare* (Evanston: Northwestern University Press, 1971), 38n15, Rupin Desai says that "Yeats is thinking of Jonson's famous swipe at Shakespeare [in *Timber*]: 'Many times hee fell into those things, could not escape laughter: As when hee said in the person of Caesar, one speaking to him; *Caesar thou dost me wrong.* He replyed: *Caesar did never wrong but with just cause* and such like: which were ridiculous.'"
3. The German composer Richard Wagner (1813–83) wrote no music between 1848 and 1854 but devoted himself instead to producing essays, plays, and poetry as well as to planning his operatic cycle *Der Ring des Nibelungen.* Count Giovanni Bardi (1534–1612) was the leader of the Florentine Camerata, a group of musicians and intellectuals who met at his palace and developed ideas important to the growth of modern secular opera. The Pléiade were a group of seven sixteenth-century French poets under the leadership of Pierre de Ronsard (1524?–85) and Joachim du Bellay (1522?–60); Yeats is probably referring here to du Bellay's *Deffence et Illustration de la Langue Françoyse* (1549).

4. The great German writer Johann Wolfgang von Goethe (1749–1832) made remarks like this several times in the conversations with Eckermann, especially in relation to the effect of philosophy on Schiller. Yeats cited the remark several times, including in a late letter to Ethel Mannin, 20 October 1938 (*L,* 917). Its exact source remains uncertain but Goethe has similar remarks in *Conversations with Eckermann* (Washington and London: M. Walter Dunne, 1901), 293 (4 February 1829), where he says, for example: "I have always kept myself free from philosophy." In *The Dome* version, after the semicolon the text included another clause framed by semicolons: "and certainly he cannot know too much, whether about his own work, or about the procreant waters of the soul where the breath first moved, or about the waters under the earth that are the life of passing things."
5. Symons makes this remark in the introduction to his *The Symbolist Movement in Literature:* "Zola has tried to build in brick and mortar inside the covers of a book" (7).
6. This quotation is from Robert Burns (1759–96), "Open the Door to Me, O," a Scots song set to the tune of the Irish air "Open the Door Softly." Yeats had in his library the four-volume *Poetry of Robert Burns,* ed. William Ernest Henley and Thomas F. Henderson (London: T. C. and E. C. Jack, 1896–97; O'Shea #310), which reads "The wan moon sets behind the white wave, / And Time is setting with me, O" (other lines of the poem end "O!") (3:211). That edition's note to the poem, 3:451, indicates that "sets" was an editorial alteration for the manuscript "is setting" made by the first editor of the poem, George Thomson (1757–1851), information confirmed by James Kinsley, *The Poems and Songs of Robert Burns,* vol. 2 (Oxford: Clarendon Press, 1968). Yeats's wording here thus restores Burns's original phrase "is setting" and Yeats's only change then appears to be "wan" to "white."
7. The Blake line comes from plate 14 of *Europe a Prophecy* (Ellis-Yeats 3; Erdman, 65). Erdman reads "when the cold moon drinks the dew." The three lines by the Elizabethan writer Thomas Nashe (1567–1601) come from his best-known lyric, "Adieu; Farewell Earth's Bliss." For more information, see note to the same quotation of "What is 'Popular Poetry'?" above. The Shakespeare quotation comes from *Timon of Athens,* 5.2.100–103 (Shakespeare, 2301–2).
8. Arthur William Edgar O'Shaughnessy (1844–81) was a poet who worked in the department of printed books at the British Museum; he was a friend of Dante Gabriel Rossetti. Yeats quotes here from perhaps O'Shaugnessy's best-known poem, his "Ode" ("We are the music makers"), *Music and Moonlight* (London: Chatto and Windus, 1874), 2: "We, in the ages lying / In the buried past of the earth, / Built Nineveh with our sighing, / And Babel itself in our mirth. . . ."
9. The seer is unidentified.
10. Dionysius the Areopagite (fl. late fifth to early sixth century) sought to

combine Neoplatonic mystical elements with Christianity; he ranked the angels "in three hierarchies of three choirs each: Seraphim, Cherubim, Thrones; Dominions, Virtues, Powers; Principalities, Archangels, Angels." The phrase "the eye altering alter[s] all" comes from Blake's "The Mental Traveller," line 62 (Ellis-Yeats 2: 32; Erdman, 485).

11. Francis Thompson (1859–1907) published three volumes of verse in the 1890s, from which "The Hound of Heaven" and "The Kingdom of God" are the best-known poems. The quotation here comes from "The Heart: Two Sonnets," sonnet two, *New Poems* (London: Archibald Constable and Boston: Copeland and Day, 1897), 192.
12. The poem may have been *The Shadowy Waters,* of which Yeats thought of the 1900 version as a poem. He mentions it in a letter to George Russell, asking Russell to comment on a series of symbolic dreams that Yeats had and that may include the incident referred to in this essay (27 August 1899; *CL2*, 442–44).
13. Virgil describes the two passages leading back from the underworld to the realm of the living at the end of book 6 of *The Aeneid* as the gates of horn and of ivory; the gate of horn gives true visions but that of ivory gives false dreams.
14. Blake, "A Vision of the Last Judgment" (Ellis-Yeats 2: 400; Erdman, 560); Ellis-Yeats reads "friend and companion" rather than "friend." Ellis-Yeats also contained a section on "The Symbolism of Colour" (1: 309–14) that may be pertinent to the present paragraph.
15. In Greek myth Demeter (the Roman Ceres) was the goddess of grain and agriculture and also the mother of Persephone, who was carried off to Hades by Pluto. Persephone's return to spend part of the year with her mother and then the rest with Pluto symbolized both the natural agricultural cycle and (in cults like the Eleusinian Mysteries) the death of man and rebirth of his spirit.
16. Yeats takes this quotation from the French writer Gérard de Nerval (1808–55) as rendered in Symons's translation from *Le Rêve et la vie* in *The Symbolist Movement in Literature* (33–34). Symons recounts de Nerval's increasing loss of control over his own visions as a consequence of his growing madness (which eventually led to his suicide by hanging).
17. The Belgian writer Maurice Maeterlinck (1862–1949) and French writer Villiers de L'Isle-Adam (1838–89) were leading figures in the symbolist movement. The phrase about the sacred book of all the arts presumably echoes the thought of Stéphane Mallarmé (1842–98), another symbolist writer, about whom Yeats would have learned from Symons, among others.
18. Yeats reviewed the last book of the Victorian poet laureate Alfred Tennyson (1809–92) upon his death, writing that Tennyson was "scarce less of a visionary in some ways than Blake himself" (*EAR*, 191). Yeats may have taken the beryl stone as a symbol from Rossetti.

In Yeats's April 1898 review of "Mr. Rhys' *Welsh Ballads*" for *The Bookman,* he writes that a new religious movement is coming into art: "This movement has made painters and poets and musicians go to old legends for their subjects, for legends are the magical beryls in which we see life, not as it is, but as the heroic part of us, the part which desires always dreams and emotions greater than any in the world, and loves beauty and does not hate sorrow, hopes in secret that it may become" (*EAR,* 390–91).

19. For some of Yeats's many comments on Blake's *Songs of Innocence and of Experience,* see his two essays on Blake above.

## The Theatre

This essay grew out of a letter to the editor of the *Daily Chronicle* dated 27 January 1899 but rejected by the editor, H. W. Massingham; the text is available in *CL2,* 347–51. Both parts of the essay respond to principles and controversies growing out of the founding of the Irish Literary Theatre, which in turn became the Irish National Theatre Society. They first appeared in *The Dome:* part 1, titled "The Theatre," in the issue for April 1899, and part 2 as a section of the essay "The Irish Literary Theatre, 1900" in January 1900. Both parts then appeared with revisions in *Beltaine,* the occasional magazine of the Irish Literary Theatre, in May 1899 and February 1900, respectively, before finding their place in *Ideas of Good and Evil.* The most important revision was dropping the beginning of the first paragraph and all of the long second paragraph of part 2; a full text of *The Dome* version of that part is available in *IDM,* 161–63. The main effect of the deletions (which also include a few sentences from part 1) was to make the essay less a review of specific current work by the Irish Literary Theatre and its successor and more an enunciation of Yeats's basic theatrical principles.

1. The unnamed writer was John Todhunter (1839–1916), a friend of John Butler Yeats and of the Yeats family; Todhunter was their neighbor when they all lived in Bedford Park. The play was *A Sicilian Idyll,* which Yeats reviewed for *The Boston Pilot,* among other places (for that review, see *LNI,* 36–39).
2. *A Sicilian Idyll* was first performed in May 1890 at the Bedford Park Social Club with a cast that included Yeats's friend and later collaborator on "Speaking to the Psaltery," Florence Farr. While it succeeded in the rarified atmosphere of the artistic suburb of Bedford Park, the play did less well when Todhunter transferred it first to the St. George's Hall on 1–2 July 1890, then again at the Vaudeville in the Strand on 15–19 June 1891, along with his new play, *The Poison Flower,* a production that Yeats also reviewed (*LNI,* 111–15). He was less enthusiastic in *The Trembling of the Veil,* where he called the play one "which I have not looked at for thirty years, and never rated very high as

poetry" (*Au*, 118). Mrs. Todhunter later denied the effect of Yeats's "advice" in a letter to *The Fortnightly Review*, NS, 114 (July 1923), 163: "There is no truth in Mr. Yeats's statement that he caused Dr. Todhunter to produce the latter's *Sicilian Idyll;* the play was written and produced without any intervention on his part, though he no doubt took an interest in the production, as several of the players were personally known to him."

3. Yeats critiques here those incapable of responding fully to late nineteenth-century artists such as the English writer Dante Gabriel Rossetti (1828–82), the French sculptor Auguste Rodin (1840–1917), or the Norwegian dramatist Henrik Ibsen (1828–1906). There is a similar passage in Yeats's 1899 essay "The Irish Literary Theatre," which concluded: "It may happen that the imaginative minority will spread their interests among the majority, for even the majority becomes imaginative when touched by enthusiasm. Men who are not more intelligent than London theatre-goers listen with sympathy and understanding to quiet and sincere miracle-plays in Brittany; and the crowds who went in procession when Cimabue had the cry, or who chanted the ballad of 'Chevy Chase,' or who filled the play-houses for Shakespeare, only differed from the crowds who think Rossetti's women 'guys,' and poetry of kinds 'a bore,' and Ibsen an 'immoral' and inexpert writer, because they were touched by the fervour of religion, or by the delight of a familiar legend, or by a world-wide movement of thought and emotion" (*EAR*, 437–38).
4. Laurence Binyon (1869–1943) worked at the British Museum after graduating from Trinity College, Oxford, and wrote in various genres, including art criticism, drama, and poetry. For rhetorical purposes, Yeats takes Binyon's quotation somewhat out of context from Binyon's own previous article in *The Dome*, "Mr. Bridges' 'Prometheus' and Poetic Drama" (March 1899), which reads "the managers who bar" rather than "the manager who bars" (203). Binyon's argument about the audience for theater there is not that far from Yeats's own, though with great concession to financial realities. Nonetheless, Binyon concludes, "I see no reason why we should not supplement the main accepted type with plays of a type which should rely more largely on its poetry, plays of a simple construction developed from such a starting-point as I have suggested, and recovering much that has been usurped by opera. But if a play is to rely much on its poetry, the method of speaking verse on the stage must be wholly changed, and the scenery must be far more in tune with the piece." Binyon then cited for support Yeats's own letter to the *Daily Chronicle* of 29 January 1899 (*CL2*, 347–51; the date should be 27 January 1899).
5. Yeats invokes here three great playwrights from different countries—the classical Greek tragedian Sophocles (ca. 496–406 BC), William

Shakespeare (1564–1616), and the Spanish Calderón de la Barca (1600–1681).

Lady Gregory, whom Yeats accompanied to those Irish cabins in Connaught, describes the lovers who were drowned going to America, five (rather than three) boys drowned recently, and the old poet confessing his sins in the following passage: "Another song I have heard was a lament over a boy and girl who had run away to America, and on the way the ship went down. And when they were going down, they began to be sorry they were not married; and to say that if the priest had been at home when they went away, they would have been married; but they hoped that when they were drowned, it would be the same with them as if they were married. And I heard another lament that had been made for three boys that had lately been drowned in Galway Bay. It is the mother who is making it; and she tells how she lost her husband, the father of her three boys. And then she married again, and they went to sea and were drowned; and she wouldn't mind about the others so much, but it is the eldest boy, Peter, she is grieving for. And I have heard one song that had a great many verses, and was about "a poet that is dying, and he confessing his sins." See Lady Gregory, "West Irish Ballads," in her *Poets and Dreamers* (Dublin: Hodges, Figgis / New York: Scribner's, 1903; O'Shea #807), 48–49. Yeats had previously dealt with the story of the ancient Irish hero Oisin and his three hundred years in Tír na nÓg (the land of Youth) in his narrative poem *The Wanderings of Oisin* (*P*, 361ff).

6. *The Return of Ulysses,* one of eight plays on mostly classical themes published by the English poet and man of letters Robert Bridges (1844–1930) between 1885 and 1893, appeared in 1890 (London: Edward Bumpus). For a more extended elaboration of Yeats's views of it, see his essay "*The Return of Ulysses*" later in the present volume. In the current passage, Yeats imagines that the play might succeed if staged on the Aran Islands, off the west coast of Ireland but not if staged in a fashionable theater located in the Strand, London.
7. In "A Vision of the Last Judgment," Blake writes, "The Nature of my Work is Visionary or Imaginative it is an Endeavour to Restore what the Ancients calld the Golden Age" (Ellis-Yeats 2: 393; Erdman, 555).
8. For more on Yeats's view of Morris, see "The Happiest of the Poets" above. *Locrine,* by the English poet Algernon Charles Swinburne (1837–1909), was first produced by the Elizabethan Stage Society at St. George's Hall, London, on 20 March 1899. Locrine, or Logrin, was a son of King Brut, who inherited a third of his father's kingdom, married Gwendolen, but then abandoned her for Estrildis.
9. Yeats rendered the scene about Oedipus and Colonus in *Sophocles' Oedipus at Colonus* (*Pl,* 419–20) and included part of it as "Colonus' Praise" in *The Tower,* whose first stanza reads "Come

praise Colonus' horses, and come praise / The wine-dark of the wood's intricacies, / The nightingale that deafens daylight there, / If daylight ever visit where, / Unvisited by tempest or by sun / Immortal ladies tread the ground / Dizzy with harmonious sound, / Semele's lad a gay companion" (*P*, 222).

The phrases about Macbeth, King Duncan (an error for Banquo), and the pendent bed and martlet come from the beginning of act 1, scene 6 of Shakespeare's *Macbeth* (Shakespeare, 2573). For "the pendent" read "his pendent."

10. Like Dante Gabriel Rossetti (see note 3 above), Ford Madox Brown (1821–93) was an English Pre-Raphaelite painter, though unlike Rossetti he never became a formal member of the brotherhood.
11. The English aesthete, artist, and fine printer Charles Ricketts (1866–1931) later did design scenery for some of Yeats's plays.
12. J[ohn] F[rancis] Taylor (1850–1902) was a nationalist orator who gave the once famous speech comparing the modern Irish to the ancient "Children of Israel" that Joyce renders in chapter 7 of *Ulysses* and Yeats in *Reveries over Childhood and Youth (Au,* 101). Yeats says in *Memoirs* that "He knew nothing of poetry or of painting, though he seemed to know by heart whole plays of Shakespeare and all the more famous passages in Milton, and was deeply read in eighteenth-century literature. He understood alone eloquence, and impassioned pleading. He sometimes gave me an impression of insanity" (53).
13. According to Ellis-Yeats 1: 337, Yeats got this phrase of Dionysius the Aeropagite (the name of a disciple of Saint Paul mentioned in Acts in the Bible, but more pertinently also the name of a fifth-century Neoplatonic writer whose most important work, *The Divine Names,* first appeared in 532) from his friend Charles Johnston (1867–1931), a member of the Theosophical Society who introduced Yeats to Madame Blavatsky. The phrase was a favorite of Yeats, who also used it in "The Ainu," "Irish National Literature, II," and "The Literary Movement in Ireland" (*EAR,* 223, 271, and 461).
14. Yeats's anecdote about the Greek tragedian Euripides (ca. 485–406 B.C.) may derive from the Roman writer Lucius Annaeus Seneca (ca. 4 B.C.–A.D. 65) in the *Letter to Lucilius;* see *IDM,* 276n4.
15. The Blake quotation comes from the last two lines of plate 28 and first three lines of plate 29 of *Milton* (Ellis-Yeats 3; Erdman, 127). For "equal to" Erdman reads "equal in its period & value to," and for the closing "within a pulsation" Erdman reads "within a Moment: a Pulsation."

## The Celtic Element in Literature

This essay first appeared in *Cosmopolis: An International Review* for June 1898. Printed in London by T. Fisher Unwin, this magazine published work in English, French, and German, seeking to counteract narrow aspects of nationalism by appealing to European interests more broadly. Yeats derived much of the essay from his lecture "The Celtic Movement," delivered to the Irish Literary Society on 4 December 1897. He first told Lady Gregory in a letter dated 11–12 January 1898, that *Cosmopolis* had accepted the essay though he did not finish writing it until 9 February (*CL2*, 169, 185). The date "1897" was added for *Ideas of Good and Evil* in 1903. Included in the *Cosmopolis* version was a paragraph at the end of part 1 omitted from subsequent versions, which is reproduced at the appropriate place in the notes below. Other interesting passages only in the *Cosmopolis* version include a parenthetical description of the Donogha O'Daly quotation as "the bitterest curse in literature" and a reference to how Edmund Spenser, "living in Celtic Ireland where the faeries were part of men's daily lives, set the faery kingdom over all the kingdoms of romance" (*Cosmopolis:* 681, 684–85). The short final paragraph regarding Lady Gregory's *Cuchulain of Muirthemne* and dated "1902" was added for *IGE* in 1903. Yeats's two footnotes dated "1924" were added in *Essays* that year.

1. The French philologist Ernest Renan (1823–92) was among the most important intellectuals of his day, though his work faced increasing criticism after his death. His training as both a priest and scholar informed his many political and philosophical writings. This essay is in part Yeats's response to Renan's "The Poetry of the Celtic Races" ("La poésie des races celtiques"), published in *Essais de morale et de critique* (1859).
2. Yeats may be quoting Renan from memory, as his wording differs substantially from the standard translation in his library, O'Shea #1735: *The Poetry of the Celtic Races, and Other Studies*, trans. William G. Hutchison (London: Walter Scott, [1896]). Hutchison's translation reads: "No race conversed so intimately as did the Celtic race with the lower creation, and accorded it so large a share of moral life" (21); "a realistic naturalism, the love of nature for herself, the vivid impression of her magic, accompanied by the sorrowful feeling that man knows, when, face to face with her, he believes that he hears her commune with him concerning his origin and his destiny" (22); "it has worn itself out in taking dreams for realities" and "compared with the classical imagination, the Celtic imagination is indeed the infinite contrasted with the finite" (9); "Its history is itself only one long lament; it still recalls its exiles, its flights across the seas. If at times it seems to be cheerful, a tear is not slow to glisten behind its smile"; "Its songs of joy end as elegies; there is nothing to equal the delicious sadness of its national melodies" (7).
3. The Victorian poet and essayist Matthew Arnold (1822–88) published his long essay *On the Study of Celtic Literature* in 1867. Although he acknowledged Renan's influence on his assessment of the Celts, his own

approach was less sympathetic and more scientific than his French predecessor's.

4. Yeats had in his library the "popular edition" of Arnold's *The Study of Celtic Literature* (London: Smith, Elder, and Co., 1891; O'Shea #55, hereafter cited as "Arnold, *Study*"), though he may be quoting here from memory. A passage in section 6 of Arnold's essay refers to "the magical charm of nature" and the Celtic belief in "the magic of nature; not merely the beauty of nature" (132–33). In section 4, Arnold describes the Celts as "always ready to react against the despotism of fact," but the adjectives "passionate, turbulent, [and] indomitable" are added by Yeats (85). Yeats alludes again to Arnold's notion of the "revolt against the despotism of fact" in his review of "Mr. Lionel Johnson's Poems," also published in 1898 (*EAR*, 389).
5. Yeats quotes Arnold (*Study*, 129), which reads "the perfectly definite motive" for "a perfectly definite motive."

   Faust and Werther are the protagonists of the two most famous works by the great German Romantic Johann Wolfgang von Goethe (1749–1832): *Faust* (part 1, 1808; part 2, 1832) and *The Sorrows of Young Werther* (1774). Arnold mentions both characters, singling out Werther as the archetypal "melancholy young man" (Arnold, *Study*, 129). Many of the unspecified "passages" that Yeats refers to in the next sentence are presumably among those cited later in the essay and are glossed there.
6. This last sentence was added for *IGE* (1903). In the *Cosmopolis* version, part 1 concluded instead with the following paragraph:

   > "I am going to make a claim for the Celt, but I am not going to make quite the same claim that Ernest Renan and Matthew Arnold made. Matthew Arnold, and still more Ernest Renan, wrote before the activity in the study of folk-lore and of folk literature of our own day had begun to give us so many new ideas about old things. When we talk to-day about the delight in nature, about the imaginativeness, about the melancholy of the makers of the Icelandic Eddas, and of the Kalavala, and of many other folk literatures, and we soon grow persuaded that much that Matthew Arnold and Ernest Renan thought wholly or almost wholly Celtic is of the substance of the minds of the ancient farmers and herdsmen. One comes to think of the Celt as an ancient farmer or herdsman, who sits bowed with the dreams of his unnumbered years, in the gates of the rich races, talking of forgotten things. Is the Celt's feeling for nature, and for the 'lower creation,' one of those forgotten things? Because we have come to associate the ancient beliefs about nature with 'savage customs' and with books written by men of science, we have

> almost forgotten that they are still worth dreaming about and talking about. It is only when we describe them in some language, which is not the language of science, that we discover they are beautiful" (676).

The Icelandic Eddas are collections of Old Norse legends, consisting of *The Prose Edda* by Snorri Sturluson (1178–1241) and *The Poetic Edda,* compiled anonymously in about 1270. The *Kalevala (Land of Heroes),* or Finnish national epic, is a grouping of songs, lyrics, and charms arranged in the mid-nineteenth century by the Finnish philologist Elias Lönnrot (1802–84). John Martin Crawford published the first complete English translation, *The Kalevala: The Epic Poem of Finland,* 2 vols. (New York: John A. Berry, 1888).

7. Yeats's wording does not appear to match any pre-1898 translation of the *Kalevala,* though he clearly has in mind a passage from the "Proem": "Many birds from many forests, / Oft have sung me lays in concord; / Waves of sea, and ocean billows, / Music from the many waters, / Music from the whole creation, / Oft have been my guide and master" (Crawford, 1:3).
8. This story is told in Rune 4 of the *Kalevala.* The name of the daughter who drowns is Aino.
9. The squirrel that runs up and down the sacred ash tree is described in section 16 of "The Beguiling of Gylfi" in *The Prose Edda* by Snorri Sturluson, glossed above.
10. The *Mabinogion,* a collection of medieval Welsh tales put into modern English by Lady Charlotte Guest from 1838–49, was a book Yeats held in equal regard with *Le Morte D'Arthur* and *Nibelungenlied* (*P&I,* 225).
11. Gwydion and Math are magicians in the *Mabinogion;* in the episode Yeats recounts, they create a wife for Gwydion's pupil and name her "Flower Aspect." Yeats's quotation follows Arnold's adaptation, with one correction: Arnold reads "gave her the name of Flower-Aspect" for "called her Flower Aspect" (Arnold, *Study,* 133–34). Yeats also quotes the passage about the burning tree from Arnold (Arnold, *Study,* 135).
12. The Keats quotations are from the poems "Ode to a Nightingale" and "Bright star, would I were stedfast as thou art," respectively. Arnold cites the first as an example of Celtic power in English poetry (Arnold, *Study,* 139). In his edition of *The Poems of John Keats* (Cambridge, MA: Harvard University Press, 1978), Jack Stillinger reads "shores" for "shore" (327) (cited hereafter as "Stillinger"). The Shakespeare quotations are from *The Merchant of Venice,* act 5, scene 1. Arnold has "patines" for "patens," and "upon the wild sea-banks" for "on the wild sea banks" (Arnold, *Study,* 140–41).
13. Yeats quotes from Arnold, *Study,* 134. Olwen is a beautiful maiden in

the *Mabinogion* whom the heroic Kilhwch marries after performing a series of nearly impossible tasks with the help of King Arthur and his knights.

14. Shakespeare, *A Midsummer Night's Dream,* act 2, scene 1; quoted in Arnold, *Study,* 141, which reads "Met" for "Meet," and "in the beached" for "on the beached."
15. Yeats quotes Arnold, *Study,* 137.
16. Yeats quotes all of these passages from Arnold. The Keats lines are from "Ode on a Grecian Urn" (Arnold, *Study,* 138). Stillinger reads "peaceful citadel" where Arnold and Yeats both read "quiet citadel" (Stillinger, 373). The Shakespeare lines are from *A Midsummer Night's Dream,* act 2, scene 1 (Arnold, *Study,* 140). The Virgil quotations come from *Eclogues* 7 (line 45) and 2 (lines 47–48). Arnold translates the first as "moss-grown springs and grass softer than sleep" (Arnold, *Study,* 140). The second may be translated, "plucking pale violets and poppy-heads, blends narcissus and sweet-scented fennel-flower." See the Loeb Classical Library edition of Virgil's *Eclogues, Georgics, Aeneid I–VI,* with an English translation by H. Rushton Fairclough (Cambridge, MA: Harvard University Press, 1994), 13.
17. Yeats alludes to one of the "Proverbs of Hell" from plate 7 of Blake's *The Marriage of Heaven and Hell:* "Bring out number weight & measure in a year of dearth" (Ellis-Yeats 3; Erdman, 36).
18. Yeats may have derived the notion that "ancient chaos" was "every man's desire" from Madame Helena Petrovna Blavatsky (1831–91), the Russian spiritualist whose theosophical teachings he once followed. In his note 12 to Lady Gregory's *Visions and Beliefs in the West of Ireland* (New York: G. P. Putnam's Sons, 1920; O'Shea #811), Yeats quotes Madame Blavatsky explaining predestination to one of her followers: "a day will come when even the Akasa will pass away and there will be nothing but God, chaos, that which every man is seeking in his heart." Yeats says Mme. Blavatsky described the Akasa "as some Indian word for the astral light" (*LE,* 271).
19. Wäinämöinen is one of the heroes of the *Kalevala,* but the mystic maiden Luonnotar is his nurse, not his mother. Ilmatar, daughter of the Ether, is the one who carries Wäinämöinen in her womb all those centuries.

    *The Song of Roland* is the great medieval French epic recounting the emperor Charlemagne's defeat in 778 at the hands of the Basques; Yeats paraphrases stanza 41, lines 539–43. Most translations describe Charlemagne as *two* hundred years old, though Lady Gregory (perhaps following Yeats) also describes Charlemagne as three hundred years old in a note to her *The Kiltartan History Book* (Dublin: Maunsel and Company, 1909; O'Shea #800), 49. The "Mahomedan king" Yeats mentions is Marsilion.
20. In his poem "The Death of Cuchulain" (later "Cuchulain's Fight with

the Sea," *P*, 29–31), Yeats had retold the story of how the Irish hero, gone mad after killing his son, met his own death fighting the ocean's waves. Yeats would tell the story again in *On Baile's Strand* (*Pl*, 151–74).

21. Yeats refers to the Irish folk song "My Hope, My Love," which he may have read in Edward Walsh's *Irish Popular Songs; with English Metrical Translations, and Introductory Remarks and Notes* (Dublin: James McGlashan, 1847), 20–21: "My hope, my love, we will proceed / Into the woods, scattering the dews, / Where we will behold the salmon, and the ousel in its nest, / The deer and the roe-buck calling, / The sweetest bird on the branches warbling, / The cuckoo on the summit of the green hill; / And death shall never approach us / In the bosom of the fragrant wood!"

22. In Yeats's dramatic poem *The Wanderings of Oisin* (*P*, 361–91), the Irish hero Oisin describes to Saint Patrick his three hundred years in Tir na nÓg with his fairy bride Niamh. George Sigerson's translation of "The Blackbird of Daricarn" tells the story of Saint Patrick and the blackbird. See George Sigerson, *Bards of the Gael and Gall: Examples of the Poetic Literature of Erinn* (London: T. Fisher Unwin, 1897; O'Shea #1921), 130–32.

23. The Irish scholar and patriot Douglas Hyde (1860–1949) published his influential volume of translations from the Irish, *Love Songs of Connacht*, in 1893. Yeats quotes from Hyde's prose translation of "My Love, Oh, She Is My Love," which accompanies his verse translation in a footnote. See Douglas Hyde, *Love Songs of Connacht* (London: T. Fisher Unwin; Dublin: M.H. Gill & Son, 1893; reprinted by Irish Academic Press, 1987), 134–36. Hyde reads "from making me ill" for "for making me ill"; "eye" for "eyes"; "place a hand beneath" for "lay a hand under"; "She is my affection, Oh! she is my affection" for "She is my love, O she is my love"; and "The woman who would not pay" for "a woman who would not pay."

24. The song is "Roisin Dubh," usually translated "Dark Rosaleen" or "Little Black Rose." Yeats quotes, with variants, the translation by Samuel Ferguson that appeared in Ferguson's article "Hardiman's Irish Minstrelsy—No. II" in the August 1834 issue of *The Dublin University Magazine*. That version reads: "The Erne shall be in its strong flood—the hills shall be uptorn; / And the sea shall have its waves red, and blood shall be spilled; / Every mountain-valley, and every moor throughout Ireland shall be on high, / Some day before (you) shall perish, my Roiseen dubh"(158).

25. The folk song is "The Dirge of O'Sullivan Bear," which Yeats knew from the English translation by Jeremiah Joseph Callanan (1795–1829) (see *EAR*, 265). It can be found in *The Poems of J. J. Callanan: A New Edition, with Biographical Introduction and Notes* (Cork: Daniel Mulcahy, 1861), 103–6.

26. Yeats paraphrases the poem "The Worms, the Children, and the Devil," which Douglas Hyde translated in *The Religious Songs of Connacht* (Dublin: M. H. Gill and Son / London: T. Fisher Unwin, 1906; reprinted by the Irish University Press and published by Barnes & Noble, 1972), 51–53. The "Elizabethan Irish poet" may be the medieval religious poet Donogha O'Daly (also spelled Donnchadh Mór Ó Dálaigh, d. 1244), whom Hyde suggests as a possible author.
27. "AE" was the pseudonym of the Irish poet and mystic George Russell (1867–1935), a close friend of Yeats. Yeats quotes Russell's poem "Illusion" from the volume *The Earth Breath* (New York and London: John Lane, 1897; O'Shea #1803), 49, which reads "grows unto" for "grows into." In a letter dated 22 January 1898, Yeats told Russell, "I now think the 'Earth Breath' quite your best work. . . . you will yet out-sing us all & sing in the ears of many generations to come" (*CL2*, 175–76).
28. The Scottish man of letters William Sharp (1855–1905) is best remembered for his mystic tales in the Celtic Twilight mode, written under the female pseudonym "Fiona MacLeod." Sharp invented the pseudonym in 1894 and kept it secret until his death.
29. In his 1895 article "Irish National Literature, III," Yeats also quoted "an old Gaelic writer" who described the Celt as "'celebrated for anger and for amouresness [*sic*],'" but the writer's identity remains untraced (*EAR*, 281).
30. In his preface to Lady Gregory's *Cuchulain of Muirthemne* (1902), Yeats attributed this description of the "lyrical" old Irish temperament to William Morris: "He [Morris] spoke of the Irish account of the battle of Clontarf and of the Norse account, and said, that one saw the Norse and Irish tempers in the two accounts. . . . He said that the Norseman had the dramatic temper, and the Irishman had the lyrical" (*P&I*, 120).
31. Cassandra and Helen are well-known figures from Greek mythology. The former was a daughter of King Priam, gifted with the power of prophecy but doomed never to be heeded; the latter was the notorious beauty whose abduction by Paris started the Trojan War. Helen recurs throughout Yeats's poetry as the archetypal object of male desire. Deirdre is a Helen-like figure from Irish mythology who betrayed King Conchubar by running off with Naoise; Yeats dramatized the story in his 1907 play *Deirdre* (*Pl*, 175–200). Lear is the tragic hero of Shakespeare's play who divides his kingdom among his daughters with disastrous consequences. Tristan is the legendary lover of the Irish princess Iseult; the many stories of their love end in sorrow.
32. Yeats repeats phrases from Renan quoted in the first paragraph of this essay and glossed there.
33. Yeats may not be quoting a specific version of Oisin's lamentation but rather paraphrasing any of several renderings available to him. He

would have been immediately familiar with Sigerson's "After the Fianna" from *Bards of the Gael and Gall* cited earlier: "Long, this night, the clouds delay, / And long to me was yesternight, / Long was the dreary day, this day, / Long, yesterday, the light. // Each day that comes to me is long — / . . . No man like me in all the world, / Alone with grief, and gray. // Long this night the clouds delay — / I raise their grave-carn, stone on stone, / For Fionn and Fianna passed away — / I, Ossian, left alone" (129–30). The passage is not present in Yeats's primary source for *The Wanderings of Oisin:* Michael Comyn's *Lay of Oisin on the Land of Youth,* text and trans. Bryan O'Looney, *Transactions of the Ossianic Society for the Year 1856* 4 (Dublin: 1859), 235–79.

34. Llywarch Hen (fl. sixth century) is the main figure in a series of poems composed in ninth-century Wales and preserved in the *Red Book of Hergest,* a fifteenth-century manuscript that was one of the sources for the *Mabinogion.* Yeats follows Arnold's translation of the "Chant de Llywarc'h-Henn sur sa vieillesse" in La Villemarqué's 1860 *Les Bardes bretons* (Arnold, *Study,* 130). Arnold reads "red, the water-flag" for "red and the water flag"; "head to my teeth" for "head and my teeth"; and "night when he was brought" for "night he was brought."

35. The Elizabethan writer was the historian and classicist Richard Stanihurst (1547–1618), who compiled the "Description of Ireland" for *Holinshed's Chronicles of England, Scotland, and Ireland* (1587). The quotation comes from chapter 8, "The Disposition and Maners of the Meere Irish, Commonlie Called the Wild Irish": "They follow the dead corpse to the graue with howling and barbarous outcries, pitifull in apparance: whereof grew, as I suppose, the prouerbe: To wéepe Irish" (London: Printed for J. Johnson et. al., 1807–8), 6:67.

36. Hyde writes this in the first paragraph of his *Love Songs of Connacht,* page 3, which reads "his poor lonely" for "his own lonely."

37. Arnold does not ask how much of the Celt one must imagine in the ideal man of genius but rather asserts that "if one sets about constituting an ideal genius, what a great deal of the Celt does one find oneself drawn to put into it!" (Arnold, *Study,* 89).

38. Yeats was fond of this phrase by the landscape painter and Blake disciple Samuel Palmer (1805–81), whom he discusses frequently, including in the essay "William Blake and His Illustrations to *The Divine Comedy*" above (see note 7 there). For the phrase itself, see A. H. Palmer, *The Life and Letters of Samuel Palmer* (London: Seeley & Co., 1892): "Excess is the essential vivifying spirit, vital spark, embalming spice . . . of the finest art," and "We must not begin with medium, but think always on excess, and only use medium to make excess more abundantly excessive" (16).

39. Yeats paraphrases Arnold, *Study,* 113: "If I were asked where English poetry got these three things, its turn for style, its turn for melancholy, and its turn for natural magic, for catching and rendering the

charm of nature in a wonderfully near and vivid way,—I should answer, with some doubt, that it got much of its turn for style from a Celtic source; with less doubt, that it got much of its melancholy from a Celtic source; with no doubt at all, that from a Celtic source it got nearly all its natural magic."

40. Yeats follows Hutchison's translation but omits Renan's reference to the researchers whose work laid the foundation for his claims. Hutchison reads: "It cannot be doubted for a moment, after the able researches of Messrs. Ozanam, Labitte, and Wright, that to the number of poetical themes which Europe owes to the genius of the Celts, is to be added the framework of the Divine Comedy" (57).

Lough Derg is a small, desolate lake on the border of County Donegal and County Fermanagh. Its association as the place where Saint Patrick fasted and saw a vision of the next world has made it an important pilgrimage site to this day.

41. King Arthur is the central figure in a vast body of medieval literature concerning the exploits of his Knights of the Round Table; several of these stories involve a quest to recover the Holy Grail. Mercutio describes Mab as the "fairies' midwife," who brings strange dreams to unsuspecting victims in Shakespeare's *Romeo and Juliet,* act 1, scene 4. Her name may be derived from the Irish Queen Maeve, ruler of the *sidhe,* who figures prominently in several of Yeats's poems. Puck is the mischievous sprite of *A Midsummer Night's Dream.*

The Scottish novelist and poet Sir Walter Scott (1771–1832) was among the most popular of the early-nineteenth-century Romantics. His major works include the historical novels *Waverley* (1814), *Rob Roy* (1817), and *Ivanhoe* (1819).

42. The work of the German composer and dramatist Richard Wagner (1813–83) was both influential and extremely controversial in the late nineteenth century. His opera *Tristan and Isolde* deals with Celtic subject matter but was drawn from German sources. Many works of the Norwegian dramatist Henrik Ibsen (1828–1906), including *A Doll's House* (1879), depict tragedy in the lives of ordinary people.

43. Yeats here enumerates some of the most famous stories from Irish legend. Deirdre and Oisin are mentioned previously in this essay; see in particular notes 31 and 22 above. The "tale of the Sons of Tuireann" and "tale of the four children changed into four swans" (sometimes called "The Tragic Story of the Children of Lir") are often grouped with the story of Deirdre as the "Three Sorrowful Stories of Erin." In the former, Tuireann's three sons, Brian, Iuchair, and Iucharba, are forced to retrieve a series of magical treasures but die performing a further dangerous feat upon the hill of Miodhchaoin. In the latter story, Lir's four children are transformed into beautiful singing swans for a period of nine hundred years by their jealous and barren stepmother, Aífe.

Fand is the immortal goddess the hero Cuchulain loved, and Emer the mortal woman he returned to. The story of their love triangle is commonly called "The Only Jealousy of Emer," though Yeats's play of that name is a very loose treatment (*Pl,* 317–28). Cuchulain's reluctant three-day battle with his friend Ferdiad at the ford in the River Dee (in modern County Louth) is described in the great Irish epic the *Táin Bó Cuailnge.* Accounts of Cuchulain's death vary widely; for two of Yeats's own, see his poem "Cuchulain's Fight with the Sea" (*P,* 29–31) and his late play *The Death of Cuchulain* (*Pl,* 545–54).

The famous "tale of the flight of Grania with Diarmuid" is the only story Yeats mentions here from the Fenian Cycle. It roughly parallels the story of Deirdre from the Ulster Cycle. Grania is betrothed to Finn mac Cumhal, but her passion for Finn's follower Diarmuid leads to both their deaths. Yeats and George Moore's 1901 collaborative play, *Diarmuid and Grania,* dramatizes the tale (*Pl,* 557–607).

44. Formally known as the Pre-Raphaelite Brotherhood or "P.R.B.," the Pre-Raphaelites were a group of artists who defied the authority of Renaissance master painter Raphael (1483–1520), seeking greater fidelity to nature and often employing religious or mystical iconography. Their movement was founded in 1848 under the leadership of John Everett Millais (1829–96), Dante Gabriel Rossetti (1828–82), and Holman Hunt (1827–1910); its impact on Yeats came partly via the involvement of William Morris.

The comte de Villiers de L'Isle-Adam (1838–89), Stéphane Mallarmé (1842–98), and Maurice Maeterlinck (1862–1949) were symbolists whom Yeats greatly admired and invoked elsewhere in *IGE,* especially in "The Symbolism of Poetry." Yeats was particularly fond of the line "As for living, our servants will do that for us" from Villiers de L'Isle-Adam's play *Axël* (1890), which he used as an epigraph to *The Secret Rose* (1897).

Gabriele D'Annunzio (1863–1938) was an Italian novelist, playwright, and poet influenced by the Pre-Raphaelites and French symbolists, and associated with the latter by Yeats.

45. The Belgian poet Émile Verhaeren (1855–1916) was a major figure in the symbolist movement. However, Yeats is probably drawing the notion of a "sacred book" of the arts from Mallarmé's concept of the "Grand Oeuvre." See above, section 4 of "The Symbolism of Poetry" and accompanying note to the following sentence: "But being of our time, he [i.e., Gérard de Nerval] has been like Maeterlinck, like Villiers de L'Isle-Adam in *Axël,* like all who are preoccupied with intellectual symbols in our time, a foreshadower of the new sacred book, of which all the arts, as somebody has said, are begging to dream."

46. Yeats wrote a glowing preface to Lady Gregory's *Cuchulain of Muirthemne: The Story of the Men of the Red Branch of Ulster* (London: John Murray, 1902) that added the *Nibelungenlied* to this distinguished list of the book's companion volumes (*P&I,* 225).

## The Autumn of the Body

This essay first appeared in the Dublin *Daily Express* for 3 December 1898 under the title "The Autumn of the Flesh." It was part of an ongoing controversy among Yeats, "John Eglinton" (William Magee), George Russell, and William Larminie, whose opinions were collected in a shilling pamphlet, *Literary Ideals in Ireland,* published in May 1899. "I am going to try & widen the cotraversy [*sic*] if I can into a discussion of the spiritual origin of the arts," wrote Yeats to Lady Gregory on 6 November 1898 about the article. "In this way we will keep people awake until we announce 'The Irish Literary Theatre' in December" (*CL2*, 289). For the newspaper version, Yeats also drew upon two earlier reviews that he had done the year before for *The Bookman,* one of Maeterlinck's *Aglavaine and Sélysette* for the long first paragraph below and the other of Arthur Symons's *Amoris Victima* after that (*EAR,* 349–51 and 332–35, respectively). "Flesh" became "Body" in the title for *IGE* (1903), after which there were no major changes.

1. Yeats may be thinking here of the condemnation of "externality" at the end of Arthur Symons's introduction to his *The Symbolist Movement in Literature* (London: William Heinemann, 1899; O'Shea #2068) in which Symons talks about "this revolt against exteriority, against rhetoric, against a materialistic tradition" (10). For more on Yeats and that work, see "The Symbolism of Poetry" above, which begins with a quotation from it.
2. The French writer Gustave Flaubert (1821–80) produced three different versions of his closet drama, *The Temptation of Saint Anthony,* over a quarter of a century (in 1849, 1856, and 1874), of which he published only the last. In it the metaphysical temptations of the fourth-century saint appear before the reader in a series of visions. Yeats especially admired the play *Axël* (1890) by the French symbolist writer Villiers de L'Isle-Adam (1838–89), which he called a "Sacred Book" (*Au,* 246) and saw performed on 26 February 1894 in Paris with Maud Gonne (for Yeats's review of that performance, see "A Symbolical Drama in Paris," *EAR,* 234). In that play Prince Axël proposes to the desirable Sara that they commit double suicide to show their contempt for everyday existence.
3. The Belgian symbolist Maurice Maeterlinck (1862–1949) recurs throughout Yeats's essays of this period. Yeats presumably has in mind especially Maeterlinck's *Aglavaine and Sélysette,* the subject of his review in *The Bookman,* which he draws on for this part of the present essay. He writes there that "M. Maeterlinck has called himself a disciple of Villiers de L'Isle-Adam" (*EAR,* 350).
4. Yeats refers repeatedly in *IGE* to the English poets Robert Browning (1812–89), Alfred Tennyson (1809–92), the slightly later Algernon

Charles Swinburne (1837–1909), and the slightly earlier Percy Bysshe Shelley (1792–1822), including in the essay on Shelley, above.

5. The Pre-Raphaelite poet and painter Dante Gabriel Rossetti is one of Yeats's recurrent touchstones in *IGE*. The man of letters and fellow of Merton College, Oxford, Andrew Lang (1844–1912) published several volumes of poetry, beginning with his first book of verse *Ballads and Lyrics of Old France* (1872) and also collaborated with S. H. Butcher on a translation of *The Odyssey* much used by Yeats. The translator and man of letters Sir Edmund William Gosse (1849–1928) is better known for his prose writings, especially *Father and Son* (1907) but did produce several volumes of lyrics. The poet, biographer, and historian (of the eighteenth century) Henry Austin Dobson (1840–1921) was a colleague and close friend of Gosse at the Board of Trade, where they both worked. Robert Bridges (1844–1930), a poet and close friend of Gerard Manley Hopkins, produced numerous volumes of verse beginning with *Poems* (1873). Yeats's essay on his play *The Return of Ulysses* (1890) appears below in *IGE*.
6. In addition to his novels, the Victorian chronicler of the British empire Rudyard Kipling (1865–1936) produced several volumes of verse, including *Departmental Ditties* (1886) and *Barrack-Room Ballads* (1892).
7. The term "the decadence" was frequently applied to the French Symbolists and the English aesthetic school that followed them. Arthur Symons wrote the essay "The Decadent Movement in Literature" (*Harper's New Monthly Magazine,* November 1893; reprinted in collections like *Aesthetes and Decadents of the 1890's,* ed. Karl Beckson, rev. ed. [New York: Academy Chicago, 1981], 134–51), and he originally planned to use the title *The Decadent Movement in Literature* for the book known eventually as *The Symbolist Movement in Literature.* For more on Yeats and Symons, see note 1 of the present essay and also "The Symbolism of Poetry" above in the present collection.
8. The Irish poet is Yeats's friend the poet, mystic, and social reformer George Russell (1867–1935) also known as AE. Stanza 3 of his poem "The Gates of Dreamland" (1898; later revised and retitled "Carrowmore") reads "'Come away,' the red lips whisper, 'all the earth is weary now. / 'Tis the twilight of the ages and it's time to quit the plough. / Oh, the very sunlight's weary ere it lightens up the dew, / And its gold is changed and faded ere its falling down to you.'" The only print version that Yeats could have seen before writing the essay is that contained in *The Internationalist* 1 no. 6: (1897–98) 104. For a later version, see AE, *Collected Poems* (London: Macmillan, 1926), 106–7.
9. The *Kalevala* (Land of Heroes) is the national epic of Finland, a group of ancient poems that were transmitted orally until a collection was published in 1822 by Zacharias Topelius; the poem was translated into English by John Martin Crawford in 1888. Yeats here considers the

*Kalevala* to be older and to show less preoccupation with the material world than the work of the ancient Greek poet Homer and classical Latin poet Virgil (70–19 B.C.).

10. For more on Yeats's views on Dante and on Shakespeare, see among other works in the present volume the essays "At Stratford-on-Avon" and "William Blake and His Illustrations to *The Divine Comedy.*"
11. Although Yeats mentions the earlier poets Johann Wolfgang von Goethe (1749–1832), William Wordsworth (1770–1850), and Robert Browning (1812–89), the phrasing "a critic of life and an interpreter of things as they are" derives from Matthew Arnold (1822–88). Arnold famously says that the "end and aim of all literature" should be a "criticism of life" in his essay "Joubert," *The Complete Prose Works of Matthew Arnold,* ed R. H. Super (Ann Arbor: University of Michigan Press, 1980); 3:209. Arnold uses the phrase "things as they are" repeatedly in his writing, including twice in his essay "The Function of Criticism at the Present Time" with its claim "The mass of mankind will never have any ardent zeal for seeing things as they are; very inadequate ideas will always satisfy them" (*Complete Prose Works,* 3:274).
12. Yeats is apparently not quoting any specific text here but rather encapsulating the late Victorian rationalism and materialism that he has been critiquing.
13. Symons wrote this in his essay "Stéphane Mallarmé" in *The Fortnightly Review,* ns 64 (November 1898): 677–85, which became a chapter in *The Symbolist Movement in Literature.* The quotations come from pages 134–35 of that book; for "abolish" read "abolished," for "subtle pages" read "subtle paper," for "thunder in" read "thunder afloat in," for "intense" read "intrinsic," and for "word hitherto unknown" read "word, new, unknown."
14. In the same essay Symons wrote "we have realised, since it was proved to us by Poe, not merely that the age of epics is past, but that no long poem was ever written; the finest long poem in the world being but a series of short poems linked together by prose" (*The Symbolist Movement in Literature,* 137).
15. The story of an older man wandering among enchanted islands before returning home fits the plots of Homer's *The Odyssey,* and Bridges's *The Return of Ulysses,* and even Yeats's own *The Wanderings of Oisin.* The actual quotations are from Symons's chapter on Mallarmé and are identified in note 13 above.

## The Moods

As with the immediately following essay, "The Body of the Father Christian Rosencrux," Yeats selected "The Moods" from a four-part series of articles on Irish national literature that appeared monthly in *The Bookman* (London) from July through October 1895. "The Moods" was originally the opening paragraph of a longer article titled "Irish National Literature: Contemporary Prose Writers" that appeared in the August 1895 issue and reviewed work by Standish O'Grady, Emily Lawless, Jane Barlow, and Nora Hopper at some length and a number of folklore collectors more briefly. For the full text of the entire article, see *EAR*, 270–76; "The Moods" underwent no significant changes after publication.

1. In a letter to Thomas Butts, 22 November 1802, William Blake includes verses with lines mentioning "little devils who fight for themselves / Remembring the Verses that Hayley sung" (Ellis-Yeats 3: 66; Erdman, 720).

## The Body of the Father Christian Rosencrux

Like the immediately preceding essay in *IGE*, "The Moods," "The Body of the Father Christian Rosencrux" originated as the opening paragraph of one of Yeats's four articles on Irish national literature published in *The Bookman* in four successive months from July through October 1895. The present article introduced the third article, "Irish National Literature. III—Contemporary Irish Poets," which included commentary on Douglas Hyde, T. W. Rolleston, Katharine Tynan Hinkson, Nora Hopper, AE (George Russell), John Todhunter, and Lionel Johnson. For the full text, see *EAR*, 280–87; the article underwent no major changes except for the deletion of the Keats allusion mentioned below in note 2.

1. "The followers of the Father Christian Rosencrux," known as the Rosicrucians, claim to have esoteric wisdom handed down from ancient times. Rosicrucianism has obscure origins but seems to derive from the *Fama Fraternitatis, or a Discovery of the Fraternity of the Most Noble Order of the Rosy Cross* (1614) of Johan Valentin Andreae (1586–1654), with its account of the legendary late medieval founder of the order, Father Christian Rosenkreuz. He was purported to be born in 1378 and lived for 106 years; his tomb was allegedly rediscovered in 1604. Yeats's friend and sometime mentor in magic MacGregor Mathers drew on the *Fama* for the Golden Dawn initiation ritual, which deeply impressed Yeats, who adapted Rosicrucian lore for numerous poems such as "A Song of the Rosy-Cross" (*P*, 544), "To a Sister of the Cross and the Rose" (W. B. Yeats, *Under the Moon: The Unpublished Early Poetry*, ed. George Bornstein [New York: Scribner, 1995], 94), and especially the section of his collected poems known as *The Rose* (1893).
2. Arthur is the legendary sixth-century king of the Britons. Perhaps the two most famous members of his court were his Queen Guinevere and her lover, the great knight Lancelot. The evil Count Guido and the good Pompilia are the major opposing characters in Robert Browning's

long poem *The Ring and the Book* (1868), which consists largely of a series of interlinked dramatic monologues. Yeats particularly admired the monologue of the pope there, of which he wrote: "I like to think of the great reveries of the Pope in *The Ring and the Book,* with all its serenity and quietism, as something that came straight from Browning's own mind, and gave his own final judgment on many things" (*LNI,* 27). In *The Bookman* version, the next sentence began "It seems to a perhaps fanciful watcher of the skies like myself that this age of criticism . . ." a presumed allusion to John Keats's sonnet "On First Looking into Chapman's Homer": "Then felt I like some watcher of the skies" (*The Poems of John Keats,* ed. Jack Stillinger [Cambridge, MA: Harvard University Press, 1978], 64).

3. The first two phrases come from William Blake: "phantoms of the earth and water" comes from Blake's "Annotations to Lavater" (Erdman, 596), which reads "man is either the ark of God or a phantom of the earth & of the water"; "uncurbed in their eternal glory" comes from Blake's "A Vision of the Last Judgment" (Ellis-Yeats 2: 26; Erdman, 564). "The wind bloweth where it listeth" comes from John 3:8 in the New Testament.

## The Return of Ulysses

This commentary on Robert Bridges's play *The Return of Ulysses* first appeared in *The Bookman* (London) for June 1897 under the title "Living Poets. IV.—Mr. Robert Bridges." Yeats and Bridges were in the early stages of becoming acquainted at the time. Yeats wrote to Bridges on 16 March 1897, "I am just renewing my recollection of your plays, as a prelude to an article, which the Bookman asked me to do some time ago, but which has got postponed through my dislike of reading in the British Museum" (*CL2,* 82). Bridges responded on 17 March, saying that "you wd please me very much if you wd in your review say two things (1) whether the plays are readable—amusing, i.e. whether you want to put them down after you have begun them—because this is the main point. And (2) I should be glad of a plain statement that my plays are for sale at 2/6 each because the papers always make out that they cannot be bought or are privately printed, or out of print, or all three" (*The Correspondence of Robert Bridges and W. B. Yeats,* ed. Richard J. Finneran [London and Toronto: Macmillan, 1977], 9). Yeats duly added the statement about availability at the end of his review for *The Bookman,* though he dropped it in revising for *IGE,* and he also made clear that Bridges's plays (especially *The Return of Ulysses*) were readable though also "that they might be perfect in the theatre." In its original form, the essay included discussion of other plays of Bridges and also of his shorter poems; Yeats deleted those for *IGE* (1903) to focus the essay more on *The Return of Ulysses.* An endnote below records a deleted postscript; two more extensive deleted passages are reproduced in appendix F of the present volume.

1. Yeats alludes several times in *IGE* to Maurice Maeterlinck (1862–1949), the Belgian dramatist and essayist important to the symbolist movement. The *Treasure of the Humble* is a volume of essays that Maeterlinck first published in French in 1896 and in English translation in 1897 (see note 2 below). Yeats reviewed it in *The Bookman* for July 1897, where he said that it "lacks the definiteness of the great mystics, but it has countless passages of this curious pathetic beauty, and shows us common arts and things, with the light of the great mystics, and a new light that was not theirs, beating upon them"; see *EAR*, 340–41, for the full text of that review.
2. The quotation comes from the essay called "The Tragical in Daily Life" from Maeterlinck's *The Treasure of the Humble,* trans. Alfred Sutro (London: George Allen and Unwin 1897), 101–2; "door open" should read "open door" instead. Gaius Marius (ca. 157–86 BC) rose to the office of consul, to which he was elected repeatedly. He and Quintus Lutatius Catulus defeated the Cimbri at Vercellae in northern Italy in 101. The first three of the seven dukes of Guise were assassinated. The first duke of Guise, Claude de Lorraine (1496–1550), was poisoned in 1550; the second, François de Lorraine (1519–63), died by a Huguenot assassin in 1563; and the third, Henri I de Lorraine (1550–88), was stabbed by the king's bodyguard in 1588. Maeterlinck refers to the third duke, whose assassination at Blois on 23 December 1588 served as the subject for such nineteenth-century painters as Pierre-Charles Comte (1823–95) and Paul Delaroche (1797–1856).
3. Robert Bridges (1844–1930) attended Eton and Corpus Christi College, Oxford, studied medicine at St. Bartholomew's Hospital, and practiced medicine until 1881. A friend of Gerard Manley Hopkins, whose collected poems he published in 1918, Bridges began his own poetic career with *Poems* (1873) and published numerous volumes of poetry and verse drama. He became poet laureate in 1913. For an overview of the relationship between Yeats and Bridges, see the introduction to *The Correspondence of Robert Bridges and W. B. Yeats.*
4. Bridges's "passionate poetry to be sung" included *Eden: An Oratorio* (1891), *Ode for the Bicentenary Commemoration of Henry Purcell* (1895), *Chants for the Psalter* (1897), and an edition of *Hymns: The Yattendon Hymnal* (1895). Bridges prefaced the Purcell ode with his essay "On the Musical Setting of Poetry," which may have affected Yeats's project described in "Speaking to the Psaltery" earlier in *IGE*. The passionate poetry "to be spoken" presumably includes Bridges's eight verse plays, including *The Return of Ulysses.*
5. Bridges's play *The Return of Ulysses,* the main subject of the present article, was published separately as *The Return of Ulysses: A Drama in Five Acts in a mixed manner* (London: Edward Bumpus, 1890) and then subsumed into *Eight Plays* (London: G. Bell and Sons, and Edward Bumpus, 1885–94), which binds together the eight separately

published plays in their original paper covers. *The Return* then appeared in the *Poetical Works of Robert Bridges,* 6 vols. (London: Smith, Elder and Co., 1898–1905), 4 (1902): 161–300. Bridges's own note to the play there calls it "a dramatizing of the chief scenes in Homer's *The Odyssey,* and not a recast of the story in dramatic form" (4:303). The closing books of *The Odyssey,* in which the hero Odysseus returns to his house in disguise, kills the suitors, and reunites with his wife, Penelope, occupy the last eight books of Homer's epic. Further quotations from *The Return of Ulysses* are cited from the *Eight Plays* gathering, which Yeats apparently used.

6. *The Return of Ulysses,* lines 2686–97 (*Eight Plays,* 98). For "now what can I see?" read "now what see I?"; for "That slay the suitors" read "That slay the wooers"; and for "his curlèd locks" read "his curling locks."
7. Yeats may be remembering here an earlier scene from act 1 when Athene takes off her helmet to speak to Ulysses in the guise of a delicate youth and conflating it with the present scene from act 5.
8. *Achilles in Scyros* is a play by Bridges (1890); on 24 March 1897 Yeats wrote Bridges that it was one of his three plays that "delight me most" (*CL2,* 84–85). The play is included in *Eight Plays* and the lines quoted (1594–1600) are spoken by the chorus (*Eight Plays,* 143).
9. *Nero: Second Part* (1894) is the third of the three plays by Bridges that Yeats said delighted him most (see previous note) and centers on the Roman emperor Nero (AD 37–68) and his tutor and adviser the philosopher Seneca (4 BC–AD 65), who was forced to commit suicide.
10. Yeats anticipates the sentiments of this final paragraph in a letter that he wrote to Bridges on 10 January 1897, shortly before starting work on this essay, in which he discussed his "dramatic poem" *The Shadowy Waters:* "I am trying for a more remote wisdom, or peace, for they are much the same, & find it hard not to lose grip on the necessary harvest of mere exterior beauty, in seeking for this visionary harvest" (*CL2,* 70).
11. The date 1896 first appeared in *IGE* in 1903 and is an error for 1897. *The Bookman* version of this essay concluded with the following two sentences: "P.S.—It is a common idea that Mr. Bridges' poems are published privately, and are not in the market. They can all be bought cheaply enough from Messrs. George Bell and Sons."

## Ireland and the *Arts*

After Yeats presented a version of "Ireland and the Arts" to the National Literary Society on 23 August 1901 as a lecture, the essay itself first appeared in the 31 August issue of Arthur Griffith's *The United Irishman,* perhaps the most important organ of the Irish nationalist movement. Griffith edited it from 1898 to 1906 and along with political articles published work by Yeats, Edward Martyn, Oliver St. John Gogarty, Padraic Colum, and others, though Griffith became increasingly critical of Synge and of the Irish national theater movement. The essay underwent no major revisions after publication in *The United Irishman* but numerous minor ones, of which the most important was the adding of the footnote about Robert Gregory for 1924.

1. The image of the charioteers may derive from Plato's famous myth in *Timaeus,* but may also come from the *Kena Upanishad* as translated by Yeats's friend Charles Johnston in *From the Upanishads* (Dublin: Whaley, 1896), 12–13, of which Yeats had a 1913 reprint in his library (O'Shea #716): "Know that the Self is the lord of the chariot, the body verily is the chariot; know that the soul is the charioteer, and emotion the reins. . . . [F]or the unwise, with emotion ever unrestrained, his bodily powers run away with him, like the unruly horses of the charioteer. . . . He whose charioteer is wisdom, who grasps the reins—emotion—firmly, he indeed gains the end of the path, the supreme resting-place of the emanating Power." G. R. S. Mead and J. C. Chattopadhyaya also did a translation in *The Upanishads* (London: Theosophical Publishing Society, 1896), 1:60–62.
2. For more extended presentation of Yeats's views on William Morris (1834–96), see the essay "The Happiest of the Poets" above in the current collection.
3. In classical Greek mythology, Persephone, daughter of Demeter, is raped and taken to the underworld by Pluto. Demeter attempts to rescue her, but Persephone cannot leave and as a compromise is allowed to spend six months of the year with Pluto and the other six with Demeter. After his death Shelley's body was burned on the beach of the Gulf of Spezia in Italy; paintings and drawings of the scene enjoyed a vogue especially in late Victorian England. Yeats alludes to the phenomenon again in his essay "Prometheus Unbound" (*LE,* 121): "When I was in my early twenties Shelley was much talked about, London had its important 'Shelley Society,' *The Cenci* had been performed and forbidden, provincial sketching clubs displayed pictures by young women of the burning of Shelley's body."
4. Yeats studied at the Metropolitan School of Art in Kildare Street, Dublin, from May 1884 until April 1886, the same month that he met William Morris.
5. The story of Queen Maeve carrying off the Brown Bull of Cuailnge is a raid told in the *Táin Bó Cuailnge* (*The Cattle Raid of Cooley*), the central saga of the Ulster Cycle of ancient Irish myths. Saint Patrick (d. ca. 493) came to Ireland to convert it to Christianity in the fifth century; his dates and many of his activities remain uncertain, though he was born in Britain and confronted the Druidic order at the court of the high king of Ireland.
6. The Young Ireland societies were founded in the 1880s but looked

back to the Young Irelanders of the 1840s, such as Thomas Davis. For more information, see "What is 'Popular Poetry'?" above, note 1; Yeats also mentioned the Young Ireland societies in "Poetry and Tradition" below. The poet and patriot Thomas Davis (1814–45) was a leader of the Young Ireland movement of the 1840s and published numerous articles and poems in *The Nation*, which he helped to found. Yeats's library includes an edition of Davis early enough for him to have read by the date of the present article, *Prose Writings*, ed. T. W. Rolleston (London: Walter Scott, 1890; O'Shea #498), though Yeats's mentor John O'Leary may have given him an edition at an earlier date. Yeats recalls O'Leary lending him books in *Au*, 104 ("From these debates, from O'Leary's conversation, and from the Irish books he lent or gave me, has come all I have set my hand to since") and specifically ones by Davis in *Au*, 100 ("he lent me the poems of Davis and the Young Irelanders").

7. Brian Bórumha (Brain Boru, 941–1014) became king of Munster in 987 and by military action against first the Vikings and then Irish rivals made himself king of Ireland, an event that shaped Irish history until the Norman invasion.
8. The American poet Walt Whitman (1819–92) did several revisions of his master collection *Leaves of Grass*. The lines quoted come from "A Song of the Rolling Earth" in the "Calamus" section of that work. Yeats's library contained John Butler Yeats's copy of *Poems by Walt Whitman*, ed. William Michael Rossetti (London: John Camden Hotten, 1868; O'Shea #2260), which prints the poem under its earlier title, "To the Sayers of Words"; for the lines that Yeats quotes, see page 330.
9. In *The United Irishman* version of this essay, Yeats misattributed the remark about beauty and strangeness to Ben Jonson. It is actually from "Of Beauty" by Francis Bacon (1561–1626), Lord Chancellor and author. Yeats may have encountered it in A. H. Palmer, *The Life and Letters of Samuel Palmer* (London: Seeley & Co., 1892), which reads: "There is no excellent beauty that hath not some strangeness in the proportion" (183).
10. The sentiment about "The end of art is peace" but not the exact phrasing derives from "Peace in Life and Art" by the English poet Coventry Patmore (1823–96) in his *Religio Poetae* (London: George Bell and Sons, 1893). Patmore revised the volume under the same title in 1898, when he also moved part of it to his *Principle in Art,* thus creating a tangled textual situation. "*Sero te amavi* . . ." is a phrase from Saint Augustine's *Confessions,* book 10. In the translation in Yeats's library, Arthur Symons translated it as "Too late loved I Thee, O Thou Beauty of ancient days, yet ever new! too late I loved Thee" (London: Walter Scott, 1898; O'Shea #68, 271). Yeats used the Latin again as the epigraph to "The Rose" section of his *Poems* (1895) and afterward, which is dedicated to Lionel Johnson.

11. Edwin John Ellis (1848–1916) was a longtime friend of John Butler Yeats who became WBY's coeditor of William Blake in the three-volume Ellis-Yeats edition of 1893 (see above, under the two essays on Blake). The celebration honoring the unnamed poet was almost certainly for Blake.
12. For Yeats's early view of the English Romantic poet Percy Bysshe Shelley (1792–1822), see the essay "The Philosophy of Shelley's Poetry" above in the current collection. For his later movement away from Shelley, see Bornstein, chapter 5, "The Aesthetics of Antinomy."
13. Lady Gregory's son, Robert (1881–1918), was her only child; he was killed in action on the Italian front on 23 January 1918. See Yeats's elegy "In Memory of Major Robert Gregory," especially stanza 9, which begins "We dreamed that a great painter had been born / To cold Clare rock and Galway rock and thorn" (*P*, 134). The Burren is an austere, fascinating countryside in County Clare.
14. Cuchulain is the best-known hero of the Red Branch Cycle of Irish legends; Yeats wrote five plays and several poems about him. The tragic story of the lovers Baile, heir to the throne of Ulster, and Aillinn, granddaughter of the king of Leinster (or in some sources Munstor), was included by Lady Gregory in her *Cuchulain of Muirthemne* (1902); Yeats published a long narrative poem about them in 1902 (*P*, 403–9).
15. Yeats met the Irish artist John Hughes (1864–1941) at the Metropolitan School of Art, where they both studied. Hughes's painting *Orpheus and Eurydice,* also known as *The Finding of Eurydice,* now hangs in the Hugh Lane Municipal Gallery of Modern Art, Dublin.
16. For the quotation, see John 3:8 in the Bible: "The wind bloweth where it listeth . . . so is every one that is born of the Spirit." In an 1895 note to *The Wanderings of Oisin,* Yeats called Aengus "the god of youth, beauty, and poetry" and Edain (Adene) "a famous legendary queen who went away and lived among the Shee" (*VP*, 794; *P*, 694). Some legends imagine their union; others describe Edain as turned by magic into a fly who took refuge with Aengus. Yeats refers to them several times in his work, including in "The Harp of Aengus" from *The Shadowy Waters* (*P*, 415). They also were invoked in the initiation rites for the occult Order of Celtic Mysteries.

## The Galway Plains

This article began as a review of Lady Gregory's *Poets and Dreamers* published in *The New Liberal Review* for March 1903 under the title "Poets and Dreamers." Yeats also reviewed the volume under the title "A Canonical Book" for *The Bookman* two months later, for May 1903 (*EAR*, 95–98). The delay in publication of *IGE* enabled Yeats to include "The Galway Plains" and the following essay along with "The Happiest of the Poets."

Yeats made numerous minor revisions to the review when incorporating it into *IGE;* after the present fifth paragraph he also dropped a ten-stanza quotation, whose first stanza is quoted below in note 8.

1. The article is a review of Lady Isabella Gregory, *Poets and Dreamers: Studies and Translations from the Irish* (Dublin: Hodges, Figgis, 1903; O'Shea #807), copublished that same year in an English edition by John Murray in London and in an American edition by Charles Scribner's Sons in New York; the London and the New York editions list Hodges, Figgis in Dublin as copublishers.

   Slieve Echtge is a range of mountains that runs from Loughrea in County Galway to near Lough Derg in County Clare; Echgthe or Echtge was a Dé Danaan lady who received Slieve Echtge as a marriage dowry. Yeats's story "The Death of Hanrahan" opens there: "Hanrahan, that was never long in one place, was back again among the villages that are at the foot of Slieve Echtge, Illeton and Scalp and Ballylee, stopping sometimes in one house and sometimes in another, and finding a welcome in every place for the sake of the old times and of his poetry and his learning" (*SR,* 117).
2. The Burren Hills are a chain of hills located in the rocky and desolate Burren landscape of northwest County Clare. Bald Conan (also known as Conan mac Morna and Conan Maol) is an often comic figure in the Fenian Cycle of Irish legends. Fat, greedy, and sometimes foolish, he has been compared to Shakespeare's character Falstaff.
3. Cruachmaa or Knockmaa is a hill about three miles from Tuam in County Galway. In his own note to his poem "The Hosting of the Sidhe," Yeats wrote: "The gods of ancient Ireland, the Tuatha de Danaan, or the Tribes of the goddess Danu, or the Sidhe . . . the people of the Faery Hills, as these words are usually explained, still ride the country as of old. Sidhe is also Gaelic for wind, and certainly the Sidhe have much to do with the wind" (*P,* 600).
4. Anthony Raftery (ca. 1784–1835) was a blind poet in County Mayo who wandered the countryside there and in County Galway near Gort and Kiltartan. *Poets and Dreamers* begins with a chapter about him, and Yeats invoked him often, as in the three stanzas beginning "Some few remembered still when I was young / A peasant girl commended by a song" from "The Tower" (*P,* 199–200).
5. The Battle of Aughrim in County Galway was the bloodiest battle fought in Ireland during the Jacobite Wars. The adherents of William defeated those of James there on 12 July 1691. Lady Gregory mentions it in her chapter on "Jacobite Ballads."
6. "Ochone" is an old Irish word signifying sorrow or regret, roughly analogous to the English word "alas."
7. Lady Gregory records some examples in her chapter "Mountain Theology" in *Poets and Dreamers.*

8. *The New Liberal Review* version of this essay included here a ten-stanza excerpt from a ballad of "Fair-haired Donough." After "men who have died upon the gallows," there was an additional phrase, "in the fight with the stranger," wording that suggests that those executed were fighters for Irish independence rather than common criminals. The first stanza reads:

   "It was bound fast here you saw him, and you wondered to
   see him,
   Our fair-haired Donough, and he after being condemned;
   There was a little white cap on him in place of a hat,
   And a hempen rope in the place of a neckcloth.[”]

   Yeats is quoting from the ten stanzas of the "West Irish Ballads" chapter of *Poets and Dreamers* (49–51).
9. Yeats quotes the lines by Douglas Hyde (1860–1949) about the people and the law from Lady Gregory's chapter "An Craoibhin's Poems," *Poets and Dreamers,* 87.
10. Lady Gregory titles her translation of this poem "A Sorrowful Lament for Ireland" and says: "The Irish poem I give this translation of was printed in the *Revue Celtique* some years ago, and lately in *An Fior Clairseach na h-Eireann,* where a note tells us it was taken from a manuscript in the Gottingen Library, and was written by an Irish priest, Shemus Cartan, who had taken orders in France; but its date is not given" (98). Yeats included the poem in *The Oxford Book of Modern Verse* (1936) under the title "A Poem written in Time of Trouble by an Irish Priest who had taken Orders in France" (98).

## Emotion of Multitude

This essay first appeared in *The All Ireland Review,* edited by Standish O'Grady, for 11 April 1903. Other than the elision of the phrase "long leagurered Troy, much-enduring Odysseus" from the subjects called up by the Greek chorus mentioned in the third sentence, there were no major changes.

1. In his *Yeats's Shakespeare* (Evanston: Northwestern University Press, 1971), Rupin Desai says that in the present essay "Yeats draws to some extent on his reading of [Victor] Hugo on Shakespeare" (43). Yeats began his 1890 essay "A Scholar Poet" with a quotation from Hugo (*LNI,* 102) and once told Maud Gonne that he "wished to become an Irish Victor Hugo" (*Mem,* 41).
2. Yeats has alluded to the Norwegian dramatist Henrik Ibsen (1828–1906) and the Belgian symbolist writer Maurice Maeterlinck (1862–1949) in several of the preceding essays in *IGE. The Wild Duck* is the title of a play by Ibsen in which Lieutenant Ekdal keeps a prized

wild duck in his attic; most critics associate the wild duck with fantasy in some way. Maeterlinck's *Pelléas and Mélisande* has a wedding ring that falls into a fountain.

3. The carved emerald is likely the Smaragdine Tablet of Hermes Trismegistus in European reconstructions of Egyptian magical lore. He was an important figure in theosophic and Hermetic teachings. Madame Blavatsky, for example, writes of Isis in her *Isis Unveiled:* "See what Hermes, the thrice-great master, says of her: 'Her father is the sun, her mother is the moon'" (*Isis Unveiled: Collected Writings,* 2 vols. [1877; repr. Pasadena: Theosophical University Press, 1972], 1:506).

## Certain Noble Plays of Japan

First published by the Cuala Press (Churchtown, Dundrum) on 16 September 1916 as the introduction to *Certain Noble Plays of Japan: From the Manuscripts of Ernest Fenollosa, Chosen and Finished by Ezra Pound, With an Introduction by William Butler Yeats.* Quotations from this volume in the present essay are indicated by the short title *Certain Noble Plays of Japan* followed by the page number. A slightly earlier version appeared as the lead essay in *The Drama: A Quarterly Review* 24 (November 1916). The most significant revision for the 1919 *Cutting of an Agate* was the elimination of the opening two sentences: "In the series of books I edit for my sister I confine myself to those that have I believe some special value to Ireland, now or in the future. I have asked Mr. Pound for these beautiful plays because I think they will help me to explain a certain possibility of the Irish dramatic movement." The text in *Essays* (1924) was subject to a number of minor revisions.

1. Yeats's friend the English artist Edmund Dulac (1882–1953) illustrated *Stories from the Arabian Nights, Retold by Laurence Housman* (London: Hodder and Stoughton, 1907).
2. Dulac designed the masks for *At the Hawk's Well,* first produced privately on 2 April 1916 in the drawing room of Maud Alice (née Burke), Lady Cunard (1872–1948). Dedicating *The Winding Stair and Other Poems* (1933) to Dulac, Yeats noted,

> I saw my *Hawk's Well* played by students of our Schools of Dancing and of Acting a couple of years ago in a little theatre called 'The Peacock,' which shares a roof with the Abbey Theatre. Watching Cuchulain in his lovely mask and costume, that ragged old masked man who seems hundreds of years old, that Guardian of the Well, with your great golden wings and dancing to your music, I had one of those moments of excitement that are the dramatist's reward and decided there and then to dedicate to you my next book of verse (*P,* 607).

3. The American scholar Ernest Fenollosa (1853–1908) had taught at Tokyo University and the Tokyo Fine Arts School; in 1890 he became curator of Oriental art at the Museum of Fine Arts, Boston. After his death his widow gave his unpublished materials on Chinese poetry and Japanese Noh drama to Yeats's friend the American writer Ezra Pound (1885–1972).
4. Yeats had depicted events from the life of Cuchulain in *On Baile's Strand,* first produced at the Abbey Theatre on 27 December 1904, and in *The Golden Helmet,* first produced at the Abbey Theatre on 19 March 1908. The latter was revised as *The Green Helmet* and first produced at the Abbey Theatre on 10 February 1910.
5. Edward Gordon Craig (1872–1966) was an English actor, producer, and stage designer. He designed a set of screens for the Abbey Theatre, first used on 12 January 1911, for the production of Lady Gregory's *The Deliverer* and a revival of Yeats's *The Hour-Glass.*
6. Coleridge's "Kubla Khan" was first published in 1816; Shelley's "Ode to the West Wind," in 1820.
7. The dancers have not been traced; the drawing room was perhaps Lady Cunard's.
8. The Japanese dancer Michio Ito (1893–1961) met Yeats and Pound in London; he provided the choreography and played the part of the Guardian of the Well for the first production of *At the Hawk's Well.* Shortly thereafter, he settled in New York, where he remained until he was deported back to Japan in 1941.
9. The Greek sculptor Callimachus (fl. late fifth century B.C.) was renowned as the first to employ the running drill, which enabled him to simulate the folds of drapery in marble. Phidias (ca. 490–ca. 430 B.C.) was the most famous sculptor of ancient Greece. The Egyptian statue is that of Ka-Aper (Fifth Dynasty, ca. 2500 B.C.), discovered by the French Egyptologist François-Auguste-Ferdinand Mariette (Mariette Pasha, 1821–81) at the excavation of Saqqara in 1860. The Egyptian workers were taken aback by the resemblance of the statue to the "headman" (mayor) of their village and thus gave it the nickname "Sheikh-el-Beled" (Head of the Village).
10. The Venetian painter Jacopo Robusti Tintoretto (1518–94) sought to combine the coloring of Titian with the draftsmanship of Michelangelo; Yeats mentions his *Origin of the Milky Way* in both "Symbolism in Painting" and the "Blind Man" section of *Discoveries* in the present collection. The Spanish painter Diego Rodríguez de Silva y Velásquez (1599–1660) developed a more naturalistic style of religious art than his predecessors.
11. The English neoclassical poet, dramatist, and critic John Dryden (1631–1700) was often seen as inaugurating a more polished style than that of his predecessors.
12. By the mid-fourteenth century in Japan, puppet dramas were per-

formed by the Ebisukaki, groups of performers in Kyoto. This activity later centered on Awaji Island and is commonly called Awaji puppet theater. The Awaji tradition is assumed to have influenced the development in the seventeenth century of the Bunraku (also called *Ningyo Joruri*) marionette theater.

13. Feodor Chaliapin (1873–1938) was a Russian bass singer. It is not known when Yeats heard him sing one of the arias from *Prince Igor* by the Russian composer Alexander Porphyrevich Borodin (1833–87).
14. In Shakespeare's *Antony and Cleopatra* (written ca. 1606–7; published 1623), a clown brings in the basket with the asp that Cleopatra uses to kill herself (5.2.240–77). Pierre Corneille (1606–84) is one of France's greatest dramatists.
15. Girolamo Savonarola (1452–98) was an Italian Dominican friar and religious reformer; he lamented the grandeur of arts in Renaissance Florence as indicative of pervasive depravity and immorality. Declared a heretic and accused of treason, he was executed by hanging and his body burned.
16. "Lethe wharf" is from act 1, scene 5, line 33, of Shakespeare's *Hamlet* (written ca. 1599–1601; first published 1603). The second quotation is derived from Shakespeare's *The Merchant of Venice* (written ca. 1596–98; published 1600): "In such a night / Stood Dido with a willow in her hand / Upon the wild sea banks . . ." (5.1.11–13).
17. Yeats's lecture on "The Theatre of Beauty" to the Dramatic Club at Harvard University on 5 October 1911 was published in *Harper's Weekly*, 11 November 1911 (*LAR*, 129–33).
18. Lines 5–12 of "Thrasymedes and Eunöe" (1846) by the English writer Walter Savage Landor (1775–1864), in *Poems, Dialogues in Verse, and Epigrams*, ed. Charles G. Crump, 2 vols. (London: J. M. Dent, 1909; O'Shea #1083), 2:282–83 (correctly "Pour'd" and "grasp").
19. Shinto was the earliest Japanese religion. Yeats's account of the development of the Noh draws on that in "Fenollosa on the Noh" in Ernest Fenollosa and Ezra Pound, *'Noh' or Accomplishment: A Study of the Classical Stage of Japan* (London: Macmillan, 1916; O'Shea #1637): "The Shinto god dance, the lyric form of court poetry, the country farces, and a full range of epic incident, in short, all that was best in the earlier Japanese tradition, was gathered into this new form, arranged and purified. The change came about in this way. The Zen parish priests summoned up to Kioto the Dengaku troupe from Nara, and made it play before the Shogun. The head actor of the Nara troupe, Kwan, took the new solo parts, and greatly enlarged the scope of the music of the other acting. During the lifetime of his son and grandson, Zei and On, hundreds of new plays were created. It is a question to what extent these three men, Kwan, Zei, and On, were the originators of the texts of these new dramas, and how far the Zen priests are responsible" (118).

Although only a few plays by Kanami Kiyotsugo (1333–84) survive, there are nearly one hundred extant by his son, Zeami Motokiyo (1364–1443)—almost one-half of the Noh repertory. Nara had been the capital of Japan for most of the eighth century; Kyoto was the capital from 1338–1597. Shogun was the title of the military dictators who ruled Japan from the twelth to the nineteenth century. The mikado, the emperor of Japan, had little power. Fenollosa notes that by the early tenth century "the passion for composing and reciting . . . Japanese poetry became so powerful among the educated classes, especially in the cultured aristocracy at Kioto, where men and women met on equal terms, that the old court entertainments of dance and music had to be modified to admit the use of poetic texts" (111). Chaucer was born circa 1343 and died in 1400.

20. *Hamlet* was first produced in 1602.
21. The Japanese protected cruiser *Takasago* was constructed at the Armstrong Works in Elswick, Wales, and launched on 18 May 1897. Measuring 360 feet with a displacement of 4,300 tons and a speed of twenty-four knots, she was sunk by a mine on 13 December 1904, during the Russo-Japanese War. *Takasago* is a Noh play by Zeami Motokiyo.
22. In the introduction to *'Noh' or Accomplishment,* Pound quotes from a 1900 program note on the genealogy of the performers: "The twenty-eighth descendant was Hiogu no Kami Kagehisa. His mother dreamed that a Noh mask was given from heaven; she conceived, and Kagehisa was born. From his childhood Kagehisa liked music and dancing, and he was by nature very excellent in both of these arts. The Emperor Gotsuchi Mikado heard his name, and in January in the 13th year of Bunmei [1481] he called him to his palace and made him perform the play. Ashikari Kagehisa was then sixteen years old. The Emperor admired him greatly and gave him the decoration (Monsuki) and a curtain which was purple above and white below, and he gave him the honorific ideograph 'waka' and this made him change his name to Umewaka. By the Emperor's order, Ushoben Fugiwara no Shunmei sent the news of this and the gifts to Kagehisa. The letter of the Emperor, given at that time, is still in our house. The curtain was, unfortunately, burned in the great fire of Yedo on the 4th of March in the third year of Bunka [1807]" (7–8).
23. In the introduction to *'Noh' or Accomplishment,* Pound notes that there were "five chartered and hereditary companies of court actors" (10). One was headed by Kanze: "The Kanze method of acting was made the official style of the Tokugawa Shoguns, and the tayus, or chief actors, of Kanze were placed at the head of all Noh actors. To the Kanze tayu alone was given the privilege of holding one subscription performance, or Kanjin-No, during his lifetime, for the space of ten days. And for this performance he had the right to certain dues and

levies on the daimyos [feudal lords] and on the streets of the people of Yedo. . . . The privilege of holding one subscription performance was later granted to the Hosho company also" (13–14). The "revolution" refers to the collapse of the Tokugawa reign and the establishment of the Meiji reign in 1867–68.

24. The Japanese dramatist Chikamatsu Monzaemon (1653–1725) in fact wrote for both the Kabuki theater and the puppet theater (Bunraku), but his reputation rests on his work for the latter.

25. In the introduction to *'Noh' or Accomplishment,* Pound noted that the Noh offers "a stage where every subsidiary art is bent precisely upon holding the faintest shade of a difference; where the poet may even be silent while the gestures consecrated by four centuries of usage show meaning" (6).

26. Yeats mentions working on this essay in a letter to Lady Gregory of 28 March 1916 (*L,* 611–12).

27. This anecdote is not included in *'Noh' or Accomplishment.*

28. *Nishikigi* by Zeami Motokiyo was included in *Certain Noble Plays of Japan.* In "West Irish Ballads" (1902), published in a revised form in *Poets and Dreamers: Studies and Translations from the Irish* (Dublin: Hodges, Figgis / New York: Scribner's; 1903; O'Shea #807), Lady Gregory notes, "Another song I have heard was a lament over a boy and girl who had run away to America, and on the way the ship went down. And when they were going down, they began to be sorry they were not married; and to say that if the priest had been at home when they went away, they would have been married; but they hoped that when they were drowned, it would be the same with them as if they were married" (48–49).

29. Little remains of Castle Hackett, near Tuam in County Galway. In "Kidnappers," first published in *The Scots Observer* for 15 June 1889, and included in *The Celtic Twilight: Men and Women, Dhouls and Faeries* (London: Lawrence and Bullen, 1893), Yeats notes, "Sometimes one hears of stolen people acting as good genii to the living, as in this tale, heard also close by the haunted pond, of John Kirwan of Castle Hackett" (*Myth,* 74).

30. Yeats's *On Baile's Strand* was first published in *In the Seven Woods* (Dundrum: Dun Emer Press, 1903) and first produced at the Abbey Theatre, Dublin, on 27 December 1904. His *The King's Threshold* was first published privately in New York in 1904 and then in *The King's Threshold: and On Baile's Strand: Being Volume Three of Plays for an Irish Theatre* (London: A. H. Bullen, 1904); it was first produced by the Irish National Theatre Society at the Molesworth Hall, Dublin, on 8 October 1903.

31. *Certain Noble Plays of Japan:* "Among the orchids and chrysanthemum flowers / The hiding fox is now lord of that love-cave . . ." (7).

32. *Certain Noble Plays of Japan:* "I go about with my heart set upon no

particular place whatsoever, and with no other man's flag in my hand, no more than a cloud has. It is a flag of the night I see coming down upon me. I wonder now, would the sea be that way, or the little place Kefu that they say is stuck down against it?" (1).

33. *Certain Noble Plays of Japan,* 1.
34. *Certain Noble Plays of Japan:* "These bodies, having no weft, / Even now are not come together. / Truly a shameful story, / A tale to bring shame on the gods." (5).
35. *Certain Noble Plays of Japan:* "Pushing aside the grass / From the overgrown way at Kefu" (6); "cutting grass on the hill" (7); "A dream-bridge over wild grass, / Over the grass I dwell in" (8); "From under the shadows of the love-grass" (9).
36. *Certain Noble Plays of Japan:* "The plumage of heaven drops neither feather nor flame to its own diminution"; "Nor is this rock of earth over-much worn by the brushing of that feather-mantle, the feathery skirt of the stars: rarely, how rarely" (26).
37. Yeats refers to *The Wave-beaten Rock* by the Japanese painter Ogata Korin (1658–1716), which was exhibited at the British Museum in 1914. As noted in the *Guide to an Exhibition of Japanese and Chinese Paintings principally from the Arthur Morrison Collection* ([London]: British Museum, 1914), the screen depicts "A favourite motive of the master" (13).
38. Yeats describes these and other image patterns in Shelley's poetry above in "The Philosophy of Shelley's Poetry."
39. The English writer Walter Pater (1839–94) was a major influence on the aesthetic movement of the 1880s. Achilles is one of the leading warriors in *The Iliad.*
40. Yeats's "Minoan" should probably be Cretan. Few images of warriors from that Bronze Age period survive, and none correspond to his description. The helmet with the winged horse (Pegasus, best known through Greek mythology but of pre-Greek origin) is the Axos Helmet in the Heraklion Museum, reproduced as plate 14 in Herbert Hoffman, *Early Cretan Armor* (Mainz on Rhine: Verlag Phillip von Zabern, 1972). The shield with the dove has not been traced.
41. Saint Kobo (774–835) was one of the most important Buddhist priests in Japan. The famous portrait of him as a child is of uncertain origin but dates from around the period of the Japanese painter Fujiwara no Nobuzane (1176–1265?).
42. Yeats regarded the Scots writer Thomas Carlyle (1795–1881) as "the chief inspirer of self-educated men in the 'eighties and early 'nineties" (*Au,* 179). Yeats ranked the French novelist Victor-Marie Hugo (1802–85) among the greatest nineteenth-century writers but given to rhetorical excess.
43. In the introduction to *'Noh' or Accomplishment,* Pound notes, "In the eighth century of our era the dilettante of the Japanese court estab-

lished the tea cult and the play of 'listening to incense'" (4); the term comes from ancient Buddhist texts that suggest that all the perceptive senses work together. Puvis de Chavannes (1824–98) was the leading French mural painter of the later nineteenth century. Yeats discusses the French poets Stéphane Mallarmé (1842–98) and Paul Verlaine (1844–96) in *IGE*.

44. Slievenamon, a mountain in County Tipperary, is associated with the Tuatha Dé Danann (the people or tribe of the goddess Dana/Danu). Cro Patrick is a mountain in County Galway, associated with Saint Patrick.
45. The "fairy stories" of the Irish writer Oscar Wilde (1854–1900) consist of *The Happy Prince and Other Tales* (London: D. Nutt, 1888), written for his sons; and *A House of Pomegranates* (London: James R. Osgood, McIlvaine and Co, 1891), often described as fairy tales for adults. Charles Ricketts (1866–1931) was an English designer and painter who, along with the English painter Charles Hazelwood Shannon (1863–1937), designed many of Wilde's books, including *A House of Pomegranates.* Wilde's popularity in Arabia has not been traced.

## The Tragic Theatre

First published in *The Mask: A Quarterly Illustrated Journal of the Art of the Theatre* (Florence) 3 (October 1910). A revised version, eliminating the first three paragraphs and the first sentence of the fourth, was printed as the preface to *Plays for an Irish Theatre* (London and Stratford-upon-Avon: A. H. Bullen, 1911). There were also some verbal revisions: for example, in *The Mask* Yeats refers to "Henry the Fifth whose poetry, never touched by lyric heat, is oratorical like a speech at a general election, like an article in some daily paper"; in the 1911 volume the description ends with "oratorical." For *The Cutting of an Agate* (1912), Yeats restored the original opening but omitted the conclusion of the essay (see appendix G). There were minor revisions for *Essays* (1924).

1. John Millington Synge's *Deirdre of the Sorrows,* unfinished at the time of his death on 24 March 1909, was arranged for production by Yeats and others and first produced by the Irish National Theatre Society at the Abbey Theatre, Dublin, 13 January 1910. It was included in the Abbey's English tour of May–June 1910.
2. The French painter Louis-Gustave Ricard (1823–73) based his celebrated portrait style on the adaptation of the old masters. The French composer Claude Debussy (1862–1918) helped pioneer musical impressionism, as in his famous "Clair de Lune."
3. In act 2, Deirdre overhears Naisi telling Fergus "I'll not tell you a lie. There have been days a while past when I've been throwing a line for

salmon, or watching for the run of hares, that I've had a dread upon me a day'd come I'd weary of her voice [*very slowly*] . . . and Deirdre'd see I'd wearied" (*Plays* 2: 227; ellipsis in text). The review is perhaps that in *The Athenaeum* for 4 June 1910: 684, although the critic did note another dramatic moment in act 3.

4. From a speech by Deirdre in act 3: "We've had a dream, but this night has waked us surely. In a little while we've lived too long, Naisi, and isn't it a poor thing we should miss the safety of the grave, and we trampling its edge?" (*Plays* 2: 255).
5. Deirdre was played by Molly Allgood (Maire O'Neill, 1887–1952), who had been engaged to Synge at the time of his death.
6. In *Deirdre of the Sorrows,* Naisi is killed by Conchubar's men. The published text does not include the detail of Deirdre touching Conchubar just before her suicide.
7. Pierre Corneille (1606–84) and Jean Racine (1639–99) are usually thought of as the two major French classical dramatists.
8. Yeats presumably refers to Timon's speech in Shakespeare's *Timon of Athens,* 4.3.370–73. "Then, Timon, presently prepare thy grave. Lie where the light foam of the sea may beat / Thy grave stone daily. Make thine epitaph, / That death in me at other lives may laugh." In *Hamlet,* Hamlet tells Horatio "If thou didst ever hold me in thy heart, / Absent thee from felicity a while" (5.2.288–89). In *Antony and Cleopatra,* Antony tells Cleopatra "I am dying, Egypt, dying. Only / I here importune death awhile until / Of many thousand kisses the poor last / I lay upon thy lips" (4.16.19–22) (Shakespeare 2293, 1755, 2693). The English writer Coventry Patmore (1823–96) refers to the "integrity of fire" in his poem "Eros and Psyche," line 73, part of *The Unknown Eros* (1877–78), included in *Poems* (London: George Bell, 1906; O'Shea #1540): "My Darling, know / Your spotless fairness is not match'd in snow / But in the integrity of fire" (339).
9. Falstaff is a character in Shakespeare's *Henry IV, Part 1, Henry IV, Part 2,* and *The Merry Wives of Windsor;* Yeats also refers to Shakespeare's *King Henry V.*
10. A translation by Lady Gregory of *Les Fourberies de Scapin* (1671) by the French dramatist Molière (1622–73) as *The Rougeries of Scapin* was produced by the National Theatre Society at the Abbey Theatre, Dublin, on 4 April 1908.
11. The first two quotations are found in "Congreve to John Dennis," a letter of 10 July 1695, in William Congreve (1670–1729), *Letters & Documents,* ed. John C. Hodges (New York: Harcourt, Brace & World, 1964), 182–83. Hodges reads: "A singular and unavoidable manner of doing, or saying any thing, Peculiar and Natural to one Man only; by which his Speech and Actions are distinguish'd from those of other Men" for the first quotation and "that Sex" for "the sex" in the second quotation. The third allusion remains untraced.

12. William Makepeace Thackeray (1811–63), English writer best known for the novel *Vanity Fair* (1847–48).
13. Édouard Manet (1832–83) was a French painter. Although the cocottes are sitting indoors, the "big picture" by one of his followers is perhaps *Brasserie au Quartier Latin, Paris* by the French painter Charles Léroy Saint Aubert (1852–1907), included in the exhibition at the Royal Hibernian Academy in Dublin, which opened on 2 March 1885, and reproduced in the *Illustrated Art Supplement* to *The Dublin University Review* (March 1885). Yeats presumably took a class at the Royal Hibernian Academy while he was enrolled in the Metropolitan School of Art in Dublin from May 1884 to April 1886.
14. Manet's *Olympia,* in the Luxembourg Museum in Paris, dates from 1863.
15. Sir Hugh Lane (1875–1915), art collector and critic (and nephew of Lady Gregory), owned Manet's 1869–70 portrait of his student Eva Gonzalès. It is reproduced in the Municipal Gallery of Modern Art *Illustrated Catalogue with Biographical and Critical Notes* (Dublin: Dollard, 1908), plate no. 122. In *The Lame Devil* (*Le Diable boiteux,* 1707; enlarged edition, 1726) by the French writer Alain-René Lesage (1668–1747), the "devil upon two sticks" explains to the main character a quarrel between a tragic poet and a comic author.
16. Yeats refers to a work in the National Gallery in London by the Venetian painter Titian (1488–1576) once called *Ariosto* but now known as *Portrait of a Man* (ca. 1508; possibly a self-portrait). In *The Trembling of the Veil* (1922) Yeats describes it as a work that he "loved beyond other portraits" (*Au,* 115). Titian's *Bacchus and Ariadne* dates from 1522.
17. In Shakespeare's *Antony and Cleopatra,* a clown brings in the basket with the asp that Cleopatra uses to kill herself (5.2.240–304).
18. Quotations untraced.
19. In the Bible, the tree of life and the tree of knowledge of good and evil are found in the Garden of Eden (Genesis 2:9). The fruit of the latter tree was forbidden to man; the disobedience of Adam and Eve causes the fall of man and the expulsion from the garden.

## Poetry and Tradition

This essay first appeared in two different publications on 1 December 1908. One was *The Collected Works in Verse and Prose of William Butler Yeats* (Stratford-on-Avon: Shakespeare Head Press, 1908), where it formed part of the eighth volume, *Discoveries. Edmund Spenser. Poetry and Tradition; and Other Essays.* The other was *Poetry and Ireland: Essays by W. B. Yeats and Lionel Johnson* (Dundrum: Cuala Press, 1908), the first book published by Cuala Press after it was reorganized from the Dun Emer Press; the essay was there titled "Poetry and Patriotism." Both versions supplied the date

"August 1907," which carried over into *The Cutting of an Agate* and *Essays*. "Poetry and Tradition" was used as the title in the 1912 *The Cutting of an Agate* and subsequent printings; that was the most significant difference among the versions.

1. The Fenian leader John O'Leary (1830–1907) became Yeats's mentor in politics after his return from exile in 1885. In *Reveries over Childhood and Youth,* Yeats recalled of a Young Ireland Society, "From these debates, from O'Leary's conversation, and from the Irish books he lent or gave me has come all I have set my hand to since" (*Au,* 104). Yeats memorialized him in "September 1913" as the type of large-minded Irish romantic nationalism (*P,* 107).
2. John F[rancis] Taylor (1850–1902), Irish barrister and journalist, was Yeats's chief rival among O'Leary's disciples. In *Reveries,* Yeats called him "an obscure great orator" and, like James Joyce in *Ulysses,* recorded part of his famous speech invoking for Irish nationalists the precedent of Moses before Pharaoh (*Au,* 101). Yeats's friend and Olivia Shakespear's cousin Lionel Pigot Johnson (1867–1902) was a poet and essayist who joined Yeats in the Rhymers' Club and in cultural nationalist activities. Yeats mentioned Johnson in his poetry and dedicated "The Rose" section of his *Poems* to him.
3. The young Irish poet Rose Kavanagh (1859–91) was a close friend of John O'Leary and his sister Ellen. Yeats commemorated her passing in "Rose Kavanagh: Death of a Promising Young Irish Poet" (*LNI,* 40–44). The point of the anecdote here is that the religious adviser confuses Giuseppe Mazzini (1805–72), the Italian nationalist and founder of the revolutionary society Young Italy, with the Italian writer Alessandro Manzoni (1785–1873), whose novels have affinities with those of Sir Walter Scott.
4. Henry Grattan (1746–1820) and Thomas (Osborne) Davis (1814–45) were both Irish Protestant patriots. The orator and politician Grattan became the moving spirit of the Irish parliament until it was dissolved by the Act of Union, which Grattan opposed; thereafter he worked for Catholic Emancipation. Davis became leader of the Young Ireland movement and cofounded *The Nation* in 1842. Yeats initially applauded Davis for his nationalism, but later agreed with O'Leary that he was too propagandist as a poet. Yeats mentions Davis in his poem "To Ireland in the Coming Times" and Mangan in the poem "The Tower" (*P,* 46 and 202, respectively), among other places. The phrase "European revolutionists of the mid-century" refers to the series of generally liberal and nationalist European revolutions occurring from 1848 to 1851 in France, Italy, Germany, and the Austrian Empire.
5. The Fenian movement was an association of Irish nationalists, founded in New York in 1857 and taking its name from the semimythical band of warriors who fought under Finn MacCool. The association soon

spread across the United States and Ireland and became the forerunner of the Irish Republican Brotherhood. O'Leary was imprisoned for a twenty-year sentence in December 1865 in Pentonville, and transferred in May 1866 to the Isle of Portland. He was released in 1871 as part of a general amnesty, but exiled from Ireland until his return in 1885. Of the four remarks by O'Leary, Yeats quotes two again in section 28 of *Reveries* (*Au,* 100–101). The remark "I have but one religion, the old Persian . . ." was not original with O'Leary but rather one that he quoted from the narrator of Charles Kingsley's novel *Westward Ho!* (London: Macmillan, 1881): "his training had been that of the old Persians, 'to speak the truth and to draw the bow'" (13). Yeats liked the remark well enough to cite it again in *Au,* 177.

6. The Irish poet and novelist Katharine Tynan (1859?–1931) became a close friend of Yeats after their meeting in 1885; in 1893 she married his sometime schoolmate Henry Hinkson. They shared the Irish literary and political nationalism of the circle around John O'Leary; Yeats's early letters to her contain important statements of his literary aims.
7. Said to descend from Hercules, Lycurgus was the legendary founder of ancient Sparta who reformed its laws. John Bunyan (1628–88) was the author of the immensely popular prose allegory *The Pilgrim's Progress.* Besides serving in the Cromwell government, the poet John Milton (1608–74) helped shape English culture through works like his epic *Paradise Lost.* The Irish patriot and journalist John Mitchel (1815–75) founded *The United Irishman;* Yeats invokes his *Jail Journal* at the beginning of section 3 of "Under Ben Bulben" (*P,* 334).
8. The Irish poet and editor William Allingham (1824–89) influenced Yeats through his lyric treatment of fairy lore and depiction of west Irish life around his native Ballyshannon. Yeats also knew his long poem *Laurence Bloomfield in Ireland* (1864), with its analysis of tensions in Irish society during the Land War. For Yeats's review of his six-volume collected poems, see "A Poet We Have Neglected" (*EAR,* 149–52). The nationalist poet and translator Edward Walsh (1805–50) influenced Yeats through his renditions of poems from the Gaelic. His *Reliques of Irish Jacobite Poetry* (1844) and *Irish Popular Songs* (1847) were both known to Yeats. The work of the poet and scholar Sir Samuel Ferguson (1810–86) helped introduce the young Yeats to the possibilities of utilizing Irish mythological material in poetry, especially through his epic poem *Congal* (1872) and his *Lays of the Western Gael, and Other Poems* (1864). Yeats's first two published articles were memorial reviews of his work (*EAR,* 3–27).
9. For more on Yeats's assessment of his sometime mentor William Morris (1834–96), see "The Happiest of the Poets" above in the current collection. The Victorian cultural and social critic John Ruskin (1819–1900) influenced Morris and Yeats through both his aesthetic views and his closely related critique of Victorian society.

10. The essayist, historian, and translator Thomas Carlyle (1795–1881) was another major critic of Victorian society; he also translated Goethe and other German writers, and helped introduce German thinking into Victorian England.
11. Frederic (William Henry) Myers (1843–1901) was one of the Cambridge founders of the Society for Psychical Research and wrote a number of influential books on spiritualism, including *Science and a Future Life* (1893) and *Human Personality and Its Survival of Bodily Death* (1903). In a note to "Swedenborg, Mediums, and the Desolate Places," Yeats included Myers on a list of those who had influenced his own thinking on psychical research (*LE*, 323).
12. The great love of Yeats's youth after he met her in 1889, Maud Gonne (1866–1953) was a leading nationalist orator and organizer who also shared some of Yeats's beliefs in psychical and occult matters. Yeats came increasingly to distrust her politics, which he saw as founded on argument and opinion. Yeats wrote about her in his poetry, his autobiography, and elsewhere; for one account of her as orator, see his "The New Speranza" (*LNI*, 61–64). The phrase "Mother Ireland with the crown of stars about her head," which Yeats also uses about Gonne in *Memoirs*, 107, remains untraced.
13. Yeats gives a slightly different recollection of O'Leary's remark in *Reveries over Childhood and Youth*, where he writes: "Neither Ireland nor England knows the good from the bad in any art, but Ireland unlike England does not hate the good when it is pointed out to her" (*Au*, 104).
14. The original Young Ireland was a romantic nationalist movement of the 1840s led by Thomas Davis, Charles Gavin Duffy, and John Blake Dillon. Nationalists revived the societies in the 1880s; in 1885 John O'Leary gave the inaugural address of the Young Ireland Society that Yeats joined in 1886. The Scottish Romantic poet Robert Burns (1759–96) both translated and wrote original poetry about the folk; "The Cotter's Saturday Night" and "Highland Mary" are two of his best-known poems.
15. Yeats quotes (in roman rather than italics) the last five lines of his poem "To his Heart, bidding it have no Fear" (1896) from the version first printed in *The Wind Among the Reeds* (1899); the semicolon after "ways" should be a comma (*VP*, 158).
16. In his edition of Yeats's *Selected Criticism* (London: Macmillan, 1964), A. Norman Jeffares identifies Charles V as Charles the Wise, who "was born at Vincennes and reigned from 1364 to 1380; he was a patron of art and literature and collected a large library at the Louvre" (283). However, Yeats may be referring instead to the Charles V (1500–1558), who was the grandson of Queen Isabella of Spain and became both king of Spain and Holy Roman emperor in the early sixteenth century; he summoned the Diet of Worms. Perhaps a painting

from this period, *The Court Jester Pejeron* by Anthonis Mor van Dashorst (ca. 1517–1576), depicts the jester in question.

Duke Frederigo da Montefeltro (1422–82) ruled the Renaissance city-state of Urbino from 1444 onward. A famous patron of the arts, he turned Urbino into a leading center of art and humanism and accumulated a famous library. He was succeeded by his physically feebler son Guidobaldo (1472–1508), who continued his patronage and was praised by Castiglione in *The Book of the Courtier.* Yeats invoked Guidobaldo in "To a Wealthy Man" (*P,* 106–7).

17. Yeats misquotes and condenses one of the "Proverbs of Hell" from plate 8 of William Blake's *The Marriage of Heaven and Hell* (Ellis-Yeats: 3, Erdman, 36), presumably from memory. Erdman reads: "The roaring of lions, the howling of wolves, the raging of the stormy sea, and the destructive sword are portions of eternity too great for the eye of man." Tristan and Iseult are the famous ill-fated lovers of medieval romances such as Sir Thomas Malory's *Le Morte D'Arthur,* of which Yeats owned a copy with designs by Aubrey Beardsley (O'Shea #1214).
18. Although Yeats repeatedly attributed this thought to the French writer and literary critic Charles-Augustin Sainte-Beuve (1804–69), in fact it comes from *Dreamthorp: A Book of Essays Written in the Country* (London: Strahan, 1863) by the Scottish writer Alexander Smith (1829–67): "And style, after all, rather than thought, is the immortal thing in literature" (43).
19. Among the poets who compared their beloved to Helen of Troy in Homer was Yeats himself in poems like "No Second Troy" (*P,* 89).
20. Yeats refers to Marvell's "An Horatian Ode: Upon Cromwell's Return from Ireland" (1650), which celebrates Cromwell's execution of Charles I (1600–1649) and his conquest of Ireland.
21. Yeats refers to the famous death scenes of Shakespeare's tragic protagonists in *Timon of Athens* (correctly "beachèd verge of the salt flood," Shakespeare, 2301) and *Antony and Cleopatra.*
22. The Italian diplomat, writer, and courtier Baldassare Castiglione (1478–1529) wrote *The Book of the Courtier* (1528; translated into English in 1561), which influenced English Renaissance writers such as Sidney and Spenser, as well as Yeats himself when he first read it in 1903 or 1904. He was especially attracted to Castiglione's concept of *sprezzatura,* which the book's first English translator, Sir Thomas Hoby, had rendered as "recklessness."
23. Yeats particularly admired the nineteenth-century Irish poet James Clarence Mangan (1803–49) and named him, along with Thomas Davis (1814–45) and Sir Samuel Ferguson (1810–86) (see notes 4 and 8 above), in "To Ireland in the Coming Times": "Nor may I less be counted one / With Davis, Mangan, Ferguson" (*P,* 46). For more on Yeats's views of Mangan, see "Clarence Mangan (1803–1849)" and

"Clarence Mangan's Love Affair" in *EAR*, 39–44 and 134–38, respectively.

24. The nationalist politician and journalist Sir Charles Gavan Duffy (1816–1903) was one of the leaders of Young Ireland and cofounder of *The Nation* and became MP for New Ross before immigrating to Australia and becoming prime minister of Victoria. After his return, he served as the first president of the Irish Literary Society in London and clashed repeatedly with Yeats, who wanted to move Irish verse beyond what he saw as the merely patriotic and sometimes philistine verse of anthologies such as Duffy's *The Ballad Poetry of Ireland* (1845). Yeats reviewed Duffy's *Young Ireland* for *The Bookman* in January 1897 (*EAR*, 326–28). On his death bed Duffy recited the poem "Dear Land" by his fellow Young Irelander writer John O'Hagan (1822–90). It was published under O'Hagan's pseudonym, "Sliab Cuilinn," in *The Spirit of the Nation: Ballads and Songs by the Writers of "The Nation"* (Dublin: James Duffy, 1845), 22–23.
25. Yeats refers to his first visit to Italy with Lady Gregory and her son in April and May 1907, three weeks after O'Leary's death in mid-March, when besides Siena they also visited Urbino, Ravenna, Venice, Florence, and other notable sites.
26. "Ireland" is the title poem of Lionel Johnson, *Ireland, with Other Poems* (London: Elkin Mathews / Boston: Copeland and Day, 1897; O'Shea #1019), 1–9. The quotation from "Ireland's Dead" comes from Lionel Johnson, *Poems* (London: Elkin Mathews / Boston: Copeland and Day, 1895, O'Shea #1020), 51; for "they do" read "thou dost."
27. "Ways of War," from Johnson, *Poems* (1895), 48–49; for "armed hands" read "armed minds."
28. When O'Leary returned to Ireland in 1885 after his twenty-year exile, he and Patrick Neville Fitzgerald (1851–1907), a prominent figure in both the Irish Republican Brotherhood (IRB) and the Gaelic Athletic Association, went on a speaking tour of Ireland. The tour concluded on 22 August 1885, with a stop in the temporary village of Mullinahone, which may be the occasion of Yeats's anecdote. Yeats's original note (1908) contained the following additional sentence: "I have known but one that had his moral courage, and that was a woman with beauty to give her courage and self-possession."
29. Charles Stewart Parnell (1846–91) led the Irish Parliamentary Party and for Yeats exemplified broad-minded romantic Irish nationalism and the personality of a great leader. Yeats refers to him repeatedly in both prose and poetry. The "new class" that Yeats deprecates by contrast was primarily Catholic, associated with towns, and included the small shopkeepers and clerks mentioned later in the paragraph.
30. The image of the fox and the badger's hole refers to lines 216–17 of

Edmund Spenser's "The Ruines of Time," which Yeats included in his edition *Poems of Spenser* (Edinburgh: T. C. and E. C. Jack, 1906), 72: "He now is gone, the whiles the Foxe is crept / Into the hole, the which the Badger swept." Yeats used the same image at the end of the fifth stanza of "The Municipal Gallery Re-visited": "And now that end has come I have not wept; / No fox can foul the lair the badger swept" (*P*, 328).

31. In his introduction to his one-volume *Poems of William Blake*, Yeats calls Blake "one of those great artificers of God" (*P&I*, 91).

## Discoveries

### Prophet, Priest and King

First appeared as "(1)" of "My Thoughts and my Second Thoughts" in the September 1906 issue of *The Gentleman's Magazine*. There were no significant revisions in later printings. For discussion of *Discoveries* as a whole, see Editors' Introduction, pp. xxiii, xxx, and xlv*f*.

1. The Irish National Theatre Society performed at the Town Hall, Loughrea, County Galway, on 13 April 1903.
2. Yeats had been staying with Lady Gregory at Coole Park.
3. The Reverend Jeremiah O'Donovan (1871–1942) was the administrator of Loughrea parish and was in charge of the construction of Saint Brendan's Cathedral, then in progress. He was committed to the revival of Irish crafts; Yeats's friend Edward Martyn (1859–1923) was providing financial backing for the involvement of the crafts movement with Saint Brendan's. After this visit, Yeats became involved in the design for the banners of the cathedral, which were made by the Dun Emer Industries (*CL3*, 348n4). The cathedral was completed in 1905, by which time O'Donovan had left both Loughrea and the priesthood; he later settled in London and wrote several novels.
4. George Meredith (1828–1909) was an English poet and novelist, perhaps best known for his novel *Diana of the Crossways* (1885).
5. The Irish National Theatre Society had also performed at the Court Theatre, Galway.
6. Auguste Rodin (1840–1917) was a major French sculptor. The Irish sculptors were John Hughes (1865–1941), who did a white marble Madonna and Child and a bronze altarpiece, and Michael Shortall (1868–1951), who did the capitals in the nave, among other contributions.
7. Portumna is a town in County Galway.
8. The play was AE's *Deirdre*, first performed in full by the Irish National Dramatic Company at Saint Teresa's Hall, Dublin, on 2 April 1902.
9. The farce was *The Pot of Broth* by Yeats and Lady Gregory, first pro-

duced by the Irish National Dramatic Company at the Antient Concert Rooms, Dublin, on 30 October 1902. The comedian was the Irish actor and producer W. G. Fay (1872–1947).

### Personality and the Intellectual Essences

First appeared as "(2)" of "My Thoughts and my Second Thoughts" in the September 1906 issue of *The Gentleman's Magazine.* There were no significant revisions in later printings.

1. Founded in 1831 and intended to encourage religious harmony, the National Schools educated primarily the lower classes and grew steadily throughout the century.
2. François Villon (ca. 1431–after 1463), the most autobiographical of the medieval French poets. On Christmas in 1456 he was part of a group which burgled the Collège de Navarre.
3. Yeats often mentions the Scottish poet Robert Burns (1759–96), frequently as a foil to or diminished version of another writer. See "What is 'Popular Poetry?'" note 11 above.
4. Yeats had met the Belgian poet Émile Verhaeren (1855–1916) in late 1898 or early 1899 in London. Yeats's main source of knowledge of Verhaeren was the English teacher, critic, and translator Osman Edwards (1864–1936), whose "Emile Verhaeren" had appeared in the November 1896 issue of *The Savoy* (65–76), preceding Yeats's "The Tables of the Law."
5. Yeats could have found the reference to the "crown of living and melodious diamonds" (correctly "diamond") in "Prayer of the Gnomes," in *Transcendental Magic: Its Doctrine and Ritual* (London: George Redway, 1896; O'Shea #1109), 220, a translation by the English writer and occultist Arthur Edward Waite (1857–1942) of *Dogme et rituel de la haute magie* (1856) by the French writer Éliphas Lévi, the pen name of Alphonse-Louis Constant (1810–75), also known as the Abbé Constant. Yeats has apparently confused him with Pierre, abbé de Villiers (1648–1728), a French Jesuit priest and writer.
6. Compare the end of "The Philosophy of Shelley's Poetry" above, in which Yeats imagines Shelley "lost in a ceaseless reverie, in some chapel of the Star of infinite desire" (p. 71). Burns's "John Barleycorn: A Ballad" (1782) praises whisky made from barley; Yeats apparently suggests that a praise of beer would be more appropriate for Burns's audience.

### The Musician and the Orator

First appeared as "(3)" of "My Thoughts and my Second Thoughts" in the September 1906 issue of *The Gentleman's Magazine.* There were no significant revisions in later printings.

1. In "The School of Giorgione" in *Studies in the History of the Renaissance* (1873), Pater claimed, "*All art constantly aspires towards the condition of music.*" See Walter Pater, *The Renaissance: Studies in Art and Poetry,* ed. Donald L. Hill (Berkeley: University of California Press), p. 106. The importance of oratory was a commonplace in classical tradition.
2. For the "melodious crown," see "Personality and the Intellectual Essences," note 5 above.

### A Guitar Player

First appeared as "A Banjo Player," "(4)" of "My Thoughts and my Second Thoughts" in the September 1906 issue of *The Gentleman's Magazine.* The instrument was changed for the 1908 *Collected Works in Verse;* there were no other significant revisions in later printings.

1. The girl is untraced.
2. François Villon (ca. 1431–after 1463) was the most autobiographical of the medieval French poets, often presenting a gritty realism about his experiences.
3. The portative organ and the positive organ of the Middle Ages were relatively small and could be moved from place to place. The development of the large and immovable organ dates from the tenth century, when it became an accepted part of Christian worship. The organ constructed circa AD 950 for Winchester Cathedral had four hundred pipes and twenty-six bellows and required two players.

### The Looking-Glass

First appeared as "(5)" of "My Thoughts and my Second Thoughts" in the September 1906 issue of *The Gentleman's Magazine.* There were no significant revisions in later printings.

1. The girl has not been identified.
2. The quotation (correctly "where") is from section 12 of Robert Browning's "A Toccata of Galuppi's": "The soul, doubtless, is immortal—where a soul can be discerned." *The Poems,* ed. John Pettigrew and Thomas Collins (New Haven and London: Yale University Press, 1981), 1:552.

### The Tree of Life

First appeared as "(6)" of "My Thoughts and my Second Thoughts" in the October 1906 issue of *The Gentleman's Magazine.* For the 1908 *Collected Works in Verse and Prose,* Yeats revised "banjo player" to "guitar player."

For the 1912 *The Cutting of an Agate,* he revised "The Devil on Two Sticks" to *Diable Boiteux* and recast the final sentence. There were no other significant revisions in later printings.

1. "Except ye be converted, and become as little children, ye shall not enter into the kingdom of heaven." Matthew 18:3.
2. Yeats met the French poet Paul Verlaine (1844–96) during his visit to Paris in February 1894. Yeats told this anecdote several times, beginning with "Verlaine in 1894," published in *The Savoy* for April 1896 (*UP1,* 397–99). Verlaine admired Tennyson's *In Memoriam* (1850) more than the anecdote suggests (*LE,* 342n9).
3. In "Shakespeare and Racine," *The Fortnightly Review* 62, no. 1 (September 1894), Verlaine notes "I am writing without books (I no longer have any), and a more or less slight attack of gout prevents me from going to the libraries within reach. This is therefore absolutely sincere, crude, outspoken, scribbled in a sick-room between two crises and some cries, and it serves for nearly my sole distraction and diversion" (440).
4. Verlaine lectured in Oxford in the autumn of 1893. As noted in the *Oxford Magazine* for 29 November 1893,

    > Last Thursday [23 November 1893] a small number of enthusiasts met in the room behind Mr. Blackwell's shop to hear M. Verlaine lecture on "Contemporary French Poetry." Fortunately M. Verlaine was persuaded to deal more largely with his own work than with that of poets with whom Oxford men are but little acquainted. He practically gave an autobiography, illustrating the varied phases of his life, by reciting his own poems, intensely dramatic and pathetic alternately. "Le poète doit vivre beaucoup, vivre dans tous les sens." This was his text, his justification; and upon it he founded a lecture of great interest and originality. His audience was small—too small, but it thoroughly appreciated seeing and hearing the eminent French poet (106).

    Yeats was in Dublin at the time, but as the visit had been arranged by Frederick York Powell and Verlaine had stayed with Arthur Symons in London (Foster 1: 139), he doubtless received a full report of the lecture.
5. François Villon (ca. 1431–after 1463), the most autobiographical of the medieval French poets.
6. Yeats refers to "A Guitar Player" and to the description of the actress in "The Looking-Glass" above.
7. Bloomsbury is a district in London, near the British Museum; Connacht, a province in the west of Ireland.
8. In his 1899 note to "He mourns for the Change that has come upon Him and his Beloved and longs for the End of the World," Yeats

recalled a remark of 23 July 1827, from the *Table Talk* of the English poet and critic Samuel Taylor Coleridge (1772–1834): "The man's desire is for the woman; but the woman's desire is rarely other than for the desire of the man" (*P,* 601). *Table Talk, and The Rime of the Ancient Mariner, Christabel Etc.* (London: George Routledge, [1884]; O'Shea #406), 65.

9. *Le Diable boiteux* (1707; enlarged edition, 1726) by the French writer Alain-René Lesage (1668–1747), translated by Joseph Thomas as *Asmodeus, or the Devil upon Two Sticks* (London: J. C. Nimmo and Bain, 1881), includes this exchange: "'I heartily pity the poor fellow,' said Cleofas, 'for I find he loves in earnest.'—'Had he not,' replied the demon, 'she had been his own before now; but it is the frailty of that weak sex to prefer an acted passion to a real one.'—'That is a fraility,' says the student, 'into which they may naturally fall. A personated lover can assume all the graces, and avoid all the imperfections of the passion. Disquietudes, jealousies, and expostulations always accompany, but very ill recommend, a heart thoroughly enamoured'" (170–71).
10. In the Bible, the tree of life is found in the Garden of Eden (Genesis 2:9). The mythical phoenix is reborn from its ashes.

### The Praise of Old Wives' Tales

First appeared as "(7)" of "My Thoughts and my Second Thoughts" in the October 1906 issue of *The Gentleman's Magazine.* Yeats added the note in the 1912 *The Cutting of an Agate;* there were no other significant revisions in later printings.

1. References to the main characters in Cervantes's *Don Quixote,* Homer's *The Odyssey,* Shakespeare's *Hamlet* and *King Lear,* and Sophocles' *Oedipus Rex.*
2. Falstaff appears in two of Shakespeare's chronicle plays, *Henry IV,* part 1, and *Henry IV,* part 2, as well as in the comedy *The Merry Wives of Windsor.*
3. *War and Peace* (1863–69) by the Russian writer Count Lev Nikolaevich Tolstoy (1828–1910) is an epic novel of the Napoleonic invasion and the lives of three aristocratic families. Launcelot is one of the main characters in the Arthurian tales.

### The Play of Modern Manners

First appeared as "(8)" of "My Thoughts and my Second Thoughts" in the October 1906 issue of *The Gentleman's Magazine.* There were no significant revisions in later printings.

1. In *Hedda Gabler* (1890; first produced in London at the Vaudeville Theatre on 20 April 1891), Hedda has a vision of Lovborg "with vine-leaves in his hair—flushed and fearless." In *The Master Builder* (1892; first produced in London at the Trafalgar Square Theatre on 20 February 1893), Hilda remarks of Solness's singing that "It sounded like harps in the air."
2. At the end of Ibsen's *Little Eyolf* (1894; first produced in London at the Avenue Theatre on 23 November 1896), the Allmers hoist a flag to signal their new resolve to solve their marital problems.
3. The characteristics of the "well-made play" were developed primarily in the work of the French dramatist Eugène Scribe (1791–1861).

### Has the Drama of Contemporary Life a Root of its Own?

First appeared as "(9)" of "My Thoughts and my Second Thoughts" in the October 1906 issue of *The Gentleman's Magazine*. There were no significant revisions in later printings.

1. Yeats refers to Dr. Thomas Stockmann in Ibsen's *An Enemy of the People* (1882; first produced in London at the Haymarket Theatre on 14 June 1893) and the title character in Shakespeare's *Coriolanus*.
2. The Famine of 1845–48, caused by the failure of the potato crop, resulted in widespread death and emigration. Many of the participants in the Rebellion of 1798 against British rule were executed by hanging.

### Why the Blind Man in Ancient Times Was Made a Poet

First appeared as "(10)" of "My Thoughts and my Second Thoughts" in the October 1906 issue of *The Gentleman's Magazine*. Prior to the 1919 *The Cutting of an Agate*, the essay concluded " . . . Noah and Deucalion, and in Joshua's moon at Ascalon." There were no other significant revisions in later printings. For the biblical allusion to Joshua, see the book of Joshua 10:12–13: "Then spake Joshua to the Lord in the day when the Lord delivered up the Amorites before the children of Israel, and he said in the sight of Israel, Sun, stand thou still upon Gibeon; and thou, Moon, in the valley of Ajalon [also Ascalon or Askalon]. And the sun stood still, and the moon stayed, until the people had avenged themselves upon their enemies."

1. *The Iliad* and *The Odyssey* were epics by Homer; *The Aeneid*, by Virgil.
2. In *The Odyssey*, Odysseus is captured by the Cyclops but escapes by getting him drunk and blinding him. In *The Iliad*, Achilles sacks the kingdom of Lyrnessus, kills the king, and takes his widow, Briseis, as his prize.

3. François Villon (ca. 1431–after 1463), Paul Verlaine (1844–96), French poets. Both suffered from various "impediments," including Villon's criminal activities and Verlaine's imprisonment for shooting his protégé, Arthur Rimbaud (1854–91).
4. In *Adonais* (1821), Shelley writes that "Life, like a dome of many-coloured glass, / Stains the white radiance of Eternity, / Until Death tramples it to fragments" (Hutchinson, 443).
5. Augustus, Gaius Julius Caesar Octavianus (63 BC–AD 14), first Roman emperor.
6. In *Poetaster* (performed 1601; published 1602) by the English playwright Ben Jonson (1572?–1637), Caesar tells Gallus and Tibullus that "You both have virtues, shining through your shapes; / To shew your titles are not writ on posts, / Or hollow statues which the best men are, / Without Promethean stuffings reached from heaven!" (5.1.13–16). *The Works of Ben Jonson,* ed. Francis Cunningham, 3 vols. (London: Chatto and Windus, 1910–12; O'Shea #1033), 1:248.
7. Yeats mentions the Venetian Renaissance painter Tintoretto (1518–94) several times in *IGE* and *COA*; see, for example, "Certain Noble Plays of Japan," note 10 above.
8. Tintoretto's *Origin of the Milky Way* (ca. 1575) is in the National Gallery, London. In "Symbolism in Painting" above, Yeats criticized the picture as "Allegory without any Symbolism" and argued that it "is, apart from its fine painting, but a moment's amusement for our fancy."

   Yeats quotes the last line of act 3, scene 2, in Shakespeare's *King Lear* (performed 1606; published 1608). In act 5, scene 3, of Shakespeare's *King Richard III* (performed 1591; published 1597), the tents of Richmond (later Henry VII) and Richard III are placed onstage together.
9. *The Knight of the Burning Pestle* (performed 1607–8?; published 1613) is a comedy by the English playwright Francis Beaumont (1584–1616), although in Yeats's time it was generally thought to be a collaboration with the English playwright John Fletcher (1579–1625). Philip Carr (1874–1957), English drama critic and producer, attempted to revive Elizabethan and Jacobean plays in authentic productions. His staging of *The Knight of the Burning Pestle* was produced by the Mermaid Society at the Royalty in London on 14–19 November 1904, and 26 December 1904–4 January 1905; and by the Mermaid Repertory Company at the Great Queen Street in London on 18–20 May, 25 May, and 1 June 1905. Jasper, the apprentice of Venturewell, was played by the English actor King Fordham (1881–1922) in the first production and by the English actor Milton Rosmer (Arthur Milton Lunt, 1882–1971) in the second.
10. *Epicene, or The Silent Woman* (performed 1609–10; published 1616) by Ben Jonson was produced at the Great Queen Street on 8–13 May

1905, by the Mermaid Repertory Company. One of the journalists referred to is the English drama critic, writer, and caricaturist Max Beerbohm (1872–1956), who reviewed the play in *The Saturday Review* for 13 May 1905: "When Ben Jonson props up a dummy . . . for the sole purpose that a practical joke shall be played on it, I (as owing my duty to my readers) sit the play out; but smile I really cannot; and indeed, as the joke happens to be a barbarous one, even according to Elizabethan standard, I should be rather ashamed of smiling at it. . . . I shall make haste to forget 'The Silent Woman'. And so, I trust, will our very admirable Mermaid Society" (623–24). The commentary by E. F. S. ("Monocle") in *The Sketch* for 17 May 1905, also complained that the play "will not serve the practical politics of our stage" and that "it was wisely deemed necessary to emasculate its chief element of humour" (142).

In a letter to Lady Gregory on 18 May 1905, Yeats described *The Knight of the Burning Pestle* (see note 9 above) and *The Silent Woman* as "just such extravagant joyous comedy as we are trying to make."

11. Perhaps *Le Antichità di Ercolano,* engraved by Tommaso Piroli, 5 vols. (Rome, 1789–94). The eruption of Vesuvius in AD 79 buried the Italian towns of Herculaneum and Pompeii.
12. In Greek mythology, Perseus, son of Zeus and Danaë, rescues Andromeda from a sea monster and marries her. The engraving may be that in volume 3 of *Le Antichità di Ercolano* (1790), plate 19.
13. Both the biblical figure Noah and his family, like Deucalion (son of Prometheus and father of Helen) and his wife, Pyrrha, in Greek mythology, survive a massive flood.

### Concerning Saints and Artists

First published as "(11)" of "My Thoughts and my Second Thoughts" in the November 1906 issue of *The Gentleman's Magazine.* Prior to the 1912 *The Cutting of an Agate,* the essay concluded "immemorial impartiality and simpleness." The "woman in evening dress" was not accompanied by "two young girls," "her husband's sisters," until *Essays* (1924); the revised account conforms to that in "The Tragic Generation" (*Au,* 264–65).

1. In "The Tragic Generation," Yeats also noted that "I take hashish with some followers of the eighteenth-century mystic Saint-Martin" (*Au,* 264); the event occurred on 17 December 1896. Louis-Claude de Saint-Martin (1743–1803) was a French writer of occultism and mysticism. Martinism combined influences from Rosicrucianism, Swedenborg, Boehme, and, to some extent, a purely spiritual version of Roman Catholicism; it enjoyed a significant following in the nineteenth century (*Au,* 480 n.100).
2. The poet is untraced.

3. Max Simon Nordau (1849–1923) was a German writer best known for *Entartung* (*Degeneration,* 1892), which attempted to establish a relationship between genius and degeneracy.

### The Subject Matter of Drama

First published as "(12)" of "My Thoughts and my Second Thoughts" in the November 1906 issue of *The Gentleman's Magazine.* Prior to the 1912 *The Cutting of an Agate,* the last sentence read in part "what art moulds religion accepts." There were no significant revisions in later printings.

1. Ibsen died 23 May 1906. The obituary has not been traced.
2. Keats's *Endymion* was published in 1818. *Mary Magdalene at the Door of Simon the Pharisee* (1853–59) by Dante Gabriel Rossetti is in the Tate Gallery, London.
3. One of the "Proverbs of Hell" in *The Marriage of Heaven and Hell* (ca. 1790–93) (Ellis-Yeats 3; Erdman, 37).
4. Quotation untraced. In a letter to *The Leader* (Dublin) on 30 November 1907, Yeats noted, "I chose rather to follow those old rules of courtesy in which, as Balzac has said, we are all Conservatives" (*UP*2, 356).
5. Pierre Corneille (1606–84) and Jean Racine (1633–99), French classical playwrights. The Roman poet Virgil (70–19 BC) is Dante's guide in the *Inferno* and *Purgatorio* sections of *The Divine Comedy.* In the Bible, Peter's denial of Christ is accompanied by the crowing of a cock (see Matthew 26 and Luke 22).
6. Lough Derg is a religious site of pilgrimage associated with the legendary fast of Saint Patrick for forty days on Oiléan na Naomh, a lake-island in County Donegal.

### The Two Kinds of Asceticism

First published as "(13)" of "My Thoughts and my Second Thoughts" in the November 1906 issue of *The Gentleman's Magazine.* Prior to the 1919 *The Cutting of an Agate,* Yeats was less uncertain of a reference in the opening paragraph: "I am not quite sure of my memory, but I think that Mr. Ricketts has said in his book on the Prado . . ."

1. The sculpture of *Moses* by the Italian artist Michelangelo Buonarroti (1475–1564), in the Church of San Pietro in Vincoli (Saint Peter in Chains), Rome, was executed circa 1513–16. The Spanish artist Diego Rodríguez de Silva y Velásquez (1599–1660) was court painter to Philip IV (1605–65), king of Spain (not to his grandfather, Philip II, 1527–98). Velásquez made several portraits of the monarch: Yeats is

perhaps thinking of one of the two in the National Gallery in London, *Philip IV of Spain in Brown and Silver* (ca. 1631–32) or, more likely, *Philip IV of Spain* (ca. 1656). The National Portrait Gallery in London does have two portraits of *Philip II, King of Spain,* one after Titian (1555) and the other unattributed (ca. 1580).

2. Quotation untraced.
3. Charles Ricketts (1866–1931) was an English illustrator, designer, and painter. Commenting on Velásquez in *The Art of the Prado* (London: John Hamilton, 1907), Ricketts argued, "The young painter was in his attitude and aim the first of the moderns, waiting more humbly upon Nature, measuring her tones, analysing and selecting; his art is almost criticism, a noble criticism of what is to hand. Where the Renaissance had divined, remoulded, and created, Velasquez stood ready to measure and observe, not without emotion or power of selection; yet by the side of Rubens the creative draughtsman and creative colourist, he was but a student of art and nature, a recorder, a weaver, a man of unwearied watchfulness and tact" (159–60). James Abbot McNeill Whistler (1834–1903) was an American painter who moved between London and Paris; he also wrote a body of criticism on art, notably his *Mr. Whistler's Ten O'Clock* (1888). Hilaire-Germain-Edgar Degas (1834–1917) was a French painter.
4. In "To the Accuser Who is The God of This World," the epilogue to *For the Sexes: The Gates of Paradise* (ca. 1818), Blake refers to "The lost Travellers Dream under the Hill" (Ellis-Yeats 3: 63; Erdman, 269).

### In the Serpent's Mouth

First published as "(14)" of "My Thoughts and my Second Thoughts" in The November 1906 issue of *The Gentleman's Magazine.* Prior to the 1919 *The Cutting of an Agate,* the essay began "There is an old saying that God is a circle whose centre is everywhere. If that is true, the saint goes to the centre. . . ." There were no other significant revisions in later printings.

1. The concept of "God as a circle whose center is everywhere and whose circumference is nowhere" is a commonplace in many religious and mystical traditions.
2. Although best known for his writings on religion and for *The Idea of a University Defined and Illustrated* (1873), the English theologian John Henry, Cardinal Newman (1801–90), also published two novels (anonymously) and a body of sacred poems, including *Lyra Apostolica* (1836).
3. The symbol of the *ouroboros,* a snake eating its own tail, is common in many cultures and in occult tradition.

### The Black and the White Arrows

First published as "(15)" of "My Thoughts and my Second Thoughts" in The November 1906 issue of *The Gentleman's Magazine.* There were no significant revisions in later printings.

1. In his *Descriptive Catalogue* (1809), Blake argued that "The Ugly man represents the human reason" (Ellis-Yeats 2: 374; Erdman, 543).

### His Mistress's Eyebrows

First published as "(16)" of "My Thoughts and my Second Thoughts" in the November 1906 issue of *The Gentleman's Magazine.* There were no significant revisions in later printings.

1. Yeats was a student at the Metropolitan School of Art in Dublin from May 1884 to April 1886. The "older student" is perhaps John Hughes (1865–1941), later a well-known Irish sculptor (see *IDM,* 88).
2. Quotations from the obituary of Ibsen cited in "The Subject Matter of Drama" above.
3. The English writer Thomas Percy (1729–1811) published *Reliques of Ancient English Poetry,* a collection of ballads, sonnets, historical songs, and metrical romances, in three volumes in 1765. Coleridge's "The Rime of the Ancient Mariner" was first published in *Lyrical Ballads* (1798).

   Yeats refers to sculpture #1780 in the British Museum, a first-century BC Roman head of an athlete in a classisizing style. At this time the statue was displayed in the Third Graeco-Roman Room and was described as a Greek archaising work. Yeats refers to the same work in *The Trembling of the Veil* (1922), writing of Lionel Johnson that "He had the delicate strong features of a certain filleted head of a masterpiece in the British Museum, an archaistic Graeco-Roman copy of a masterpiece of the fourth century . . ." (*Au,* 184).
4. In Greek mythology, Jason and the Argonauts sail to Colchis to obtain the Golden Fleece, the magic fleece of a ram given by Hermes to Nephele, the wife of Athamas.

### The Tresses of the Hair

First published as "(17)" of "My Thoughts and my Second Thoughts" in the November 1906 issue of *The Gentleman's Magazine.* There were no significant revisions in later printings.

1. Hafiz (Shams ed-Din Muhammad, d. ca. 1388), the greatest of the Persian lyric poets. Although the concept is common in his work, the exact

passage has not been traced. A manuscript in the Yeats Papers headed "From Hafiz" reads in part "From unbeginning eternity my heart made a bargain with your ringlets [?] to unending eternity it will not be broken" (NLI, 30,049; SB, 1201593). Yeats may have later learned that the hair of the beloved in Hafiz's poetry is black, as in his 1930 diary he quotes the passage as simply "I made a bargain with that hair before the beginning of time" (*Ex,* 300).

*A Tower on the Apennines*

First published in *The Shanachie: An Irish Illustrated Quarterly* 2, no. 5 (Autumn 1907) under the title "Discoveries." There were no significant revisions in later printings.

1. Yeats visited Italy in May 1907 with Lady Gregory and her son, Robert. The Apennines is a mountain system that traverses the length of the Italian peninsula. San Sepolcro and Urbino are towns in central Italy.
2. As in "The Tree of Life" above, Yeats is quoting from a lecture that Verlaine gave at Oxford in November 1893.
3. In "Happy and Unhappy Theologians," first published in *The Speaker* for 15 February 1902, and included in the 1902 edition of *The Celtic Twilight,* Yeats ascribed this notion to a "Mayo woman": "Christ Himself was not only blessed, but perfect in all manly proportions in her eyes, so much do beauty and holiness go together in her thoughts. He alone of all men was exactly six feet high, all others are a little more or a little less" (*Myth,* 43). Yeats also notes in the 1902 version of *The Speckled Bird* that: "Christ, being the perfect man, had alone the perfect measurements. . . . It is an idea the people have" (*SB,* 75).
4. In ancient Greece, Delphi was the home of the supreme oracle; Eleusis was renowned for the mysteries celebrated in honor of Demeter and Persephone.

   The quotation has not been traced in the Irish ecclesiastic and missionary Saint Columbanus (543?–615). Yeats's poem "The Dancer at Cruachan and Cro-Patrick" (1932) begins "I, proclaiming that there is / Among birds or beasts or men, / One that is perfect or at peace . . ." (*P,* 272). In Yeats's introduction to Shri Purohit Swami's autobiography, *An Indian Monk* (1932), the quotation is ascribed to "Some Irish saint, whose name I have forgotten . . ." (*LE,* 133). The passage is also quoted without attribution in the 1937 introduction to the unpublished Scribner edition (*LE,* 207). Yeats's first use of the idea is in the 1902 version of *The Speckled Bird,* where in a vision Margaret hears it spoken by Jesus: "There is among the birds one that is perfect and among the fish one that is perfect and among the beasts one that is perfect, and I were not among men none would know the perfect, and the foundations of things would be broken up" (*SB,* 77).

### The Thinking of the Body

First published in *The Shanachie: An Irish Illustrated Quarterly* 2, no. 5 (Autumn 1907) under the title "Discoveries." There were no significant revisions in later printings.

1. The Venetian artist Antonio Canaletto, properly Canale (1697–1768), painted a series of views of Venice. The Flemish painter Frans Francken II (1581–1642) had studied in Italy. The specific paintings and the house have not been traced.
2. The *Winged Victory of Samothrace,* in the Louvre, is one of the finest extant Greek sculptures. The Parthenon, a temple sacred to the goddess Athena, is on the Acropolis in Athens. Most of its friezes are in the British Museum.
3. In "On Virgil" (ca. 1820), Blake claims that "Grecian is Mathematic Form / Gothic is Living Form / Mathematic Form is Eternal in the Reasoning Memory. Living Form is Eternal Existence" (Ellis-Yeats 3; Erdman, 270).
4. "The Ballad of Little Musgrave and Lady Barnard" is included in *Reliques of Ancient English Poetry* (1765) by the English writer and translator Thomas Percy (1729–1811). Lord Barnard discovers his wife and Little Musgrave in adultery and kills them both.
5. *The Book of the Courtier (Il libro del cortegiano,* 1528) by the Italian humanist Baldassare Castiglione (1478–1529) describes the aristocratic life at the court of Urbino in Italy. The duchess was Elisabeth Gonzaga (1471–1526), who had married Duke Guidobaldo in 1489; Lady Emilia was Emilia Pia (d. 1528), a widow since 1500 and her close companion.

### Religious Belief Necessary to Religious Art

First published in *The Shanachie: An Irish Illustrated Quarterly* 2, no. 5 (Autumn 1907) under the title "Discoveries." There were no significant revisions in later printings.

1. "Siren there / Winds her dizzy hair and sings," lines 27–28 of Dante Gabriel Rossetti's "Love's Nocturn" (1870), in *The Collected Works of Dante Gabriel Rossetti,* ed. William Michael Rossetti, 2 vols. (London: Ellis and Elvey, 1897; O'Shea #1789), 1:288.
2. Dante's *The Divine Comedy* (*La Divina Commedia*) was finished shortly before his death.
3. In "Shelley," originally a review of Edward Dowden's *The Life of Percy Bysshe Shelley* (1886) in the *Nineteenth Century* for January 1888 and then included in *Essays in Criticism: Second Series* (1888),

Arnold wrote of Shelley: "And in poetry, no less than in life, he is 'a beautiful and ineffectual angel, beating in the void his luminous wings in vain.'" The last phrase is in quotation marks because Arnold is citing his own earlier description of Shelley in an essay on Byron.

For the "one Star," see the extensive discussion of Shelley's star as representing both desire and Intellectual Beauty in "The Philosophy of Shelley's Poetry" above in the present edition.

4. *Endymion* was published in 1818.
5. Shelley's "Prince Athanase: A Fragment" was published in 1817. The title character roams the world searching for perfect love, "like lights & sounds, from haunted tower to tower" (line 69).
6. Yvette Guilbert (1865–1944) was a French singer and model, a favorite subject for the French artist Henri Toulouse-Lautrec (1864–1901). She performed at the Duke of York's Theatre in London on 8, 12–13, 15, 19–20, 22, 26–27, and 29 June 1906. Describing the first performance, the anonymous critic of *The Times* (London) complained of "a tendency to exaggerate, and especially in facial expressions. She 'made faces'—sometimes appropriate faces, . . . sometimes very inappropriate and inartistic faces . . ." (9 June 1906: 8).

## The Holy Places

First published in *The Shanachie: An Irish Illustrated Quarterly* 2, no. 5 (Autumn 1907) under the title "Discoveries." For the 1912 *The Cutting of an Agate,* Yeats made two important changes. In the earlier printings the penultimate sentence ended " . . . European mind that would not have been had Constantinople wall been built of better stone," referring to the conquest of the city in 1453 by Mohammed II (1429–81), who had constructed the largest cannons then known; and the essay concluded by invoking "Supernal Eden and the White Rose over all."

A note at the end of the essay reads

> These chapters are the last of a book called "Discoveries," Ben Jonson's old title, now printing at the Dun Emer Press. The sentence in the first chapter ["A Tower on the Apennines"] beginning "that dignity, . . . the perfection of form," is an incomplete quotation from Paul Verlaine, quoted in full in an earlier chapter ["The Tree of Life"]. His argument was that a man should put all of himself into his work, but without forgetting style, "that dignity."

Jonson's *Timber: or, Discoveries* (1640) was a commonplace book. The printing of *Discoveries* was completed on 12 September 1907; the volume was not published until 15 December 1907, perhaps so as not to precede the publication of *The Shanachie.*

1. The story of Cambuscan, king of Tartary, is included in Chaucer's *Canterbury Tales,* but in the unfinished "The Squire's Tale," not "The Miller's Tale." Cruachmaa, a hill near Tuam in County Galway, is the legendary home of Finnvarra, king of the fairies of Connacht; Olympus was the home of the supreme gods in ancient Greece.
2. Hesiod was a Greek epic poet of the eighth century BC, best known for his *Works and Days.*
3. Yeats thought of the Victorian novelist Charles Dickens (1812–70) as a realist and of the Romantic poet Percy Bysshe Shelley as an idealist.
4. Yeats admired the writer Walter Savage Landor (1775–1864) and compared him to Shelley again in his description of Phase 17 in *A Vision* (*AV-B,* 140–45).
5. One of Yeats's favorite quotations, from part 4, scene 2, of *Axël* (1890) by the French playwright Villiers de L'Isle-Adam (1838–89). Yeats saw a production of the play at the Théâtre de la Gaîté in Paris on 26 February 1894. Yeats uses the translation by Arthur Symons in "Villiers de L'Isle-Adam," *The Symbolist Movement in Literature* (London: William Heinemann, 1899; O'Shea #2068), 56.
6. Yeats refers to Shakespeare's *Antony and Cleopatra* (written 1606–7; published 1623) and *The Two Gentlemen of Verona* (written ca. 1592–93; published 1623). John Palaeologus VIII (1390–1448) was the penultimate Byzantine emperor. *King Cophetua and the Beggar Maid* (1884) is one of the best-known works by the English painter and designer Sir Edward Coley Burne-Jones (1833–98). The king resembles one of the depictions of John Palaeologus VIII in the *Journey of the Magi to Bethlehem* (1458–60), frescos in the Palazzo Medici-Riccardi in Florence by the Italian artist Benozzo Gozzoli (1420–97).
7. In Ptolemaic astronomy, the primum mobile is the outermost concentric sphere, carrying the spheres of the fixed stars and the planets in its daily revolution. Yeats refers to "supernal Eden" in a note to the 1900 version of *The Speckled Bird* (*SB,* 224). In *A Vision* (1925), Yeats cites "the Great Yellow Rose of the Paradiso" (p. 76), a reference to canto 30, line 113, of Dante's *Paradiso.*

## Preface to the First Edition of The Well of the Saints

First published in *The Well of the Saints. By J. M. Synge. With An Introduction by W. B. Yeats. Being Volume Four of Plays for an Irish Theatre* (London: A. H. Bullen, 1905). For the 1908 *Collected Works* (in which the essay is titled "Mr. Synge and His Plays"), Yeats revised the concept that Lady Gregory "had listened with somewhat different ears" to simply "with different ears." Prior to the 1919 *The Cutting of an Agate,* Yeats referred to preserving "the innocence of good art" rather than "the integrity of art." For *Essays* (1924), Yeats revised "why it is all, as it were, flat" to "why it is all like a decoration on a flat surface." There were no other significant revisions in later printings.

1. Yeats was staying at the Hôtel Corneille in Paris, when he met Synge on 21 December 1896. Yeats was never very adept at mathematics: "six years" should be nine years.
2. Yeats indicated that *The Secret Rose* was "in the press" as of 19 March 1896, although page proofs were not produced until early November 1896 (*CL2*, 15). The volume was eventually published on 5 April 1897.
3. This note was added in the 1919 edition of *The Cutting of an Agate.* Yeats extracted the Red Hanrahan stories from *The Secret Rose* (1897) and revised them with Lady Gregory's assistance as *Stories of Red Hanrahan* (1904). Yeats's reference that the stories were revised "Since writing" this essay is incorrect, as the revised text was in the press before 25 April 1904 (*CL3*, 586). Yeats also misdated the revision in *Early Poems and Stories* (1925), claiming that the stories were "rewritten in 1907 with Lady Gregory's help."
4. Yeats had visited the Aran Islands from 5 to 7 August 1896.
5. Sir Thomas Malory (ca. 1408–71) was the author of *Le Morte D'Arthur,* a cycle of Arthurian legends finished in 1470 and published in 1485.
6. Yeats refers to Lady Gregory's *Cuchulain of Muirthemne* (1902), *Gods and Fighting Men* (1904), and *Poets and Dreamers: Studies and Translations from the Irish* (1903).
7. *The Shadow of the Glen* was first produced (as *In the Shadow of the Glen*) by the Irish National Society at the Molesworth Hall, Dublin, 8 October 1903. In *The Splendid Years: Recollections of Maire Nic Shiubhlaigh* as told to Edward Kenny (Dublin: J. Duffy, 1955), the actress who played Nora Burke recalled

   > At first I found Synge's lines almost impossible to learn and deliver. Like the wandering ballad-singer I had to 'humor' them into a strange tune, changing the metre several times each minute. It was neither verse nor prose. The speeches had a musical lilt, absolutely different to anything I had heard before. Every passage brought some new difficulty and we would all stumble through the speeches until the tempo in which they were written was finally discovered. I found I had to break the sentences—which were uncommonly long—into sections, chanting them, slowly at first, then quickly as I became familiar with the words (42–43).

8. The plays referred to are *The Well of the Saints, Riders to the Sea,* and *The Shadow of the Glen.*

9. Founded in 1831 and intended to encourage religious harmony, the National Schools educated primarily the lower classes and grew steadily throughout the century.
10. The main characters in Shakespeare's *King Lear* (performed 1606; printed 1608) and Cervantes's *Don Quixote de la Mancha* (published in two parts in 1605 and 1615).
11. The first two plays have not been identified. The third play mentioned is *Die versunkene Glocke* (The Sunken Bell) (produced 1896; published 1897) by the German playwright Gerhart Hauptmann (1862–1946); Yeats owned a translation by Charles Henry Meltzer (New York: R. H. Russell, 1899; O'Shea #857). At the beginning of the play a wood sprite tells how he toppled a bell on its way to be installed in a mountain chapel (Yeats's "tower") down into a lake.
12. Yeats refers to Ibsen's *Emperor and Galilean* (*Keiser og Galilæer*), published in 1873 and the first of his plays to be translated into English (1876). The work was not performed until 1896 (and then not in its entirety). The quotation is from Blake's "Public Address" (1809–10): "Princes appear to me to be Fools Houses of Commons & Houses of Lords appear to me to be fools they seem to me to be something Else besides Human Life" (Erdman, 580).
13. Quotations presumably invented by Yeats.
14. Falstaff is a character in several plays by Shakespeare.
15. From "Oisin and Patrick" in Lady Gregory's *Gods and Fighting Men* (London: John Murray, 1904; O'Shea #795), 456.
16. In *The Shadow of the Glen,* Nora tells Michael, ". . . I was a hard child to please, and a hard girl to please, and it's a hard woman I am to please this day . . ." (*Plays* 1: 49). At the end of *The Well of the Saints,* Martin and Mary Doul choose to return to their blindness, Martin explaining, "I'm thinking it's a good right ourselves have to be sitting blind, hearing a soft wind turning round the little leaves of the spring and feeling the sun, and we not tormenting our souls with the sight of the grey days, and the holy men, and the dirty feet is trampling the world" (*Plays* 1: 149).
17. At the end of *The Shadow of the Glen,* Nora leaves her husband and her suitor and goes off with the tramp: ". . . you've a fine bit of talk, stranger, and it's with yourself I'll go" (*Plays* 1:57).
18. *The Well of the Saints* was first produced by the Irish National Society at the Abbey Theatre, Dublin, on 4 February 1905. The production was designed by the artist Pamela Colman ("Pixie") Smith (1878–1951) and Edith Craig (1869–1947), actress and costume designer and the sister of Gordon Craig.

## Preface to the First Edition of John M. Synge's Poems and Translations

First published as "John M. Synge" in *Poems and Translations by John M. Synge* (Churchtown, Dundrum: Cuala Press, 1909). For the 1912 *The Cutting of an Agate,* Yeats deleted the first part of section 2 (see appendix H). He also revised the quotation in the penultimate sentence of section 3 from "And what it is but desire of ardent life, like that of Usheen who cried 'tears down but not for God, but because Finn and the Fianna are not living,'" doubtless because the same quotation was used in the "Preface to the First Edition of *The Well of the Saints*" (see p. 220). See also note 12 below.

1. The quotation is derived not from the Neoplatonic philosopher Proclus (410?–485) but rather from the conclusion of the *Enneads* (6.9.11) of the Neoplatonic philosopher Plotinus (205?–270), which Yeats would have read in the translation by Thomas Taylor, as in *Select Works of Plotinus,* ed. G. R. S. Mead (London: George Bell, 1895; O'Shea #1595a): "This, therefore is the life of the Gods, and of divine and happy men, a liberation from all terrene concerns, a life unaccompanied with human pleasures, and a flight of the alone to the alone" (322).

   Yeats draws on Lionel Johnson's allusion to the same passage in the conclusion to his "The Dark Angel," *Poems* (London: Elkin Mathews, 1895; O'Shea #1020), 69:

   > Do what thou wilt, thou shall not so,
   > Dark Angel! triumph over me:
   > *Lonely, unto the Lone I go;*
   > *Divine, to the Divinity.*

   In his 1930 diary, Yeats noted that Plotinus "thought of man as re-absorbed into God's freedom as final reality" (*Ex,* 307).
2. Synge's *Poems and Translations* was published by the Cuala Press on 5 June 1909; Synge had died on 24 March 1909.
3. As Yeats indicated in his journal and in *The Death of Synge and Other Passages from an Old Diary* (1928), the friend was Lady Gregory, the sister Elizabeth Corbet ("Lolly") Yeats (1868–1940) (*Mem,* 200; *Au,* 375).
4. In *A Vision* (1937), Yeats explains that the *Daimon* ("divine spirit" in Greek) is the "ultimate self" of man and that it "contains within it, co-existing in its eternal moment, all the events of our life, all that we have known of other lives" (*AV-B* 83, 192). Other descriptions offered include the "buried self" (*Au,* 279) and the "permanent self" (*Ex,* 331). After his trial and conviction, Socrates was forced to drink the poison hemlock. In the entry in his journal just before he learned of

Synge's death, Yeats noted, "One's daimon is silent as was that of Socrates before his own death" (*Mem,* 199).

5. In the preface, dated December 1908, Synge claims that: "The poems which follow were written at different times during the last sixteen or seventeen years, most of them before the views just stated, with which they have little to do, had come into my head." Among the "views just stated" was the axiom that "before verse can be human again it must learn to be brutal" (*Poems,* xxxvi).
6. "Epitaph" cannot be dated precisely but is believed to have been written before 1900 (*Poems,* 31). Robin Skelton, the editor of *Poems,* describes "On an Anniversary" as "undatable" and comments: "According to Yeats this poem is an early one. Stylistically, it appears to have more in common with the poems written after 1900 than with those before. This may, however, be due to Synge's revision of an earlier version now lost" (*Poems,* 33).
7. Yeats refers to the Greek poet and soldier Archilochus (ca. seventh century BC), whose canon in fact consists of some three hundred items (all or almost all fragments) and about forty paraphrases and indirect quotations. The quotation is a translation of fragment 1. A literal version would be "I am a follower of my Lord Enyalios and I know the Muses' lovely gift," Enyalios being the cult name of the war god Ares. Yeats's source for the translation or the misstatement as to the extant canon has not been traced.
8. Yeats later translated and expanded the Latin epitaph on the tomb of Swift in Saint Patrick's Cathedral, Dublin, as "Swift's Epitaph" (*P,* 250):

   Swift has sailed into his rest;
   Savage indignation there
   Cannot lacerate his breast.
   Imitate him you dare,
   World-besotted traveller; he
   Served human liberty.

   The allegory was *Gulliver's Travels* (1726).
9. In "A Question," written in 1908 and implicitly addressed to Molly Allgood ("Maire O'Neill"), Synge suggests that her attitude toward the mourners at his funeral would be to "rave and rend them with your teeth" (*Poems,* 64).
10. Yeats recorded this statement in his journal shortly after Synge's death and included it in *The Death of Synge:* "In Paris Synge once said to me, 'We should unite stoicism, asceticism and ecstasy. Two of them have often come together, but the three never" (*Mem,* 202; *Au,* 376).
11. "The Passing of the Shee" begins "Adieu, sweet Angus, Maeve and Fand, / Ye plumed yet skinny Shee" (*Poems,* 38).

12. This title has not been traced, although Irish literature offers numerous laments by Oisin over the death of the Fenians.

    In the 1909 edition the next sentence read "The two blind people of *The Well of the Saints* arise from the loveliness of their dreams to a foul reality; and that woman of *The Shadow of the Glen* who 'was a hard girl to please' and is 'a hard woman to please' has to spend her life between a drunken tramp, an angry hateful husband, a young milksop, and a man who goes mad upon the hills." The quotations are from a speech by Nora Burke (*Plays* 1: 49). Yeats deleted the sentence on the galley proofs of the 1912 *The Cutting of an Agate* (Berg).
13. Fionn or Finn, hero of the Ossianic Cycle of Irish mythology, is described as "golden salmon of the sea, clean hawk of the air" in "Oisin's Laments" in Lady Gregory's *Gods and Fighting Men* (London: John Murray, 1904; O'Shea #795), 457.
14. From a speech by Martin Doul in act 2 of *The Well of the Saints* (*Plays* 1: 113).
15. Synge was engaged to the Irish actress Molly Allgood ("Maire O'Neill," 1887–1952). She told Yeats on 2 April 1909 that Synge knew for a year that he was dying.

## J. M. Synge and the Ireland of His Time

First published in *Synge and the Ireland of His Time by William Butler Yeats with a Note Concerning a Walk Through Connemara with Him by Jack Butler Yeats* (Churchtown, Dundrum: Cuala Press, 1911). For the 1912 *The Cutting of an Agate,* Yeats subsumed part 7 (which began "Synge seemed by nature unfit to think a political thought") into part 6; he also revised the last sentence of the original section 6 from "But it became possible to live when" to "But life became sweet again when." For *Essays* (1924), Yeats deleted what had been the second sentence of part 4: "An old man with an academic appointment, who was a leader in the attack upon Synge, sees in the 11th century romance of Deirdre a re-telling of the first five act tragedy outside the classical languages, and this tragedy from his description of it was certainly written on the Elizabethan model; while an allusion to a copper boat, a marvel of magic like Cinderella's slipper, persuades him that the ancient Irish had forestalled the modern dockyards in the making of metal ships." In a popular fairy tale, Cinderella alone can wear the glass slipper. The "old man" is untraced but is perhaps Robert Atkinson (see note 58 below).

Yeats did not reprint the preface to the 1911 volume (see appendix I).

1. Hosted by Sir Herbert Grierson (1866–1960), professor of English at the University of Aberdeen, Scotland, Yeats's lecture on Irish affairs included a commentary on Synge's *The Playboy of the Western World.*
2. *The Playboy of the Western World* opened at the Abbey Theatre on

26 January 1907, and ran until 2 February 1907. At the first performance, Christy Mahon's reference to "drifts of chosen females standing in their shifts [underclothes]" (*Plays* 2: 167) provoked considerable hissing. Many of the reviewers attacked the play as a libel upon the Irish character. Only about eighty people were present for the second performance on 28 January 1907, but the protests continued during the week, with the police being called in to maintain order. An open debate was held at the Abbey Theatre on 4 February 1907, with Yeats vigorously defending Synge.

The popular poet and patriot Thomas Osborne Davis (1814–45) was one of the founders of the Young Ireland movement. Much of his verse was published in *The Spirit of the Nation* (1843–44; enlarged edition, 1845); a fiftieth edition was published in 1870. Charles Joseph Kickham (1828–82) was a novelist, poet, and political activist, best known for his novel *Knocknagow* (1873).

3. Synge's *The Shadow of the Glen* was produced (as *In the Shadow of the Glen*) by the Irish National Theatre Society at the Molesworth Hall, Dublin, on 8 October 1903. The opposition to the play was led by the nationalist politician Arthur Griffith (1871–1922) in his *United Irishman,* arguing in the issue for 17 October 1903 that the play was "a corrupt version of the old-world libel on womankind—the 'Widow of Ephesus'" (1), a story best known from the version included in the *Satyricon* by the Roman writer Petronius Arbiter (first century A.D.). The reference to "a writer of the Roman decadence" has not been traced but is consistent with Griffith's views. When the controversy flared up again in 1905, Griffith described the story as "invented by the wits of decadent Greece" and Petronius as "the pander of Nero" (*The United Irishman* [4 February 1905]: 1).
4. The opening sentences of John Mitchel's *Jail Journal; or, Five Years in British Prisons* (1854; 2nd ed. [New York: P. M. Haverty, 1868]) reads as follows: "England has been left in possession not only of the soil of Ireland, with all that grows and lives thereon, to her own use, but in possession of the world's ear also. She may pour into it what tale she will; and all mankind will believe her" (9).
5. "The Memory of the Dead" (1843) is a famous ballad on the 1798 Rebellion by the Irish writer and social philosopher John Kells Ingram (1823–1907), beginning "Who fears to speak of Ninety-Eight?"
6. Founded in 1831 and intended to encourage religious harmony, the National Schools educated primarily the lower classes and grew steadily throughout the century.
7. The English politician and soldier Oliver Cromwell (1599–1658) was lord protector of Britain and Ireland from the end of 1653 until his death; especially in Ireland, he is remembered for his harsh treatment of Irish Catholics. Invasions by Danes and Norsemen began in 795; at various times they controlled much of the country until their defeat at

the Battle of Clontarf in 1014. The "Penal Laws," enacted in the years following the defeat of the Catholic James II (1633–1701) by the Protestant William of Orange (1650–1702) at the Battle of the Boyne in 1690, severely restricted the rights of Catholics. The rebellion by the United Irishmen in 1798 against British control of Ireland was short-lived and unsuccessful. The catastrophic Great Famine of 1845–48, caused by the failure of the potato crop, resulted in widespread death as well as emigration.

8. The concept of "recklessness" (*sprezzatura*) is important in *The Book of the Courtier* (*Il libro del cortegiano,* 1528) by the Italian humanist Baldassare Castiglione (1478–1529). Translated into English as early as 1561, the work was much admired by Yeats. In *The Bounty of Sweden* (1924), Yeats recalled that "twenty years" ago Lady Gregory "read out to me at the end of each day's work Castiglione's commendations and descriptions of the Court of Urbino . . ." (*Au,* 400). The Greek philosopher Democritus (ca. 460–ca. 370 BC) envisioned Truth as a goddess lying at the bottom of a well.
9. Yeats quarreled with the Dublin barrister and famed orator John Francis Taylor (1850–1902) about the literary quality of the poetry of the Young Ireland movement. Yeats once commented that "I braved Taylor again and again as one might a savage animal as a test of courage, but always found him worse than my expectation" (*Au,* 101). Both were disciples of the Fenian patriot John O'Leary (1830–1907).
10. *Owen Roe O'Neill* (London: T. Fisher Unwin, 1896; O'Shea #2112). The legendary O'Neill (Eoghan Ruadh O'Neill, 1584?–1649) was commander of the native Irish forces in the Confederation of Kilkenny.
11. In chapter 2 of his epic *Jerusalem* (1804), Blake argued that "Art & Science cannot exist but by Naked Beauty displayd" (Ellis-Yeats 3; Erdman, 179).
12. In Christian tradition, the archangel Gabriel is usually depicted as sounding the trumpet that heralds the Last Judgment. The archangel Michael is usually depicted as the warrior angel, the conqueror of Satan. Yeats also refers to Michael's trumpet in "The Happy Townland" (*P,* 84).
13. The *Book of Invasions* (*Lebor Gabála Érenn*), a medieval chronicle, recounts the legendary history of Ireland and its inhabitants from the Creation to the twelfth century.
14. In 1805 Blake produced a set of drawings for *The Grave* (1743) by the Scottish poet Robert Blair (1699–1764), one of which was "The Soul Exploring the Recesses of the Grave." The Amazons were women warriors in Greek mythology.
15. Yeats met Synge in Paris on 21 December 1896. On 1 January 1897, Yeats and Synge attended the inaugural meeting of *L'Association Irlandaise,* the Paris branch of the Young Ireland Society, founded by Maud Gonne with Yeats's assistance.

16. The productions of the Irish National Theatre Society in 1903 and in January–February 1904 were held in the Molesworth Hall, Dublin. Synge composed the scenario in response to a request from the Irish actor Frank J. Fay (1870–1931) in a letter of 5 April 1904, responding on 10 April 1904, "By all means have 98 plays—I will do one if I can . . ." (*Letters* 1: 82). For the scenario and a fragment of dialogue, see "Bride and Kathleen: A Play of '98" (*Plays* 1: 215–17). François Rabelais (ca. 1494–ca. 1553) was a French physician, humanist, and satirist, renowned for his earthiness and comic inventiveness.
17. Henry VIII (1491–1547), king of England from 1509, broke with Pope Clement VII (1478–1534) and the Catholic Church and established the Church of England. Elizabeth I (1533–1603), daughter of Henry VIII and Anne Boleyn (1507?–36), became queen of England in 1558, on the death of her half sister, Mary I (1516–58), daughter of Henry VIII and Catharine of Aragon (1485–1536). Mary, queen of Scots (Mary Stuart, 1542–87), who was Catholic, was next in line to the throne of England after the children of Henry VIII; she was accused of plotting against Elizabeth and was beheaded on 8 February 1587.
18. In a memorandum dictated to Lady Gregory on 2 December 1906, Yeats proposed that the Abbey should include "selections from foreign masterpieces" in its repertoire and that the "final object" of the theatrical movement should be "to create in this country a National Theatre something after the Continental pattern" (*TB,* 169). In a letter to Lady Gregory on 13 December 1906, Synge argued, "To turn this movement now . . . into an executive movement for the production of a great number of foreign plays of many types would be, I cannot but think, a disastrous policy" and urged that "we keep our movement local" (*TB,* 177, 178).
19. From Synge's early lyric "Prelude" (written 1890s; revised 1907; published 1909) (*Poems,* 32).
20. In Greek mythology, Hephaestus, the god of fire and metalwork, was lame. In 1897 Synge suffered the first attack of the Hodgkin's disease which would eventually cause his death.
21. In a letter to Yeats about his unpublished works on 4 May 1908, Synge noted that he did not want "my bad things printed rashly,—especially a morbid thing about a mad fiddler in Paris, which I hate" (*Letters,* 2: 155). Synge was referring to "Étude Morbide" (*Prose,* 25–36). See also appendix I.
22. The first poem is "Rendez-vous Manqué dans la rue Racine" (written 1898; revised 1906–8) (*Poems,* 21), the second "(The Conviction)" (written 1896; revised ca. 1907) (*Poems,* 19). Neither was published by Synge.
23. The Irish novelist Maria Edgeworth (1767–1849) published her best-known work, *Castle Rackrent,* in 1800.
24. From the first stanza of the seventh song in *Astrophel and Stella* (ca. 1582) by the English poet, statesman, and soldier Sir Philip Sidney

(1554–86), in *The Poems of Sir Philip Sidney,* ed. John Drinkwater (London: George Routledge, 1910; O'Shea #1917), 174; correctly "fools, if."

25. The English writer George Henry Borrow (1803–81) traveled in Spain as a distributor of Bibles for the British and Foreign Bible Society from 1835–40, describing his adventures in *The Bible in Spain; or, The Journeys, Adventures, and Imprisonments of an Englishman in an Attempt to Circulate the Scriptures in the Peninsula* (London: John Murray, 1843). Yeats is apparently misremembering Borrow's "Honour to Ireland and her 'hundred thousand welcomes!' Her fields have long been the greenest in the world; her daughters the fairest; her sons the bravest and most eloquent. May they never cease to be so!" (277).
26. The remote Aran Islands (Inishmoore, Inishmann, and Inisheer) are off the coast of County Galway; Synge first visited them in 1898. The Blasket Islands, also remote, are off the coast of County Kerry; Synge visited them in 1905.
27. From part 4 of *The Aran Islands* (Dublin: Maunsel, 1907; O'Shea #2071) (*Prose,* 162), Synge's account of his stays there.
28. The Black Forest is a mountainous district in southwest Germany. Synge, who was an accomplished violinist, had traveled in Germany in 1893–94 and again in 1894.
29. From part 1 of *The Aran Islands* (*Prose,* 103).
30. Quotation untraced. The other playwright was presumably the Irish playwright and novelist Norreys Connell (Conal Holmes O'Connell O'Riordan, 1874–1948), whose *Time: A Passing Phantasy in One Act* was produced at the Abbey Theatre, 1 April 1909.
31. *Riders to the Sea* was first published in 1903 and first produced by the Irish National Theatre Society at the Molesworth Hall, Dublin, on 25 February 1904.
32. *The Well of the Saints* was first published in 1905 and first produced at the Abbey Theatre on 4 February 1905. In *The Aran Islands,* Yeats's "couple" are in fact "near relations who lived side by side and often quarrelled about trifles": "little boys and girls were running along the lanes towards the scene of the quarrel as eagerly as if they were going to a race-course" (*Prose,* 152).
33. From part 4 of *The Aran Islands* (*Prose,* 163). Christy Mahon is the main character in *The Playboy of the Western World,* first published in 1907 and first produced at the Abbey Theatre on 26 January 1907. Martin Doul is the main character in *The Well of the Saints.*
34. Source untraced. In "The Poetry of Sir Samuel Ferguson" (*The Irish Fireside,* 9 August 1886), Yeats noted that "'The food of the passions is bitter, the food of the spirit is sweet,' say the wise Indians" (*EAR,* 9); and in "If I Were Four-and-Twenty" (*Irish Statesman,* 23–30 August 1919), he remarked that "'The passionate-minded,' says an Indian saying, 'love bitter food'" (*LE,* 40).

35. In *The Aran Islands,* the old man is Pat Dirane (*Prose,* 100).
36. Synge discussed his single visit to the Blasket Islands in "In West Kerry," published in three installments in *The Shanachie* in 1907. However, that published version did not include the account here of "a middle-aged and simple-minded man from an inland district," Yeats's "lame pensioner." Yeats also omits the conclusion of the anecdote: "I was walking about my room in extravagant rage when I heard his step on the stairs, and he told me he had been out for a ride only" (*Prose,* 259).
37. In a notebook of circa 1895–98, Synge commented that "Lyrics can be written by people who are immature, drama cannot. There is little great lyrical poetry. Dramatic literature is relatively more mature. . . . Lyrical art is the art of national adolescence" (*Prose,* 350).
38. Synge began *The Tinker's Wedding* in 1902, but it was not published until the end of 1907 and was not produced in his lifetime. See *Plays* 2: 1–49 and 271–92 for the revisions. There is no evidence that he altered the play to make it less popular. In a letter to James Paterson on 27 March 1908, Synge explained, "I am sending you a little play which I wrote some years ago but did not publish till the other day—The Tinkers Wedding—as you will understand we think it too dangerous to put on in the Abbey—it is founded on a real incident that happened in Wicklow a few years ago" (*Letters* 2: 145).

The play about the Irish tragic heroine Deirdre was unfinished at the time of Synge's death; it was first produced at the Abbey Theatre on 13 January 1910. Yeats's preface to *Deirdre of the Sorrows: A Play* (Churchtown, Dundrum: Cuala Press, 1910) is dated "April, 1910":

> It was Synge's practice to write many complete versions of a play, distinguishing them with letters, and running half through the alphabet before he finished. He read me a version of this play the year before his death, and would have made several more always altering and enriching. He felt that the story, as he had told it, required a grotesque element mixed into its lyrical melancholy to give contrast and create an impression of solidity, and had begun this mixing with the character of Owen, who would have had some part in the first act also, where he was to have entered Lavarcham's cottage with Conchubor. Conchubor would have taken a knife from his belt to cut himself free from threads of silk that caught in brooch or pin as he leant over Deirdre's embroidery frame, and forgotten this knife behind him. Owen was to have found it and stolen it. Synge asked that either I or Lady Gregory should write some few words to make this possible, but after writing in a passage we were little satisfied and thought it better to have the play performed, as it is printed here, with no

word of ours. When Owen killed himself in the second act, he was to have done it with Conchubor's knife. He did not speak to me of any other alteration, but it is probable that he would have altered till the structure had become as strong and varied as in his other plays; and had he lived to do that, 'Deirdre of the Sorrows' would have been his masterwork, so much beauty is there in its course, and such wild nobleness in its end, and so poignant is an emotion and wisdom that were his own preparation for death.

39. From part 3 of *The Aran Islands* (*Prose,* 138).
40. The crowd on the train for the commemoration of the Irish political leader Charles Stewart Parnell (1846–91), who had died eight years earlier on 8 October 1891, is described in part 2 of *The Aran Islands* (*Prose,* 122–24). The mother cursing her son who had become a bailiff occurs in part 1 (*Prose,* 92); the old woman keening at the death of her son occurs in part 4 (*Prose,* 160–61).
41. From part 1 of *The Aran Islands* (*Prose,* 99–100).
42. The opening of Sophocles' tragedy *Oedipus Rex* in the 1887 translation by Sir Richard Jebb reads "My children, latest-born wards of old Cadmus." Yeats's version in *Sophocles' King Oedipus* (1928) offers "Children, descendants of Cadmus."
43. The blinding of Gloucester by Cornwall occurs in act 3, scene 7, of Shakespeare's tragedy *King Lear* (performed 1606; published 1608). Euphuism involves an excessive use of certain stylistic devices, including antithesis and allusion; the term derives from *Euphues* (1578–80) by the English writer John Lyly (1554?–1606).
44. The Belgian dramatist and essayist Maurice Maeterlinck (1862–1949), who wrote in French, was a leading figure in the symbolist movement.
45. In his "Argument with Whisky," the Gaelic poet Anthony Raftery (Antoine Raiftearai, ca. 1784–1835) claims, "And the world knows it's not for love of what I drink, but for love of the people that do be near me," as translated by Lady Gregory in her *Poets and Dreamers: Studies and Translations from the Irish* (Dublin: Hodges, Figgis / New York: Scribner 's, 1903; O'Shea #807), 23.
46. From the speeches of Mary Byrne in act 1 of *The Tinker's Wedding* (*Plays* 2: 23, 25, 27).
47. François Villon (ca. 1431–after 1463), an important autobiographical poet of medieval France. The Spanish novelist and dramatist Miguel de Cervantes Saavedra (1547–1616) is best known for his novel *Don Quixote de la Mancha* (published in two parts in 1605 and 1615).
48. Lady Gregory's *Cuchulain of Muirthemne* was published in 1902. Yeats refers to *Love Songs of Connacht* (1893) by the Irish writer, scholar, and cultural activist Douglas Hyde (1860–1949).

49. *Of the Imitation of Christ,* a mystical work, is traditionally ascribed to the German monk Thomas à Kempis (1380–1471). Synge mentions the work in *Étude Morbide,* written about 1899 and partly revised circa 1907 (*Prose,* 30–31).
50. From "An Old Woman's Lamentations" (written 1908; published 1909) (*Poems,* 80).
51. Swinburne's version of "An Old Woman's Lamentations" is "The Complaint of the Fair Armouress," which refers to "Eyes wide apart and keen of sight, / With subtle skill in the amorous air" ("Translations from the French of François Villon," *The Bibelot* 5 [July 1899]: 231; O'Shea #165). Synge's translation from Petrarch is "He understands the great cruelty of Death" (written 1907; published 1909) (*Poems,* 93).
52. Matthew Arnold withdrew his dramatic poem *Empedocles on Etna,* published anonymously in 1852, a year later, arguing in the preface to *Poems* (1853) that the work was "poetically faulty" because in it "the suffering finds no vent in action" and "a continuous state of mental distress is prolonged, unrelieved by incident, hope, or resistance."
53. Shelley's lyric "The Cloud" was published in 1820.
54. From Synge's preface to *The Playboy of the Western World* (*Plays* 2: 53). Geesala is a small Irish-speaking village on Blacksod Bay, County Mayo; Carraroe is an Irish-speaking district in Connemara, County Galway; Dingle Bay is in County Kerry.
55. The fanciful Irish account of the Battle of Clontarf, fought on 23 April 1014 between the forces of Brian Boru (Brian Bórumha, 941–1014), king of Munster, and the forces of the Leinstermen and their Viking allies, is found in *The War of the Gaedhil with the Gaill* (*Cogadh Gaedhel re Gallaibh,* ca. 1100–1110); the contrasting Norse version is included in the thirteenth-century *Brennu-Njálssaga* (*The Saga of Burnt Njal*).
56. Based on the opening stanza of "The Worms, the Children, and the Devil" in Douglas Hyde's *Religious Songs of Connacht* (Dublin: M. H. Gill and Son / London: T. Fisher Unwin, 1906), 1:51. Yeats had included another version as a song in the play *The Unicorn from the Stars* (1908), written in collaboration with Lady Gregory (*Pl,* 230).
57. In part 1 of *The Aran Islands,* Synge also recounts this story of parricide and escape (*Prose,* 95).
58. The Gaelic League, founded in 1893, promoted the learning and speaking of Irish. The "old Fellow" was perhaps Robert Atkinson (1839–1908), professor of Romance Languages, Sanskrit, and Comparative Philology at Trinity College, Dublin, who argued against the teaching of Gaelic. Yeats discussed Atkinson in "The Academic Class and the Agrarian Revolution" (*UP2,* 148–52).
59. Perhaps a reference to Thoth, the Egyptian god of writing, who is often equated with the Greek god Hermes (Mercury in Roman mythology), usually depicted with winged sandals.

60. From a speech by Naisi in act 1 of *Deirdre of the Sorrows* (*Plays* 2: 205).
61. Adam is the first man in the Bible; the account in Genesis 2–3 makes several references to vision and seeing.
62. Villon mortally wounded a priest during a student riot in 1455, and at Christmas 1456, he was part of a group that burgled the Collège de Navarre. Yeats often contrasted Villon with Dante.
63. Cino da Pistoia (Guittoncino dei Sinibaldi, or Sighibuldi, 1270–1337?), Italian jurist and poet, was a friend of Dante and Petrarch. Some of his poems were translated by Dante Gabriel Rossetti, who was likely Yeats's source for his statement about Cino's view of Dante. In "The Phases of the Moon," Yeats also refers to "True song, though speech: 'mine author sung it me'" (*P*, 165).
64. The famous Benedictine abbey at Mont-Saint-Michel, off the Normandy coast, was founded in 708. The church sits atop a series of six buildings constructed from 1203–28. Yeats visited Mont-Saint-Michel with Maud Gonne and her family on 11–12 May 1910.
65. Yeats also wrote his father, John Butler Yeats, on 19 May 1910 that "the Pope had to make a special edict to keep them [the monks] from drinking out of cups standing upon feet of gold, and carrying jewelled studded daggers in their belts." However, no such ordinances have been traced.
66. The "dead language" is Latin, the traditional language of the Roman Catholic Church.

## John Shawe-Taylor

First published in *The Observer* (2 July 1911) as "John Shawe-Taylor. An Appreciation." For the 1912 *The Cutting of an Agate,* Yeats revised the end of the fourth paragraph, originally "ten, and their simplicity and their triumph, which has always something of miracle, are the bewilderment of their associates." Yeats also revised the final paragraph for the 1919 *The Cutting of an Agate,* adding "young" before "man's moral genius" and recasting the last sentence from "And yet it may be that, although he died in early manhood, his work was finished, that the sudden flash of his mind was of those things that come but seldom in a lifetime, and that his name is as much a part of history as though he had lived through many laborious years."

1. The portrait in the Dublin Municipal Gallery of Captain John Shawe-Taylor (1866–1911), a nephew of Lady Gregory and a County Galway magistrate, was painted in 1908 by the English artist Sir William Orpen (1878–1931).
2. Queenstown (now Cobh) is in County Cork. In *Hugh Lane's Life and Achievement, with some account of the Dublin galleries* (London: John Murray, 1921; O'Shea #796), Lady Gregory recalls Yeats recount-

ing this anecdote in the course of a conversation about Shawe-Taylor and Hugh Lane:

> And Yeats in talking to me of these two, said: "Hugh said to me once, 'Everybody loves John, he has personality, but I am only an eye and a brain.' Yet his talent was just as much rooted in character as John Shawe-Taylor's. To begin with there was the same audacity. You will remember how when John was returning from America the boat reached Queenstown in a storm and he was the only man who left it in a tender, he had leaped into it before the ships were swept apart" (72).

3. On 2 September 1902, Shawe-Taylor published a letter in the Dublin papers calling for a conference to settle the Irish Land Question. The conference was held in December 1902, and its recommendations were incorporated into the Wyndham Land Act of 1903, which offered favorable terms for tenants to buy and inducements for landlords to sell, and so led to the redistribution of land in Ireland.
4. In Tennyson's "Sir Galahad," included in *English Idyls, and Other Poems* (1842), Galahad claims, "My strength is as the strength of ten, / Because my heart is pure." *The Works of Alfred Tennyson*, vol. 3, *Locksley Hall, and Other Poems* (London: Henry S. King, 1874; O'Shea #2115), 89.
5. Synge had died on 24 March 1909.

## *Art and Ideas*

First published in parts in *The New Weekly* for 20 and 27 June 1914. Yeats made numerous revisions for the next printing in *Essays* (1924). He revised the opening sentence from "I was at the Tate Galleries last summer to see the early Millais's . . ."; he also revised the last sentence of section 1, originally "when the adventure of uncommitted life and still dreaming sex changes all to romance." Section 2 originally began "I ask myself," and the first paragraph ended "but who can deny that he was not quite respectable." The second paragraph originally began "I developed these principles to the rejection of elaborate description, that I might not envy the painter's business, and, indeed, I was always seeking for some art or science that I might be rid of it"; and the reference to Balzac was in the text rather than in a footnote. The second paragraph of section 3 originally read "altar, that we may not forget the little round of poetical duties and imitations . . ." Several other sentences in the essay were recast.

1. Paintings in the Tate Gallery in London by the English painter Sir John Everett Millais (1826–96)—*Ophelia* (1851–52)—and the English poet and painter Dante Gabriel Rossetti (1828–82)—*Mary Magdalene*

*Leaving the House of Feasting* (1857) and probably *The Girlhood of Mary Virgin* (1849), though possibly *Ecce Ancilla Domini* (1850).

2. Richard Wilson (1714–82), English landscape painter; Frank Huddlestone Potter, English painter (1845–87).
3. *Little Dormouse,* given to the Tate Gallery by Lady Tate in 1908. In *Reveries over Childhood and Youth* (1916), Yeats also recalled that "Potter's exquisite *Dormouse,* now in the Tate Gallery, hung in our house for years" (*Au,* 67).
4. The Pre-Raphaelite movement, named for its admiration for art preceding that of the Italian painter Raphael (1483–1520), began in England in the late 1840s but had run its course by the time of Yeats's childhood.
5. *The Pilgrim's Progress* (1678–84) is an influential prose allegory by the English writer John Bunyan (1628–88). The Danish writer Hans Christian Andersen (1805–75) was famous for his fairy and folk stories.
6. Yeats is referring to a character in *Les Petits Bourgeois* (1854) by the French novelist Honoré de Balzac (1799–1850), translated as *The Middle Classes* by Clara Bell in the Temple edition (1901; O'Shea #96), but the character is a man, not a woman. In describing the dinner parties at the Thuillier home, Balzac notes of Louis-Jerôme Thuillier, "in mind and manners, Thuillier had relapsed into the porter's son; he would repeat his father's jests, and at last, in his declining years, allowed some of the mud of his earlier youth to come to the surface" (55–56). *King Cophetua and the Beggar Maid* (1884) is one of the best-known works by the English painter and designer Sir Edward Coley Burne-Jones (1833–98).
7. Quotation untraced in the work of the German philosopher Arthur Schopenhauer (1788–1860). In 1857–58 a group of artists organized by Dante Gabriel Rossetti, including William Morris and the English painter and designer Sir Edward Coley Burne-Jones (1833–98), set out to decorate the new Oxford University Museum and Union Society debating hall with murals. However, the project proved more complicated than expected, and only the Union was completed. Worse, since Rossetti failed to prepare the walls properly, the paint flaked off. The murals were further damaged by the gas lighting.
8. The essay by the English writer Arthur Henry Hallam (1811–33) on the work of Tennyson, "On Some of the Characteristics of Modern Poetry, and on the Lyrical Poems of Alfred Tennyson," was published in *The Englishman's Magazine* for August 1831. In his journal for 9 March 1909, Yeats noted, "The doctrine of what the younger Hallam called the Aesthetic School was expounded in his essay on Tennyson, and when I was a boy the unimportance of subject was a canon" (*Au,* 361).
9. Presumably Mary Magdalene, traditionally associated with the repentant prostitute who anointed the feet of Jesus, and the Virgin Mary.

10. In *Pierre Grassou* (1840), Balzac indicates that Grassou became famous for his 1829 *Death-toilet of a Chouan, condemned to execution in 1809*. Balzac comments that although the picture was clearly second-rate, it was much admired. The Chouans were a counterrevolutionary peasant movement, active from early in the Revolution of 1789–99 until 1815.
11. Yeats refers to a series of poems addressed to Saint Teresa of Avila (1515–82), a Spanish writer and mystic, by the English poet Richard Crashaw (1612–49); and to the French poet François Villon (ca. 1431–after 1463).
12. Algernon Charles Swinburne (1837–1909), English poet known for his skillful metrics and provocative expansion of subject matter. Academic form refers to art that emphasizes a technically rigid adherence to form and line over sentiment, inspiration, or color; often used as a pejorative, indicating that technique takes precedence over innovation and expression.
13. Yeats refers to the Rhymers' Club, a group of writers and artists who met at the Cheshire Cheese, a pub in London, in the 1890s. The American painter James Abbott McNeill Whistler (1834–1903) lived in London from 1859 to 1891 and returned there in 1902; his dictum has not been traced.
14. In the Bible, Joseph, the Virgin Mary, and Jesus flee to Egypt to escape the decree by Herod the Great for the death of infants aged two or below. The province of Connacht in the west of Ireland includes the counties of Mayo, Sligo, Leitrim, Roscommon, and Galway; Connemara is a region in County Galway. Many of Yeats's early essays urge the use of Irish materials, but this particular recommendation has not been traced. For Yeats's criticism of *Prometheus Unbound,* see both "The Philosophy of Shelley's Poetry" in *IGE* above and *"Prometheus Unbound"* in *LE*.
15. Saint Brendan (fl. 580) is best known for the popular tale of his journey westward to wonderful islands, *Navigatio Sancti Brendani* (Voyage of Saint Brendan), composed possibly as early as the eighth and not later than the tenth century. The Connemara chapel is Saint Brendan's in Loughrea, County Galway, discussed by Yeats in the second paragraph of "Prophet, Priest and King" (in *Discoveries* above). Augustus John (1878–1961) was an English painter and a friend of Yeats. Neither the quotation nor the Phallic Temple has been traced.
16. The Temple of Jupiter Ammon, a ram-shaped god worshipped by ancient Libyan desert tribes that later became synonymous with the Egyptian supreme god Amun, was located in the oasis at Siwa and was described by William George Browne in *Travels in Africa, Egypt and Syria* (1799), supposedly the first European to visit the site. The Romans rechristened the god Jupiter Ammon.
17. There was considerable debate about Rossetti's attitude toward reli-

gion. In his *Recollections of Dante Gabriel Rossetti* (London: Elliot Stock, 1882), T. Hall Caine devotes part of a chapter to Rossetti's Catholicism, claiming that Rossetti in his later life "was by religious bias of nature a monk of the middle ages" (141). However, that claim is refuted by William Michael Rossetti in *Dante Gabriel Rossetti: His Family-Letters with a Memoir,* 2 vols. (London: Ellis and Elvey, 1895), noting that his brother "may indeed have been so by 'bias,' but clearly not by implicit belief" (1:382). But William Michael Rossetti does claim that his brother came to "believe in a future life" in the closing years of his life (1:380–81). Modern biographical work on Rossetti tends to dispute this claim altogether.

Caine and William Michael Rossetti also disagree about Dante Gabriel Rossetti's dislike of Wordsworth. Caine argues that Rossetti believed Wordsworth was too concerned with treating nature philosophically, rather than appreciating or loving nature, and thus thought that Wordsworth's poetry lacked a desired "vital lyric impulse" (148–51). William Michael Rossetti, while not denying that the comment was made, plays down the intensity of the supposed dislike, suggesting that Caine "was concerned with minor details" instead of the entire truth of Dante Gabriel Rossetti's critical views (1:359).

18. Yeats draws on a quotation from the sketchbook of the English artist Samuel Palmer (1805–81) in A. H. Palmer, *The Life and Letters of Samuel Palmer* (London: Seeley, 1892), 16: "Excess is the essential vivifying spirit, vital spark, embalming spice . . . of the finest art. Be ever saying to yourself 'Labour after the excess of excellence'" (ellipsis in original). Yeats drew on the same passage for "Palmer's phrase" in "Under Ben Bulben": "Prepared a rest for the people of God" (*P,* 335).
19. In the Bible, Abraham is the progenitor of the Hebrews and the founder of Judaism.
20. Guillaume de Lorris (fl. thirteenth century) was the author of the first 4,058 lines of the allegorical romance *Roman de la Rose.* The first 1,705 lines of the Middle English translation are usually attributed to Chaucer.
21. In "Gods in Exile," the German poet and essayist Heinrich Heine (1797–1856) recounts the story of a fisherman/ferryman at Tyrol who ferried a group of monks across the lake at every autumnal equinox for seven years. In the seventh year, overtaken by the mystery of the monks, he followed them to a "wide forest-glade which he has never before seen," where there were half-naked men and women covered in flowers. When the monks disrobe, the first two were balding, fat, middle-aged men; but the third was revealed as a "marvelously beautiful youth" almost feminine in appearance—and the women "caressed him with wild enthusiasm." Heine comments that "a most cultured and well-informed reader" "would only give way to a slight volup-

tuous shudder, an aesthetic awe, at sight of this pale assemblage of graceful phantoms, who have risen from their monumental sarcophagi, or from their hiding-places amid the ruins of ancient temples, to perform once more their ancient, joyous, divine service; once more, with sport and merry-making, to celebrate the triumphal march of the divine liberator, the Saviour of the senses; to dance once more the merry dance of paganism, the *can-can* of the antique world—to dance it without any hypocritical disguise, without fear of the interference of the police of a spiritualistic morality, with the wild abandonment of the old days, shouting, exulting, rapturous. Evoe Bacche!" *The Prose Writing of Heinrich Heine,* ed. Havelock Ellis (London: Walter Scott, 1897), 270–74. Yeats knew the English physician and writer Henry Havelock Ellis (1859–1939) and may have heard the story directly from him.

22. Yeats refers to Shelley's *The Revolt of Islam* (1818), Wordsworth's *The Excursion* (1814), *Gebir* (1798) by the English poet Walter Savage Landor (1775–1864), Tennyson's *The Idylls of the King* (1859–85), and Browning's *The Ring and the Book* (1868–69).
23. Swinburne's "Faustine" and "Dolores (Notre-Dame des Sept Douleurs)" were included in his *Poems and Ballads* (1866).
24. Matthew Arnold withdrew his dramatic poem *Empedocles on Etna,* published anonymously in 1852, a year later, arguing in the preface to *Poems* (1853) that the work was "poetically faulty" because in it "the suffering finds no vent in action" and "a continuous state of mental distress is prolonged, unrelieved by incident, hope, or resistance." His "Sohrab and Rustum" was also included in the 1853 volume.
25. Works by Shakespeare and Dante, respectively.
26. In his journal for 9 February 1909, Yeats refers to "that fall into the circumference the mystics talk of" (*Au,* 355). Although the quotation has not been traced, it is a common idea in mystical tradition that man's loss of unity with God moves him from the center to the circumference, God being a circle whose center is everywhere but whose circumference is nowhere.

    The only photograph of a painting by the French artist Paul Gauguin (1848–1903) known to have been owned by Yeats is *Three Tahitians* (also known as *Conversation in Tahiti,* 1897 or 1899). This does not correspond very well with Yeats's description, as one of the three figures is a boy and none wears a crown of lilies (though there are flowers of some sort in the hair of one of the girls). Yeats had seen some Gauguin paintings in the Post-Impressionist exhibition at the United Arts Club in Dublin on 27 January 1911 (a small selection from a London exhibition, "Manet and the Post-Impressionists," Grafton Galleries, 8 November 1910–15 January 1911). He told Lady Gregory on 1 February 1911, "There is an exhibition of the principle post-impressionist pictures here at the arts club. I find seeing them as I do more constantly they grow on me greatly. I am buying some larger photographs, through Mrs. Duncan who brought the collection over" (Berg Collection). Ann Saddlemyer notes in *Becoming George: The Life of Mrs. W. B. Yeats* (Oxford and New York: Oxford University Press, 2002), "It was probably now [October 1936] that he brought home with him a large reproduction on canvas of Paul Gauguin's *Ta Matete* which they hung in the dining room over the fireplace" (515). As one of the girls in that painting (*The Market,* 1892) is wearing a crown of flowers (though whether of lilies is an open question), it is possible that one of the 1911 photographs was of *Ta Matete* and that it is the one mentioned in "Art and Ideas." The original painting is in the Kunstmuseum in Basel.

27. Rajput painting flourished in northern India from roughly 1500 to 1900; it became well known in the West only with the publication in 1916 of A. K. Coomaraswamy's two-volume *Rajput Painting* (Oxford University Press). Yeats was acquainted with Coomaraswamy, inviting him to dinner and in an unpublished letter of [21?] June 1913 telling him "I greatly admire your work," probably referring to his *Art and Swadeshi* (Madras: Ganesh, 1912), reviewed by Ezra Pound in *Poetry* 2, no. 6 (September 1913): 226–27. Coomaraswamy and his family dined with Yeats on 27 June 1913. In a letter to Lady Gregory on 17 August 1913 or thereabouts, Yeats noted, "I am finishing an essay for Coomaraswamy which I think good," almost surely a reference to "Art and Ideas." The Rajput paintings, which have not been traced, were most likely in Coomaraswamy's collection. Lovers on a rooftop is a relatively common motif in Rajput painting, especially those from the Kangra region.

    The Chinese painting is possibly the diptych entitled *The Sage in the Forest* in *Painting in the Far East* (1908) by Yeats's friend the English writer Laurence Binyon (1869–1943). Yeats owned a copy of the second edition (London: Edward Arnold, 1913; O'Shea #194), where the diptych is reproduced as plate 21.

## Edmund Spenser

This essay first appeared as the introduction to *Poems of Spenser: Selected and with an Introduction by W. B. Yeats* (Edinburgh: T. C. and E. C. Jack, 1906). In January 1902, Yeats wrote to Lady Gregory, "I have had a letter from an Edinburgh publisher asking me to edit a book of selections from 'Spenser' for £35. It is good pay & I am writing to ask when it will be wanted. I may do it if I have not to do it at once. I have a good deal to say about Spenser but tremble at the thought of reading his six books" (*CL*3, 148). Yeats accepted the assignment and worked on it throughout 1902, completing a first draft of the introduction by 22 October, when he called it "a somewhat elaborate essay," but did not finish it until the last day of 1902, when he told Lady Gregory that he had "Just dictated last word of Spenser" (*CL3*, 240, 291). The next week he wrote to her that "It is all founded now on a single idea—the contrast between Anglo-French England & Anglo[-] Saxon England"; but ten days later he offered the disconcerting news that the publishers had sent him £20 on account but "they say that owing to the delay of several authors about the sending in of MSS. They have had 'to reconsider' the series or the publication I forget which and that they cannot publish for some time" (*CL3*, 294, 302). In the event, T. C. and E. C. Jack did not publish *Poems of Spenser* until October 1906 and Yeats revised the essay as late as March of that year. There were no major changes after 1906 but several minor ones, including identifying the author of "Oh, deep, dissembling heart, born to great weal or woe of thy country" as William Camden (1551–1623) rather than simply "an English historian," and the addition of Yeats's footnote to section 1 in 1924 for *Essays* and to section 9 in 1908 for the *Collected Works*. In preparing his essay and edition, Yeats used and annotated extensively the five-volume *Works of Edmund Spenser,* ed. J. Payne Collier (London: Bell and Daldy, 1862; O'Shea #1978), presented to him by Lady Gregory; that edition has been used in the notes below, indicated as "Collier." For more information, see George Bornstein, "The Making of Yeats's Spenser," in *Poetic Remaking: The Art of Browning, Yeats, and Pound* (University Park: Pennsylvania State University Press, 1988), 97–105.

1. Lancashire is a county in northwestern England. Spenser writes that his family descended from "An house of auncient fame" in "Prothalamion," line 131 (Collier 5:261); "belonging to" should not be in quotation marks. The home estate of the Spensers (also Spencers) is Althorp, in Northamptonshire.
2. Lodovico Ariosto (1474–1533) and Torquato Tasso (1544–95) were two of the most important poets of the Italian Renaissance. Ariosto is best known for his epic about the medieval hero Roland, *Orlando Furioso*. Tasso, whose work also directly influenced Spenser, is best known for his *Gerusalemme Liberata*.
3. Sir Thomas Malory (ca. 1408–71) wrote *Le Morte D'Arthur,* widely considered the finest medieval prose collection of Arthurian romance. He was a member of parliament in 1445 and spent the final twenty years of his life in prison while working on his masterpiece. Minstrels were professional performers of medieval lyric or narrative poetry; the term is sometimes applied to the troubadours of medieval Provence or the minnesingers and Meistersingers of the German courts.
4. Victor Hugo (1802–85) was the leading French Romantic novelist of his day and author of *Les Misérables* (1862), among other works.
5. Though an ancient and illustrious university, Cambridge was in something of a decline when Spenser matriculated in Pembroke College in 1569. The Italian scholar and poet Francesco Petrarca (Petrarch),

1304–74, was a major shaper of the European Renaissance and gave his name to what we call the Petrarchan sonnet. Spenser translated canzone 323 from Petrarch's *Rime sparse* in 1569 and republished it as *The Visions of Petrarch* in *Complaints* (1591). Joachim Du Bellay (1522–60) was a French poet and contemporary of Ronsard. Spenser published an unrhymed translation of his *Songe* along with the Petrarch in 1569, and later translated Du Bellay's sonnet sequence *Les Antiquités de Rome* (*Ruins of Rome*).

6. Paul Verlaine (1844–96) was a leading French symbolist poet who influenced Yeats (see *Au,* 261, for Yeats's sketch of him). The Belgian symbolist poet Émile Verhaeren (1855–1916) was an important exponent of free verse. The earlier French poet Pierre de Ronsard (1524?–85) was a contemporary of Du Bellay and leader of the Pléiade, a group of sixteenth-century French poets who drew on the Greek and Roman classics as models.
7. Spenser's *Shepheards Calendar* (1579) was Spenser's first independent publication. It consists of twelve eclogues, one for each month, together with considerable paratextual material. Hobbinol is a character in the *Shepheards Calendar* modeled on Gabriel Harvey (ca. 1550–1631), a fellow of Pembroke Hall who became Spenser's mentor and longtime friend. Harvey came from the town of Saffron Walden, in Essex.
8. *The Faerie Queene* is Spenser's greatest work, a long epic of which three books were published in 1590 (1589 Old Style) and three more in 1596. By the *Nine Muses,* Yeats presumably means Spenser's "Complaint: The Tears of the Muses," from his *Complaints,* which Collier prints as "The Tears of the Nine Muses"; but it is possible that Yeats intends rather a more general contrast between the folk-derived figure of the Faerie Queen and the classical Muses. Yeats's source for this information was a letter from Gabriel Harvey to Spenser that includes the following remarks: "I will not stand greatly with you in your own matters. If so be the *Faery Queen* be fairer in your eye than the Nine Muses, and Hobgoblin runne away with the garland from Apollo, mark what I say . . ." (Collier, 1:xlvi). The same page refers to a lost work of Spenser called "Nine Comedies."
9. John Milton (1608–74) wrote in a headnote to his epic poem *Paradise Lost:* "The measure is English heroic verse without rhyme, as that of Homer in Greek, and of Virgil in Latin; rhyme being no necessary adjunct or true ornament of poem or good verse, in longer works especially, but the invention of a barbarous age, to set off wretched matter and lame metre; graced indeed since by the use of some famous modern poets, carried away by custom, but much to their own vexation, hindrance, and constraint to express many things otherwise, and for the most part worse than else they would have expressed them." *John Milton,* the Oxford Authors series, ed. Stephen Orgel and Jonathan Goldberg (Oxford and New York: Oxford University Press,

1991), 355. Yeats had a copy of *Paradise Lost* with illustrations by Blake in his library (O'Shea #1321), but its publication date of 1906 makes it unlikely, though just barely possible for the composition of the present essay.

10. Spenser included a poem titled "Iambicum Trimetrum" in a letter to Harvey printed in 1580 but written several years earlier. It begins, "Unhappy verse, the witness of my unhappy state" (Collier 1:clxii); in Yeats's quotation, for "for thy" read "of thy" and for "to my love" read "unto my love."
11. From Keats's *Isabella; or, The Pot of Basil,* lines 324–26: "Thinking on rugged hours and fruitless toil, / We put our eyes into a pillowy cleft, / And see the spangly gloom froth up and boil." See *The Poems of John Keats,* ed. Jack Stillinger (Cambridge, MA: Harvard University Press, 1978), 257.
12. Yeats quotes the first nine lines of "Iambicum Trimetrum." (See note 10 above.)
13. See *The Shepheards Calendar,* "April," lines 25–28: "But now from me hys madding mynd is starte, / And woes the Widdowes daughter of the glenne; / So nowe fayre Rosalind hath bredde hys smart; / So now his frend is changed for a frenne" (Collier 1:44). In the poem Colin is in love with Rosalind, whose actual identity remains uncertain. The poem's own gloss to "January" states that "*Rosalinde,* is also a feigned name, which, being wel ordered, wil bewray the verie name of hys love and mistresse" (Collier 1:20). The "College friend" is the person identified as "E. K." in *The Shepheards Calendar.* He is credited with writing the prefatory epistle to Harvey, the "general argument," the glossary, and the explanatory notes for the first edition. J. Payne Collier writes, "We are now in a position to be able to assert pretty distinctly that they were all contributed by Edward Kirke" (Collier 1:xxiv). Scholars currently remain skeptical of a definite attribution and besides Kirke have also suggested Gabriel Harvey and even Spenser himself.
14. Menalcas is a rival suitor for Rosalind in *The Shepheards Calendar.*
15. Robert Dudley (1532?–88) was the first Earl of Leicester and a favorite courtier of Elizabeth I. Sir Philip Sidney (1554–86) became an Elizabethan prototype of the accomplished gentleman, skilled in literature, politics, and war. Both were leaders of the Elizabethan political faction that favored aggressive foreign intervention on behalf of Protestant interests.
16. The English Renaissance playwrights Christopher Marlowe (1564–93) and William Shakespeare (1564–1616) were thus slightly younger than Spenser (1552?–99), and Ben Jonson (1572?–1637) was another decade younger still.
17. Yeats quotes from Spenser's poem *The Ruines of Time,* lines 216–17: "He now is gone, the whiles the Foxe is crept / Into the hole, the

which the Badger swept" (Collier 4:303). The passage was a favorite of Yeats, who invoked it in "The Municipal Gallery Re-visited": "And now that end has come I have not wept; / No fox can foul the lair the badger swept. / (An image out of Spenser and the common tongue.)" (*P*, 328).

18. Kenilworth is a castle and town in north Warwickshire and was the country estate of Robert Dudley, Earl of Leicester. A pamphlet written by the pseudonymous "Robert Laneham" (thought to be William Patten) describes the "festivals" to which Yeats refers, a series of entertainments put on by the Earl of Leicester for Queen Elizabeth when she visited Kenilworth in 1575. The pamphlet influenced Walter Scott's 1821 novel *Kenilworth,* with its description of those festivals.
19. In 1580 Spenser became the private secretary to Lord Arthur Grey de Wilton (1536–93), who served as lord deputy of Ireland from 1580 to 1582.
20. Spenser's castle in Ireland, Kilcolman Castle, is located roughly halfway between the cities of Limerick and Cork in County Cork. The Fitzgerald earldom of Desmond played an important role in the Desmond Rebellions of 1569–73 and 1579–83 against Tudor centralization in Ireland. Yeats may have in mind particularly the eighth earl, Thomas Fitzgerald (d. 1477), who was executed for treason at Drogheda.
21. The Aubeg is a small river flowing past Kilcolman Castle. Spenser writes of it as "Mulla mine, whose waves I whilom taught to weep," in *The Faerie Queene,* book 4 canto 11 (Collier 3:287). "Old Father Mole," who numbers Mulla among his daughters, is mentioned several times in Spenser's poetry, including *Faerie Queene,* book 7, canto 6 (the "Mutability Cantos"): "Amongst the which there was a Nymph that hight / Molanna; daughter of old Father Mole, / And sister unto Mulla faire and bright" (Collier 4:255). The Ballyvaughan Hills are in the nearby Burren region of County Clare. The fourteen lines come from Spenser's poem "Colin Clout's Come Home Again" (Collier 5:42), Spenser.'s autobiographical eclogue based on his visit with Sir Walter Raleigh to London and the court of Elizabeth in 1589.
22. Spenser's only lengthy piece of prose, his *View of the Present State of Ireland,* defended harsh Tudor measures in Ireland and made suggestions for dealing with Irish resistance. Artegall is the Knight of Justice and hero of book 5 of *The Faerie Queene,* where the Iron Man serves as his instrument for finding and punishing malefactors.
23. For Spenser's first return to England and his poem "Colin Clout's Come Home Again," see note 21 above. His later return for the publication of the second installment of the three books of *The Faerie Queene* took place in 1596–97.
24. The Elizabethan writer, courtier, and adventurer Sir Walter Raleigh (1554–1618) also served in the retinue of Lord Grey de Wilton in Ireland and met Spenser there; they became friends and neighbors.

William Cecil, Lord Burleigh (1520–98), served as lord treasurer under Queen Elizabeth and her chief minister. First recorded by Thomas Birch in his three-volume 1751 edition of *The Faerie Queene* (London: Printed for J. Brindley and S. Wright), 1:xii, Burleigh's famous deprecation of a grant to Spenser as "All that [or this] for a song" is widely known. He and Spenser were antagonists, and Spenser's description of him as a "rugged forehead" occurs in the first stanza of the preface to book 4 of *The Faerie Queene:* "The rugged forehead, that with grave foresight / Welds kingdomes causes and affaires of state, / My looser rimes (I wote) doth sharply wite / For praising love as I have done of late, / And magnifying lovers deare debate" (Collier 3:831).

25. The "fair woman" was Elizabeth Boyle (d. 1622), whom Spenser married on 11 June 1594. She was a cousin of Richard Boyle (1566–1643), who established the family in Ireland. Spenser's *Amoretti* is a unified sequence of eighty-nine sonnets in tribute to her. The *Epithalamiun* (derived from a Greek phrase meaning "before the marriage chamber") is a poem of twenty-three stanzas and an envoy also in tribute to her; it and the sonnets were first published together in 1594. The passage in the sixth book of *The Faerie Queene* where Colin Clout pipes to the Graces comes from canto 10, especially stanzas 15–16 (Collier 4:196). The three Graces in Greek myth are Aglaia (splendor or elevation), Euphrosyne (mirth), and Thalia (abundance).

26. *Two Cantos of Mutabilitie* are usually read as the fragmentary book 7 of *The Faerie Queene.* The phrase "the wandering companies that keep the wood" may derive from the following passage about a hypothetical Irish rebel from *A View of the Present State of Ireland:* "the wood is his house against all weathers, and his mantle is his couch to slepe in. Therein he wrappeth himself round, and coucheth himselfe strongly against the gnates which in that countrey doe more annoy the naked rebels, whilst they keepe the woods . . ." (Collier 5:359).

27. Lough Swilly, located in Donegal, is in fact not a lough but an estuary thirty miles long. Red Hugh is Hugh O'Donnell or Aodh Ruadh Ó Domhnaill (1572–1602), who in 1587 was lured by an invitation to drink on a ship at Rathmullen and imprisoned four years in Birmingham Tower of Dublin Castle. The earls of Tir Conaill were an Irish clan consisting most notably of members of the O'Donnell and Talbot families.

28. Hugh O'Neill (ca. 1550–1616) was the second Earl of Tyrone and last inaugurated O'Neill; he won the battle at Yellow Ford in 1598 but was defeated at Kinsale and surrendered at Mellifont in 1603. The Elizabethan historian William Camden (1551–1623) described O'Neill in book 4 of *The Historie of the Most Renowned and Victorious Princesse Elizabeth, Late Queene of England* (London: Benjamin Fisher, 1630), 23: "much knowledge hee had in Military skill and a

minde most profound to dissemble: insomuch, as some did then foretell, that hee was borne to the very great good or hurt of *Ireland*."

29. J. Payne Collier quotes Ben Jonson's phrase in his "Life of Spenser" (Collier 1:cl); for "of" read "for."
30. For Spenser's poem on the Nine Muses, see note 8 above. "Whether on Ida's shady brow" is the first line of Blake's "To the Muses" (Ellis-Yeats 3: 29; Erdman, 417).
31. Shakespeare's *Richard III* was first acted in 1592–93, his *Richard II*, in 1595, and his *Romeo and Juliet*, also in 1595. All the plays of Christopher Marlowe (1564–93) had also been acted by that time.
32. Spenser died in 1599 and was buried near Chaucer in Westminster Abbey. The story of the poets at his funeral casting their pens into his grave derives from William Camden (see note 28 above); Collier retells it and speculates that one of the poets may have been Ben Jonson (Collier 1:cxlvi).
33. Yeats refers here to the aftermath of the Norman Conquest after William the Conqueror's victory at the Battle of Hastings in 1066. The Angevins were the royal dynasty that began in the twelfth century with Henry II (reigned 1154–89) and his immediate successors, Richard I and John; they were called the Angevin kings because Henry's father was their Count of Anjou.
34. "Marprelate pamphlets" refer to a controversy associated with the pen name Martin Marprelate, pseudonymous author of seven pamphlets published in 1588–89 that satirized the bishops of the Church of England and championed Presbyterianism.
35. "Lollards" is a pejorative term for religious heretics applied in fourteenth-century England to the Wycliffites. Yeats then contrasts two contemporary poets: Geoffrey Chaucer (ca. 1343–1400) at the king's court at Westminster with William Langland (1330?–1400?), author of *Piers Plowman*, at Saint Paul's Cathedral in London.
36. Bunyan (1628–88) wrote a large portion of *The Pilgrim's Progress* while in prison in 1676. In it the Delectable Mountains are within sight of the Celestial City. See John Bunyan, *The Pilgrim's Progress from This World to That Which is to Come*, ed. James Blanton Wharey, rev. Roger Sharrock (Oxford: Clarendon Press, 1960), 119.
37. The doctrines of the ancient Greek philosopher Plato (ca. 427–ca. 348 BC) were rediscovered and popularized in the Renaissance by Italian philosophers in the Florentine courts, especially Marisilio Ficino (1433–99) and Pico della Mirandola (1463–94).
38. For the connection between beautiful soul and beautiful body, see Spenser's "Hymne in Honour of Beautie," lines 127–140:

    So every spirit, as it is most pure,
    And hath in it the more of heavenly light,

So it the fairer body doth procure
To habit in, and it more fairely dight
With chearefull grace and amiable sight:
For of the soule the bodie forme doth take;
For soule is forme, and doth the bodie make.

Therefore where ever that thou doest behold
A comely corpse, with beautie faire endewed,
Know this for certaine, that the same doth hold
A beauteous soule, with fair conditions thewed,
Fit to receive the seede of vertue strewed;
For all that faire is, is by nature good:
That is a signe to know the gentle blood (Collier 5:200).

39. For the woman named Wisdom or Beauty, see "An Hymne on Heavenly Beautie," for instance, lines 183ff: "There in his bosome Sapience doth sit . . ." (Collier 5:223). The seraphim and cherubim are ranks of angels in Judeo-Christian tradition; Venus and Adonis are famous lovers from classical tradition.

40. For Yeats's views on Shelley's "worship of Intellectual Beauty," see his essay "The Philosophy of Shelley's Poetry" above. Shelley wrote a "Hymn to Intellectual Beauty" (Hutchinson, 529).

41. Yeats's comments here follow the letter to Sir Walter Raleigh that Spenser attached to *The Faerie Queene* as an explanation of the poem. There he writes, "I chose the historye of King Arthur, as most fitte for the excellency of his person. . . . in the person of Prince Arthure I sette forth magnificence in particular; which virtue, for that (according to Aristotle and the rest) it is the perfection of all the rest, and conteineth in it them all, therefore in the whole course I mention the deedes of Arthur applyable to that verture . . . But of the xii. Other vertures, I make xii. Other knights the patrones, for the more variety of the history" (Collier 1:148–49).

42. Calidor, the Knight of Courtesy, appears in book 6 of *The Faerie Queene,* cantos 1–3 and 9–12. His great antagonist is the Blatant Beast, identified with Puritanism but also with the misuse of language in general.

43. The author of the first section of *The Romance of the Rose,* a medieval allegory about courtly love, was Guillaume de Lorris (fl. thirteenth century).

44. Emerson refers to Shakespeare as "master of the revels to mankind" in his essay "Shakespeare; or, the Poet," in Ralph Waldo Emerson, *Essays and Lectures* (New York: Library of America, 1983), 725.

45. Dante, *Paradiso,* canto 3. Like most English-speaking poets from Coleridge up to his own day, Yeats read Dante in Cary's translation. See *The Vision; or, Hell, Purgatory, and Paradise of Dante Alighieri,*

trans. Henry F. Cary (London and New York: Frederick Warne and Co., 1890; O'Shea #476), 224: "in his will is our tranquility." Among nineteenth-century translations, Henry Wadsworth Longfellow's comes closest to Yeats's wording in his translation of *The Divine Comedy* (Boston and New York: Houghton-Mifflin, 1867), 502: "his will is our peace." The sentence from Thomas à Kempis (1380–1471) comes from *De Imitatione Christi* (*Of the Imitation of Christ*), book 1, chapter 3: "He to whom the Eternal Word speaketh, is delivered from a world of unnecessary conceptions" (London: Griffith Farran Okeden & Welsh, n.d. but 1880s), 5. The original Latin reads, "Cui aeternum Verbum loquitur, a multis opinionibus expeditur." Hamlet refers to the bare bodkin in his famous "To be, or not to be" soliloquy, *Hamlet,* act 3, scene 1 (Shakespeare 1706).

46. The English poet laureate receives a stipend for being an officer of the Royal Household and would originally perform such duties as writing court odes. In 1616 Ben Jonson was the first poet awarded these duties, but John Dryden became the first to officially hold the title of poet laureate in 1668.

47. In *The Faerie Queene,* Phaedria is the figure of Immodest Mirth whom Guyon meets on her Idle Lake in the second book. Acrasia is the enchantress in the same book; she presides over the Bower of Bliss. "La Belle Dame Sans Merci" is a ballad by Keats in which the Belle Dame similarly creates a distracting paradise for the knight. The line "perilous seas in faery lands forlorn" comes from Keats's "Ode to a Nightingale," *The Poems of John Keats,* ed. Jack Stillinger (Cambridge, MA: Harvard University Press, 1978), 371. *Water of the Wondrous Isles* is the title of an 1897 novel by William Morris mentioned by Yeats in "The Happiest of the Poets" above.

48. For Sir Philip Sidney, see note 15 above. Yeats often took derogatory views of the Roman poet Virgil (70–19 BC) and his epic *The Aeneid.*

49. The cento of phrases comes from "April" in *The Shepheards Calendar* (Collier 1:45–48) and is presumably quoted from memory. For "the image of the heavens" read "her heavenly haveour," for "without mortal blemish" read "No mortal blemish," for "an angelic face" read "her angelic face," for "a fourth Grace" read "a Grace to fyll the fourth place," and for "above all her sex that ever yet has been" read "which in her sex doth all excel."

50. See lines 211–13 of Spenser's poem "Daphnaida": "In purenesse and in all celestiall grace, / That men admire in goodly womankind, / She did excel, and seem'd of Angels race" (Collier 5:240).

51. The passage from the French novelist Gustave Flaubert (1821–80) comes from a letter Flaubert wrote to Louise Colet dated 27 March 1853. Yeats's source was most likely Walter Pater's essay "Correspondance de Gustave Flaubert," first published in *The Athenaeum* on 3 August 1889. Pater translates several excerpts from Flaubert's letters

without mentioning when or to whom Flaubert wrote them, which might account for Yeats's vague phrase "Flaubert says somewhere . . ." The passage as Pater translates it reads: "What could be worse built than many things in Rabelais, Cervantes, Molière, Hugo? But, then, what sudden thrusts of power! What power in a single word!" See Walter Pater, *Uncollected Essays* (Portland, ME: Thomas B. Mosher, 1903), 107–8. François Rabelais (ca. 1494–ca. 1553) was a French physician, humanist, and satirist best known for his *Gargantua and Pantagruel.*

52. Theocritus (ca. 310–ca. 250 BC) was the Greek poet of classical antiquity credited with inventing pastoral poetry.

53. For Spenser's *View of the Present State of Ireland,* see notes 22 and 26 above. For "sure it [is] yet a most beautiful and sweet country as any [is] under heaven," see Collier 5:315. For the passage about the four garrisons issuing forth, see Collier 5:414; for "creete, or" read "creete in or"; for "moste sustenance" read "cheife sustenance"; for "killed in" read "killed with"; for "short space" read "short time"; for "winters" read "winter"; for "following of" read "followed upon." For the passage about consuming themselves, see Collier 5:418–19; for "they would" read "they should"; for "eate of the dead" read "eate the dead"; for "happy were they if they" read "happy where they"; and for "man or beast" read "man and beast."

54. The *Annals of the Four Masters* is the English version of the *Annála Ríoghachta Éireann,* undertaken by the Franciscan friar Míchéal Ó Cléirigh (Michael O'Clery) (ca. 1580–1643) and three assistants and completed in 1636.

55. Tristan and Iseult were famous medieval doomed lovers; Guinevere was the wife of King Arthur and the beloved of Sir Lancelot.

56. The "Great Demagogue" is Oliver Cromwell (1599–1658), who subdued Ireland harshly. Yeats slightly modifies a passage from volume 1, chapter 11, of the George Borrow (1803–81) novel *Lavengro* in *The Scholar—The Gypsy—The Priest,* 3 vols. (London: John Murray, 1851), 148. The original passage reads:

> "Is this your house, mother?" I at length demanded, in the language which I thought she would best understand.
>
> "Yes, my house, my own house; the house of the broken-hearted."
>
> "Any other person's house?" I demanded.
>
> "My own house, the beggar's house—the accursed house of Cromwell!"

57. Caibry (Cairbre) Cathead is a legendary figure in the *Lebor Gabála* (Book of Invasions). When the more plebeian Aithech-Tuatha overthrow the Milesians, they set Cairbre to rule over them, and he is

sometimes therefore referred to as a usurper. During his reign there is only one grain on each stalk of wheat and one acorn on each oak, the rivers are empty of fish, and the cattle milkless, as nature refuses to condone his wrongful succession.

58. Dido and Helen are beautiful queens in classical antiquity, Helen in Homer's *The Iliad* and *The Odyssey,* and Dido in Virgil's *The Aeneid.*
59. The quotation is from the opening lines of "Sephestia's Song to Her Child" by Robert Greene (1558–92). See Robert Greene and Thomas Lodge, *Menaphon by Robert Greene and A Margarite of America by Thomas Lodge,* ed. G. B. Harrison (Oxford: Basil Blackwell, 1927), 29.
60. This catalog of trees occurs in *The Faerie Queene,* book 1, canto 1 (Collier 1:178–79).
61. "Claude's 'Mill'" is a 1648 oil painting by the French landscape painter Claude Lorrain (1600–1682). The painting, also known as both *Landscape with Dancing Figures* and *The Marriage of Isaac and Rebecca,* depicts several rustics participating in a pastrol dance in front of a river with a mill. In 1816 the English painter J. M. W. Turner (1775–1851) did two paintings of the Temple of Jupiter Panellenius. The first, *Temple of Jupiter Panhellenius, Restored,* represents the temple as it might have originally looked in ancient Greece. The second, *View of the Temple of Jupiter Panellenius, in the Island of Aegina, with the Greek National Dance of the Romaika: the Acropolis of Athens in the Distance. Painted from a sketch taken by H. Gally Knight, Esq. in 1810,* shows the temple in its current state of ruin. Yeats presumably refers to the first of the two Turner works.
62. Yeats mistakenly assigns this name to the anonymous hero of Shelley's poem *Alastor.* In actuality, Alastor is a transliteration from Greek, meaning "evil spirit or demon of solitude." See "The Philosophy of Shelley's Poetry" above.
63. Christopher Smart (1722–71), English poet, whose religious mania landed him first in a mental hospital and then in a private madhouse, wrote a bold new sort of visionary poetry grounded in biblical lore and later associated with that of Blake. His most famous works are *Jubilate Agno* (1759–63) and the rhapsodic *Song to David* (1763).
64. *Laon and Cythna* is the first-published version of the twelve-canto poem by Percy Bysshe Shelley (1792–1822) that was revised and republished as *The Revolt of Islam. Adonais* is Shelley's elegy upon the death of John Keats (1795–1821). Yeats discusses both works in "The Philosophy of Shelley's Poetry" above. The stanza quoted is stanza 34 of canto 6 from *The Revolt of Islam* (Hutchinson, 102).
65. *Endymion* is a four-book narrative poem published by John Keats in 1818. It tells the story of the love of the shepherd Endymion for the moon goddess Cynthia.
66. *The Earthly Paradise* is a poem by William Morris (1834–96), consisting of a prologue followed by twenty-four tales in Chaucerian

meters. Yeats mentions it in his own essay "The Happiest of the Poets" above.

67. The English poet Matthew Royden (ca.1580–1622) wrote an elegy on the death of Sir Philip Sidney called "An Elegy or Friend's Passion for His Astrophill" that is often bound up with Spenser. The lines quoted may be found in Collier 5:99.
68. In "A Vision of the Last Judgment," Blake writes, "Fable or Allegory is Formd by the Daughters of Memory" (Ellis-Yeats 2: 393; Erdman, 554).
69. All three references come from *The Faerie Queene.* Sir Guyon visits the cave or treasure house of Mammon in book 2, canto 7; the Red Cross Knight encounters Despair in book 1, canto 9; and the vision of Scudamour (the lover of Amoret) takes place in book 4, canto 10. Yeats includes all three passages in the "Emblems and Qualities" section of his *Poems of Spenser,* see pages 86–106, 75–86, and 126–143, respectively.
70. Board Schools were established by the Elementary Education Act of 1870 and were under the management of a school board.
71. Amoret is the bride of Sir Scudamour in *The Faerie Queene,* books 3 and 4; the enchanter Busirane imprisoned her until she was released by Britomart.
72. In *Poems of Spenser,* Yeats reprints the descriptions of the islands of Phaedria and Acrasia from book 2 of *The Faerie Queene* on pages 183–220 and of the Garden of Adonis from book 3 on pages 220–26.
73. The erotic narrative poem *Hero and Leander* by Christopher Marlowe (1564–93) tells the story of the tragic love of Hero and Leander, which leads to the drowning of Leander while trying to swim the Hellespont and the resultant suicide of Hero.
74. For the Keatsian source of "perilous seas," see note 47 above.

## Preface to The Cutting of an Agate (1912)

1. Yeats worked on the Spenser essay for a volume in The Golden Poets series not during "a couple of summers" but throughout 1902, announcing its completion in a letter to Lady Gregory on 31 December 1902 (*CL*3, 290) and sending it to the publishers on 2 January 1903 (*CL*3, 290, 294). However, on 13 January he told Lady Gregory of the publisher's response: ". . . owing to the delay of several authors about the sending in of MSS. they have had 'to reconsider' the series or the publication I forget which and . . . they cannot publish for some time," repeating this information in a letter to her the next day (*CL*3, 302–4). Yeats revised the Introduction in late March 1906. *Poems of Spenser: Selected and with an Introduction by W. B. Yeats* was eventually published in October 1906 (Edinburgh: T. C. & E. C. Jack).

   The Irish National Dramatic Company was formally constituted on

9 August 1902. The first productions at the Abbey Theatre were offered on 27 December 1904.

2. Volume 4 of the *Collected Works in Verse and Prose* (Stratford-on-Avon: A. H. Bullen, 1908) included *The Irish Dramatic Movement,* a selection of Yeats's contributions to *Samhain* (1901–6) and *The Arrow* (1906–7), as well as two items first published in the *United Irishman,* for a total of 153 pages (see *IDM*).

The Cuala Press (formerly the Dun Emer Press) in Dundrum, County Dublin, was managed by Yeats's sisters, Susan Mary Yeats ("Lily," 1866–1949) and Elizabeth Corbet Yeats ("Lolly," 1868–1940). *The Cutting of an Agate* included *Discoveries* (Dundrum: Dun Emer Press, 1907) as well as Yeats's contribution to John Millington Synge's *Poems and Translations* (Churchtown, Dundrum: Cuala Press, 1909).

## Preface to The Cutting of an Agate (1919, 1924)

This preface was first published in the 1919 edition of *The Cutting of an Agate* and was reprinted without change in *Essays* (1924).

1. Yeats worked on the Spenser essay for a volume in The Golden Poets series not during "a couple of summers" but throughout 1902, announcing its completion in a letter to Lady Gregory on 31 December 1902 (*CL3*, 290) and sending it to the publishers on 2 January 1903 (*CL3*, 290, 294). However, on 13 January he told Lady Gregory of the publisher's response: "owing to the delay of several authors about the sending in of MSS. they have had 'to reconsider' the series or the publication I forget which and . . . they cannot publish for some time," repeating this information in a letter to her the next day (*CL3*, 302–4). Yeats revised the Introduction in late March 1906. *Poems of Spenser: Selected and with an Introduction by W. B. Yeats* was eventually published in October 1906 (Edinburgh: T. C. & E. C. Jack).

## Dedication of Essays (1924)

1. The one-act play *Crabbed Youth and Age* (1924) by the Irish playwright and theatre manager [Esmé Stuart] Lennox Robinson (1886–1958) was first produced at the Abbey Theatre on 14 November 1922 and became one of his most popular plays. Robinson resigned as Manager of the Abbey on 1 December 1923, becoming a co-director with Yeats and Lady Gregory.

In addition to *Ideas of Good and Evil* and *The Cutting of an Agate, Essays* (1924) included *Per Amica Silentia Lunae.* The Dedication is found on both the 14 June 1949 proofs of *Essays* (BL Add. Ms. 55894) and the 22 September 1959 proofs of *Essays and Introductions* (BL

Add. Ms. 55895). However, on the later set it is queried "Is this to be kept?" and is then cancelled. The corrected copy of *Essays* prepared for the Scribner edition also has the Dedication cancelled. It was not included in *Essays and Introductions* (1961).

# INDEX